MARGARET BRAZIER

Medicine, Patients and the Law

Third Edition

PENGUIN BOOKS

In memory of
L. T. Jacobs 1914–85
and
Harry Street 1919–84

PENGUIN BOOKS

Published by the Penguin Group
Penguin Books Ltd, 80 Strand, London WC2R ORL, England
Penguin Putnam Inc., 375 Hudson Street, New York, New York 10014, USA
Penguin Books Australia Ltd, 250 Camberwell Road, Camberwell, Victoria 3124, Australia
Penguin Books Canada Ltd, 10 Alcorn Avenue, Toronto, Ontario, Canada M4V 3B2
Penguin Books India (P) Ltd, 11, Community Centre, Panchsheel Park, New Delhi – 110 017, India
Penguin Books (NZ) Ltd, Cnr Rosedale and Airborne Roads, Albany, Auckland, New Zealand
Penguin Books (South Africa) (Pty) Ltd, 24 Sturdee Avenue, Rosebank 2196, South Africa

Penguin Books Ltd, Registered Offices: 80 Strand, London WC2R ORL, England

www.penguin.com

First published in Pelican Books 1987
Second edition published in Penguin Books 1992
Third edition published 2003
1

Copyright © Margaret Brazier, 1987, 1992, 2003
All rights reserved

The moral right of the author has been asserted

Set in 9.5/11.5pt Linotype Minion
Typeset by Palimpsest Book Production Limited, Polmont, Stirlingshire
Printed in England by Clays Ltd, St Ives plc

PENGUIN BOOKS

Medicine, Patients and the Law

Margaret Brazier was born in 1950. She graduated from the University of Manchester in 1971 and was called to the Bar in 1973. She has lectured at Manchester University since 1971 and was appointed Professor of Law in 1990. Her publications include several articles on torts and medico-legal problems, *Autonomy and Healthcare: Protecting the Vulnerable* (with Mary Lobjoit) (eds.) and several editions of *Street on Torts*; she is General Editor of *Clerk and Lindsell on Torts*. She chaired a review of laws relating to surrogacy from 1996 to 1998, and currently chairs the NHS Retained Organs Commission.

Contents

Preface

Writing a book about medicine and law these days is rather like chasing a moving target. No sooner is one chapter completed than some novel development throws the process into disarray. Any book on medical law is at least in part out of date before it is on the shelf. Rarely a day passes without the media highlighting some new controversy surrounding medical practice, or medical ethics. The Law Reports regularly feature cases relating to health. The medical profession finds itself in the limelight. Its image undergoes drastic changes. One day the doctor is hailed as a saviour. The next he is condemned as authoritarian or uncaring. The past decade has witnessed more of the latter than the former. The rapid progress of medical science, extending life at one end and bringing new hope to the childless at the other, has thrown up intricate problems of ethics and morals. At every level of medical practice the law plays a part. The number of claims for malpractice against doctors continues to grow. Doctors fear an epidemic of US proportions. Yet patients still find the English legal system obstructive and cripplingly expensive. Nor are patients' and their families' grievances limited to the lack of provision for compensation for medical mishap. Increasingly patients demand a greater say in their treatment. They are no longer prepared to be patient. The extent to which it is their right to have such a say becomes ultimately a question for the law. Research on embryos, cloning, abortion, euthanasia and organ retention excite lively legal and moral debate. The impact of the Human Rights Act 1998 is beginning to be felt.

The purpose of this book is to examine the regulation of medical practice, the rights and responsibilities of patients and their doctors, the provision of compensation for medical mishaps and the framework of rules governing those delicate questions of life and death when medicine, morals and law overlap. It is intended to provide a picture of the role of the law in medical practice today and to highlight those areas where the law is inadequate. So in Part I, I consider the general legal framework within which medicine is practised today. In Part II, I look at legal remedies available to the patient injured by, or unhappy with, treatment he has received. And finally in Part III, I examine some specific dilemmas relating to the treatment of the living, the dying, and the dead that pose awkward problems of law, morals and medicine. Throughout the book I concentrate, primarily, on the provision of health care for the mentally competent patient. In Chapter 5, I consider the problems arising when a patient is temporarily or permanently mentally incapacitated. I do not attempt any systematic coverage of mental health law. To do so would be to double the length of the book. The reader should refer to the specialist works on that topic. This book is intended for a wide audience. It is designed to be read by lawyers and law students seeking an introduction to the law relating to medical practice, by members of the medical profession, and above all by the lay public, looking for a guide through the maze of current issues confronting them every day in their daily newspaper. I make no judgements about medical practice in the twenty-first century. I am not qualified to do so. I do evaluate the state of the law and too often find it sadly wanting.

The first edition of this book was to have been a joint project of Professor Harry Street, Professor Gerald Dworkin and me. Professor Street died in April 1984. He inspired the writing of the book. His example as colleague and teacher created a debt that I can never repay. Gerald Dworkin's many commitments prevented him from completing his planned share of the work. For that first edition, he kindly allowed me to use the drafts he prepared of Chapters 17, 18 and 19. His wise advice and meticulous reading of other chapters assisted me greatly in 1987. For this edition, I am indebted to Dr Emma Cave of the University of Leeds who prepared the first draft of Chapter 16 on Medical Research. Chapter 16 is a joint enterprise. Emma Cave is the primary author of that challenging chapter.

I should like to acknowledge the help given to me by many of my colleagues in Manchester and elsewhere, from the disciplines of law, philosophy and medicine. Their patience in listening to me as I chewed over awkward problems, and advising me as the work progressed has been invaluable. In particular I thank my friends and colleagues Diana Kloss, Maureen Mulholland, Sara Fovargue, Caroline Bridge, Marie Fox,

Kirsty Keywood, Jean McHale, John Harris and Charles Erin, who have given me invaluable advice and support. I must also thank my students, who challenged my views on several occasions and forced me to think again on many issues. I acknowledge the especial efforts of Catherine Yates and Vicky Clark in helping me with research. Most of all I thank Shirley Tiffany who struggled with my appalling handwriting and kept me going through a difficult couple of years.

No criticisms made in the book are the result of any personal experience of medical practice. The care which I and my family have received from our general practitioners at the Bodey Medical Centre, from Central Manchester NHS Trust and from Withington hospital, where my daughter was born, has always been of the highest standard.

I submitted the typescript for this edition to the publishers in April 2002. I have been able to make some minor amendments in February 2003, plus one or two changes at proof stage in June. I have been able only to deal very superficially with the recent reforms of the General Medical Council, which will gradually take effect throughout 2003. A number of crucial decisions of the courts are very briefly noted. Between my last opportunity to amend my work and publication, the White Paper on Clinical Negligence is likely to surface. A draft Human Tissue Bill may well make an appearance. CHAI will be born and revolutionize complaints procedures. At long last reforms to the law relating to mentally incapacitated patients will (I hope) reach Parliament. As will be evident, I did not catch up with the moving target which is medical law today.

Margaret Brazier

Introduction

The law of England, in contrast to that of most European countries, is not to be found neatly encapsulated in any code. The task of the non-lawyer seeking to establish her rights, or ascertain his duties is far from easy. The law relating to medical practice is to be discovered from a variety of sources. Parliament has enacted a number of statutes governing medical practice. The regulation of medical practice and the disciplining of the defaulting doctor have traditionally been entrusted to the General Medical Council by virtue of the Medical Act 1983. The organization of the health service is governed by a series of statutes on the National Health Service, notably the National Health Service Act 1977, the Health Act 1999 and the Health and Social Care Act 2001. The Medicines Act 1968 is concerned with the safety of drugs. A number of other Acts of Parliament, such as the Abortion Act 1967 and the Human Fertilization and Embryology Act 1990, are crucially relevant to questions about medicine, patients and the law. An Act of Parliament only creates a general framework of legal rules and therefore commonly empowers government ministers to make subsidiary regulations known as statutory instruments. These regulations may determine the answers to crucial questions. For example, most of the duties of general practitioners within the NHS are dealt with by regulations and not by Act of Parliament.

It is impossible today to understand the legal rules governing the practice of medicine without reference to European law. In matters within the jurisdiction of the Treaty of Rome and subsequent treaties, notably the Treaty of Amsterdam, the European Union is empowered to make laws affecting all Member States. This may be by way of *regulations*, which immediately and directly become law in the United

Kingdom, or by way of *directives*, which oblige the United Kingdom government to introduce an appropriate Act of Parliament to give effect to the directive. In 1985 a Community directive on liability for unsafe products resulted in the Consumer Protection Act 1987, which, as we shall see in Chapter 8, introduced strict liability for defective drugs. The *Clinical Trials Directive*, promulgated in April 2001, will oblige the United Kingdom to introduce reforms of the law governing medical research. Provisions of the EU treaties themselves may be invoked to make a case for greater rights for patients. Diane Blood was able to persuade the Court of Appeal that while it would be unlawful for any fertility clinic in England to inseminate her with her dead husband's sperm, EU law allowed her to take his sperm abroad to be inseminated in another member state. Mrs Blood received treatment in Belgium and is now the mother of two sons born as a result of posthumous insemination with their father's sperm. It must be noted, though, that the European Union is primarily concerned with economic and commercial matters. The extent of the European Union's powers to pronounce on ethical questions such as embryo research or abortion is limited and much disputed.

The European Union must not be confused with the European Convention on Human Rights. That Convention is a separate treaty to which the United Kingdom is a party. The Convention seeks to establish the rights of the individual and directly addresses questions such as rights to life, to privacy, and to found a family. The Human Rights Act 1998 renders rights granted by the Convention enforceable against public authorities in the United Kingdom. As we shall see, the Act has the potential to transform medical law and offer a clearer articulation of patients' rights.

Conventions, statutes and statutory regulations alone, be they British or European legislation, by no means paint the whole picture of English medical law. Much of English law remains judge-made, the common law of England. Decisions, judgments handed down by the courts, form the precedents for determining later disputes and define the rights and duties of doctors and patients in areas untouched by statute. The common law governs questions of compensation for medical accidents, the patient's right to determine his own treatment, parents' rights to control medical treatment of their children and, as we shall see, several other vital matters. I deal with English law. The common law is not confined to England. Decisions of courts in the USA, Canada and elsewhere are mentioned from time to time. Such judgments do not bind an English court. They can be useful as examples, or warnings, showing us how the same basic principles of law have developed elsewhere. Finally it must be remembered that, for the lawyer, Scotland counts as a foreign country. Scotland maintains its own independent legal system and post-devolution will have the power to legislate independently on most issues relating to medical care. I confine myself to stating the law as it applies in England and Wales. On many of the questions dealt with in this book English and Scottish law coincide, but occasionally the law in England and Scotland diverges. The problems of law and medicine embodied in the book are, however, common to Britain as a whole.

The internal organization of the NHS has undergone a series of seismic changes in the past thirteen years. Yet further reforms began to be implemented in October 2002.* This work does not attempt to describe the structure of the NHS, but readers do perhaps need to understand that the modern NHS will depend largely on three principal sorts of institutions. Primary Care Trusts (PCTs) will be responsible for securing services for patients. This means not only ensuring and sometimes providing primary care, now renamed personal medical services, but also commissioning hospital care and all the specialized services patients may need. The PCT in effect becomes the gatekeeper for access to health care. Hospital care and specialized services will in most cases be delivered by NHS Trusts, very much as has been the case for the past decade. PCTs may, however, in certain circumstances commission treatment from the private sector. Twenty-eight Strategic Health Authorities (StHAs) will performance manage PCTs and NHS Trusts, seeking to develop a coherent strategic framework within the NHS.

What does all this mean in the context of legal disputes arising with the NHS? NHS Trusts, both acute hospital trusts and mental health trusts, are the most likely targets of litigation. The overwhelming majority of clinical negligence claims, or disputes about consent, arise in relation to hospital patients. Very many of the heart-rending ethical dilemmas that end up in court involve hospitals. Decisions about whether to treat a very disabled infant, or whether to switch off a ventilator at an adult's request, rarely surface in the community. The responsibilities of PCTs to commission services mean they may become vulnerable to claims relating to access to health care. While most general

---

* See http://www.doh.gov.uk/shiftingthebalance/nextsteps2.htm

practitioners will continue to be self-employed, so that any legal claim by a patient lies against the practice itself, some personal medical services will now be provided directly by the PCT. In such cases the PCT may be liable for the employed doctor's negligence or other wrongdoing.

Table of Cases

The date in brackets after the reference to a case in this Table refers to the date at which the case was decided. In a number of instances the case is actually reported at a later date, as will be apparent in the full case reference given in the relevant note.

If no clear citation is given on a page where a case is discussed, the relevant note number appears in square brackets after the page reference.

Table of Statutes

Where no clear citation appears in the text, the relevant note number appears in square brackets after the page reference.

Table of Statutory Instruments

Where no clear citation appears in the text, the relevant note number appears in square brackets after the page reference.

Part One:
Medicine, Law
and Society

1

The Practice of Medicine Today

Few professions once stood so high in public esteem as that of medicine. Popularity polls of professionals regularly resulted in doctors at the top of the poll and lawyers near the bottom! The final years of the twentieth century dealt a body blow to the reputation of the medical profession in the United Kingdom. Scandal after scandal beset doctors. Surgeons carrying out cardiac operations on infants in Bristol were found to have continued to operate despite incurring higher death rates for such surgery than their peers. The subsequent Inquiry[1] uncovered a 'club culture'. Vulnerable children were not the hospital's priority. Care was poorly organized, the standard of care was poor and openness non-existent.

In Bristol,[2] and in Liverpool,[3] evidence emerged of hospitals retaining children's organs and parents not being told that only parts of their children's bodies were returned to them for burial. Subsequently it became apparent that organ retention, of both children and adults, was a widespread practice. A gynaecologist was struck off the medical register after years of gross malpractice involving bungled operations, removing women's ovaries without their consent and a record of appalling rudeness to patients. Harold Shipman, the infamous general practitioner, was convicted of the murder of fifteen of his patients and suspected of hundreds of other killings. Nor were the doctors alone in their misery. The conviction of Beverly Allitt of the murder of four of her child patients dented the reputation of nurses too. As 2000 began, health professionals felt under siege. Previously regarded as national treasures, doctors were often reviled in the media as pariahs.

Ironically, the very popularity of doctors and nurses within the National Health Service explains their current plight. Praised to the skies for their triumphs, few individuals attract greater public odium than the doctor or nurse who falls from her pedestal. The revulsion occasioned by Nazi atrocities in the concentration camps was nowhere as marked as in the case of Dr Josef Mengele. That he used his skills as a doctor, taught to him that he might heal and comfort the sick, to advance torture and barbarism still causes horror, more than half a century after the end of the Nazi era. The transformation of a supposed angel of mercy into an angel of death makes the blood run cold.

Public passion is rightly aroused by the likes of Mengele and Shipman. Passion is never far away from everyday relationships between doctor and patient. Clients usually remain unemotional about their solicitor. If he does a good job they may appreciate him. If he is incompetent they sack him. He will rarely be loved or hated. The family doctor arouses more intense feelings. For many patients the doctor is almost a member of the family. He is expected to feel for them as well as provide professional care. When doctors meet their patient's expectations, they are rewarded by admiration and affection. Woe betide them if they do not. One error, one moment of exasperation or insensitivity, may transform a beloved doctor into a hate figure. The hospital consultant enjoys or endures a similarly ambivalent role. Consultants, until comparatively recently, were accorded godlike status. They inspired awe in the patient, visiting the ward attended by a retinue of junior doctors and nurses. Their exalted status insulated them from personal contact with patients and protected them from the sort of complaints voiced freely to nursing staff. They paid a price. Gods are expected to work miracles. They are not expected to be subject to human error. When a consultant proved to be human, when medicine could not cure, the patient found it hard to comprehend failure and rightly or wrongly, often wrongly, regarded the doctor as personally incompetent.

Medical attitudes are changing, if slowly. Family doctors are becoming a different breed. Many try hard to persuade patients to see their doctor as a partner in promoting good health. Doctors are urged to prescribe less freely and to talk more to their patients. The good GP is as interested in the prevention of ill-health as its cure. A new generation of consultants is taking over in the hospitals. They are (in most cases) less grand and more prepared to listen to patients and nursing staff. Entrenched attitudes take time to change. Although doctors may attempt to shed any image of omnipotence, the perceptions of many patients remain the same. They still want to regard the doctor as a miracle worker. The publicity attaching to, and money poured into, high-technology medicine reinforce that perception. Stories rarely appear in the press applauding the good work of the geriatrician or praising the community health physician. Doctors in such unglamorous specialities rarely win the coveted NHS merit awards that could boost the senior doctor's salary. Money, fame and publicity are often reserved for the transplant surgeon, the fertility specialist or gene therapy expert. The medical marvels with which the public are bombarded reinforce the image of the doctor as 'superman'.[4] When a member of the public becomes a patient and 'superman' lets him down, he is unsurprisingly aggrieved.

Doctors cannot entirely blame the media for their image, as they themselves played a role in deciding who got merit awards. Doctors make their own decisions as to which branch of medicine they enter and many continue to vote for the glamorous world of 'high-tech' medicine. Nor can the medical profession deny its own internal difficulties. The scandals emerging at the end of the 1990s were not invented by the media. While, unsurprisingly, leaders of the profession basked in good publicity incontrovertible evidence condemned a number of doctors as incompetent, callous and even criminal.

One, or even several 'bad apples', should not destroy the reputations of thousands of other medical practitioners who do their job diligently and compassionately. The most serious charge levelled against doctors is not that individuals betrayed patients' trust but that too little was done by doctors to identify and remedy other doctors' failings. The medical profession as a whole should not be punished for Shipman's bizarre and apparently motiveless murders. Nor should the reputation of surgery be tarnished just because two of their number in Bristol were culpably incompetent. It seems amazing that no colleague noted or acted on the evidence of the number of apparent healthy patients on Shipman's list who died suddenly, in certain cases even in his surgery. An anaesthetist who worked with the Bristol surgeons tried several times to raise his concerns about their competence with his superiors. His complaints were cavalierly dismissed. His career in Britain stalled and he emigrated to Australia. None the less as the Bristol Inquiry Report put it, events even at Bristol did not disclose

. . . an account of bad people. Nor is it an account of people who did not care, nor of people who wilfully harmed patients. It is an account of people who cared greatly about human suffering, and were dedicated and well-motivated. Sadly some lacked insight and their behaviour was flawed. Many failed to communicate with each other, and to work together effectively for the interests of their patients. There was a lack of leadership, and of teamwork.[5]

Evidence that the profession has not tried hard enough to maintain its standards mounts up. However, the challenges confronted by doctors should not be underestimated. Denigrating bad doctors may have become a national pastime, but there are certain inescapable features of the profession of medicine that will always render doctors more vulnerable to attack than fellow professionals. The doctor deals with the individual's most precious commodities, life and health. On a mundane level she may determine whether patient X is to be sanctioned to enjoy seven days off work for nervous exhaustion brought about by overwork, or classified as another malingerer.[6] At the other end of the scale, the doctor may hold in his hands the power of life and death. He is the man with the skill and experience. In his hands, as the patient sees it, rests the power to cure. As Ian Kennedy has said, the patient appears before the doctor '. . . naked both physically and emotionally'. However unwilling we may be to acknowledge the fact, however well-intentioned the doctor, it is hard to overstate the power that this vests in the doctor.[7] The price of power is that those who exercise it must expect constant scrutiny from those subject to it and from the public at large. The age of deference is past.

The power inevitably held by the doctor in our society is matched by the human cost of any error he may make. When an overstretched accountant makes a mistake, she will probably get a chance to put it right next day. When a trainee solicitor's inexperience lets him down, the likelihood is that his principal will notice and correct the error. The junior doctor who has been working continuously for over thirty-six hours may get no second chance. Nor is there a second chance for the patient. The accountant or the solicitor may cause her client to lose money or property. Monetary compensation paid for out of the professional's insurance cover will go some way to placate the client. For the patient whose doctor's mistake resulted in disability or death, money is poor compensation. Finding out why things went wrong may be more important to the patient and the family. The difficulties in finding out 'why' may explain the bitterness that attends many claims against the medical profession.

When the price of error is so high, it follows that concern to prevent error is acute. Every profession has its black sheep, not just medicine.

Some are merely incompetent, others are venal. The failure of the Law Society to pursue and discipline its members effectively is well recorded.[8] There is no evidence that the medical profession is any better or worse than its brethren in other disciplines in maintaining and policing standards, but medicine's failures attract greater attention. A solicitor who grossly overcharges, fails to keep proper records or conducts his client's business dilatorily will arouse public concern as well as private anger, but the outcry will not reach the same level of passion as that occasioned by reports of a doctor failing to visit a child who later dies, or of hospitals 'deceiving' parents about the retention of their dead child's organs. It is meaningless for the medical profession to claim that doctors make no more mistakes, that there are no more 'bad' practitioners, than in any other profession. The cost of a medical error is such that doctors will always be expected to be better, in every sense, than other mortals, and the standards of the profession as a whole will be expected to be of the highest.

The consequences of a failure in medical skill are not the only reason for the medical profession's susceptibility to virulent attack. The decisions that face the doctor often touch on sensitive areas of moral and religious concern. This is nothing new. For example, until the advent of safe Caesarean surgery doctors were often called on to decide whether to save the life of mother or baby in a difficult confinement. Three developments have intensified the modern doctor's dilemma. First, technology has given doctors power to save and prolong life that was undreamed of thirty years ago, but they now have to decide when to use that technology. In many cases life can be prolonged; the question is whether that life is worth prolonging. Secondly, until relatively recently decisions about life and death were usually made in the privacy of the patient's home. The midwife attending the birth of a grossly disabled baby decided with the parents whether to attempt to save the infant's life. Only she and the family ever knew that the supposedly stillborn baby struggled to breathe. Today such scenes are played out in the publicity of a busy labour ward. Finally, there is no longer consensus on the sanctity of life, when life begins, or when it ends, or should end. Abortion, once illegal and hazardous to the mother, can now be carried out safely and cheaply in the early months of pregnancy. The debate on the morality of abortion has not abated, however. The divide between pro- and anti-abortion campaigners is greater than ever, to the extent that in the USA abortion clinics have been bombed and doctors carrying out abortions have received death threats. In Northern Ireland, pickets of family planning clinics, and personal abuse hurled at doctors and others who support women's choice in relation to abortion are common. In 1981, Dr Leonard Arthur stood trial for murder as a result of his management of the care of a severely disabled baby. His ordeal ended in acquittal. At the core of the issue was a dispute between medical professionals and within society itself about how such babies should be treated. In what other profession would an ethical and professional dispute result in a criminal prosecution?

The power vested in the hands of the doctor explains the concern that the public has in its exercise. It places the medical profession in the limelight, a limelight some doctors relish. Doctors cannot be surprised when failure, incompetence or controversy attract equal notoriety. Unfortunately, representatives of the profession often react in an over-defensive manner, exacerbating the original criticism or complaint. What the profession, patients and the public have in common is a need for:

(1) the medical profession to be properly regulated and controlled,
(2) where possible, a clear definition of the rights and obligations of patients, doctors and other health professionals,
(3) an adequate and rational system of compensation for patients suffering injury,
(4) effective means of investigating medical accidents and errors,
(5) provision for doctors and patients to be given comprehensible guidance on those areas of medical practice of moral and ethical sensitivity.

The extent to which the law does and can meet those needs is at the heart of this book.

Regulating medical practice

The Medical Act 1983 entrusted the regulation of the medical profession to the profession itself acting through the General Medical Council. The GMC controls medical education and maintains a register of qualified practitioners. Unfettered self-regulation was ended by the National Health Service Reform and Health Care Professions Act 2002 which created a supra-regulatory council, the Council for the Regulation of Health Care Professionals, to supervise the GMC and all other health care regulators. At the time of writing, radical reform of the way in which medical practice is regulated is making rapid progress.

Surprisingly, no law expressly prohibits any unregistered or unqualified person from practising most types of medicine or even surgery. A criminal offence is committed only when such a person deliberately and falsely represents himself as being a registered practitioner or having a medical qualification.[9] The rationale of the criminal law is that people should be free to opt for any form of advice or treatment, however bizarre, but must be protected from rogues claiming a bogus status and from commercial exploitation of untested 'alternative' medicine. On its own the penalty for falsely claiming to be qualified is not much of a deterrent, a maximum fine of £5,000. The fraudulent 'doctor' out to make money is deterred in other ways. He will not be able to recover his fees in a court of law.[10] If money has been handed over voluntarily where the 'doctor' led the patient to believe he was qualified he may face additional charges of obtaining property by deception and conviction may result in imprisonment.[11] The herbalist and the faith-healer are left free to practise, but they must be honest with those who come to them for help and not pretend to be registered doctors. The growing popularity of complementary or alternative medicine has led to calls, often by practitioners themselves, for the regulation of complementary therapies.[12] Osteopaths[13] and chiropractors[14] now practise within a system of statutory regulation based on the 'medical' model. The Secretary of State for Health is looking for ways to integrate complementary medicine within the NHS. Practitioners of complementary medicine seek to make a sharp distinction between themselves and the amateurs and charlatans. Co-operation with 'conventional' medicine is becoming more common.[15] The policy adopted by the law, albeit developed haphazardly, is that patients should have choices about what kind of medicine they seek. The law should ensure patients are not deceived about what is on offer and minimum standards of regulation should be set where possible.

Few would quarrel with the liberality of the law where the unqualified 'practitioner' limits himself to advice. What if an unqualified person practises surgery? Any physical contact with a patient permitted under the impression that he is dealing with a 'real doctor' will be a criminal assault. A biology teacher who set himself up in private practice in Lancashire was imprisoned for assault causing grievous bodily harm for carrying out gynaecological operations on unsuspecting women.[16] A more difficult question is raised where the patient agrees to surgery by an unregistered practitioner knowing full well that he is not dealing with a registered medical practitioner. I would tentatively suggest that a prosecution for assault would still succeed even if nothing went wrong with the 'operation'. The consent of the 'victim' of an assault is not always a defence when bodily harm is done.[17] The public interest in preventing unqualified persons from engaging in surgery may be sufficient to render the 'doctor's' conduct punishable as a crime.

The General Medical Council

The General Medical Council remains the governing body of the medical profession. Its composition will change radically in July 2003. From 1983 the GMC was composed of fifty-four doctors elected by the profession at large, twenty-five members appointed by universities and the Royal Colleges of Medicine, and twenty-five persons, nominated by the Queen on the advice of the Privy Council.[18] The Medical Act 1983 requires that elected members constitute a majority on the GMC, and that a majority of the nominated members must be lay people. As elected and appointed members are required to be doctors, the lay element was fairly minimal at less than 25 per cent. Doctors chosen by their peers dominated the Council. In so far as the GMC acts as the supreme representative of medical interests, the predominant position of doctors within the Council was explicable. However, the central function of the modern GMC is to regulate the profession in the public interest. Some of the difficulties that beset the GMC arose from the conflict of interests between doctors and patients. Neither lobby was happy. In 2000, the British Medical Association passed a motion of no confidence in the GMC. The Council, the BMA declared, was failing to protect doctors' interests. Patients' representatives accuse the GMC of just the opposite bias. The Council in their view fails to protect patients from poor practice or even outright abuse. The election to the GMC of a doctor who had some years earlier been struck off the register for misconduct triggered outrage. Whether even a reformed GMC can continue to ride two horses must be debatable but the GMC is not the only professional regulatory body that combines the role of protector of the profession and the public. The Law Society and the Bar Council both seek to achieve the same awkward balance between their own members and their clients. Lay representation on those bodies is even more token than is the case with the GMC.

The GMC developed proposals for reform.[19] A council of 104 people was on any analysis an unwieldy organization to govern the profession. From July 2003 the Council will comprise just thirty-five members, nineteen of them directly elected by the profession, two doctors appointed by the Royal Colleges and the universities, and fourteen lay people appointed by an independent commission. Lay representation on the reformed Council rises to 40 per cent. A wider pool of elected and appointed doctors, and nominated lay people will gradually be established to provide members for committees and working groups of the GMC. These reforms were given legal effect by virtue of Orders in Council made under section 60 of the Health Act 1999.[20] No new Medical Act was required.

Whatever the merits or otherwise of its composition, what does the GMC do? The Council's duties include maintaining the register of practitioners,[21] and providing '. . . advice for members of the medical profession on standards of professional conduct or on medical ethics'.[22] The Medical Act 1983, which defines and delimits the Council's powers, illustrates the importance of the Council's role in relation to medical education and in ensuring that registration is granted only to suitably qualified and experienced aspirants. Over half of the statute deals with this issue. Extraordinarily, until relatively recently, no formal provision at all was made in the United Kingdom to recognize or accredit specialist qualifications. A person registered as a medical practitioner and was then free to practise in the specialty of his choice. The specialist Royal Colleges offered qualifications and accreditation in their particular disciplines. Patients understanding the 'system' would check that their surgeon was a Member or Fellow of the Royal College of Surgeons. The body entrusted by Parliament with the regulation of medical practice left such matters with the ancient and powerful Royal Colleges. The GMC established a Specialist Register within which medical practitioners are identified by their specialities, accreditation and qualifications. A non-statutory committee, the Joint Committee on Higher Medical Teaching (JCHMT) undertook the actual accreditation of specialists. Equivalent qualifications from other member states of the European Union must now be recognized by the JCHMT and the Committee must conform to rules of due process. Practising in a specialty outside the specialism on the Register is not prohibited. The Specialist Register provided a source of information rather than a 'guarantee' of the specialist's competence. Reforms are imminent.

Registration is evidence that the doctor on entry to the register satisfied criteria for medical competence. Twenty years after the doctor leaves medical school, is he still competent? In response to the scandals that have overwhelmed the profession the GMC adopted proposals to ensure monitoring of medical practice. Doctors now have to submit to five-yearly tests and inspections to revalidate their competence and performance.[23] The GMC recognized that it is not enough to maintain standards by acting after complaints are made about a doctor's practice. It had to develop a more proactive role and this the Council has sought to do in the past decade. Consider its role in providing advice to doctors on standard and ethical conduct. Before 1995 that advice was little more than the famous 'Bluebook', a pamphlet containing some basic rules of professional ethics and etiquette, with an emphasis on the latter. As will become apparent when we delve further into key issues of consent, confidentiality, and the care of patients, the GMC has put considerable effort into developing, at least in embryo, a code of ethical conduct for its members. The irony is that the GMC left internal reform too late. Events conspired to overwhelm good intentions.

Fitness to practise

I shall not look further at the details of medical education and registration. Public concern focuses on the Council's powers to remove inadequate doctors from the register. Three different sorts of cases are dealt with by the GMC. First, there are provisions to deal with doctors whose own ill-health renders them unfit to practise. Next, there are the traditional powers to discipline doctors found guilty of serious professional misconduct. In 1997, procedures were introduced to deal with doctors whose professional performance was inadequate; doctors who were just not up to the job. Both the disciplinary and performance procedures are about to change.[24] A brief outline of the shape of these changes is offered later. The reader must gauge how substantial these are likely to prove to be.

Doctors whose health endangers patients used to be dealt with by the Health Committee, which can suspend a doctor unfit to practise by reason of physical or mental illness or make his registration conditional on compliance with certain conditions, for example, obliging him to accept medical treatment himself.[25] Elaborate safeguards ensure that a doctor alleged to be unfit to practise is treated fairly.

Complementary to the Health Committee was the Professional Conduct Committee whose function was to deal with 'bad' doctors. With this Committee lies the power to discipline any doctor who has been found guilty of a criminal offence in the British Isles or who '. . . is judged by the Professional Conduct Committee to be guilty of *serious professional misconduct*'.[26] Such a doctor may have his name erased from the register, or be suspended from the register for one year, or have his registration made conditional on compliance with conditions set by the Committee, for example undergoing additional training or attending a refresher course. Once again the procedure is designed to be scrupulously fair to the accused doctor and the doctor has a right of appeal.[27] Amendments to the Medical Act 1983, which came into force in August 2001, gave the GMC powers to suspend doctors swiftly pending the outcome of investigations into their conduct.

What amounts to serious professional misconduct?[28]

The efficacy of the General Medical Council's disciplinary powers as a means of maintaining standards of competence and good practice within the profession and protecting patients depends on what the Council treats as 'serious professional misconduct', in the penalties imposed on guilty doctors and how efficiently the disciplinary process proceeds. The GMC was bitterly criticized for its failure for many years to treat professional negligence as serious professional misconduct.[29] Times have changed and the GMC has recognized that grossly negligent practice equals misconduct. Two constraints necessarily limit any interpretation of what constitutes misconduct. First, it must be recognized that error alone does not equal misconduct. Good doctors make bad mistakes. Second, the GMC can act only within the limits set by Parliament and the courts. Earlier legislation defined punishable misconduct as 'infamous conduct in a professional respect'. Echoes of that wording persisted. Adultery, drug abuse, alcoholism and fraud were the most common charges brought against delinquent doctors. The Privy Council acted to cast off the shackles of an earlier age. To constitute serious professional misconduct, it is no longer necessary to show that the doctor was morally blameworthy.[30] It must be demonstrated both that he fell short of the standards to be expected from his profession and that his failures were serious in nature or degree.[31] The change in language must be given substance. Disastrously incompetent doctors deserve to be disciplined.

Since 1995,[32] GMC advice to doctors clearly places the patient at centre stage. Doctors are advised that they must (*inter alia*) take suitable and prompt action to ensure adequate assessment of a patient's condition, arrange further investigation where required and refer a patient to another doctor where indicated. Doctors must recognize the limits of their own professional competence and keep their knowledge and skills up to date. Injunctions about professional competence today outnumber rules about sexual and personal conduct. Doctors are rightly instructed to respect patients' privacy and dignity and listen to their views. It is difficult to fault the theory of what constitutes good professional conduct. Yet suspicion persists that doctors who fail their patients are let off lightly. Are there any grounds for this suspicion? First a high degree of proof is demanded before a doctor will be 'convicted'.[33] The charge against the doctor must be proved beyond all reasonable doubt. This is no different from the standard pertaining in any other professional disciplinary committee, for the doctor may well stand to lose his livelihood and reputation. Current dismay at the parade of incompetent and downright dangerous doctors appearing before the GMC have resulted in calls for a lower standard of proof.

There was a further cause for disquiet. Patients' organizations complained about the small number of cases that ever reached the Professional Conduct Committee. Elaborate screening procedures sought to eliminate supposedly 'frivolous' complaints. All letters from aggrieved patients were first scrutinized by GMC staff. If a complaint relates to an NHS doctor and concerns poor practice rather than personal misconduct such as sexual misbehaviour, the patient was told that he must first pursue his complaint through the NHS complaints procedures. Only if the doctor is found culpable within the NHS system is the matter then dealt with by the GMC. The second stage within the GMC is that a complaint is examined by the Preliminary Screener. If the Preliminary Screener, a medical member of the Council consulting with a lay member, considers that there is a case to answer, the evidence is placed before the Preliminary Proceedings Committee (PPC) if evidence of professional misconduct is forthcoming. The PPC decides whether to 'commit' the doctor for a full disciplinary hearing before the Professional Conduct Committee. The numbers of complaints to the GMC continues to escalate. In 2000 the total rose by 49 per cent to 4470. About a quarter of these complaints were said to be wrongly directed and referred on to the appropriate body by the GMC. Of the remainder, 1386 were dismissed in the interim stages of the process and only 753 proceeded to a formal hearing before a GMC committee. Patients find the proportion of complaints dismissed in the early stages of the process suspicious. After the Alder Hey Inquiry sixteen doctors were referred to the GMC. In only two instances has evidence gone forward to the Preliminary Proceedings Committee. Parents whose children were the subjects of organ retention at Alder Hey are challenging the validity of GMC decision making. They and others seek greater transparency and assurances that every complaint is fully investigated.

One initiative by the GMC itself may help. Discipline used to be an all or nothing process. There was either enough evidence that the doctor has been guilty of serious professional misconduct, in which case he can be disciplined, or there was not, and he escaped scot-free. Imminent reforms allow for a 'yellow card' procedure in which the GMC could make a finding that there were serious deficiencies in the doctor's practice, issue a warning and take other appropriate action.

The GMC has sought to respond to public concerns. It has acted on a number of malpractices, notably unsafe prescribing practices. Doctors who failed to warn the parents of a child who subsequenty died of the dangers of surgery were suspended swiftly. Disregard of professional responsibilities led to erasure from the register of two doctors in 1989. In one case a hospital doctor failed twice to attend a new mother and her baby when junior doctors became concerned about their condition. When she did attend she failed to make an adequate examination of the baby, whose heart had stopped beating, and failed to take any adequate steps to resuscitate him. Two gynaecologists whose bungling left patients with permanent injury were struck off. The senior of the two British surgeons whose deficiencies were exposed at the Bristol Inquiry was struck off, as was the doctor who, as Chief Executive, failed to take action to prevent inadequate surgery continuing.[34]

The Medical (Professional Performance) Act 1995

All but the most aggrieved patients would concede that there may be doctors, just like any other professionals, who do their best but whose performance is sub-standard. There is no wilful disregard of their patient's welfare and they are not guilty of misconduct. They may in fact be unaware of their own deficiencies. The Medical (Professional Performance) Act inserted a new section 36A into the Medical Act 1983 that deals with poor performance short of misconduct. As with misconduct procedures, the process of dealing with performance complaints was labyrinthine. Performance complaints, like misconduct complaints, were first screened by GMC staff and then by the equivalent of Preliminary Screeners. If there was evidence of seriously deficient performance the complaint was referred to the Assessment Referral Committee (ARC) which decided whether to send the case on to the Committee on Professional Performance (CPP). The CPP determines whether or not seriously deficient performance has been proven. If the case is made out the CPP may suspend the doctor from the register for up to twelve months or make his registration conditional on undergoing further training or supervision for up to three years.

The whole disciplinary process is set to change dramatically.[35] The Preliminary Proceedings Committee, the Professional Conduct Committee, the Assessment Referral Committee, the Committee on Professional Performance and the Health Committee will be swept away. A new Investigation Committee will consider any allegation that a doctor is unfit to practice whether by virtue of misconduct, deficient professional performance or ill-health. If that Committee judges that there is substance in the allegation, the matter will be referred to a Fitness to Practise Panel. The Panel will have strong lay representation and broad powers to act to discipline the doctor and protect the public. The details of this new system will have to await the next edition of this book. The spirit of the enterprise is represented by an amendment to section 1 of the Medical Act 1983. A new sub-section will state plainly:

The main objective of the General Council in exercising their function is to protect, promote and maintain the health and safety of the public.[36]

Appeals to the High Court and the Council for Regulation of Health Care Professionals

Traditionally doctors had a right to appeal against any decision of the Professional Conduct Committee to the Privy Council. In 2000 sixteen doctors did so. There was a complete rehearing of the evidence. The system again was designed to ensure total fairness to the doctor. The Privy Council examined the evidence in detail, but was usually unwilling to interfere with penalties or to take a lead in condemning any particular variety of misconduct.[37] The complainant had no right of appeal if dissatisfied with the GMC decision. The Medical Act 1983 also entrusted to the Privy Council default powers to require the General Medical

Council to exercise any powers or duties conferred on it. The ability of the Privy Council to supervise medical regulation effectively has long been doubted.

The National Health Service Reform and Health Care Professions Act 2002 abolishes the role of the Privy Council. It transfers the doctor's right of appeal to the High Court.[38] Acting on proposals in both the NHS Plan and the Bristol Inquiry Report,[39] sections 25 to 29 of that Act establish the Council for the Regulation of Health Care Professionals. This Council will have over-arching powers to control the regulatory bodies of all the health care professions. Among its most important powers is the power (in section 29) to refer decisions by the GMC in disciplinary cases to the High Court. The Council can in effect appeal on a patient's behalf both against a decision that serious professional misconduct was not proven or against too lenient a penalty. The Council will become the final arbiter of medical regulation.

Doctors' responsibilities: patients' rights

The first part of this chapter focused on how doctors are regulated; how the profession itself seeks to monitor responsible practice. This is only part of the picture of medicine today. Certainly, patients want to be treated by competent, reasonable doctors. Increasingly, they also assert their own rights, especially in the context of decision-making. Patients are no longer content to be passive recipients, even of 'good' care. They want a say in what that care comprises. The pace of medical developments is such that, particularly in the fields of reproductive medicine and genetics, new questions surface daily regarding the implications of certain kinds of treatment. These may concern such issues as entitlement to treatment, patient choice of treatment, the role of the State, or the interests of commerce. How does the law begin to address patient rights in 2003?

Human rights and medicine

Medical law, Ian Kennedy and Andrew Grubb, two of England's most influential experts, declared[40] is essentially '. . . a sub-set of human rights law'. The fundamental nature of the relationship between doctors and patients amply proves their point. At stake within the realm of medical law, is my right to make my own decisions about how I live my life and how I die. My interests in privacy and in family life, in having or not having children, are central to my dealings with health professionals. So the Human Rights Act 1998 will undoubtedly affect health care law and the importance of the Act should not be under-estimated. Lord Irvine, the Lord Chancellor, reflected thus:

Which Convention rights may be relevant in the medical field? The answer here, and I suspect elsewhere, is 'more than you might guess.'[41]

The European Convention on Human Rights addresses only a limited range of rights. There is no *positive* right to health care; there is no equivalent to Article 25 in the Universal Declaration of Human Rights. For the most part what the Convention confers are *negative* rights – i.e. prohibitions against certain kinds of infringement of basic freedoms. Moreover the 1998 Human Rights Act does not (whatever the media says) incorporate the Convention into English law. It renders the Convention enforceable against *public authorities*. The Act is relevant to disputes over enforced treatment or arguments that the *government* is violating patients' privacy. Where what is at stake is a failure by the NHS to provide certain sorts of care, or concerns about allowing, for example, insurers to demand medical details about you, the utility of the Act will need to be tested. We shall see that the European Court of Rights has interpreted the Convention as imposing *positive* obligations in some cases. The extent of such positive obligations remains unclear.

Even when a patient can bring her claim squarely within the ambit of the Convention she may find that the violation of her right is found to be justified. Many Convention rights are qualified. A good example is Article 8 (1) – the right to respect for private and family life. In certain circumstances, Article 8 (2) provides that infringement of the right may be justifiable; a violation of a patient's privacy could be held justified on grounds of public health, or for the protection of health or morals, as long as that infringement is proportionate. That means that interference with the individual's right must be shown to be 'necessary in a democratic society'. Moreover, Articles of the Convention may 'contradict' each other in certain circumstances, for example, Article 2 (life) and Article 8 (privacy). Finally the jurisprudence of the European Court of Human Rights expressly endorses a doctrine oddly entitled the 'margin of appreciation'. That is, national jurisdictions will be allowed a degree of freedom in defining their own criteria of public policy (morality). English courts will still enjoy some degree of discretion to determine English views of ethical dilemmas in medicine.

Nor should you expect the European Court of Human Rights itself to be startlingly radical in relation to health care. Many European countries adopt a conservative approach to health care rights. For example, France restricts access to fertility treatment to heterosexual couples where the woman is of normal childbearing age, and Germany bans embryo research and pre-implantation diagnosis. Be wary of arguments that English law violates the Convention where a consequence would be that other European countries are also in breach. Remember that as the supreme arbiter of the Convention, the European Court of Human Rights is an international court with judges representing several jurisdictions.

It should be also noted that, in practice, English Courts have referred to and deferred to the Human Rights Convention for several years in developing the common law. The Human Rights Act does not replace or eliminate existing common law principles. Albeit the common law relating to health care has developed piecemeal, with an apparent emphasis on wrongs rather than rights, in many instances the existing law may suffice to vindicate rights endorsed in the Convention. Decisions of the English courts so far that address the Human Rights Act tend not to declare new rights but review whether the existing common law 'rights' are sufficient in the light of the Convention.

How the Human Rights Act works [42]

Understanding how the Human Rights Act works is crucially important in assessing how it may affect health care law. As we have noted, the Act does not directly incorporate the Human Rights Convention. In a claim against a private litigant, the claimant cannot sue for violation of Convention rights. The Act requires that primary and subordinate legislation be interpreted where possible in a way that is compatible with Convention rights [43] and renders it 'unlawful for a public authority to act in a way which is incompatible with a Convention right'. [44]

'Convention rights' are the fundamental rights and freedoms [45] set out in Articles 2 to 12 and 14 of the Convention, Articles 1 to 3 of the First Protocol (concerning rights to property, education and free elections) and Articles 1 and 2 of the Sixth Protocol (abolishing the death penalty). Section 11 of the Human Rights Act makes it crystal clear that Convention rights are in addition to, not in substitution for, rights and freedoms already endorsed at common law. It may seem odd that no express provision of the Act requires that judges develop the common law in a manner consistent with Convention rights. However, as noted above, English judges already, wherever possible, seek to ensure that the common law is consistent with such rights. More importantly, section 6 of the Act, which makes it unlawful for any public authority to act in a way incompatible with Convention rights, provides that courts are classified as public authorities. A judge hearing a patient's claim must, by virtue of section 6, consider compatibility with Convention rights and ensure consistency between common law and Convention rights.

Where a claim alleging violation of a Convention right involves legislation, section 3 of the Act requires any court or tribunal to seek to interpret that rule in a way that is compatible with the relevant Convention right. However, if such an interpretation is not possible, the courts are not granted powers to strike down legislation. The judicial role remains limited by doctrines of Parliamentary sovereignty.[46] Section 4(2) provides that:

If the court is satisfied that the provision is incompatible with a Convention right, it may make a declaration of that incompatibility.

The government should then act to amend legislation to 'cure' the relevant incompatibility. Section 10 enables it to do so by secondary legislation making a 'remedial order'. Failure to act to remove the stated incompatibility would give rise to a claim against the United Kingdom before the European Court of Human Rights at Strasbourg. The dissatisfied patient could bring another claim suing the government itself.

This can be illustrated by considering the controversial provisions of the Human Fertilisation and Embryology Act 1990 concerning access to fertility treatment. Section 13(5) requires that licensed clinics take account of '. . . the welfare of any child who may be born as a result of the treatment (including the need of that child for a father)'. Imagine that a single woman is denied treatment at an NHS clinic on the grounds of her lack of a male partner and/or sexual orientation. She challenges the decision as a violation of Article 8 (which requires respect for her private and family life) or Article 12 (the right to found a family). The court will first seek to interpret section 13(5) (and the HFEA Code of Practice) in a manner compatible with Convention rights. Only if (an unlikely if) the court decides that any restriction on access violates Convention rights will they issue a declaration of incompatibility forcing Ministers to amend the 1990 Act or face a claim before the Strasbourg Court. However another provision of the Human Fertilisation and Embryology Act has been the subject of a declaration of incompatibility. Section 28 (6) (b) provides that if the sperm of any man is used after his death he is not to be treated as the father of the child. Diane Blood[47] fought a long battle to be able to undergo insemination with her deceased husband's sperm. She ultimately gave birth to two sons after fertility treatment abroad. Section 28 (6) (b) meant that the boys' birth certificates recorded the father as 'unknown'. Mrs Blood and her sons succeeded in their contention that the Act violated their rights to respect for private and family life endorsed by Article 8.

For the health care professional, the most crucial element of the Act is the provision that Convention rights are directly enforceable against public authorities, and that an individual who considers that his rights have been violated by a public authority can sue for damages. Where an individual considers that a public authority has acted in breach of Convention rights, a number of rather different outcomes must be considered. First, in many cases, the self-same rights conferred by the Convention are already recognized by the law of torts. For example, Article 5 provides for a right to liberty and security and protects the citizen against arbitrary detention. The ancient tort of false imprisonment protects that same fundamental interest. A patient alleging unlawful detention in hospital may not need to resort to claiming a breach of Article 5. He can sue for false imprisonment. In determining whether his detention was lawful, the court will be mindful of the provisions of Article 5 and the jurisprudence of the European Court of Human Rights.

The position is more complex when a Convention right is not so well established in domestic law. Privacy was not,[48] though the common law is developing rapidly. The claimant might then choose to bring his claim directly under the Act alleging breach of Article 8, which requires respect for private and family life. If he elects for a Convention remedy alone, he can sue under the Act only if the defendant is a *public authority*. Were I to discover that the Department of Health was bugging my office, suing a government department would be straightforward. What if a tabloid newspaper splashed my medical history all over its front page? There is an argument[49] that the newspaper, too, might be classified as a public authority, for section 6(3)(b) classifies as a public authority '*any person certain of whose functions are functions of a public nature*'.

Suppose, however, a private individual, a colleague, for example, invades my privacy by steaming open my private correspondence and finds letters from my doctors revealing an embarrassing medical complaint. What then? In practical terms, often some common law remedy may be found within which to frame a cause of action to be reinforced by reference to Convention rights. The 'snooper' who peers through windows or opens my mail could be liable for harassment or trespass to goods. If no common law remedy can be identified, and the defendant appears to be immune from liability, Article 6 of the Convention comes into play. Article 6 grants a right that, in determination of his civil rights and obligations, everyone is entitled to a fair trial. It grants a right of access to justice. If no remedy for violation of Article 8 (right to privacy) appears to exist, the court must in effect develop a remedy (as the Court of Appeal at times seems to have sought to do in relation to privacy),[50] or it will be acting unlawfully in failing to implement Article 8.

Article 6 will affect the development of the English law in two ways. Relatively rarely, Article 6 will come into play because the common law offers *no* remedy for violation of a Convention right. More commonly, the Article will be invoked in order to overcome some restriction on the claimant's common law right. The common law recognizes a right to life and freedom from bodily harm. However, consider the following case. It is a well-established principle of common law that there is no duty to be a 'Good Samaritan'. A doctor who passes by and does nothing to help a road accident victim commits no tort. Could the victim's family argue that the absence of any obligation to rescue violated their relative's right to life (under Article 2)? Long established principles of common law may have to be revisited and revised.

Who can be sued?

As we have seen, the Human Rights Act does not define public authority. Section 6(3) provides that public authority includes: (a) a court or tribunal, and (b) any person certain of whose functions are of a public nature. What does this mean for the NHS? National Health Service Trusts, including Primary Care Trusts, are public authorities. So are bodies such as MRECs (Multi-Research Ethics Committees) and LRECs (Local Research Ethics Committees). Quangos such as HFEA (Human Fertilization and Embryology Authority) are equally clearly public authorities, as are regulatory bodies such as the GMC. Individual health professionals, doctors and nurses working within the NHS are performing functions of a public nature and face potential claims under the Act (although normally such claims would be brought against their employer). GPs and other non-employed NHS personnel might be more directly in the firing line.

Professionals in private practice and private hospitals raise tricky questions. Wadham and Mountfield[51] say rightly, 'Doctors would be public authorities in relation to their NHS functions, but not in relation to their private patients . . .' So if patient A contracts with Dr B to carry out surgery at Clinic C paying out of his own pocket, or via private health insurers, the relationship is entirely private. However, if patient A later sues Dr B or Clinic C, in determining the nature of his redress the court must seek to develop the common law consistently with the Convention on Human Rights. If this is not possible, patient A may have redress against the government under Article 6 for violation of his right to a fair trial to determine his civil rights and obligations. Do private clinics treating NHS patients perform functions of a public nature? It has been held that a charity responsible for providing a home and care paid for by the local authority for a number of disabled people was not a public authority for the purpose of the Human Rights Act. It was created by private individuals. It was not obliged to accept publicly funded residents nor was it closely regulated by the State.[52] This limited definition of public functions will severely restrict the scope of the Act.

Who can sue?

Only a person who is a 'victim' of an alleged violation of the Convention can bring a claim under the 1998 Act. The concept of victim derives from the Convention and jurisprudence of the ECHR. A victim must be actually and directly affected by the act or omission that is the subject of the complaint. There is no direct provision for interest groups to sue to vindicate Convention rights.

What does this mean in practice? Obviously a claimant who is detained in hospital against her will can ground a claim on Article 5 (although a claim in false imprisonment will suffice). A person who alleges that he has been experimented on without consent may have a claim under Article 3 (prohibiting inhuman or degrading treatment) or Article 8. However, for individuals to fund claims about important principles may be difficult. Interest groups will want to use the Convention to challenge and change existing law (for example the ban on voluntary euthanasia). Will they be able to do so, given that interest groups cannot sue as groups?

It is not necessary to show that a claimant has actually already suffered from the consequences of an alleged violation. 'Victims' need only show a real risk of being directly affected by a breach. Gay men in Northern Ireland were allowed to challenge laws criminalizing all homosexual conduct.[53] Abortion centre counsellors acting with women wishing to receive advice successfully challenged Irish laws prohibiting dissemination of any information about abortion.[54] Representative interest groups *involving groups of victims* are able to gain standing under the Act.

Convention rights

Reference will be made to relevant Convention rights throughout the chapters that follow. All that I do now is give a brief overview of those Convention rights which I judge are likely to have the most significant impact in the rights and obligations of doctors and patients in England.

Article 2 provides that 'Everyone's right to life shall be protected by law.' This might be invoked to challenge a number of entrenched principles of English law. Consider the following question. Could a patient whose life (health) is endangered by refusal of treatment (e.g. denied expensive chemotherapy) use Article 2 to obtain a court order demanding that he be given priority in treatment? Article 2 does impose on the State a *positive* obligation to intervene to protect people whose lives are at real and immediate risk.[55] Assuming that this is the case, what limits may or must be placed on such a right? When does such a right crystallize? Is it an absolute right entitling the patient to any possible treatment? How are the competing rights of other patients to be addressed? Remember that such a right would necessarily impose an obligation to provide *publicly funded* care. The European Court of Human Rights has made it clear that where protection from disease requires use of State resources, individual countries are allowed considerable freedom to assess their own aims and priorities.[56]

Article 2 will also affect legal issues surrounding allowing patients to die. It was suggested that Article 2 might render decisions that it is lawful to withhold/withdraw treatment unlawful in certain circumstances, in particular that Article 2 might alter the law on withdrawing artificial nutrition and hydration from patients in persistent vegetative state.[57] However in *NHS Trust* v. *M.*,[58] the President of the Family Division (Elizabeth Butler Sloss P.) has ruled that Article 2 does not impose an obligation to prolong life in such cases.

Finally could Article 2 affect laws permitting abortion or case-law denying foetuses any legal personality? Could the judgment in *St George's Healthcare NHS Trust* v. *S.*[59] be subjected to a foetal life challenge? Refusing to strike down national abortion laws, the European Commission has not applied Article 2 to foetuses in the first trimester of pregnancy and ruled that states have discretion in this delicate area of policy. There has (to my knowledge) been no decision relating to viable foetuses and the ECHR has rejected arguments that decisions on termination are entirely within the sphere of private life (Article 8).[60]

Article 3 provides that 'No one shall be subjected to torture or inhuman or degrading treatment or punishment.' It has been suggested that this could be used to challenge failure to provide treatment or poor quality treatment. Does being left on a trolley constitute degrading treatment? It seems unlikely.[61] We should never forget the original evils that the Convention was framed to prevent.

Are laws prohibiting voluntary euthanasia contrary to Article 3? An argument might be framed linking Articles 3 and 8. The case could be put, for example, that a patient dying of some terrible degenerative disease or suffering acute pain from terminal cancer was, by being denied the option of active euthanasia, subjected to inhuman and degrading treatment, contrary to Article 3. Moreover if her doctor, or some other third party, was willing to help her die preventing patient and doctor implementing her choice violated her privacy contrary to Article 8. We shall see that when Diane Pretty,[62] a woman dying of motor neurone disease, sought to invoke Articles 3 and 8 to support her claim that her husband should be granted immunity from prosecution if he helped her to commit suicide, her claim failed. The House of Lords refused to interpret Article 3 in such a way as to affirm the right to die with dignity. Her further appeal to the Strasbourg Court also failed.[63]

Article 3 will raise other questions about our existing common law. Might certain forms of non-consensual treatment fall foul of Article 3?[64] Consider cases relating to feeding anorexic patients. What effect might Article 3 have on principles relating to consent to clinical research and research involving patients incapable of giving consent?

The relevant parts of Article 5 provide:

Everyone has the right to liberty and security of person. No one shall be deprived of his liberty save in the following cases and in accordance with a procedure prescribed by law . . .

(f) the lawful detention of persons for the prevention of the spreading of infectious diseases, or persons of unsound mind, alcoholics or drug addicts or vagrants.

I shall argue later that Article 5 (f) will radically affect common law powers to detain/treat mentally incapacitated patients.[65]

Article 6 could have significant effect on malpractice claims. It provides that:

In the determination of his civil rights or obligations or of any criminal charge against him, everyone is entitled to a fair and public hearing within a reasonable time by an independent and impartial tribunal established by law.

Article 6 could impede attempts to reduce litigation, for example excluding any right to sue within a no-fault scheme.[66] Might Article 6 include the rights of health professionals facing disciplinary procedures?[67]

Article 8 will have far-reaching effects. Article 8 (1) provides: 'Everyone has the right to respect for his private and family life, his home and his correspondence.' Note the wording, the right is a right to *respect*. Does that connote an absolute claim to privacy? As with Article 2, the question arises as to what kind of obligations Article 8 creates. Does it impose positive obligations on the State to act to promote a right to privacy or simply a duty not to interfere with privacy?[68] It is clear that some sort of positive obligation is imposed by Article 8. Therefore we have to define the parameters of private and family life. Prohibition of contraception, for example, obviously constitutes an interference with that right as it involves intimate relationships. However, does the regulation of third parties involved in assisted conception fall into the same category?

In some cases one person's right to private life may conflict with another's right to family life. Imagine person A tests positively for an inherited form of bowel cancer. A's children have a one in four chance of inheriting the condition also, but A refuses to inform her estranged daughter of this possibility. Does respecting A's privacy violate her daughter's right to family life or her right to life under Article 2?

Most excitingly, could Article 8 be used to prevent certain information ever being sought from individuals? The government recently conceded that insurers could require applicants for insurance to give results of certain genetic tests, including tests for Huntington's Chorea. Does such a policy violate Article 8? Could it be justified under Article

8(2)? Article 8(2) graphically illustrates the qualified nature of certain Convention rights. It provides:

There shall be no interference by a public authority with the exercise of this right except such as is in accordance with the law and is necessary in a democratic society in the interests of national security, public safety or the economic well-being of the country, for the prevention of disorder or crime, for the protection of health or morals, or for the protection of the rights and freedoms of others.

Note the width of potential exceptions to Article 8 (1).[69] The jurisprudence of the European court illustrates both the complexity of Article 8 and judicial conservation on the part of the ECHR.[70]

Article 9 protects religious freedom providing:

Everyone has the right to freedom of thought, conscience and religion; this right includes freedom to change his religion or belief and freedom, either alone or in community with others and in public or private, to manifest his religion or belief, in worship, teaching, practice and observance.

Freedom to manifest one's religion or beliefs shall be subject only to such limitations as are prescribed by law and are necessary in a democratic society in the interests of public safety, for the protection of public order, health or morals, *or for the protection of the rights and freedoms of others.*

Nor must Article 10 be overlooked. Article 10 guarantees freedom of expression, a right embracing freedom of the press. All too often Articles 8 and 10 conflict and the courts must embark on a delicate balancing exercise.[71]

As we shall see, English courts have on a number of occasions overruled parental objections to treatment of their children that runs contrary to their faith. The classic example is where a court orders that a blood transfusion is given to a child of Jehovah's Witness parents. The parents might argue that requiring that their child undergo a transfusion violates the family's religious freedom and their right to respect for their family life (Article 8). Do the rights of the child, especially her right to life under Article 2, trump the parents' claims?

Finally Article 12 might be thought to guarantee a right to reproduce as it states that:

Men and women of marriageable age have the right to marry and found a family according to the national laws governing the exercise of that right.

Could Article 12 be used to challenge limitations on access to fertility treatment? For example, refusals to treat a single woman or a lesbian couple? First, consider whether Article 12 confers a single right to marry and (having married) found a family, or does it confer two discrete and separate rights, the right to marry and the right to found a family (irrespective of marital status)? If it is the latter then perhaps Article 12 could be used in conjunction with Articles 8 and 14 (prohibition of discrimination) to challenge the exclusion of single parents or gay couples from access to fertility treatment.

The Convention on Human Rights and Biomedicine

It will be apparent that patients' rights are not centre-stage in the European Convention on Human Rights. To raise a question about patients' rights, the relevant dispute must somehow be fitted into the pigeonhole of general rights. A further European convention, the European Convention on Human Rights and Biomedicine,[72] the Bioethics Convention, directly addresses doctor/patient relationships. This convention, agreed in 1997 by states party to the Human Rights Convention, has not been signed or ratified by the United Kingdom. Even if and when the United Kingdom does ratify this convention it will not have direct force. A patient will not be able to sue for violation of a right granted by the convention. Nor is there any right of individual petition to the European Court of Human Rights at Strasbourg. None the less, articles of the Human Rights Convention may be interpreted with reference to the much fuller explanations and definitions of human rights offered in the Bioethics Convention.

Access to health care[73]

If the European Convention on Human Rights fails to endorse a direct unequivocal right to health care, can we construct such a right from other sources? Before looking at the case-law, let us reflect for a moment what a right to health care might involve. Article 25 of the Universal Declaration of Human Rights provides:

Everyone has the right to a standard of living adequate for the health and well being of himself and his family including food, clothing and medical care.

Other rights within Article 25 can be easily defined and quantified. Basic needs for food and clothing differ little from one person to another. Desires may vary widely, but no one would argue that I have a fundamental human right to caviar and champagne every day. Basic needs for medical care vary widely. A baby born prematurely at twenty-four weeks may consume as much health care resource in his first week of life as others do in a lifetime. What constitutes need is hotly debated. Treatment for pneumonia falls comfortably into a definition of need. Where would you place surgery to eliminate varicose veins? What if my restricted height causes me emotional distress and stops me becoming an air stewardess? Do I need 'treatment' to make me taller? Note the World Health Organization definition of health as '. . . a state of complete physical, mental and social well-being and not just the absence of disease or infirmity'. What would a right to health so defined involve and whose duty is it to ensure that I enjoy such health?

Ultimate responsibility for the health of the NHS lies with the Secretary of State for Health. The National Health Service Act 1977 provides in section 1:

It is the Secretary of State's duty to continue the promotion in England and Wales of a comprehensive health service designed to secure improvement:

(a) in the physical and mental health of people of those countries and
(b) in the prevention, diagnosis and treatment of illness and for that purpose to provide or secure effective provision of services in accordance with the Act.

Section 3 of the Act imposes on the Secretary of State a further duty to provide, to such extent as he considers necessary to meet all reasonable requirements, services including hospital accommodation, medical, dental, nursing and ambulance services and such other services as are required for the diagnosis and treatment of illness. High-sounding sentiments and expressions of political will, but is there any legal significance in this 'duty' imposed on the Secretary of State? Do patients have a right to health care? The case-law was unpromising. Judges have been wary of involving the courts in disputes over allocation of resources or priorities for treatment. Three developments signal change. First, there are signs of greater judicial activity in relation to access to health care. Second, the European Court of Justice has established a limited right to access to other national health systems if your own cannot provide the care you need without undue delay. Finally, once again government ministers are offering 'guarantees' of speedier, fairer treatment.

I will look first at the 'unpromising' case-law. In 1979 four patients who had spent long periods vainly awaiting hip-replacement surgery went to court alleging that the Secretary of State had failed in his duty to promote a comprehensive health service and to provide hospital accommodation and facilities for orthopaedic surgery. The patients alleged that their period on the waiting list was longer than was medically advisable, and that their wait resulted from a shortage of facilities, caused in part by a decision not to build a new hospital block on the grounds of cost. The patients asked for an order compelling the Secretary of State to act, and for compensation for their pain and suffering. The Court of Appeal[74] held that the financial constraints to which the Secretary of State was subject had to be considered in assessing what amounts to reasonable requirements for hospital and medical services; and that the decision as to what was required was for the Secretary of State, and the court could intervene only where a Secretary of State acted utterly unreasonably so as to frustrate the policy of the Act. An individual patient could not claim damages from the Secretary of State for pain and suffering. The patients lost the immediate legal battle, but they gained valuable publicity. The courts did not entirely abdicate control over the Secretary of State. A public-spirited patient, resigned to getting no damages himself, could (by way of an application for judicial review) challenge a Secretary of State whom he alleges had totally subverted the health service, for example one using his position and powers exclusively to benefit private medicine at the expense of the NHS. Chances of success are not high, and of course the government of the day could always change the law, but they can be made to do it openly and not be permitted to pay lip service to a duty to a health service that may have been abandoned.

None the less, the Court of Appeal clearly rejected any legally enforceable right to health care actionable by a patient for his own benefit. Does any such right exist against local health providers? In 1987 the parents of two sick babies who needed cardiac surgery sought to enforce such a right on their sons' behalf. They applied to the Divisional Court for a court order that their sons be operated on. The health authority explained that lack of resources and lack of trained nurses meant that each baby kept missing out on his operation to other more urgent cases. The court refused to make an order that the operation be carried out immediately.[75] The parents had no right to demand immediate treatment for their sons.

The health authority could do only what was reasonable within their limited resources, human and financial. It is difficult to see what else the court could have done in these cases. The court could not provide the resources needed to operate on all sick babies. In effect, the judges were being asked to decide that baby X needed surgery more urgently than baby Y, and judges are not qualified to make clinical judgements.

In *R* v. *Cambridge District Health Authority ex p. B.*[76] the Court of Appeal again demonstrated its reluctance to become involved in questions of allocation of resources. B was a ten-year-old girl suffering from non-Hodgkin's lymphoma. In 1994 she received a bone marrow transplant from her sister. In 1995 she became ill again. The doctors treating her considered no further treatment should be given to prolong B's life. B's father was advised that with further intensive chemotherapy, B stood a 10 to 20 per cent chance of remission sufficient to allow a second bone marrow transplant to be attempted. The transplant itself stood a 10 to 20 per cent chance of success offering B at best a 4 per cent chance of recovery. The treatment package would cost about £75,000 and the health authority refused to fund B's treatment. They argued that such 'experimental' treatment was not in B's best interests and that given the minimal prospects of success the cost could not be justified. Other demands on their limited budget took priority.

The trial judge, Laws J, was not convinced by the authority's case. He issued an order requiring the authority to reconsider the evidence in support of their decision not to treat B. They must do more than 'merely toll the bell of tight resources'. The authority appealed. The Court of Appeal backed them unequivocally, rejecting Laws J's attempt to require greater transparency in decisions about allocating resources.

The appeal court decision rested largely on clinical grounds, on evidence from the doctors that the aggressive treatment proposed was not in B's interests, despite the contrary view of B's father and the child herself. Sir Thomas Bingham MR, however, summed up judicial attitudes to problems in allocation of health care resources when he commented:

Difficult and agonizing judgements have to be made as to how a limited budget is best allocated to the maximum advantage of the maximum of patients. That is not a judgement which the court can make. In my judgement, it is not something that a health authority can be fairly criticized for not advancing before the court.

Will the courts ever intervene to question decisions about whom to treat or what treatment patients may be entitled to? Judges do assert the power to assess the reasonableness of decision-making by NHS bodies, just as they will hold other public bodies to account for the reasonableness of their decision-making processes. In *R* v. *St Mary's Hospital Ethical Committee ex p. Harriott*,[77] Mrs Harriott had been refused treatment by the IVF (test-tube baby) unit. The unit's informal ethical advisory committee had supported the doctors' decision not to treat Mrs Harriott because she had been rejected by the local social services department as a potential adoptive or foster mother and because she had convictions for prostitution offences. She challenged their decision. The judge held that the grounds for refusing her treatment were lawful. But he said refusal of treatment on *non-medical* grounds could be reviewed by a court. It would be unlawful to reject a patient because of her race or religion or other irrelevant grounds. A patient denied renal dialysis or surgery because the consultant in charge refuses to treat divorced people, or New Labour Party members, might well have a remedy. However, judges, it must be remembered, tend to be conservative. In *R* v. *Sheffield Health Authority ex p. Seale*[78] the judge refused to interfere with the health authority's decision to refuse fertility treatment to older women, defined as any woman over 35.

Successful challenges to decisions regarding provision of health care have so far required that patients identify some obvious flaw in the decision-making process. In *R.* v. *North Derbyshire Health Authority ex p. Fisher*[79] the health authority refused to fund the costly drug beta interferon for any patient with multiple sclerosis. They operated a blanket ban on provision of the drug, failed to make any assessment of individual patients' needs and ignored a circular from the Department of Health advising that serious consideration be given to providing beta interferon to certain categories of patients with multiple sclerosis. The judge held that the authority failed to take a reasoned decision after consideration of all the relevant factors.

The most notable 'victory' for patients denied access to treatment is found in *R* v *North West Lancashire Health Authority ex p. A. & B.*[80] The defendant health authority refused to pay for gender-reassignment surgery for the applicants. Such surgery was classified by the authority as a low priority along with cosmetic procedures such as facelifts or hair transplants. Transsexuals should be provided with psychiatric and psychological services but the authority would not 'commission drug

treatment or surgery that is intended to give patients the physical characteristics of the opposite gender'. Statements in the policy document
about exceptional cases based on overwhelming clinical need made it
abundantly clear that in reality such a case would never be conceded. No
one would be a sufficiently exceptional case to qualify. The Court of
Appeal quashed the decision to refuse treatment to the applicant as 'irrational'. The authority had failed to evaluate the medical evidence relating to transexuality. They paid lip service to the notion that the applicant's
condition constituted illness, but dismissed forms of effective treatment
without proper consideration. The authority did not:

... in truth treat transexualism as an illness, but as an attitude or state of mind
which does not warrant medical treatment ... [T]he ostensible provision that
it makes for exceptions in individual cases and its manner of considering them
amount effectively to the operation of a 'blanket policy' against funding treatment because it does not believe in such treatment.

The courts are beginning to show themselves prepared to scrutinize
the process by which health care providers make decisions about what
kinds of treatment they will provide and who will have access to such
treatment. However, if the health care provider can demonstrate that it
has fully considered the case made to it and addressed all the relevant
considerations but ultimately determined that other treatments and other
claims must be given priority, courts remain unlikely to intervene. Nor
is going to court likely to take you to the head of the waiting list.

Much publicity was given to the decision of the European Court of
Justice[81] that if a patient living in one member state of the European
Union faced undue delay in receiving treatment in his home country, his
state insurance system must be prepared to pay for him to have treatment in another member state where treatment is available more speedily. A patient forced to wait years for a hip-replacement in England might
demand to be sent to Germany, where such surgery can be performed
within weeks. Do we now enjoy a 'European' right to health care? Several
questions bedevil any such 'right'. What constitutes 'undue delay' remains
undefined. Treatment must be normal; a treatment tried and tested by
international medical science. Nor is it clear what expenses the NHS
must meet. Assume I am to have my hip replacement in Germany. The
NHS must pay for the surgery and it seems will pay my air fare. What
about the cost of my husband accompanying me? Who will cover child-
care at home? Even if treatment in Europe is generously funded, for most

people it will be far from ideal. Patients complain if they have to have their operation in a different city a short distance from their home. The cost to the NHS of sending patients abroad will drain resources here and exacerbate existing difficulties.

Unsurprisingly the government is exploring other strategies. Strict limits are placed on waiting times. A concordat with the private sector seeks to allow the NHS to clear waiting lists by resort to the private sector. If a patient has to wait more than the prescribed maximum time for treatment, the NHS should pay for that treatment in the private sector. NHS hospital trusts with waiting lists exceeding government targets will be penalized. Some doctors are dubious about strategies based on waiting lists. Hospitals anxious to avoid sanctions will find themselves treating less urgent cases first just because that patient has been waiting longer. 'Guarantees' of timely treatment or surgery raise other questions too. Unless enshrined in statute, will this still fall short of a legal *right* to health care? Against whom might any right be enforceable? The Health Care Act 1999 moves responsibility for arranging NHS care, primary or secondary care to Primary Care Trusts.[82] Section 18 of the 1999 Act imposes a duty of quality:

It is the duty of each Health Authority, Primary Care Trust and NHS Trust to put and keep in place arrangements for the purpose of monitoring and improving the quality of health care which it provides to individuals.

Failure to address provision of timely treatment on the part of a PCT is an obvious breach of section 18. Good care is timely care. Will the courts offer a remedy to patients aggrieved by the failure of their PCT to provide timely treatment, or to provide the treatment of their choice? The remedy many patients may seek is compensation. Imagine that a patient is told that she will have to wait another twelve months for her hip replacement, in contravention of Department of Health guidelines. She borrows money from the bank and pays £8000 to have her operation privately. If she is to recover that sum from her PCT, the courts will have to overrule *ex p. Hincks* and allow a claim for breach of statutory duty against the NHS. Once again money to compensate patients will deplete funds to treat patients. If the patient cannot raise the costs of private treatment herself will the court grant an order requiring the PCT to arrange her operation immediately, if need be in the private sector, but paid for by the NHS? Perhaps they may. A court will at least require from a PCT a cogent explanation for delay. This scenario does not involve a judge saying, treat this patient and not some other patient in greater need. It entails a court requiring the PCT, a public body, to establish that in *not* using the powers they have to arrange this patient's care, they acted *reasonably*. Budgets remain relevant factors. A right to treatment 'on demand' is unlikely to emerge. What we may see develop in the next few years is a legal right to an equitable process of decision-making about NHS treatment. In other contexts, one positive impact of the Human Rights Act has been to encourage the judges to scrutinize public authority decisions more vigorously, particularly where life may be at stake.[83]

2

Medicine, Moral Dilemmas
and the Law

Medical ethics makes news today but it is far from new. From the formulation of the Hippocratic Oath in Ancient Greece to the present day, doctors have debated among themselves the codes of conduct that should govern the art of healing. These days philosophers, theologians, lawyers and journalists insist on joining the debate. Outside interest, or interference as doctors sometimes see it, is not new either. Hippocrates was a philosopher. The Church through the centuries has asserted its right to pronounce on medical matters of spiritual import, such as abortion and euthanasia, and to uphold the sanctity of life.

The Hippocratic Oath makes interesting reading. Its first premise is that the doctor owes loyalty to his teachers and his brethren. Obligations to exercise skill for the benefit of patients' health come second. Abortion, direct euthanasia and abetting suicide are prohibited. Improper sexual relations with patients are banned. Confidentiality in all dealings with patients is imposed. In 2500 years these basic precepts of good medical practice changed little. Dramatic changes in the kinds of moral and ethical problems confronting the doctor came only in the last fifty years. The art of the Greek philosopher physician became a science for many practitioners. Science has given the doctor tools to work marvels undreamed of by earlier generations. Women whose blocked Fallopian tubes prevent natural conception can be offered the hope of a test-tube baby. Women who have never ovulated can become mothers via egg donation. Creating a human clone looks technically feasible now mammalian cloning has proved possible. Babies born with spina bifida and other disabling handicaps can be saved from early death by delicate and complex surgery. Some forms of foetal handicap are correctable by surgery carried out while the baby is still in the womb, and certain genetic disorders may be curable by means of genetic manipulation of the embryo. Ventilators keep alive accident victims whose heart and lungs have given up. Dialysis and transplant surgery save kidney, liver and heart patients from certain death. The list of technological miracles is endless. They have placed in the hands of the doctors powers that humanity once ascribed to God alone.

Technological progress has been matched by social change. People are less willing to accept without question the decisions of those who exercise power, be they judges, politicians or doctors. Paternalism is out of fashion. Feminists ask why doctors should determine which infertile women receive treatment. Lawyers and philosophers, not to mention parents, wonder why the doctor is best qualified to judge whether a damaged baby's quality of life is such as to make life-saving surgery desirable. The power of the doctor to end life, whether by switching off a ventilator or by deciding not to give a patient a place in a dialysis unit, disturbs us all. These moral dilemmas are just as acutely felt by doctors. Their difficulties are accentuated by the fact that the new technology cannot be made available to all those in need. There is just not enough money or resources in the National Health Service.[1] Above all, the medical profession in 2003 faces a society more deeply divided on virtually every moral question than ever before. The public demands a say in medical decision making on sensitive ethical issues. Yet from the hot potato of whether doctors should help lesbians to have children by artificial insemination, through the debates on abortion to euthanasia, the doctor who seeks guidance from public opinion will discover division, bitterness and confusion.

Questions of medical ethics arise throughout the whole field of medical practice. Increasingly medical students receive education in ethics as an integral part of their studies. Several texts address medical ethics in detail.[2] The ethics of the doctor/patient relationship are touched on throughout this book, but it is not and does not purport to be a book about medical ethics. Two fundamental issues of ethics do need to be introduced at this juncture, however. Are ethics more than etiquette? How does society today understand and implement concepts of the sanctity of human life?

Ethics not etiquette

Were you to peruse the ethical guidance provided for doctors in the nineteenth and early twentieth centuries, what you might find would have scant relationship to what most of us today think of as medical ethics.

Two sorts of advice predominated. First, the physician was envisaged as an English gentleman.[3] As long as he behaved in a gentlemanly and benevolent fashion, his own conscience and integrity would guide him towards ethical solutions in dilemmas surrounding how to treat a patient.[4] Formal advice from professional bodies, notably the GMC, offered somewhat more concrete advice. Doctors were prohibited from sexual relationships with their patients or their patients' wives. They should not take advantage of their privileged access to patients' homes. They must avoid misuse of alcohol or drugs. They were not to tout for custom, nor must they disparage other doctors. They must refrain from any sort of collaboration with unqualified practitioners.[5] Both sorts of advice centred on gentlemanly behaviour and without doubt some of the injunctions issued in earlier days had beneficial effects on patient care. However, what was styled ethics had at its core a code of etiquette. Doctors should conduct themselves in a particular way, they should show professional solidarity and practise benevolent paternalism.

The scale of grossly unethical abuse of medicine revealed in the wake of the Second World War destroyed any complacent culture of paternalist medicine. A series of codes of medical ethics were promulgated internationally. Moral philosophers began to subject medicine to a much more rigorous critical analysis. 'Critical' medical ethics emerged offering a framework within which ethical dilemmas could be the subject of debate and reflection. Beauchamp and Childress's seminal book *Principles of Biomedical Ethics* proved especially influential.[6]

Beauchamp and Childress formulated four basic principles as a framework for ethical conduct. The four principles are now a fashionable subject for attack by modern ethicists.[7] They do not and never sought to provide easy answers to particular questions or to offer a comprehensive ethical analysis. They do, as Gillon says,[8] '. . . help us bring more order, consistency and understanding to our medico-moral judgements'. The influence of the four principles and their delicate relationship with legal principles make it important that in any study of the law relating to health care at least a brief account is given of the four principles – autonomy, beneficence, non-maleficence and justice.

Respect for autonomy – self-determination

Autonomy literally means self-rule, as opposed to heteronomy – rule by others. Respect for autonomy demands that we respect autonomous choices made by other people. Crude paternalism is the antithesis of respect for autonomy. Non-consensual treatment of a patient, even for her own good, violates her autonomy. Gradually, as we shall see in Chapters 4 and 5, English law via principles governing consent to treatment has clothed the moral principle of autonomy in legal reality.

Respect for autonomy does not demand unthinking deference to any choice made by another human being. To demand respect, a choice must be a maximally autonomous choice – an informed and free choice made by someone capable of making such a choice. A very young child will 'choose' not to go to the dentist and 'choose' not to be injected with antibiotics. His choice will be dictated by the nastiness of the procedure involved. He is not able to weigh the benefits of good dental care, or antibiotics to cure his streptococcal infection, against the immediate unpleasantness. An older person with severe mental disabilities may be similarly unable to make any real choice. A paranoid schizophrenic may be constrained by his 'voices' to refuse treatment because he knows that the doctor is Satan. The preferences expressed in such cases are not autonomous choices.

In setting boundaries of mental capacity the law struggles with the concept of what constitutes an autonomous choice. The temptation is strong to regard a choice you disagree with as non-autonomous. The outcome of the choice should be irrelevant. A woman who rejects surgery for breast cancer because she cannot tolerate any mutilation of her breast makes a decision that I see as bizarre. The Jehovah's Witness rejecting blood transfusion does so on the basis of an interpretation of the Bible that I do not share. However, their choices remain autonomous choices, made by people able to reason and on the basis of adequate information.

Beneficence – do good

An injunction to act beneficently requires doctors to frame their actions to benefit their patients. The needs of the patient should be the professional's pre-eminent concern. Patients should never be a means to an end. But what does such a pious hope mean in practice? The ethics of clinical research have attracted an undue amount of philosophical attention. The failure of doctors to act beneficently and to treat human subjects as little more than research tools explains that emphasis on research ethics. Ethical professionals put the individual's welfare first even if to do so conflicts with their own interests.

Another problem with beneficence might be that it could be seen as just another name for paternalism. The beneficent doctor does what he thinks is best for me. If natural childbirth is dangerous for me and the child I carry, must the beneficent doctor perform a Caesarian section whether I like it or not? The answer is no because beneficence demands respect for autonomy. The professional should offer his judgement on what is good for me, but ultimately he must accept *my* decisions on what is good for me.

Translating the ethical imperative of beneficence into legal principle is tricky. The law imposes a duty of care owed by doctor to patients. That duty, however, generally involves not doing me any harm. English law does not impose any duty to be a Good Samaritan. Once a patient is admitted to hospital, staff must provide him with adequate and competent care. However, a doctor or nurse who witnesses a road accident but passes by on the other side commits no legal wrong. Yet if she fails to help when she could easily do so, she fails to act beneficently.

Beneficence illustrates an important point about law and ethics. Ethics demands a higher standard of behaviour than the law requires. A competent surgeon who removes my gallstones without mishap fulfils his legal duty of care. If he dismisses my complaints of pain with scorn, makes me feel like a child, and treats me as just another patient number, is he acting ethically?

Non-maleficence – do no harm

Raanan Gillon[9] says of non-maleficence: 'Among the shibboleths of traditional medical ethics is the injunction *Primum non nocere* – first (or above all) do no harm'. Gillon does not challenge the principle of non-maleficence as such. Its importance is self-evident; what he rightly points out is that this principle cannot be absolute. Medicine often involves doing harm. Removing an inflamed appendix inevitably involves a degree of harm – risk, pain and scarring. The benefits obviously outweigh the harm in that case. Practices that avoid all risk have ultimately done more harm than good. Sometimes agonizing dilemmas confront us as was the case in relation to the conjoined twins, Jodie and Mary, separated by surgeons in Manchester in 2000.[10] Without surgery both girls would die. Separating Mary from her sister would and did result in her death. Doing no harm to Mary meant doing harm to Jodie.

Justice[11]

'[T]he idea that justice is a moral issue that doctors can properly ignore is clearly mistaken.'[12] Few would dissent from a proposition that doctors should treat patients justly. Justice in this context might be interpreted as meaning that patients are entitled to be treated fairly and equally by their doctors. The Queen should be treated no differently from a tramp brought into casualty after he is found unconscious in a doorway. Health professionals should not show preference for patients who enjoy a particular status or provide sub-standard care for patients of whom they disapprove.

Alas justice is much more complex than this. Within the NHS resources are limited. Not every treatment can be offered to every patient who may derive clinical benefit from such treatment. Imagine that the Queen and the tramp both needed a liver transplant. The demand for donor livers far exceeds supply. How should a just decision be made about whether either of them should receive a transplant? The Queen is seventy-six but in otherwise good health. The tramp is thirty-five, but an alcoholic. His general health is poor. Other contenders compete for livers, a number of them younger than the Queen and in better health than the tramp.

We might agree then the Queen should not get a transplant just because she is the Queen.[13] We might agree that the tramp should not be refused a transplant just because he is a tramp. Is it relevant that if he continues to drink after surgery, the transplant is likely to fail? Even if he overcame his addiction his lifestyle may militate against success. Poor diet and no settled home will make it difficult for him to comply with the post-operative regime necessary to avoid rejection of the donor liver. There is a lively debate about how far lifestyle and/or 'fault' should affect access to NHS resources.[14]

The complexity of notions of justice in health care have resulted in health economists entering the debate. They have advanced the merits of an exercise based on 'quality adjusted life years' (QALYs). QALYs embody an attempt to provide an objective framework to assess how society should determine priorities for treatment. The QALYs approach seeks to ascertain:[15]

... (i) to what extent, and for how long, will a treatment improve the quality of a patient's life and (ii) how much does the treatment cost. In this way it seeks to compare the cost of generating QALYs, regardless of the particular treatment in question. In this theory, there is a sliding scale on which each year of full health counts as one, and each year of declining health counts as less than one; death scores 0. Thus, if the improvement in health after treatment is both significant and long lasting the patient accumulates units and scores high on the quality of life measure. If the treatment is relatively inexpensive, then the cost per unit of quality is low. The theory favours treatment which achieves the greatest increase in the quality of life, over the longer period for the least cost.

Both the Queen and the tramp may do badly on a QALY test. Life post-transplant is unlikely to generate years of full health for anyone. Let us award the Queen ten years[16] of 0.75 health and the tramp twenty years at 0.25 health, the cost being the same for both patients. The Queen scores 7.5; the tramp scores 5; both will almost certainly lose out to younger, fitter patients. QALYs then triggers another question. Should anyone get a liver transplant? Compare liver transplants with hip replacements. A woman of fifty having a hip replacement for arthritis may generate 15 to 20 QALYs at lower cost. Yet arthritis is not life-threatening. It is perhaps not surprising then, as we have seen, that the English courts shy away from active involvement in questions of health resources.

To whom (or what) do we owe ethical obligations?[17]

All too often principles of medical ethics conflict. If an obstetrician performs a Caesarian section without the woman's consent, she violates her autonomy. If she does not intervene and the child dies or is born severely disabled, she has done harm to the child. Withdrawing treatment from a patient in a persistent vegetative state may be seen to harm him. Yet continuing to keep him alive can equally be classified as harming him. Money spent on sustaining such a patient over several years deprives others of treatment in a cash-strapped NHS. Keeping X alive may be an injustice to Y. The trump card invoked to demand that the foetus and the patient in PVS be accorded priority centres on beliefs in the sanctity of life. What we mean by sanctity of life, and whether it is in fact a trump card, is now hotly debated.

The sanctity of life: Judaeo-Christian tradition[18]

For the devout Roman Catholic sanctity of life is straightforward. Human life is a gift from God and thus is literally sacred. Any act that deliberately ends a life is wrong. Life begins at conception and therefore abortion, and research on, or disposal of, an artificially created embryo, a test-tube embryo, is never permissible. The truly obedient Catholic will abstain from any form of non-natural contraception. Life ends when God ends it. No degree of suffering or handicap justifies a premature release effected by us.

Yet even so there remain grey areas in the application of the belief that life is sacred. Abortion is banned because the only intent of that operation is to kill the child. The Roman Catholic Church forbids abortion even when pregnancy threatens the woman's life. However, a pregnant woman with cancer of the womb may be allowed a hysterectomy even though the child will then die. This is called the doctrine of double effect. The operation for cancer incidentally destroys the child but that was not its primary purpose.

At the other end of life, the Church, while condemning euthanasia, does not demand that extraordinary means be taken to prolong life. Where is the line drawn? Should a severely disabled baby be subjected to painful surgery with a low success rate? Must antibiotics be administered to the terminal cancer patient stricken with pneumonia? The doctrine of double effect, the application of a distinction between ordinary and extraordinary means to preserve life, has generated substantial literature and debate.[19] Even accepting that areas of doubt exist, the orthodox Roman Catholic remains fortunate in the security of her beliefs on the sanctity of life, beliefs shared by many fundamentalist Christians of the Protestant tradition.

Other practising Christians, who subscribe in essence to the doctrine of the sanctity of life, see further problems once they seek to apply their faith. Contraception is morally acceptable to the majority, and to many Roman Catholics now. The exact point when life begins and becomes sacred then becomes of the utmost importance in determining the morality of certain contraceptive methods. Abortion to save the mother's life is accepted by many Christians, as it always has been in the Jewish faith. The child's life may deserve protection but not at the expense of his mother's. This step taken, the extent to which the child's life may be sacrificed to his mother's has to be ascertained. Is a threat to the mother's mental stability sufficient? What about a woman who suffers rape and conceives as a result? Today there is the question of the status of the early embryo created in the test-tube. These and many other issues have caused dissent within the Church of England and the other Christian traditions.

For example, a number of eminent Anglican theologians[20] have found that research on the early embryo is acceptable and raises no conflict within their Christian faith. This stance received the support of the Archbishop of York[21] in debates in the House of Lords. Other Anglicans remain adamantly opposed to any form of destructive research on embryos. None the less, the Christian, Jew, or adherent of any religious faith at least enjoys a framework of belief. The sanctity of life has meaning for them because that life was given by God.

The sanctity of life in a secular society

Many still subscribe to some form of belief in a divinity or higher power. Churches are still popular for weddings and funerals and thriving communities of Jews and Muslims remain committed to their traditions. Yet Britain today is an overwhelmingly secular society where the majority of the population is uncommitted to any religious creed and those people practising any religious faith are in a minority. How many people retain a residual belief in God as the Creator is open to question. For those who do not, what meaning has the sanctity of life? If life is not bestowed by God, on what grounds is it sacred?

There can be no doubt that belief in the sanctity of life does survive the death or absence of religious belief. Taking life is as reprehensible to many agnostics and atheists as it is to the Christian or the Jew. Indeed very many non-believers have been more consistent in upholding and fighting for the sanctity of life than have certain warmongering Christian priests or those 'Christians' who in the USA gather round the jails to celebrate the death penalty's return.[22] What in a secular society is the basis of the sanctity of human life? To most people who are not philosophers the answer is simple. There is a deep and embedded instinct that taking human life is wrong. Life is a most precious possession. All other possessions, all potential joys, depend upon its continued existence. An unchecked attack on one individual's right to life threatens us all. Our autonomy is undermined. Our security becomes precarious. The move away from a concept of life as God-given, however, has certain consequences. If at the basis of belief in the sanctity of life is a perception of the freedom of the individual, of the joy that life can bring, then the quality of life comes into account. The right of the foetus to come into possession of his own life, his own freedom, must be balanced against his mother's rights over her own life and body. When pain and disability cause an individual to cease to wish to live, then he may be free to end that life. It is his to do with as he wishes. Individual choice becomes central to applying the concept of the sanctity of life. No one must interfere with an adult's choices on continued life.[23] Whether any other adult can be compelled to assist a fellow to end his life raises more difficult questions. The concept of freedom of choice offers little guidance where an individual is incapable of choice. Nevertheless this uncertain position commands a fair degree of generous support. People have an intrinsic right to life. Life is sacred, but not 'absolutely inviolable'.[24] This is the view occupying the 'middle ground'.

Sanctity of life: a different perspective[25]

The latest stage in the debate on the sanctity of life involves an attack on the whole idea that 'taking human life is intrinsically wrong'. Life is seen as having no inherent value. Life has value only if it is worth living. Taking life is wrong because 'it is wrong to destroy a life which is worth living'.[26] Side by side with a move to concentrate attention on the quality of life alone comes a redefinition of human life deserving of protection. It is *persons*,[27] not all human animals, whose lives have value. Unless there is a capacity for self-awareness, for the individual to recognize himself as a functioning human person able to relate to other persons, he has no life of the quality and kind that must be preserved. Certain consequences follow from this. A person who can reason must be allowed to judge for himself whether continued life is worth it. A human who cannot reason for himself, who is not a person, may have that judgement made for him by others. Providing painless release for a person who considers his life not worth living, or an individual whose capacity for self-awareness has gone, so that he has ceased to be a person, becomes a moral action. The unborn are not persons. They have no rights against their mothers who are persons. Abortion is moral and it may even be considered immoral not to abort a seriously damaged foetus. Research on embryos to benefit existing persons, whether by improving treatment for infertility or seeking a cure for congenital disease, is not only morally permissible but almost a moral imperative. Euthanasia of the hopelessly brain-damaged with no hope of recovery is entirely acceptable and may, in strictly controlled circumstances, be non-voluntary.

Sanctity of life and the medical profession[28]

No doubt the disparity of views among the general population is reflected in the personal views of many doctors. Doctors, however, actually have to take decisions on the sorts of matters others merely debate. How far and in what fashion is the sanctity of life a central medical ethic? The Declaration of Geneva[29] includes the following undertaking:

I will maintain the utmost respect for human life from time of conception; even under threat, I will not use my medical knowledge contrary to the laws of humanity.

When the Declaration was first formulated in 1947, 'the utmost respect for human life' no doubt imported to most doctors a prohibition on abortion, at any rate where the mother's life was not in danger, and a complete ban on any form of euthanasia. The Declaration was amended and updated in Sydney in 1968. By 1968 abortion on grounds other than immediate danger to the mother had been legalized in Britain and parts of the USA. Within a decade debate was flourishing within respected medical circles as to whether keeping alive all disabled babies was right, and whether prolonging the life of the sick and elderly had not been taken to extremes by modern medicine. What then does the utmost respect for human life entail?

What it does not entail, and what has never existed in any code of medical ethics, is an injuction to preserve life at any price.[30] The prevention of suffering is as much the doctor's task as the prolongation of life. Alas, the two cannot always be complementary. The doctor struggling to interpret and apply his obligation to respect life faces a number of quandaries.

The beginning and end of life

An admonition to respect human life would be easier to adhere to if there was agreement as to when life begins and ends. Few biologists now see the fertilization of the egg as the beginning of a new life. They argue that egg and sperm are living organisms and point out that many fertilized eggs fail to implant. The fertilized egg may still split into two, and in rare cases grow not into a baby but a hydatiform mole. Fertilization, is just one further step in a continuing process. Acceptance of that view renders acceptable the use of contraceptive devices and post-coital contraception, including the 'morning-after' pill, that prevent implantation.[31] At what stage then does life begin and attract respect? We have noted the argument that the foetus has no status because it is not a person. From observation of medical practice this appears to attract little support among doctors. A growing view is that the foetus attracts greater and greater status as it grows to full human likeness.[32] In 1990 this gradualist perception of the embryo has resulted in support for embryo research from most doctors' organizations. No doubt such 'official' and prestigious support for research helped to ensure that Members of Parliament eventually voted to permit research on embryos up to fourteen days old in the Human Fertilization and Embryology Act 1990.

The influence of the medical profession is discernible too in the current debate on human cloning. Nuclear substitution is a technique in which a nucleus with its complete complement of DNA is removed from a cell taken from the organism to be cloned. The nucleus is inserted in an egg cell that has had its nucleus removed. The egg cell, now carrying the DNA from the first organism is encouraged to divide and develop into an embryo that is genetically identical to the donor of the DNA. Experiments on mammals, such as those that produced Dolly, the most famous sheep in the world, suggest that it will be possible to produce human clones using this process. It need not be taken as far as producing a new person, termed reproductive cloning. It is also possible to collect stem cells, undifferentiated cells with the potential to divide indefinitely and give rise to more specialized tissue cells, from the cloned embryo. These could be used to provide tissue grafts, or ultimately transplant organs, to treat the donor of the DNA. This is called therapeutic cloning, or stem cell therapy. Doctors and scientists mostly oppose reproductive cloning but back therapeutic cloning. Their views carried the day with the British government.

The end of life too has no definite marker any more. It can no longer be equated with the cessation of breathing and heartbeat. Resuscitation techniques to restart the heart still enthrall the press, with tales of the 'man who came back from the dead'. The development of life-support machines to replace heart and lung functions during surgery or after traumatic injury demonstrates that life can go on although the heart has stopped. When then does death occur? A definition of death as the irreversible cessation of all activity in the brain stem[33] is generally accepted within the medical professions although some doctors still occasionally express public doubts. For the lay public the decision to agree to switch off the life-support machine of a relative causes individual anguish, and anxiety occasionally surfaces that a desire for organs for transplantation might prompt too swift a pronouncement of death.[34] These are problems solved by procedures designed to ensure that no anticipation of death is allowed, by reassurance and sympathy offered by medical staff to waiting relatives. The moral dilemma relating to dying arises a stage before brain stem death. A person may suffer irreversible brain damage, be irreversibly comatose and yet still show signs of some activity in the brain stem. He is not dead according to the current definition of death. Some argue that this definition should be extended to include the irreversibly comatose. For those who regard human life as of value only where the individual can recognize himself as a person, loss of consciousness is equated with physical death.[35] If a patient is in PVS having lost all cortical function should we regard him as dead? Was Tony Bland alive in any real sense?[36] Is such a move really euthanasia by the back door? The question of continuing to keep alive the unkindly named 'human vegetable' will not go away. It must be faced, not by a surreptitious moving back of the moment of death but by addressing ourselves to the question of whether the doctor may ever kill.[37]

Killing and letting die

Caring for a patient as he dies in peace and dignity may be the last service his doctor can perform for him. Doctors and nurses tending the terminally ill in hospices are accorded the highest respect. The doctor's obligation to relieve suffering may on occasion cause him to refrain from prolonging life. Asked whether a doctor should invariably invoke every weapon of medical progress to prevent death, people of every shade of opinion would answer, no. For the Roman Catholic the test would be whether 'extraordinary means' must be resorted to in order to prolong that life. Extensive surgery on a dying cancer patient offering him only weeks more life would be ruled out. Antibiotics to cure a sudden, unrelated infection pose a more difficult moral dilemma. Nevertheless for most of us, religious or irreligious, this satirical rhyme sums up our attitude;

> Thou shalt not kill; but needst not strive
> Officiously to keep alive.

We revolt at the thought of a doctor killing a patient directly. We accept and are content to leave to the medical profession a liberty to refrain from further treatment in a hopeless case.

Scratch the surface of this popular attitude and problems and doubts emerge. What amounts to 'officiously' keeping alive? Is the doctor alone to judge when a life is worth living, for example to decide when a patient with kidney disease qualifies for dialysis? Lawyers and philosophers enjoy the endless argument these issues generate, doctors on the whole do not. They have to provide answers.[38] Where a patient is sane, conscious and an adult, the dilemma has today a relatively easy answer, albeit no less painful. The patient should decide whether treatment continues (see Chapter 18). Indeed the doctor, if he has been frank with the patient, has little choice but to leave the decision to him. He cannot lawfully give treatment without the patient's consent. Once a patient has decided to reject further treatment the doctor must normally desist. Suicide, if refusing treatment can be so classified, is no longer a crime. The freedom of the individual to make his own moral choices where he is able to is largely unquestioned.

A more acute dilemma arises where the patient cannot make his own decision. Here the distinction between killing and letting die takes a central role. Asked if a doctor, or anyone else, should be allowed to smother a brain-damaged patient, the average person recoils in horror. When a parent at the end of his tether does the same to his dying disabled child he may attract public sympathy and understanding. Public attitudes to 'mercy killing' are not consistent.[39]

Not surprisingly then, the distinction between killing and letting die has not been allowed to go unchallenged. It is subject to a three-pronged attack: (1) Technology makes the distinction between letting die and killing difficult if not impossible to put into practice. (2) It is argued that there is no valid moral distinction between killing and letting die. (3) Some writers have maintained that directly and painlessly killing a patient is a morally superior decision to leaving him to a slow undignified death.[40]

The problems posed for the doctor by the technology at his disposal cannot be sidestepped. An accident victim rushed into hospital is put on a life-support machine. All that can be done is done. He proves to be irreversibly brain-damaged but not brain dead. Failing to put him on the machine would have meant allowing him to die. Is disconnecting the machine killing him[41] (though comatose patients disconnected from life-support machines have lived on for several years in some cases)?[42] Into which category, killing or letting die, does not feeding the patient fall? A newborn baby with severe disabilities may never demand food, may be unable to feed naturally from breast or bottle. Is omitting to tube-feed that baby killing or letting die? What about failing to operate to remove a stomach obstruction? Into which category does failure to perform delicate and painful surgery to relieve hydrocephalus (water on the brain) fall? The difficulties of applying the distinction in practice can be enumerated endlessly.

So, why not abandon the distinction altogether? Several apparently persuasive arguments can be made in favour of such a change of direction.[43] The concept of the value of human life as dependent on self-awareness and the quality of life renders it moral to end a life once self-awareness has gone, or, as in the case of a newborn baby, where it has never developed. A patient still able to reason but living in pain, distress and handicap retains the right to make his own judgement on his quality of life. If he is unable to reason the decision may be taken from him. Once quality of life, not life itself, is the determining factor, it follows that directly killing the patient may be a moral imperative. For if the patient's quality of life is such that life has no intrinsic value, is it not kinder to end that life painlessly than let him drag on for days, weeks or months in undignified 'sub-human' misery? If one accepts the basic premise that the value of human life is solely dependent on life being objectively 'worth living', then in pure logic acceptance that a doctor may sometimes kill his patient must follow.

Pure logic does not, however, govern most human reactions. Voluntary euthanasia, assisting a patient who desires to die, has a growing number of committed advocates. Involuntary euthanasia, involving the doctor directly killing patients whose prospects are hopeless, has very, very little support and virtually none among doctors themselves.[44] The arguments against are dismissed with some scorn by the philosopher proposing a change of attitude. Suggestions that doctors are 'playing God' ought to cut little ice unless you believe in God. Fear that powers to kill may be misused could be alleviated by proper controls. Instinctive revulsion is seen as an uninformed response.

The distinction between killing and letting die will not go away. Three factors at least impede any introduction of involuntary euthanasia. First, the conception of life as in some sense 'sacred' has a greater hold on the population as a whole than its detractors appreciate. Few may now subscribe to belief in the God of the Bible, the Talmud and the Koran, but belief in a Creator of sorts is still widespread. Belief that humanity must set limits on what humanity may do is deeply ingrained. Killing those who cannot speak for themselves remains taboo. Second, the vision of the slippery slope to euthanasia for the unfortunate and the dissenter operates to deter acceptance of involuntary euthanasia. Today the hopelessly brain damaged, tomorrow the mentally disabled, the day after opponents of the government, is the fear of many. No elaboration of controls devised by lawyers and politicians will drive away the fear. Finally, and practically most importantly, even if the exercise of judging quality of life objectively is carried out in all good faith, how can it be achieved? Who will sit in judgement? Occasionally that task falls even now to certain doctors. There is insufficient provision for the treatment of kidney failure within the NHS and not all patients who need it can be offered dialysis. The doctors decide which are left to die. In Oxford doctors decided to terminate dialysis for a mentally disabled patient. His quality of life did not justify continuing to treat him while denying others treatment. The public outcry was overwhelming. The doctors responsible were branded as 'murderers' and 'barbarians'. How much greater would that outcry have been had the decision been to kill the patient despite the fact that on one view killing him quickly and painlessly might be seen as 'kinder' than leaving him to die as his system was slowly poisoned by blood that his failed kidneys could not purify?[45]

Sanctity of life and the law[46]

Legislating on moral and ethical issues created fewer problems for the Victorian parliamentarian. Applying the common law posed no dilemma for the judge. He knew what was right and what was wrong. The Victorian judge was unperturbed by doubt, unconcerned by any feeling that his decision should mirror the moral attitudes of society as a whole. Women and the 'lower classes' were deemed incapable of making moral judgements in any case. Additionally divisions in moral attitudes, although they did exist, were not as deep as those pertaining today. Nor were the problems of medicine as complex. Death remained then an independent agent largely beyond the doctor's skill to combat.

Yet, despite the plethora of ethical problems created daily by modern medicine and the changed moral climate, the law changes slowly. No statute expressly addresses the fate of the newborn infant with multiple disabilities who in an earlier age would have died whatever had been done for her. Every attempt to legislate on euthanasia has stalled early in its progress through Parliament. Governments shy away from legislating, or even pronouncing on medical ethics. The first test-tube baby, Louise Brown, was born in July 1978. It was not until twelve years later that Parliament finally enacted the Human Fertilization and Embryology Act regulating IVF. Before that Act, the Abortion Act 1967 stood alone as a legislative attempt specifically designed to tackle developments in medicine and altered moral outlooks. The Abortion Act was piloted through parliament not by the government of the day, but by David Steel MP by means of a Private Member's Bill. The troubled history of that Act, a compromise that pleases few, perhaps explains why governments of all political colours shy away from entering the battlefields on sanctity of human life. Attempts to amend the Human Fertilization and Embryology Act, which originally sought to reduce the time-limit for abortion,[47] (see page 329) unleashed a bitterness and an outburst of vitriolic abuse unknown in even the most hard-fought party political battle.

Political disinclination to engage in debate on the sanctity of life means that to a large extent the regulation of the medical profession on issues of life and death is left to the common law. In drawing up and applying codes of practice on the treatment of the disabled newborn, the brain-damaged and the dying, the medical profession acts within the constraints of the criminal law of murder and manslaughter. The doctor's exposure to the law can be brutal. The law holds its hand from laying down the code of practice within which he works. Struggling to decide on whether treatment should continue he acts within guidelines agreed by his own profession but lacking any statutory force. Ninety-nine times out of a hundred he can comfort himself with the thought that no one will question his decision in these grey areas between living and dying. On the hundredth occasion he may face the spectre of prosecution for murder or attempted murder. The distinction between killing and letting die does not operate in the criminal law to debar a charge of murder. Allowing a patient to die when it was the doctor's duty to treat him, when the doctor knew that and intended that death would ensue, is as much murder in the eyes of the law as stabbing the patient to death.

The crucial issue once more is what is the content of the doctor's duty? When is it his obligation to prolong life? Left to decide that issue according to conscience and professional opinion most of the time, doctors not unnaturally are resentful that intervention when it comes may take the form of criminal prosecution for murder. Doctors do not see themselves as murderers. Even the most vehement and passionate member of *Life*, believing as he will that medical decisions as to the care of the newborn are frequently wrong, and err too often on the side of withholding treatment, would not place the doctor on the same moral plane as the man murdering in the course of robbery.

The reaction of the medical profession has often been that the law should keep out of medical ethics. Proposals to replace the existing and hazy common law with detailed legislative rules attract little enthusiasm (see Chapter 18).[48] Procedural rules about consultation, reference to codes of practice and the keeping of records of decision making appear more acceptable. What doctors might really welcome is legislation that additionally promises immunity from prosecution to the doctor following the correct process. Such legislation would check the maverick and would ensure that no one doctor whose standards deviate markedly from his fellows could pursue a course of treatment or non-treatment of patients that was unacceptable to the majority. However, it would enshrine in the law a principle that such decisions are for the doctors alone. The rest of us would be excluded from any right to a say on these matters of life and death.

'The ultimate decisions about life and death are not simply medical decisions.' This was the view expressed in an editorial in the *British Medical Journal* in 1981.[49] I concur wholeheartedly. The meaning and application of the sanctity of life is not a matter to be left for doctors to decide and for philosophers to argue over. The law's involvement to ensure that society's expectations are met is inevitable. The law is very far from perfect in its operation. Reform in a society divided in its moral judgements is hard to formulate. Detailed legislation is probably undesirable even if such legislation were to be agreed on. The variations in the circumstances confronting the doctor are too great. Rules cannot be invented that would meet every possible dilemma the doctor may face. The doctor's judgement cannot and should not be excluded. What can be done, if there is a will to do so, is to stimulate greater debate on the codes of practice under which the doctor works. Greater legal and lay involvement in their development should be encouraged. The gap between lawyer and doctor needs to be bridged. Perhaps amendment of the law of homicide should be considered, so that a doctor alleged to have stepped beyond the bounds of the acceptable in his professional sphere remains subject to society's judgement but avoids an inappropriate murder charge. Doctors complain that lay people do not understand the full implications of the problems presented by the disabled and the dying, and do not appreciate the complexity of modern medical technology. Only greater openness and a greater willingness to involve those outside the medical profession in decision making will bring about better understanding. Only better understanding of the problems of medicine will bring about better lawmaking.

However much any government might prefer to remain aloof from debates on medicine and morals, developments in embryology and assisted conception have forced the British, and other European and Commonwealth governments, to legislate. There are perhaps four main aspects to the problem of legislating on the implications of reproductive medicine. (1) Legislation may be designed to protect patients from possible abuses, to prevent what is generally perceived as an undesirable practice creating risks of exploitation. An example of such legislation in England might be the Surrogacy Arrangements Act 1985 prohibiting commercial exploitation of surrogacy. (2) Legislation may be needed because gaps in the existing law place certain patients and their families in a legal limbo. For example, if A donates an egg that is fertilized and implanted in B, who carries and gives birth to the child, who in law is the child's mother? Such questions of family law and status, may be complex and sometimes controversial. Clear answers are essential to safeguard the interests of the child. (3) Developments in genetics and biotechnology create or exacerbate several legal problems. Who owns genetic information, and how should access to that information be controlled? What property rights accrue from body products? If cells from my body are used to develop a remedy to some disease, can I claim the ensuing profit made by a drug company? If a healthy gene taken from my embryo is used to replace a defective gene from my sister's embryo, to whom does the gene belong? Can human genes be patented? All these questions require a legal answer and if legislation does not provide the answer expensive litigation proliferates. Inadequate, unclear laws also generate distrust and anger. The fuzzy toothless provisions of the Human Tissue Act 1961 contributed immensely to the outrage and agony occasioned by revelations of organ retention practices (see Chapter 19). (4) Finally, the most difficult of all aspects of legislation in this area is to decide what kinds of procedures are acceptable in our society. Are there medical possibilities whose implications are such that, though possible, they should be prohibited by law? The United Kingdom is to allow stem cell therapies, i.e. therapeutic cloning. Most of Europe outlaws cloning altogether.

Legislating on what is permissible is fraught with difficulty. Emotions run high. In 1990 anti-abortion campaigners flooded Parliament with model foetuses. Pro-embryo research lobbies played to the cameras with touching and well-timed stories of the joy brought to previously infertile women by their 'test-tube' babies. The scientific possibilities are hard to grasp and science fiction scenarios abound. Test-tube-baby technology creates fears of Aldous Huxley's *Brave New World*. But above all, each side in the moral debate is convinced they are right and the other is irretrievably wrong. What tends to be overlooked is this: in many ethical debates today there is no answer that will be accepted as unchallengeably right. I may believe that from fertilization my embryo is a human entity endowed with the same moral status as I am and endowed with an immaterial, immortal soul. I cannot prove my contention but nor can that contention be disproved. The question for legislators is not to find a right answer, to achieve a moral consensus, but to determine how in a liberal, democratic society legislation can be formulated in the absence of such consensus. To evade that task is to give the scientists free rein to do as they see fit. To criticize them with hindsight is unfair and unproductive. Theologians, ethicists, lawyers and indeed all citizens must be prepared to grapple with these awkward moral dilemmas and, probably, be ready to compromise.

3
A Relationship of Trust and Confidence

Whatever, in connection with my professional practice, or not in connection with it, I see or hear in the life of men, which ought not to be spoken of abroad, I will not divulge, as reckoning that all such should be kept secret.

The Hippocratic Oath

I will respect the secrets which are confided in me, even after the patient has died.

Declaration of Geneva (as amended Sydney 1968)

Doctors, like priests and lawyers, must be able to keep secrets. For medical care to be effective, for patients to trust their doctor, they must be confident that they can talk frankly to him. An obligation of confidence to patients lies at the heart of all codes of ethics. Comparison of the quotations above shows that the obligation is not always absolute. The Ancient Greek physician undertook not to divulge that which ought not to be spoken of abroad. He presumably judged what fell into that category. The Declaration of Geneva is more stringent. *Any* information given by a patient in confidence must be kept secret for ever. A moment's reflection reveals the problems inherent in both absolute and relative obligations of confidence. An absolute obligation leaves the doctor powerless to do anything but try to persuade his patient to allow him to take action when the patient tells him he is HIV positive but is still sleeping with his wife, or when a mother confesses her violent impulses towards her baby, or when examination reveals that the patient may be a rapist sought by the police. Examples could be elaborated endlessly. On the other hand, a relative obligation, which leaves the doctor free to breach confidence when he judges that some higher duty to another person or to society applies, may deter patients from seeking necessary treatment. This may damage not only the patient but also those very people at risk when the doctor treats and does not 'tell'. The wife whose husband receives no advice about 'safe sex' and HIV, and the baby whose mother seeks no counsel may be more vulnerable if fears of breach of confidence prevent the husband and the mother getting any help at all.[1]

In this chapter I look at the law on confidentiality as it affects doctors and adult patients, and I examine the role of the medical profession in enforcing the ethical obligation of confidence. The special problems affecting confidentiality and parents and children are considered in Chapter 14. The vagueness and complexity of the law may surprise some. The number of occasions when the law compels the doctor to breach confidence may shock many. The present chapter also explores what the patient is entitled to be told. From the patient's viewpoint the doctor's obligation of confidence exists to prevent the doctor passing on information about the patient to third parties. A relationship of trust requires that this should not happen. It also requires that the doctor be frank with the patient. Information about the patient should generally not be withheld from him. How far is the patient entitled to frankness from his doctor?[2]

Breach of confidence: the common law[3]

The present law on breach of confidence has developed in a haphazard fashion. The core obligation requiring doctors to respect patient confidence derives from the common law. However, any attempt to understand the law governing medical confidentiality must take account of the Data Protection Act 1998 and Article 8 of the European Convention on Human Rights.

The precise legal nature of the common law obligation of confidence remains uncertain.[4]

What is clear is that judges have shown themselves willing to act to prevent the disclosure of confidential information in a wide variety of circumstances. A duty to preserve confidences has been imposed in settings as diverse as trade or research secrets confided to employees,[5] marital intimacies,[6] intimate disclosures to close friends[7] and Cabinet discussion.[8] Very often the obligation of confidence arises as an implied term of a contract, as is the case with the employee bound by his contract of employment to keep his employer's business to himself. But the obligation of confidence can equally arise where no contract exists, or has ever existed, between the parties. The basic general principles of the law on breach of confidence amount to these. The courts will intervene to restrain disclosure of information where (1) the information is confidential in nature and not a matter of public knowledge, (2) the information was entrusted to another person in circumstances imposing an obligation not to use or disclose that information without the consent of the giver of the information, and (3) protecting confidentiality of that information is in the public interest.[9] As well as acting in advance to prevent the disclosure of confidential information, the courts may, where appropriate, award compensation after information has been improperly disclosed. Finally, once an obligation of confidence is created it binds not only the original recipient of the information, but also any other person to whom disclosure is made by the recipient when that other person knows of the confidential status of the information.

Applying the general law to the specific issue of medical confidentiality, no problem arises from the requirement that the information given by the patient himself, or that deduced by the doctor on examination, is confidential in nature. Most people do not broadcast their medical problems from the rooftop. Equally it is unchallenged that the relationship of any doctor with any patient, NHS or private, imports an obligation of confidence. In a very early case, action was taken to prevent publication of a diary kept by a physician to George III.[10] Much later, in 1974, a judge put the doctor's duty thus:

. . . in common with other professional men, for instance a priest and there are of course others, the doctor is under a duty not to disclose, [voluntarily] without the consent of his patient, information which he, the doctor, has gained in his professional capacity, save . . . in very exceptional circumstances.[11]

The difficult area of medical confidentiality does not lie in establishing a *general* duty of confidence, but in determining what amounts to 'very exceptional circumstances' justifying breach of that duty. First, disclosure will always be justified legally when the doctor is compelled by law to give confidential information to a third party. This may be by way of an order of the court to disclose records in the course of some civil proceedings, or may be under some statutory provision such as those

Acts of Parliament requiring that specified diseases be notified to the health authorities. Doctors, unlike lawyers, enjoy no professional *privilege* entitling them to refuse to give evidence in court. I shall return to this later. Second, it is clear that the doctor may voluntarily elect to disclose information in certain circumstances. The general law on confidence requires that preserving confidentiality be in the public interest. In early judgments the public interest 'defence' tended to concern disclosure of crime; 'there is no confidence in the disclosure of iniquity'.[12] It is clear now, though, that that defence is not limited to crime, or even misconduct. In *Lion Laboratories Ltd* v. *Evans* (which considered the disclosure of confidential information suggesting that a breathalyser device, the Intoximeter, was unreliable), Griffiths LJ said:

I can see no sensible reason why this defence should be limited to cases where there has been wrongdoing on the part of the plaintiffs . . . it is not difficult to think of instances where, although there has been no wrongdoing on the part of the plaintiff, it may be vital in the public interest to publish a part of his confidential information.[13]

The exact ambit of the public interest defence as it affects doctors remains difficult to ascertain, despite key judgments of the High Court[14] and the Court of Appeal.[15] Should, or rather may, the doctor inform on any patient whom he suspects of any crime, however trivial? What other circumstances justify the invocation of the public interest to override the patient's interest in confidentiality? The guidance available to doctors comes primarily from the General Medical Council and I shall consider that guidance a little later, for despite the underlying authority of the *law* of confidence, the enforcement of medical confidentiality often rests in practice with the GMC.

The civil action for breach of confidence is an excellent weapon for restraining threatened breaches of confidence. It is less effective in compensating the victim of a breach of confidence outside a commercial setting. If a trade secret is revealed by an employee and the employer loses profits, his loss can be measured by the courts and appropriate compensation ordered. A breach of medical confidence rarely results in monetary loss, but will give rise to indignity and distress for the patient. It is not clear whether damages for mental distress can be awarded in an action for breach of confidence. In 1981, the Law Commission recommended reforms that would allow the award of such damages.[16] Their recommendations have never been acted on. Even if damages are available for distress, such damages may be costly to obtain, and complaining to the GMC is likely to remain the preferred remedy in many cases of breach of confidence, although the GMC is not the sole arbiter on issues of confidence. A patient dissatisfied with the finding of the GMC has no appeal from the GMC decision. What he does have is a concurrent right to take the matter to the courts by way of an action for breach of confidence. In this way the GMC definition of the duty of confidentiality is on every occasion susceptible to review by the courts. In any event the GMC will pay due regard to whatever principles the courts develop in analogous cases. The courts, not the GMC, are the ultimate arbiters of the scope of the doctor's duty of confidentiality. However, the judges have tended to look to the GMC's guidelines on confidentiality in formulating the legal rules.[17]

Breach of confidence: the GMC

Any improper disclosure of information obtained in confidence from or about a patient can constitute serious professional misconduct on the part of the doctor. Again the crucial issue is: when is a disclosure improper? The GMC gives detailed guidance.[18] I consider first information where the identity of the patient is disclosed, what the GMC describes as *personal* information. The doctor's duty is to maintain strict confidentiality. The GMC recognizes that patients have a 'right' to confidentiality. The death of the patient does not absolve the doctor from this duty.[19] In this respect the doctor's ethical obligation is stricter than his legal duty. The law of confidence probably does not protect the patient's secrets after death. Any doctor deciding to disclose information 'must always be prepared to justify [his] decision in accordance with this [GMC] guidance.' The most recent guidance warns doctors to be vigilant in protecting confidential information. It rightly notes that many improper disclosures of information are accidental, as for example when consultations with patients are overheard by other patients or by staff not directly involved in the care of the patient.

Where a considered decision is made to disclose information about a patient voluntarily,[20] disclosure would be justifiable in the following categories of cases:

(1) The patient, expressly consents to disclosure. The doctor must ensure that the patient understands what is to be disclosed, the reasons for disclo-

sure and the consequences thereof. The patient must be told to whom information will be given and how much information will be disclosed.

(2) Information is shared within a health care team caring for the patient. The GMC makes it clear that every effort must be made to ensure that the patient is aware that information about him may be disclosed to other health professionals working with his doctor and that if a patient does not want certain information about him revealed to others his wishes must be respected. Doctors must make sure that everyone within the team to whom information is disclosed understands that they are bound by a legal obligation of confidence.

(3) In circumstances of emergency, and when the patient cannot be consulted directly, information may, and should, promptly be passed on to those involved in her care. If a patient is brought unconscious into casualty, staff may properly share all relevant information about her and, for example, her GP could properly disclose her relevant medical history to hospital staff.

(4) Difficult questions arise when doctors believe that a patient is incapable of giving consent to disclose information because of 'immaturity, illness or mental incapacity'. The GMC advises doctors to try to persuade the patient to allow appropriate persons, including family members, to be involved in the consultation. If the patient refuses but the doctor is 'convinced that it is essential, *in their medical interests*, [the doctor] may disclose relevant information to an appropriate person or authority'.

(5) '[E]xceptionally, in cases where patients withhold consent, personal information may be disclosed in the public interest where the benefits to an individual or to society of the disclosure outweigh the public and the patient's interest in keeping the information confidential. In all such cases [the doctor] must weigh the possible harm (both to the patient and the overall trust between doctors and patients) against the benefits which are likely to arise from the release of information.'

The most recent guidance from the GMC narrows and structures the discretion granted to doctors to disclose information about their patients. Confidentiality is given the emphasis it deserves and, as we shall see, much more specific guidance about potentially difficult dilemmas for doctors is spelled out in some detail. Awkward questions still

bedevil the extent to which doctors may lawfully[21] disclose information
without consent in, first, the patient's own interests and, second, the
public interest.

Disclosure in the patient's interests

Let us consider cases (3) and (4) above. Both suggest that a doctor should
be free to speak to some proper person, when he judges that the patient
is unable to make decisions as to his own treatment. He should act in
the patient's interests. Two points must be made clear. Relatives of an
adult patient have no special status as regards his treatment. Acting in
the patient's medical interests is not in itself a defence to a breach of
confidence. However, if the patient is temporarily or permanently incapable of making any decisions for himself, whether in relation to treatment, or disclosure of information, the law sanctions doctors taking
whatever action they judge necessary to promote their patient's welfare
(see pages 117–21).[22] Discussing the condition of an unconscious patient
in casualty and seeking advice on her treatment with colleagues and
family members is proper and lawful.

Case (4) is trickier. It suggests that where a patient is very ill, but not
necessarily mentally incapacitated by her illness, relevant information
may be disclosed in her medical interests. The extent of permissible
disclosure in such cases is not clear. Does it mean, for example, that if
the patient is terminally ill at home and unable to care for herself, the
GP may alert the district nurse to her condition? Does it allow disclosure to a patient's family? Earlier GMC guidance expressly allowed
doctors, albeit rarely, to bypass the patient and entrust information that
might be damaging to her to her family. Information could even be withheld from the patient. That now appears to be outlawed by the GMC
but the poignant dilemmas doctors may still face remain. A doctor may
believe that it is kinder to spare the patient pain by not telling him how
close he is to death. If the patient retains the capacity to make his own
decisions,[23] i.e. he remains mentally competent, the legal basis for
compassionate paternalism is shaky (see pages 121–5). Doctors might
argue that consent to talk to family or close friends could be presumed
in such cases. No doubt most people would be only too ready to let their
family be consulted and involved in decisions about whether and how
to tell them of their plight. But if a patient places a ban on communication with any third party then, as the GMC now acknowledges, the

doctor must respect that ban. The patient is entitled to confidentiality and entitled to require that it be maintained even when it is *contrary* to his interests. The doctor may seek to persuade him to change his mind, but he may *not* override his decision. The difficulties such a rule may pose for doctors should not be underestimated. Imagine treating a nineteen-year-old girl for terminal cancer in circumstances where the girl appears terrified and frail. The intuition that someone close to her should know how ill she is and help break the news to her will be strong. A desire to protect her is properly beneficent. May doctors not protect patients from themselves? The law affords doctors no such privilege.

Disclosure in the public interest

Case (5) invokes the general 'public interest' defence available in any action for breach of confidence. These issues generate the most sensitive questions surrounding medical confidentiality, seeking to justify breaching the patient's confidences to protect the public interest and safeguard other people. Let us look first at the most obvious public interest defence given to justify breach of confidence, the prevention or detection of a serious crime. When may, or even should, a doctor inform the police about criminal conduct on the part of a patient? Contrary to popular myth a doctor is under no general obligation enforced by the criminal law to contact the police. Unless a statute specifically so provides, a doctor does not commit any offence by failing to tell the police of any evidence he may have come across professionally that suggests that a patient may have committed or is contemplating some crime.[24] A criminal offence is committed only when a doctor or anyone else accepts money to conceal evidence of crime.[25] Section 18 of the Terrorism Act 2000 imposes a duty on everyone, including doctors, to inform the police if they believe or suspect certain offences concerning funding terrorist activity have been committed. Unlike its predecessor, the Prevention of Terrorism (Temporary Provisions) Act 1989, there is no longer an absolute obligation to inform the police about suspected terrorist *acts*. Draconian though the Terrorism Act is in other respects, it relieves the burden on doctors to volunteer their suspicions of terrorist activity on the part of patients or risk prosecution. Although many statutes require doctors to disclose information if asked to do so by police[26] they are not compelled to volunteer that information. Of course, in many cases, a doctor will none the less judge that he should do so where others are at risk.

So in the case of most crimes, the choice is the doctor's. The criminal law will not penalize him for not informing the police. Will he be in breach of confidence if he elects to do so? Early last century judges were divided on the issue of whether a doctor was justified in going to the police after attending a woman who had undergone a criminal abortion. Hawkins J condemned such a course as a 'monstrous cruelty' and doubted whether such a breach of confidence could ever be justified,[27] whereas Avory J saw the doctor's duty to assist in the investigation of *serious* crime as always outweighing his duty to his patient.[28] More recent judgments appear to support Avory J's view, although they deal with confidential relationships outside the medical field. Lord Denning has suggested that the public interest justifies disclosure of *any* crime or misdeed committed or contemplated.[29]

Within the doctor/patient relationship freedom to disclose in the public interest should be more limited in scope. Unless commission of any crime disentitles the criminal from normal standards of medical care, disclosure should be strictly limited. Doctors who suspect that another person is at risk of physical injury at their patient's hands must be free to act to protect that person. Preventing harm to others outweighs the private and public interests in confidentiality. Volunteering evidence of less serious crimes committed by patients to the police may be seen as less straightforward. The GMC takes a firm stance. Disclosure is only ethically defensible in relation to serious crime.[30] Serious crime is defined as crime that '. . . will put someone at risk of death or serious harm and will usually be crimes against the person such as abuse of children'. What the doctor should not do is hand over to the police information on each and every patient who transgresses the law. Parliament has legislated in numerous cases to compel breach of medical confidence. The courts should not be zealous to add to that list. The law should limit justifiable breach of confidence to *serious* crime and interpret the term *serious* strictly.

The flaw in this argument may be that a doctor found to be in breach of confidence for disclosing a crime could be condemned by a court or the GMC for performing a moral duty cast on every citizen. The doctor is distinguished from other citizens by the presence of a positive legal duty to his patient. Enforcing his duty to his patient benefits the public as well as the patient. The Court of Appeal has expressly recognized a public interest in the maintenance of medical confidentiality.[31] Medical confidentiality is at the root of good health care. Should the courts, however, find that as upholders of the law they cannot condemn those who help bring lawbreakers to justice, the alternative solution is to fall back on the ethical standard set by the GMC, that breach of confidence is justified only in case of grave or serious crime. The doctor may not break the law if he discloses details of petty crimes, but he may be punished for professional misconduct. The legal and ethical standards do not need to be exactly the same.

Next arises the question of disclosure where crime is not an issue. The law no longer limits the concept of public interest disclosure to crime alone, nor does the GMC in its ethical guidance to doctors. Defining exactly when the doctor may disclose on this more general basis is exceptionally difficult. May he tell a wife that her husband is HIV positive? What if a doctor is treating a fellow health professional who is HIV positive but continues to carry out risky surgery? Suppose a general practitioner knows that a patient continues to drive even though epilepsy renders her a danger on the roads. In all cases, the doctor must first do his utmost to obtain the patient's consent to disclosure. If persuasion fails, what may the doctor do? He must balance his duty to the patient against the risk threatening other individuals. It is clear then that he may in an appropriate case inform an appropriate public body.[32] The GMC expressly addresses the case of patients unfit to drive who refuse to accept medical advice. A doctor may lawfully contact the Driver and Vehicle Licensing Centre (DVLC) if a patient unfit to drive absolutely rejects advice to surrender his licence. Similarly where colleagues are medically unfit to practise, the GMC puts the safety of patients first.

How would the law address such cases?

The boundaries of lawful disclosure are explored in two important precedents. In *X* v. *Y*[33] a tabloid newspaper acquired, through a breach of confidence by a health authority employee, information identifying two general practitioners who were continuing to practise after having been diagnosed as HIV positive. The authority sought an injunction prohibiting publication of the doctors' names. The newspaper argued that the public at large, and the doctors' patients in particular, had an interest in knowing that doctors were HIV positive. Rose J reviewed the evidence about transmission of HIV from doctor to patient where the doctor had received proper counselling about safe practice. He found that the risk to patients was negligible. Far greater risks arose from the possibility that people with AIDS, or who feared they might have AIDS, would not seek medical help if they could not rely on confidential treatment. The judge, granting the injunction, said:

In the long run, preservation of confidentiality is the only way of securing public health; otherwise doctors will be discredited as a source of education, for future individual patients will not come forward if doctors are going to squeal on them. Consequently, confidentiality is vital to secure public as well as private health, for unless those infected come forward they cannot be counselled and self-treatment does not provide the best care . . .[34]

By contrast in *W. v. Egdell*[35] the Court of Appeal sanctioned a breach of confidence by a psychiatrist. *W.* had been convicted of the manslaughter of five people and of wounding two others. He was ordered to be detained indefinitely in a secure hospital. He could be released only by order of the Home Secretary if he were found to be no longer a danger to public safety. As a step towards eventual release he sought to transfer to a regional secure unit. The transfer was not approved by the Home Secretary and *W.* then applied to a mental health review tribunal for a conditional discharge. In support of his application his solicitors arranged for an independent psychiatric report from Dr Egdell. Dr Egdell's report was not favourable. He judged that *W.* was still a dangerous man with a psychopathic personality, no real insight into his condition and a morbid interest in explosives. Unsurprisingly *W.*'s solicitors withdrew their application for his discharge but they did not pass on the report to the tribunal or the hospital where *W.* was detained. Dr Egdell was concerned by the fact that his report was not passed on. He ultimately sent his report to the medical director of *W.*'s hospital and agreed that a copy of the report should be forwarded to the Home Secretary. *W.* sued Dr Egdell for breach of confidence.

The Court of Appeal made it crystal clear that Dr Egdell did owe *W.* a duty of confidence. Had he sold his story to the press or discussed the case in his memoirs Dr Egdell would have been in breach of confidence. But the duty of confidentiality is not absolute. The public interest in medical confidentiality must be balanced against the public interest in public safety. If Dr Egdell's diagnosis was right, *W.* remained a source of danger to others and he was entitled to communicate his findings to the director of the hospital now detaining *W.* and to the Home Secretary, who would have the final say on if and when *W.* should be released into the community.

X. v. Y. and *W. v. Egdell* do not mean that a doctor may *never* disclose that a patient is HIV positive, or that he may always disclose his concerns about a patient's mental health. In each case the powerful interest in maintaining confidentiality must be balanced against the danger ensuing if confidentiality is not breached. Only where there is a clear and significant risk of the patient causing harm to others that cannot be abated by any other means may confidence be breached. Consider this example. It is not uncommon for surgeons to cut themselves in the course of surgery so that there is blood-to-blood contact between surgeon and patient, and in fact a number of doctors have contracted HIV from patients in this way. Certain forms of surgery, now styled exposure-prone procedures, carry a real risk of cross-infection between surgeon and patient. Public concern about health workers transmitting HIV to patients prompted the GMC to give further and specific guidance on the ethical issues surrounding not just HIV and AIDS, but all serious communicable diseases.[36] Hepatitis B[37] for instance is much more infectious than HIV but transmitted in the same manner. A doctor reporting a colleague who refuses to avoid endangering patients when he risks transmitting such a disease acts lawfully. The GMC expressly advises that 'when a doctor knows, or has good reason to believe that, a fellow health worker is infected with a serious communicable disease and that that person has not sought or followed advice to modify his practice to protect his patients the doctor must inform the appropriate regulatory authority and an appropriate person in that health worker's employing authority'. A surgeon, or, for example, a midwife, carrying out procedures where there is an unavoidable risk of transmitting a blood-borne disease poses such a risk of harm to her patient that the public interest in confidentiality is outweighed by the need to safeguard the patient.[38]

Can this *public* interest justify disclosure, not only to a public body or official, but also to an individual at risk? If an HIV positive surgeon refuses to refrain from unprotected intercourse or to tell his wife of his condition, can she be warned of the danger she faces? The GMC advises that doctors *may* disclose such information to known sexual contacts. Doctors are urged to do all they can to persuade the infected person himself to inform sexual partners. If persuasion fails then the doctor should consider whether he should inform any sexual partner at risk of infection. Would the law support a doctor who did so? In defamation a defence of qualified privilege protects any communication that the maker has a duty to impart and the recipient a legitimate interest in receiving.

No defence of qualified privilege as such exists in breach of confidence.[39] The defence is that the *public* interest demands disclosure. Private interests alone are not usually enough. However, where a genuine risk of physical danger, of injury or disease is posed to any third party, the public interest in individual security is sufficient to justify disclosure to that person so that she can protect herself appropriately. When the doctor reasonably foresees that nondisclosure poses a real risk of physical harm to a third party he ought to be free to warn that person, especially if that person too is his patient. Courts should not be over-zealous in proving him wrong. Similarly, in such cases, if the doctor thinks it more appropriate to contact the third party's GP he should not be condemned. None the less risk of harm must be established. A simple belief that someone else, spouse or relative, is entitled to information is insufficient. A husband has no 'right to know' if his wife asks to be sterilized. Parents have no 'right to know' if a daughter seeks an abortion. They may have a legitimate interest in the matters at stake but that is not enough. The balance of public interest in favour of preserving confidentiality should be displaced only by a significant danger of physical harm.

Openly identifying a healthcare worker who is HIV positive will thus rarely be lawful. A more delicate and difficult question arose in *H. (A Healthcare Worker)* v. *Associated Newspapers Ltd and N (A Health Authority)*.[40] H. tested positive for HIV while working as a healthcare professional for a health authority, identified in court proceedings only as N. The health authority proposed to carry out a 'look back' exercise to notify patients treated by H. and invite them to undergo HIV testing if they so chose. H. first sought an injunction to prevent N from notifying his patients and carrying out the 'look back' study. He provided details of at least some of his NHS patients with the utmost reluctance and refused to supply any information about his private patients. H. argued that, in his particular case, the risk to patients of HIV was so low that it did not justify breach of his, or his patients' clinical confidentiality.

Before H.'s case against the health authority could be heard, the *Mail on Sunday* heard about the case. The newspaper planned to publish a story about H.'s condition and his dispute with the health authority. He sought a second injunction to prevent publication of any details identifying him personally, or identifying either the health authority that employed him or his medical specialty. A temporary injunction was granted to him in the terms he sought. The newspaper retaliated with the headline 'Judge's gag over Aids threat to patients'.

Gross J upheld the ban on publishing details of H.'s identity, but would have allowed publication of the health authority's identity and H.'s speciality. H. appealed. He argued that if the nature of his specialty and the name of his employing authority were in the public domain, he himself would be readily identifiable by a significant number of people, including some of his patients. The Court of Appeal acknowledged that H.'s case involved a difficult balancing exercise. They concluded that a ban on identifying the health authority should be imposed. Disclosing N's (the health authority's) identity would be likely to '. . . set in train a course of events' that could result in disclosure of H.'s identity and compromise his first action against the health authority to prevent the health authority conducting the 'look back' study. Patients might also be harmed by discovering the risk to themselves without immediate access to proper advice and counselling. The appeal court, however, was not convinced that a ban on identifying H.'s specialty was necessary. Such a restraint would inhibit legitimate debate on a matter of public interest. The Court of Appeal in *H.* granted more legitimacy to the interest in freedom of expression and public debate about the risks of HIV transmission and infected health workers than Rose J did in *X.* v. *Y.* The influence of Article 10 of the Human Rights Convention (guaranteeing freedom of expression) is plainly seen.

Especially difficult questions touching on confidentiality arise in relation to genetic screening and genetic counselling. Tests that reveal that the individual patient suffers from or is a carrier of a genetic disease often indicate that other family members are at risk from the same disease.[41] Consider a simple example. Jenny, a medical student, having completed her initial course in genetics, becomes concerned about her family history. There appears to be a pattern of paternal relatives succumbing to dementia and premature death. After counselling she consents to a test for Huntington's Chorea. The test proves positive. Huntington's is an autosomal dominant genetic disease, which means that if a parent has the affected gene, any child has a 50 per cent chance of inheriting Huntington's. The disease does not manifest itself until early middle age when the affected person succumbs over several years to progressive dementia and early death. Jenny's diagnosis necessarily means that one of her parents must also have the affected gene, and that each of her siblings is at 50/50 risk, as will be any child whom Jenny may bear. If Jenny refuses to consent to genetic counsellors contacting her family, would the interests of those family members justify a breach of confidence? If Jenny's elder brother had just married and he and his wife were hoping to start a family, would the potential harm to any child justify disclosure?

Whatever the problem before him, a doctor must not forget that the law ultimately determines when overriding interests justify a breach of confidence. Moreover, the role of the law of defamation must not be overlooked. Disclosure of *any* confidential information, albeit every word is true, may be the subject of an action for breach of confidence. If the doctor is mistaken and information disclosed by him proves to be untrue, he may face a further action for defamation. Any statement causing responsible citizens to think less of a person or to avoid his company may be defamatory. Diagnoses of alcoholism, venereal disease and HIV are all examples of possible defamatory remarks. Suspicion of child abuse is another. In defamation the doctor has a complete defence if what he has stated is true. Additionally he has a defence of qualified privilege if first he reasonably believed his statements to be true, and second he communicated with a person with a legitimate interest in the relevant information. Informing the police of suspected violence to a child is privileged even if the doctor's suspicions prove to be unfounded. Informing an employer that an employee is an alcoholic is generally not. The issue of whether communication was justified is one and the same in the law of confidence and defamation.

A duty to disclose?

There are clearly circumstances where the doctor's duty of confidence to his patient may be overridden by his duty to safeguard a third party from physical harm. If he mistakenly decides the question of this conflict of duty in the patient's favour, and the risk of harm to someone else materializes, is the doctor at risk of a lawsuit by the injured party? Normally where a risk of injury is readily foreseeable and a person has the ability to eliminate that risk, or at any rate to minimize it, a duty to take the necessary action will arise. An education authority that failed to ensure that small children could not get out of their nursery school and on to a busy road was found liable, not just to any child on the road, but to a lorry driver injured in an incident caused by a straying child.[42]

The student medical centre at the University of California was held liable for failing to warn a young woman of the risk posed to her by one of their patients.[43] The girl's rejected lover sought psychiatric help at the centre. He told staff there of his violent intentions towards the girl and that he had a gun. The staff warned the police, who decided to take no action and the medical centre said nothing to the girl. She was murdered by their patient soon afterwards. Her family sued the university for negligence. The medical centre was found liable for failing to breach their patient's confidence and warn the girl of the threat to her life.

On similar facts an English court would be less likely to find a doctor negligent. First the court would have to determine whether in the special circumstances of medical confidentiality a duty to breach confidence could be countenanced. In the case of the education authority held liable for the escape of the infant, their duty to child and to lorry driver was one and the same. The doctor is faced with a stark conflict of duty. If the doctor *may* lawfully breach his patient's confidence, does he have a duty to do so to safeguard the individual at risk? The courts in England are reluctant to make A liable for a wrong committed by B.[44] So the injured individual would have to satisfy the court that the doctor's knowledge of the risk to him was sufficient to make it 'just and reasonable'[45] for the doctor to be required to act to protect him. At its highest, the doctor's duty may be set as an obligation to consider and assess the risk to the third party. The Californian medical staff did their best. They informed the police. The extent of the doctor's duty to third parties in England would appear to be this. He must not ignore any risk to other people created by his patient. He must weigh his duty to his patient against his duty to society and other individuals. If he acts reasonably on the evidence before him in the most awesome of dilemmas, the court will not penalize him if he proves to be wrong.

Breach of confidence: law reform

In 1981 the Law Commission, a body appointed to review the current state of the law and recommend reform, published a report on *Breach of Confidence*[46] proposing detailed reforms. Twenty years later the government has still not acted on the report. The proposals are to some extent technical and will have more impact in the field of commercial confidence than medical confidentiality. Proposals relevant to doctors and patients include the following. The action for breach of confidence should be an action in tort, a civil wrong. An obligation of confidence will attach both to information entrusted by the patient to his doctor and to information about the patient confided to the doctor by a third party, for example, reports to a general practitioner from a consultant to whom the patient has been referred. Compensation ordered where an action for breach of confidence is successful should include damages for mental distress and any consequent physical or mental harm. The Law Commission rejected arguments that the doctor's duty of confidence should survive the patient's death. They took the view that a law protecting the individual's interest in information entrusted by him to his doctor could not be stretched to embrace his family's privacy and freedom from distress after that person's own death. The ethical obligation imposed by the GMC might properly be more stringent than the legal obligation enforced by the law on confidence.

Compulsory disclosure

The circumstances in which doctors may choose to disclose information about their patients may worry some patients and creates difficult problems for doctors. The doctor's legal dilemma is solved when the law compels him to disclose information. The number of instances in which this is the case is worryingly high.

First, a doctor must give any information required by a court of law. Privilege, in the sense of being free to refuse to give evidence relating to professional dealings with clients, is something usually enjoyed by lawyers alone and not shared by any other professional colleagues.[47] A doctor can be subpoenaed to give evidence just like anyone else. Nor can he withhold anything from the court. He does not have to volunteer his views or expertise but whatever questions he is asked he must answer. Just as he can be called to the witness box, so his records can be called up before the courts. The only protection for medical confidentiality lies in the judge's discretion. Judges will try to ensure that confidence is breached only to the extent necessary for the conduct of the trial. The doctor may be unhappy at having to break trust with his patient, but he can at least be reassured that he is at no legal risk. Any breach of confidence made as a witness in court is absolutely privileged.

In exercising their powers to order disclosure of evidence or documents, courts strive to balance justice and confidentiality. In *D.* v. *NSPCC*[48] the plaintiff sought to compel the NSPCC to disclose who had mistakenly accused her of child abuse. The court refused to make the order. The public interest in people feeling free to approach appropriate authorities to protect young children outweighed the plaintiff's private interest in unearthing her accuser. Thus there will be some cases where the courts may refuse to help a party seeking to discover who gave damaging information about him to the police or some other body. The courts may find that the public interest outweighs the private rights of the affected party. A similar balance of public versus private interest may also apply where the doctor is not a potential defendant but merely a witness. Particularly sensitive information may be allowed to be withheld from the court in the public interest. So in *AB* v. *Glasgow and West of Scotland Blood Transfusion Service* [49] a Scottish court refused to order disclosure of the identity of a blood donor who had allegedly supplied infected blood. The doctor's protection depends on the judge's discretion.

Next, the doctor may be compelled to hand over information to the police or other authorities before any trial commences. Several statutes demand that the doctor answers questions if the police come and ask him. If a statute imposes a duty on 'any person' to answer police questions, any person includes a doctor.[50] His profession confers no exemption or privilege upon him. Where no specific statutory power aids the police in their investigation of a crime the question becomes whether, if they believe a doctor holds records or other material constituting evidence of a crime on the part of a patient, they can search the doctor's premises and seize the relevant material. The Police and Criminal Evidence Act 1984 grants police access to medical records but imposes certain safeguards. A search warrant to enter and search a surgery, hospital or clinic for medical records or human tissue or fluids taken for the purposes of medical treatment may be granted only by a circuit judge[51] and not, as is usually the case, by lay magistrates. The judge is directed to weigh the public interest in disclosure of the material against the general public interest in maintaining confidentiality.

Beyond the scope of the criminal law several further examples of compulsory disclosure must be noted. Provision is made for compulsory notification of certain highly infectious diseases and of venereal disease.[52] Interestingly, AIDS is not a notifiable disease in the United Kingdom. The Public Health (Control of Disease) Act 1984 expressly states that cholera, plague, relapsing fever, smallpox and typhus shall be notifiable diseases and makes provision for other diseases to be so categorized at times of epidemic. The government has resisted pressure to make HIV/AIDS a notifiable disease. Again the question is one of balancing the competing public interests, the interest in patients seeking advice and treatment for disease, and the interest in protecting the health of those at risk from infection. HIV is not in the same league as diseases such as cholera. The cholera carrier immediately places his casual contacts at risk. If he is untreated he can do little to minimize that risk. Cholera spreads like wildfire. HIV is much, much less infectious and by acting responsibly the patient can reduce the risk to others. To act responsibly he needs professional help and should not be deterred from seeking help by fear that his doctor will be forced to 'squeal' to the authorities. It should be noted though that the provisions for compulsory detention in the 1984 Act do extend to AIDS patients and HIV carriers, though, to my knowledge, they have been invoked only once.[53]

Accidents at work and instances of food poisoning are notifiable. Abortions must be reported. Details of drug addicts are required under the Misuse of Drugs Act. Births and deaths have to be notified by doctors as well as registered by families.

Finally, a number of bodies concerned with health administration may require information in the course of performing their functions. These include the NHS Ombudsman, the Department of Health and other NHS authorities.[54] Examining the individual items on the long list of circumstances when a doctor can be forced to hand over information concerning his patients, many can be justified on grounds of public interest. The trouble is that the list grows haphazardly. Only in the case of HIV has the question of competing public interests and private rights been expressly addressed. What is needed is a review of medical confidentiality to examine all instances of compulsory disclosure and clarify when the public interest overrides the general benefit of preserving confidentiality. Legislation compelling disclosure should be express rather than simply including the doctor in a general requirement for any person to give information. Parliament should address the problem directly and not leave it to the judges to interpret ambiguous statutory provisions.

An opportunity for such a review might by offered by the highly controversial section 60 of the Health and Social Care Act 2001. Section 60 (1) provides that:

The Secretary of State may by regulation[55] make such provision for and in connection with requiring or regulating the processing of prescribed patient information for medical purposes as he considers necessary or expedient –

(a) in the interest of improving patient care, or
(b) in the public interest

As the Health and Social Care Bill progressed through Parliament, fears were voiced that Ministers would use this power to undermine the Data Protection Act and other common law protection of medical privacy. In a concession to opponents of the move, a Patient Advisory Group was established with whom the Secretary of State must consult on any regulations to be made under section 60. How the extensive powers in section 60 for mandatory or authorized disclosure of patient information will be used remains to be seen. Would it be too much to hope that government will establish new exceptions to the principle of confidentiality sparingly and use its new powers to bring about a structured approach to the balance between individual interest and the public good?

Data Protection Act 1998 [56]

The Data Protection Act 1998 offers statutory protection to control the use and processing of all forms of 'personal data'. This includes all medical and health records whether the records are manual or computerized. The individual about whom information is held is designated the 'data subject', and the person or organization responsible for holding that information is styled the 'data controller'. The 1998 Act applies to all kinds of information held about us, not just health records. I am, however, concerned here only with its application to health records.

'Health records' are defined as:

any record which:

(a) consists of information relating to the physical or mental health or condition of an individual, and
(b) has been made by or on behalf of a health professional in connection with the care of an individual.[57]

Health professional[58] is broadly defined to include doctors, dentists, nurses and most kinds of other 'conventional' health professionals, but not most complementary medicine practitioners.[59] The Act is lengthy, complex and not compelling reading. The fundamental points to emphasize are these. Any processing of data, including alteration of health records, retrieval of or use of records, disclosure or erasure of records must be done in conformity with the Act. Any 'personal data' from a health record that is information relating to a living and identifiable patient is subject to stringent controls. Whenever such data is processed one at least of the conditions of Schedule 2 of the Act must be met. These include that the patient gave consent to processing, or that processing is necessary to protect the 'vital interests' of the patient, or necessary in the administration of justice, or for the purpose of the legitimate interests of the data controller. Consent need not be explicit. Notices in GP surgeries and clinics about possible uses of information may suffice. A broader range of justifications for disclosure than the common law allows is sanctioned by Schedule 2.

However, health records fall within the category of 'sensitive personal data' and are thus granted additional protection by the Act. Sensitive personal data includes any information about a person's physical or mental health or condition and may only be processed, and therefore only disclosed, either with the *explicit* consent of the patient or in the following circumstances. (Specific provision is made in relation to research and I address this later in Chapter 16.) What follows is not an exhaustive list:

(1) to protect the vital interests of a patient who cannot consent on his own behalf, or where the data controller cannot reasonably be expected to obtain consent, or to protect the vital interests of another person where the patient has unreasonably withheld consent to disclosure;

(2) in connection with the administration of justice, or disclosure is required by law;

(3) for medical purposes by a health professional and only where disclosure to another person is bound by a similar duty of confidentiality.

The Secretary of State is empowered to add further conditions allowing the lawful processing of sensitive personal data. He has done so *inter alia* to allow the disclosure of health records in professional disciplinary proceedings involving health professionals and to allow various NHS authorities to investigate mismanagement or malpractice. A wide all-embracing provision allows processing without consent where it is in the substantial public interest and necessary for the discharge of any function designed to protect the public against dishonesty, malpractice or service failure and must necessarily be carried out without the explicit consent of the patient 'so as not to prejudice the discharge of that function'.

The range of exceptions to the duty of non-disclosure under the Data Protection Act mean that its scope is little greater than the obligation of confidentiality imposed by common law. The force of the 1998 Act lies in its remedies. A patient suspecting misuse of his health records can apply to the data controller to cease processing records when what is being done is or is likely to cause him substantial and unwarranted damage or distress.[60] A person who has suffered damage or distress as a consequence of violation of the Act has a right to compensation. He does not need to prove financial loss. However the data controller may in defence of such a claim establish that he had taken all reasonable care to comply with the Act.[61] Most crucially section 14 of the Act allows a patient to apply to the court to correct inaccurate health records. He can act to ensure that misinformation about his health is not perpetuated for all time.

Patients' access to records[62]

I turn now to the opposite side of the coin. Patients expect their doctors to keep their secrets. Can the doctors have secrets from their patients? The law of confidence prevented doctors from improperly disclosing information from or about their patients. What if the patient seeks information about herself? When can a patient demand to see his records?

Until November 1991, the answer to this simple question was confusing. A patient who started legal proceedings was able to obtain a court order giving her and her advisers access to her health records. The difficulties in getting access to health records by any other means prompted patients who only wanted to know what had gone wrong with their treatment to bring legal action even though they did not particularly want or need monetary compensation. From 1987, the Data Protection Act 1984 gave patients limited access to computerized health records. Then the Access to Health Records Act 1990 offered access to manual records,[63] but only records compiled after November 1991. An attempt to assert a common law right of access to all records, including records compiled before 1991, failed.[64] The Data Protection Act 1998 repeals and replaces most of these prior rules. Section 7 of the 1998 Act establishes a right for data subjects to have access to all personal data relating to them held by the data controller. For our purposes this means that patients have a *prima facie* right to access of all their health records whether manual or computerized. However, the 1998 Act, like its predecessors, allows the Secretary of State to exempt or modify rights of patient access to health records.[65]

Access is not unlimited. Certain sorts of information held for research, historical or statistical purposes are exempted from access. Special rules are laid down where information about a patient also includes information about some third party. A host of other exemptions and limitations apply. Most crucially access to health records may be refused where release of information would be likely to cause serious harm to the physical or mental health or condition of the patient or any other person.[66] In deciding whether to refuse access, NHS authorities are required to consult the health professionals currently responsible for the patient's care.[67]

On the face of it such exclusions from rights of access seem reasonable. A patient whose mental health is fragile and who may be devastated by a full account of his diagnosis and prognosis may be thought to be 'better off' not knowing the true state of affairs. Of course, when he is refused access he may imagine an even worse scenario! The crux of the problem is the way in which relevant NHS authorities, and doctors in particular, will use the exclusions. Suppose a patient has been diagnosed as having terminal cancer. His doctor decides not to tell him, and advises the health authority to refuse access to records because *he* judges that the patient could not cope with the truth. What can the patient do? Section 7 of the Data Protection Act allows him to apply to the court, so a judge can decide if access has been improperly refused.

In the past ten years medical and legal attitudes to patients' 'right to know' have altered. The GMC expressly acknowledges the importance of sharing information with patients. Doctors are admonished that patients '. . . have a right to information about any condition or disease from which they are suffering'.[68] The Court of Appeal has moved away from its previously entrenched position that doctors decide what patients have a right to know. Lord Woolf has asserted that patients should be told about any '. . . significant risk which would affect the judgement of a reasonable patient'[69] (see pages 107–8). With luck the Data Protection Act will provide a legal framework within which a culture of openness will flourish. Fears that such a culture will result in patients being forced to cope with unwanted information are misplaced. No one is obliged to seek access to his records.

Finally the access provisions of the Data Protection Act 1998 apply only to living patients. Consequently a small part of the Access to Health Records Act[70] is preserved to enable executors of a deceased person's estate or member of his family to gain access to his records in an appropriate case.

Anonymized data

Most of what has been said so far relates to information from which the identity of the patient can be ascertained. For many purposes however anonymized data about patients and their diseases is needed or wanted by diverse bodies. Anonymized information may be necessary to carry out clinical audits, or to compile statistics about health needs, or for epidemiological purposes. Many of us might applaud such purposes. Commercial organizations such as drug companies may also seek access to such information to help them with marketing or product development. The GMC gives extensive advice on anonymizing data and its disclosure.[71] It urges doctors to explain to their patients how such data is used and what benefits flow from exchange of information. Does the confidentiality apply to anonymized information?

In *R* v. *Department of Health ex p. Source Informatics Ltd*[72] the applicants were a data collection company. They persuaded GPs and pharmacists to supply them with anonymized information about prescribing habits. They then sold this information to drug companies. The Department of Health issued a document ruling that to disclose such information without patient consent constituted a breach of confidence. The company challenged the ruling. The trial judge found that anonymization did not remove the obligation of confidence. Transfer of anonymized data might in certain cases be justifiable, for example, to ensure clinical audit, but information about patients was in all cases confidential, whether the patient was identifiable or not. The Court of Appeal disagreed, ruling that disclosure of anonymized information did not violate the interests that obligations of confidentiality protect. The patient's privacy is not violated. He is not vulnerable to any harm. Patients have no property in information about them. Ethical safeguards now surround anonymized data. The law restricts itself to controlling information about us only where we can be identified. GPs, pharmacists, and drug companies may still profit from information derived from us.

NHS practice

It is important to note that within the NHS crucial decisions on patient confidentiality and access to records may be made not by health professionals but by health service administrators. A manager, not a doctor or nurse, may decide, for example, to allow police access to patient records.[73]

I have already examined the role of the GMC in enforcing the ethic of confidentiality. Their jurisdiction is limited to medical practitioners. The Nursing and Midwifery Council (NMC) enforces similar stringent ethical rules for nurses. Doctors as well as patients have expressed concern that a patient's notes are seen by an unnecessary number of persons. They complain that decisions as to when to disclose records are taken too often by administrators, and that administrators are not subject to the control of the GMC or the NMC. Doctors fear they may be less concerned about confidentiality.

Such fears should be misguided. All NHS staff are subject to the law on confidence. Information confided by the patient to her doctor remains legally confidential when passed by the doctor to NHS clerks for filing and preserving in NHS files. Department of Health Guidelines[74] make it clear that confidentiality binds everyone working within the NHS. Disclosure within the service is justified only if required in the context of the patient's health care. Disclosure to third parties outside the service is permissible only with the patient's consent, save in exceptional cases. The exceptions, for example, where disclosure is required by law or in the case of serious crime, correspond closely to the exceptions sanctioned by the GMC. Generally decisions on disclosure should always be taken by a medically qualified person and where possible it should be the doctor caring for the patient. Guidelines are enforced by the sanction of disciplinary action or even dismissal against staff members who break them.

A right to medical privacy?

Everyone has the right to respect for his private and family life, his home and his correspondence.

Thus runs Article 8 of the European Convention on Human Rights. There is no doubt Article 8 embraces medical privacy. What is more debatable is how much further the privacy right encapsulated in Article 8 extends than the right to confidentiality endorsed at common law. The two overlap, reinforcing each other. An NHS doctor improperly disclosing confidential information violates Article 8. The key becomes again, when is disclosure improper? Article 8, like the common law, imposes only a relative obligation of confidence. Consider the scope of Article 8 (2).

There shall be no interference by a public authority with the exercise of this right except such as is in accordance with the law and necessary in a democratic society in the interests of national security, public safety or the economic well-being of the country, for the prevention of disorder or crime, for the protection of health or morals, or for the protection of the rights and freedoms of others.

When medical privacy is covered by an obligation of confidence the conditions justifying violation of Article 8 may even be wider than judicial interpretation of the public interest defence in breach of confidence. The European Court of Human Rights has upheld seizure of medical records in criminal proceedings[75] and use of records in connection with social security benefits.[76] Article 8's importance may lie principally in its utility in establishing a right of privacy separate from obligations of confidence.

Laws governing confidentiality only prevent others from disclosing information about you without your consent. They do not enable you to protect your privacy as such. Imagine this scenario. X undergoes genetic tests to establish whether she has a gene rendering her susceptible to breast cancer. The test proves positive. A potential employer or insurer seeks to ascertain if she has undergone such a test and to find out the results. Doctors breach confidence if they release test results without the patient's consent. So the employer or insurer will simply demand that information from the patient herself. She is free to refuse to divulge her test results, but the consequence may be that she is turned down for the job, or refused insurance. Her 'right' to privacy means little.

Could Article 8 establish a right to keep personal information secret unless the other party has a justifiable claim to that information within Article 8 (2)? The possible emergence of such a right can be discerned in two highly publicized judgments of the English courts.

In *Douglas* v. *Hello Ltd* and *Venables* v. *News Group Newspapers Ltd*, the courts extended the protection afforded to private life, acknowledging the impetus to do so derived from the Human Rights Act. In *Douglas* v. *Hello Ltd*[77] two film stars sought to sue a magazine which had published unauthorized photographs of their wedding. The Court of Appeal unanimously held that their claim could proceed, albeit suggesting that there might in any case be a sufficient relationship of confidentiality between the parties. However Sedley LJ gave powerful support to the recognition of a discrete right of privacy not dependent on any prior confidential relationship. He said that recognition should be given:

. . . to the fact that the law has to protect not only those people whose trust has been abused but those who simply find themselves subjected to an unwanted intrusion into their personal lives. The law no longer needs to construct an artificial relationship of confidentiality between intruder and victim; it can recognise privacy itself as a legal principle drawn from the fundamental value of personal autonomy.[78]

In *Venables* v. *News Group Newspapers Ltd*,[79] Butler-Sloss P issued an injunction to prevent the media disclosing new identities given to, or the whereabouts of, the two boys convicted of killing James Bulger. Not quite as radical as Sedley LJ in her argument, she acknowledged an extended duty of confidence '. . . independent of a transaction or relationship between the parties.'[80] The English courts seemed to be feeling their way to a fully-fledged right of privacy.[81] Progress however is slow and the Court of Appeal[82] seems unwilling to grant any final seal of approval to Sedley LJ's bold proposition. Their Lordships prefer to see how far the law on confidentiality can be adapted to meet the demands of Article 8.

Could a right assist patient X seeking to protect her genetic privacy? Private employers and insurers will argue that the Human Rights Convention itself cannot be used directly against them because they are not *public authorities*.[83] However the courts can invoke the principles of the Human Rights Convention to develop existing causes of action, as the *Douglas* and *Venables* judgments well illustrate. Should the common law not prove sufficiently flexible, a claim under the Human Rights Act against the government for failing to implement effective laws on privacy could be contemplated.

Alas, X's case faces a further hurdle. An employer or insurer may seek to invoke one of the justifications for violating privacy set out in Article 8(2). In X's case, where what is established by tests is a susceptibility to breast cancer, a 'defence' based on the protection of the health or freedom of others invoked by an employer is unlikely to succeed. Were she a potential airline pilot with a genetic susceptibility to heart failure the balance of the argument might be different. Another argument that might be advanced in X's particular case might be on protection of 'economic well-being'. Can employers or insurers be forced to take on poor risks? Note though that Article 8(2) speaks of the economic well-being of the country, not of individual businesses. A further twist to the tale is this. Does X's daughter have any right to information about X? Could she argue that her right to life (Article 2) and 'family life' (Article 8(1)) impose an obligation on X to disclose information to her, to inform her decisions about whether to seek genetic testing? Defining the scope of a right to medical privacy will prove more difficult than establishing that such a right exists.

In the context of genetic privacy, the Human Genetics Commission (HGC) was established to develop policy and advise the government on the regulation of genetics. The HGC is reviewing whether individuals applying for insurance policies have a right to genetic privacy and what such a right entails. In May 2001 the HGC advised that there should be a three-year moratorium, except in relation to tests for Huntington's chorea, preventing insurers seeking access to genetic test results in relation to policies worth less than £500K. Subsequently, in October 2001, the insurers themselves, via the Association of British Insurers, agreed a voluntary five-year moratorium in relation to life insurance policies worth less than £500K, and other insurance policies worth less that £300K. The HGC is pressing for laws to protect genetic privacy.[84] Would it make sense to legislate more generally to safeguard medical privacy?

Part Two:
Medical Malpractice

Introduction

In this Part, I examine what remedies the law affords a patient dissatisfied with the medical care that he has received. He may feel that he has not been fully consulted or properly counselled about the nature and risks of treatment. He may have agreed to treatment and ended up worse, not better. Consequently the patient may seek compensation from the courts. Or he may simply want an investigation of what went wrong, and to ensure that his experience is not suffered by others.

The law relating to medical errors, often described as medical malpractice, operates on two basic principles. (1) The patient must agree to treatment. (2) Treatment must be carried out with proper skill and care on the part of all the members of the medical profession involved. Any doctor who operated on or injected, or even touched, an adult patient against her will might commit a battery, a trespass against the patient's person. A doctor who was shown to have exercised inadequate care of his patient, to have fallen below the required standard of competence, would be liable to compensate the patient for any harm he caused her in the tort of negligence. In short, to obtain compensation the patient suing for negligence must show that the doctor was at fault and that the doctor's 'fault' caused her injury. Three overwhelming problems are inherent in meeting these apparently simple conditions.

First, how do courts staffed by lawyer-judges determine when a doctor is at fault? We shall see that the judges in England used to defer largely to the views of the doctors. Recent case-law suggests judges are now more ready to scrutinize medical practice. Establishing what constitutes good practice will still cause the court some difficulty. Each side is generally free to call its own experts and a clash of eminent medical opinions is not unusual.

Second, as liability, and the patient's right to compensation, is dependent on a finding of fault, doctors naturally feel that a judgment against them is a body blow to their career and their reputation. Yet a moment's reflection will remind the reader of all the mistakes she has made in her own job. A solicitor overlooking a vital piece of advice from a conference with a client can telephone the client and put things right when he has a chance to check what he has done. A carpenter can have a second go at fixing a door or a cupboard. An overtired, overstrained doctor may commit a momentary error that is irreversible. He is still a good doctor despite one mistake.

Finally, the doctor's fault must be shown to have caused the patient harm. In general, whether a patient is treated within the NHS or privately, the doctor only undertakes to do his best. He does not guarantee a cure. The patient will have a legal remedy only if he can show that the doctor's carelessness or lack of skill caused him injury that he would not otherwise have suffered. So if I contract an infection and am prescribed antibiotics that a competent doctor should have appreciated were inappropriate for me or my condition, I can sue the doctor only if I can show either (1) that the antibiotic prescribed caused me harm unrelated to my original sickness, for example, caused an allergic reaction, or (2) that the absence of appropriate treatment significantly delayed my recovery. In both cases I must prove that had the doctor acted properly the harm to me would have been avoided.

We shall see therefore that the law is a remedy only for more specific and serious grievances against a doctor. It is in any case an expensive and unwieldy weapon. Many patients have complaints, particularly about hospitals, that do not amount to actionable negligence. They complain about being kept waiting, inadequate visiting hours, or rudeness on the part of NHS staff. I shall look in this Part at extra-legal methods of pursuing complaints against a hospital or a doctor, and in particular I examine the role of the National Health Service Ombudsman. Nor do I limit my examination to faults alleged against medical practitioners. Many medical mishaps arise from the dangers inherent in certain drugs. I consider the liability of the drug companies and attempts by government to ensure that available medicines are safe. In the last chapter of this Part, I ask whether the whole basis of the present law of negligence as it applies to medical practice is due, or indeed overdue, for radical reform.

Finally, I should say a word about legal 'language' today. The person who initiates a legal action, for example the patient suing a doctor for battery or negligence, used to be referred to as the *plaintiff*. When Lord Woolf recommended radical reforms of the civil justice system, some of which are discussed in Chapter 7, he also proposed that old-fashioned language should be changed into plain English. So today the patient bringing a claim against a doctor is simply called the *claimant*. Where I discuss cases decided before 1999, I use the old term *plaintiff*. In discussion of contemporary cases and problems, I use the new approved style of claimant. Defendants, thankfully, remain just that, defendants.

4
Agreeing to Treatment

Medical treatment normally requires the agreement of the patient. There would be little support today, even from the most paternalistic doctor, for the proposition that every sick adult should be compelled to accept whatever treatment his doctor thought best. No one suggests that adults who stay away from dentists out of childlike fear and to the detriment of their dental and general health should be rounded up and marched to the nearest dental surgery for forcible treatment. Few would deny the right of the adult Jehovah's Witness to refuse a blood transfusion even if by doing so she forfeits her life. The right of the patient, who is sufficiently rational and mature to understand what is entailed in treatment, to decide for herself whether to agree to that treatment is a basic human right. The right to autonomy, to self-rule rather than rule by others, is endorsed by ethicists as a right to patient autonomy. How far is patient autonomy recognized and protected by the law in England?

This chapter considers only the relatively easy case of mentally competent adults. Such an adult has an inviolable right to determine what is done to his or her body. I shall look at the law in relation to mentally incapacitated patients and children later, and also address circumstances where legislation may endorse compulsory medical treatment.

The tort of battery is committed where any non-consensual contact takes place. A person who intentionally touches another against that other's will commits a trespass to that person just as much as coming uninvited on to the person's land is a trespass to his land. Where a person consents to the contact no battery is committed. So a boxer entering the ring cannot complain of battery when he is hit on the chin by his opponent. Conduct that constitutes the tort of battery will generally also amount to the crime of assault.

How does this relate to doctors? Any doctor examining a patient, or injecting or operating on a patient, makes contact with that patient's body. Normally he commits no wrong because he does so with the patient's agreement. Should the doctor fail to obtain the patient's agreement he commits the tort of battery, and the crime of assault. That scenario is extremely unlikely. What of the surgeon who correctly decides to treat cancer of the bone in the right leg by amputating that leg but by error amputates the wrong leg? Once the error is discovered the poor patient has to endure a further operation to remove the right leg. Or a patient's notes are mixed up and a woman who was scheduled for and consented to an appendectomy is given a hysterectomy. Both unfortunate victims can sue the surgeon in battery as they did not consent to the operation performed. In a Canadian case a woman who expressed her wish to be injected in her right arm was injected by the doctor in her left. She sued in battery and succeeded.[1]

In all these examples the surgeon or some other member of the hospital staff has been careless. So the patient could normally sue in negligence too. However, there are certain differences between the two torts. In battery, a patient need not establish any tangible injury. The actionable injury is the uninvited invasion of his body. This is important. A doctor may, on medically unchallengeable grounds, go ahead with an operation that he decides is in the patient's best interests. Yet if the operation was done without consent a battery has still been committed even if the patient's health improves. A doctor who discovered that his patient's womb was ruptured while performing minor gynaecological surgery was held liable to her for going ahead and sterilizing her there and then, because she had not agreed to sterilization.[2] A woman whose ovaries were removed without her express consent similarly recovered for battery.[3] The essence of the wrong of battery is the unpermitted contact. There is no requirement that the patient prove that if he had been asked to consent to the relevant treatment he would have refused.

Two further points should be noted. First, battery may be alleged by a patient who *says* he did not consent. On whom does the onus of proof lie? It has been held in England that the onus of proof lies on the patient. He must establish that he did not agree to the procedure.[4] Second, for what will the patient be compensated? In negligence we shall see that a defendant is only liable for the kind of damage that he reasonably ought to foresee. In battery the test may be more stringent. The defendant may be liable for all the damage that can factually be shown to flow from his wrongdoing. A doctor who injected a patient in the 'wrong' arm would be liable in battery *and* negligence for any unwanted stiffness in that arm, and for any adverse reaction that he ought to have contemplated in view of the patient's history. He would not be liable in negligence for a 'freak' reaction. In battery he might be so liable. None the less judges in England seem eager to limit the scope of battery when it overlaps with negligence. They strive to avoid subjecting a surgeon to liability in battery. A significant disadvantage with the tort of battery as a means of vindicating patients' rights is that for a claim to lie in battery there must be *physical* contact between doctor and patient. A patient who agreed to take a drug orally, having been totally misled as to the nature of the drug, could not sue in battery. Had the doctor injected him with that self-same drug, a claim in battery would lie. Law is not always logical!

A right to say no?

Will the law ever set limits to a person's right to refuse treatment? Are we free to reject life-saving treatment that others might consider it 'wicked folly'[5] to refuse. The theory is clear. In *Re T. (Adult: Refusal of Medical Treatment)*,[6] Lord Donaldson declared: An adult patient '. . . has an absolute right to choose whether to consent to medical treatment, to refuse it or to choose one rather than another of the treatments being offered'.[7]

Such an absolute right to autonomy '. . . exists notwithstanding that the reasons for making the choice are rational, or irrational, unknown or even non-existent'. In *Re T.* a young woman of twenty had suffered serious injuries in a road accident. She was thirty-four weeks pregnant and consented to a Caesarian section on the following day. Later that evening she was visited by her mother, a devout Jehovah's Witness. T. was not herself a baptized Witness. After her mother's visit, T. told doctors that she would not agree to any blood transfusion before or during surgery. She first enquired whether alternatives to whole blood were available, and was assured that such alternatives exist. She was given a form to sign evidencing her refusal of transfusion and absolving the hospital from liability for failing to administer blood should she haemorrhage. After delivery of a stillborn child, T. lapsed into a coma and suffered life-threatening internal bleeding. The hospital argued that they could not lawfully give her a blood transfusion. Her boyfriend and father sought a court-order authorizing a life-saving transfusion. Notwithstanding his ringing endorsement of patient autonomy, Lord Donaldson and his brethren in the Court of Appeal granted that order.

The Court of Appeal held that on the facts of the case T.'s refusal of treatment was not an autonomous judgement. Her decision was 'flawed'. The combination of the effect of her injuries and the medication she was taking impaired her mental capacity to decide whether or not to agree to blood transfusions. T. lacked sufficient information to make a decision to refuse transfusion. While she was told there were alternatives to whole blood, she was not advised about their limited utility or warned that there were circumstances where, without transfusion, her life would be at risk. Lord Donaldson criticized doctors, whom he suggested were more anxious to disclaim any possible legal liability than to ensure that T. was given comprehensible and comprehensive information.[8] Pressure from T.'s mother may have constituted undue influence[9] rendering her purported refusal of blood transfusion less than independent and voluntary. These several factors clouding the nature of T.'s decision caused the Court of Appeal to conclude that T.'s rejection of blood could be disregarded. The right of the individual to decide whether to accept medical treatment was paramount but in '. . . cases of doubt, that doubt falls to be resolved in favour of preservation of life, for if the individual is to override the public interest, he must do so in clear terms'.

It may be tempting to regard *Re T.* as judges saying one thing, upholding the rhetoric of autonomy, and doing another, rejecting an unusual belief that caused a young woman to risk sacrificing her life. *Re T.* requires careful scrutiny. The unusual facts support judicial doubts as to whether T. ever made a truly voluntary and sufficiently informed choice to reject life-saving treatment. Subsequent judgments have upheld the principle of autonomy articulated in *Re T*.[10] In *B. v. An NHS Trust*,[11] Butler-Sloss P ruled that it was unlawful for doctors to refuse to switch off a ventilator keeping Ms B. alive. The judge unequivocally endorsed the value of patient autonomy. The crux of the matter will always turn on the capacity of the individual to make a valid choice – a subject explored further in the next chapter.

Lord Donaldson's recognition of an unqualified right to refuse treatment as long as the adult patient was competent to make that decision was subject to a controversial caveat. He contended that an exception to that right might exist in '. . . a case in which the choice may lead to the death of a viable foetus'.[12] Pregnant women and women in labour might be excluded from the normal right to self-determination. A series of cases followed *Re T.* in which judges ordered women to submit to Caesarean sections. In *Re S.*,[13] Sir Stephen Brown P invoked Lord Donaldson's dictum to authorize Caesarian surgery to save the life of the woman's unborn child. Other judgments[14] tended to rely more heavily on the judge's ruling that, at the time she refused 'necessary' surgery, the woman's capacity to make decisions was impaired. Ultimately the Court of Appeal clarified the law. An adult woman 'of sound mind' retains exactly the same rights to accept or refuse treatment as any other adult. The unborn child enjoys no legal personality that entitles the court to force its mother to submit to any form of intervention she elects to decline.[15] The mother's right to autonomy is not diminished or reduced merely because her decision may '. . . appear morally repugnant'.[16] Adults can say no to treatment.

What is meant by consent?

Consent is mandatory, but what is meant by consent? Consent may be implied from the circumstances and need not be written. If a patient visits his general practitioner complaining of a sore throat and opens his mouth so that the doctor can examine his throat, he cannot complain that he never expressly said to the doctor: 'You may put a spatula on my tongue and look down my throat.' A patient visiting casualty with a bleeding wound implicitly agrees to doctors or nurses cleaning and bandaging the wound. In an American case an immigrant to the USA complained that he had not consented to vaccination. It was found that he had bared his arm and held it out to the doctor. His action precluded the need for any verbal consent.[17]

Patient identifier/label

Name of proposed procedure or course of treatment (include brief explanation if medical term not clear). . . . .
. . . .

Statement of health professional (to be filled in by health professional with appropriate knowledge of proposed procedure, as specified in consent policy)

I have explained the procedure to the patient. In particular, I have explained:

The intended benefits . . . .
. . . .

Serious or frequently occurring risks . . . .
. . . .

Any extra procedures which may become necessary during the procedure:

blood transfusion . . . .

other procedure (please specify) . . . .

I have also discussed what the procedure is likely to involve, the benefits and risks of any available alternative treatments (including no treatment) and any particular concerns of this patient.

The following leaflet/tape has been provided . . . .

This procedure will involve:
general and/or regional anaesthesia ☐ local anaesthesia ☐ sedation ☐

Signed . . . . Date . . . .
Name (PRINT) . . . . Job title . . . .

Contact details (if patient wishes to discuss options later) . . . .
. . . .

Statement of interpreter (where appropriate)

I have interpreted the information above to the patient to the best of my ability and in a way in which I believe s/he can understand.

Signed . . . . Date . . . .
Name (PRINT). . . . .

Top copy accepted by patient: yes/no (please ring)

Statement of patient **Patient identifier/label**

Please read this form carefully. If your treatment has been planned in advance, you should already have your own copy of page 2 which describes the benefits and risks of the proposed treatment. If not, you will be offered a copy now. If you have any further questions, do ask – we are here to help you. You have the right to change your mind at any time, including after you have signed this form.

I agree to the procedure or course or treatment described on this form.

I understand that you cannot give me a guarantee that a particular person will perform the procedure. The person will, however, have appropriate experience.

I understand that I will have the opportunity to discuss the details of anaesthesia with an anaesthetist before the procedure, unless the urgency of my situation prevents this. (This only applies to patients having general or regional anaesthesia.)

I understand that any procedure in addition to those described on this form will only be carried out if it is necessary to save my life or to prevent serious harm to my health.

I have been told about additional procedures which may become necessary during my treatment. I have listed below any procedures **which I do not wish to be carried out** without further discussion.

. . . .
. . . .
. . . .
. . . .

Signed . . . . , Date . . . .
Name (PRINT) . . . .

A witness should sign below if the patient is unable to sign but has indicated his or her consent. Young people/children may also like a parent to sign here (see notes).

Signed . . . . Date . . . .
Name (PRINT) . . . .

Confirmation of consent (to be completed by a health professional when the patient is admitted for the procedure, if the patient has signed the form in advance)

On behalf of the team treating the patient, I have confirmed with the patient that s/he has no further questions and wishes the procedure to go ahead.

Signed . . . . Date . . . .
Name (PRINT) . . . . Job title . . . .

Important notes (tick if applicable)

See also advance directive/living will (eg Jehovah's Witness form)
Patient has withdrawn consent (ask patient to sign/date here)

. . . .

A patient for whom surgery or any form of invasive investigation is proposed will normally be asked to sign a consent form. The Department of Health issues guidance on consent to treatment and produces model forms for use within the NHS. The Department's aim is to ensure that health care professionals appreciate the need to give patients the information to which they are entitled. A model form for routine surgery, investigation or treatment is shown on pages 95–7.[18]

The current form is much more detailed than its predecessors. It attempts to ensure that patients appreciate that they are entitled to ask questions and to demand explanations about what is to be done to them, and covers anaesthetic procedures as well as surgery. Patients are not passive recipients of what the doctor thinks best. However, a form is no more than some evidence of what the patient has agreed to. What is important is the substance of what the patient is entitled to be told and has been told, and what is then done to him. Clearly any action expressly prohibited by the patient, that is, additional procedures which on the form he states '*I do not wish to be carried out without further discussion*' would constitute a battery if imposed on the patient.

What sort of authority does the provision in the form regarding additional procedures necessary to save life or serious injury to health confer on the doctor? This would not affect liability in the cases discussed earlier of the doctor who sterilized a patient in the course of minor gynaecological surgery or the surgeon who removed a woman's ovaries without her consent. Neither measure was immediately necessary to preserve the woman's health. The doctor is only authorized to carry out further surgery without which the patient's life or health is immediately at risk. A surgeon discovering advanced cancer of the womb while performing a curettage may be justified in performing an immediate hysterectomy as delay might threaten the woman's life. A doctor discovering some malformation, or other non-life-threatening condition, must delay further surgery until his patient has the opportunity to offer her opinion.

The use of the model form is not compulsory within the NHS and practice varies widely. In private hospitals and clinics a quite different form may be used. What would be the effect of a form within which the patient consented to any procedure that the surgeon saw fit to embark on? In the absence of the clearest evidence that the patient fully understood the 'blank cheque' that he handed to his doctor, such a form will be virtually irrelevant. Any consent form is no more than one piece of evidence that the patient did, in fact, consent to what was done to him.[19]

If the patient can show that despite the form he did not give any real consent to the procedure carried out, the surgeon will be liable in battery.

How much must the doctor tell the patient?

We have seen that for consent to be real the patient must be told what operation is to be performed and why it is to be done. The doctor certifies on the consent form that he has explained the proposed operation, investigation or treatment to the patient. What exactly must the doctor explain? All surgery under general anaesthetic entails some risk. Many forms of surgery and medical treatment carry further risk of harm even if they are carried out with the greatest skill and competence. Patients have argued that if they are not informed of the risks inherent in an operation then they have inadequate information on which to make a proper decision and cannot, therefore, be said to have granted real consent to the procedure. As informed consent was not given a claim in battery should lie. Alternatively they argue that if a claim in battery does not lie, they ought to be able to sue for negligence. The doctor's duty of care encompasses giving adequate information and advice. If he has given the patient inadequate information and the patient agreed to a risky procedure from which injury ensued, the doctor, it is argued, is responsible for that damage.

Let us look first at the argument that if risks or side-effects inherent in an operation are not disclosed then the patient has not really consented at all, and the surgeon is liable for battery. In *Chatterton* v. *Gerson*[20] Miss Chatterton pursued such a claim. She suffered excruciating pain as a result of post-operative scarring and Dr Gerson proposed a second operation to relieve her symptoms. The second operation also failed and Miss Chatterton subsequently lost all sensation in her right leg and foot with a consequent loss of mobility. She claimed that while Dr Gerson was in no way negligent in his conduct of the surgery, he failed to tell her enough for her to give her 'informed consent'. Her claim in battery failed. The judge said that a consent to surgery was valid providing that the patient was 'informed in broad terms of the nature of the procedure which is intended'. Any claim in relation to inadequacy of information about the risks or side-effects of treatment, or availability of alternative treatment, should be brought in negligence.

By contrast, a patient who agreed to an injection that she understood to be a routine post-natal vaccination but which was in fact the controversial long-acting contraceptive Depo-Provera succeeded in battery. Her doctor failed the test set in *Chatterton* v. *Gerson*. He obtained her agreement to the injection leaving her totally unaware and indeed misleading her, albeit in good faith, as to the nature of what was being done to her.[21] A dentist who deliberately misled patients to persuade them to agree to unnecessary dental treatment was also held liable in battery. His fraud vitiated the apparent consent given him by his unfortunate patients.[22] A bogus doctor who persuaded several women to allow him to examine their breasts, claiming that he was conducting research into breast cancer, was convicted of indecent assault.[23] The women's 'consent' depended on their belief that he had medical qualifications and that the contact to which they agreed had a proper medical purpose. Similarly an embryologist was convicted and jailed for a criminal assault when he deceived women into believing they were being implanted with their embryos when in fact they received a saline solution. The women agreed to a medical procedure, not an empty sham.

Other attempts to claim in battery, where the nature of what was to be done was honestly explained but the risks of the procedure were not, have failed just as Miss Chatterton's claim failed.[24] In *Sidaway* v. *Royal Bethlem Hospital* in the Court of Appeal, Lord Donaldson said:

> It is only if the consent is obtained by fraud or misrepresentation of the *nature* [my italics] of what is to be done that it can be said that an apparent consent is not a true consent.[25]

The House of Lords unanimously endorsed his views.[26] The Canadian courts also view battery as an inappropriate remedy for inadequate counselling. The Canadian Chief Justice has said:

> I do not understand how it can be said that the consent was vitiated by failure of disclosure of risks as to make the surgery or other treatment an unprivileged, unconsented to and intentional invasion of the patient's bodily integrity . . . unless there has been misrepresentation or fraud to secure consent to the treatment, a failure to disclose the attendant risks, however serious, should go to negligence rather than battery.[27]

It is easy to understand why courts shy away from finding doctors liable in battery. The word itself is emotive. Doctors resent being accused of 'battering' their patients. Conduct constituting the tort of battery might constitute the crime of assault.[28] Inadequate information given in good faith may not be seen as so reprehensible as to warrant criminal punishment.

However, distinguishing between battery and no battery on the *Chatterton* v. *Gerson* test is not easy. Consider the example of a patient tested for HIV without his consent. He agrees to a blood test preparatory to surgery but is never told that among the tests to be carried out on his blood is a test for HIV. Did he understand the nature and purpose of the test? He understood what would be done to him and that several tests would be carried out on his blood. Opinion about whether such a practice constitutes battery is divided.[29] Normally, express and detailed information on exactly what tests are proposed when blood is given is rarely sought or offered. Patients agree to tests so that doctors can find out what problems they may encounter and treat them safely. It is difficult to say that such patients, including the patient tested for HIV, do not understand in broad terms what is going on. Of course, were some ruse employed to obtain consent the picture might be different. Imagine that a doctor suspects a patient is HIV positive and wants a test for that sole purpose. Fearing that the patient would refuse consent if asked outright, the doctor uses a pretext, for example, a suspicion of anaemia. Would you argue that the patient falls within the *Chatterton* v. *Gerson* test, that his consent was obtained by fraud or misrepresentation? The difficulty is that what constitutes fraud is complex. In the context of criminal law, the courts have tended to say that the fraud must deceive the victim about the very nature of what is being done to her.[30] The patient agreeing to the blood test, albeit believing the test is designed to check his red blood count, still understands what is being done. It may be that civil and criminal law adopt different tests of fraud. In the case where a dentist was prosecuted for assault because, unbeknown to her patients, she continued to practise when suspended from the dental register the Court of Appeal quashed her conviction for criminal assault.[31] The patients were not misled about what was being done to them or as to the identity of the accused. None the less, Otton LJ condemned the accused's conduct as reprehensible and suggested a civil claim for damages might well succeed.

What is clear is that, where no question of misrepresentation arises, a claim based on failure to give a patient adequate information about proposed treatment lies in negligence, although until recently patients fared little better here. The doctor's duty of care to his patient undoubtedly includes a duty to give him careful advice and sufficient information upon which to reach a rational decision whether to accept or reject treatment. The problem is when the doctor is in breach of that duty. In the famous (or infamous) case of *Bolam* v. *Friern Hospital Management Committee*,[32] Mr Bolam agreed to electroconvulsive therapy to help improve his depression. He suffered fractures in the course of the treatment. The risk was known to his doctor, but he had not told Mr Bolam. Mr Bolam alleged that the failure to warn him of the risk was negligent. The judge found that the amount of information given to Mr Bolam accorded with accepted medical practice in such cases and dismissed his claim. He added that even if Mr Bolam had proved that the doctor's advice was inadequate, he would only have succeeded if he could have further proved that had he been given that information, he would have refused consent to the treatment. The test of negligence was the test of responsible medical opinion. Other cases were even more favourable to the doctors. Lord Denning held it to be entirely for the individual doctor to decide what to tell his patient, even if the doctor went so far as to resort to what his Lordship termed 'a therapeutic lie'![33]

The underlying trend in the English courts was that 'doctor knew best'. Across the Atlantic matters took a startlingly different turn. The doctrine of 'informed consent' was born. In *Canterbury* v. *Spence*[34] a US court said that the 'prudent patient' test should prevail. Doctors must disclose to their patients any material risk inherent in a proposed line of treatment.

A risk is material when a reasonable person, in what the physician knows or should know to be the patient's position, would be likely to attach significance to the risk or cluster of risks in deciding whether or not to forgo the proposed therapy.

The Canadian Supreme Court also rejected the 'professional medical standard' for determining how much the doctor must disclose. Emphasis was laid upon 'the patient's right to know what risks are involved in undergoing or forgoing surgery or other treatment'.[35] The Canadian court did allow that a particular patient might waive his right to know and put himself entirely in the hands of the doctors. They said that cases might arise where '. . . a particular patient may, because of emotional factors, be unable to cope with facts relevant to the recommended surgery or treatment and the doctor may, in such a case, be justified in withholding or generalizing information as to which he would otherwise be required to be more specific'. The doctor could rely on a defence of therapeutic privilege. The High Court of Australia several years later followed Canada in rejecting the *Bolam* test of professional opinion. In *Rogers* v.

Whittaker[36] failure to disclose a 1 in 14000 chance of blindness in both eyes inherent in surgery was held negligent. The patient had made clear her concerns about the risks of losing her sight altogether.

In England lawyers invoking the transatlantic doctrine of informed consent tried for years to breach the walls of medical silence. Miss Chatterton, who as we saw lost in battery, also failed in negligence. The doctor, the judge said, did owe her a duty to counsel her as to any real risks inherent in the surgery proposed. He did not have to canvass every risk and in deciding what to tell the patient he could take into account '. . . the personality of the patient, the likelihood of misfortune and what in the way of warning is for the particular patient's welfare'. This standard Dr Gerson had met.

So what amounted to a 'real risk of misfortune inherent in the procedure'? The case that eventually went to the House of Lords concerned Mrs Sidaway. For several years, following an accident at work, Mrs Sidaway had endured persistent pain in her right arm and shoulder. Later the pain spread to her left arm too. In 1960 she became the patient of Mr Falconer, an eminent neurosurgeon at the Maudsley Hospital. An operation relieved the pain for a while but by 1973 Mrs Sidaway was again in pain. She was admitted to the Maudsley Hospital in October 1974 and Mr Falconer diagnosed pressure on a nerve root as the cause of her pain. He decided to operate to relieve the pressure and Mrs Sidaway gave her consent to surgery. As a result of that operation Mrs Sidaway became severely disabled by partial paralysis.

Mrs Sidaway sued both Mr Falconer and the Maudsley Hospital. She did not suggest that the operation had been performed otherwise than skilfully and carefully. Her complaint was this. The operation to which she agreed involved two specific risks over and above the risk inherent in any surgery under general anaesthesia. These were damage to a nerve root, assessed as about a two per cent risk and damage to the spinal cord, assessed as less than a one per cent risk. Alas for Mrs Sidaway, that second risk materialized and she suffered partial paralysis. She maintained that Mr Falconer never warned her of the risk of injury to the spinal cord. Throughout the long and expensive litigation Mrs Sidaway's greatest handicap was that Mr Falconer died before the action came to trial. The courts were deprived of vital evidence as to exactly what the patient was told by her surgeon and what reasons, if any, he had for withholding information from her. The case had to proceed from the inference drawn by the trial judge in the High Court that Mr Falconer would have followed his customary practice, that is, he would have warned Mrs Sidaway in general terms of the possibility of injury to a nerve root but would have said nothing about any risk of damage to the spinal cord.

Ten years after the operation that left Mrs Sidaway paralysed, and seven years after Mr Falconer's death, the case reached the House of Lords.[37] The paucity of evidence about what actually happened when Mrs Sidaway and Mr Falconer discussed the proposed surgery rendered the case, as Lord Diplock put it, 'a naked question of legal principle'. What principle governed the doctor's obligation to advise patients and to warn of any risks inherent in surgery or treatment recommended by the doctor? The majority of their Lordships endorsed the traditional test enunciated in the case of Mr Bolam nearly thirty years before. The doctor's obligation to advise and warn his patient was part and parcel of his general duty of care owed to each individual patient. Prima facie, providing he conformed to a responsible body of medical opinion in deciding what to tell and what not to tell his patient, he discharged his duty properly. There being evidence that while some neurosurgeons might warn some patients of the risk to the spinal cord many chose not to and Mrs Sidaway's case was lost.

The *Sidaway* judgment, some of their Lordships said, should not be seen as endorsing the view that providing a doctor follows current medical practice in deciding what information to give his patients he will be immune from legal attack. The courts retain ultimate control of the scope of the doctor's obligation. First, for Lords Bridge and Templeman, a crucial issue in Mrs Sidaway's case was that the risk of which she was not advised was a less than one per cent risk, and all the medical expert witnesses were agreed that it was a risk that many responsible neuro-surgeons elected not to warn patients of. Had the risk been of greater statistical significance, their Lordships *might* have held in Mrs Sidaway's favour, even if expert medical witnesses supported non-disclosure. Lord Bridge gave as an example '. . . an operation involving a substantial risk of grave adverse consequences, for example [a] ten per cent risk of a stroke from the operation'.[38] He went on to acknowledge more generally that there might be cases where '. . . disclosure of a particular risk was so obviously necessary to an informed choice on the part of the patient that no reasonably prudent medical man would fail to make it'.[39] Second, for Lords Diplock and Templeman a further vital question in the case was that Mrs Sidaway had not expressly inquired of Mr Falconer what risks the surgery entailed. For Lord Diplock the case concerned solely what information the doctor must *volunteer*. Lord Templeman said Mr Falconer could not be faulted for failing to give Mrs Sidaway information for which she did not ask.

What four out of five of the Law Lords in *Sidaway* unequivocally agreed on was the rejection of the transatlantic test that what the patient should be told should be judged by what the reasonable patient would want to know. Lord Scarman alone rejected current medical practice as the test of what a patient needs to be told. He dissented, and in a powerful judgment asserted the patient's right to know. The patient's right of self determination, his right to choose what happened to his body, was the factor that to Lord Scarman made the issue of advice given to the patient distinct from other aspects of medical care. The doctor should be liable '. . . where the risk is such that in the court's view a prudent person in the patient's situation would have regarded it as significant'.[40] But, albeit the patient's right of self-determination distinguishes advice given from other stages in medical care, advice before treatment cannot be totally separated from the doctor's general duty to offer proper professional and competent service. Doctors, in Lord Scarman's view, should be to a certain extent protected by 'therapeutic privilege'. This would permit a doctor to withhold information if it can be shown that 'a reasonable medical assessment of the patient would have indicated to the doctor that disclosure would have posed a serious threat of psychological detriment to the patient'.[41] Lord Scarman recognized the right of a patient of sound understanding to be warned of material risks save in exceptional circumstances, yet he too found against Mrs Sidaway. He held that she failed to establish on the evidence put forward by her counsel that the less than one per cent risk was such that a prudent patient would have considered it significant.

After *Sidaway*

Much was made in *Sidaway* of evidence that Mrs Sidaway did not expressly ask Mr Falconer about the risks and side-effects of the proposed operation. Mrs Blyth asked a lot of questions. She suffered prolonged bleeding after an injection of the long-term contraceptive Depo-Provera. Despite her questions, she was not given comprehensive information on the potential side-effects of that controversial drug. She sued for negligence. The trial judge held that in the circumstances he did not have to follow the *Sidaway* judgment.[42] Mrs Blyth had made express requests for full information, and was entitled to *all* the relevant information about Depo-Provera. The Court of Appeal[43] allowed the health authority's appeal. The test of what Mrs Blyth must be told was to be judged by good professional practice. It seemed that asking questions made little difference to the degree of information the patient was entitled to!

The Court of Appeal reiterated its support for the 'professional' standard for disclosure in *Gold* v. *Haringey Health Authority*.[44] Mrs Gold agreed to be sterilized. She was never warned that sterilization might be reversed naturally, nor was she told that male vasectomy carried a lower risk of reversal. She sued for negligence after the birth of her unplanned child.[45] Again the trial judge said that he did not have to follow *Sidaway*.[46] *Sidaway*, he argued, applied to therapeutic treatment only. Mrs Gold was not sterilized because of any medical problem but as a convenient means of permanent contraception. In cases of non-therapeutic interventions, the patient should be given all the information a sensible and reasonable patient would be likely to want to know. The test should be the 'prudent patient' test not the professional standard. Mrs Gold fared no better than Mrs Blyth in the Court of Appeal.[47] Any distinction between therapeutic and non-therapeutic treatment was resoundingly rejected. The provision of any health care advice or treatment demanded the exercise of professional skill and so the *Bolam* test must apply. Whether or not the doctor was negligent was to be judged by whether or not he conformed to a responsible body of professional opinion in deciding what to tell the patient. Some gynaecologists did warn of the risks of reversal and discuss the comparative 'safety' of vasectomy as against female sterilization. Others, however, did not, so Mrs Gold's claim was doomed to fail. In *Gold* the patient's right to decide for herself on treatment virtually disappears.[48] Lloyd LJ said:

. . . a doctor's duty of care in relation to diagnosis, treatment and advice, whether the doctor be a specialist or a general practitioner, is not to be dissected into its component parts. To dissect a doctor's advice into that given in a therapeutic context and that given in contraceptive context would be to go against the whole thrust of the decision of the majority of the House of Lords in [*Sidaway*].[49]

Autonomy renascent?

The judgment in *Gold* left patient autonomy woefully thin in substance. Uninformed consent is a hollow vessel. Several factors suggest that doctors and courts are beginning to attach greater value to ensuring patients receive adequate information. Professional practice has changed markedly. Doctors themselves now endorse much more open disclosure of risks. Guidance from the General Medical Council directs doctors to '. . . take appropriate steps to find out what patients want to know and ought to know about their condition and its treatment'.[50] The professional standard endorsed in *Sidaway* may, in a number of cases, now demand that professionals provide patients with the information which prudent patients might want.

The courts are also more ready to require a fuller disclosure of information about treatment risks and options for patients. In *Smith* v. *Tunbridge Wells Health Authority*[51] a claim was brought by a twenty-eight-year-old man who was not warned of the risk of impotence inherent in rectal surgery. His claim succeeded despite expert evidence that a body of surgeons did not warn patients of that risk. The judge, citing Lord Bridge in *Sidaway*, found that failure to warn such a patient of a risk of such importance to him was 'neither reasonable nor responsible'. Mere evidence of a medical practice did not counter allegations of negligence. That practice must be reasonable in the context of providing patients with an informed choice. As we shall see in Chapter 6, in *Bolitho* v. *City & Hackney Health Authority*[52] the House of Lords has stressed that, in relation to all claims of negligence against doctors, expert evidence advanced to support the defendant's case that he acted without negligence must be shown to be responsible. To rebut negligence a practice must have a 'logical and defensible' basis. In *Bolitho*, Lord Browne-Wilkinson seemed at one stage to suggest that in his clarification of the *Bolam* test he was not concerned with cases about informed consent.[53] That statement was not designed to exempt consent claims from judicial scrutiny, simply to acknowledge that case-law stretching back to Lord Bridge in *Sidaway* already allowed scrutiny of information disclosure practice.[54]

That the *Bolitho* approach is applicable to informed consent claims is amply confirmed in *Pearce* v. *United Bristol Healthcare NHS Trust*.[55] Mrs Pearce, who was expecting her sixth child, was two weeks past her due date of delivery. She discussed the possibility of induction with her obstetrician who warned her of the risks of induction and caesarian surgery, but did not tell her that there was a 0.1 to 0.2 per cent risk of stillbirth associated with non-intervention. Mrs Pearce's child was still-born and she alleged that failure to warn her of the risk of stillbirth was negligent. The Court of Appeal held that she had not established negligence. The very slight risk of stillbirth arising from non-intervention, compared to the risks of intervention, was not a risk that the defendants were negligent in failing to disclose, especially in the light of Mrs Pearce's distressed condition at the time of the consultation. What is of interest in *Pearce* is that Lord Woolf's judgment in the doctors' favour departs radically from a simple test of whether the information offered Mrs Pearce conformed to a reasonable body of expert opinion. Relying on both Lord Bridge in *Sidaway* and Lord Browne-Wilkinson in *Bolitho*, Lord Woolf declares that '. . . if there is a *significant risk which would affect the judgement of a* reasonable patient, then in the normal course it is the responsibility of a doctor to inform the patient of that significant risk, if the information is needed so that the patient can determine for him or herself as to what course she should adopt' (my emphasis). Lord Woolf suggests that the reasonable doctor must tell the patient what the reasonable patient would want to know.

There will be cynics who view Lord Woolf's judgment in *Pearce* rather differently. He might be charged with using 'politically correct' language to conceal continuing deference to medical opinion. In future cases how will significant risk be defined? Ultimately Mrs Pearce's claim failed as have so many others. None the less *Pearce* is a step in the right direction especially in Lord Woolf's conflation of what reasonable doctors and reasonable patients should seek in order to achieve partnership rather than conflict.

Establishing that the reasonable doctor ought to have disclosed the relevant risk to her reasonable patient does not conclude the case for compensation. A problem of causation arises. The doctor can only be liable for the injury caused by the relevant risk materializing if the patient can show that had she been properly warned of the risk, she would not have consented to the procedure. In *Chester* v. *Afshar*[56], the claimant consented to surgery for the removal of three intra-vertebral discs. She suffered nerve damage leading to paralysis. Her surgeon had not warned her of the admittedly small risk of such disastrous consequences of surgery. The claimant's evidence was that had she been so warned she would have not agreed to surgery without at least seeking further opinions on the necessity and risks of surgery. She did not seek to maintain that in no circumstances would she ever contemplate surgery. Her back pain was considerable and incapacitating. The Court of Appeal held that none the less she succeeded in her claim. She had demonstrated that if she had been properly advised of the risks of surgery, she would not have had that operation at that time. Her paralysis was caused by the defendant's inadequate advice.

Does informed consent really matter?

Judicial reluctance to overrule medical opinion and doctors' fears of litigation[57] surrounding 'consent' are understandable. The sheer difficulty of recalling, reviewing, and interpreting conversations that took place years ago in a context far removed from a courtroom should not be underestimated. None of these factors should be allowed to override the importance of providing patients with comprehensible and comprehensive information. Lord Diplock in *Sidaway*,[58] in a judgment echoed by others of his brethren in subsequent cases, suggested information might be counterproductive. Patients, he contended, did not want more information and could not understand that information even if they were offered it. More information would lead to patients 'irrationally' refusing much-needed treatment. None of these reasons are sound.[59] Surveys show that most patients do in fact want more information. A right to more information does not mean information will be forced on the unwilling patient. If a patient says, 'Doctor, it's up to you. I don't want to know any more about this operation,' he is not going to be held down and forced to listen. Patients do have difficulties understanding medical details. The remedy is to teach doctors how to communicate more effectively. As for 'irrational' treatment refusals, there is no evidence to support the contention that more information leads to more patients refusing treatment. In any event how is 'irrationality' to be judged? A woman is told that radical mastectomy will maximize her prospects of recovery from breast cancer. Psychologically she is unable to cope with the necessary mutilation and she also knows that if she loses a breast her husband will leave her. Who can say she is 'irrational' if she opts for the statistically less 'safe' option of lumpectomy?

Undue emphasis on statistical risk bedevils debate on how much and what sort of information patients should be given about proposed treatment. The likelihood of a risk materializing is just one factor in a decision about what treatment to undergo if you are ill. The impact of the risk on the way that an individual lives her life is equally significant. It might be thought that an elderly man facing rectal surgery of the same sort as the operation involved in *Smith* v. *Tunbridge Wells Health Authority* would contemplate a small risk of impotence with greater equanimity than the twenty-eight-year-old Mr Smith. Who but the gentleman in question can judge that risk to his own remaining hopes in life?

The standard determining how much patients should be told about treatment needs to be patient-centred. Preferably it should relate not to the mythical reasonable patient but to that particular patient. The tort of negligence remains a clumsy mechanism for vindicating a patient's right to information. Battery is inappropriate both because of its emotive language and because it excludes oral drug therapies. In Canada, courts have sought to reclassify doctor–patient relationships by adapting the legal concept of the fiduciary relationship to embrace the doctor and her patient.[60] Within such a relationship of trust the doctor's duty would be to make available to the patient the information that it seems likely that individual patients would need to make an informed choice on treatment. Such a change is desirable not only to endorse patient's rights but also to enhance patient care.[61] An alliance between patient and doctor, in which the patient is fully involved improves the quality of health care.[62] Interestingly, growing numbers of doctors are moving towards this view. So far English courts have found little to recommend a departure from established torts to a more innovative fiduciary approach.[63]

Does it matter who operates?

As important to many patients as what the operation entails may be the question of who operates. If a patient agrees to surgery believing eminent consultant X will operate on him, is his consent invalidated if registrar Y operates? Where a private patient contracts with consultant X that he will operate, the consultant is in breach of contract if he substitutes someone else. Within the NHS the patient would have to show that his consent was conditional on X operating. He would not have agreed to the surgery if anyone else proposed it. In practice, consent forms used within the NHS provide that no assurance is given that any particular doctor will operate. He cannot complain if the registrar operates. If the registrar lacks the experience to perform a particular operation the patient will be able to sue him and the consultant if harm ensues. He can sue the registrar for his lack of competence and the consultant for failure to provide proper supervision and for allowing an inadequately qualified member of the team to operate.

On a number of occasions stories have appeared in the press that medical students are being allowed to carry out minor operations. A story from 1984 told of a vet who was allowed by a surgeon friend to remove a patient's gall bladder. A patient operated on by a vet will have a claim against the vet however competent he may have proved to be. He agreed to a qualified doctor operating on him.[64] He no more agreed to surgery by a vet than to surgery by the author of this book. If the vet proves to be not up to the job, the patient can also sue the surgeon who allowed him into the theatre and the hospital that permitted such an event. His action will lie in negligence. An operation performed by a medical student will give rise to a claim in negligence if the student is not competent. A claim in battery may also lie if the patient was not informed about the proposal to allow a student to operate. He consented to an operation and accepted, if he signed the standard form, that no particular practitioner undertook to operate. However, he consented to surgery performed by a practitioner, not an 'apprentice'. Teaching hospitals play a vital role and the public interest requires that medical students train on real people. Nevertheless, any contact with a patient on the part of a medical student requires the patient's consent.

Recent accounts of medical incompetence, notably the sad state of affairs in Bristol, cause patients to be concerned about the record and experience of whoever operates on them, even lofty consultants. How does their surgeon's record of success compare to that of his peers? Do his mortality rates exceed the norm? Has he been fully trained in this procedure? Evidence that surgeons have begun to practise laparascopic procedures ('keyhole surgery') without adequate training is depressingly common. Should the law oblige each doctor to provide information about his own background and experience? Patients are entitled to competent care. The medical profession has an obligation to monitor the standards attained by doctors launching into, or continuing to perform, procedures that they are not able to carry out with competence. 'Informed consent' is unlikely to be a fruitful means of attaining these ends. If Dr X has a four per cent failure rate in relation to procedure A, and Dr Y a five per cent rate, those who are able to make choices will opt for X. The difference in failure rates do not mean that Y is necessarily the poorer doctor. If Y works in a deprived area, a one per cent difference in outcome may be more than explained by the poorer state of health of his patients before they enter hospital. None the less the Government has promised that by 2004 'league tables' will be published that will include each surgeon's mortality rate.[65]

Emergencies

So far in this chapter, I have discussed the patient in a fit state to give consent. When the patient is unconscious, treatment may have to be given immediately, before the patient can be revived and consulted. She may have been wheeled into casualty after an accident. He may have agreed to operation X, in the course of which the surgeon discovers a rampaging tumour needing immediate excision. Where there is no available evidence of the patient's own wishes in such circumstances, the law authorizes doctors to do whatever is immediately necessary to preserve the life and prevent any deterioration in the health of the patient.[66] The doctor can invoke the defence of necessity. Such a defence is not exclusive to doctors.[67] The bystanders who rush to the aid of the unconscious accident victim and administer first aid, the ambulance crew who bring him into casualty, are equally protected from any claim in battery. Emergency treatment is lawful as long as it can be demonstrated to be administered in the best interests of the patient and in conformity with responsible medical practice.

In practice when a patient is unconscious or otherwise incapable of consenting to treatment himself, the response of the hospital staff is to consult, where possible, with the patient's relatives or friends. What legal validity has consent given by the relatives of an adult? The answer is none. Consulting relatives is courteous, but is legally significant solely in that as a matter of evidence it establishes that the doctor's consideration of the patient's interests has been adequately informed (see pages 117–21).[68] Only if the patient dies and his dependants seek to sue the doctor for performing the operation do their views become directly relevant.

One difficult problem arises when some evidence is forthcoming about the unconscious patient's own wishes. An unconscious patient is wheeled into hospital needing an immediate blood transfusion. His wife says, truthfully, that he is a Jehovah's Witness and would refuse a transfusion. Can the doctor lawfully give a transfusion? The procedure is necessary but the doctor knows the patient would be likely to refuse it. In *Malette* v. *Shulman*,[69] a Canadian case, a young woman was brought unconscious into casualty. She carried with her a card clearly stating that she was a Jehovah's Witness and that she would in no circumstances consent to a blood transfusion even if her life was in danger. The Canadian court held that the doctor who administered a transfusion committed a battery. There was in that case no room for doubt that the patient had taken pains to ensure that doctors should know of her refusal of blood in any contingency. Attempts to argue that a refusal of treatment must be 'informed' by knowledge of the actual circumstances of treatment were rejected by the court.[70] As we have seen in *Re T.*,[71] the English Court of Appeal overruled an apparent objection by T. to transfusion (see page 93). The facts of the cases are markedly different. The evidence that T. truly and independently objected to transfusion was shaky. Mrs Malette's convictions were beyond doubt.

The problems posed for doctors treating Jehovah's Witnesses look set to get worse. The ruling body of the Witnesses appears to have relaxed its doctrine by suggesting that refusal of blood is a matter for the conscience of the individual believer. Doctors who know a patient is a Witness must seek evidence as to whether that particular patient maintains an immovable objection to blood. People who out of religious faith or other conviction have implacable objections to certain forms of treatment should ensure that, like Mrs Malette, they carry cards indicating their views. Doctors cannot be expected to be mind readers. Such advance directives are discussed further in the next chapter and in Chapter 18.

5

Competence, Consent
and Compulsion

In Chapter 4, the principles relating to consent to treatment were examined. This chapter looks at two further dimensions of consent to medical
treatment. When an adult is incapable of deciding for herself whether
or not to agree to treatment, how can treatment be lawfully authorized
on her behalf? If an adult refuses to agree to treatment, can that refusal
ever be overruled, either on the grounds that the patient 'irrationally'
refused treatment that was in her interests, or because, untreated, her
physical or mental condition threatens the safety of other people?

The law relating to decision making on behalf of mentally incapacitated people has been reviewed by the Law Commission. In 1995, in their
Report *Mental Incapacity*[1] the Law Commission made extensive and practical proposals to reform the existing law. They proposed a new statute
to provide a statutory 'code' addressing the many complex questions
raised by the care of people who cannot care for themselves. This 'code'
would look at all the different needs of patients, not just health care
needs. If an elderly person develops dementia, decisions have to be made
about where he should live, and what happens to his home, just as much
as what medical treatment he receives. Social care and medical care cannot
be divorced from each other. Controversy surrounding just a few of the
Law Commission's recommendations deterred politicians from implementing their proposals.[2] The incoming Labour Government launched
a fresh consultation exercise in 1997.[3] In 1999 the Lord Chancellor's
Department decided that in principle much of what the Law Commission
suggested should be accepted.[4] Legislation is now said to be imminent.
Meanwhile, NHS guidance has been introduced to implement, in part,
what the Law Commission sensibly proposed. The overall picture of the
law governing the care of mentally incapacitated people is made yet more

difficult to draw by the fact that separate proposals to reform the Mental Health Act 1983 are in the pipeline. A draft Mental Health Bill has attracted considerable controversy. Those proposals would make more extensive provision than previously for the use of Mental Health Act powers in the community.

Doctors and nurses caring for a mentally incapacitated patient confront an awkward dilemma. Once a person reaches eighteen, the age of majority, no one else, be he next of kin or a professional carer such as a social worker, can consent to treatment on his behalf.[5] What does the law allow and require a doctor to do when a patient is chronologically thirty but has severe learning disabilities? The doctor is faced with a patient who cannot himself give the consent required to make treatment lawful and so not a battery, and there is no one else who can lawfully act as the patient's proxy. Not to treat the patient at all would be inhumane and a breach of the duty of care owed to every patient. If a patient's physical condition threatens her life, or grave injury to her health, a defence of emergency might justify necessary treatment, just as it does when an otherwise competent patient is wheeled unconscious into casualty. What if there is no grave emergency? Neither an elderly demented lady suffering from cataracts, a severely mentally impaired middle-aged patient with a hernia, nor a pregnant, mentally-disabled nineteen-year-old face life-threatening emergencies, yet both the patients' families and their doctors will agree that they would be 'better off' for treatment.

A legal limbo

Those caring for and treating mentally incapacitated patients confront a dilemma. The patient himself is not capable of authorizing his own treatment, and no one else has the legal authority to act for him. How has this state of affairs come about? Contrast the position of adult patients whose mental condition disables them from deciding on treatment for themselves with that of children whose immaturity similarly disables them. Parents are able to authorize treatment in the best interests of their child. If there is doubt, or some dispute, about whether a particular treatment is in the best interests of the child, the Family Division of the High Court can intervene (see Chapter 15). Before 1983, section 34(1)[6] of the Mental Health Act 1959 allowed a guardian, appointed to care for a mentally disabled adult, to consent to treatment on behalf of the patient just as a parent does on behalf of her child. Section 8 of the Mental

Health Act 1983, which replaces the provisions of the 1959 Act, restricted the powers of guardians substantially, so that a guardian could no longer consent to treatment of his 'adult ward' for any physical ill. Adult guardianship in any case has been little used in this country.[7]

What of the powers of the court? Can adults with mental disability be made wards of court as children can? Again, no. The Mental Health Act 1983 makes provision for applications to court for a judge to manage the property and affairs of a patient.[8] That power has been interpreted as restricted to the management of the patient's financial affairs and to exclude the management of his person or his everyday care.[9]

The courts' jurisdiction over children is not exclusively statutory. The courts enjoy an inherent jurisdiction derived from the prerogative powers of the Crown as *parens patriae*. An analogous, though *not* identical, *parens patriae* jurisdiction over adults fell into disuse long ago, but survived in theory until 1960.[10] The Mental Health Act 1959 was considered to be a comprehensive code for the proper care of mentally disabled and mentally ill patients. Consequently the Royal Warrant under which *parens patriae* powers could be exercised was revoked in 1960.[11] Perhaps that did not matter too much in 1960 because under section 34(1) of the 1959 Act the patient's guardian, if he had one, could authorize treatment for him. Then, the 1983 Act destroyed that power removing guardians' powers to give proxy consent to medical treatment.

Part IV of the Mental Health Act 1983 is entirely devoted to consent to treatment. Section 63 dispenses with any requirement for consent to treatment for *mental disorder* on the part of patients detained under the Act. It is of limited use as few patients are detained under the Act. The majority of mentally disabled or ill patients live in the community or are voluntary patients in hospital. Even when a patient is detained under the Act, section 63 authorizes non-consensual treatment for mental disorder. It authorizes psychiatric treatment only, not treatment for any physical injury or disease.[12] Doctors may require a detained patient to accept medication for schizophrenia but they would appear to have no power to authorize surgery for a hernia, or an abortion or sterilization of a mentally disabled woman. A number of recent judgments have given mental disorder a wide meaning. Judges have held that forcible feeding of anorexic patients constitutes treatment of their mental disorder.[13] Controversially caesarean surgery has been found to be treatment necessary to alleviate a detained woman's schizophrenia.[14] The correctness of such judgments may be questioned. Even the broadest reading of section

63 cannot allow the Mental Health Act to be used to authorize treatment of mentally disabled people not detained in hospital or the treatment of most physical complaints.

Patients and doctors find themselves in a legal limbo, created by a series of legislative blunders. I suspect that until relatively recently no one gave much thought to the law governing treatment of such patients – they just went ahead on the paternalistic theory that 'doctors know best'. The rise in medical litigation and increased concern for patients' rights caused health care professionals understandable concern. Doctors and nurses not only feared litigation if they went ahead with unauthorized treatment, but also feared litigation if a patient suffered because they did nothing.

F. v. West Berkshire Health Authority

The trigger for judicial action to clarify the legality of treatment of mentally disabled patients came in a series of cases relating to the sterilization of mentally disabled women over eighteen.[15] If the girl was under eighteen, she could be made a ward of court and the court, if it agreed with her parents and her doctors that sterilization was in her best interests, could authorize that radical surgery.[16] Whether or not they should do so is discussed further in Chapter 11. T. was nineteen years old. Somehow, despite her mother's care, she became pregnant. She was described as having a 'mental age' of two-and-a-half, she could barely communicate and she was doubly incontinent. Her mother and her doctors applied to Wood J for a declaration that to terminate T.'s pregnancy and then sterilize her would not be unlawful. He granted that declaration, finding that where a patient was suffering from such mental abnormality as *never* to be able to consent to proposed treatment a doctor was justified in 'taking such steps as good medical practice demands'.[17]

In 1989 a similar case reached the House of Lords. F. was a thirty-six-year-old woman, said to have a mental age of five to six. She was a voluntary patient in a mental hospital and had entered into a sexual relationship with a male fellow patient. The House of Lords in *F. v. West Berkshire HA*[18] granted a declaration stating that F. might lawfully be sterilized. Lord Brandon declared:

. . . a doctor can lawfully operate on, or give other treatment to, adult patients who are incapable, for one reason or another, of consenting to his doing so, provided that the operation or other treatment concerned is in the best interests of the patient.[19]

Doctors, lawyers and patients had mixed reactions to *F*. Their Lordships had made it clear that mentally disabled adults can lawfully receive medical care and treatment. The confused elderly lady with cataracts can have those cataracts removed. However *F*. empowers doctors to decide on what treatment a patient receives with no formal restriction imposed on the exercise of that power. Operating on an old lady with cataracts is one thing, sterilizing a mentally disabled woman is an intervention of a different order of magnitude. The Court of Appeal in *F*. tried to meet such concerns.[20] If a radical, irreversible intervention such as sterilization, or use of the patient as an organ donor was proposed, the Appeal Court said that doctors *must* apply to the High Court for a declaration that the intervention was in the patient's best interests. The House of Lords concluded by a majority of four to one[21] that they had no jurisdiction to *require* doctors to apply for a declaration before any form of surgery or treatment on mentally incompetent patients. As a matter of practice a doctor contemplating radical and/or irreversible treatment should normally *choose* to make an application to the court.

Protecting doctors: protecting patients?

Disquiet about the decision in *F*. v. *West Berkshire HA* arose from a suspicion that the judgment benefited doctors rather more than patients.

If doctors are not *required* to seek a declaration, however radical the proposed intervention, when will they choose to do so? Obviously a gynaecologist concerned about the propriety of sterilizing a young woman is very likely to seek a declaration that he acts lawfully in so doing. If he 'gets it wrong' acting on his own initiative, he might subsequently face an action for battery. A declaration from a High Court judge protects him from subsequent litigation.[22] Particularly if there is some dispute between the woman's relatives, or relatives and carers, the *doctor* benefits from the court's intervention.

More importantly, how is the propriety of the proposed intervention to be evaluated? The judgment in *F*. directed that the *Bolam* test[23] be applied. Treatment would be lawful if it conforms with a reasonable and competent body of professional opinion, albeit there may be another reasonable and competent body of professional opinion that would take a contrary view. The *Bolam* test is the traditional test for professional negligence. A doctor should not perhaps be found negligent because he conforms to one professional school of thought in a disputed area of treatment. It is not an appropriate test when judging whether to sanction compulsory treatment of incompetent patients.[24] Gynaecologists have sharply differing views about the circumstances in which non-consensual sterilization is justified. The application of the *Bolam* test to determine whether a doctor acts lawfully in the patient's 'best interests' could mean that women afflicted with exactly the same degree of mental disability would be sterilized in Brighton but not in Manchester. Moreover, whose professional opinion is to be evaluated? Do we look to the views of the doctors carrying out treatment or of those whose expertise lies in assessing the patient's mental capacity? Using the example of sterilization again, is it responsible opinion in gynaecology or psychiatry that is the touchstone? Lord Goff in *F.* stressed the need for an interdisciplinary approach.[25] The Law Commission criticized the use of *Bolam* in this context. Their Report declares that it '. . . should be made clear beyond any shadow of a doubt that acting in a person's best interests amounts to more than not treating a person in a negligent manner'.[26] They proposed to retain a 'best interests' test to assess the lawfulness of treatment of mentally disabled people, but identify verifiable criteria to determine that person's best interests (see pages 131–3).

After a decade of simply rubber-stamping medical opinion, the courts have recently adopted a much more proactive approach to best interests. Refusing to authorize a vasectomy on a mentally disabled man, Thorpe LJ[27] emphasized that the decision about the patient's interests was one that the judge must make. It encompasses 'medical, emotional and other issues'.[28] In assessing the pros and cons of treatment the judge should embark on a balancing exercise. Before authorizing major invasive and irreversible procedures, the judge must be satisfied that the case for such treatment will be significantly in credit.

In Re S. (Adult Patient: Sterilization)[29] concerned an application to carry out a hysterectomy on a twenty-nine-year-old woman with severe learning difficulties. Doctors and her mother were concerned about the risk of pregnancy and the woman also suffered from severe menstrual problems. She had a phobia about hospitals. Overturning the trial judge's decision that hysterectomy would be lawful, the Court of Appeal held that other less invasive alternatives should be tried first. Butler-Sloss P said this:

The *Bolam* test [is] irrelevant to the judicial decision, once the judge [is] satisfied that the range of options was within the range of acceptable opinion among competent and reasonable practitioners.[30]

Thorpe LJ emphasized that what the medical expert witnesses offered was expert advice on the options for treatment. The court then must exercise the choice the patient was unable to make. Her welfare in its broadest sense must be the paramount consideration.

When doctors seek a declaration relating to a patient's care, at least a public forum is available in which an independent evaluation of what is proposed is possible. Judgments subsequent to *F*. caused disquiet about its practical implications. Seeking judicial sanction for every intervention involving a mentally disabled adult is obviously impractical. The Family Division would drown in a flood of cases. The High Court has issued procedural rules standardizing how applications to court should be made. However, a series of cases ruled that where treatment was essentially *therapeutic* in intent, to relieve the patient from pain or illness, no declaration from a court need be sought. If her doctors and family believed that a mentally disabled woman should be sterilized because sterilization was the only effective means of protecting her from pregnancy they should seek the court's sanction; if it were proposed to carry out a hysterectomy to alleviate 'menstrual disorder', no independent review of that judgement was called for.[31] Yet hysterectomy is a much more radical operation with exactly the same effects as sterilization, removing the woman's fertility. What constitutes a therapeutic intervention? Were a mentally disabled woman of forty-six to be suffering from irregular heavy bleeding and acute pain, conditions that had proved resistant to non-surgical treatment, accepting that hysterectomy might be the best option to protect her welfare is not difficult. What of the much younger woman whose 'menstrual disorder' is essentially that her mental state renders her unable to cope with the effects of menstruation, leading to problems of hygiene and an added burden on her carers? Just as in recent decisions, the courts have adopted a more interventionist approach to best interests. So the Court of Appeal has made it clear that where there is real dispute about the best means to protect the patient's welfare, an application to court should be made regardless of whether the disputed procedure could arguably be labelled 'therapeutic'. So in *In Re S*. (discussed earlier), Thorpe LJ made it clear that '. . . if a particular case lies anywhere near to the boundary line it should be referred to the court'.[32] Hysterectomy in a young woman where there is no evidence that her condition poses a serious threat to her physical health is just such a case.

The most alarming development in this field of health care surfaced in *R. v. Bournewood Community and NHS Trust ex p. L.*[33] The House of Lords ruled that the common law powers derived from *F.* could be invoked to authorize the *detention* of mentally disabled patients. L. was forty-eight years old, autistic and severely mentally disabled. He could not speak and had very limited understanding. There is no doubt that L. was incapable of making any of his own decisions about his health or personal care. From 1994, after nearly thirty years in mental hospitals, L. lived with paid carers. One day in 1997 he became extremely agitated at his day centre. His carers could not be contacted and L. was taken by ambulance to Bournewood hospital were he was ultimately admitted as a 'voluntary' informal patient. He was not formally detained under the Mental Health Act 1983, however he remained in hospital for several months despite his carers' wish for him to return to their home. An action was brought on L.'s behalf accusing the hospital of false imprisonment. The essence of the case was whether or not L. had been unlawfully detained. The Court of Appeal ruled in L.'s favour. He had been detained against his will and no lawful grounds for his detention justified his treatment. The Law Lords by a bare majority held that L. was not imprisoned in the hospital. He was kept in an unlocked ward and not actually restrained from leaving. The majority considered that evidence that he would have been restrained had he attempted to leave, did not establish that he was detained against his will. All their Lordships agreed, however, that L. was 'imprisoned' in the ambulance. All their Lordships ruled that his detention was in any event lawful. Given his inability to consent to admission to hospital himself, any necessary removal and detention in hospital, plus whatever consequent treatment was called for, was lawful in his best interests. L. found himself subjected to a regime of compulsory detention without any of the safeguards offered by the Mental Health Act. Their Lordships emphasized the urgent need for reform of the law. L.'s carers are taking the case to the European Court of Human Rights.[34]

Criteria for competence

The broad discretion entrusted to doctors to decide what is best for their mentally disabled patients makes the criteria by which we determine who is, and is not, mentally capable of making their own decisions crucial. The competent patient may do as she wishes, however morally repugnant her reasons may appear to be (see page 95).[35] The incompetent patient will have done to him what others think is good for him. The early cases outlining the legality of treating such patients in their 'best interests' did not even touch on the boundaries of competence. In a case like *T. v. T.*[36] (discussed above, page 117) this is not surprising. T. was said to have a mental age of two-and-a-half and could hardly communicate at all. F. communicated at the level of a two-year-old and was said to have a 'mental age' of four or five. Much is made in the judgments of 'mental age'. That concept triggers a picture of a real child. Were I to propose that a child of seven should be allowed to consent to sterilization or organ donation, I should be laughed out of court. Yet the adult in question is not a real child and will have experience, and hopefully education, the child has not yet enjoyed. 'Mental age' infantilizes the patient with mental disability and obscures proper consideration of that individual's own abilities.

Not until 1994, in *Re C. (Adult: Refusal of Treatment)*,[37] did the English courts address the criteria defining mental capacity for consent to treatment. Before examining the cases, we need to be clear that in English law competence depends on the particular transaction in issue. There are no rigid criteria that decide that X is competent or incompetent for all legal purposes. The relevant question is rather whether X enjoys the necessary degree of understanding to embark on that particular enterprise, be it entering into a contract, or getting married, or making a will. The law adopts a 'functional' test of competence. The illuminating case of *In the Estate of Park*[38] highlights the flexible nature of the concept of mental capacity in English law. Mr Park, an elderly man who had previously suffered a severe stroke, married his second wife one morning and that afternoon he executed a new will. He died soon afterwards. His family challenged the validity of the marriage. His widow challenged the will. He was found to be mentally competent to marry, but to lack the necessary mental capacity to make a will. His impaired understanding and reasoning power remained sufficient for him to grasp what was entailed in marriage, but his confusion and loss of memory disabled him from having the necessary recollection of his properties and his obligations to make a will.

In *Re C.*,[39] C. was a sixty-eight-year-old patient detained in a special hospital. He had been diagnosed as suffering from chronic paranoid schizophrenia. In 1993, he developed severe problems with a grossly infected leg. Doctors judged his life might be at risk if they did not amputate the leg below the knee. Conservative treatment had no better than a fifteen per cent prospect of success. C. refused to consent to surgery. He sought an injunction preventing doctors amputating the leg without his express consent. There was no doubt C. was mentally ill. He suffered from a number of delusions, including a fixed belief that he himself had had a glittering career in medicine. None the less Thorpe J. found that C. was competent to make his own decision on the surgery in question and granted the injunction C. sought. The test for mental capacity in medical treatment involved three stages:

(1) Can the patient take in and retain treatment information?
(2) Does he believe it?
(3) Can he weigh that information and *make* a decision?

Despite his delusions, C. remained capable of understanding what he was told about the proposed treatment and, in particular, he comprehended the risk of death consequent on refusing surgery. *Re C.* was approved by the Court of Appeal in the subsequent case of *Re MB (An Adult: Medical Treatment).*[40] Butler-Sloss LJ stressed that there is a presumption that every patient has the capacity to consent to or refuse treatment. It is for those who argue that a patient's capacity to decide matters for herself is impaired to prove their case. *Re MB* is a case with a sting in the tail. MB suffered from acute needle phobia. While she was in principle prepared to agree to the Caesarian section that obstetricians thought necessary to deliver her child safely, she refused to agree to any form of anaesthetic involving an injection. The Court of Appeal held that she lacked the requisite capacity to refuse treatment. Her phobia disabled her from *making* a decision. Althought she suffered from no mental illness or impairment, temporary factors could erode a patient's capacity. Such temporary factors might include confusion, shock, pain or drugs. 'Fear may also . . . paralyse the will and thus destroy the capacity to *make* a decision.'

Re MB neatly illustrates a number of tricky questions surrounding capacity to consent. Capacity will generally only become a live issue when a patient refuses treatment that others consider that she *ought* to agree to. The Law Commission, broadly approving of the *Re C.* criteria, acknowledged that the test of capacity adopted by English law is a *functional* test.[41]

They reject an *outcome* test whereby capacity to consent would be judged by others' judgement of the rationality of the decision. Yet outcomes play an inevitable role in capacity. Capacity is unlikely to be disputed unless others disagree with the outcome.[42]

Re MB highlights the complexity of the third stage of the *Re C.* test, the ability to make a decision.[43] Butler-Sloss enumerates 'temporary' factors eroding decision-making powers that are common to many patients facing surgery. She stresses that the '. . . graver the consequences of the decision, the commensurately greater the level of competence is required to take the decision.' The cynic may wonder if, outside the context of childbirth, doctors or courts will be assiduous to find evidence of such temporary incapacity. Legal theory declares that English law does not recognize foetal interests as justifying interference with a competent woman's right to autonomy.[44] In practice, may judges, understandably, be more ready to find evidence of incapacity in a woman in labour endangering herself and her child than in a panic-stricken man of forty-four refusing prostate surgery?

In *B. v. An NHS Trust*[45] a tetraplegic patient sought to have the ventilator keeping her alive switched off. Her doctors challenged her capacity, citing alleged ambivalence in her views, her lack of understanding of the options open to her, and supposed depression. In an incisive judgment, Butler-Sloss P held Ms B. retained full mental capacity. She warned that:

. . . it is most important that those considering the issue should not confuse the question of mental capacity with the nature of the decision made by the patient, however grave the consequences. The view of the patient may reflect a difference in values rather than an absence of competence.

The threshold for mental capacity in English law is not set high. Highly publicized lawsuits such as *Re MB* may sometimes obscure the questions of patient capacity surfacing every day in routine treatment decisions.[46] The importance of effective communication between patients and professionals cannot be underestimated. It is too easy to assume incapacity.

Consider these examples. An elderly demented patient needs dental treatment for an abscessed tooth. He has little concept of time, sometimes does not recognize his wife and engages in bizarre behaviour. Is he incompetent to consent to dental treatment? What does he need to be told and to understand? His tooth hurts. The tooth can be removed so the hurt will be 'cured'. Despite his dementia he is almost certainly competent to authorize that simple procedure. He meets the *Re C.* test. A woman of twenty-one is said to have a 'mental age' of seven. She plays with dolls and if she could choose her companions she would choose 'real' children. She might appear incompetent to consent to sterilization but what does she have to understand? It is not a good idea for you to have a baby. An operation on your tummy can stop you having a baby. Most seven-year-olds understand enough about how babies are born to comprehend that information. While she may enjoy only the limited reasoning capacity of the seven-year-old, she has the experience of a woman. She has experienced puberty and menstruation and should have been educated to understand and care for her body.

The *Re C.* test of competence in theory enables many patients with some degree of learning disability to remain competent to authorize their own treatment. It also entails the risk that, although the patient understands enough to authorize her own treatment, she may none the less refuse to do so. The elderly patient with toothache may allow fear of the dentist to overrule his desire to be rid of the toothache. The woman may think that she would quite like a baby to 'play with'. Both outcomes will be seen by others as undesirable. Those others will be tempted to say the patients are unable to *make* a decision. Care should be taken before rushing to enforce treatment in the patient's 'best interests'. Many indubitably competent people damage their dental health by staying away from the dentist. Just because a patient is labelled demented or mentally disabled, should we enforce his visit to the dentist? Many women who others might consider to be unfit mothers will have babies. If we decide that, whatever she wants, the twenty-one-year-old with a mental age of seven must be sterilized, are we really acting in *her* interests alone, or to protect the interests of an unborn child, and safeguarding society from yet another child whose mother cannot care for it herself?

Mental health legislation[47]

This book does not attempt to deal in detail with the provisions of the Mental Health Acts. However, some reference needs to be made here to both the Mental Health Act 1983 and the Mental Health (Patients in the Community) Act 1995. Both Acts may soon be replaced by a new Mental Health Act granting more extensive powers to detain 'dangerous' patients. A draft Mental Health Bill[48] was published in 2002 but, temporarily at least, withdrawn in a storm of controversy. A further attempt to legislate is likely this year. At present the Mental Health Act 1983 grants statutory authority to dispense with patients' consent to certain treatment and treat such patients in their best interests. The scope of express mental health legislation does not, as we shall see, answer all the dilemmas posed in relation to the care of individuals who cannot care for themselves.

Part II of the 1983 Act makes provision for the detention in hospital of certain mentally disordered patients. Only a tiny minority of patients with mental disorder are in fact detained in hospital under the Act. An application for admission for assessment (observation and tests) must be based on the written recommendations of two medical practitioners who testify that the patient is suffering from mental disorder of a nature warranting his detention in hospital, at least for a limited period, and ought to be so detained in the interests of his own health or safety, or to protect others.[49] Admission for the assessment authorizes the patient's detention for twenty-eight days. If he is to be detained for longer an application for admission for treatment must be made.[50] Such an application made under section 3 of the Act must be founded on grounds that the patient:

(a) ... is suffering from mental illness, severe mental impairment, psychopathic disorder or mental impairment and his mental disorder is of a nature or degree which makes it appropriate for him to receive treatment in a mental hospital; *and*

(b) in the case of psychopathic disorder or mental impairment, such treatment is likely to alleviate or prevent a deterioration in his condition; *and*

(c) it is necessary for the health and safety of the patient or for the protection of other persons that he should receive such treatment and it cannot be provided unless he is detained under this section.

'Severe mental impairment' is defined as 'a state of arrested or incomplete development of mind which includes severe impairment of intelligence and social functioning'. 'Mental impairment' is similarly defined, save that impairment need not be severe. Where the grounds for detention are based either on degree of mental impairment or on psychopathic disorder there must additionally be evidence of 'abnormally aggressive or seriously irresponsible conduct'.

The number of mentally disabled individuals eligible to be detained under the 1983 Act is thus small for a number of reasons. In the case of mental impairment, whether existing since birth or as a result of accident or disease, condition (b) (treatability) is unlikely to be met. Being shut up in hospital will not do them any good.[51] A mentally disabled person is unlikely to be a danger to others and can be protected from herself by means other than detention, so condition (c) may not be met. Government policy for several years was to promote care in the community, and all over the country long-stay mental hospitals were closed down. Psychiatrists maintain that there are insufficient beds in mental hospitals even for patients who indubitably meet the criteria set out in the 1983 Act. Only the most dangerously disordered or profoundly disabled patients are detained in hospital under the 1983 Act.

Compulsory treatment under the 1983 Act

Part IV of the Mental Health Act provides for the compulsory treatment of that minority of patients detained under the Act. Section 63 provides that:

The consent of a patient shall not be required for any medical treatment given to him for the mental disorder from which he is suffering, not being treatment given within section 57 or 58 [of the Act].

Section 63 applies to detained patients only. It cannot be used on voluntary patients, or on an out-patient basis. At one hospital doctors admitted patients under section 3, gave them long-term medication, then released them on licence until their next dose of medication was due. That practice was found to be unlawful.[52] Section 63 could be used to dispense with a patient's consent to treatment only where that patient actually needed to be detained, the conditions laid down in section 3 for admission for treatment were not met, and the use of section 3 to enforce treatment was an unlawful fiction.

On the face of it section 63 authorizes psychiatric treatment, not treatment for physical illness. Yet it has been interpreted by judges as allowing the forcible feeding of anorectic patients and justifying non-consensual Caesarian surgery on a detained patient. The first example is perhaps the less curious. In *B. v. Croydon Health Authority*[53] the Court of Appeal authorized the nasogastric feeding of a woman of twenty-four. She suffered from a borderline personality disorder, including among its symptoms a compulsion to self harm. She was dangerously anorexic and was detained in hospital under the 1983 Act. The appeal court held that feeding constituted treatment for her mental disorder as this alleviated the symptoms of her disorder. Refusing food was such a symptom. Forcible feeding thus constituted a 'cure'.[54] Understanding the outcome of *Tameside and Glossop Acute Services Trust* v. *CH*[55] requires an even more imaginative approach to section 63. CH suffered from paranoid schizophrenia and was detained in a mental hospital. On admission to hospital she was discovered to be pregnant. At thirty-seven weeks the retarded growth of the foetus caused doctors to suspect placental failure and they wanted to deliver the child swiftly by Caesarian section. Wall J. held that such surgery was justified under section 63 as treatment for CH's mental disorder. CH maintained a belief that medical staff were malicious and out to harm her child. She could not be given the medication most appropriate to treat her mental illness while still pregnant. The judge ruled that '. . . a successful outcome of her pregnancy is a necessary part of the overall treatment of her mental disorder'.

Whether B. or CH should have been compelled to submit to treatment is something reasonable people might disagree on. The extended use of section 63 as a device to compel them to do so is disturbing.

Whatever reservations judicial interpretation of section 63 of the Mental Health Act may provoke, other aspects of the 1983 Act offer a model of decision-making that is instructive in considering how the general law relating to mentally disabled patients might be reformed. Within its original and intended context, section 63 empowers doctors to determine what routine psychiatric treatment detained patients should receive. Sections 57 and 58 provide important safeguards both for patients' welfare and autonomy.

Section 57 is unusual in that it applies to *all* patients and not just those detained in hospital. Any form of psychosurgery,[56] such as lobotomy, and any surgical implantation of hormones to reduce male sexual drive will be unlawful[57] unless (1) the patient consents *and* (2) an independent doctor (appointed by the Mental Health Commission) certifies that (a) the patient is capable of understanding the nature and purpose of the treatment proposed and its likely effects; and (b) the treatment is likely to benefit the patient. The role of the Mental Health Act Commission is crucial. The Commission acts as a watchdog for patients' interests. It has a lay chair and a mixed professional/lay membership.

Section 58 applies to detained patients only.[58] Electro-convulsive therapy[59] or any long-term medication (administered for longer than three months[60]) are authorized only if either (a) the patient consents and a doctor certifies that he is competent to do so or (b) an independent doctor certifies that the patient is incapable of giving consent or has refused to do so but that none the less '. . . having regard to the likelihood of the [treatment] alleviating or preventing a deterioration of his condition the treatment should be given'.

The 1983 Act only applies to patients actually in hospital. Insufficient hospital beds, coupled with a desire to help rehabilitate patients into everyday life, means that many patients are discharged from hospital while still ill and needing to continue to take medication. The Mental Health (Patients in the Community) Act 1995 grants powers to supervise patients returned to the community and, if the patient refuses to comply with his supervised after-care, to return him to hospital. Much more radical proposals including powers to impose compulsory treatment in the community are envisaged in the proposals for reform of the Mental Health Act.[61]

Law reform: some order out of chaos?

From 1989 to 1995 the Law Commission conducted an extensive analysis of existing law relating to decision-making on behalf of mentally incapacitated adults. Despite further consultation that endorsed most of the Law Commission's proposals, legislation has been a long time coming. The government perhaps hoped that NHS guidelines and judicial decisions could fill any gaps in the law and avoid Ministers having to introduce possibly controversial legislation. Now it appears that a Bill will be introduced in 2003. So an examination of the Law Commission's proposals, likely to form the basis of that Bill, is called for. It is not possible to cover all the issues covered in the Law Commission's consultation papers and final report so I shall address four key questions. How should mental incapacity be established? What general rules determine how decisions should be made when patients cannot decide for themselves? When, if at all, should others enjoy proxy powers to consent on behalf of a patient? What role should the courts play?

The proposed definition of the threshold for mental capacity differs little from the common law.[62] A Mental Incapacity Act (or Lack of Capacity Act) would reinforce a presumption in favour of capacity. It would be incumbent on doctors or relatives who claim a patient lacks capacity to decide for herself to prove their case. A person would be without capacity if 'by reason of mental disability' he is at the material time

. . . unable to understand or retain the information relevant to the decision, including information about the reasonably foreseeable consequences of deciding one way or the other or of failure to make the decision; or (b) he is unable to make a decision based on that information.

Additionally a person will be without capacity if he is unable to communicate his decision because he is unconscious or *for any other reason*. Two factors need to be noted. First, proof of mental disability is a precondition for establishing incapacity in most cases. But mental disability is broadly defined to embrace any 'disability or disorder of mind or brain, whether permanent or *temporary*, which results in impairment or disturbance of mental functioning'. Would the notion of 'temporary incapacity' promulgated by Butler-Sloss LJ in *Re MB* survive a new Mental Incapacity Act? Second, patients whose disease or injury deprives them of capacity to communicate are treated as mentally incapacitated. A patient who retains her mental faculties but whose injuries render her unable to speak or move is deemed incapable. Yet what other solution could the law adopt? The safeguard for the autonomy and dignity of such patients lies in the mandatory duty imposed in the draft Bill to use all practicable measures to assist such a patient to communicate. It will not be enough to conclude that because a patient's larynx has been destroyed he cannot communicate. Body language, computers, eye contact and other avenues must all be explored before removing decision-making powers from the patient himself.[63]

In relation to how decisions may lawfully be taken on behalf of persons who do lack mental capacity, the Law Commission recommended significant changes to the common law. First a new Act would establish a general authority[64] to '. . . do anything for the personal welfare or health care of a person who is, or is reasonably believed to be, without capacity . . . if it is in all the circumstances reasonable for it to be done by the person in question'. In the exercise of that authority, the person in question must act and/or make any relevant decision in the *best interests* of the patient. At first glance the statutory scheme might look like a simple endorsement of *F. v. West Berkshire Health Authority*. Where an adult cannot make her own decisions and her welfare is in jeopardy the neighbour who takes her arm and leads her way from the middle of a busy road, the paramedic who helps her into an ambulance and perhaps sedates her, and the doctor who treats her in hospital all act lawfully, as long as they act in her best interests. The best interests test survives the process of reform. Given the stringent criticism of the operation of that test at common law should a different standard have been proposed? In the USA, courts have sought to adopt a test of 'substituted judgment'. The court attempts to discern what that patient himself, had he been able to decide for himself, would have desired. Karen Quinlan's father was held entitled to authorize doctors to switch off her ventilator because that was what Karen herself would have wanted.[65] In cases where a patient once enjoyed mental capacity, his known preferences and even idiosyncrasies, the views that he has expressed to family and friends of what he would hope for were he ever to be severely disabled, are useful and crucial factors on which to base treatment decisions. In the majority of cases where a patient has been afflicted by mental disability from birth 'substituted judgment' is a myth. The unfortunate young woman in *T* v. *T* was never capable of communicating her preferences and choices to others – she was never able to make autonomous choices at all.

Rejecting 'substituted judgment' the Law Commission strove to give force where appropriate to the prior preferences of a now incapacitated patient. First, they recommended giving statutory force to advance directives.[66] Living wills, whereby a person gives directions about which treatment he should, and should not, receive if he becomes unable to decide such matters for himself, should be enforced.[67] I could today set out my decisions about continuing treatment in circumstances where for me death would become preferable to life. The government rejected that proposal considering that the judge-made law gives adequate force to advance refusals of treatment. Second, and more important, is the Law Commission's definition of best interests, a radically different formulation of best interests from that developed by the judges initially.[68]

In determining best interests any decision-maker must have regard to:

(1) the ascertainable past and present wishes and feelings of the person concerned, and the factors that person would consider if able to do so;

(2) the need to permit and encourage the person to participate, or to improve his or her ability to participate, as fully as possible in anything done for and any decision affecting him or her;

(3) the views of other people whom it is appropriate and practicable to consult about the person's wishes and feelings and what would be in his or her best interests;

(4) the purpose for which any action or decision is required can be as effectively achieved in a manner less restrictive of the person's freedom of choice.

That definition, endorsed by government,[69] requires decision-makers to focus on the individual patient and make a judgement to promote her welfare that takes proper account of any prior views she may have expressed and involves the people most likely to know of such a view. Substituted judgement becomes an integral part of best interests where such judgement can practically be discerned. The dignity of every patient, including those mentally disabled from birth, is given due regard. The patient in *T. v. T.* never had the capacity to make judgements. None the less she would have preferences and feelings. Perhaps she may have displayed particular aversions or special pleasures. Treatment that transgressed those aversions or removed those pleasures could only be in her interests if strong evidence supported its continuation despite the distress occasioned to T.

A statutory best interests test would no longer conflate best interests with non-negligent care. None the less doctors remain proxy decision-makers for their patients. The Law Commission's initial proposals, following the Mental Health Act model, placed further safeguards against cavalier or [paternalist] decision making. The general authority to make decisions in a patient's best interests was to be subjected to restrictions.[70] Certain controversial radical and/or irreversible treatments would normally demand authorization by a court. These would include sterilization and organ or bone marrow donation. Other debatable treatments, including abortion and hysterectomy for menstrual management, would require a certificate from an independent doctor who would review the best interests criteria in each case.

Alas the government rejected restrictions on the general authority.[71] Doctors carrying out such procedures would not be required to seek an independent judgement of the benefits of the procedure to the patient nor would they be *obliged* to seek court approval in any case. The current practice, whereby doctors may choose to seek a declaration of the legality of what they propose to do, would continue. Indeed it could be that by categorizing all potential treatments as within the *general authority* to act in the interests of incapacitated patients, resort to court in any instance becomes otiose. Statute sanctions the procedure without limitations. Law reform granting unfettered general authority to doctors may paradoxically restrict, not enhance, legal safeguards protecting mentally disabled patients.

In the consultation process that led to the Law Commission's original Report, proposals were put forward to remove decision making regarding mentally disabled patients from doctors altogether. Decisions about the treatment of mentally incapacitated patients should be entrusted to an appropriate 'guardian', often a family member.[72] Intuitively many people may feel that if a person cannot make decisions for himself his family are the best substitute decision-makers. The Law Commission and the government rejected both granting automatic proxy powers to families and a system whereby mentally disabled people are routinely subjected to guardianship.

Laws granting automatic decision-making powers to 'next of kin' would be fraught with difficulty and danger. Identifying *who* the decision-maker should be is not straightforward. Imagine X, who is suffering from dementia at eighty-four, has lived for forty years with Y, her female partner. Y is better placed to act as X's 'guardian' than X's only niece Z who may in the strict sense be her next of kin. Envisage A, who is a widow with three children. The 'next of kin' do not agree how their mother should be treated. Perhaps B has just one son, who has visited her no more than once or twice a year in the past five decades. He will not be the ideal 'guardian' of his mother's interests. Her interests and his may conflict if questions of inheritance arise.

Such difficulties might be overcome if laws allowed the express appointment of a guardian. In the case of X, Y (her partner) could be appointed her guardian. Wholesale appointment of guardians for every person unable to make decisions for themselves is simply impracticable, however. The courts would sink under a flood of applications. Nor is guardianship necessarily beneficial to patients. It imposes a childlike status on an adult. Given that English law endorses a 'functional' test of capacity the law's aim is that the person herself should take as many decisions as she is capable of making.

The Law Commission proposals do provide exceptionally for the appointment of a manager.[73] Where serious issues arise about the continuing treatment and welfare of a mentally incapacitated patient, a manager may be appointed who will be authorized within strict limits,[74] and for as short a time as possible, to act on the patient's behalf generally. Managers' functions would be broadly similar to those currently exercised by receivers appointed by the existing Court of Protection. Their powers would not be limited to medical care, but extend to all questions of personal welfare, health care, property and finance.

Appointment of a manager might be envisaged in the following example: A forty-five-year-old barrister who is the single father of small children is severely injured in a road accident. He has substantial shareholdings in several companies and owns three properties. Injuries to the brain have deprived him of mental capacity and other injuries may necessitate several further operations. A number of decisions need to be made over a period of a couple of years. Should he sue? How can his property and money best be used to benefit him and his children? How should decisions be taken about further surgery? Appointing a suitable relative or colleague as a manager in such a case could make good sense.

Reform proposals also put forward another means to appoint a proxy decision-maker on behalf of the patient. It is already possible for someone to execute an enduring power of attorney[75] to appoint a nominee to take decisions for him in relation to his property and financial affairs. An elderly person who fears that his mental faculties are declining can appoint a relative or friend to act as his agent in managing his property and finance. If he subsequently loses mental capacity, the agent can continue to act on his behalf. As the law stands it is not possible to execute such a power appointing a proxy decision-maker for health care decisions. Reform will allow the execution of a Continuing Power of Attorney (CPA)[76] so that if I decide that should I lose mental capacity I want my daughter to act for me, I can authorize her to make decisions about my intimate welfare and medical treatment as well as looking after my money and property.

CPAs overcome many of the difficulties inherent in automatically entrusting decisions about health care to next of kin. The patient actively chooses her preferred 'agent'. If in thirty years, I am estranged from my daughter I will not grant her power of attorney. If I suspect that she is over-anxious to receive her inheritance, I will not give her power over my life and death. As long as the requisite rules about the execution and registration of CPAs ensure that the grant of a CPA is a free and informed decision of the patient, CPAs are an attractive option to people who choose to entrust their future health to relatives, friends or self-chosen professional advisers.

Central to the Law Commission proposals was the creation of a new court[77] with wide-ranging jurisdiction to oversee the care of mentally incapacitated adults and adjudicate on disputes about what form such care should take. At present, the Court of Protection has jurisdiction to deal with the financial and property affairs of mentally incapacitated adults. The new court will be based on the model provided by the Court of Protection, but embrace in a single jurisdiction *all* the decision-making processes involving such people, including health care and welfare matters. To ensure accessibility, the court would be established on a regional basis. The court would hear any disputes between the several parties involved in the care of an incapacitated person. It would inherit the jurisdiction to issue declarations about the legality of proposed treatment. It would appoint managers where appropriate, and register and supervise CPAs. But, as we have noted, resort to the court to oversee especially controversial or problematic procedures would not be mandatory. Does this matter? Can we not trust the good sense of doctors and families to seek judicial oversight of what they propose to do in cases where, and only when, such oversight is truly needed? The difficulty is this, when doctors and families disagree either with each other or among themselves, an application to court is likely to be made. However, where either there is consensus among the several people involved with the patient, or perhaps an absence of involved family or friends, resort to court is less likely. In such circumstances the patient, lacking an advocate, is deprived of any voice to speak on his behalf.

Some reform is better than no reform?

The government's initial response to the Law Commission's proposals for new laws to address decision-making on behalf of mentally incapacitated adults was disappointing. No legislation at all was a dire prospect. Well intentioned NHS guidance will not suffice.[78] It is good that sooner, not later, legislation is to be introduced to create a coherent system to underpin the proper care of mentally incapacitated patients. Some reform is better than no reform. The common law may well violate the Human Rights Act 1998. Article 5 of the European Convention on Human Rights provides that every person has a right to liberty and security of person. A number of cases justifying the infringement of that right are acknowledged in Article 5(f), including the lawful detention of persons of unsound mind. Article 5 requires, however, that any deprivation of liberty be 'in accordance with a procedure prescribed by law'. The extension of *F.* v. *West Berkshire Health Authority* (see page 117) to sanction admission to hospital in *R.* v. *Bournewood Community and NHS Trust ex p. L.* (see page 121) obviously violates Article 5. A statutory basis clearly defining the rights of patients and the powers of others is the minimum needed to comply with Article 5. Then there is Article 8 requiring respect for privacy. How far might 'compulsory' sterilization or even 'compulsory' tonsillectomy violate Article 8, or even Article 3? Doubts about the current law are exacerbated if we seek guidance from the Convention on Human Rights and Biomedicine. Article 5(3) of that Convention clearly states that any intervention involving a mentally incapacitated adult '. . . may only be carried out with the authorization of his or her representative or an authority or a person or a body provided for by law'.

Compulsory treatment

Whatever the final outcome of proposals to reform the law relating to mentally incapacitated people, the question remains as to whether compulsory treatment of a competent patient could ever be legally justifiable. Can an elderly, confused yet still competent patient be required to submit to dental treatment in his own 'interests'? Should a patient who refuses to bathe, yet remains competent, be compelled to do so in the interests of those who share a ward with him?

In England, unlike the USA,[79] legislation has never enforced sterilization on those seen as mentally or physically unfit to reproduce. Also in England, unlike in many countries in Europe, childhood vaccination has never been compulsory. Compulsory treatment outside the sphere of mental health law has been confined to the control of infectious disease. The Public Health (Control of Disease) Act 1984 provides that patients suffering from 'notifiable diseases', for example cholera or typhus,[80] lose not only their right to confidential treatment, but may also lose their liberty. Magistrates may order such a patient to be removed to hospital,[81] and they may require suspected carriers of the disease, or a patient thought to be incubating the disease, to submit to medical examination.[82] AIDS is not a notifiable disease under the 1984 Act. However, the Public Health (Infectious Diseases) Regulations 1985 apply the provisions of the Act giving magistrates powers to order compulsory detention and testing to people who have, or are suspected of having, AIDS. To my knowledge these powers have only once been invoked in the case of a patient with AIDS.

British laws governing control of communicable diseases have developed in a fairly haphazard manner since the Victorian era. Designed to deal with plague diseases where infection swiftly robbed the victim of both his physical health and mental capacity, legislation addresses a situation where the patient deprived of his liberty is likely either to die or recover in short order. The diseases that were first designated as notifiable carried a high risk of spreading potentially deadly infection to others with little possibility of protecting others from infection if the sufferer continued to live a normal life. Diseases such as HIV, hepatitis B (and even tuberculosis) do not fit neatly into that pattern. A person may be seropositive for HIV or hepatitis B but not ill and certainly not suffering from any mental impairment or confusion. If he amends his lifestyle in conformity with medical advice the risk he poses to others is minimal. Using public health powers to force his compliance with 'safe living' necessarily involves a massive invasion of his liberty. A person with hepatitis B will never cease to be a carrier of that disease. How long could society justifiably detain such a person?

The dilemma posed by infectious disease prompts the question of whether a 'patient' who fails to protect other people from herself and recklessly disregards the welfare of others commits a criminal offence.[83] If a midwife who knows that she is infected by hepatitis B conceals her condition and infects several patients is her conduct significantly different from the train driver who, knowing that he is over the alcohol limit, still takes the controls and endangers his passengers? Identifying a pigeonhole in which to fit criminal liability for spreading diseases is tricky. If our hypothetical midwife's patients have consented to her ministrations, their consent is unlikely to be vitiated by lack of information about her infection, so no criminal assault is committed.[84] In one case a surgeon continued to operate, fraudulently concealing that he had hepatitis B. Several of his patients contracted the disease. The surgeon was ultimately convicted of the antiquated common law offence of causing a public nuisance.[85] Proposals for reform of the law governing offences against the person include a new crime of *intentionally* transmitting disease.[86] They miss the point. Very, very few people set out to infect others. The revenge campaign of the person determined that if he is to die of AIDS others must join him is part of HIV mythology. What the law should seek to deter, and ultimately punish, is acting with reckless disregard of others' health and welfare.[87] Scottish law already makes such provision to deter reckless transmission of disease. In *HM Advocate* v. *Kelly*[88] a man who infected his lover with HIV was convicted of culpably and recklessly engaging in sexual intercourse to the danger of the woman's health and life.

There are circumstances where private interests should rightly be subordinated to the public good. This reasoning lies at the heart of public health laws. The basis of enforced treatment under public health legislation is the protection of the public. A person can be removed to hospital if precautions to prevent infection spreading are not being taken and a 'serious risk of infection is thereby caused to other people'. There is no pretence that the compulsory powers are exercised solely in the 'best interests' of the patient. Where someone, albeit through no fault of his own, poses a threat to the health of others, his autonomy cedes to others' interest in health and safety. Is this a doctrine applicable outside the confines of the Public Health Acts?

At common law an individual enjoys a right to self-defence. This is a common-law right that almost certainly survives the enactment of a public right to use force to prevent crime in section 3 of the Criminal Law Act 1967. If I am attacked by a person so mentally disordered that he could not be found guilty of any crime, I am still lawfully entitled to fend off my attacker using whatever degree of force is necessary. Might there then be circumstances in which treatment of a competent but confused or disturbed patient could be justified because of the harm his untreated condition poses to others? Can a patient who refuses to bathe be washed to prevent him becoming a hazard to hygiene? Such a suggestion sounds like heresy. Apart from the provisions in the Public Health Acts, the Mental Health Acts (discussed earlier), and special provisions in the National Assistance Act 1948 concerning elderly patients,[89] treatment of patients whose competence is disputed is in theory lawful only if in the patient's 'best interests'.

'Best interests': a pious fiction[90]

In practice there can be little doubt that health care professionals are imposing 'treatment' on patients that cannot be shown to be *exclusively* in the patients' interests. I am not suggesting that gynaecologists are sterilizing women for eugenic reasons, or that surgeons are experimenting on unfortunate patients. But patients are washed against their will or given medication they would rather not have. Without such stratagems, nurses struggling to care for wards catering for confused geriatric patients, or working in long-stay institutions for voluntary mental patients, might give up the struggle. Should such miscreants be tracked down and prosecuted for assault? Or should we look carefully at the 'best interests' test?

It is dubious whether it is ever possible to divorce the interests of the individual entirely from the interests of the carer. The example that follows is unpleasant but is an instance of the sort of dilemma that doctors have to face and parents may have to live with. A young woman lives at home with her father. She is physically adult and normal but has the mind of a two-year-old. She is sexually provocative and fertile. She is incontinent and it is her father who every month has to cope with her periods. None of this distresses her any more than it would a two-year-old child. Sterilization by hysterectomy could never be said to be in her best interests even if sterilization *per se* could. Yet her father may find that he cannot cope much longer. Is that young woman better off without a uterus but with her father, or with her uterus intact but in an institution? Her interests and her father's are inextricably intertwined.

The interests of the patient must take precedence, but perhaps other interests should also be taken into account. Individuals live as part of society. Society has obligations to the individual, especially the vulnerable individual. Individuals, though, have reciprocal obligations to society. Moreover, a careful review of all the decided cases on non-consensual treatment may suggest that courts do in fact take note of interests other than the patient's. If nineteen-year-old T. had never been properly aware of her pregnancy, or the birth and removal of a child, that experience may at any rate not have harmed her. Her mother and the child would certainly suffer, however. Would it be wrong to consider their interests? If the interests of others are to be considered, would it not be better to do so openly and not hide behind a pious fiction of best interests?

6

Clinical Negligence[1]

The civil law of negligence is designed to provide compensation for one individual injured by another's negligence. Gross negligence may be punished by the criminal courts. I will consider any possible criminal liability incurred by doctors at the end of this chapter. A person seeking compensation for negligence has to establish (1) that the defendant owed him a duty of care, (2) that he was in breach of that duty, and (3) that the harm of which the victim complains was caused by that carelessness. He must satisfy all these tests to succeed. A widow succeeded in establishing that a hospital doctor was careless in not coming down to casualty to examine her husband. He was admitted to hospital in an appalling state that eventually proved to be the result of arsenical poisoning and died within hours. She failed to recover any compensation from the hospital in respect of her husband's death because the evidence was that, even had he been properly attended, he would still have died.[2]

The bare bones of the law of negligence outlined above are general to everyone, in the conduct of their everyday activities and in carrying out their job. They are not special to doctors. Certain special factors about clinical negligence claims need to be introduced here. I have already mentioned the factual difficulty of proving negligence where there is a clash of medical opinion, and the effect that the need to prove fault has on the medical profession's reaction to claims against them. For a long time English judges were unwilling to find against a 'medical man'. A brotherly solidarity bound the ancient professions of law and medicine together. However judicial attitudes are changing while at the same time patients are less deferential. Claims against doctors and damages awarded against NHS hospitals have risen dramatically. The medical profession is haunted by the spectre of a malpractice crisis and doctors have been put on the defensive. In the next chapter I explore whether the spectre has any substance. I go on now to examine the basic principles governing a claim for negligence against a doctor.

Duty of care

A patient claiming against his doctor or a hospital generally has little difficulty in establishing that the defendant owes him a duty of care. A general practitioner accepting a patient on to his list undertakes a duty to him. A hospital and all its staff owe a duty to patients admitted for treatment. If the patient is an NHS patient the duty derives from the law of tort, which imposes a duty wherever one person can reasonably foresee that his conduct may cause harm to another. Where the patient is a private patient the duty arises from his contract with the doctor or the hospital. It is the same duty regardless of its origins. I will look later at the circumstances in which the private patient is owed duties other than that of care.

Difficulty arises where a person has not been accepted as a patient. English law does not oblige anyone to be a Good Samaritan. If someone has a coronary attack on an express train, and a doctor fails to respond to the guard's call, 'Is there a doctor on the train?' the doctor incurs no liability to the victim who dies for lack of medical treatment. Indeed, the law almost discourages the Good Samaritan. For if the doctor comes to the sick man's aid she undertakes a duty to him and may be liable if her skill fails her.[3]

A practical problem arises from the increasing practice of centralizing casualty facilities in the larger hospitals. More and more hospitals have notices on their gates stating that they do not accept emergencies and accident victims. The notice refers the injured person to another named hospital. An accident victim whose injuries worsened because of the delay in reaching a casualty department is unlikely to succeed in a claim against the hospital that refused him admission as it never assumed any duty to him. By contrast, a hospital that operates a casualty department is responsible for the patients who come within its doors, regardless of whether they have been formally admitted to hospital. By running a casualty department an NHS hospital undertakes to treat those who present themselves and will be liable in negligence if any failure on the part of their staff causes the patient to be sent away untreated.[4] Similarly a GP owes a duty to emergency patients as well as to those on his own list. His contract with the NHS provides that he will treat visitors to his practice area who fall suddenly ill. Like the hospital with the casualty ward he undertakes to treat the genuine emergency as much as his regular patients.

In *Kent* v. *Griffiths*[5] the duties owed to patients by the ambulance services came before the courts. The claimant was asthmatic. She was also pregnant. She had been exceptionally wheezy on the day in question and called her GP who telephoned for an ambulance. The ambulance took forty minutes to arrive despite two further anxious phone calls from the claimant's husband. On the journey to the hospital, the claimant was given oxygen. Shortly before arrival at the hospital she suffered a respiratory arrest resulting in serious brain damage and a miscarriage. The ambulance service denied negligence. They contended that their only duty to the claimant was not by their own actions to cause her any additional injury. They had no duty to come to her aid, to 'rescue' her from the danger her illness placed her in. Earlier cases[6] involving police and fire services had found that (generally) simply failing to respond to, or respond sufficiently promptly to, a 999 call did not render those services liable in negligence. The Court of Appeal were adamant that the ambulance service was different. It is an NHS service owing equivalent responsibility to patients in need as that of doctors and nurses. Where an identifiable patient needed and summoned the ambulance service, there was a duty to respond. Due care on the part of an ambulance service demands a reasonably prompt response. There might be cases of conflicting priorities. For example, the call of an elderly flu patient may be given lower priority than the victims of a road accident but he is still owed a duty by the ambulance service. In the circumstances, there may be no breach of duty because confronted by competing demands the ambulance service responded reasonably.

One sadly common scenario poses a tricky question relating to a hospital's duty to a patient. A patient is referred by her GP to an outpatients clinic at the local hospital. The consultant who examines her decides that she needs surgery as soon as possible. Lengthy waiting lists mean that surgery is delayed and the patient's condition deteriorates. Could she sue the hospital for negligence, arguing that she was owed a duty as a patient from the time she was first given an appointment to attend the hospital clinic? The courts have refused to order hospitals to operate on patients, refused to review waiting-list priorities,[7] but if she can prove actual damage from delay might she have a claim in negligence? Determining what constitutes negligence would be awkward.[8]

Another possible avenue of redress for patients whose health deteriorates because treatment is delayed may be to sue their Primary Care Trust (PCT). PCTs are now responsible for arranging secondary care for all NHS patients within their jurisdiction. If a PCT fails to arrange a cardiac by-pass for a patient with clogged arteries sufficiently promptly, and he dies, could his family bring a claim in negligence? I would argue that PCTs, like the ambulance service, do owe a duty to all their patients for arranging reasonably prompt and adequate secondary care for patients in need of such care. That does not mean a PCT will be liable to compensate every patient who does not obtain the treatment he needs. The demand for secondary care may outstrip what the PCT can supply. The PCT must act reasonably, however. If the unfortunate cardiac patient did not get his operation quickly enough because the PCT lost his notes, or simply bungled the arrangements, his family should succeed. If difficult decisions about priorities for treatment have to be made, resulting in other sick patients having first call on the PCT budget, proving negligence will be trickier.

One recent phenomenon should be noted. Increasingly, patients seek to sue, not just in respect of physical harm, such as brain damage in the course of surgery, but also in cases of psychiatric injury. Where psychiatric harm ensues directly from bungled treatment of the claimant herself, such claims have a fair chance of success.[9] In *Farrell* v. *Merton, Sutton and Wandsworth Health Authority*[10] the claimant suffered a horrific childbirth. She remained aware during an emergency caesarian section; she contracted a post-operative infection and her child was born with serious brain damage. News of her child's sad condition was communicated inadequately and totally insensitively. She recovered compensation to include the adverse effects on her mental health of all that had happened to her.

Claims where one person alleges that negligent treatment of someone else, a close relative, for example, caused them to suffer mental illness are harder to sustain. The law regards such people as *secondary* victims of psychiatric injury, akin to those who witness some horrific disaster such as the events at Hillsborough Football Stadium when fans were crushed to death as a result of negligence on the part of the police.[11] Just because a relative suffers injury from inadequate treatment and the effect of distress and grief make you ill, does not suffice to create a duty owed by the defendant hospital to you. Only if you actually suffer psychiatric injury from the trauma and shock of *witnessing* or *discovering* what has happened to your relative are you likely to be owed any duty.[12] A husband who was present and watched his wife screaming in agony because she remained awake during Caesarean surgery might well succeed. A mother, coming to visit her daughter who had had routine surgery, and who, with no warning, is simply abruptly told that her child is dead and directed to the mortuary might be owed a duty. If, in either case, husband or mother were not in any sense at the scene of the 'accident' to their beloved, but simply learned of their fate, or were told of the tragedy insensitively, they will not recover compensation, even if, not unnaturally, the original injury to wife or daughter drives them into clinical depression.

Finally a number of recent cases consider how far doctors examining patients not for the patient's benefit, but on the instruction of a third party, owe a duty to the patient being examined. Imagine that you had to have a medical examination before a job offer was confirmed. The doctor who examined you failed to inform you that you were showing early signs of cancer with the result that your cancer is now inoperable. Did the doctor owe you a duty to alert you to your dangerous condition? There is no case directly in point but such a duty may well be found.[13]

Now imagine that the doctor carries out the examination negligently and wrongly concludes that you are unfit for the job. Does the doctor owe you a duty to protect you from the financial (economic) loss of not getting the job? One case suggests such a duty is owed.[14] A later judgment of the Court of Appeal is to the contrary.[15] The examining doctor owed no duty to the job applicant to protect him from economic loss. He was not responsible for looking after his job prospects.

The medical standard of care

The second matter that any claimant in negligence has to prove is that the defendant was careless. The onus of proof is on the claimant. He must show that the defendant fell below the required standard of care. The basic standard is that of the reasonable man in the circumstances of the defendant. A professional person must meet the standard of competence of the reasonable professional doing his job. A woman who went to a jeweller to have her ear pierced developed an abscess because the jeweller's instruments were not aseptically sterile. The woman's claim failed because the jeweller had done all a jeweller could reasonably be expected to do.[16] If she wanted the standard of care a surgeon could offer she should have consulted a surgeon.

Is the standard of care demanded of the doctor, then, the standard of the reasonably skilled and experienced doctor? In *Bolam* v. *Friern HMC* the judge said:

The test is the standard of the ordinary skilled man exercising and professing to have that special skill. A man need not possess the highest expert skill, it is well established law that it is sufficient if he exercises the ordinary skill of an ordinary competent man exercising that particular art.[17]

The defendant doctor will be tested against the standard of the doctor in his particular field of medicine. The general practitioner must meet the standard of the competent general practitioner; the consultant gynaecologist the standard of the competent consultant in that specialty. As Lord Scarman put it: '. . . a doctor who professes to exercise a special skill must exercise the ordinary skill of his specialty'.[18]

A patient who attends her general practitioner complaining of an eye disorder cannot require him to have the skill of a consultant ophthalmologist. She can complain if the GP fails to refer her on to a consultant when her condition should have alerted a reasonable GP to the need for further advice or treatment.

No allowance is made for inexperience. The Court of Appeal has consistently rejected the idea that standards of care should vary to allow for the degree of experience possessed by the defendant. They held an L-driver liable where, although she had done the best that could be expected of a learner, she fell short of the standard of the reasonably competent and experienced motorist.[19] In *Wilsher* v. *Essex AHA*[20] the appeal court considered the liability of junior hospital staff. Martin Wilsher was born nearly three months prematurely. He was admitted to a neo-natal unit managed by the defendants where skilled treatment probably saved his life. He needed extra oxygen to survive. Sadly, junior doctors made an error in monitoring the oxygen levels in Martin's blood, and on two occasions he received an excess of oxygen. It was argued by Martin's lawyers that excess oxygen caused him to develop retrolental fibroplasia (RLF), a retinal condition that left Martin nearly blind. Ultimately the House of Lords held that the plaintiff had failed to prove that excess oxygen caused RLF in Martin and ordered a retrial.[21] The importance of the Court of Appeal's judgment lies in their exposition of the rules on negligence by junior staff. Argument by the defendants that staff concerned did their best in view of their inexperience was rejected. The law requires all medical staff in such a unit to meet the standard of competence and experience society expects from those filling such demanding posts. Their Lordships recognized the need for medical staff to train 'on the job'. They stressed that a finding of negligence on one occasion did not imply incompetence or any degree of moral culpability. Legal and moral tests of negligence may differ, although doctors may find the distinction hard to understand. One point must be made clear here. A junior doctor who, recognizing his inexperience, calls in his consultant will have discharged his duty. Responsibility in law will move to the consultant.[22]

Note too that just as no allowance is made for youth so none will be made for age. The eighty-year-old GP continuing his private practice must meet the same standard of alertness and dexterity as his thirty-year-old colleague.

Ascertaining the standard of care

How does a court ascertain the standard of skill that the doctor should have met? As I have said earlier, they begin by asking the doctors. Let us consider the case of Mr Bolam again. He was given electro-convulsive therapy and sustained fractures. He argued that the doctor was negligent in not giving him relaxant drugs, in failing to provide adequate physical restraints as drugs were not given, and in not warning him of the risks involved in the treatment. We have seen that he failed in his argument that he should have been warned. As to the absence of relaxant drugs or restraints, the evidence was that while some doctors would have thought them necessary many did not. The judge found the doctor not guilty of negligence for he acted:

. . . in accordance with a practice accepted as proper by a responsible body of medical men skilled in that particular area . . . a man is not negligent, if he is acting in accordance with such a practice, merely because there is a body of opinion who would take a contrary view.[23]

The *Bolam* test was destined to become [in]famous. At first sight, it is unexceptionable. Courts cannot decide whether a doctor was negligent without expert evidence of 'accepted medical practice'. Within any profession, genuine differences of opinion may surface. In obstetrics, doctors have quite radically different views about how best to deliver a premature breech baby. Some doctors consider that, in every case, the woman should be strongly advised to agree to an elective caesarian section. Others believe that a trial of labour should be permitted and, only if complications ensue, should surgery be resorted to. Both sides of the debate advance logical reasons for their respective judgements. Judges are not well placed to resolve such questions.

The *Bolam* test focusing on 'accepted practice' came to be applied to all claims for professional negligence. 'Responsible professional opinion' was the litmus test of liability for solicitors, accountants and architects just as much as for doctors. There was a crucial difference. In claims against other professionals, the courts rigorously scrutinized expert evidence to ensure that evidence of professional opinion could be demonstrated to be responsible and reasonable.[24] In claims against doctors it appeared that as long as suitably qualified expert witnesses endorsed the defendant's conduct, English judges simply deferred to the doctors. Providing expert testimony was seen to be truthful, the courts assumed that it must also be responsible.[25] The key to successfully defending a claim in negligence was to find expert witnesses who would be impressive in the witness box.[26]

Trial judges who took it upon themselves to scrutinize and evaluate medical evidence faced reprimands from above. In *Maynard* v. *West Midlands* RHA,[27] the plaintiff had consulted a consultant physician and a surgeon with symptoms indicating tuberculosis, but she also displayed symptoms that might indicate Hodgkin's disease. The doctors decided on mediastinoscopy, a diagnostic operation. It carried a risk of damage to the vocal cords and Mrs Maynard's vocal cords were in fact damaged. She proved to have tuberculosis. She alleged that the defendants were negligent in subjecting her to the operation. Her expert witness, Dr Hugh-Jones, argued that the operation should never have been done. He would have regarded her condition as almost certainly a case of tuberculosis. The defendants called a formidable number of experts who testified that the fatality rate for Hodgkin's disease if treatment was delayed justified the defendants in exposing Mrs Maynard to the risk of the mediastinoscopy. The original judge preferred Dr Hugh-Jones's evidence. The Court of Appeal and the House of Lords overruled him. Lord Scarman said:

. . . a judge's 'preference' for one body of distinguished professional opinion to another also professionally distinguished is not sufficient to establish negligence in a practitioner . . .[28]

At least in *Maynard*, the defendants had numbers on their side! In *De Freitas* v. *O'Brien*,[29] the expert evidence established that only a tiny minority of neurosurgeons endorsed the defendant's practice, just four or five out of 250 doctors in that specialty. The Court of Appeal ruled that the body of opinion supporting the defendant need not be large. The perception arose that English judges would not cross swords with the doctors, however thin the evidence advanced in defence of a claim. Michael Jones expressed the state of play as a football score. In six medical negligence claims before the House of Lords between 1980 and 1999 the score stood at Plaintiffs 0, Defendants 6.[30]

In fairness, it must be noted that individual judges did on occasion attempt to assert judicial authority over medical evidence. Sir John Donaldson MR[31] emphasized that professional opinion must be '... *rightly* accepted as proper by a body of skilled and experienced medical men'. In 1968, the Court of Appeal in *Hucks* v. *Cole*[32] rejected expert evidence in the defendant's favour. Evidence that other doctors would have followed the same practice as the defendant was 'a very weighty matter', but such evidence could not be conclusive. Such challenges to the supremacy of medical evidence tended to be ephemeral, apparently forgotten in the next flurry of cases.

The decision of the House of Lords in *Bolitho* v. *City & Hackney Health Authority*[33] heralds a new dawn. Lord Browne-Wilkinson reasserts the proper authority of the courts. *Bolitho* involved questions of causation as much as breach of duty. The facts, briefly, were these. Patrick Bolitho, aged two, was admitted to the defendant's hospital suffering from respiratory difficulties. On the second afternoon of this hospital stay Patrick was in respiratory distress. A nurse summoned the paediatric registrar who promised to attend as soon as possible, but did not do so. Patrick appeared to recover. At 2.00 pm, Patrick was once again having breathing problems. The registrar was called a second time, but again failed to attend. At 2.30 pm, the boy collapsed; he stopped breathing and suffered a cardiac arrest causing catastrophic brain damage. The hospital admitted negligence on the part of the paediatric registrar. She should have come to examine the child, or arranged for a suitable deputy to do so. They denied liability, however, arguing that even if the doctor had attended Patrick prior to 2.30 pm, she would not have intubated him. Intubation offered the only prospect of averting the respiratory distress and cardiac arrest that Patrick suffered at 2.30 pm.

The trial judge accepted the doctor's evidence of fact that she would not have intubated Patrick. The question then became whether or not a competent doctor who had attended Patrick *should* have intubated the child. The *Bolam* question became the key to resolving causation. The experts were sharply divided. The plaintiff's five experts testified that Patrick's history of breathing problems was such that responsible practice required that he be intubated to prevent just the sort of catastrophe that materialized. The defendants' three experts argued that, apart from the two episodes of respiratory difficulty, Patrick seemed generally well. Intubation was distressing and not risk free for so young a child. A responsible doctor would not have intubated Patrick prior to 2.30 pm. The judge ruled that, as both sets of experts represented a body of professional opinion espoused by distinguished and truthful experts, he was bound to conclude that Patrick's injury did not result from the defendants' admitted negligence. In effect, the judge asserted that he was disqualified from any form of scrutiny of expert medical evidence.

The Court of Appeal upheld the trial judge. The case proceeded to the House of Lords. Two issues fell to be resolved by their Lordships. The first, whether the *Bolam* test ever applies in determining causation, will be addressed later. The second is our present concern. Does the *Bolam* test require a judge to accept without question truthful evidence from eminent experts? Their Lordships, speaking with one voice through Lord Browne-Wilkinson, answered that question with a firm and forceful no. Reviewing precedents relating to claims of negligence against other professionals, his Lordship declared that

... the court has to be satisfied that the exponents of the body of opinion relied on can demonstrate that such opinion has a logical basis. In particular, in cases involving as they so often do, the weighing up of risks against benefits, the judge before accepting a body of opinion as being reasonable, responsible or respectable, will need to be satisfied that, in forming their views, the experts have directed their minds to the questions of comparative risks and benefits and have reached a defensible conclusion on the matter.[34]

Expert evidence after *Bolitho* remains of the highest importance to the success or failure of clinical negligence claims. Lord Browne-Wilkinson acknowledged that in '... the vast majority of cases the fact that distinguished experts in the field are of a particular opinion will demonstrate the reasonableness of that opinion'. None the less he went on to say '. . . if in a rare case, it can be demonstrated that the professional opinion is not capable of withstanding logical analysis, the judge is entitled to hold that the body of opinion is not reasonable or responsible'.

Bolitho returns *Bolam* to its proper limits.[35] Doctors, like solicitors and all other professionals, are subject to legal scrutiny. The courts, not the medical profession, are the ultimate arbiters of the standard of care in clinical negligence claims. How influential *Bolitho* will be remains to be seen. Pessimistic commentators point out that Lord Browne-Wilkinson speaks of 'rare' cases and later notes that it will be 'very seldom' that it would be right to conclude that views genuinely held by competent experts were unreasonable. *Bolitho*, some fear, will do little to aid patients.[36] Others are concerned that *Bolitho* might stifle innovative medicine. Mason and McCall Smith suggest:

Bolam provides some protection for innovative or minority opinion. If this protection is removed then the opinion which the cautious practitioner will wish to follow will be that which involves least risk. This may have an inhibiting effect on medical progress . . .[37]

I hope that both fears will prove unfounded. The proclamation of judicial authority over medical practice in *Bolitho* comes at last from the Law Lords. It comes at a time when several other developments in the manner in which medical practice is regulated and audited are placing limits on unfettered clinical autonomy.[38] Cases decided after Bolitho send mixed messages.

In *Marriott* v. *West Midlands Health Authority*,[39] the plaintiff had suffered head injuries. He was discharged from hospital but remained unwell at home. Eight days after the fall he was visited by the defendant general practitioner. The GP carried out some basic neurological tests, prescribed painkillers and told the plaintiff's wife to telephone him again if her husband's condition got worse. Four days later the plaintiff collapsed and was readmitted to hospital. A large extradural haemotoma was operated on and surgery revealed a skull fracture and internal bleeding. The plaintiff was left paralysed and afflicted by a speech disorder. In the claim against the GP, the crucial question was whether a responsible GP would have judged that a full neurological examination was called for and readmitted the plaintiff to hospital. The defendant's expert acknowledged that the defendant should have recognized that there was a risk that the plaintiff had a clot on the brain but contended that the risk was so small that it was not negligent to fail to refer the plaintiff for further tests. The trial judge evaluating that evidence held that albeit the risk was small '. . . the consequences, if things go wrong are disastrous to the patient. In such circumstances, it is my view that the only reasonable prudent course . . . is to readmit for further testing and observation.' The Court of Appeal upheld the judgment. Beldam LJ endorsed the judge's exercise in risk assessment. Whatever the expert witnesses might say, the devastating nature of the consequences of a clot on the brain were such that no responsible doctor would have subjected the plaintiff to that risk. Nor is *Marriott* the only case utilizing the *Bolitho* approach to scrutinize medical evidence.[40] Extra-judicially both the Lord Chancellor[41] and the Lord Chief Justice[42] have indicated that no longer should judges blindly defer to medical opinion. A less optimistic view of *Bolitho*'s impact on clinical negligence claims emerges from Alastair Maclean's research.[43] Out of sixty-four subsequent cases (before November 2001), he finds *Bolitho* was only even mentioned in twenty-nine. A tendency to assume eminent experts must necessarily give logical evidence is to be discerned in *Wisniewski* v. *Central Manchester Health Authority*.[44]

If *Bolitho* heralds a new dawn for patient-claimants will it endanger innovative medicine? Will doctors simply retreat into defensive practice? Will guidelines and protocols replace a sensitive and imaginative approach to the needs of particular patients? This should not happen. *Bolitho* does not seek to usurp judgements that properly rest with doctors. Post *Bolitho*, judges are not empowered to decide what constitutes good medical practice. What *Bolitho* does is to require expert witnesses to justify and explain the basis of their judgements.[45]

'Responsible practice' means current practice

It is no defence for a doctor to say that a practice was widely accepted when he was at medical school when current medical opinion has rejected it.[46] A doctor clearly cannot '. . . obstinately and pig-headedly carry on with some old technique if it has been proved contrary to what is really substantially the whole of informed medical opinion'.[47] Doctors must keep up to date with new developments and incorporate them in their practice. But there is an inevitable 'time-lag' between the making of new findings by researchers and the percolation of ideas through to doctors in the field. The doctor will be judged by the standard of awareness and sophistication to be expected of a doctor in his sort of practice. Great emphasis is placed on the professional position and the specialty of the defendant.[48] A patient who suffered from brachial palsy as a result of his arm being kept extended in a certain position while he was given a blood transfusion in the course of a bladder operation brought a claim against the anaesthetist. Six months before the operation an article had appeared in the *Lancet* condemning this practice because of the risk of brachial palsy. The claim failed. Failure to read one recent article was not negligent.[49] Another doctor made a mistaken diagnosis of cancer of the bladder. If he had used a cystoscope he would not have made such a mistake. But at that time cystoscopes were not freely available. Few doctors outside the major teaching hospitals had one. He was not negligent.[50]

It must be stressed that the relevant date to judge current practice must be the date of the operation or treatment and not the date the claim comes to trial. In *Roe* v. *Ministry of Health* a patient had become permanently paralysed after an injection of the spinal anaesthetic Nupercaine, administered in 1947. His claim against the doctors and the hospital came to trial in 1954. Before the operation the drug had been kept in glass ampoules in a solution of phenol. The accident to the patient occurred because phenol percolated through invisible cracks in the ampoules and contaminated the Nupercaine. No one had ever known this to happen and so the claim in negligence failed because such an eventually could not have been anticipated. Lord Denning said: 'We must not look at the 1947 accident with 1954 spectacles.'[51] Once a tragic incident of this nature has occurred and has been attended by publicity then of course a further incident would easily be proved to be the result of negligence. Current practice would have been shown to be wanting.

Protocols and guidelines[52]

The buzz-words in medicine today are evidence-based medicine and clinical governance. Within the NHS the government seeks to ensure that treatment provided to patients is soundly based on good practice derived from concrete evidence. The Health Act 1999 imposes on Primary Care Trusts and Hospital Trusts a duty to monitor and improve the quality of health care provided.[53] The National Institute of Clinical Excellence (NICE) is expressly instructed to investigate medical practice and provide authoritative guidelines on good practice. The Royal Colleges of

Medicines and other doctors' organizations increasingly draw up protocols for treatment and issue guidelines on good practice.

Evidence of good practice as defined by protocol and guidelines will clearly play a role in any claim for clinical negligence. The considered judgement of NICE, or the profession itself, will be evidence of what constitutes responsible practice. Does this mean any doctor departing from official guidelines will be proven negligent? Some doctors fear guidelines enforced by the courts will lead to a 'tick-box' approach to patient care.[54] Doctors will cease to exercise professional judgement based on the needs and circumstances of the individual patient. This should not happen. Where departure from the guidelines can be justified in the interests of the patient, the doctor discharges his duty of care. Blind adherence to guidelines or protocols would itself be negligent. *Bolitho* requires that responsible practice be demonstrably logical and defensible. Guidelines will offer some evidence of what constitutes proper treatment for the patient's condition. Evidence that the patient requires a different mode of care is not excluded by the presence of such general guidance.[55]

Diagnosis

A mistaken diagnosis is by itself no evidence of negligence on the part of the doctor. As a Scottish judge said:

In the realm of diagnosis and treatment there is ample scope for a genuine difference of opinion and one man is clearly not negligent merely because his conclusion differs from that of other professional men . . .[56]

A patient alleging that a diagnosis was negligent must establish either that the doctor failed to carry out an examination or a test that the patient's symptoms called for, or that his eventual conclusion was one that no competent doctor would have arrived at. Although the myth of infallibility of 'clinical judgement' has been exploded, a patient who relies solely on an allegation that the doctor's conclusions were mistaken will rarely succeed. Not surprisingly a doctor who failed to diagnose a broken knee-cap in a man who had fallen four metres on to a concrete floor was found to be negligent.[57] Other examples are hard to find.[58]

The courts are readier to find negligence when a patient and his experts can point to a specific failure on the part of the doctor. A casualty doctor, who failed to examine or X-ray a drunken patient admitted after he had been seen under a moving lorry, was found to be negligent when, after his death next day, the man was discovered to have sustained eighteen fractured ribs and extensive damage to his lungs. It was no defence that the patient never complained of pain. The doctor should have known that alcohol would dull the patient's reaction to pain.[59] The doctor must be alert to the patient's background. A GP who failed to test for and diagnose malaria in a patient who had recently returned from East Africa was held liable for the patient's death. The doctor was consulted nine days after the patient's return to Britain. A relative suggested malaria but the doctor diagnosed flu. Six days later malaria was diagnosed in hospital, where the patient died that day.[60] Failure to diagnose diabetes where the symptoms complained of by the patient should have alerted the doctor to this possibility may lead to liability.[61] Too hasty a diagnosis of hysteria or depression will often be negligent.[62] By dismissing the patient as 'neurotic', physical symptoms may go uninvestigated.[63]

In all the above examples the doctor was negligent because he failed to act on information available to him and/or to perform routine tests. Where a diagnostic procedure is not routine, is costly, or painful, or risky, an additional factor has to be considered. Do the symptoms displayed by the patient justify subjecting him to the procedure? The doctor faces a legal as well as a medical dilemma. If he does not arrange for the test and the patient does suffer from some condition that the test would have revealed, the doctor may be sued for that failure. If he does arrange the test and an inherent risk of the test harms the patient the patient may sue if the test reveals that the doctor's suspicions were groundless. We saw that that is what happened with Staff Nurse Maynard (see page 147).[64] The defendants were *not* liable to her because they had followed accepted practice in going ahead with the test despite its dangers. Doctors argue forcefully that alacrity to pin liability on them for every diagnostic error may cause patients to be submitted to more expensive and potentially risky procedures than may be strictly medically desirable.

Treatment

A claim in respect of negligent treatment may be based on an allegation that the treatment chosen was inappropriate, or that while the treatment embarked on was correct it was negligently carried out.

Doctors must ensure that they act on adequate information. A GP prescribing drugs must check what other medication the patient is on.

In 1982 the Medical Defence Union settled a case where a powerful painkiller prescribed to an elderly patient for pain in the wrist and fingers reacted with long-term anticoagulants also prescribed for the patient and caused neurological problems.[65] Doctors must be alert to common drug reactions and actively seek relevant information from patients. A clinic that injected a woman with penicillin was held liable for her death an hour later.[66] Had they inquired of her, or examined her records, they would have been aware of her allergy to the drug. A GP arranging for the admission of a pregnant patient to hospital while he was treating her for a septic finger was found negligent in not so informing the hospital. She contracted septicaemia. Had the hospital known of the state of her finger they would have put her on antibiotics straight away.[67] Doctors must be wary of relying entirely on information supplied by their colleagues. In 1984 the Medical Defence Union settled the claim of a patient who was admitted to hospital for a gynaecological operation. The gynaecologist asked a general surgeon to remove what he said was a ganglion from the patient's wrist, thus sparing the patient two separate operations. However, it was not a ganglion. Surgery of that sort was inappropriate and the patient's hand was permanently paralysed. The MDU settled because the general surgeon should have made his own pre-operative assessment and not relied on a colleague from another specialty.[68]

Once the doctor is properly informed and has selected his course of treatment he must ensure that he carries it out properly. He must check the dosage of any drug. Prescribing an overdose will readily be found to be negligent.[69] He must be sure that his handwriting is legible. In *Prendergast* v. *Sam and Dee*[70] the defendant doctor's handwriting was so appalling that the pharmacist dispensed the wrong drug to the plaintiff patient. Care must be taken to read drug labelling properly. In a tragic case,[71] a senior house officer misread a label and administered potassium chloride instead of saline to a newborn infant. The baby died.

Where surgery is called for, the risk of injury is increased. Especially risky is the administration of anaesthetic. The anaesthetist would be found to be negligent if he failed to make a proper pre-operative assessment of the patient, failed to check his equipment, failed to monitor the patient's blood pressure and/or heartbeat in the course of surgery or if, an inevitable accident having occurred, the anaesthetist failed to invoke adequate resuscitation measures. Some specific failure on the defendant's part must be pinpointed. A disturbing number of claims have arisen from failure to intubate the patient properly (putting the tube in the wrong place) or attaching tubes to the wrong gas so that the patient fails to receive essential oxygen.[72] Several claims have arisen from failure to anaesthetize the patient completely. Patients are paralysed and unable to communicate, but remain awake and feel pain throughout surgery.[73]

An anaesthetic tragedy of itself is generally not evidence of negligence. An anaesthetist who failed to check equipment and ended up administering carbon dioxide instead of oxygen was put on trial for manslaughter in New Zealand.[74] An anaesthetist who injected cocaine instead of procaine was found negligent in this country,[75] as was the junior doctor who injected pentothal into an anaesthetized patient, causing his death.[76] If the wrong drug, or the wrong dosage, or a contaminated drug, is used, the patient's claim will generally be made good. The exception will be where the error cannot be laid at the anaesthetist's door. So, as we saw in *Roe* v. *Ministry of Health*[77] a patient who was paralysed as a result of the then unknown risk of phenol percolating into the ampoules of local anaesthetic recovered no compensation.

Surgery itself must be performed with the utmost care. One judge has suggested that the more skilled the surgeon the higher the standard of care.[78] Some errors advertise their negligence. Leaving swabs and equipment inside the patient is a good example. The surgeon must accept responsibility for such matters and not pass it on to nursing staff.[79] Nor does the surgeon's responsibility end with the careful completion of surgery. He must give his patient proper post-operative care and advice. A surgeon who performed a cosmetic operation just below the eye told his patient to inform him if bleeding occurred within forty-eight hours. It did, and the patient tried to contact the surgeon but was unable to do so. The surgeon was held to be negligent.[80]

Overtired, overworked doctors

Any account that lists the claims that succeed against, or are settled by, doctors distorts the true picture and appears unfair. While rising steadily the proportion of claims in relation to visits to GPs, hospital admissions and successful surgery remains low. No account is taken of the hours some doctors work. Despite restrictions on working hours many junior hospital doctors still work more than eighty hours a week. Who would not occasionally make a mistake faced with such pressure? If a doctor makes a mistaken diagnosis because she is intolerably weary, or makes a surgical error because her dexterity fails her, will the patient's rights be in any way affected? No, the courts rightly will not accept any argument that the doctor's duty is fulfilled if he provides an adequate service generally and only occasionally falls below the required standard of competence.[81] Judges sympathize with hard-pressed doctors, but a doctor who carries on beyond the point when fatigue and overwork impair her judgement remains liable to an injured patient. The fact that the doctor was required by his employer to work such hours will not affect the patient's rights.

The patient might more appropriately proceed against the doctor's employers, the hospital. He would allege that the hospital undertook to provide him with adequate care.[82] Requiring their doctors to work to the point of utter exhaustion is a breach of that duty. The essence of the patient's claim would become not that the hospital was vicariously liable for an individual doctor's negligence, but that there was a breach of a primary duty to ensure an adequate and competent service. In the Court of Appeal's judgment in *Wilsher* v. *Essex AHA*,[83] Browne-Wilkinson VC suggested that in many cases this was a more appropriate analysis of clinical negligence claims that avoided stigmatizing overworked doctors for understandable errors. There is a risk, however, that even fewer patients may obtain compensation if this analysis were accepted. The defendant hospital might plead in its defence the problems it faces arising from lack of resources. If patient A suffers an injury because the surgeon who operated on him was too tired to perform the surgery properly and no other surgeon was available, the hospital may argue that it could not afford to employ more, or more senior, surgeons. It will be contended that although far from ideal the level of service was reasonable in the light of the defendants' limited budget. In one judgment a judge expressly said that lack of resources must be taken into account in medical negligence claims.[84] The 'wrong' inflicted on the overworked junior doctor should not be remedied at the expense of the patient. The doctor must have a remedy against the employer who demands that he work impossible hours. The decision of the Court of Appeal that young doctors whose health is threatened by the impossible demands made on them may bring their own action in negligence against their employer is much to be welcomed.[85]

General practice

At first sight, legal problems concerning patients and their general practitioners appear less prevalent than claims against hospital doctors. Patients visit their GP on average four or five times a year and make one or two hospital visits in a lifetime. Malpractice actions against GPs are becoming more common, but still are far less likely than lawsuits against hospitals. There are several reasons for this. NHS arrangements for general practice and the consistant quality of care offered by the majority of GPs are such that many family doctors still enjoy high esteem. Patients have traditionally enjoyed a longstanding personal relationship with their GP. A mistake is more likely to be forgiven and forgotten in the context of a GP's continuing care than in an impersonal hospital atmosphere. The patient is less likely to want to put a man or woman he knows well 'into the dock'. There are other reasons too. Proving negligence, and that the patient's injury resulted from that negligence, is always difficult. Against a GP the problems multiply. How do you prove that a child's sudden deterioration resulted from the GP not visiting at once? Would immediate treatment have arrested the condition? Added to these difficulties, the common run of complaints about general practice do not tend to be the sort that make litigation with its expense, pomp and ceremony worthwhile. Patients may object to unhelpful receptionists, difficulty in getting home visits, or a lack of sympathy, but rarely do these irritations cause injury serious enough to merit litigation.

Every GP must attain that standard of skill and competence to be expected of the reasonably skilled and experienced GP. It is no defence that he has just entered practice or that he is elderly and infirm.[86] As we have seen, he is not expected to have the skill or qualifications of a consultant specialist. He must exercise his judgement about when to refer a patient to a specialist or admit him to hospital with due care.[87] Should a GP offer additional services to his patients, for example, if he is on the obstetric list and is prepared to attend home confinements, then he must be able to demonstrate the skill that he claims to possess. He must attain the standard not of the consultant obstetrician but of the specially qualified and experienced GP.

In reported cases where negligence has been proved against GPs, certain danger areas stand out. The maintenance of proper records and ensuring adequate communication with hospitals and other doctors sharing the care of a patient is one. A failure to record and pass on to a hospital information on a patient's allergy to certain drugs is a clear case of negligence.[88] Similarly, a failure to check exactly what treatment has been given by the hospital may result in liability. In *Coles* v. *Reading and District HMC*[89] a man had gone to a cottage hospital after a lump of coal had fallen on him and crushed his finger. A nurse dressed the wound and instructed him to go to another larger hospital. Either because this was not properly explained to him or because he was in shock he did not go. He went later to his own doctor, who did not inquire as to his earlier treatment and simply put on a new dressing. At no stage did the patient receive an anti-tetanus injection and he died of toxaemia. The cottage hospital and the GP were both found to be negligent and responsible for the youth's death. The judge made his views emphatically clear:

the National Health Service had been developed on the basis that a patient might well be transferred for treatment from one person to another so that the responsibility for the patient shifted . . . Any system which failed to provide for effective communication was wrong and negligently wrong.

Prescribing medicines is another area where GPs must be ultra-cautious, not just out of professional concern for the patient but also in order to safeguard themselves. In 1982, a GP prescribed the drug Migril for a Mrs Dwyer. Carelessly he wrote out a prescription for a massive overdose of the drug. A pharmacist dispensed the drug as prescribed with the result that Mrs Dwyer became ill. A partner in the same practice attended her at home. The Migril was on a table in her bedroom but the second doctor did not notice the bottle. Mrs Dwyer suffered gangrene as a result of the overdose. She sued both doctors and the pharmacist. All were originally found to be liable but the second doctor was exculpated on appeal. Mrs Dwyer received £100,000 in damages, 45 per cent of which was paid by the GP whose slip caused the over-prescription and 55 per cent by the pharmacists.[90] In *Prendergast* v. *Sam and Dee*[91] a general practitioner prescribed Amoxil, a common antibiotic, for the plaintiff who was suffering from a chest infection. The doctor's handwriting was so atrocious that the pharmacist read the prescription as an instruction to dispense Daonil, an anti-diabetic drug. The plaintiff succumbed to hypo-glycaemia and brain damage. The Court of Appeal upheld Auld J's finding that both the doctor and the pharmacist were negligent. The doctor was liable because he should have foreseen that his careless writing of the prescription might mislead the pharmacist into a dangerous error. The pharmacist was liable because the dosage prescribed and other indications on the prescription should have alerted him to the fact that the doctor did not intend to prescribe Daonil. Both judgments operate as timely warnings against sloppy practice. Doctors must exercise great care in writing out prescriptions. Pharmacists must exercise even greater care in checking on the doctors.

Duty to attend

A frequent complaint about GPs is that patients have difficulty getting appointments or home visits and that receptionists take it upon themselves to decide when and if someone can see the doctor. What exactly is the GP's duty to attend his patients and who in law are his patients? GPs' terms of service[92] provide that his patients are firstly those who are accepted on his list.[93] Provision is made to ensure that no patient is ever without a GP. Most importantly, the doctor's patients include persons accepted as 'temporary residents' and 'persons to whom he may be requested to give treatment which is immediately required owing to an accident or other emergency at any place in his practice area',[94] providing that *inter alia* the doctor is available and the patient's own doctor is not able to give immediate treatment. The doctor's obligation to the health service is to provide an umbrella of cover. Wherever an NHS patient goes he should be able to see a GP. If he falls ill on holiday and can get to a doctor himself, he can go temporarily on to the local doctor's list. In dire emergency he or his friends can call on and count on any GP practising in the area to come to his aid. Changes to general practice may, alas, dilute this valuable service.

Is there any obligation directly to the patient? Could a patient sue if his condition deteriorated because he was denied treatment? The GP has a continuing duty to the patients on his list. A failure to attend such a patient where a competent GP would recognize the need for attendance is as much a breach of duty as giving wrong and careless treatment. Patients accepted as 'temporary residents' by a GP are in the same position for as long as they are registered with that GP.

What about 'emergency cases'? The GP on the express train is as immune from responsibility for fellow passengers as her consultant colleague. However, the GP's terms of service oblige her to treat such cases *in her practice area* when she is available to provide medical care. In 1955 lawyers acting for a doctor being sued by a patient on his NHS list conceded that the creation of the NHS had created a legal duty on a doctor to treat any patient in an emergency, whether or not the patient was on his list.[95] A commentator has doubted the correctness of this decision, stating that such a state of affairs reflects '... the standards by which the medical profession regards itself as bound and would wish to be judged [but] from the strictly legal point of view [is] too wide'.[96] I cannot see why it is 'too wide'. The doctor has undertaken to provide an emergency service within an area and under circumstances that are closely defined. The obligation on him is not unbearably onerous. Emergency patients within his practice area when he is on duty are a foreseeable class of persons to whom, by accepting the position of GP within the NHS, he has undertaken a duty, and a duty that should be legal and not merely moral.

Establishing a duty to treat will rarely be difficult, except in emergency cases. A patient suing a GP will find that his problems start when he seeks to prove, as he must, that the GP's failure to treat him was negligent. Some patients make intolerable demands on their doctors. The doctor is not obliged to respond immediately to every call. He may indeed be in breach of duty to his more patient patients if he always responds to the most insistent call on his services. He has to exercise his judgement. In 1953 a GP was sued when he failed to visit a child whose mother reported that the child had abdominal pains, and that she had previously been examined by a hospital casualty officer who had sent her home. The child proved to have a burst appendix. The judge found that the casualty doctor was negligent and the GP was not. He had acted reasonably on the information available to him.[97]

The information available to the doctor is vital in assessing his obligation to the patient. When a patient changed his address without telling his doctor the doctor was found not negligent when after an attempt to visit the old address he left to complete other calls. The judge found that he acted reasonably in assuming that if urgent treatment was needed he would be contacted again. The doctor could not be expected to mount a search for his missing patient.[98] Similarly, information as to the patient's condition must be full and accurate. A patient may fail in any action for failure to attend if all he said to the doctor was that he felt sick and had a headache, when in fact he was feverish, vomiting and had severe abdominal pains. The courts will condemn the doctor who fails to act on information from his patient, but the patient must give the doctor the information to act on.

Information about requests for visits and appointments is usually channelled via the receptionist. This makes not a jot of difference to the doctor's legal obligation. His terms of service will require that he provide treatment during approved hours or, if he operates an appointments scheme, that the patient be offered an appointment within a reasonable time. If the patient's condition so requires, he must be visited at home. He is responsible for his staff and must ensure that their service as well as his is efficient. His liability for them is absolute. Let us imagine a perfect GP whose receptionist abuses the mother of a seriously ill toddler and refuses to ask the doctor for a visit. The child has peritonitis and dies for lack of immediate treatment. The receptionist, not the doctor, was negligent, but as her employer he is legally responsible for her negligence.[99]

Relating the injury to medical negligence

So far the majority of the cases examined involved something going wrong as a result of a medical mistake. The patient's problem has been to prove that what was done, or not done, amounted to actionable negligence. Proving negligence by the doctor does not conclude the case in the patient's favour. He must also show that his injury, his worsened or unimproved condition, was caused by the doctor's negligence. He must prove causation. In practice, proving causation is often the most problematic aspect of a patient's claim. The difficulties of causation in medical malpractice cases fall into two main categories. First, can the patient convince the court that it was the relevant negligence that caused his injury, rather than the progress of his original disease or condition? Second, how should the courts proceed when the essence of a claim is, not that clinical negligence caused any fresh or additional injury to the patient, but that that negligence deprived him of a chance of full recovery from his original disease or condition? A number of attempts by trial judges to ease the burden of causation for patients were squashed by the House of Lords. It remains to be seen whether the more claimant-friendly 'modified approach to causation' adopted by the House of Lords in *Fairchild* v. *Glenhaven Funeral Services Ltd*[100] in industrial disease claims will be extended to benefit patients bringing claims in clinical negligence. The omens are not favourable.

Two decisions of the House of Lords illustrate the difficulty of proving that negligence, and not the pre-existing condition of the patient, caused his injuries. In *Kay* v. *Ayrshire and Arran Health Board*,[101] a two-year-old boy, Andrew Kay, was rushed into hospital suffering from pneumococcal meningitis. He was negligently given a massive overdose of penicillin and nearly died as a result. Intensive efforts by hospital staff saved Andrew's life and he recovered from both the toxic overdose and from the meningitis. But he was found to be profoundly deaf. His parents acting on his behalf sued the Scottish health board responsible for the hospital where Andrew had been treated. The board admitted negligence, but denied that Andrew's deafness resulted from that negligence. Deafness is often a complication of meningitis even where the disease has been correctly treated. Massive overdoses of the sort that Andrew was given are mercifully rare. So there was little available evidence of whether such an overdose materially increased the risk that Andrew would become deaf as a result of his disease. The House of Lords quashed the trial judge's finding in Andrew's favour. Lord Keith commented that the lack of recorded cases demonstrating the effect of an overdose of penicillin '. . . cannot in itself make good the lack of appropriate evidence'.[102]

As we have seen, in *Wilsher* v. *Essex AHA* junior doctors were found to be negligent in administering excess oxygen to a very premature baby, Martin Wilsher. Martin succumbed to retrolental fibroplasia (RLF), an incurable condition of the retina causing gradual blindness. The question that went to the House of Lords was whether Martin's lawyers could prove that RLF resulted from that negligent administration of excess oxygen. The scientific evidence suggests that RLF *may* result from excess oxygen, but there are five other possible causes of RLF in very sick, very premature infants. The trial judge had held that as negligence had been proved the burden of disproving that that negligence caused Martin's injuries moved to the defendants. He said that as the evidence showed that the doctors were in breach of their duty to Martin and failed to take a precaution expressly designed to safeguard Martin from RLF, it was then up to them to prove that Martin's condition resulted from one of the other possible causes. The House of Lords[103] roundly condemned such an approach, and ordered a retrial. The burden of proving causation rests on the claimant alone, and does not move to the defendant even though negligence has been proved or admitted.[104]

What is crucial for the claimant is the quality of the expert scientific evidence presented on his behalf. That evidence must at the very least demonstrate that it is more likely than not that the defendants' negligence materially contributed to the claimant's condition or materially increased the risk that the claimant would succumb to such a condition. Where the scientific evidence is ambivalent or suggests a variety of competing causes for the claimant's state, the action for negligence will fail.

Uncertainty about causation is likely to be common in many claims that essentially relate to whether the defendants' negligence caused or exacerbated disease. In *Fairchild* v. *Glenhaven Funeral Services Ltd*,[105] claims were brought by workers who had been exposed to asbestos dust or fibres during their working lives and developed the fatal lung disease mesothelioma. The men had worked for several different employers so pinpointing which defendant employer was responsible for the onset of the disease was nigh on impossible. Mesothelioma can result from a single asbestos fibre entering the lung. The greater your exposure to asbestos fibres, the more likely it is this will occur. The Law Lords allowed the claim, holding all the defendant employers liable, as each of them had materially increased the risk of harm to their employees. The judges overtly invoked policy considerations to support their modified approach to, and departure from, the usual strict rules of causation. Might the harsh decision in *Wilsher* thus be reconsidered? It seems unlikely. Lord Hoffmann expressly endorses *Wilsher*. He not only declares *Wilsher* to be correctly decided in principle, but also suggests that policy reasons to protect NHS budgets could play a part in denying patient-claimants a more favourable approach to causation. He says:

> ... the political and economic arguments involved in the massive increase in the liability of the National Health Service which would have been a consequence of the broad rule favoured by the Court of Appeal in *Wilsher's* case are far more complicated than the reasons ... for imposing liability upon an employer who has failed to take simple precautions.[106]

The House of Lords' decision in *Bolitho* v. *City & Hackney Health Authority*[107] raised a rather different question of causation. You will recall (see page 148) that Patrick Bolitho stopped breathing and suffered a cardiac arrest that resulted in serious brain damage. The hospital admitted negligence in relation to the failure of the paediatric registrar to attend Patrick when she had been summoned to do so earlier. They denied liability because, they said, the registrar would not have intubated Patrick, had she attended him prior to his collapse. Intubation, however, was the only means by which Patrick's respiratory failure and cardiac arrest might have been averted. The plaintiffs argued that, had Patrick been intubated, he would not have suffered injury. The defendants responded that attendance would have made no difference, medical opinion would support *not* intubating the child. The key question became whether or not the *Bolam* test plays a role in causation.

Lord Browne-Wilkinson agreed with counsel for the plaintiff that 'in the generality of cases' *Bolam* plays no role in causation. *Bolitho* exemplifies an unusual problem. How do the courts address causation when the essence of the matter is whether something should have been done which has not been done? The factual inquiry proceeds into the 'realms of hypotheses'. The court has to ask two questions.[108] First, what would the defendant have done if she had attended the boy? This is a purely factual question to which *Bolam* has no relevance. Second, if the answer to that first question is that she would *not* have intubated, would that have been negligent?

In addressing the second question, *Bolam* is central. The court had to decide if non-intubation conformed to responsible professional practice applying their Lordships' caveat that responsible practice must be demonstrated to be 'logical and defensible'. In the event, their Lordships were convinced by evidence from the defendants' experts that intubation of a child of Patrick's age in his circumstances was itself far from risk-free.

When the unfortunate claimant complains not of some new injury inflicted by the defendants, but of a lost chance of recovery, his claim is even more difficult to prove. In *Hotson* v. *East Berkshire HA*[109] the plaintiff, a schoolboy of thirteen, fell heavily from a rope on which he had been swinging to the ground four metres below, He was taken to hospital, where his knee was X-rayed but no injury was revealed. No further examination was made and the plaintiff was sent home. Five days later the boy was taken back to the same hospital and an injury to his hipjoint was diagnosed and subsequently swiftly and correctly treated. The injury had traumatic consequences. The boy suffered a condition known as avascular necrosis. This condition, caused by a restriction of the blood supply in the region of the original injury, leads to misshapenness of the joint, disability and pain, and later in life almost certainly brings on osteoarthritis in the joint. The plaintiff's disability might have ensued from the accident in any case, but there was a 25 per cent chance that given the correct treatment immediately the plaintiff might have avoided disability and made a nearly full recovery.

The defendant hospital admitted negligence in failing to diagnose and treat the plaintiff's injury on his first visit. Both parties agreed that prompt treatment would have offered a 25 per cent chance of avoiding permanent disability. The trial judge awarded the boy 25 per cent of full compensation for his condition, that is a sum of money to compensate him for a 25 per cent lost chance of full recovery.[110] The House of Lords quashed his judgment.[111] Their Lordships held that the plaintiff had failed to prove that it was more likely than not that avascular necrosis resulted from the negligent delay in treatment, because there was a 75 per cent chance he would have suffered from avascular necrosis in any event, even if the treatment had been given promptly. To recover damages for the avascular necrosis the plaintiff needed to establish a better than fifty/fifty likelihood that 'but for' the negligent delay in treatment he would have made an uncomplicated recovery from his original injury. Had he succeeded in so doing he would have been entitled to 100 per cent compensation for his disability. Their Lordships declined to say that loss of a less than 50 per cent chance of full recovery was never recoverable in a medical negligence claim. They left that question open.

So might a patient who seeks compensation for loss with a less than 50 per cent chance of recovery be able to do so in the following sort of circumstances?[112] Expert evidence suggests that the relevant negligent mismanagement of, or delay in, treatment diminished his statistical prospects of recovery by an ascertainable percentage.[113] For example, if a doctor negligently failed to diagnose cancer and a further period elapsed before a proper diagnosis was made and treatment begun, might the patient be allowed to recover damages for diminished prospects of survival and recovery?[114] Perhaps at the time when the diagnosis should have been made the patient would have had a 75 per cent chance of recovery, but by the time it was in fact made that chance had diminished to 50 per cent. Such a case differs from *Hotson* in this way. On the evidence available in *Hotson* no one could say whether or not but for the relevant negligence the plaintiff would or would not have suffered avascular necrosis at all. In the example of the unfortunate cancer patient scientific and statistical evidence strongly indicates that 'but for' the relevant negligence the patient would have enjoyed a much greater chance of prolonged survival. The complex judgment of the Court of Appeal in *Gregg* v. *Scott*[115] suggests that 'the reduced prospect of a good outcome' is not recoverable. Their Lordships, however, still refuse to rule loss of a chance entirely out of court. And once again, like Lord Hoffman in *Fairchild*, they note '. . . powerful policy arguments for not extending the scope of liability within the field of health treatment'.

Private patients

A patient who pays for treatment enters into a contract with his doctor. They are free to set the terms of that contract, save that the doctor cannot exempt himself from liability for any injury to his patient arising from his negligence.[116] There is rarely a written contract between them. The terms will be implied from their relationship. This usually means that the doctor undertakes a duty of care to the patient. His duty of care to his private patient is indistinguishable from his duty to his NHS patient.

In private practice could a doctor be found to have contracted to *guarantee* the desired result of treatment? This can never happen in the NHS. The doctor can only be liable in tort for a failure in care. Only rarely however will a private doctor be found to have guaranteed a result in contract either. Where a patient is ill and seeks a cure, unless the doctor foolishly and expressly promises success in his treatment, no court will infer any term other than that the doctor will exercise skill and care. So far, for example, claims by patients who have undergone private sterilization have ultimately failed in attempts to argue that the surgeon guaranteed permanent sterility.[117]

Criminal liability

Negligence is normally a matter for the civil, not the criminal, law. However gross, however culpable an act of negligence, negligence will generally not be criminal in England unless made so by an Act of Parliament, as in the case of careless driving. The picture changes if the victim dies. Gross negligence causing death can lead to a conviction for manslaughter. Much more than ordinary negligence, of the sort that would found a civil action for negligence, must be proved. Prosecution of doctors used to be rare. In older cases the negligence will be seen to derive from morally disgraceful conduct – a doctor operating while drunk or under the influence of drugs. In *R.* v. *Bateman*[118] the Court of Appeal overruled a conviction for manslaughter of a doctor whose ignorance and failure to send a woman to hospital resulted in his patient's death. The judge at the trial had failed to direct the jury properly. Criminal liability required more than the degree of negligence needed to establish civil liability. The doctor must be shown to have demonstrated '. . . such disregard for the life and safety of others as to amount to a crime against the State and conduct deserving of punishment'.

The last ten years have seen a sharp rise in the number of doctors prosecuted for manslaughter albeit many cases ended in acquittal. In *R* v. *Prentice, R* v. *Adomako and R* v. *Holloway*[119] the Court of Appeal considered two[120] appeals by doctors against conviction for manslaughter. In the first case, two junior doctors, Drs Prentice and Sulman, were convicted of manslaughter after they had wrongly injected a potent chemotherapeutic drug (vincristine) into the patient's spine, when it should have been administered intravenously. Their sixteen-year-old patient was suffering from leukaemia. Every month he received an intravenous injection of vincristine. Every other month he received a spinal injection of another powerful drug, methotextrate. The drug came down to the ward on the same trolley. Neither Dr Prentice nor Dr Sulman had ever administered such drugs before and they were left unsupervised.

The second case involved Dr Adomako, an anaesthetist. During surgery to reattach a detached retina, Dr Adomako failed to notice, for over four minutes, that the tube administering oxygen to his patient had become disconnected. He neither noted the evidence before his eyes that the tube was no longer in place nor did he respond to the alarm raised by the operating theatre's monitoring system. One prosecution expert described his standard of care as abysmal. The appeal court reversed the convictions of Drs Prentice and Sulman but upheld Dr Adomako's conviction.

The Court of Appeal set the following test for gross negligence manslaughter:

(1) Did the doctor show obvious indifference to the risk of injury to his patient?
(2) Was he aware of the risk but none the less (for no good reason) decided to run the risk?
(3) Was an attempt to avoid a known risk so grossly negligent as to deserve punishment?
(4) Was there a degree of inattention or failure to have regard to risk, going beyond mere inadvertence?

Only if at least one of these questions could be answered affirmatively should a doctor be convicted of manslaughter. In the case of Dr Prentice and Dr Sulman there was insufficient evidence of gross negligence deserving punishment. Dr Adomako, the Court of Appeal declared, failed to perform:

. . . his essential and in effect sole duty to see that his patient was breathing satisfactorily and to cope with the breathing emergency . . . his failure was more than mere inadvertence and constituted gross negligence of the degree necessary for manslaughter.

Dr Adomako appealed to the House of Lords without success. His conviction was upheld.[121] The Law Lords offered no precise definition of 'medical manslaughter'. Lord MacKay endorsed the trial judge's warning to the jury:

You should only convict a doctor of causing death by negligence if you think he did something which no reasonably skilled doctor would have done.[122]

When should doctors face criminal prosecution? The increasingly common demand that doctors be punished for tragic mistakes causes great anxiety within the profession. Some argue that only if there is evidence of indifference or total disregard for the patient's welfare should a doctor face criminal liability.[123] The civil law should compensate victims of mistakes. Incompetent doctors should be dealt with by the GMC. Patients may lack trust in the GMC and perceive monetary compensation that comes from the NHS, not the doctor's pocket, as inadequate redress for the death of a relative. Doctors are not the only workers who risk prosecution for negligence. Train drivers and electricians, for example, meet the same fate. In all these cases the crux of the difficulty is to determine when a mistake is so bad that an otherwise good citizen deserves to be branded a criminal.

The principles of the law of negligence applicable to the medical profession have long been criticized as leaning too far in favour of rubber-stamping professional practice. Judicial attitudes have changed. Courts are more ready, though still reluctantly, to find against the doctor. Two problems bedevil medical litigation. First, the medical profession becomes increasingly resentful of what they see as judicial interference and damage done to medical careers. While compensation for injured patients depends on proof of fault on the part of medical staff, judicial 'interference' is inevitable and likely to increase. A judgment that a doctor on one day was liable for actionable negligence is not a finding that that doctor is a bad or incompetent doctor. It is merely a decision that in one instance his conduct was such as to warrant a fellow citizen's claim for compensation. That is not how the doctors see it. Second, the issue of judging when a doctor falls below an acceptable standard remains a thorny problem. It must not be forgotten that litigation after the event is always no more than applying sticking plasters to a wound. Even if the claimant succeeds, the wound remains. Efforts to prevent medical error, to learn from past errors must be given due weight. Apportioning blame may inhibit that learning process.[124]

7

Malpractice Litigation

So far I have examined the principles governing liability for clinical negligence. Now I look at the process of litigation. Formidable practical problems confront the patient.[1] How can he fund a lawsuit? Whom should he sue? How quickly must he act? How do you prove negligence? What level of compensation is available? Is it worth it? As we shall see, recent years have witnessed radical changes in the process of litigation. The way in which patients fund claims, how the NHS meets the cost of claims and the fundamental rules of civil procedure (the Woolf reforms) have all altered since the last edition of this book. Before addressing the detail of the litigation process, I first explore the debate about a malpractice crisis. Critics of medical litigation argue that escalating rates of claims against doctors are damaging medicine. The spectre of the malpractice crisis haunts the colleges of medicine, the courts of justice and the corridors of Whitehall. Is it a spectre with any substance?

Malpractice crisis: reality or illusion?

Those who contend that the United Kingdom faces a malpractice crisis advance the following evidence. (1) The numbers of claims made are escalating dramatically. (2) Doctors are held negligent on 'unfair' grounds. (3) The cost of compensation awards to patients is rapidly becoming prohibitive to the NHS. (4) Consequently doctors are practising 'defensive medicine'. That is to say, a doctor will choose the treatment for the patient most likely to be 'legally safe' to ensure that he will not be sued by the patient, even though that treatment may not necessarily be medically best for the patient, and may be unnecessarily expensive and time-consuming. A common example of alleged defensive medicine is a decision to carry out a Caesarean section as soon as there is any sign of difficulty in the course of labour, rather than to run the legal risk of continuing to attempt a natural delivery. (5) The rising tide of clinical negligence claims is destroying doctor/patient relationships and driving promising young doctors away from specialties such as obstetrics, which are seen as 'high-risk' for negligence claims.

Previous editions of this book expressed scepticism about the reality of any crisis. The evidence is still inconclusive and equivocal. Arguments that experiences in the USA are soon to be repeated this side of the Atlantic should be viewed with caution. We must not forget that the USA is a litigious nation and malpractice claims are big business. Even today patients leaving NHS hospitals are more likely to return with a box of chocolates for the staff than with a claim form! Moreover, there remain differences in the organization of both health care and legal services in the USA that should make us wary of relying too heavily on experiences in that country.

Assessing the evidence for and against the existence of a malpractice crisis in the United Kingdom is difficult. The evidence of escalation in claims for negligence is incontrovertible. A comprehensive study of medical litigation[2] published in 1988 demonstrated that numbers of claims against doctors doubled between 1983 and 1987. The average cost of compensation also doubled. Ten years later the picture looked bleaker still. In 1996, 36 per cent of consultants and senior registrars were sued at least once and litigation cost the NHS £300m.[3] In 2001 an even more worrying picture was painted by the National Audit Office.[4] About 10,000 new claims were initiated against the NHS in 1999–2000. In March 2000, £2.6 billion was set aside to meet the cost of claims and an estimated £1.3 billion was estimated as needed to meet claims not yet reported. Since 1995–6 the cost of litigation to the NHS had increased seven-fold. Yet only 24 per cent of legally aided claims succeeded.[5] In claims of above £10,000, the time from making the claim to settlement or an award of damages was on average five and a half years. In claims worth less than £50,000 in 1999–2000, in 65 per cent of cases costs exceeded compensation. No wonder one Secretary of State for Health was provoked to declare: 'The only place for a lawyer in the NHS is on the operating table.'[6] Frank Dobson obviously believed that there is a medical malpractice crisis and that lawyers are to blame for it.

What of claims that doctors are unfairly treated? The evidence does not substantiate such claims. First, although the rise in the number of claims has been dramatic, 76 per cent of legally aided claims fail. A 'success' rate of 24 per cent might rather indicate a system that fails to do justice to patients. Nor does an argument that doctors are unjustly judged by lawyers stand up to scrutiny. For in deciding whether a doctor is negligent, in the vast majority of cases the court relies on expert professional opinion.[7] A doctor can normally only be found to be negligent if his peers testify to his negligence. The House of Lords in *Bolitho* v. *City & Hackney Health Authority*[8] has endorsed judicial power to disregard expert testimony in exceptional cases. Evidence of adequate practice to rebut a claim of negligence must be shown to be 'logical and defensible'. Doctors cannot really complain if courts refuse to accept evidence of 'illogical or indefensible' practice.

The cost of clinical negligence claims is a cause for concern. Where a claim is made by an NHS patient, that money comes from the NHS budget. Money to compensate an injured patient and money to defend claims brought in respect of alleged negligence must come out of funds that might otherwise have been used to employ an extra surgeon, or pay for a new neo-natal unit, or support a programme of preventive medicine. When that money is used to compensate an injured patient, at least some benefit to society can be discerned.[9] Given that 76 per cent of claims fail, a large proportion of the cost to the NHS may be seen to be eaten up by lawyers' fees. The gross disproportion reported between costs and compensation, even where settlements are agreed, is acutely disturbing.

The prospect that doctors will base decisions concerning treatment not on their professional judgement of what is best for the patient but on what is 'legally safest' for the doctor does sound appalling. Is there hard evidence that doctors are being forced to practise defensive medicine?[10] The classic example given of defensive medicine – the rise in the rate of Caesarean sections – has often been found to be explicable by many other factors. Caesarean rates are rising in several countries, not all of which have experienced rising litigation rates.[11] None the less the steady rise in Caesarean rates continues with 21.5 per cent of mothers in England now giving birth by surgery. Obstetricians have voiced a subjective belief that fear of litigation makes them more ready to move swiftly to surgery rather than allow a difficult labour to proceed.[12] Then there is the question of what is meant by defensive medicine. In the House of Lords, Lord Pitt eloquently argued that the rising tide of litigation meant that doctors ordered unnecessary and sometimes painful tests, and he predicted '. . . an increase in defensive medicine with an alarming waste of resources'.[13] The difficulty is to decide when further tests and cross-checks cease to be a sensible precaution in the interests of the patient and simply become a waste of resources.[14]

What is undoubtedly true is that many doctors have become so frightened by the spectre of a malpractice crisis that doctor/patient relationships have been damaged. Evidence of defensive medicine may be disputable, defensiveness in medicine is a sad fact.[15] Doctors in 'high-risk' specialties such as obstetrics and anaesthetics are the worst affected among the profession. Doctors, and indeed all health care professionals, in England need to be aware of the reality of the current state of malpractice litigation here. Claim rates remain substantially less than in the USA and awards of compensation are minimal compared to the highest US awards. Before concluding that England will necessarily follow the US pattern to its extreme, three differences between the two countries must be noted.[16] What will concern doctors is that those differences are rapidly diminishing.

In the USA virtually all medical care is provided by the private sector. If your treatment goes wrong and you suffer a medical accident, you will have to pay out more money for corrective treatment. Naturally an aggrieved patient is going to be looking to the doctor whom he perceives as responsible for the accident for the money to pay for the necessary corrective treatment. Most patients will carry private health insurance. Their insurers will be as keen as the patient to ensure that any costs arising from medical negligence are recovered from the doctor and his insurers. In a private health system such as that of the USA, health care is charged on a fee-for service basis. The more tests a doctor carries out the more money he makes. Perhaps some of the apparent evidence for 'defensive medicine' is better explained as 'expensive medicine'? Finally, it may be that patients who pay directly for treatment will tend to be more aggrieved by medical accidents than those treated within a public health system. Doctors who charge their patients may lose some of their professional aura and become just businessmen to be sued if their 'goods' fall short of customers' expectations.

Legal services in the USA are organized on a different basis from those in the UK. Lawyers acting for the clients in negligence actions in the USA act on a *contingency* fee basis. If the case fails, the client pays nothing; if the claim succeeds the lawyer takes a percentage of the damages, normally about one third. Such a system makes it much easier for patients to litigate, and gives lawyers a direct interest in the levels of damages awarded. As we shall see, English lawyers are now allowed to take on clinical negligence claims on a *conditional* fee basis.[17] Solicitors can agree to provide legal services on the basis that they charge no fee if the claim fails, but are permitted to increase their fee by up to 100 per cent if the claim succeeds. However, the claimant remains at risk of having to meet the defendant's legal costs should she lose her case. That significant risk can only be contemplated if the claimant is able to obtain insurance cover against losing her case. Premiums charged in complex clinical negligence claims are considerable. Access to the courts to litigate a clinical negligence claim remains difficult. Unlike most personal injury claims, those whose income is low enough to qualify may see legal aid (now styled community legal service funding). However, the majority of adults fall outside that very limited category of eligibility. Funding a case by way of conditional fee agreements means finding a lawyer who judges your case to be a good enough 'gamble' to take on. The reward for the lawyer of an enhanced fee remains less alluring than the full-blown contingency fee system of the USA. However, the numbers of lawyers campaigning to allow true contingency fees in England is steadily growing.

Awards of damages in the USA are decided not by the judge, as is the case in England, but by the jury. Even though the Court of Appeal[18] has recently raised the tariff for compensation for pain and suffering in this country, levels of such compensation remain infinitely more generous in the USA. Moreover, currently damages in this country are awarded solely for the purpose of compensating the patient for what he has lost as a result of the defendant doctor's negligence. A US jury is empowered in certain circumstances to double, or even treble, compensatory damages by making a further award of punitive damages, to punish the defendant for negligence. The Law Commission has proposed that in exceptional cases punitive damages should be awarded here.[19]

The spectre of a malpractice crisis has haunted us for many years. I used to believe that it was a spectre without substance conjured up by doctors aggrieved by how the system seemed to treat them. The last five years have given our ghostly crisis greater reality. The financial burden on the NHS is crippling; incremental changes in law and practice brings us closer to US experience; the distrust between doctors and patients and between doctors and the legal system brings litigation into disrepute. The current crisis is of such concern to government that a White

Paper proposing reform of the whole system is now due to be published in the summer of 2003.

There are no true winners, no beneficiaries in this current climate of crisis. Where did the system go wrong?

Funding a lawsuit[20]

Few people are rich enough to meet the costs of clinical negligence claims out of their own income and savings. The majority of clinical negligence claims in the past were funded by legal aid. The success rate of such claims remains low. The cost to the public purse of legal aid in personal injury claims generally became astronomical. Unsurprisingly, the government sought to find ways to reduce the legal aid bill. The Access to Justice Act 1999[21] removes legal aid from most personal injury claims but, at least at present, legal aid remains available in clinical negligence claims. However, gaining legal aid is not an easy task. Claimants must meet a stringent means test; only adults with a very low income and minimal capital will qualify. Children under 18[22] are assessed on their own, not their parents' income, so child-patients are still likely to qualify for legal aid. Even if the potential claimant passes the means test, her case must be strong on its merits. Given that 80 per cent of the total value of claims made against the NHS relate to cerebral palsy and brain damage, the legal aid bill will remain substantial.[23]

The state will only fund claims likely to succeed. Solicitors able to act for legally-aided clients must be approved by the Legal Services Commission. Only firms which hold a franchise to do legally-aided clinical negligence work can act, and they must be members of a clinical negligence franchise panel. The franchise system has advantages for aggrieved patients. Clients can be assured that their case is in the hands of a solicitor judged competent to handle such cases. They are receiving specialist care. However the numbers of franchised solicitors may not meet demand, and Harpwood[24] notes concern about whether the system will allow sufficient young solicitors to train in the speciality. Might a complacent monopoly be established?

Whether legal aid for clinical negligence claims will survive is another pressing question. Conditional fees have become the norm in other personal injury claims. Under a conditional fee agreement (CFA)[25] the solicitor agrees to provide legal services on the basis that unless the claim is successful the client will pay nothing for her services. If the case is won, legislation allows the solicitor to charge up to twice the normal fee.[26] Conditional fees are often styled '*no win no fee*' agreements. The major problem for clinical negligence claimants are two-fold. (1) Conditional fees involve risk to the lawyers. They will only take on claims if satisfied that the majority of the claims on their books will succeed. Otherwise the firm will lose money. (2) The 'no win no fee' provision only covers the patient's own solicitor's costs. If the case fails he becomes liable for the defendant hospital's or doctor's costs. These may be crippling. In most personal injury claims, claimants can buy insurance to cover them against the risk of liability for the defendants' costs. The complexity and expense of clinical negligence claims is such that insurers have been wary about entering this field. However, if the claimant wins her case she can recover the cost of insurance premiums from the defendant, the losing party, providing the premium is set at a reasonable rate.[27]

Defending claims

Until 1990, the medical defence organizations, principally the Medical Defence Union and the Medical Protection Society, indemnified individual doctors against personal liability for clinical negligence. Each hospital, health authority or other NHS body met its own costs. The medical defence organizations were powerful players in deciding whether to and how to defend claims because they paid the doctors' bills. NHS Indemnity, introduced in 1990,[28] provides that hospital trusts indemnify hospital doctors against liability now and trusts took over the financing and managing of all claims. The medical defence organizations continue to meet claims against GPs and claims arising in the private sector. From 1990 to 1995 individual hospital trusts, health authorities and the defence organizations dominated the defence of NHS claims. Different sets of legal advisers might adopt different policies about settling claims and how aggressively a claim was defended. Where a case succeeded, the cost fell on an individual hospital. A large compensation award could force a hospital to make budget cuts, immediately affecting patient care in that hospital. In 1995 a more sensible system was put in place. The Clinical Negligence Scheme for Trusts (CNST) was established.[29] NHS trusts may choose to join the CNST and it creates a pooling arrangement to meet liability arising out of patient claims. Premiums for trusts are worked out depending on the service they offer and their scale of operations.

Membership of the CNST is conditional on trusts complying with risk management procedures prescribed by the CNST. It offers a mutual assurance system so that no individual trust risks devastation of its service because of a clutch of unfortunate losses in the courts.

Complementary to the CNST is the National Health Service Litigation Authority[30] (NHSLA). The NHSLA now administers the CNST.[31] It also advises the Department for Health about controversial or complex claims, and any claim where the total value is over £1 million. The NHSLA is the driving force behind the defence of claims against the NHS today. It exercises significant control over all claims, seeking to ensure swift resolution of indefensible claims and to minimize the cost to the NHS. Greater efficiency and uniformity should benefit patients as much as hospitals. The NHSLA plays an active role, not just in advising on defence of individual claims, but also in seeking to ensure that the whole litigation system is regularly kept under review.

Whom should the patient sue?

Once funding is assured, one of the first practical matters that the patient and his legal advisers must consider is whom they should sue. The legal doctrine of vicarious liability provides that when a person who is an employee commits a tort in the course of his employment, his employer is also responsible to the victim. The employer will often be better able to pay compensation than an individual employee.

Let us look first at a claim by a patient who alleges that he suffered injury in the course of treatment as an NHS patient in an NHS hospital. If he can identify a particular individual as negligent he may, of course, proceed against him, be he consultant, anaesthetist, house officer, nurse, physiotherapist or hospital porter. However, he may also sue the person's employer, in the case of an NHS trust hospital, the NHS trust itself. Where a hospital doctor is a defendant in the action, payment of any award of compensation made against him is guaranteed because, as we noted earlier, NHS Indemnity ensures that any liability incurred by an NHS hospital doctor will be met by his employer. NHS trusts indemnify doctors directly just as they have always done for nurses and other hospital employees. There is no practical need to bring a claim against the doctor personally. Patients who bring a claim based on the alleged negligence of a nurse rarely bother to name the nurse personally as a defendant. Patients and their lawyers should ponder the wisdom of suing a doctor personally. As his employer will meet in full any award of compensation there is little to gain from naming the doctor in the claim. A doctor who sees his reputation on the line may seek to pressure his employer to fight the case tooth and nail. NHS trusts, and the NHSLA, may be more prepared to settle swiftly. However, suing a doctor individually may be designed not to obtain compensation but to ensure accountability. As long as complaints and review procedures in health care are perceived by patients as inadequate, patients may go on using clinical negligence claims to name individuals as a means to ensure accountability.[32]

The employer to sue, as vicariously liable, in the case of NHS hospital treatment will normally be the NHS trust. As privatization creeps into the health service this must be examined carefully. Take this example: an elderly, confused patient slips and falls on a highly polished floor. Who, if anyone, is responsible? The relevant negligence may be that a nurse failed to supervise the patient, or it may be that the cleaners were careless. The nurse will be employed by the hospital but the cleaner may be the employee of a private contractor. If the patient can rely only on the doctrine of vicarious liability to make someone other than the individual nurse or cleaner liable, he may have difficulty in selecting the correct defendant. Hospital and contractor may each blame the other's employee.[33] What of the case where an NHS patient is treated in a private hospital by virtue of an arrangement between the NHS trust and a private hospital? What we need now to examine is the direct, primary liability of the health authority to an NHS patient. First, the hospital will be liable for any failure of its own. A patient may suffer injury not because any particular doctor or nurse is careless but because the system provided by the authority is inadequate. There may be insufficient medical staff to cope swiftly enough with injured patients admitted to the casualty ward. Lack of experienced staff on night duty may cause injury to a patient whose condition deteriorates rapidly, and whom the staff on duty cannot, with the best will in the world, treat sufficiently promptly. For such faults an action will lie directly against the hospital.[34]

Direct responsibility to NHS patients may go an important step further. When a patient is admitted for hospital treatment under the NHS, the NHS trust undertakes to provide him with reasonably careful, competent and skilled care. Should his treatment fall below that standard, the hospital is directly, not just vicariously, responsible to the patient.[35] So if an elderly patient falls on a slippery floor the hospital is liable. It does not matter whether a nurse employed by the hospital or a cleaner employed by a contractor was the individual personally at fault. The hospital undertook to care for the patient. It failed and it is directly liable. Similarly a patient offered a hip replacement on the NHS need not be concerned if the operation is contracted out to a private hospital, as quite often happens now. The hospital undertook to provide the care and treatment. If anything goes wrong through negligence the NHS trust is liable. The patient can lie back and enjoy the trimmings of the private hospital. The importance of direct liability in today's NHS can clearly be seen. Until about ten years ago it hardly ever mattered whether a hospital was sued vicariously or directly as practically everyone working in NHS health care was an NHS employee. Contracting out vital services and increasing reliance on agency staff make it crucial.

The implications of direct liability could be far-reaching. In *M.* v. *Calderdale Health Authority*,[36] M. became pregnant and consulted an NHS doctor at an NHS community health centre. The doctor arranged an abortion at a private hospital but it was negligently performed and the woman went on to give birth to a baby boy. The health authority was found liable in negligence to M. Although no NHS employee was negligent nor was the health authority negligent in selecting the private clinic to which they contracted out abortions, they were in breach of a direct non-delegable duty to their patient. The judge summed up the position.

[M] never left the care of the first defendant. She was its patient. She never had an opportunity to divert from the route of treatment arranged on her behalf. In these circumstances she is entitled in my view to remain in the same position as a patient who remains in house relying upon the expectation of an effective provision of services.[37]

This does not mean that if an NHS trust seeks to clear its waiting list by an arrangement to contract out, for example, tonsillectomies, to a local private clinic, it will bear the full cost of the private clinic's negligence. The NHS trust will be able to make arrangements to ensure that the private clinic indemnifies them against any liability. It does mean NHS patients can always seek redress from the NHS.

Our next concern is the private patient. A private patient who engages a private bed in an NHS hospital contracts individually with the surgeon and anaesthetist for the surgery and the administration of the anaesthetic, and contracts separately with the hospital trust for nursing and ancillary care. Even if the surgeon and the anaesthetist are employed by the trust when caring for NHS patients, when they act for a private patient they are acting on their own behalf and not in the course of their NHS employment. If an error by surgeon or anaesthetist causes the patient injury he can sue only the responsible individual. If the carelessness is that of nursing or other medical staff he may sue the trust. As we shall see (page 193), this may cause problems of proof of negligence. Identifying who was the responsible individual may be nigh on impossible, leaving surgeon and hospital to blame each other and the patient to go uncompensated.

A patient entering a private hospital needs to consider carefully the nature and scope of his contract. The usual arrangement is similar to that entered into by a private patient taking a private bed within the NHS. The patient engages his own surgeon and anaesthetist who will not be employees of the private hospital. The hospital contracts to provide other medical and nursing care. Like the private patient within the NHS, the patient must proceed against the surgeon for any error of his, and against the hospital for error by their staff. Some private hospitals and clinics will contract to provide a whole 'package' of care and treatment. When the hospital undertakes to provide total care, the operation, anaesthetic, post-operative care, etc., and fails to do so then it is in breach of contract and liable for its failure to meet the required standard of care.[38] It is irrelevant that the surgeon, anaesthetist, or anyone else is not an employee of the hospital. The hospital is not vicariously liable for any fault of a particular person. It is directly responsible for its own breach of contract.

What of claims against general practitioners? First of all, most general practitioners are not employees of any NHS authority. A claim relating to negligence by a GP operating a single-doctor practice lies against that GP alone. General practitioners are not covered by NHS Indemnity and are not obliged to belong to a medical defence organization. The majority do, but a slight risk remains that a GP sued may be personally impecunious and professionally 'uninsured'. Where a GP is a member of a partnership his partners may be sued as jointly responsible for any negligence. If it is not the doctor himself who is at fault but a receptionist or nurse employed by the practice, the GP and his partners are vicariously liable as employers.

A thorny question of whom to sue in relation to general practice arises out of the use of locums and deputizing services. Locums and deputies are not employed by the regular general practitioner as a hospital doctor is employed by the health service. Therefore the general practitioner is not vicariously liable for any and every act of negligence on their part.[39] Of course, he may be liable for any personal carelessness of his in selecting a locum or deputizing service. Failing to check the qualifications of a locum, or engaging a deputizing service notorious locally for its incompetent doctors, will be negligence on the part of the GP. It is arguable too that engaging a locum or deputy without checking whether he carries professional indemnity insurance may equally be a breach of duty to the patient. A GP selecting another doctor to care for his patients must consider not only the stand-in's medical skill but also his ability to meet any claim against him. Doctors know all too well that such a claim can arise out of the occasional error made by even the most skilled practitioner.

When must proceedings be started?[40]

A patient contemplating an action for clinical negligence must act relatively promptly. The general rule is that all actions for personal injuries must be brought within three years of the infliction of the relevant injury. This is known as the limitation period and is laid down in the Limitation Act 1980. A claim form must be served no later than three years from the date of the alleged negligence. Sections 11 and 14 of the 1980 Act provide, however, that where the patient was originally either unaware that he had suffered significant injury,[41] or did not know about the negligence that could have caused his injury, the three-year period begins to run only from the time when he did discover, or reasonably should have discovered, the relevant facts. Where the patient knew all the relevant facts, but was ignorant of his legal remedy, the three-year limitation period runs from the time when he was or should have been aware of the facts.

All is not quite lost for the patient who delays beyond three years or who is ignorant of the law. A judge may still allow him to start an action later. Section 33 of the 1980 Act gives to the court a discretion to override the three-year limitation period where in all the circumstances it is fair to all parties to do so. The courts will examine the effect of allowing the action to go forward on both parties, taking into account, among other things, the effect of delay on the cogency of the evidence, the conduct of the parties, and the advice sought by and given to the patient by his lawyers and medical advisers.[42] The three-year (or longer) limitation period applies only to *starting* legal proceedings. Once started, an action may drag on for years before it is settled or finally decided.

One further aspect of the rules on limitation must be noted. Where the injured patient is under a legal disability at the time he suffers injury, that is to say he is under age (under eighteen) or mentally incapacitated, the limitation period does not begin to run until he reaches the age of majority or ceases to be mentally incapacitated. This means that, for example, a baby might be injured at birth and the obstetrician could face an action in respect of the injury up to twenty-one years after the event! Of course, the child's parents are free to bring the action earlier on their child's behalf. Until 1990, legal aid rules provided that if they did so their income would be taken into account in assessing their child's eligibility for legal aid. Now the child's income alone (if any) is relevant. Parents no longer face a financial deterrent to taking action at the earliest possible stage to obtain compensation for their child.

Civil justice reform: the Woolf Report

Cost, complexity and delay bedevilled not just clinical negligence claims, but all actions for compensation in the latter part of the twentieth century. The civil justice system was perceived as inadequate. One of England's most senior judges, Lord Woolf, was commissioned to conduct a comprehensive review of the civil justice system and to recommend radical reform. He issued his Final Report in 1996.[43] Lord Woolf set out a number of admirable objectives for the civil justice system. It should be just in its results, and the operation of the system should be fair to all parties. Costs should be proportionate to the nature of the case. Claims must be dealt with reasonably swiftly. The process should be understandable to everyone using it, including any litigant who chooses not to engage a lawyer but to sue in person. The system should be responsive to the needs of litigants. There should be certainty in the way the process works. Civil justice should be adequately resourced and reasonably funded.

Four key features of the Woolf reforms are central to malpractice litigation. (1) In December 1998, the *Pre-Action Protocol for the Resolution of Clinical Disputes*[44] (the *Clinical Negligence Protocol*) was issued. The Protocol seeks to find less adversarial and more cost-effective ways of resolving disputes about health care. (2) In April 1999, the Civil Procedure Rules 1998[45] came into force. These Rules introduce a unified set of procedures for claims regardless of whether a claim is heard in the county court or the high court. (3) Integral to the Rules is the concept of case-management. Judges are given infinitely greater powers to manage cases. (4) The rules governing expert witnesses are altered, seeking to abolish the misuse of expert evidence too often evident in the pre-Woolf era.

The Clinical Negligence Protocol

The Protocol sets out what it describes as '. . . "ground rules" for handling disputes at their early stages'. It seeks to encourage a greater climate of openness, to provide guidance as to how this more open culture can be achieved, and recommends a timed sequence of events when disputes do arise. The Protocol aims to maintain or restore the relationship between the aggrieved patient and health care professionals and providers, and to resolve as many disputes as possible without litigation. Communication between the parties lies at the heart of the Protocol. Cases should be investigated swiftly and records volunteered to the claimant for a reasonable period of time. Full consideration needs to be given to early settlement and whether, if agreement between the parties cannot be reached, resort might be had to mediation or some other form of alternative dispute resolution.

The Protocol promotes a 'cards on the table' approach. Ideally, when a patient believes that she has a case in clinical negligence, in a matter of months she will be able to judge whether her belief is well founded. The defendant doctor or hospital will also be in a position to settle any sustainable claim quickly. Means other than litigation for resolving genuine disputes will be reviewed and only the truly intractable case will go to court. Once in the court system, the case will be resolved efficiently.

What does the *Clinical Negligence Protocol* actually do? It focuses on pre-action events, before any claim form is issued and formal litigation begins. Requests for health records should be met within forty days at a cost no greater than if the patient requested her records under the Data Protection Act 1998. The request must provide sufficient information for the doctor or hospital to know if the injury of which the patient complains is serious and has serious consequences, and the request must be as specific as possible about which records are required. Just as the potential defendant must not keep the claimant in the dark, so too the Protocol aims to ensure that claimants and their lawyers are open and frank and do not set traps for unwary defendants. Where appropriate, on receipt of a request for records, the hospital should start to investigate the case fully.

A patient who is considering initiating litigation should send a letter of claim identifying any alleged negligence, her injuries and any consequential financial losses. The letter or claim must identify relevant documents and give sufficient information to enable the defendant to commence investigations and evaluate the claim. The patient may choose to include an offer to settle the case stating his valuation of what would constitute satisfactory compensation. No formal legal proceedings should be issued until three months after the letter of claim.

The potential defendant must acknowledge the letter of claim within fourteen days, and within three months must provide a reasoned answer. That letter of response must make it clear if the claim or part of the claim is admitted, and if admissions are binding. If the claim is denied, specific answers must be given to the patient's allegations. If additional documents are relied on, they must be disclosed. Where the patient made an offer to settle the doctor or hospital must respond to that offer. Every opportunity to resolve the case without going to court must be explored.

The Protocol also aims to ensure that NHS hospitals, and their staff, understand the law. It encourages proper risk management, prompt action when adverse outcomes occur, and good communication with patients. When the Protocol works, patients should have no incentive to rush into litigation and both sides should have every incentive to work together and not to engage in trial by battle. What happens, however, if parties do not co-operate and comply with the Protocol? Breaches of the Protocol can result in sanctions against the parties and their solicitors. Parties may be refused extension of time to serve claim forms or take various other steps in litigation, i.e. they will not be allowed to delay proceedings. Costs may be disallowed for unnecessary proceedings, for example if a patient rushes off to start formal proceedings before the three-month period has elapsed and before receiving a response from the defendants. Opinions vary on how effective sanctions are.[46] One matter is clear. If the defendant refuses or fails to provide records, the patient still has to resort to formal proceedings to force disclosure of records; he must seek an order for pre-action disclosure.

Compulsory disclosure of records

The patient seeking to compel disclosure of records will rely on section 33[47] of the Supreme Court Act 1981. He can apply for a court order requiring the doctor or hospital whom he plans to sue to disclose any records or notes likely to be relevant in forthcoming proceedings. Section 34[48] goes further. The court may order a person *not* a party to proceedings to produce relevant documents. So if the patient has started proceedings against a GP or a private medical practitioner, but believes that the hospital or clinic holds notes of value to his claim, the hospital or clinic can be made to hand over the notes. This will help the private patient in a dilemma as to whether he should properly proceed against doctor or hospital. It may also lead to the clinic being brought into the proceedings.

Hospitals still fear fishing expeditions by aggrieved patients. As we have seen, the *Clinical Negligence Protocol* urges voluntary disclosure of records. Initially hospitals preferred to disclose records to the patient's medical adviser alone, and not to the patient or his lawyers. Indeed, they sought to argue that this was the limit of their obligation. The House of Lords disagreed.[49] Under the 1970 statute, then in force, the patient himself was entitled to see the documents produced. Pleas that patients would be unduly distressed and fail to understand medical data cut little ice. The Supreme Court Act 1981 is less favourable to patients. It allows terms to be imposed on disclosure by the court. A court may limit disclosure to (a) the patient's legal advisers, or (b) the patient's legal and medical advisers, or (c), if the patient has no legal adviser, to his medical or other professional adviser. It is up to the court to decide whether the patient sees the records. As long as he has retained a lawyer, his lawyer must be permitted to examine the documents.

Three important matters on disclosure need a mention. First, the intention to bring proceedings and the likelihood that they will go ahead must be real before the court will order disclosure. The patient must have some solid ground for thinking he has a claim. He cannot use an application for disclosure to mount a fishing expedition on the off-chance that some evidence of negligence will come to light.[50] Resort to compulsory disclosure ought now to be rare. Documents truly relevant to a sustainable claim should have been volunteered under the Protocol. Other avenues to discover records and information may also be pursued. A patient simply wondering if he has a claim, but not yet even ready to approach a solicitor, may apply to see his records under the Data

Protection Act 1998. Or he may use the complaints procedure to explore whether he has any legal entitlement to pursue a compensation claim (see page 224).

Second, will the patient be able to see notes of any inquiry ordered by the hospital into his misadventure? The position is complex. If the inquiry was held mainly to provide the basis of information on which legal advice about the authority's legal liability is based, the records are protected by legal professional privilege. If the dominant purpose of the inquiry was otherwise, for example to improve hospital procedures or to provide the basis of disciplinary proceedings against staff, then the patient may be allowed access to the notes of the inquiry.[51] That is the legal position. The Court of Appeal has expressed its disquiet about the effect such claims of legal professional privilege may have on the patient's claim. Claims of privilege can be used to frustrate the patient's attempt to find out what happened. In *Lee* v. *South West Thames RHA*[52] a little boy, Marlon Lee, suffered a severe scald at home. He was taken to a hospital run by health authority A and then transferred to a burns unit controlled by health authority B. The next day he developed breathing problems, was put on a respirator and sent back to A in an ambulance provided by health authority C, the South West Thames RHA. When three days later the boy was taken off the respirator he was found to have suffered severe brain damage, probably due to lack of oxygen. In her attempts to find out what went wrong, the child's mother sought disclosure of records and notes on her son prepared by staff of all three authorities. Health authority A asked South West Thames RHA to obtain a report from their ambulance crew. South West Thames RHA compiled and forwarded the report to A. It was this report that the plaintiffs went to court to obtain access to. South West Thames RHA had revealed the report's existence but refused to hand it over to the family. They claimed it had been prepared in contemplation of litigation and to enable legal advice to be given in connection with that litigation. So it had, but it had been prepared on the request of health authority A to assess A's liability to the child. Reluctantly the Court of Appeal held that the privilege attaching to the document was enjoyed by health authority A. South West Thames could not be ordered to disclose the report. Even had they been prepared to do so they could not have handed over the report without A's agreement. The principle was that defendants or potential defendants should be '. . . free to seek evidence without being obliged to disclose the result of his researches to his opponent'. So a child was damaged for life in circumstances pointing to negligence on someone's part, and the law was powerless to help his mother find out what exactly caused his brain damage. The Court of Appeal expressed their disquiet and called for reform of the law. Within the doctor/patient relationship Sir John Donaldson MR said there was a duty to answer questions put before treatment was agreed to. Why should the duty to be frank with the patient be different once treatment was completed? In 1987 he again emphasized the importance he placed on what he termed a duty of candour.[53]

Third, the court retains the power to refuse to order disclosure where to do so would be injurious to the public interest.[54] This is unlikely to be the case where what is asked for is the patient's own medical notes. An attempt by the Secretary of State for Health to plead public interest immunity to avoid disclosure of records in the actions brought by several haemophiliac patients who had contracted HIV and AIDS from contaminated blood products failed.[55]

Going to court: case-management[56]

If attempts to resolve the claim fail, and the patient starts formal proceedings, the conduct of the case will now be strictly controlled, with an emphasis on enforcing strict time-limits and keeping costs down. The claim will be allocated to a *track*. A clinical negligence claim worth less than £1,000 would theoretically be allocated to the *small claims track*. Most such claims ought never to result in proceedings but will rather be resolved within complaints procedures. Claims worth between £1,000 and £15,000 are allocated to the *fast track*. This means that the case should be resolved within thirty weeks. The actual hearing should take one day or less and oral expert evidence is limited. Claims worth more than £15,000, or where the issues are especially complex, go on to the *multi-track*. Judges control the allocation process. Most clinical negligence claims will be multi-track. None the less the process should be speedier than before. At every point, opportunities to resolve the case without further proceedings must be seized. Time-wasting and unnecessary manoeuvres by lawyers will be penalized.

Proving negligence: the role of the expert

I come now to the heart of the problem. How does the patient prove negligence? The onus lies on him. He must demonstrate that it is more likely than not that his deterioration in health or his injury resulted from the negligence of the defendant. Mrs Ashcroft underwent an operation on her left ear. In the course of the operation she suffered damage to a facial nerve and her face was left permanently partly paralysed. The judge found the evidence finely balanced. There was formidable evidence that this should not have happened if proper care was taken. There was equally formidable evidence that in such delicate surgery damage to the nerve might occur even where the utmost skill and care were used. The judge held that the patient must fail.[57] There were, he said, 'no winners in such circumstances'.

How does the claimant discharge the onus of proof laid on him? In the majority of cases he will be heavily reliant on expert testimony. He will need to put forward medical evidence to demonstrate first that there was negligence on the part of the defendant, or a person for whom the defendant was responsible and second that the relevant negligence caused the harm of which he complains. Obtaining expert evidence used to be a nightmare for patients. Doctors are naturally unhappy about voicing public criticism of a colleague. Doctors in the same hospital may be unwilling to testify against each other. However greater openness does mean that today most patients should be able to obtain legal advice fairly locally. The patients' pressure group Action for Victims of Medical Accidents (AVMA) maintains a comprehensive list of reliable, truly expert, expert witnesses.

Until the Civil Procedure Rules came into force unrestricted freedom for each side to call its own experts made a mockery of justice. *Whitehouse* v. *Jordan*[58] illustrates the worst excesses of the 'old' system. In this case (which we have already looked at in the context of principles of liability) a claim was brought on behalf of a baby born disastrously and irretrievably brain-damaged. His mother, who was aged thirty and 4ft 10ins, had refused to submit to any internal examination or to an X-ray of her pelvis. The consultant in charge of her pregnancy put on her notes that 'trial of forceps delivery' should be attempted. However, when Mrs Whitehouse went into labour he was not there as he was ill with flu. The young doctor on duty summoned help. Mr Jordan, a senior registrar who had never seen the patient before, came to his aid. Mr Jordan made five or six attempts to deliver the baby by forceps. He then discontinued the attempt and proceeded swiftly and efficiently to deliver the baby by Caesarean section. The baby was born damaged. The mother alleged that this resulted from Mr Jordan's continued attempts to deliver by forceps and that he had persevered in those attempts beyond the point where a competent obstetrician would have desisted. He had pulled too hard and for too long. He was negligent, she said, in not proceeding sooner to deliver by Caesarean section. On the central issue of the extent to which it is correct practice to pursue an attempt to deliver by forceps, the trial judge was faced with a galaxy of 'stars' from the field of gynaecology and obstetrics. For the child, there appeared Professor Sir John Stallworthy (past president of the Royal College of Obstetricians and Gynaecologists) and Professor Sir John Peel (former gynaecologist to the Queen). For Mr Jordan, there lined up Professor Sir John Dewhurst (past president of the RCOG), Professor L. B. Strang, Professor J. P. M. Tizard, and Dame Josephine Barnes (past president of the RCOG). Mrs Whitehouse's witnesses put in a joint report, originally prepared by them but 'settled' by counsel, that is, her lawyers prepared the final draft! Lord Denning in the Court of Appeal criticized the report as wearing 'the colour of a special pleading rather than an impartial report'.[59] Not surprisingly, the opinions of the experts as to how far an attempt at forceps delivery could be pursued were miles apart. It is disturbing for the lay person to discover how large a gap can exist as to what constitutes proper obstetric practice.

Faced with the contradictions offered by the experts, the trial judge based his decision on a report by Professor Maclaren, the head of the unit, that the child's head had become impacted. The judge interpreted this as meaning that the head was in the pelvis and that Mr Jordan continued to pull with the forceps, thus subjecting the head to undue pressure. Professor Maclaren subsequently said that 'impacted' did not carry this meaning, and the defence experts supported him. Subsequently so did the House of Lords. The claim in *Whitehouse* v. *Jordan* dragged on for eight years from the issue of the proceedings. The child was nearly eleven before his claim was finally dismissed. The cost of three Queen's Counsel, two junior counsel, the solicitor's and experts' fees must have been astronomic.

The excesses of *Whitehouse* v. *Jordan* should never be repeated. Reform of the rules governing expert evidence are fundamental to the Woolf reforms. The Civil Procedure Rules are explicit and emphatic: the expert's primary duty is owed to the court to assist the court in matters involving his expertise, and this duty to the court '... overrides any obligation to the person from whom instructions were received or by whom the expert is paid'.[60] The Civil Procedure Rules also impose limits on the use of expert evidence. Expert testimony must be restricted to what is reasonably required to resolve the case.[61] The court has power to direct the appointment of a single joint expert rather than each party choosing their own experts.[62] Obviously if a single expert is to be appointed it makes sense for the parties themselves to agree on such an expert. Lord Woolf saw no reason why in straightforward clinical negligence up to a value of £10,000 parties should not be able to agree on a single expert. Such cases may necessarily not be all that common. They are likely to be limited to cases where there is no substantial medical dispute about causation or prognosis and perhaps all that is in issue is the appropriate measure of compensation. Many clinical negligence cases will involve disputes about whether there was any negligence at all, whether the negligence caused the injuries of which the claimant complains, and what the likely prognosis for the claimant will be. Such issues may well require separate experts.

Imagine a claim alleging that a child was brain-damaged as the result of a mismanaged delivery. Multiple experts may be unavoidable. Obstetric evidence will be needed to establish if the obstetrician was negligent. Neurologists may have to be called to testify to the likely cause of the brain damage. Paediatricians and rehabilitation experts will be required to assess how the child can best be cared for into adulthood. None the less control over the proliferation of expert evidence will be asserted by the court. Where practical, a single joint expert must be agreed in relation to any particular issue. So if there is a real and substantive dispute about whether the obstetrician was negligent, each party will probably be allowed to call its own obstetric expert, but save in the most exceptional case not more than one expert each. If there is no especial complexity about causation, a single expert should be agreed to address that issue. As much of the expert evidence as possible should be in writing. Oral testimony is allowable only with the permission of the court.

Where there are multiple experts, all letters, documents and instructions must be disclosed to the experts and there must be mutual disclosure of all experts' reports. Experts' meetings are encouraged. The hope may be that at such a meeting, the experts will resolve the differences between them and promote resolution of the case without proceeding to a hearing. Initially it was envisaged that experts would meet alone and conduct a quasi-scientific seminar. Lawyers and their clients were uncomfortable with such a process, which could be seen as surrendering the judicial process to the doctors. Additionally the objective of resolving proceedings more speedily might well be frustrated. The parties would not accept the experts' conclusions as binding. Consequently it is now agreed that the parties' lawyer may be present at experts' meetings.[63]

It is too early to judge the success of the new rules on experts. It does seem that fewer experts are being instructed and that costs have fallen.[64] As Lord Woolf recognized, the quality of expert evidence is crucial. Training for experts is available and all experts are encouraged to take advantage of this. Mandatory training and formal accreditation of experts cannot be far away.

Where the burden of proof shifts to the doctor

While in the majority of cases the patient must prove negligence and the doctor is not called on to prove his 'innocence', are there ever occasions when that burden shifts to the doctor? There is a general rule of the law of negligence that where the defendant is in complete control of the relevant events, and an accident happens that could have been avoided if proper care had been taken, then the fact of the accident itself affords reasonable evidence of negligence. The defendant will be held liable unless he can advance an explanation of the accident consistent with the exercise of proper care by him. This rule is known as *res ipsa loquitur* (the thing speaks for itself).[65]

Res ipsa loquitur can be applied in clinical negligence cases, but the courts are reluctant to do so. At first it was argued that *res ipsa loquitur* applied only where everyone of reasonable intelligence would know that that sort of accident did not ordinarily happen without negligence. As most people are not medically qualified, how could they know whether the accident to the patient was one which could or could not happen, if proper care was taken? The Court of Appeal said that expert medical evidence was admissible to establish what should and should not occur if ordinary care was exercised.[66] *Res ipsa* proved to be a boon in the following kind of case. Sometimes after an abdominal operation a swab or even a pair of forceps is discovered in the patient's body. Without evidence of a quite exceptional nature, it is clear someone has been careless. *Res ipsa* is also of value to the NHS patient who has undoubtedly suffered because someone was negligent either in the theatre or in the course of post-operative care, but he cannot identify that someone. If every member of the staff who might be responsible is employed by the hospital then an inference of negligence is raised against the hospital, who are necessarily vicariously liable for whoever may be the culprit.[67]

So in *Cassidy* v. *Ministry of Health*[68] a patient was operated on for Dupuytren's contraction, a condition affecting two of his fingers. After the operation the patient's hand and lower arm had to be kept rigid in a splint for up to fourteen days. When the splints were removed the plaintiff's whole hand was paralysed. Upon finding that all the staff involved in Mr Cassidy's care were NHS employees, the court held that there was evidence of negligence against their common employer. The onus shifted to the hospital to explain how this disaster might have struck without *any* of its employees being negligent.

Beyond this kind of obvious bungling, *res ipsa* has limited use in clinical negligence claims. In many operations the source of greatest danger for the patient lies not in the surgery itself, but in the anaesthetic. An anaesthetic mishap will not usually be of itself evidence of negligence, although *res ipsa* was applied in *Saunders* v. *Leeds Western HA*.[69] The patient was a four-year-old girl in otherwise perfect health who was undergoing surgery to correct a congenitally displaced hip. She suffered a cardiac arrest and consequent brain damage. Mann J. said:

It is plain from evidence called on her [the child's] behalf that the heart of a fit child does not arrest under anaesthesia if proper care is taken in the anaesthetic and surgical processes.

The Court of Appeal[70] has however made it very clear that *res ipsa* will rarely be applicable in such cases and indeed criticizes the phrase itself. It can arise only when either what happened simply cannot normally happen without negligence (e.g. the patient went into theatre for surgery on his left foot and comes out with unnecessary surgery having been performed on the right foot) or where expert evidence *agrees*, that without negligence, such an adverse outcome is highly unlikely. An unexpected outcome in itself will not raise any inference of negligence.

Even in those cases of apparently obvious negligence (such as the forceps left in the abdomen) where the facts give rise to an inference of negligence, problems surface if one of the staff caring for the patient is not an employee of the hospital. For example, the theatre sister may be an agency nurse. Can the hospital say, 'No inference of negligence is raised against *us* because the negligent actor may well have been that nurse for whom we are not responsible'? Once again it depends on whether the hospital's liability is solely vicarious, or whether the hospital is (as I have argued earlier) directly liable for any failure to measure up to the required standard of skill and care (see page 179). If the hospital is directly liable it matters not to the patient who actually employs the negligent individual.

The private patient may be less fortunate. As we have seen, whether he enters an NHS or a private hospital he will usually contract separately with the surgeon and the anaesthetist for surgery and anaesthetic. The surgeon and the anaesthetist will not be acting as employees of the hospital. If something goes wrong in the operating theatre or post-operatively and it is not clear who is to blame, *res ipsa* probably cannot be invoked. The hospital is not liable for any negligence on the part of the surgeon or anaesthetist. The patient can raise an inference of negligence against the hospital only if he can trace the relevant negligence to one of their staff. He can raise an inference of negligence against the surgeon or anaesthetist only if he can pin the relevant act on one of them personally.

If the surgeon, anaesthetist and hospital are all sued, none of them can be compelled to testify against the others. The patient will not be able to identify who was negligent. However, hope lies in the following statement made long ago by Lord Denning:

... I do not think that the hospital and [the doctor] can both avoid giving an explanation by the simple expedient of throwing responsibility on to the other. If an injured person shows that one or other or both of two persons injured him, but cannot say which of them it was, then he is not defeated altogether. He can call on each of them for an explanation.[71]

Thus robust common sense would force open any 'conspiracy of silence'.

Awards of compensation[72]

Once a patient has overcome all the formidable hurdles in his path and has satisfied the court that there has been negligence by the defendant as a result of which he suffered harm, what damages will he receive? There are no special rules governing clinical negligence awards. The patient's damages will be assessed to compensate him for any actual or prospective loss of earnings and for the pain, suffering and disability that he has endured and will endure. His compensation for loss of earnings will include a sum representing any period in which he would, if not for his injuries, have expected to be alive and earning.[73] Additionally to these sums to represent what he has lost, the patient will be awarded an amount to cover extra expenses that he and his family will incur. If he requires intensive nursing care, or his house needs adapting to his invalid needs, or he requires constant attendance so that his wife has to give up her job, all these expenses will be reflected in the award of damages. If the patient himself is dead, the damages awarded to his family will reflect the loss to them of the moneys he regularly expended on them. They recover for their loss of dependency.[74] It takes little imagination to see that if the patient dies, the burden of compensation will often be reduced. Dead he suffers no pain. Dead he incurs no expenses.

Returning to the living patient, thorny problems bedevil the question of damages. The first is this. The patient must usually sue within three years (see page 181). At that stage a prognosis about future health is speculative. All his medical advisers may be able to say is something like this. The patient has a degree of brain damage and is mildly disabled now. There is a 20 per cent chance that within ten years he may deteriorate to become paralysed and totally unable to do anything for himself. The process of assessing damages for such a patient used to be ludicrous. The courts would work out what he should receive if he did deteriorate and award him 20 per cent of that sum! The patient was grossly under-compensated if his condition did in fact deteriorate. If it did not, the doctor had paid out a sum to compensate for damage that had never happened. Section 32A of the Supreme Court Act 1981[75] cures this absurdity. The court now has power to make an award of provisional damages based on the assumption that the prospect of further damage or deterioration will *not* materialize. Should it do so at some later date, the patient may return to court to ask for a further award to compensate him for the consequences of that damage or deterioration.

Save for that provision in section 32A of the Supreme Court Act, unless the parties agree to set up a structured settlement, damages have to be assessed on a once and forever basis, as a lump sum. The court cannot order periodic payments that could be varied to suit the claimant's changing circumstances.

The need to award a lump sum poses particular difficulty in estimating claims for future expenses. This is especially acute where the patient is so badly injured as to be unable to manage his own affairs.[76] Large sums of money can be claimed to cover the cost of future care in expensive nursing homes, but there is no guarantee that the money will be so spent. The patient may be consigned to the NHS and the money invested to provide a windfall for relatives on the patient's death. The courts are alert to this danger. They will seek to ensure that the sum awarded is such as will be wholly exhausted by care of the patient, with no surplus left over as a bonus for relatives. Plans for care must be realistic, and section 5 of the Administration of Justice Act 1982 provides that 'any saving to the injured person that is attributable to his maintenance at public expense . . . in a hospital . . . or other institution shall be set off against any income lost . . .'

A further anomaly in the law is that the claimant may be able to claim for the full cost of *any* private medical care he selects regardless of whether such facilities are available free on the NHS.[77] Even where exactly identical surgery to alleviate the patient's condition could have been performed without charge, the claimant may demand the full cost of private care.

Before exploring how the law compensates pain and suffering, one other matter must be touched on. What happens if the defendant argues that the claimant could have avoided serious disability, and consequent loss of income, by undergoing further surgery or other medical treatment? For example, a patient is injured by a negligently performed spinal operation. Doctors recommend corrective surgery but the patient refuses to agree and is left unable to walk. The Privy Council[78] has now made it clear that a court should only reduce the compensation payable to the patient for her disability if the defendant hospital can prove that the decision to refuse further surgery was unreasonable.

Once the patient's monetary losses have been quantified, consideration must then be given to how to compensate his pain and suffering. Levels of compensation for those non-monetary losses have traditionally been much lower in this country than in the USA. In 1986 in *Housecroft* v. *Burnett*[79] the Court of Appeal ruled that £75,000 was the 'tariff' to compensate the suffering of a young woman left tetraplegic (paralysed from the neck down). Incrementally that sum crept up to about £100,000. Claimants felt that £100,000 for a lifetime of suffering was ludicrously low. The Law Commission conducted a review of compensation for pain and suffering and recommended that compensation for pain and suffering should be increased dramatically, in some instances of catastrophic injury by as much as 100 per cent.[80] In *Heil* v. *Rankin*[81] the Court of Appeal considered the Law Commission's proposals. An especially enlarged court agreed that more generous compensation for suffering and disability was justified but settled on a lesser increase than that envisaged by the Law Commission. No increase should be offered in claims of less than £10,000. Graduated increases would be allowed thereafter to a maximum of about 50 per cent above prior levels of awards. Their Lordships acknowledged that the impact on the NHS of increased levels of damages played a role in motivating their caution.[82]

Other changes in the law relating to damages have also contributed to the increase in compensation payable in negligence claims against the NHS.[83] Awards of over £3 million are no longer uncommon.[84] Improved medical skills mean that patients who suffer injury as a consequence of medical mistakes live much longer. Greater opportunities exist to improve their quality of life. Such benefits escalate costs, however. The concern generated by spiralling awards of damages is exacerbated by the fact that compensating people for injury can never be an exact science.

When negligence results in a patient's death, compensation for the bereavement occasioned to their family is only available to parents of children under eighteen, or to spouses. The level of compensation is now set at £10,000 in relation to deaths after 31 March 2002. The child left desolate at the loss of her father receives no compensation for her emotional loss. The parent losing a child is told her child is worth £10,000, an insulting assessment. Can any sum compensate for bereavement? Was the old rule that bereavement damages were never available preferable? When a patient is paralysed from the waist down, will £150,000 heal her pain?

Defendants also feel badly done by. *Who* the patient is may be crucial to the extent of their liability. Should I be left paralysed from the waist down by an anaesthetist's mistake, the defendant hospital will have to cover my cost of future care and of equipment I will need, such as wheelchairs and alterations to my house. Providing that I can still go on lecturing, even if seated, my loss of income will be minimal. Should England's football captain suffer an identical mishap at the height of his career, his claim for loss of income could easily exceed £5 million! When a child suffers birth injuries, who her parents are may be a factor in this compensation lottery. If the unfortunate infant is the son of a university vice chancellor, the assumption may be made that he would have a substantial earning capacity and he may be awarded greater compensation than if he were the offspring of a poorly educated unemployed couple.

The lottery element in compensation awards is graphically illustrated by the case of Hollie Calladine.[85] Nine-year-old Hollie was awarded £700,000 in respect of brain damage caused by negligence during her birth. Much of this sum was to cover the expense of her future care. Days after the award was made Hollie died suddenly. The hospital tried unsuccessfully to recover their damages. This sad case must suggest lump sum payments are not accurate or fair. The only equity of the system is that both sides suffer. For every case like Hollie Calladine's there is another where claimants go grossly under-compensated. For example, suppose a young man of twenty-three is injured in the course of surgery. Doctors estimate he will live a further ten years, but he survives for twenty-five years. His compensation will be less than half of what he required.

Structured settlements[86]

Some of the uncertainties generated by having to assess compensation as a lump sum, are avoidable by resort to structured settlements. The settlement is devised to meet the actual needs of the patient over time. He will receive an initial capital sum to cover actual losses already quantifiable and such matters as compensation for pain and suffering. The remainder of the money will be used by the defendant to purchase an annuity for the claimant's benefit. The annuity will be flexible to adapt to the changing circumstances of the patient. The income received by the patient is not taxable. The money paid out will be what he requires and no more. Should he die earlier than anticipated payments stop. Structured settlements avoid cases like that of Hollie Calladine.

In ordinary personal injury claims the defendant's insurer arranges the settlement and negotiates the purchase of annuities. As we have seen, the NHS does not insure against liability for clinical negligence on the commercial market. NHS structured settlements are usually self-financed. They use their own income to arrange periodical payments building the settlement into budgets. Tax concessions aid this process. Structured settlements in large claims save the NHS money. However, not all claimants agree to such a settlement. Distrust may cause them to be suspicious or to want control over the investment of their own money. Courts as yet have no powers to order structured settlements.[87] Should they have?

8

Medical Products Liability[1]

The pharmaceutical industry once basked in the warm glow of public acclaim. The development of antibiotics, of drugs to combat high blood pressure and heart disease, of medicines to alleviate the pain of rheumatism, and later the invention of the contraceptive pill, brought benefits to many and life itself for some.[2] Events were to change the drug companies' image. Starting with the thalidomide tragedy, a series of disasters taught us the painful lesson that drugs can be dangerous and their use must be paid for. The list of drugs enthusiastically promoted in the first place and withdrawn from the market a few years later, amid bitter allegations that the drug in question caused injury and even death, is long.[3] Opren, the benzodiazepine tranquillizers such as Valium, human growth hormone, and even the Pill itself are but a random sample of the better-known cases. Allegations of gross profit-making by multinational drug companies have proliferated.[4] Concern about the safety of drugs has extended today to anxiety about the safety of medical devices (such as breast implants) and, most worrying of all, to the risks posed by contaminated blood supplies[5] and other body parts.

Thalidomide was originally developed by West German manufacturers, Chemie Grunenthal. A British company, Distillers, bought the formula and manufactured and marketed the drug here under licence from Chemie Grunenthal. The drug was promoted as a safer alternative to existing sedatives and was expressly claimed to be suitable for pregnant and nursing mothers. Thalidomide was alleged to be the cause of gross foetal deformity. All over Europe, wherever thalidomide had been available, babies began to be born suffering from startlingly similar deformities, notably phocomelia (flipper limbs). After a bitter campaign, Distillers and the children's parents reached a settlement to provide compensation for children recognized as damaged by thalidomide.[6] The anti-rheumatic drug Opren, withdrawn here in 1982, is alleged to have caused kidney and liver damage, and even death, in some of its elderly users. Claims arising out of the misuse of benzodiazepines met little success.

Patients who suffered injury as a result of taking Opren took legal action on both sides of the Atlantic. In the USA, Opren sufferers secured substantial compensation payments. British victims found themselves entangled in lengthy and complex litigation. They won some preliminary skirmishes,[7] but ultimately the cost of litigation forced many of them to accept an out-of-court settlement offering only meagre compensation.[8] Other Opren victims fought on in the courts. The defendant drug company successfully contended that they took legal action too late and were barred from either benefiting from the settlement or pursuing their case further in the courts.[9] Costly litigation ending in minimal compensation payments was for decades the pattern for virtually all claims for drug-induced injury in England.[10]

In 1987, Parliament enacted the Consumer Protection Act, imposing on all producers of goods strict liability for unsafe products. This Act was based on a European Community Directive that required all Member States to introduce such strict liability for products. In part the intention of the Directive was to ensure fair competition between businesses in the Community. If France required French producers to meet more stringent safety laws than other Member States, French businesses competed at a disadvantage to their rivals. However, much of the impetus for strict liability for unsafe goods in Europe and the United Kingdom arose from a desire to give more effective protection and remedies to people who suffered injury as a result of defects in goods.

The Consumer Protection Act might be thought to make the law on drug-induced injury straightforward. A drug that causes kidney damage or foetal abnormality would be perceived by most lay observers as 'unsafe'. Defining 'defective' under the Act will be seen to be more problematical. The damage caused by some drugs takes years to manifest itself. No action under the Act is allowed more than ten years after the drug in question was put on the market. Nor is a drug company's liability under the Act wholly strict, for the Act permits producers to plead a 'development risks' defence and so escape liability. Victims of drug-induced injury often still resort to prior common-law remedies in contract and the tort of negligence. Negligence liability for drug-induced injury needs to be understood to evaluate how far strict liability under the Act is a real advance on the bad old rules that thalidomide and Opren victims had to play under. For well over a decade the Act seemed almost irrelevant. A trio of judgments in 2000 and 2001 have breathed life into strict liability. None the less applying the Consumer Protection Act to drugs is far from straightforward.[11]

Product liability and drugs

Whatever scheme for compensation is in operation there are problems relating to drug-induced injury that will not go away. The law, here and in the USA, purports to treat drugs as just another product.[12] For legal purposes a defective drug is little different from a defective electric blanket or kettle. In practice there are vital distinctions affecting both user and manufacturer if litigation is started. Defects in products can be of two sorts; in *design*, which means that every example of the product will prove defective, or in *construction*, which means that some but not all of the products will be faulty simply because they have not been put together properly.[13] Faults in electric blankets, kettles, or even aircraft, are usually construction faults. Defects in drugs are mostly design flaws. That means that a drug company facing a claim alleging their product to be defective, is facing a disaster. There are going to be not just one or two claimants but a host of embittered and injured users. The cost to the company may put it out of business. It should be no surprise that the company fights back with equal vigour.

From the user's viewpoint, the greatest difficulty in any claim against the drug company is proving that the drug caused her injury. Should a new brand of electric blanket suffer a design defect, and within a week of purchase 5 per cent of users suffer an electric shock, the link between cause and effect is clear. With a new drug the process will be nothing like so swift or sure. Consider the case of diethylstilboestrol, a drug prescribed over fifty years ago to women threatening to miscarry. Evidence has emerged that women *in utero* when their mothers took the drug were affected in disproportionate numbers by vaginal and cervical cancer.[14] Delay in effect is only one of the problems. There may be uncertainty as to whether injury resulted from the drug taken, the original disease, or some other natural cause. When a drug is alleged to cause foetal deformity this is a particular difficulty. Was the child's disability the result of the drug, or of some inherited disorder or disease in the mother, or one of a number of other possible causes? Then in all claims there is the problem of proving that the drug was taken by the patient in the proper dosage, and as often the same drug is manufactured under different brand names, it must be shown which brand the patient actually used.[15] Medical records are often far from perfect; memory is fallible. Finally, there is the intractable difficulty of personal idiosyncrasy. A drug that is beneficial to 99.9 per cent of us may be lethal to the other 0.1 per cent. Is that drug defective? Should the company, or anyone else, compensate the 0.1 per cent who suffer injury?

The drug companies refuse to let government and legislators forget these special problems. They press other claims for special treatment. Drugs are intrinsically dangerous. Patients should accept that there is a balance of benefit and risk. The pharmaceutical industry argues that laws that weigh too onerously on it may inhibit research. Medicine would be held back and British companies would suffer loss of competitiveness. Some view this claim sceptically. Much of the competition appears aimed at producing new brands of the same basic drugs. The pace of innovation has slowed down.[16] Doctors are moving away from prescribing as freely as they did in the past. Any decline in the pharmaceutical industry is as likely to be due to these factors as it is to be the result of law reform to help drug-injured patients.

Consumer-buyers: most favoured claimants

A victim of drug-induced injury who bought the offending drug himself, or acquired the drug in the course of a contract, has a more effective remedy than any of his fellow sufferers. Despite the Consumer Protection Act, consumer-buyers remain the most favoured claimants in England.

Two conditions are implied in every contract for the sale of goods. First, the goods must be of satisfactory quality.[17] This means they must meet the standard that a reasonable person would regard as satisfactory. Second, the goods must be reasonably fit for the purpose for which they are sold.[18] When drugs are bought over the counter they must meet these conditions just like any other goods. To take a simple example, a patient buying a bottle of cough mixture suffers internal injury because the medicine is contaminated by powdered glass. That patient recovers full compensation for his injuries from the pharmacist who sold him the medicine even though the pharmacist may be entirely without fault. The medicine may have been supplied by the manufacturer in a sealed, opaque container. That does not matter. The medicine is neither of satisfactory quality nor fit to be sold, and the pharmacist is in breach of contract. This simple and effective remedy has a defect, however. It is normally available only when the person suffering injury from the defective drug bought it himself. Had the contaminated medicine in our example been purchased by a husband and taken by his wife, she may well have had no remedy in contract.[19] She cannot benefit from a contract to which she is not a party.

How useful is the contractual remedy in practice? Recent developments in the regulation of medicines may increase the usefulness of contractual remedies. In the past ten years, a growing range of medicines have ceased to be available by prescription only. They have been reclassified to allow their sale in pharmacies, or in many cases just in ordinary shops.[20] Antihistamines to alleviate hayfever, similar drugs to aid sleep and a host of medicines to help digestive problems can now be bought over the counter. These newly 'deregulated' drugs are more likely to carry inherent risks of harm than the sort of cough and cold remedies that were available over the counter in 1992. More patients may choose to look to their pharmacist or local supermarket for redress. Patients prescribed their medicines on the NHS remain less favoured. Such medicines will not attract conditions of satisfactory quality and fitness for purpose because there is no contract between the pharmacist and the patient into which such conditions can be implied, even though the patient will often pay for his prescription.[21] The pharmacist dispenses the drug as part of his obligation under his contract with the Primary Care Trust to provide pharmaceutical services in the area. The patient pays a statutory charge. He does not buy the drug; he pays a tax for NHS services.

By contrast, when drugs are dispensed under a private prescription a contract does exist between the pharmacist and the patient. The patient pays the full cost of the drug directly to the pharmacist. It matters not whether the contract is one of simple sale or a contract of service under which the pharmacist provides a skilled service and incidentally supplies the drug. Quality conditions are imposed in identical terms regardless of whether goods are supplied in the course of a service or in an ordinary sales transaction.[22] The number of private prescriptions is rising. The pharmacist is exposed on the front line of liability for defective drugs. When more potent drugs become the subject of conditions of fitness, whether by prescription or an over-the-counter sale, problems of applying those conditions are likely. The question may arise as to whether a drug perfectly safe for all but pregnant women is fit to be supplied. Clearly if it is specifically aimed at pregnant women then it is not fit for the purpose for which it is supplied if it damages the woman or her baby. If it is a general medicine, such as a hayfever remedy, it could be argued that if it carries risk to a substantial section of the community, for example pregnant women, then it is not of satisfactory quality, nor fit to be on general sale. This immediately raises further questions. Did the manufacturer warn of the risk to pregnant women? Is such a warning sufficient? Should the woman herself be aware of the dangers of taking drugs and avoid drugs while pregnant?

These sorts of problems inevitably plague questions of liability for defective drugs. Where a remedy lies in contract, once a court finds the drug unsafe, the claim for compensation is established. It is no defence for the retailer of the drug, or the pharmacist dispensing the drug, to argue that he personally was blameless. Nor is it any answer to the patient's claim that the state of scientific and technical knowledge at the time when the drug was produced was such that the defect could not have been discovered. There is no 'development risks' defence against a claim in contract. The liability imposed on the retailer or supplier is truly strict.

The remedy in negligence

Patients who suffer injury as a result of drugs prescribed within the NHS must look outside contract for a remedy. Prior to the Consumer Protection Act 1987 that remedy would have to be found in the tort of negligence. The 1987 Act applies only to products marketed *after* 1 March 1988, so that any claim arising out of a drug put on the market *before* that date (albeit taken by the patient at some later date) will still lie exclusively in negligence. Gaps in the Consumer Protection Act mean that victims of drug-induced injury cannot ignore the tort of negligence.

An action in negligence arises where one person suffers injury as a result of a breach of a duty of care owed him by another. His doctor may be the first person to whom the patient turns for a remedy when he believes a drug prescribed by that doctor has harmed him. The doctor will be liable for drug-induced injury if the drug caused damage because she prescribed an incorrect dosage, or because she ought to have appreciated that that drug posed a risk to a particular patient in the light of his medical history, or where drugs have been prescribed in an inappropriate and harmful combination. Similarly if the injury to the patient results from a negligent error by the pharmacist in, for example, dispensing the wrong drug, or indicating the wrong dosage, an action in negligence lies against the pharmacist. In a number of cases, it is the cumulative negligence of both doctor and pharmacist that causes injury, as where a doctor's atrocious handwriting misled the pharmacist into dispensing entirely the wrong drug (see page 159).[23] The problem for the patient is that all he knows is that he is ill and he believes the drug to be the cause. He will have no means of knowing whether an inherently 'safe' drug was prescribed for him in an unsafe and careless fashion, or whether the drug is inherently defective and harmful, however careful his doctor may be. Hence patients contemplating litigation for drug-induced injury often have to start by considering suing the doctor, the pharmacist *and* the manufacturer, and hope that evidence of who was actually to blame will emerge in the course of the litigation.

Turning now to the liability in negligence of drug companies manufacturing drugs, the manufacturer of any product,

. . . which he sells in such a form as to show that he intends them to reach the ultimate consumer in the form in which they left him with no reasonable possibility of intermediate examination, and with the knowledge that the absence of care in the preparation or putting up of the products will result in injury to the consumer's life or property, owes a duty to the consumer to take that reasonable care.[24]

There is no doubt that this duty to take care attaches as much to the manufacturer of drugs as to the manufacturer of ginger beer or any other product. The duty covers the design and formulation of the drug as well as its construction. Nor is the duty limited to the original manufacturer. Thalidomide, as we have seen, was initially developed by a West German company and manufactured under licence here by Distillers. Distillers still owed a duty to British patients to take steps to check on the safety of the drug by testing and monitoring the formula before putting the product on the UK market.[25]

Establishing a duty to avoid negligence is not the problem. Determining what amounts to negligence is a formidable task. The potential harm caused by a defective drug is such that a very high standard of care will be imposed on the manufacturer. This is generally acknowledged. However, in England no action for personal injuries against a drug company has yet resulted in an award of damages by a court although a claim against the National Blood Authority has, as we shall see, succeeded. What are the obstacles confronting claimants? First, the drug company must be judged by the standards for drug safety pertaining at the date when the drug was put on the market, not at the date proceedings are taken against them. Drug companies, like doctors, must not be judged negligent on hindsight alone. Today the risk to the developing foetus of drugs taken by the mother is well known to all lay women. When thalidomide was first on the market it is far from clear that the dangers of drugs to the foetus were widely appreciated even by gynaecologists and scientists.

Consideration of the history of the thalidomide claim[26] leads us into the second difficulty for litigants. How does a claimant obtain the evidence he will need to prove the company careless? The thalidomide story is instructive, albeit depressing. The charge against Distillers was that they should have foreseen that the drug might harm the foetus and therefore should have conducted adequate tests before promoting it as safe for use in pregnancy, and/or that once adverse reports on the drug reached them they should have withdrawn it at once. In retrospect, the available evidence that Distillers was negligent falls into three categories. First, there was material available from 1934 onwards to suggest that drugs could pass through the placenta and damage the foetus. Second, in the 1950s a number of drug companies marketing new products had carried out tests to check the effect on the foetus, mainly by way of animal experiments. Such evidence would need to have been given by experts and might not have been conclusive. The burden of proof lies on the claimant. The defendant's experts would have argued that when thalidomide was developed it was by no means universally accepted that drugs could damage the foetus, the efficacy of animal tests would have been disputed, and it would have been strongly submitted that in any case such tests were not then current general practice.

The third and final category of evidence might have been more damning if the claimants could have got hold of it. Reports of the original testing of thalidomide in West Germany by Chemie Grunenthal suggest that it may have been a pretty hit and miss affair. Fairly early on, adverse reports on the drug and concern over the risk to the foetus were in the hands of Chemie Grunenthal. Some considerable time elapsed before they withdrew the drug there. Distillers acted faster, taking the drug out of circulation soon after adverse reactions were reported to them. The contents of adverse reports on a drug, and the sequence and exact dates on which those reports are received, are of crucial importance to a claimant. No drug company is going to hand the reports over voluntarily. The process of discovery, of compelling a defendant to hand over documents, was seen to be complex enough in a malpractice claim against an individual doctor. In claims against a drug company the process often became an insuperable obstacle race. It remains to be seen how far reforms of the civil justice system discussed in Chapter 7 will assist future claimants.

One general point on the law of negligence as it affects drug claims can be made by way of illustration from the thalidomide case. It may ultimately prove to be the case that there is insufficient evidence that the company were negligent when they originally marketed the drug. There may be evidence, however hard to come by, that they were negligent in failing to act on adverse reports and recall the drug. Is that a breach of the manufacturer's duty? Two separate situations must be examined. Had it been proved that a child was injured by thalidomide when the drug taken was put on the market by Distillers *after* a date by which they should have known it to be dangerous, there is no problem. The drug that injured that child was negligently put into circulation. Difficulty would arise where the drug taken by the mother had been put into circulation before Distillers should have known it was dangerous but was actually prescribed to her and taken by her after that date. There is a strong case that a manufacturer owes a further duty to monitor his product and to take reasonable steps to withdraw it if it proves unsafe.[27] Proving breach of that duty could be a nightmare. Stories of doctors continuing to prescribe, and pharmacists retaining stocks of, withdrawn drugs recur. The patient bringing such a claim may falter and sink in a sea of allegation and counter-allegation between drug company, doctor and pharmacist.

The inadequacy of negligence as an effective means of compensating victims of drug-induced injury has been demonstrated time and time again. Successive reviews of negligence as a means of remedying personal injuries resulting from any unsafe product concluded that the reform of product liability laws was essential.[28] What must now be evaluated is how effective reform by way of the Consumer Protection Act 1987 has proved to be.

Strict liability: the Consumer Protection Act[29]

The concept of strict liability is simple. A claimant seeking compensation from the manufacturer of a product need prove only that the product was defective *and* that the defect in the product caused his injury. Strict liability is fairer to claimants because it establishes that responsibility for an injury caused by a defective product is borne by the person creating the risk and benefiting financially from the product, that is the manufacturer. The manufacturer is in the best position to exercise control over the safety and quality of the product, and can more conveniently insure against the risk of injury posed by the product. Proponents of strict liability for products also argued that prolonged, expensive and complex litigation was likely to be less common with a strict liability regime. Does the Consumer Protection Act achieve the aims of strict liability for patients injured by defective drugs?

The Act imposes liability for personal injury arising from defective products on all *producers* of goods. 'Producers' embraces a wider category of businesses involved in the marketing of drugs than simply the companies manufacturing the finished products.[30] Manufacturers of components are liable for any defect in the components. Companies importing drugs into the European Union are as liable under the Act as if they manufactured the drug in England. If the drug in question was manufactured in Japan, the aggrieved patient need not concern himself with the potential difficulties of suing the Japanese company abroad: he can bring his claim in England[31] against the European Union company who brought the drug into the EU. A company that brand-names a drug is a producer within the Act. Companies cannot use their name to claim the credit and the profit for a drug and then when something goes badly wrong disclaim any responsibility for that drug. Finally, any supplier[32] of a drug will be deemed to be a producer unless he identifies the source of his supply. This provision is crucial for patients. The patient may well receive his prescription or injection in a form such that he cannot possibly identify the original producer of the drug. The community pharmacist or hospital pharmacy supplying the drug must assist him to identify the producer or bear liability for the patient's injuries themselves. The intention of the European Directive,[33] on which the Act is based, and of the Act itself, is that there should, as far as humanly possible, always be an identifiable producer on whom liability must rest. No company can hide behind a smokescreen.

So far so good, but how do you establish that the drug is defective? Section 3(1) provides that

... there is a defect in a product ... if the safety of the product is not such as persons generally are entitled to expect;

Section 3(2) goes on to direct the judge to take into account all relevant circumstances pertaining to the safety of a product including

(a) the manner in which, and purposes for which, the product has been marketed, its get-up, the use of any mark in relation to the product and any instructions for, or warnings with respect to, the doing of anything with or in relation to the product;

(b) what might reasonably be expected to be done with or in relation to the product; and

(c) the time when the product was supplied by its producer to another;

and nothing in this section shall require a defect to be inferred from the fact alone that the safety of a product which is supplied after that time is greater than the safety of the product in question.

Determining when a drug falls within the definition is far from easy.[34] Drugs are by their nature dangerous. They are designed to do damage to the bacteria or diseased cells or whatever caused the original disease. How much safety are persons generally entitled to expect? Side-effects are often unavoidable. The court has to try to balance the potential benefit against the risk when deciding if an unwanted side-effect renders a drug defective. Distinctions may be drawn based on the condition that the drug was designed to combat. A minor tranquillizer that carried an unforeseen 5 per cent risk of liver damage could be deemed defective where an anti-cancer drug carrying an identical risk would not. Relief of moderate anxiety may be seen as an insufficient benefit to warrant the risk of liver damage, whereas the battle against cancer may justify that degree of inherent danger. Anticipated risks raise different issues. An anticipated risk must be warned against. Will the tranquillizer be deemed *not* defective if its potential danger is outlined to doctors and patients, leaving the choice to them? Clearly the warning must be taken into account. An antibiotic harmful only to the foetus will almost certainly not be deemed defective if a warning of its risk is clearly given. Less essential drugs may remain defective even if risks are detailed in the literature supplied to doctors. The patient may never have the warning passed on to him. In such a case, though, a heavy share of liability would rest with the doctor prescribing the drug in contravention or ignorance of warnings from the producer.

Other problems in applying this definition of defective beset the patient. What of the patient who suffers injury because of an allergic reaction to the drug? The drug is perfectly safe and effective for you, but lethal to me. So might it be argued that the drug is safe for 'persons generally'? Such an argument will fail. Society, 'persons generally', demands that regard be had for the safety of all of us where, as in the case of drugs, allergic and idiosyncratic reactions are a well-known risk of the product. If risk to an individual or group is foreseeable and *not* warned of in the presentation of the product, it is defective. An individual is entitled to expect that the manufacturer will not simply ignore an identified danger to however small a group. When the risk is not foreseeable, the size and predictability of the affected group will be crucial. A sedative that causes damage to the foetus or liver damage in 10 per cent of the over-seventies will be defective. Pregnant women and the elderly are large groups of potential consumers known to be vulnerable to drug-induced injury. But what if the sedative injured only a handful of users out of millions?

Guidance on defining 'defective' is to be found in three recent judgments. In *Abouzaid* v. *Mothercare Ltd*[35] a twelve year old boy was trying to attach a fleece-lined sleeping bag to his baby brother's pushchair. The sleeping bag had to be clipped on to the pushchair by passing elasticated straps round the back of the chair joined by a metal buckle. There were no instructions provided. As the boy struggled to fasten the sleeping bag to the chair, one of the straps slipped from his grasp and the metal buckle flew up and hit him in his left eye. The injury caused him to lose significant vision in that eye. The Court of Appeal found that the product was defective. There was a failure to provide instructions and the design of the product was unsafe because it could not be secured without risk. Consumers would properly expect that such a product could be used without that degree of risk. Relatively minor alterations in design would eliminate that risk.

The *Mothercare* judgment can be applied to make two key points about liability for drugs. (1) Instructions about the use of, and warnings concerning possible adverse effects of, drugs are crucial. Failure to warn of a known risk will, as argued earlier, render a drug defective. (2) *Common sense* will play its part in determining what 'people generally' may expect from a product. That latter point is reinforced in *Richardson* v. *LRC Products Ltd*.[36] The plaintiff became pregnant after a condom split. She sued the manufacturers arguing that the condom failure demonstrated that the product was defective. She was unable to identify any particular construction defect in the condom or point to a risk of damage that the manufacturers should have avoided. The judge found no evidence of unsatisfactory testing of the product. The evidence was simply that in actual use an inexplicable number of condoms fail. Dismissing the plaintiff's claim, the judge held that the manufacturers made no claims that their (or any method) of contraception was 100 per cent safe. The fallibility of contraception was well known.

Returning to drug-induced harm, consider the following examples in the light of the above cases. You purchase Ibuprofen in a supermarket. The packet clearly warns you *not* to take the medicine if you suffer from asthma. You ignore that warning and, despite your asthma, take several tablets. An acute attack of asthma lands you in hospital. Is that pack of Ibuprofen defective? You are prescribed a cream to cure acne. No warning accompanies the product. The cream causes the eruption of a rash all over your body. Evidence emerges that that product will produce just such an allergic reaction in about 2 per cent of female users if they use the cream during pregnancy. Neither you nor your GP was aware you were pregnant at the time. Is the product defective?

A. v. National Blood Authority[37]

The judgment in *A.* v. *National Blood Authority* is by far the most important case yet to interpret the Consumer Protection Act. It breathes new life into strict liability. The case addresses claims by patients infected with hepatitis C from blood and blood products through blood transfusions after 1 March 1988. Two important points must be made. First, the defendants (rightly) conceded that blood and body parts fell within the regime of strict liability imposed by the Consumer Protection Act. Secondly, the judge ruled that the provision of the British legislation (the 1987 Act) must be interpreted in the light of the European Product Liability Directive. Where there were apparent inconsistencies between the two, the Directive should be preferred. The importance of this will be highlighted later.

Moving to the substance of the claims, the judge held that in determining whether the contaminated blood products were defective what must be decided is what the *legitimate expectations* of the public were in relation to that product. People expected blood to be 100 per cent clean. Whether the relevant 'defect' in the product was *avoidable* was not the issue. The defendants had tried to argue that the public could only expect they would have done what was possible to screen blood and avoid contamination. In more diplomatic language, the judge effectively declared this to be nonsense. He said

. . . it is as inappropriate to propose that the public should not 'expect the un-attainable' – in the sense of tests and precautions which are impossible – at least unless it is informed as to what is unattainable or impossible as it is to refor-mulate the expectation as one that the producer will not have been negligent or will have taken all reasonable steps.[38]

The judge marked a clear boundary between negligence and strict liability. He went on to say a distinction needs to be made between *standard* and *non-standard* products, a distinction analogous to design and construction defects. Establishing that a standard product was defective would continue to be difficult. The infected batches of blood were non-standard. They could only not be defective if it could be shown the public were made aware of the risks. In this instance, this was not the case. Unlike condoms, which most people know do and can split for no apparent reason, most of us assume that blood will not cause us to succumb to serious, even fatal, disease.

Development risks

The Blood Authority had another weapon. If the contaminated blood was defective, they argued, they were not liable because they could invoke the development risks defence.[39] A development risks defence amounts to this. The manufacturer will not be liable if he can prove that the state of scientific and technical knowledge at the time when he put the product into circulation was not such as to enable the existence of the defect to be discovered.[40]

The scope of the development risks defence in the United Kingdom looks broad. The European Directive on Product Liability framed the defence in terms of the scientific and technical knowledge generally available. Section 4(1)(e) of the Consumer Protection Act provides '. . . *the state of scientific and technical knowledge was not such that a producer of products of the same description as the product in question might be expected to have discovered the defect.'* The test in the Act appears to be what was the knowledge and practice of the pharmaceutical industry at the time. The European Commission challenged the British Act alleging that the UK had improperly sought to broaden the defence allowed by the Directive. The challenge failed.[41] The European Court of Justice allowed the British interpretation of the Directive. The result might have been depressing.[42] Academic research may reveal significant concerns about the safety of a novel drug. If that research has not permeated industry the 'development risks' defence could still be cited by the drug companies, creating a test little different from 'old' negligence rules. So, in *A. v. National Blood Authority* the defendants argued (1) that as at the relevant time there was no effective test to screen blood for hepatitis C the development risks defence applied, and, (2) that the 1987 Act provided that producers of analogous products must at the relevant time have been aware of and able to eliminate the relevant risk. Construing the Act in the light of the Directive, the judge dismissed both arguments. The defence applies only where the very existence of the defect was unknown and undiscoverable.[43] Bodies responsible for blood supplies at the relevant time were aware of the risks of contamination. That no method of screening for hepatitis C had yet been developed was irrelevant. The wording of section 4(1)(e) of the 1987 Act was inappropriate. The Directive made it clear that once knowledge of a risk was accessible to manufacturers, the risk was known. A single article in an obscure Chinese journal ('the Manchurian exception') might not suffice,[44] but general knowledge accessible to the academic and commercial communities would.

If *A. v. National Blood Authority* is followed in the higher courts, the Consumer Protection Act will make a difference. A producer invoking the development risks defence will have to establish that the defect in the drug, or device, or bodily product, was undiscoverable and the onus will lie on him to prove this.

Why was the British government so insistent on the development risks defence? All the bodies that recommended product liability reform rejected such a defence. The Pearson Commission said:

. . . to exclude development risks from a regime of strict liability would be to leave a gap in the compensation cover, through which, for example, the victims of another thalidomide disaster might slip.[45]

The government allowed itself to be swayed by counter-arguments from industry. They claim that innovation would be discouraged and that the cost of insurance against development risks would be crippling.[46] There is another disquieting feature of the acceptance of a development risks defence. Germany, which boasts a thriving pharmaceutical industry, rejected the development risks defence specifically with regard to drugs while adopting it in relation to other products. Germany did not want to become a testing ground for risky drugs. Does Britain?

Causation

The claimants in *A.* v. *National Blood Authority* were lucky in one respect. They knew who had supplied the 'defective' blood. Where a claim relates to a drug, a potential claimant may well have taken the drug over several years and not be able to trace which of several drug companies manufactured the drug that caused his injury. An analogous problem arose in *Fairchild* v. *Glenhaven Funeral Services Ltd*[47] facing workers who contracted the industrial disease, mesothelioma. They could show that their illness was caused by exposure to asbestos dust or fibres. They established that their employers were negligent in exposing them to asbestos. However, as they had worked for several companies during their working life, they could not pinpoint which employer was actually responsible for their disease, which can be caused by a single fibre entering the lung. The Law Lords ruled that as each defendant employer had increased the risk to the affected workers, causation was established against all of them. In the USA, in *Sindell* v. *Abbot Laboratories*,[48] it has been held that where patients are exposed to risk from a defective drug manufactured by several different companies, each company is held liable in proportion to its market share. Lord Hoffmann in *Fairchild* did not consider that the industrial disease claims before the Law Lords and claims against drug companies were the same. He said that the risk from consuming a drug bought in one shop is not increased by the fact it can be bought in another shop. With respect he overlooks the possibility of drug-induced injury caused by prolonged or incremental use of a medicine. However, more importantly, he signals that, even if *Fairchild* does not conclusively determine that the *Sindell* rule prevails in England, he looks at the possibility with some favour. He describes the market share approach against several drug companies as 'imaginative' and suggests such a possibility would be looked at if a claim came before the House of Lords.[49]

Prevention better than cure?[50]

The thalidomide tragedy prompted new laws to vet drugs before they could be marketed in the UK. The Medicines Act 1968 provided for the licensing and monitoring of drugs.[51] In 1998 a similar system was set up to regulate medical devices. The two systems have recently been amalgamated into one single agency, the Medical and Healthcare products Resources Agency (MHRA). The licensing process (described below) remains (as yet) broadly the same.

The 1968 Act entrusts the licensing of new drugs and the scrutiny of drugs already on the market to the Secretary of State for Health.[52] In practice, the Medicines Control Agency acted on his behalf. No medicine may be manufactured, imported or marketed without a licence. When a new product is developed, a clinical trial certificate must be obtained before it can be tested on patients, and a product licence is required before the drug can be marketed.[53] The Medicines Commission and its specialist sub-committees provide advice to the Secretary of State. The Commission's powers are general in nature. It is directed to advise the Secretary of State on (*inter alia*) the practice of medicine and pharmacy, and the operation of the pharmaceutical industry.[54] The Committee on Safety of Medicines (CSM), one of the sub-committees established by the Medicines Commission, has the more specific, central role in licensing new drugs. The CSM is empowered to advise on the safety, quality and efficacy of drugs, and to promote the collection of information on adverse reactions and advise on action to be taken as a consequence thereof.[55] It is to the CSM that applications for clinical trial certificates and product licences are first referred. The Medicines Control Agency cannot refuse a licence without first consulting the CSM.[56] When deciding whether to grant a licence the Medicines Control Agency and the CSM are directed to consider:

(1) the safety of the drug to which the application relates;
(2) the efficacy of the drug for the purpose for which it is to be administered; and
(3) the quality of the drug, having particular regard to its method of manufacture, and arrangements proposed for its distribution.[57]

They are expressly *excluded* from taking into account any question of whether other existing drugs are equally or more efficacious for the purpose proposed.[58] The Medicines Control Agency cannot reject an application for a product licence for a new tranquillizer simply because it considers there are already sufficient effective drugs of that sort available. Their remit is to protect the consumer from injury, not from a plethora of expensive close-copy drugs. Where a licence is granted, a product licence is operative for five years[59] and a clinical trial certificate for two.[60] At the end of those periods the manufacturer must apply for renewal of his licence. The Medicines Control Agency is also responsible for monitoring adverse reaction to drugs in use. Section 28 of the Medicines Act 1968 empowers the Secretary of State to revoke an existing licence. Several grounds for revocation are established, of which the most important is where:

. . . medicinal products of any description to which the licence relates can no longer be regarded as products which can safely be administered for the purposes indicated in the licence, or can no longer be regarded as efficacious for those purposes . . .

The decision to withdraw a drug from the market is no longer solely a matter for the manufacturer.

A manufacturer aggrieved by the refusal or revocation of a product licence may seek a review by the Medicines Commission. No product licence can be refused or revoked without consultation with the CSM and/or the Medicines Commission. A manufacturer whose product has been approved by the CSM and/or the Commission but who is refused a licence by the Secretary of State has a right to a further hearing. If he chooses, as he may, to reject their advice, he must set up an independent inquiry before which the manufacturer may state his case.[61] The Secretary of State rejected the advice of the CSM to license the injectable contraceptive Depro-Provera for long-term use. After receiving a report from the independent inquiry panel set up, the Secretary of State licensed the drug under strict conditions.

The pharmaceutical industry is an international business. Regulation is increasingly a matter for European Law. Gradually the British licensing system described above is being replaced by an EU system. The European Medicines Evaluation Agency was established in 1993. One of its sub-committees, the Committee for Proprietary Medicinal Products (CPMP) has the power to license medicines across Europe. Companies can opt to go directly to the CPMP rather than seek individual product licences in each Member State. Where it is proposed to withdraw a medicine from the British market, the CPMP must be consulted. European legislation has influenced the licensing of medicines in a number of other ways too. Since 1998 all medical devices (for example diagnostic tests or intra-uterine devices) are regulated in a manner broadly similar to medicines.[62] An increasing range of medicines have been deregulated to become available in pharmacies or ordinary shops.[63]

An elaborate framework for licensing drugs has existed for thirty-five years. The MHRA will bring further change. Detailed provision is made for the submission of applications, and a great deal of work and manpower is expended both by the companies and the MCA. The pharmaceutical industry claims that the process is over-burdensome and bureaucratic. Drug companies in the UK are suffering, they say. They dare not innovate. They cannot compete. The drug companies' well-orchestrated self-pleading has been vigorously resisted. Consumer groups counter-attack. In particular, concern has been voiced over the links between many members of the CSM, and the pharmaceutical industry. With the spectre of several drug disasters hanging over us, today does not seem to be the time to weaken existing consumer protection laws that have not in themselves proved entirely adequate.[64]

Claims against the regulators

The possibility of governmental liability for drug-induced injury was aired even in the thalidomide days. Then Secretary of State for Health Sir Keith Joseph dismissed suggestions that the government could be liable. He argued further that even when the elaborate licensing provisions of the 1968 Act were in force, the legal liability for any defect in the drug rested on the manufacturers alone.[65] The patients injured by the anti-arthritic drug Opren sought compensation from the Secretary of State and the CSM as well as from the drug company.[66] They contended that the government and the CSM had been negligent both in originally licensing the drug and for continuing to allow it to be marketed after its dangers should have become apparent to the Department of Health and the CSM. The Opren case against the government was ultimately abandoned.

Could a claim against the Medicine Control Agency, in effect for negligently monitoring drugs and/or blood products, succeed? The claimants would have to persuade the court that it was 'just, fair and reasonable' for the MCA to be subjected to a duty of care to individual patients.

Two particular questions will pose problems for claimants. The court will seek to ask whether the scheme of regulation established by the Medicines Act and now heavily influenced by European legislation, was designed to provide a right to compensation to those injured by unsafe drugs. Given that the primary responsibility in the medicine still rests with the drug company why should the government be liable for their wrongdoing?

Claims brought abroad

The majority of drug companies are multinationals. Drugs are not confined within national borders. British women who suffered injury as a result of using the Dalkon Shield IUD sued the manufacturers in the USA and recovered compensation from a settlement fund set up when the company went bankrupt.[67] When can an injured patient resort to a foreign court and why should he want to?

When a claim has a foreign element a set of rules known as private international law, or conflict of laws, comes into play. These are excessively complex and I give only the barest outline of the relevant law. Essentially, when a claim for negligence is brought the claimant can sue in any country where a relevant act of negligence occurred, or in the country where the drug company is based.[68] There may be more than one such country. So in the case of a defective drug, negligence may have occurred both in the country where it was carelessly manufactured and in the country where it was carelessly marketed as safe[69] and injured the claimant. It was on the basis of the careless manufacture of the device in the USA that the women suing over the Dalkon Shield were able to go to court in the USA. Where there is a dispute over whether an action should be allowed to go ahead, the law of the country where the claimant is trying to sue determines whether it should do so.

Why should anyone want to sue abroad? After all, if they took the drug here and were injured here they can bring their claim in their homeland on the basis that it was here the drug caused them harm. There are two reasons why claimants may opt for the hassle of a foreign lawsuit. First, the procedural rules in the foreign courts may be more favourable to claimants. They may be able to conduct a 'class action' more effectively than in England. That is to say, the group of claimants will be able to bring their action co-operatively, sharing expenses and expertise. Second, there remain financial incentives to sue in the USA if you can. Not only is liability for drugs strict, but awards of damages are made by juries, and are generally much higher than English judge-made awards. The contingency fee system may offer more favourable access to the courts than conditional fees do here. Finally, a threat to sue in the USA may prompt the defendants into offering a more generous settlement than would otherwise have been the case!

Vaccine damage: a special case

Vaccine damage has received special treatment because of the distinction in social effect between vaccines and other drugs.[70] Generally the benefit and risk of taking a drug fall on the individual patient alone. No one else suffers directly if he does not take the drug. No one else benefits directly if he does. With a vaccine the position is different. If a child is immunized against contagious disease, the child himself benefits from the immunity conferred and his friends and schoolfellows benefit from the elimination of the risk that he will pass that disease on to them. Consequently vaccination of young children against tetanus, diphtheria, polio, measles and whooping cough is actively promoted by the Department of Health. The whooping cough vaccine caused the greatest outcry and distress, although the concerns about MMR vaccine now look set to generate similar controversy. A number of children healthy before vaccination have, their parents claim, suffered severe and lasting brain damage as a consequence of receiving the vaccine.

What remedies have the parents of a vaccine-damaged child? First they may, as a number of parents of children allegedly damaged by whooping cough vaccine have done, seek to use the tort of negligence to obtain compensation. The advantage of this course is that if the claim is successful their children will receive full compensation for any disability caused by the vaccine. The problem for the parents is whom to sue. The crux of the question is often whether the risk of the vaccine to a child is greater than the risks posed by contracting the disease itself. An action against a doctor for negligently using a reputable vaccine is likely to fail because even if some doctors and experts condemn its use, a substantial body of informed opinion still backs the vaccine. A malpractice action is usually only viable if some special feature of the child's history should have ruled out routine vaccination or if symptoms at a first vaccination, indicating that further vaccination was unwise, were missed. Suing the manufacturers will run into the problem of the risk/benefit ratio of the product. The manufacturers will dispute the level of risk from the vaccine and will argue that the overwhelming benefit to the community of vaccination outweighs any risk to a very few. They will contend that, properly used, the vaccine is not defective. In relation to the whooping cough vaccine the companies deny that the vaccine does indeed cause brain damage. In relation to MMR the alleged link to autism and bowel disease is bitterly contested. Attempts to recover compensation for vaccine injuries through claims in negligence have generally proved unsuccessful in England.[71] In *Loveday* v. *Renton*[72] a judge held that the claimants failed to prove that the pertussis (whooping cough) vaccine caused the child's brain damage.

The problems of litigation deter many parents from going to court. Successive reviews of the issue of compensation for vaccine damage recognized that it is an example of injury where compensation via the tort of negligence, or the Consumer Protection Act, may be totally inappropriate. There may at the end of the day prove to be no negligence on anyone's part because the benefit to the majority is held to justify the risk to a small minority. Yet it is scarcely fair that those who suffer damage should bear the whole burden of disability alone. On the recommendation of the Pearson commission, Parliament enacted the Vaccine Damage Payments Act 1979 to provide for a no-fault compensation scheme for vaccine-damaged individuals. It provided originally for an award of £10,000 only where a person suffers 80 per cent disablement as a result of vaccination against a disease to which the Act applied. In June 2000 the amount payable was raised to £100,000 and the requirement of 80 per cent disability was reduced to 60 per cent. Claims for payments under the Act are made initially to the Department of Health. If the department official responsible is not satisfied that the claim is made out, the claimant may ask for the decision to be reviewed by an independent medical tribunal. The decision of the tribunal is final. The making of a payment under the 1979 Act does not debar a claimant from also suing for negligence in respect of the vaccination.

The Act remains a target of criticism. £100,000 may sound a substantial amount, but if a child is so damaged that he will never be able to care for himself and earn his own living, it falls far short of his needs. A successful tort claim would result in a multi-million pound award. The Act remains a compromise. It has not replaced tort with an adequate compensation mechanism. Critics complain that the ever-present problem of causation of drug-induced injury is simply ignored in the Act. The claimant must establish on the balance of probability that his disablement resulted from the vaccine.[73] Disputed cases go to the independent tribunals. Statistics seem to show that establishing cause and effect is not a precise science. It is difficult to see what factors accounted for a 39 per cent success rate in disputed cases before the Manchester tribunal in contrast to only a 12 per cent success rate in Belfast.[74]

What of the future?

The future looks brighter as long as the higher courts do not draw back from *A. v. National Blood Authority*. Strict liability will improve the claimant's lot. Establishing that a drug is defective will still not be easy. The problems of proving causation remain formidable. Further hope for patients seeking compensation in future is to be found in changes not in the substantive law governing liability but in improved procedures. Solicitors acting for patients are better at their job. They act together and coordinate their work for their separate clients. The example of the Opren Action Campaign provides a model for solicitors acting in later claims. As we saw in Chapter 7, judges are more willing to order disclosure of evidence, be it the patient's medical records or expert advice given to drug companies. The cards are not stacked so heavily against the patient. None the less, drugs will always be dangerous substances and society should not forget to put as much effort into preventing injury as it does into dealing with the consequences of injury.

9

Hospital Complaints Procedures

Litigation is traumatic for both parties. In the majority of cases where legal aid is not available to the aggrieved patient, he will have to find a solicitor willing to act on a conditional fee basis. This means that, normally, the evidence that the doctor or hospital has been negligent must be strong and hold out a reasonable prospect of substantial compensation. This is often not the case. Moreover, money may not be the patient's primary concern. Many patients simply want an explanation of what went wrong and an apology. A recent survey showed that when they first began to pursue their grievance over 50 per cent of patients primarily sought an admission of fault and action to prevent what happened to them happening to others, and an investigation of their complaint. Only 30 to 39 per cent of aggrieved patients initially wanted monetary compensation.[1] Despite the clumsy and inadequate nature of a lawsuit as a means of investigating medical error, some patients still sue simply to find out what really happened.

Effective complaints procedures in which patients have trust generate many benefits. Fewer patients will sue. Allegations of inadequate care are fully investigated and swiftly resolved. Lessons can be learned that help to avoid future mistakes. Before 1996 there was an assortment of complaints procedures within the National Health Service. Separate procedures dealt with complaints against GPs and hospital doctors. This could cause problems when a complaint embraced both the initial conduct of the GP and subsequent hospital treatment. The Hospital Complaints Procedures Act 1985 imposed a duty on the Secretary of State for Health to give directions to health authorities to ensure that every NHS hospital set in place adequate arrangements to handle complaints. It achieved little, and in 1993 the government set up a committee, chaired by Sir Alan Wilson, to review NHS complaints procedures and propose reforms. The Wilson Committee reported in 1994[2] and its recommendations were largely implemented in 1996.[3] Dissatisfaction with NHS complaints systems endures.[4] Further reforms are imminent. Nor is the NHS the only focus of concern. The private patient had limited options in pursuing any grievance.[5] He might conclude that going to court was his only effective means of redress. New provisions requiring private hospitals and clinics to set up complaints procedures are about to come into force.

Complaints procedures provide redress after the event. Effective complaints procedures generate lessons for the future. However, for the aggrieved patient it would have been better never to have had cause for complaint. The NHS has recently set up a bewildering range of new bodies laudably designed to minimize medical accidents. Every NHS organization is subject to a statutory duty of quality[6] '. . . to put and keep in place arrangements for the purpose of monitoring and improving the quality of health care which it provides for individuals'. A system requiring mandatory reporting of adverse incidents in health care has been established. If an error is made it must be reported, even if happily no harm is done to any patient. The National Patient Safety Agency was set up to monitor the system.[7] The National Clinical Assessment Authority reviews doctors' performance.[8] The Commission for Health Improvement[9] (CHI) started work in 1999. The Commission has extensive powers (*inter alia*) to develop principles of clinical governance, to provide advice and information on monitoring arrangements, to investigate specific issues touching on health care, and to conduct national reviews of particular kinds of health care. Just four years later CHI is to be replaced by a more powerful inspectorate, the Commission for Healthcare Audit and Inspection (CHAI). This new authority will play a major role in addressing NHS complaints.

This chapter will focus on hospital complaints procedures. It considers how satisfactory the means provided for individuals to have their complaints heard now are.[10] The reader must be aware that reform in this field is likely to come very soon so this chapter outlines the position in January 2003 only.

NHS complaints procedures

The NHS complaints system initiated by the Wilson Report was based on a number of fundamental objectives. Procedures should be responsive to complainants and seek to answer their grievances. They should enhance the quality of care and be cost effective. All processes should be accessible, be seen to be impartial, be simple and swift. Complainants should be assured of confidentiality. NHS authorities must be accountable for the operation of complaints procedures. No one would dissent from these sentiments. Putting principle into practice proved a harder task.

Three key features govern the current scheme and differentiate it from the procedures in place before 1996. (1) There is now one single procedure applicable throughout the NHS. Hospital doctors, GPs and other community-based health professionals are now dealt with within a unified complaints system. (2) A three-step process was introduced so that complaints are first subject to 'local resolution', which may be followed by an 'independent review' of the case, with an ultimate right to resort to the Health Service Commissioner, popularly known as the NHS Ombudsman, (3) The NHS Ombudsman, at long last, is empowered to investigate complaints about clinical judgement and his jurisdiction is extended to cover GPs.

NHS hospital trusts, Primary Care Trusts and other relevant NHS bodies are obliged to establish and publicize complaints arrangements. Hospital trusts must appoint designated complaints managers to oversee complaint procedures.[11] At least one person must be appointed to act as a 'convenor' for the second stage of the complaints process where a complaint goes to 'independent review'. Larger NHS trusts obviously need more than one person. Where there is a single convenor, that person must be a non-executive director of the trust. Where there are a number of convenors, one at least must be a non-executive director.

Initiating a complaint: local resolution

A complaint may be initiated by any NHS patient or former patient, or by a third party with the patient's consent. Where a patient is a child or for some other reason is unable to act on his own behalf, once again someone else, usually a parent or relative, can act for him. However, if a complaints manager considers that the person initiating a complaint on someone else's behalf is an inappropriate person he may refuse to deal with the complaint or nominate another person to act on the patient's behalf.

Any complaint must normally be submitted within six months of the incident giving rise to the complaint. There is a discretion to allow complaints managers to extend that period.[12] A refusal to extend the six months limit can itself be challenged by a request for a review of the complaints manager's decision and if the review fails to satisfy the patient by referral to the NHS Ombudsman.

The complaints procedure is not intended to deal with disciplinary matters.[13] Sometimes a disciplinary process will need to be initiated separately. Any evidence of a criminal offence must be referred to the police. Both these sort of cases may delay the complaints process. Most crucially and controversially the '. . . complaints procedure should cease if the complaint explicitly states an intention to take legal action in respect of the complaint'. If the complaints manager judges that there is a likelihood of legal action, he must inform the trust department responsible for risk management. Only an explicit statement that the patient will sue should terminate the complaints process. Defensive reaction to the possibility of lawsuits should be avoided. As the Guidance makes clear:

A hostile, or defensive, reaction to the complaint is more likely to encourage the complainant to seek information and a remedy through the courts. In the early part of the process, it may not be clear whether the complainant simply wants an explanation and apology, with assurance that any failures in service will be rectified for the future, or whether the complainant is in fact seeking information with formal litigation in mind.[14]

Complaints managers must not assume that patients will sue, or use litigation as an excuse to terminate the complaints process. They may fear that shrewd patients (or their lawyers) will use the process to get information that will assist a legal claim. Is this misusing the system? Or in a climate where litigation itself is supposed to be prompted by a 'cards on the table' approach, why should complainants be denied the benefit of information disclosed in the investigation of a complaint, if they discover good grounds to seek compensation through the courts?

Once a complaint is accepted, every attempt must be made to achieve 'local resolution'. How this is done is largely left to individual hospital trusts, and Primary Care Trusts. Basic rules are laid down. All written complaints should be fully investigated. Oral complaints must be considered and the complainants fully advised of their options to pursue the complaint. Where 'front-line staff' such as receptionists, ward sisters or department managers receive complaints, they must ensure that the patient's immediate health care needs continue to be met. They must be responsive and ensure that, where appropriate, oral complaints are passed on to the complaints manager.

Complaints must be resolved swiftly. Oral complaints should be dealt with within two working days and the target for local resolution of any complaint is twenty working days. To emphasize the importance of an effective complaints mechanism the chief executive must respond in writing to all written complaints. Response to complaints about clinical judgement should be, in the words of the Guidance, '. . . agreed by the clinician concerned'.[15] As Montgomery comments this would appear to give clinicians a veto on any response they dislike!

Local resolution places a heavy responsibility on complaints managers. While the Guidance suggests[16] that the complaints manager may be the Chief Executive and, if not, should be a senior manager, in many hospital trusts complaints managers are quite junior personnel. Training and support for complaints managers is essential if local resolution is to work.

Independent review

When a complainant is dissatisfied with the outcome of local resolution of his complaint, he has twenty-eight days in which to request an independent review of his complaint. We have seen that all trusts are obliged to appoint at least one convenor for such reviews. The complainant must submit a statement setting out remaining grievances and explain why he is dissatisfied with the outcome of local resolution. There is no *right* to an independent review. The convenor has broad discretion whether or not to convene a panel to review the complaint, although he must consult an independent lay chair of an NHS review panel. The convenor should not convene a panel if he judges that there are further local measures that the trust could take without a review. He should in such cases refer the matter back to the trust. If the convenor judges that the complaint has already been fully investigated and appropriately dealt with, he should not convene a panel. If a complaint involves clinical judgement he should take appropriate clinical advice. The subject of any complaint must be informed. When a convenor refuses a request for independent review, a dissatisfied complainant may put his case to the NHS Ombudsman.

If it is decided to hold a review the convenor will establish a review panel. The panel will be chaired by a lay chair from a list established by the Department of Health. The convenor will be a member of the panel and a third layperson will complete the panel. In clinical cases, two clinical assessors will be appointed to advise the panel. The terms of reference of the review are set by the convenor. Complainants must be given every opportunity to put their case. They may be accompanied by a friend, but not by a lawyer acting as advocate. The panel must have access to all records and where appropriate will interview health care staff. If clinical judgements are in question, at least one of the assessors must be present at interviews with staff. There is an emphasis placed on informality and flexibility. The Guidance directs:

The panel should be proactive in its investigation, always seeking to resolve the complainant's grievance in a conciliatory manner. The panel should be flexible in the way it goes about its business, choosing a method of procedure appropriate to the circumstances of the complaint. It should not allow confrontational situations to arise . . . It is a matter for the panel whether the complainant and complained against should be brought together at the same meeting . . .[17]

Just as the complaints manager is the focal point of local resolution so the convenor sits at the centre of the independent review process. He decides if there will be a review. He sits on the panel. If the lay chair of the panel is not a person of weight, the convenor will be the dominant figure in the process. As he is a director (albeit a non-executive director) of the trust, patients may have misgivings about how *independent* the independent review is. Where separate hearings mean that complainant and complained against are heard separately, patients may fear that they never have an adequate chance to put their case.

At the conclusion of the process, the panel must issue a full report. Panels may choose to prepare a draft report allowing each side to check their findings for factual accuracy and offer comments. The chief executive must inform the patient of any action taken consequent to independent review. The complainant who remains dissatisfied may next pursue his final remedy, a complaint to the NHS Ombudsman.

Is the system working?

I noted above that the 'new' complaints system introduced in 1996 continues to attract criticism, and is about to be overhauled yet again. A substantial number of complaints to the NHS Ombudsman are complaints about complaining. A survey in 1997 showed that 40 per cent of patients were unhappy with the way their complaint had been dealt with.[18] Particular criticisms[19] focus on poor handling of the initial complaint, a perception that the convenor is not independent, lack of consistency between trusts, lack of training for complaints managers and inadequate monitoring of complaints procedures and their outcomes. The Select Committee on Health[20] reviewed the evidence of complaints about complaints procedures. Their recommendations emphasize the key role of training. They call for measures to ensure that independent review panels are, and are seen to be, truly independent. Greater formality in procedure and extended powers for review panels are suggested. One fundamental difficulty bedevils NHS complaints procedures. There is great merit in such procedures giving attention to speed, informality and low cost. Patients want complaints dealt with swiftly, in a manner in which they can explain their grievance without the need for lawyers, and in an atmosphere that is friendly and welcoming. An overstretched NHS needs processes that do not consume a disproportionate part of the health care budget. Poorly handled, however, an informal low cost service can present itself as 'cheap and nasty' failing to pay proper regard to the complainant's case.

The NHS Ombudsman

The post of NHS Ombudsman, or more correctly Health Service Commissioner, was established in 1973.[21] The Ombudsman's powers are set out in the Health Service Commissioners Act 1993, as amended by the Health Service Commissioners (Amendment) Act 1996, National Health Service (Primary Care) Act 1997, the Health Act 1999, and the Health Services Commissioners (Amendment) Act 2000. In theory there are three separate NHS Ombudsmen. In practice, to date the post has been held by one person who is also the Parliamentary Commissioner for Administration (the general national Ombudsman). He is supported in his NHS post by a Deputy Commissioner with experience of NHS management. The Ombudsman is empowered to investigate any complaint where it is alleged that a failure in the health service or maladministration in the service resulted in injustice or hardship. His jurisdiction has been significantly extended since 1996. He can now investigate complaints about general practitioners. Hospitals trusts, ambulance services, clinics and community nursing services are self-evidently among the bodies that he may review. He still may not pursue a complaint where the person concerned may have a remedy in the courts unless he is satisfied that it is not reasonable to expect the complainant to invoke that remedy.[22] Most crucially the Ombudsman is now empowered to investigate action taken as a result of the exercise of the professional, clinical judgement of doctors or nurses. What then is the extent of the Ombudsman's power and influence today?[23]

Investigating a complaint

The Ombudsman is the court of last resort in the complaints system. Complaints to the Ombudsman must be made in writing, normally within one year of the incident giving rise to the complaint.[24] The complaint may be made by a patient or by some responsible person acting on his behalf. Health service bodies may also refer written complaints to the Ombudsman.[25] The Ombudsman has complete control of the investigation and his powers of inquiry are extensive. He and his staff investigate in private. They will contact all hospital or primary care staff involved in complaints and seek their comments. If co-operation from hospital staff or administrators is not forthcoming, the production of records and documents may be ordered and staff may be compelled to testify to the Ombudsman.[26]

In 2000–2001,[27] 2595 complaints were made to the Ombudsman against NHS bodies and practitioners, a marginal increase on the 2526 complaints reaching the Ombudsman in 1999–2000. Only 241 complaints were accepted for investigation in 2000–2001 and 212 complaints were scheduled for investigation in 1999–2000. The huge discrepancy between complaints sent to the Ombudsman and those investigated has a number of causes. The Ombudsman only investigates complaints where the patient can show that he has 'sustained injustice or hardship'[28] as a result of maladministration or a failure in the service, except in the case of complaints about clinical judgement where this restriction does not apply. He will only investigate a complaint if all local remedies to resolve the complaint have first been exhausted. Investigations take considerable time and resources. The Ombudsman has to select the most pressing complaints to follow up.

On completion of an investigation the Ombudsman reports to the complainant, the relevant NHS body, and any individual against whom allegations were made. The report will contain a decision about whether the complaint was justified and recommend a remedy. In 2000–2001 the Ombudsman completed 204 reports and 68.8 per cent of complaints investigated were found to be justified. Of grievances investigated in 1999–2000 65.6 per cent were upheld and 61.7 per cent of those investigated in 1998–9 were upheld. A common remedy is an apology from the authority and the staff member involved. An apology should not be seen as meaningless sympathy. Many complainants value an acknowledgement of their grievances and a tangible expression of regret from those responsible.[29] The Ombudsman, however, places great emphasis on positive recommendations made to NHS trusts and the Department of Health about changes in practice to avoid a recurrence of similar complaints. For example, in 1999–2000[30] the Ombudsman reported that on the basis of his recommendations action had been taken to improve practice in relation to general practitioners treating women with breast disease and to ensure that women were fully informed about the outcome of surgery as soon as possible. Record keeping and communication between hospitals and GPs had been improved, in particular in relation to records concerning the discharge of patients from hospitals. The Ombudsman may additionally recommend the making of an *ex gratia* cash payment to a patient by way of compensation. Such payments are generally made in cases where maladministration has resulted in loss of patients' property or unnecessary expenses. The Commissioner does not normally suggest that trusts offer monetary compensation for pain and hardship suffered by patients.

Each year the Ombudsman makes an Annual Report to Parliament published by HMSO and available to the public. Additionally in the course of each year he publishes three reports summarising selected investigations with all the parties involved kept anonymous. His activities are monitored by a Select Committee of MPs who encourage him in his work and spur him on to greater efforts on behalf of NHS patients. The issue of maladministration in the NHS is kept firmly in the public eye.

The work of the Ombudsman

The reports of the Ombudsman make interesting, if sometimes depressing, reading. Certain sorts of complaints recur over the years.

In 1989–90 the Ombudsman listed seven main topics of concern:

(1) observation and management of patients, especially elderly or disabled patients;
(2) arrangements for discharge;
(3) procedures and management, in particular delayed operations;

(4) patients being led to believe they would have to opt for private treatment, as they were unlikely to receive NHS treatment promptly;

(5) the handling of complaints by hospitals;

(6) the procedures for independent professional review;

(7) the operation of Family Practitioner Committees.

In 1999–2000, the Ombudsman focused on four particular areas of disquiet: out-of-hours GP services, removal of patients from GP lists, poor communications and mishandling of initial complaints. A year later in 2000–2001 communications and complaints systems continued to trouble the Ombudsman, and he identified additional concerns in relation to the quality of nursing care and the adequacy of supervision of junior medical staff. The NHS's capacity to improve communications and deal with complaints seems to have made slow progress over the decade.

A number of examples illustrate both failures in communication and inadequate care across the years. In 1999–2000 a daughter complained about poor arrangements for her elderly father's discharge from hospital. He was known to have a pressure sore. No plan to treat his sore at home was recorded and neither his family nor community nursing services were alerted to his condition.[31] Fifteen years earlier in 1984–5 the Ombudsman castigated the inadequate arrangements to discharge an elderly lady from hospital. She had scalded herself while in hospital and fallen on the day of discharge. The hospital failed to let her GP have this crucial information or to assist her husband to care for her at home.[32] Two cases from 1998–9 concern inadequate care of the nutritional needs of elderly patients. After surgery the hospital failed to monitor Mrs F. or check how she was eating. By the time a dietician saw her she had lost several kilograms in weight.[33] Another patient was given twice as much fluid as he should have received. Nursing staff failed to note that he was being given fluid by two routes, both intravenously and naso-gastrically. Note that in 1989–90 the Ombudsman was drawing hospitals' attention to the need to observe and manage elderly and vulnerable patients with meticulous care, the very same concerns voiced by his successor at the turn of the century.[34]

Complaints about complaints continue too. In 1989–90 the then Ombudsman declared:

Sometimes an indifferent or careless local investigation or even the lack of an apology for an obvious mistake are all that is needed to send the complainant along a stressful – and perhaps increasingly exasperating – path to my door. Fear of litigation may at times lie behind defensiveness on the part of the person complained against, but that is quite possibly the last thing that the complainant had in mind when looking for an explanation.[35]

Ten years later his successor was still concerned about complaints procedures, though able to note that, as well as bad practice, he has also seen evidence of NHS bodies handling complaints well. In his Report for 2000–2001 the Ombudsman also addresses the problem of vexatious and unreasonable complaints. He finds himself receiving complaints about the complaints process not just from patients but from NHS staff too!

The Ombudsman and clinical judgement

The exclusion of clinical judgement from review by the Ombudsman was without doubt the most serious limitation on his effectiveness. In 1989–90, out of 470 complaints rejected as outside the Commissioner's jurisdiction, 204 related to clinical judgement.[36] The Health Service Commissioners (Amendment) Act 1996 extended his jurisdiction to embrace clinical judgement. By 2000–2001, 77 per cent of completed investigations concerned clinical judgement.[37]

The nature of these complaints are varied. Quite a number deal with the level of care provided by junior doctors, and the adequacy of supervision and support provided for junior staff. In one case[38] a junior doctor ordered inappropriate neurological tests on a critically ill elderly patient. Vigorous and inappropriate attempts were then made to resuscitate the patient. The patient's daughter complained, saying that had she understood the futility of the resuscitation attempts she would not have supported them. The junior's own consultant was away. The Ombudsman criticized the lack of consultant cover. Another case involved a woman readmitted to hospital after minor gynaecological surgery.[39] In the course of that day, and the following night, her condition deteriorated. The next day she was admitted to the intensive care unit where she died later in the day from a complication of surgery. Delay in transferring the patient to intensive care may have contributed to her death. Six junior doctors were involved in looking after the patient. None sought the advice of a consultant.

Dealing with complaints about clinical matters is not easy.[40] Identifying if a complaint has substance is time-consuming. Records must be obtained with the complainant's consent. Clinical advice is required and often has to be sought from specialists outside the Ombudsman's office.

The Ombudsman and the courts

Many of the complaints dealt with by the Ombudsman would not be the subject of court action for a variety of reasons. In one disgraceful case an elderly gentleman dying of terminal cancer was left to suffer from acute pain.[41] Claiming damages would not have been worthwhile for his widow. A baby was born prematurely and placed on a ventilator. Staff sought to wean him off the ventilator but soon judged that the child would not survive. A week after his birth he collapsed and died. NHS doctors were not in any sense responsible for his death; they were not negligent in their care of the infant. However staff did not explain to the child's mother what was happening. When the consultant finally spoke to her, he said 'he had decided to let [the child] go'. His parents felt excluded from his care and lack of communication left them unprepared for his sudden death.[42] The case described above of the patient who was unnecessarily and inappropriately subjected to resuscitation attempts, rather than left to die in peace and dignity gave rise to no claim for damages. The mistreatment of the patient did not cause her death.

Other investigations undertaken by the Commissioner are more likely subjects of a claim for compensation. One notorious example concerned a woman of twenty-three. She sought an abortion in 1970 and attended the hospital with her mother. The woman suffered from temporal lobe epilepsy and a degree of personality disorder. After discussion with her parents the consultant sterilized the woman with their consent. The first she learned of the operation was when some years later and married she was trying to have a baby. The Ombudsman found no evidence that sterilization was necessary for the woman's health. He judged that, acting in breach of DHSS guidance, which he had never read, the consultant was at fault.[43]

Other more routine cases, where a claim for clinical negligence looks more straightforward, come before the Ombudsman. The family of the patient who died after inappropriate delay in transferring her to intensive care might have had a tenable claim for compensation for her loss.

In another case a Caesarean section resulted in injury to a patient who had had problems with anaesthesia in earlier surgery. The complainant alleged that records of her previous difficulties were not transferred to her obstetric records, that her own warnings were ignored, and that her complaint was badly and unsympathetically dealt with. Her first two allegations are of simple negligence. The Ombudsman nevertheless agreed to investigate the case in return for an undertaking that the complainant would not take legal proceedings.[44] This has become common practice. The undertaking is not legally binding and there is nothing to stop a complainant assuring the Commissioner he will not sue and then launching proceedings on the basis of evidence uncovered by the Ombudsman.

Is the restriction on dual access to the Ombudsman and the courts justifiable? In 1980 the Ombudsman expressed his concern that he might be used to provide a free investigation service to enable potential litigants to decide whether or not to sue. Is there anything wrong with that? We have seen the tremendous difficulties faced by patients in litigation. If negligence has resulted in injury, and investigation as opposed to adversarial litigation discovers that negligence, the patient ought to get compensation. Attitudes may be changing. The Civil Procedure Rules seek to encourage litigants to explore other means of resolving grievances before resorting to litigation.[45] A patient unsatisfied by the complaints procedure should not be denied the benefit of evidence gathered in pursuing her complaint. Growing support can be seen for an integrated complaints and compensation system. If reasonable compensation were available via the complaints system, fewer people might contemplate litigation.[46]

Health service inquiries

Dissatisfaction with the outcome of the complaints procedure and the numbers of instances where preliminary investigations into one or two cases reveal fundamental defects in NHS care have fuelled a growing demand for public inquiries. Patients and patients' organizations want a comprehensive and independent review either of an inadequate service in general or of the misconduct of particular individuals. They want to see the whole picture and receive concrete assurance that action is being taken to remedy the shortcomings of the NHS and/or call to account staff whose wrongdoing caused serious harm. A number of different procedures within the NHS provide for further investigation of NHS 'scandals'. An informal local inquiry may be established.[47] In serious cases an independent team will be drafted in to conduct the investigation. Such an inquiry will be conducted by a small committee usually consisting of a legally qualified chairman and two medical practitioners, one from the same specialty as the person whose competence is in issue. All inquiry members will be unconnected with the hospital where the complaint originated. Copies of all documents are circulated to all parties. The complainant and the subjects of the complaint may be legally represented, and cross-examination of witnesses is allowed. No one can be compelled to attend the inquiry. The committee's findings of fact are then submitted to the staff concerned for further comment. Finally the committee reports its findings and recommendations.

The inquiry procedure can be effective, but if hospital staff refuse co-operation the procedure may break down altogether. For example, in 1981 a twenty-six-year-old man, David Woodhouse, entered hospital for an appendectomy. He never regained consciousness and ten months later still lay in a coma. Pressure from MPs led the health authority to set up an inquiry. On the advice of their defence organization doctors refused to testify. The inquiry was abandoned. The authority then asked three independent experts to examine the case. They reported a series of disasters. For example, the anaesthetist's command of English was poor, he could not spell the names of basic drugs, and neither he nor the duty registrar knew how to use the ventilator. Mr Woodhouse was left without oxygen for twenty minutes. The health authority promised to tighten up procedures. An out-of-court settlement was reached to pay compensation to David Woodhouse and his family.

The National Health Service Act 1977 section 84(1) empowers the Secretary of State to '. . . cause an inquiry to be held in any case where he deems it advisable to do so in connection with any matter arising under this Act'. At such an inquiry all those involved may be compelled to attend and to produce documents, and if the person appointed to hold the inquiry sees fit, all evidence may have to be given on oath. The Secretary of State used to invoke his coercive power only rarely. Successive Secretaries have argued that their power to order an inquiry was not intended for use in cases of individual error or even gross incompetence. These powers should be invoked only to protect the public at large. The most recent and famous example of a section 84 inquiry is the Public Inquiry into children's heart surgery at the Bristol Royal Infirmary.[48] Its Terms of Reference were broad:

To inquire into the management of the care of children receiving complex cardiac surgical services at the Bristol Royal Infirmary between 1984 and 1995 and relevant related issues; to make findings as to the adequacy of services provided; to establish what action was taken within and outside the hospital to deal with concerns raised about the surgery and to identify any failure to take approrpriate action promptly; *to reach conclusions from these events and to make recommendations which could help to secure high-quality care across the NHS* [my emphasis].

The Bristol Inquiry investigated a ghastly series of events at Bristol Royal Infirmary. It was instructed not simply to discover how such events came to pass and what action that trust should take; the Inquiry also had a national agenda. It achieved two aims; to seek justice and accountability for families of children who suffered death or disability because of inadequacies in the cardiac surgery service in Bristol and to learn how such a disastrous failure in the service could be avoided across the country. Its costs were considerable. The Inquiry took nearly three years and was estimated to cost over £14 million.

Bristol led to many other dissatisfied patient groups demanding similar public inquiries.[49] The government has tended to resist those demands. In July 2000, a gynaecologist, Richard Neale, was struck off the medical register after thirty-four charges of professional misconduct were proved against him. His mistreatment of patients resulted in pain, disability and infertility. A GP, Clifford Ayling, was convicted in 2001 of multiple indecent assaults on female patients. In both cases patients asked the Secretary of State for public inquiries. He refused. His decision is being challenged in the courts. Patients argue that to refuse a public inquiry in cases of such gravity is irrational and contravenes patients' rights to information.[50]

Part of the trouble with inquiry procedures seems to be that the Secretary of State's powers are reserved for national *causes célèbres* and less formal health service inquiries have no teeth. Patients will have less confidence in inquiries held behind closed doors with no powers to compel NHS staff to co-operate. Government fears the cost of public inquiries both in cash and to the reputation of the NHS. The Bristol Report[51] points out that private inquiries may be counterproductive. Holding the inquiry in private may be '. . . more likely to inflame than protect the feelings of those affected by the inquiry'. And the report emphasizes the need for transparent clear criteria determining when a public inquiry should be established.

The Wendy Savage affair[52]

Patients are not alone in their unhappiness with NHS inquiries. Events in 1985 highlighted aspects of inquiry procedures that were profoundly disturbing to doctors. Tower Hamlets Health Authority suspended Wendy Savage, a consultant obstetrician at the London Hospital. Allegations of incompetence were laid against her by her colleagues, and an inquiry was launched. Charges focused on her handling of five maternity cases, accusing Mrs Savage of allowing sympathy for women wanting a natural birth to override her professional judgement and endangering mother and child. In only one of the cases cited against Mrs Savage had a patient complained. Two patients were outraged that their treatment was used as evidence against a doctor whom they trusted and backed implicitly. They were horrified when their confidential medical records were made public at the inquiry. The Savage inquiry was, in essence, not an inquiry into complaints of unsatisfactory treatment by patients, but a public ventilation of professional disagreements.

The procedure at the inquiry left much to be desired. The initiation of the complaint by colleagues of a doctor, rather than patients, cannot be faulted in principle. Protection of patients requires that procedures exist to allow practitioners to air their concern about the practices or competence of a colleague. Fundamentally, three flaws in the inquiry procedure were revealed by the highly publicized Savage inquiry. (1) Before the start of an inquiry immense power rests in the hands of the health authority chairman. The decision to suspend a doctor is his. Allegations have continued to be made that chairs are over-free with the use of this power to suspend, hoping that, unlike Mrs Savage, the suspended doctor will simply resign quietly. (2) The inquiry is not an *investigation*. The procedure at the Savage inquiry resembled a criminal trial. A barrister engaged by the authority 'prosecuted' Wendy Savage. He called medical experts who saw her practices as unsound and leapt on any error they could discern. Mrs Savage's counsel 'defended' her. Experts favourable to her had their say. At no stage did an observer feel that a difficult problem of correct obstetric practice was being objectively investigated. (3) Mrs Savage was effectively 'on trial'. Yet she had no automatic claim to the support of her defence organization as would have been the case had she faced a civil suit for negligence. The MDU at first refused to fund Mrs Savage's 'defence' by the lawyers of her choice although they did eventually agree to assist her.

The Savage inquiry demonstrated once again that English legislators and lawyers seem incapable of devising a genuinely inquisitorial procedure. It also showed that a procedure designed to consider complaints by patients is ill-equipped for use either as a forum for debate on what constitutes good medical practice or to resolve difficulties between colleagues antipathetic to each other. Wendy Savage was acquitted of all charges of incompetence. Getting her back in her post against the continued hostility of some other doctors proved, alas, a tougher battle for her and for the health authority obliged to reinstate her.

More disturbing still though is the fact that the Savage 'affair' has been repeated in a number of instances across the country. Doctors have been suspended pending a Savage-style inquiry not because their patients have complained, but because they are in dispute with their employers or colleagues. Speaking out against inadequate and unsafe conditions in our hospitals, failure to conform to the majority view of your specialty may be more likely to result in disciplinary proceedings against a hospital doctor than failing to meet patients' needs. Female doctors seem especially vulnerable to such attacks.

10

No Fault Compensation?

In earlier chapters, I examined the present systems for compensating injured patients and for investigating patients' complaints. Despite sterling efforts to reform them, both systems remain less than satisfactory. The medical profession perceives an action for negligence against a doctor as an attack on his professional integrity and a blight on his career. Defensive attitudes engendered by the law relating to malpractice claims still carry over into the way in which the profession and NHS trusts react to complaints. To some extent doctors' fears are misplaced. The function of the tort of negligence is to compensate one individual injured by another's errors, not to adjudicate on a doctor's general competence. Complaints procedures often exonerate the doctor. Frequently all a patient wants is an explanation of what went wrong; she is not gunning for the doctor. None the less, it must be recognized that there is cause for the doctors' concern. It is all very well to say that the action for negligence has little to do with blame. To the non-lawyer the term negligence itself connotes blame, neglect, carelessness and so on. The conduct of litigation, even after the Woolf reforms, creates an atmosphere of conflict. The patient may not start out with any intention of harassing the doctor but the rules of 'the game' of litigation all too often ensure that a 'me against him' mentality exists. The spectre of a malpractice action hangs over complaints procedures. The doctor is haunted by the risk that by co-operating fully he may provide incriminating evidence against himself.

The rules of the game have long cried out for reform. Has the time in fact come to change the game? Should the action for medical malpractice be replaced by a new scheme to compensate for injuries arising out of medical misadventure? What is proposed, and receives support from many doctors,[1] is a system of no-fault compensation. Under such a system a patient who suffers injury in the course of medical treatment would receive compensation without any need to prove that the medical staff involved were at fault. No-fault compensation is suddenly on the policy agenda at the highest level. The mounting cost of malpractice litigation and the perception that lawyers are milking the system has brought attacks on the system from politicians.[2]

The Bristol Inquiry Report eloquently implored government to abolish clinical negligence litigation. The Report declares:

The system of clinical negligence litigation is now ripe to review . . . [W]e take the view that it will not be possible to achieve an environment of full, open reporting within the NHS when, outside it, there exists a litigation system the incentives of which press in the opposite direction. We believe that the way forward lies in the abolition of clinical negligence litigation, taking clinical error out of the courts and the tort system. It should be replaced by effective systems for identifying, analysing, learning from and preventing errors, along with all other sentinel events. There must also be a new approach to compensating those patients harmed through such events . . . [W]e recognize that such a radical change is likely to have wide implications not least in terms of any new system of compensation . . .[3]

In September 2001 the Chief Medical Officer initiated a comprehensive consultation process to explore potential options for reform of clinical negligence claims. He wants to develop

. . . a more responsive and patient focused approach to both complaints and clinical negligence claims handling, which provides remedies more closely tailored to individual patients' needs – including practical, financial and non-financial remedies which address concerns directly and quickly.[4]

The first of the options he seeks to explore is:

No-fault compensation, which may save time and costs in achieving settlements. A no fault system would also mean that NHS staff would not have to be 'blamed' for problems, encouraging a more open system.

Momentum in favour of no-fault compensation is building up but this is a debate in which high flown principle is easy to articulate. Putting principle into practice is much more difficult. A White Paper on clinical negligence is about to be published. It seems unlikely that given the practical problems of implementing a no-fault scheme this radical option will be endorsed by government. Anything less may amount to little more than tinkering with the current system. Thus I look at the arguments for a no-fault scheme, consider how similar schemes operate abroad, and begin to identify the practical problems of implementing no-fault. I then briefly explore other options for reform of the medical litigation system in England.

An attack on tort

Criticism of the tort of negligence as a means of compensating for personal injury however caused, whether by medical error or in a road accident or any other area of human activity, is far from new.[5] The tort system has been condemned as unpredictable, expensive and unfair.[6] These criticisms are as valid as they ever were.

The nature of the tort system is unpredictable. The injured claimant, on whom the burden of proving negligence falls, cannot know in advance whether he will receive any monetary compensation. He cannot plan his personal finances and put his life in order. For example, a person rendered paraplegic in an accident cannot know whether he will be able to afford to convert his house to meet the limitations imposed by his new disability. The uncertainty and delay as he fights his claim through the courts may even impede his recovery.

The tort system remains expensive because of the cost of litigation. A part of the cost is already borne by the State. Where the claimant is still legally aided, as is often the case in the cerebral palsy claims that form such a large proportion of clinical negligence cases, the NHS will bear the cost of defending the claim, perhaps with nothing to show for it in the end. The prohibitive price of litigation may deter some claimants with a genuine case from pursuing it if they are not wealthy, yet are sufficiently well off to fall outside provision for legal aid, and are not a good enough gamble for a conditional fee arrangement. The expense of any no-fault scheme, often given as an argument against its introduction, must be measured against the existing total cost of the tort system. In *Wilsher* v. *Essex AHA*[7] (see page 163) the costs of that action at over £200,000 exceeded the agreed damages of just over £116,000, even before any retrial! The recent report from the National Audit Office showed that in 65 per cent of claims below £50,000, costs exceeded the compensation awarded to the patient.[8]

Most of all the tort system is not fair. First, the difficulties and cost of litigation place enormous pressure on a claimant to settle for less than full compensation. Second, the dividing line between negligence and no negligence is paper thin. Think back to the controversial case of *Whitehouse* v. *Jordan*[9] (see page 188). The experts and the judges were divided on whether Mr Jordan acted wrongly when delivering the child. Mrs Whitehouse went away without a penny. The opposite outcome might have been equally unfair to Mr Jordan. He came into the case for the first time late at night. He pursued a course many distinguished experts backed. Although others disagreed, to condemn him on that basis would have been inappropriate. This feature of the law of tort, the need to apportion blame for medical accidents and the difficulty of doing so, has attracted criticism from the judiciary as well as from doctors and academics. In *Ashcroft* v. *Mersey AHA*[10] Kilner Brown J. reluctantly dismissed the plaintiff's claim for compensation after an operation on her ear left her with a degree of facial paralysis. He found the expert evidence on whether such damage could occur without negligence equally balanced and so the plaintiff failed to discharge the burden of proof. He commented:

Where an injury is caused which never should have been caused common sense and natural justice indicate that some degree of compensation ought to be paid by someone.[11]

Finally, the tort system has been attacked as unfair on the grounds that it lacks any proper moral basis. What is the justification for giving X, who can attribute his injury to human error, full compensation, and leaving Y, whose injury has some other cause, to struggle on State benefits?

The Pearson Report[12]

Criticism of the operation of the law of tort and the introduction of alternative compensation schemes elsewhere in the world led to the creation in 1973 of the Royal Commission on Civil Liability and Compensation for Personal Injury chaired by a Law Lord, Lord Pearson. The Pearson Commission was set up to consider to what extent, in what circumstances and by what means, compensation should be payable in respect of death and personal injury. They were specifically instructed to examine the tort system in the light of other provisions made for compensation, whether via insurance or social security benefits.

The Pearson Commission reported in 1978. They advised against abolition of tort as a means of compensating personal injuries. They made a number of specific proposals for more limited reforms. I will concentrate on the proposals that relate to medical and drug-induced injuries. The Commission decided against recommending a no-fault scheme for all medical injuries.[13] They did propose a scheme whereby the government became strictly liable to victims of vaccine damage[14] and those conducting medical research would be strictly liable for injury caused to volunteers in the course of clinical trials.[15] The Report further recommended the introduction of strict liability against producers of defective drugs.[16] They also urged the creation of new disability allowances for all severely disabled children irrespective of whether their disability resulted from anyone else's fault.[17] The Commission further said that although in 1978 they had decided against an overall no-fault scheme for medical accidents, some Commission members found the question difficult and saw the arguments for and against as finely balanced.[18] All agreed that circumstances might change, calling for a review of the Commission's decision. The progress of no-fault schemes elsewhere, particularly in Sweden and New Zealand, should be studied and assessed.

The Commission's Report gathered dust and many of their proposals went unheeded. A compensation scheme for vaccine damage was established, but not to universal acclaim. Strict liability for defective drugs was introduced by the Consumer Protection Act 1987. That reform came not as a result of the Pearson Report but because of pressure from Europe. Twenty-five years later the government is at last revisiting no-fault compensation for medical accidents.

The case for a medical no-fault scheme

The case for a no-fault scheme is made out in part by the manifest deficiencies of the present system. It is beyond the scope of this book to consider whether a comprehensive no-fault scheme for all types of accidents should be introduced. In an ideal society any person suffering from disability from whatever cause would receive appropriate financial support. The person paralysed by a stroke has identical needs to the person paralysed by a fall from a ladder or a bungled operation. That ideal would require not an *accident* compensation scheme but the provision of a general disability income.[19] Even in New Zealand compensation for disability continues to exclude disability arising from disease or other non-accidental cause. Radical reform can never be expected to happen instantly. It must be approached incrementally. A medical accidents scheme could operate as a pilot project for a general accidents scheme. Experience of an accidents scheme may lay the foundation for a general disability income.

So what are the arguments for and against a medical accidents scheme? One of the grounds on which the Pearson Commission rejected a scheme for all medical accidents must be given due weight. The Commission argued that tort served a valuable purpose in emphasizing the accountability and responsibility of *individual* medical staff. They could not hide behind a bureaucratic smokescreen. The principal reason for the Commission's rejection of a no-fault scheme was the problem of causation. The Commission felt that distinguishing between an injury arising from treatment given and the natural progression of disease or inescapable side-effects of treatment was too difficult. They were also anxious about the overall cost of any no-fault scheme and about the way in which it could be designed to cover public and private medicine. Moreover, the Commission seemed to be unimpressed by what they had seen of the no-fault scheme already operating in New Zealand.

Pearson's objections must be answered if the case for change is to stand up. I consider that, although the Commission's concern about causation is valid, this is insufficient reason to rule out a change to no-fault compensation. Causation presents just as much of a problem within the present system. Reform of the law introducing a no-fault principle would have the following benefits. A greater number of claimants would obtain compensation to help them adapt their lives to their disabilities, or to meet financial loss resulting from the death of a breadwinner. The damage done to relations between the medical profession and the public by bitter and protracted litigation would be removed. As the Chief Medical Officer's consultation paper[20] emphasizes, the link between compensation and blame would be broken. The patient would obtain compensation because he suffered injury as a result of treatment going wrong. The issues of *why* it went wrong and the doctor's competence would be for completely separate investigatory procedures. The problem of causation would still be present. Distinguishing between injury and the progression of disease, or whatever, would be made easier. The issue of causation would be *investigated*. It would not be part of a battle between the patient and the NHS, with the NHS having a vested interest in finding experts to deny that the patient's condition was caused by the treatment. Consideration could be given to whether the burden of proof of causation might be alleviated by requiring only proof of a reasonable possibility of causation.

The overall cost of a no-fault scheme is difficult to judge. It is not a cheap option. The lessons of the 'costs crisis' in New Zealand must be learned. The Working Party set up by the King's Fund Institute and the Centre for Socio-Legal Studies, Oxford, suggested (in its 1988 Report) that a no-fault system might cost £117 million per year as against £75 million for the current tort system.[21] The cost today would be higher. It might be reasonable to expect it to amount to at least one and a half times as much as the current system. No-fault is, however, cost-effective. In New Zealand, administrative costs prior to 1992 ran at less than 10 per cent of the cost of the system as a whole, i.e. at least 90p in every pound was paid out to victims. In Sweden, administrative costs amount to about 14 per cent of total cost.

Deterrence and accountability

The Pearson Commission placed great emphasis on accountability. One of the functions of the tort system is to make the defendant accountable for what he has done, and to deter negligent conduct. It may be costly and inefficient, may be inequitable in whom it compensates, but if it deters medical malpractice, can we afford to abandon it? I remain unconvinced that the tort system has much of a systematic deterrent effect in health care insofar as individual doctors are concerned. Moreover, the alleged deterrent impact of tort often obscures the crucial question of accountability.

Firstly, the tort system is capricious in its operation. Obstetricians are at high risk of a law suit. Eighty per cent of the total value of claims against the NHS relate to cerebral palsy in infants after an allegedly negligent delivery. Geriatricians on the other hand are hardly ever sued. This is not because obstetricians are more likely to be negligent than their colleagues in geriatrics. It is because if Granny dies as a result of a negligent overdose so little could be claimed by way of damages that it is not worth suing the responsible doctor. Remember the Legal Services Commission will not fund claims of less than £10,000. Nor would such a claim be a good risk for a conditional fee agreement.

Secondly, even where doctors are sued, the deterrent effect of tort is not direct. The damages will not come out of the doctor's pocket nor will his 'premiums' be increased. The deterrent function of tort normally operates via the insurance system. Poor drivers are deterred from carelessness and encouraged to improve because 'carelessness costs money'. NHS Indemnity means that NHS doctors do not pay any sort of insurance or indemnity. There is, of course, the emotional impact of litigation. Does the worry of being sued deter the incompetent doctor? I doubt it. Where negligence is gross and obvious, claims are settled swiftly to avoid adverse publicity. It is the cases where there truly is doubt about whether an error is negligent that drag on in the public eye. I suspect 'good' doctors worry about litigation and 'bad' doctors rarely give the possibility much thought.

Finally, there are a number of cases where, albeit there was actionable negligence, there is no moral culpability. Doctors who make mistakes after hours without sleep in under-resourced hospitals should not be blamed for their error. The tort system could operate to deter such 'negligence' only by encouraging such a doctor to refuse to treat patients at all, once he suspected he could not do so entirely competently. Such an outcome would prompt more, not less, patient suffering.

One caveat must be issued before dismissing the impact of deterrence via the tort system. PCTs and NHS hospital trusts are encouraged to be cost-conscious. Is there a risk that a hospital trust anxious to offer the lowest-cost appendectomy will cut corners and offer less than safe appendectomies? The fear of litigation might operate on the collective mind of the trust to deter economy measures that prejudice patients' safety. The impact of tort on PCTs and hospital trusts must not be overlooked in the no-fault debate. Evaluating the extent to which PCTs and hospital trusts may be influenced by the deterrent function of tort is difficult. Risk-management has a high profile within the NHS now and that is good. Hospitals review their practice and investigate adverse outcomes to try and prevent medical accidents. Currently a key player in risk-management is the Clinical Negligence Scheme for Trusts (CNST). Failure to implement adequate risk management strategies can lead to expulsion from the CNST. That will mean a hospital is left to bear all its own litigation costs. CNST is the enforcer of risk management. It operates a strategy embedded in the tort system. Put simply, NHS hospitals and other bodies are obliged to comply with risk-management or face financial disaster. Risk-management could and should survive a no-fault compensation scheme. But what would replace CNST and will it have the same teeth?

Returning to accountability, does the tort system ensure that health professionals and NHS trusts are made to account for their conduct? Tort's role in ensuring accountability is minimal. The nature of adversarial litigation militates against such an outcome. If an operation goes wrong and a patient is injured, what went wrong and why it went wrong needs investigation. The professional or professionals involved should be required to explain all they can to the patient and their conduct should be evaluated to discover whether it fell below a standard of good practice and to consider what measures might be taken to avoid such an accident in future. It may well be that even though there is no negligence in the tort sense, doctors and nurses can learn from the accident and amend standard procedures in the light of that knowledge. Adversarial litigation does not encourage such an investigation of the incident. Even after the Woolf reforms, little opportunity exists in litigation to evaluate disputed practices. Doctors and nurses in the shadow of litigation clam up; they are naturally wary of admitting any doubts they may have as to what they did or did not do. If the patient fails to prove negligence, within the tort system that is the end of the matter. Accountability is crucial but the tort system provides only token accountability. It is bodies such as the National Patient Safety Agency (see page 222) that will help ensure the NHS learns from its mistakes.

Experience abroad [22]

A growing number of no-fault compensation schemes operate abroad. I outline only two, the New Zealand accident compensation scheme, which covers medical injury within comprehensive provision for compensation for personal injury from all causes, and the Swedish Patients' Insurance Scheme, designed specifically for medical injuries. Review of New Zealand's and Sweden's experience will highlight certain problems of no-fault liability. They are problems that should be treated as an education in mistakes to avoid, rather than an indication that the concept of no-fault liability should be abandoned. In this brief review of both schemes I concentrate on how the basic principle of no-fault liability works. Space does not allow consideration in detail of the funding and administration of either scheme. It will swiftly become apparent that defining the criteria governing eligibility to compensation is the litmus test of whether no-fault compensation can be made to work.

The New Zealand scheme[23] underwent wholesale reform in 1992. It is now administered by the Accident Rehabilitation and Compensation Insurance Corporation. The scheme was first set up in 1974 to award compensation to anyone who had suffered 'personal injury by accident'. Personal injury by accident was defined as including 'medical, surgical, dental or first aid misadventure'. Damage caused exclusively by disease, infection or the ageing process was specifically excluded, a distinction criticized as unfair. There might be two elderly women side by side in a hospital ward. One suffered a stroke in the course of minor surgery and is awarded compensation for medical misadventure. The other suffered hers by Act of God and gets nothing. The New Zealand Commission, whose report led to the implementation of the accident compensation scheme, hoped that eventually the scheme would extend to disease as well as accident.

In 1974, many New Zealanders saw the scheme as not going far enough to meet the needs of social justice. Idealism was tempered by realism over the years as the costs of the scheme escalated. The Accident Rehabilitation and Compensation Insurance Act 1992 sought to prevent further expansion of the fluid boundaries of 'personal injury by accident'. The Act limited benefits payable to claimants and sought to reinforce individual responsibility, both on the part of accident victims and those whose conduct caused others injury. 'Misadventure' was further interpreted by the Accident Compensation Commission to involve

... injury or damage ... caused by mischance or accident, unexpected and undesigned in the nature of medical error or medical mishap.

A veritable flood of litigation was to ensue in which the New Zealand courts struggled to find suitable definitions of error and mishap.[24] Part of the problem was that under the New Zealand scheme, if a person qualified for compensation within the Accident Compensation Scheme, he was barred from seeking damages for negligence. Error initially seemed to be defined as virtually identical to common law negligence. A patient like Mrs Whitehouse (page 188) who failed to prove negligence in England might also fail in a claim for compensation in New Zealand. Error was said, in one early decision, to involve a failure to observe '. . . a standard of care and skill reasonably to be expected of . . .' a medical practitioner. Subsequently the New Zealand Court of Appeal was to adopt a more liberal view of error, acknowledging that a non-negligent blameless error could give rise to an entitlement to compensation. In *Polansky* v. *Accident Compensation Corporation*[25] a woman was misdiagnosed as having cancer and underwent surgery to remove her stomach and other internal organs. There was no proof of negligence on the part of her doctors. She was entitled to claim compensation for medical misadventure because something had happened '. . . which should not have happened in the course of medical or surgical treatment'. A mistake had been made albeit a blameless mistake. So after *Polansky*, Mrs Whitehouse might perhaps have had success were an equivalent scheme in place here. With hindsight Mr Jordan may have made an error in not proceeding more quickly to deliver her baby by surgery.

Polansky and similar cases expanded the scope of error. Defining mishap was to prove yet more testing for the courts. Ultimately a broad definition won the day.[26] An unsatisfactory outcome beyond the normal range of medical or surgical failure for that treatment constituted mishap.[27] It did not have to result from any untoward event actually within the course of treatment.

The Accident Rehabilitation and Compensation Insurance Act 1992 redraws the boundaries narrowing down the cases where compensation will be payable. A statutory definition of medical misadventure continues to embrace two classes of cases, medical error and medical mishap. Medical error no longer includes blameless errors. It is defined as '. . . the failure of a registered health professional to observe a standard of care and skill reasonably to be expected in the circumstances'. Medical error does now cover negligent omissions to treat and negligent failure to obtain a sufficiently informed consent to treatment.

Mishap is now defined as follows

Medical mishap means an adverse consequence of treatment by or at the direction of a registered health professional properly given if:

(a) the likelihood of the adverse consequence of the treatment occurring is rare; and

(b) the adverse consequence is severe

Rare is in turn defined as a probability that the adverse consequence would not occur in more than 1 per cent of cases where that kind of treatment is given. Severity requires that the patient's injury involved death, or extended hospitalization, or significant disability lasting more than twenty-eight days, or disability qualifying for an independence allowance. Abnormal reactions or complications of treatment will not qualify as medical mishap unless the reactions or complications occurred at the time of the procedure. New Zealand claimants, with their supposedly generous no-fault scheme, find a doorway to recompense that is now little wider than the English tort system.

Unlike the New Zealand scheme, the Swedish Patients' Insurance Scheme[28] is expressly designed to provide compensation for medical injuries. Compensation is payable in respect of any injury or illness resulting from any procedure related to health care. Injury arising from any diagnostic procedure, inappropriate medication, medical treatment or surgery falls within the ambit of the Swedish scheme. But compensation for such injury is subject to three important provisos. As in New Zealand, the injury must be proved to result from the procedure in issue, and not from the original disease. Injury resulting from a risk taken by the doctor to save life or prevent permanent disability is excluded. Most crucially, the claimant has to show that the procedure causing his injury was *not medically justified*. The test of whether the procedure was medically justified often reintroduces the question of negligence. Had Mrs Whitehouse claimed in Sweden, the central issue would have been whether Mr Jordan's delay in proceeding to Caesarean surgery was justified. Faced with balancing the risk of surgery against the risk of vaginal delivery, did he take the correct medical decision?[29] Certain claimants who lose in England will obtain compensation in Sweden. Mrs Ashcroft, who suffered paralysis when the surgeon accidentally cut a facial nerve, would recover compensation in Sweden. The surgeon was not to blame, but cutting the nerve was not medically indicated.[30] The limitation in the Swedish scheme to injury arising from acts not medically justified is as restrictive, if not more so than, 'medical misadventure' claims in New Zealand.

Examination of the problems encountered in New Zealand and Sweden should not obscure the benefits of no-fault schemes. Patients uncompensated by a tort-based system benefit in those countries. The investigation of the cause of a medical mishap may still involve questions akin to negligence, but the opportunities for scoring points, and the advantages to be gained from having the best advocate, rather than the best case, do not exist.

The way ahead for the UK

The experiences of New Zealand and Sweden must be considered carefully and learned from. The basic structure of any scheme should be aimed at redirecting claims for compensation for medical injury away from the courts and towards an independent tribunal. Tribunal staff would initially investigate each claim. They would have access to all relevant records. Provision for hearings and appeal against an unfavourable initial decision would have to be made. Care would need to be taken to prevent the lawyers taking over the process and adding to its expense, formality and technicality. The underlying problems confronted in Sweden and New Zealand in defining the criteria for compensation would have to be faced. The basic premise of any English scheme would be the same. Compensation claims for personal injury arising from medical accidents would be made not in the courts against the doctor but to an administrative tribunal. Tribunal staff would examine medical notes and see the parties involved. There would be no adversarial hearing. Provision would need to be made for the grant of a hearing to the claimant where appropriate and for appeals by claimants dissatisfied by the initial decision. The distinction between injury resulting from disease and injury resulting from medical treatment is a problem we must probably live with. Ideally a system would be devised whereby the healthy provided funds to alleviate the discomfort and disadvantage of disability and disease, however caused. This is at present an ideal unlikely to be realized, and reform must have the more limited aim of replacing the tort of negligence by a fairer and less destructive system of compensation for medical injury.

The scheme proposed in the first two editions of this work embraced two categories of medical injury. (1) Injury or illness arising from an absence of, or delay in, appropriate medical treatment[31] provided that (i) treatment would have prevented that injury or illness, and (ii) a reasonable request for medical care from a person or authority under an obligation to provide care has been made by the patient or some other person acting on his behalf. (2) Injury or illness resulting from medical treatment provided that (i) the injury or illness is not caused by the natural progression of disease or the ageing process, and (ii) the injury or illness is not the consequence of an unavoidable risk inherent in the treatment, of which the patient has received proper warning.

Category 1 would cover injury arising from failure to treat both in circumstances where the present tort of negligence would operate and where it would not. For example, a request for treatment might be made and not acted on by the GP because at the time he acted reasonably in thinking an immediate visit was not necessary. Events might prove him wrong but they do not render him negligent. Under this proposed no-fault scheme the patient's claim would succeed because he did in fact suffer as a result of lack of treatment, albeit no one was to blame.

Category 2 is more difficult to define. Careful drafting of any legislation will be called for, and I do not attempt that formidable task. The intention of category 2 is that it should extend to any damage to the patient that is neither the result of the natural progression of his original disease or condition nor a consequence inherent in that treatment and unavoidable if that treatment is to be successful. Under that last limitation the side-effects of certain surgery and therapy would be excluded. At one level the patient could obviously not recover compensation for pain and suffering ordinarily attendant on surgery. At another level unpleasant and dangerous side-effects, for example, the patient's hair falling out during chemotherapy or the risk of a stroke in some forms of brain surgery, would have to be excluded if they were inescapable in the pursuit of proper treatment. One important proviso is attached to the exclusion of unavoidable side-effects from compensation. The patient must have been properly warned. Failure to give proper warning, which results in injury unexpected and unconsidered by the patient, would remain a ground for compensation.

Avoiding definitions and drafting points may well be criticized as cowardice. The scheme above operates in a presumption of entitlement when injury follows medical treatment and ensues from lack of treatment. It seeks to avoid the linguistic complications of concepts of error or mishap. Ken Oliphant[32] has argued that the experience from New Zealand should make us cautious. Initially at least a compensation scheme should be based on evidence of 'medical error'. Where investigation and hindsight indicate that the patient received less than the optimum treatment, and with such treatment her injury could have been avoided, she would receive compensation. Simple evidence of an unexpected outcome of treatment would not suffice, however serious that outcome. If a previously healthy patient suffers a cardiac arrest in the course of minor surgery he will recover compensation if, for example, a defect is found in the anaesthetic equipment or some error was made by the anaesthetist. He will not have to show blameworthiness. If no reason for the sudden heart failure can be discovered, he has no claim in relation to that mishap.

The 'Oliphant solution' will, as he says, provide 'consistency and ease of application'. It may provoke awkward questions of causation and make it difficult to cast off the shackles of negligence. It is a notable attempt to put substance into defining 'medical misadventure'. A root cause of the inadequacy of two attempts to introduce legislation to implement no-fault compensation in the United Kingdom was their failure to define medical mishap. Harriet Harman's Compensation for Medical Injury Bill contained this partial definition only: mishap did not occur if resulting from '. . . a reasonable diagnostic error, having regard for the state of medical knowledge and best medical practice'. Rosie Barnes' National Health Service (Compensation) Bill left the definition of mishap open. Her Bill provided that . . . 'Mishap includes but is not restricted to, any act or omission which gives rise to an action at common law'.

Ways and means

My emphasis on principle rather than detail does not mean I am blind to the problems inherent in setting up a no-fault scheme or to its potential cost. Until the impetus for reform is sufficiently cogent, any examination of ways and means can become an exercise in attempting to solve insuperable problems.

The means adopted in Sweden to provide, to finance and to administer the scheme, recommend themselves. An insurance-based scheme would draw on resources already employed in making compensation payments and fighting compensation claims. Funds in Sweden are drawn from the authorities maintaining public health facilities and from doctors and clinics operating in the private sector. Similar provision could be made here for levying premiums on NHS authorities and private care organizations. The need for resources here is likely to be greater than in Sweden. Benefits paid in Sweden are limited to what is needed to 'top up' their already generous social security system.[33] A levy on individual practitioners would be required. The governing principle in determining the funding of the scheme should be that those organisations and individuals who provide health care should contribute to the funds needed to compensate those injured in the provision of that care. Additional funds will be required from general taxation, but this will be offset to some extent by a reduction in the social security payments now made to claimants outside the tort system.

The ultimate cost of a no-fault scheme will depend on the level of payments made to victims. Several hard questions need to be addressed. It would seem obvious that the payment of compensation for loss of income and cost of care should generally be by way of periodical payments rather than as a lump sum. Payments can then be adjusted to meet the claimant's current needs. Should there be a ceiling on payments? Under the tort system a high-earning solicitor rendered unable to work obtains money to make up her actual loss of income. Should no-fault compensation be limited to sufficient to provide for the claimant's needs arising from her disability up to the 'average' standard of living?[34] What about compensation for pain and suffering? The harder a no-fault scheme tries to offer generous compensation, the harder it is to fund a scheme to meet the needs of the widest possible range of claimants.

An affordable no-fault scheme will necessarily have to limit compensation payments. The New Zealand Scheme no longer compensates non-pecuniary loss. Previously wealthy victims of medical accidents will not receive full compensation for their monetary loss. Their loss of income will be capped. Medical and rehabilitation costs that could be met from other sources will not be included in compensation payments.

Consider this scenario. X and Y are both paralysed in a medical accident. X, a PE teacher, who might have got nothing from the tort system because he could not prove negligence, will benefit from no-fault whatever his prior circumstances. He will gain a reasonable income (shall we say £350 a week) if he can no longer work. He will obtain money to pay for care at home over and above what the social security system may provide, and money to adapt his house to the demands of his disability. Y who could win damages under the tort system may lose. Assume prior to his accident Y was a wealthy young football star – £350 a week could be about 5 per cent of his previous income. He will get nothing for pain and suffering. A no-fault scheme will not pay for him to have costly private care in the USA.

Proponents of social justice will argue that it is better to offer some recompense to more people than to award lottery-type damages to winners in the tort system. The problem is this. If a no-fault compensation scheme exists side by side with access to the tort system, patients such as Y will still opt for the tort system. Two options could be explored. First, claimants who opt to sue in tort do so at their peril. If their claim fails they are excluded from the no-fault scheme. That might radically lower the cost of tort claims because only the most clear cut claims will be brought and they should be swiftly settled. Second, as in New Zealand, where a claimant is entitled to claim under the no-fault scheme, a tort claim is barred altogether. No-fault becomes the exclusive route to compensation for medical accidents. Financially, and to achieve the objective of a no-fault scheme, the second option makes pre-eminent sense.

But in barring access to the courts would it violate Article 6 of the European Convention on Human Rights entitling everyone to a fair trial in determination of his civil rights and obligations?

Drugs and medical injuries[35]

What about the relationship between drug-induced injury and medical accidents? We have seen how the distinction operates at present, often denying a patient any remedy because he cannot establish whether he was damaged because the doctor prescribed negligently or because there was some inherent defect in the drug. How would a no-fault scheme for drugs operate and how would it relate to a medical accidents scheme?

Under a no-fault scheme for drugs, the first benefit to ensue would be an end to the kind of unproductive and expensive lawsuits discussed in Chapter 8. A patient injured by a drug would receive compensation without the need to prove the company negligent, or the drug defective. It would be no answer to a claim that the damage to the patient resulted from some condition peculiar to him. Questions of whether risk to a particular group was sufficiently great to be taken into account would cease to be relevant. The drug companies could save a great deal of the money now spent on lawyers. Compensation would be paid even where the manufacturer cannot be identified, for example where the patient took a generic drug and records to trace the manufacturer are unavailable. Issues of the balance of risk versus benefit of a drug would be removed from the courts. A dilemma posed by some drugs is this. They benefit 99.9 per cent of us and damage 0.1 per cent. Under no-fault the 0.1 per cent would get proper compensation. The issue of whether they should ever have been exposed to that risk would be properly and impartially investigated, not submitted to the adversarial atmosphere of a court. Causation remains an inescapable problem, but as with medical injury, I believe that investigation of a claim for no-fault compensation is more likely to reveal the truth than a battle in court with the drug company having a vested interest in disclosing as little as possible.

The central problem to be tackled in implementing a no-fault scheme will be whether it should be separate from or incorporated within a medical injuries scheme. My preference would be for incorporation and a definition of medical treatment including drug-induced damage. That way, resources for a united scheme could be maximized, with the drug companies contributing. Against unification lies the argument that the inclusion of drug-induced damage, and so potentially another thalido-mide disaster, would impose too great a strain and imbalance on the scheme's resources. Some relationship between medical and drug-induced injury must be worked out to ensure that no future patient falls between two stools, ending up admittedly injured but unable to get himself into the right scheme to obtain compensation.

Accountability and no-fault

Any consideration of a move to no-fault compensation for medical acci-dents must have at its heart the need to ensure professional accounta-bility. Opponents of no-fault have always expressed fears that removing any element of blame from compensation for medical injury could provoke a decline in standards of health care. This must not happen. The price doctors pay for freedom from the threat of malpractice litigation must be the establishment of thorough investigatory procedures into all medical accidents. Where error is revealed, action should be taken to ascertain the cause of the error. Is it a result of a failure in the system or the inadequacy of a particular doctor? One means to achieve this end is to integrate complaints and compensation systems.[36] There would be one simple route for pursuing a grievance arising out of a medical accident. The patient would initiate a complaint indicating whether or not he seeks compensation as well as investigation of his grievance. His compensa-tion claim would be reviewed to see if it meets the criteria of the no-fault scheme. The causes of and responsibility for his injury would be followed up in a parallel inquisitorial process. Recommendations would then be made as to how best (if possible at all) to avoid repetition of any error or systems failure. Evidence of professional failings would be passed on to the appropriate authority.

Doctors intimidated by such a proposal, who may fear that the medi-cine of no-fault is worse than the illness of the tort system, should not overlook the power of retribution today. A compensation system that takes no account of fault, without a vigorous complaints system identi-fying fault where fault is present, would result in further escalation of criminal prosecutions of doctors. I would agree with Merry and McCall Smith when they say:

An important barrier to progress in reducing the incidence of medical injuries and in finding better ways of handling these injuries when they occur is an undue emphasis on blame. Blame promotes an adversarial response, which in turn feeds upon blame. A sophisticated and constructive approach to the attribution of blame is required.[37]

Where blame is due none the less the system must allow its attribution. Otherwise aggrieved patients will simply seek alternative, even more adversarial, means of seeking to pursue their grievances.

Other options

No-fault is just one of the options for reform currently on the political agenda. The Chief Medical Officer[38] is floating several other options. Some focus on improving the cost-effectiveness of the current litigation system. They ask the following questions. Should courts be able to impose structured settlements? Could better means be found to fund litigation, and the gross disproportion between costs and damages be reduced? Alternative dispute resolution, including mediation, is explored. Other proposals examine means of meeting claimants' needs other than compensation in cash. Patients might be offered rehabilitation payments rather than monetary compensation. Many of the suggestions focus on limiting payments. At a more mundane level, consultees are asked whether section 2(4) of the Law Reform (Personal Injuries) Act 1948 should be repealed. This provision allows patients to opt for private care and claim the cost of private treatment as part of their damages even though the NHS could perfectly adequately provide for their needs.

Most controversially the possibility of a system of fixed tariffs for specific injuries is raised. Claimants would be offered a fixed sum only, not compensation tailored to their own circumstances. Fixed tariffs would undoubtedly assist NHS planning and reduce legal argument about levels of compensation. But would they apply only to medical accidents? Assume the fixed tariff for brain damage resulting in impaired vision and slurred speech was £20,000, plus periodic payments to bring the claimant up to the average wage should her earning capacity be diminished. Imagine a particular claimant was a well-known newsreader who could no longer do her lucrative job. Would she be awarded only the fixed tariff if her injury resulted from a medical accident, yet full compensation if she was injured in a road accident?

Part Three: Matters of Life and Death

11

Family Planning

In 1924, Marie Stopes sued for libel after her work had been described as a 'monstrous campaign of birth control', with the rider that 'Bradlaugh was condemned to jail for a less serious crime'. In the House of Lords, Viscount Finlay said of the practice of birth control:

... it is impossible to hold that the bounds of fair comment are exceeded by the expression of an opinion that such practices are revolting to the healthy instincts of human nature. There is an old and widespread aversion to such methods on this ground.[1]

In 1954, less than fifty years ago, Lord Denning MR said of vasectomy:

Take a case where a sterilization operation is done so as to enable a man to have the pleasure of sexual intercourse without shouldering the responsibilities attached to it. The operation is plainly injurious to the public interest. It is degrading to the man himself. It is injurious to his wife and any woman who he may marry, to say nothing of the way it opens to licentiousness, and unlike other contraceptives, it allows no room for a change of mind on either side. It is illegal, even though the man consents to it . . .[2]

Attitudes have changed radically. In 2002, Munby J[3] resoundingly declared that contraception was a matter for personal choice and conscience, and no business of the law. Is he right?

Can contraception be criminal?

Contraceptives were never totally banned in England, as they were in Ireland, and in France. However, not until 1967 was formal provision made for contraceptive advice and treatment to be offered within the NHS.[4] Attempts to invoke the criminal law to prohibit certain sorts of birth control go on. The boundary between prevention of pregnancy and early abortion will be fully examined in Chapter 13. In *Gillick*, prescribing contraceptives to girls under sixteen was unsuccessfully argued to be aiding and abetting unlawful sexual intercourse (see Chapter 14). After post-coital contraception was made available over the counter in pharmacies, pro-life groups unsuccessfully went to court to overturn the relevant regulations allowing such sales, expressing outrage that young girls are able to gain easy access to such a controversial form of contraception. Failure is unlikely to prevent them continuing to try to use the courts to advance their case.[5] The diversity of views concerning sexual morality, from the position that the use of contraception is always morally wrong, through the view that contraception should be solely a means of spacing a family within marriage, to the point where contraception is seen as a right for all regardless of age or status, ensures acrimonious debate.

What of sterilization? Is there any substance in Lord Denning's argument that performing a sterilization could entail criminal liability for the surgeon? That cannot now be the law. His argument was based on the principle that a victim's agreement cannot make lawful an inherently criminal act. A man who sadistically beat a seventeen-year-old girl was convicted of a criminal assault upon her despite her consent to be beaten. Inflicting violence on another person for sexual gratification is unacceptable to society.[6] Lord Denning argued that sterilization without medical cause was mutilation of the patient, and unacceptable because of its potential for risk-free immorality. Several thousands of Britons undergo sterilization every year. It is an acceptable option for birth control.[7] No judge would nowadays categorize sterilization as inherently unlawful and put the surgeon on a par with the sadist! Today, the principal controversy surrounding sterilization is how readily the courts will *impose* sterilization on young women with mental disability.

Contraception, sterilization and marriage

Two questions arise. Can the use of contraception by, or the prior sterilization of, one of the spouses affect the validity of a marriage? Does a refusal to have children give rise to grounds for divorce?

English law provides that a marriage that remains unconsummated because of the incapacity or wilful refusal of one party to consummate that marriage is voidable and may be annulled. The earlier sterilization of one of the spouses, or the use of mechanical or chemical contraception, does not prevent consummation taking place.[8] Consummation means full sexual intercourse regardless of whether or not the act is open to the procreation of children. A husband who had unwillingly used a condom when engaging in intercourse with his wife failed in his attempt to argue that the marriage had never been consummated. Neither will refusal by one spouse to have intercourse unless contraceptives are used amount to wilful refusal to consummate. This can create a knotty problem. If one party is entirely prepared to engage in normal sexual intercourse only if contraceptives are used and the other, for religious reasons perhaps, only if they are not, the marriage remains unconsummated, but neither spouse is guilty of wilful refusal to consummate and the marriage cannot be annulled.[9] Their remedy lies in divorce. Any hardship in having to await a divorce is alleviated by the Matrimonial and Family Proceedings Act 1984, which permits divorce in normal circumstances after one year of marriage only.

A divorce will be granted if the petitioner can establish that the marriage has irretrievably broken down. One means of establishing the breakdown is to show that the respondent has behaved in such a way that the petitioner cannot reasonably be expected to live with him or her. This test of 'unreasonable behaviour' is liberally interpreted by the courts. Undergoing a vasectomy after the marriage,[10] or insisting on using contraceptives,[11] was held in the past to be cruelty on the part of the husband if the effect was damaging to the wife's health. Today a wife would probably succeed in establishing unreasonable behaviour without having to show evidence of damage to her health. Equally, a husband could prima facie show it to be unreasonable for his wife to refuse, without good reason, to have children. One difficulty can be outlined. In *Archard* v. *Archard*[12] the parties were both Roman Catholics. The wife was advised on medical grounds not to conceive, and refused to have intercourse without the use of contraceptives. Her devout husband refused to have intercourse if contraceptives were used. She failed to establish that his behaviour was unreasonable, as she was aware of his faith and his views. Equally, he would have failed to establish her behaviour to be unreasonable on the grounds of her medical condition. The reasons for one party's refusal to have children must be examined in determining whether this conduct is such that the petitioner can no longer be expected to go on with the marriage. Today it may well not be limited to cases where the wife (or the husband) is medically advised against conception, but embrace the whole of the parties' lifestyle and aspirations.

Finally, there is one anomaly in the law. What if one spouse has been sterilized before the marriage and never tells the other? We have seen that that is no ground for nullity. Nor is it evidence of unreasonable behaviour so as to support a petition for divorce. The relevant conduct, undergoing sterilization, takes place before the marriage. A divorce can be granted only on the basis of conduct *after* the marriage.[13] The unhappy spouse will have to establish the breakdown of the marriage on other grounds. A divorce may be granted after two years' separation where the other party consents. Should the contesting party be obdurate, a divorce can be granted without consent after five years' separation. Five years may be enough to end an older woman's hope of having children within a future marriage. Had the Family Law Act 1996 been fully implemented allowing 'no-fault' divorce after a waiting period of one year, the law's role in disputes over a spouse's 'right' to a child would be ended. If the other party's refusal to have children in effect destroys a marriage, no longer would that refusal have to be fitted uncomfortably into the straitjacket of unreasonable behaviour. We are still bedevilled by outdated concepts of marital 'behaviour'.

Contraceptives: patients' rights

An infallible contraceptive has yet to be invented. The more sophisticated and convenient contraceptives, such as the Pill and the IUD, carry a price-tag. Contraception is very much a medical as well as a social issue that largely concerns women. Except for the experimental male 'Pill', all the more sophisticated contraceptives are used by women and pose some risk to their health. Women seek two sorts of protection from the law. First, they require a definition of the doctor's obligation to assist them to avoid pregnancy at the least possible risk to health. Second, they demand information, and greater control of their reproductive and sexual lives. The law is fairly well equipped for the first task, and almost entirely a futile weapon in the second.

A doctor advising a woman on contraception owes her the same duties as in any other area of medicine. He must offer her competent and careful advice. He must perform any technical procedure, for example inserting an IUD, skilfully. He must obtain her consent to any invasive procedure. When a woman consults her GP his obligation to her is part and parcel of his ordinary care of her. He will be aware of her medical history, prescribe in the light of that history, and take note of any symptoms of general ill-health that are revealed by any examination he undertakes. Many women prefer to consult specialist Family Planning Clinics. They feel that clinics have greater experience. Some prefer not to discuss their sexual lives with the family doctor. Clinics must beware. Their obligation is not limited to providing competent advice on how to avoid conception. Contraception cannot be divorced from general health care. The clinic must act on any indication that the woman's general health is at risk, whether from the prescription of a particular contraceptive, or otherwise. In *Sutton* v. *Population Services Family Planning Ltd*,[14] Mrs Sutton visited the defendant's clinic and was examined by a nurse preparatory to being given contraceptive advice. The nurse either failed to note, or failed to act on, evidence of early signs of cancer. The cancer was diagnosed much later, with the result that far more drastic treatment was called for and the disease was likely to recur at least four years earlier than would have been the case had it been promptly treated. Mrs Sutton was awarded damages for her additional suffering. Clinics must ensure that women receive treatment when signs of disease are present. This will usually be done by advising the patient to contact her GP. While the clinic staff may not wish to alarm a patient with what may be a tentative diagnosis, she must be given sufficient information on which to act and, if she agrees, her GP be directly notified. Of course, the clinic must respect her confidence, and should a woman refuse permission to contact her GP, say where a sexually transmitted disease is suspected, they must not breach her confidence. In such a case a clinic must take steps to advise the woman on alternative sources of treatment.

Litigation and contraception

Modern contraceptive treatments have not just generated moral controversy. They have resulted in litigation where use of contraceptive methods·has resulted in adverse effects for women. Several million dollars in compensation were paid out to women who suffered injury through use of the Dalkon shield, an IUD that caused substantial pelvic injuries to patients. The injectable contraceptive Depo-Provera led to a number of lawsuits in the United Kingdom. The use of Depo-Provera in its early years offers a classic example of how not to approach contraceptive advice and treatment.

Depo-Provera is a synthetic form of a natural hormone that acts, like most brands of the Pill, to prevent eggs developing and makes the womb hostile to any fertilized embryo. One injection is effective for at least three months. Doctors may advise the use of the drug for women for whom the Pill is a health risk, women who are considered too unreliable to be trusted to use other means of contraception and where pregnancy should be completely ruled out, for example when a woman has just been vaccinated against rubella. Increasingly women choose Depo-Provera for its convenience. Depo-Provera can produce unpredictable and unpleasant side-effects, including severe and irregular bleeding. Complaints were made that some women were injected with the drug without ever being told of its nature, and even where Depo-Provera was expressly prescribed and described as a contraceptive, inadequate explanation of its potential side-effects was given. Fears were voiced that Depo-Provera might be 'forced' on the inarticulate, or not particularly intelligent, woman.

A woman injected with Depo-Provera without being told what is in the syringe, or without being asked for her express agreement, has a claim in battery. She will get compensation for the unlawful violation of her body, and for any unpleasant side-effects that flow from the injection. She will get some compensation even if the drug does her no harm, for the doctor acted unlawfully in acting without her consent. A Salford woman, Mrs Potts, won £3,000 damages[15] after she was injected with Depo-Provera concurrently with a vaccination against rubella. She suffered severe bleeding. The injection was given days after the delivery of her third child, and she thought that it was a routine post-natal 'jab'. The aim of her doctor was laudable, to protect her from pregnancy while the vaccine might harm any unborn child. However, he had no right to deprive her of her choice of whether or not to accept or decline a controversial drug. Women must be told the nature of the drug offered to them, and if their right to choose is to be effective they must have its advantages and disadvantages explained to them. The judge awarding Mrs Potts's compensation said: 'She should have been given the choice, and she was entitled to know beforehand what the decision entailed.' The same holds true of any contraceptive treatment.

Scare stories about the Pill and risks of cancer, heart disease or thrombosis hit the headlines with monotonous regularity. Growing awareness of the potential risks has led women to demand more information about a substance that so many of us swallow every day. What can the law do for them? A doctor prescribing the Pill must be properly informed about the current stage of research and knowledge about brands of Pill and their risks to particular patients. A GP is not required to have the experience of a consultant gynaecologist specializing and researching into the control of fertility, but he must be adequately informed if he elects to offer advice personally rather than referring women to a specialist clinic. His terms of service do not oblige him to offer contraceptive services. He must take care to ensure that the Pill is 'safe' for the patient consulting him. If there are special risk factors relating to the woman's medical history, or weight, or smoking habit, he must seek to ensure that she is protected as far as possible from those risks. The most crucial question is what information is the woman entitled to? Information leaflets accompanying prescriptions of the Pill have lengthened considerably in recent years in their descriptions of side-effects and contra-indications. Clearly both her doctor and the drug company manufacturing the Pill are required to give the woman sufficient information to enable her to make an informed choice about whether to use, or continue to use, that method of contraception. I would argue that in the light of *Bolitho* v. *City & Hackney Health Authority*,[16] and *Pearce* v. *United Bristol Healthcare NHS Trust*[17], women must be advised of any risk that the Pill poses to them that a sensible woman would consider material to a reasonable decision about what sort of contraception to use.[18]

The doctor's duty to warn his patient about the risks of the Pill does not relieve the drug company of its responsibility to provide adequate information and warning about its product to both the prescribing doctor and the patient. A Canadian court expressed the manufacturer's duty in this way:

. . . the manufacturer's duty is to provide to the consumer written warnings conveying reasonable notice of the nature, gravity and likelihood of known or knowable side-effects and advising the consumer to seek fuller explanation from the prescribing physician or other doctor of any such information of concern to the consumer.[19]

In respect of any product put on the market after 1 March 1988, the drug company will be subject to strict liability under the Consumer Protection Act 1987 for injury arising from a defect in that product. Unfortunately strict liability does not make the task of suing in respect of drug-induced injury much easier. This is especially the case with the Pill – and what is said about the Pill also applies to certain mechanical methods of contraception such as the IUD. Risks associated with the Pill are well known, particularly the risk of succumbing to a stroke. Hence all manufacturers expressly warn patients of those risks, and seek to ensure that women who are specially vulnerable, for example older women or women who smoke, avoid the Pill. None the less 'at-risk' women continue to take the Pill, viewing it as a lesser evil than an unwanted pregnancy. Occasionally a woman with no identifiable risk factor falls seriously ill. The legal questions become: (1) Were the manufacturers' warnings adequate? (2) Bearing in mind the innate risk posed by the Pill balanced against its benefit as an effective contraceptive, is the Pill defective? (3) Can the woman prove that her injury was caused by taking the Pill?[20] The analysis of these questions is unlikely to be different whether the woman's claim is framed in negligence or under the Consumer Protection Act 1987. Strict liability under the 1987 Act may help a patient injured by some construction defect in a contraceptive, such as a negligently constructed IUD that damages the cervix. It will do little for the patient claiming that the inherent design of a contraceptive drug or device is defective. For such an action to succeed there will need to be overwhelming evidence that the manufacturer failed to note and act on evidence of clear risk to women's health, a risk not justified by the contraceptive benefit of the product. It should be stressed that the manufacturer's duty is a continuing duty. It is no answer for the manufacturer to contend that his product was safe by, say, 1995 standards, if evidence of its dangers has emerged from its use, and that same product is still being marketed in 2003.

What about contraceptives that simply fail? We shall see later that the House of Lords has ruled that parents cannot recover compensation for the cost of bringing up a normal, healthy child.[21] In *Richardson* v. *LRC Products Ltd*[22] it was held that evidence a condom split was not by itself sufficient to prove that product defective. The fallibility of condoms was well known. The manufacturer never guaranteed 100 per cent success.

Voluntary sterilization

When a further pregnancy or the burden of caring for more children may endanger a woman's health, therapeutic sterilization may be advised.

Non-therapeutic sterilization is increasingly sought as a method of permanent birth control, both by older couples who feel that their family is complete and by younger childless women adamant that they never wish to reproduce. Both sorts of prospective patients express disquiet about present practice. Too many doctors regard the decision to sterilize as theirs and not their patients'.[23] They are over-inclined to sterilize women whom they regard as unfit for childbearing or child-rearing and disinclined to help the fit but unwilling. The latter struggle to find a legal remedy. A plethora of private clinics has grown up offering female sterilization and vasectomy at a price. Patients refused sterilization within the NHS must resort to the private sector if they can meet the cost. Attempts to demand that the NHS provides non-therapeutic sterilization are unlikely to succeed. By contrast, any woman alleging that she was hustled into sterilization without her full consent may usefully look to the law for assistance.

A doctor undertaking sterilization must ensure that the patient understands and agrees to what is to be done. Operating without any consent is obviously a battery. Nor should sterilization be automatically performed concurrently with some other gynaecological operation to which the patient has consented. The doctor may correctly judge, in the course of some other form of surgery, that a woman should not risk pregnancy again but he cannot act 'in her best interests' without her agreement. In *Devi* v. *West Midlands AHA*,[24] a married woman of thirty-three who already had four children entered hospital for a minor gynaecological operation. Her religion outlawed sterilization or contraception. In the course of the operation the surgeon discovered her womb to be ruptured and sterilized her there and then. She received £4000 damages for the loss of her ability to conceive again and £2,700 damages for the neurosis caused by the knowledge of what had been done to her. The choice of whether to accept sterilization is the patient's. It may be more convenient to sterilize the patient on the spot but it is never so *immediately* necessary as to justify acting without consent.

A doctor who has obtained consent may still be liable for negligence if he fails to discuss properly with the patient the implications of the operation in a manner consistent with good medical practice. The doctor must not only give the patient sufficient information on which to make up her mind, but do so at a time when she is in a fit state to make a reasoned decision. A Roman Catholic woman of thirty-five was awarded £3000 damages in negligence when she was sterilized in the course of a

Caesarean operation to deliver her second child. She signed the consent form just as she was about to be wheeled into the operating theatre. The judge said that, although she consented to the additional surgery and understood what would physically be done to her, she had been inadequately counselled about its implications for her.[25] Sterilizing a woman in the course of an abortion or Caesarean saves time and money for the NHS and cuts down on pain and suffering for the patient. However, it is a course of action fraught with legal hazard unless the patient has been properly advised about the physical and emotional consequences of electing to be sterilized. The doctor must assess, not just his patient's physical condition, but also her religious and moral attitudes to enable him and her to take into account the possible emotional impact of sterilization. Moreover, if sterilization is proposed on therapeutic grounds the patient's consent must necessarily be based on adequate and careful advice as to the medical need for sterilization. In *Biles* v. *Barking HA*[26] a woman was advised to undergo sterilization on the grounds that she was suffering from a severe and probably fatal kidney complaint. That diagnosis was later proved to be mistaken and negligent. Mrs Biles recovered damages of £45,000, which included the cost of a failed attempt to reverse the sterilization and the cost of IVF treatment to try to enable her to have a child of her own, despite her surgically blocked Fallopian tubes.

A number of doctors still believe that they should seek the consent of one spouse for the sterilization of the other. There is no legal obligation to do so. If one spouse objects to consultation with the other the surgeon is obliged to respect his patient's confidence. The surgeon cannot be obliged to operate. He does not, in law, owe any duty to the patient's spouse. Nor, providing he has advised his patient properly, can he be liable to a patient whose spouse repudiates the marriage on learning of the sterilization.

Who pays for the unplanned child?

Contraception and sterilization are fallible. No doctor guarantees avoidance of conception. He undertakes to use his skill to maximize the chances of preventing pregnancy. Sterilization is often expected and intended to be final. What if it fails? This can happen if the surgeon is negligent. There is also a small but real risk inherent in both vasectomy and female sterilization that tissues will rejoin naturally and conception once again be possible. Who foots the bill for the unexpected infant?

When the surgeon admits that sterilization failed because he was negligent the only issue is the amount of damages he should pay. Should damages be limited to compensation for the mother's pain and discomfort arising from the useless operation and from the subsequent pregnancy? Or should parents be able to recover the cost of bringing up their unplanned child? In *Udale* v. *Bloomsbury Health Authority*.[27] Jupp J held that the birth of a healthy child could not be allowed to create a claim in damages. He argued that the child, when he came to know of the award, might feel unwanted and the family's relationship would be disrupted. Doctors might put pressure on women to have abortions. Children were a blessing, and any financial loss was offset by the joy of their birth.

A series of judgments from the Court of Appeal firmly rejected Jupp J's invocation of policy to refuse parents compensation in such a case.[28] Damages amounting to the cost to the family of raising an unplanned child appeared to be readily endorsed in claims for wrongful conception. The decision of the House of Lords in *McFarlane* v. *Tayside Health Board*[29] restored English and Scottish Law to the position declared by Jupp J in *Udale*, albeit on apparently different grounds. Compensation for the cost of bringing up a healthy child will not be awarded. Such a loss is categorized now as irrecoverable economic loss. *McFarlane* is difficult to analyse.[30] Five Law Lords rejected the parents' claim. Five sets of very different reasons are advanced by their Lordships.

The facts of the case are straightforward. Mr and Mrs McFarlane had four children. Mr McFarlane had a vasectomy. Six months after his operation, the surgeon told him that his sperm count was negative and he and his wife could dispense with contraception. The couple relied on that advice. Mrs McFarlane became pregnant. They alleged that the surgeon was negligent and sought compensation not only for Mrs McFarlane's pain and distress in pregnancy and labour but also for the costs of bringing up their healthy daughter, Catherine. Four out of the five Law Lords[31] held that Mrs McFarlane could recover damages for the pain and discomfort of pregnancy and any immediately consequential financial loss to her. All agreed that the more substantial claim for the cost of raising Catherine should fail. All tried to avoid Jupp J's forthright reliance on policy to categorize such claims as repugnant to the public interest.

Lord Slynn appeared to accept that the blessings conferred by healthy children come in tandem with substantial burdens. He rejected the argument that courts should regard the financial costs of raising a child as offset by the joys of parenting. He claimed not to be concerned by possible psychological consequences to a child of learning that she is unwanted because her parents received damages for her wrongful conception. His speech focused on his finding that doctors are not responsible for the economic loss entailed in child rearing. Doctors owe a duty of care to prevent pregnancy and the consequential physical effects on the mother. It is not fair, just or reasonable to extend that responsibility to the costs of rearing the child.[32] Lord Hope took a somewhat similar approach. He appeared exercised by the potential scale of claims for wrongful conception. If such a claim is allowable it would relate to the actual costs to particular parents of raising that child. Thus a claim by wealthy aristocrats might extend to the cost of nannies, ponies, public school and so on. The extent of liability would be disproportionate to the negligence.[33]

Lord Hope and Lord Steyn both, unlike Lord Slynn, adverted to the benefits of parenthood, Lord Hope declared:

. . . it would not be fair, just or reasonable, in any assessment of the loss caused by the birth of a child, to leave these benefits out of account. Otherwise the [claimant] would be paid far too much. They would be relieved of the costs of rearing the child. They would not be giving anything back to the wrongdoer for the benefits. But the value attached to their benefits is incalculable. The costs can be calculated but the benefit, which must in fairness be set against them, cannot. The logical conclusion, as a matter of law, is that the cost to the [claimant] of meeting their obligations to their child during her childhood are not recoverable as damages.[34]

Lord Steyn contended that his rejection of the parents' claim was not on policy grounds. He '. . . would avoid those quicksands'.[35] He saw the question as one of distributive justice. He stated that he was 'firmly of the view that an overwhelming number of ordinary men and women' would reject claims such as the McFarlanes'. He argued that if claims by a child for wrongful life should be rejected as repugnant to the value of human life, so should a claim by parents for its wrongful conception.[36] Lord Steyn may have sought to avoid the quicksands of public policy but he becomes immersed in them none the less.

Lord Clyde treated the claim as one of a *quantum* of damages. Like

Lord Hope, he was exercised by questions of proportionality. There could be significant differences in the level of awards depending on parental lifestyle. The expense of bringing up the child would be disproportionate to any wrongdoing and go beyond reasonable restitution.[37] Lord Millett, uniquely, sought to reject both claims by the parents, the claim for the mother's pain and suffering in pregnancy as well as the claim for the cost of raising Catherine. Lord Millett was forthright in his views.[38]

In my opinion, the law must take the birth of a normal healthy baby to be a blessing, not a detriment. In truth it is a mixed blessing. It brings joy and sorrow, blessing and responsibility. The advantages and disadvantages are inseparable. Individuals may choose to regard the balance as unfavourable and take steps to forego the pleasures as well as the responsibilities of parenthood. They are entitled to decide for themselves where their own interests lie. But society itself must regard the balance as beneficial. It would be repugnant to its own sense of values to do otherwise. It is morally offensive to regard a normal, healthy baby as more trouble and expense than it is worth.

The only damages Lord Millett would allow was a nominal sum to represent the loss of the parental freedom to limit the size of their family. He proposed £5000. Lord Millett stands alone in the openness of his opinion that it is simply unacceptable to society to compensate parents for having a child, however hard they had tried to avoid further pregnancies. His honesty should be commended. The reasons advanced by his colleagues are not convincing.

The judges in *McFarlane* expressly confined their ruling to cases where a healthy child is born.[39] Subsequent judgments at first instance,[40] and now in the Court of Appeal, have held that where a disabled child is born, his parents may recover the additional costs ensuing from their child's disability. The rationale is difficult to comprehend. Unless the defendants' negligence related to advice or treatment given to help parents avoid the birth of a disabled child, how does the child's disability result from negligent advice about, or performance of, sterilization? In *Parkinson* v. *St James and Seacroft University NHS Hospital Trust*[41] the parents' claim related to the birth of their fifth child. Sadly the baby proved to have substantial disabilities, possibly related to autism. Mrs Parkinson was sterilized after the birth of her fourth child but the operation was performed negligently. The surgeon failed to secure a clip effectively to Mrs Parkinson's left fallopian tube and she conceived again ten months after the operation. The Court of Appeal ruled that, *MacFarlane* notwithstanding, the parents could recover the special costs of raising a child with their son's disabilities.[42] A doctor who performs a sterilization negligently should reasonably foresee the birth of a disabled child as a possible consequence of his breach of duty. Only a limited group of people (parents whose children were unfortunately born disabled) could bring a claim and Brooke LJ saw no difficulty with the proposition that the doctor assumed responsibility for the disastrous economic consequences of the birth of such a child. '[O]rdinary people would consider that it would be fair for the law to make an award in such a case provided that it is limited to the extra expenses associated with the child's disability.'[43] Both Brooke LJ and Hale LJ[44] construct elegant examples to distinguish the case of the disabled child from *McFarlane*. The reader may ponder whether the appeal court did not in reality simply regard *McFarlane* as wrongly decided. Unable to say so forthrightly, the judges sought to mitigate its worst effects.

Subsequently the Court of Appeal went further in its attempt to limit the effects of *McFarlane*. In *Rees* v. *Darlington Memorial Hospital NHS Trust*,[45] they held that a seriously disabled woman could recover the additional costs to her of raising her son born after a negligently performed sterilization. The claimant suffered from retinitis pigmentosa. She had only very limited vision in one eye. She elected to be sterilized because she did not want children as she judged that her virtual blindness would prevent her looking after a child. Hale LJ[46] distinguished this case from *McFarlane* on a number of grounds. Unlike the healthy parent of a healthy child, but like the parent of any disabled child, the claimant incurred extra costs in bringing up a child. The compensation awarded to her was not compensation for the cost of the child *per se*, but the costs occasioned by her own disability.

What constitutes negligent sterilization?

It might be that another factor motivating the decision in *McFarlane* was an explosion in unmeritorious claims.[47] Where a surgeon bungles the operation by only clipping one Fallopian tube, imposing responsibility for the consequences of his carelessness seems instinctively right. Liability for failed sterilization extends beyond such examples of crass negligence, however. Consider cases where conception occurs because tissues heal naturally. Even though the operation has been performed impeccably an act of God or of nature reverses the surgery. At first sight it might appear that the surgeon is in no way responsible. What could he have done? The practice of most surgeons has been to warn patients of the risk when discussing the proposed operation with them. Can a failure to warn give rise to a claim against the surgeon? In *Thake* v. *Maurice*, Mr and Mrs Thake had five children and little money. They wanted no more children. Mr Thake decided to have a vasectomy and paid £20 for the operation. The judge found that the defendant never warned Mr and Mrs Thake of the small but real risk that nature would reverse the surgery. Mrs Thake did not discover her pregnancy until it was nearly five months advanced. The couple sought compensation from the defendant surgeon. As Mr Thake had paid for his vasectomy, unlike an NHS patient he had a contract with the surgeon. The trial judge held that Mr Thake had agreed to an operation that he understood would render him irreversibly infertile.[48] That is what he contracted for. The defendant was in breach of contract if he failed to achieve that aim. By failing to warn Mr Thake of the risk of natural reversal of the vasectomy, he *guaranteed* to make him sterile. He was responsible for the financial loss to the family occasioned by the birth of the unplanned infant.

The Court of Appeal held by a majority that the surgeon never guaranteed to make Mr Thake sterile.[49] Neill LJ found that no reasonable person would have understood the defendant as giving a binding promise that the operation would achieve its purpose. They nevertheless unanimously found for Mr Thake on grounds enabling NHS patients as well as private patients to sue if they are not warned of the risk of nature reversing sterilization of either sex. They held that failure to warn of this risk was negligent. That negligence resulted in Mrs Thake being unaware of her pregnancy until abortion was no longer a safe option. The defendant was responsible for that state of affairs and thus for the birth of the child. He was liable in contract to his private patient. He would have been liable in negligence to an NHS patient.

In *Thake* v. *Maurice*, the defendant conceded that failure to warn the patient of the risk of reversal in vasectomy was negligent. In other cases the crux of the dispute became the question of when such a failure was negligent. Practice among doctors used to differ quite substantially. Professional opinion today is clear. Patients must be told about the risks of reversal of male and female sterilization. Formal guidance from the Department of Health on consent to sterilization, male and female, stresses that such information should routinely be given. The Department's advice, based on expert gynaecological opinion, should be enough to render any failure to warn, a maverick, not a responsible, opinion.

A claim by an NHS patient based on failure to warn of the risks of reversal will succeed. Damages will be limited to the losses pregnancy occasions to the mother, when a healthy mother gives birth to a healthy child in which case bringing a claim may not be worthwhile. It remains open to question whether a private patient suing in contract can evade the bar on recovery of child-rearing costs imposed in *McFarlane*. Could it be argued that what one pays for in arranging a private vasectomy is at the least care to avoid the imposition of the financial burden of further offspring? Questions of whether it is 'fair, just and reasonable' to impose a duty of care in tort are irrelevant in contract.

Finally, who is entitled to sue in respect of failed sterilization? As was the case in *McFarlane*, when vasectomy fails, the man's wife or an established partner enjoys a claim in respect of the loss pregnancy occasions her. She is within the scope of the duty undertaken by the doctor operating on her man. In the reverse case, given that costs of childrearing are excluded from such claims now, a man whose female partner's sterilization failed would find it difficult to identify a recoverable injury to himself.

Subsequent partners are beyond the scope of any duty owed by the surgeon. In *Goodwill* v. *BPAS*[50] a woman became pregnant by a man who had had a vasectomy three years before they met and started a sexual relationship. She claimed that she relied on the expertise of the defendant's clinic who had performed her lover's vasectomy. The Court of Appeal threw out the claim with some disdain. Thorpe LJ said:

It cannot be said that [the doctor] knows or ought to know that he also advises any future sexual partner of his patient who chance to receive his advice at second-hand. Presented with such a set of facts, a doctor is entitled to scorn the suggestion that he owes a duty of care to such a band so uncertain in nature and extent and over such an indefinite future span.[51]

Sometimes, even in this litigious age, people must accept responsibility for themselves.

Involuntary sterilization

Unlike in a number of US states and European countries, no statute in England ever provided for the compulsory sterilization of mentally disabled patients. None the less, in 1987 the House of Lords in *Re B*.[52] authorized the involuntary sterilization of a girl under eighteen. Two years later, in 1989, in *F. v. West Berkshire Health Authority*,[53] their Lordships ruled that sterilization of an adult woman with mental disability was not unlawful if that operation was in her 'best interests'. In theory, a woman may not be sterilized in the interests of society, of her potential children, or on eugenic grounds. She may be sterilized only where she is incapable of making decisions on childbearing for herself, and to protect her health and welfare. In *Re B*. Lord Oliver said of the argument that sterilizing Jeanette violated her right to reproduce: '[A] right to reproduce is of value only if accompanied by the ability to make a choice . . .'[54] Where a woman lacks the ability to choose, and pregnancy may be harmful to her, any right to reproduce may be taken from her. But does it logically follow that just because the woman is incapable of making a rational decision on whether to embark on childbearing, it is in her interest to be sterilized?[55] A number of questions arise.

First, sterilizing a mentally disabled woman 'protects' her from one evil that might befall her if she is enticed or coerced into sexual intercourse. It in no way safeguards her from exploitation by men taking advantage of her, from perversion or sexually transmitted disease. Indeed it is quite likely that, knowing she cannot become pregnant, those caring for her may be less vigilant in attempts to prevent her being enticed into exploitative sexual relations.

Second, one reason advanced for sterilizing severely mentally disabled women is that they can be allowed more freedom. Free from the risk of pregnancy, the woman, although deprived of a right to reproduce, can exercise a 'right' to sexuality. Two difficulties confront this superficially attractive proposition. First, has the woman the capacity to consent to sexual intercourse? T.[56] was said to have a mental age of two. Sexual intercourse with T. would constitute rape. It may well be that other women in cases involving non-consensual sterilization like Jeanette[57] understood enough of what was entailed in sexual intimacy to give consent to intercourse and seemed to invite such contact. Yet intercourse with her would still be a criminal offence. Sexual intercourse with a mentally defective woman is an offence contrary to section 7 of the Sexual Offences Act 1956. Are women being sterilized to facilitate crime? Second, if the rationale for sterilizing mentally disabled women is to enable them to enjoy sexual pleasure, sterilization on its own is not enough. For a right to sexuality to have any meaning, positive steps need to be taken to ensure circumstances where such women could enjoy such pleasure safely and without risk of harm or disease.

The most troubling question remains how to decide who should be sterilized. Did *Re B.* represent the first step on a slippery slope to wholesale sterilization of those whom society regards as unfit to bear children? Sir Brian Rix of MENCAP greeted *Re B.* with horror, claiming that sterilizing mentally disabled girls was to reduce them to the status of pets to be neutered at will. Lord Hailsham condemned Sir Brian's remarks as intemperate. Some decisions subsequent to *Re B.* provide *post facto* justification for Sir Brian's outrage. In *Re M.*[58] Bush J authorized the sterilization of a girl whose limited mental capacity was similar to Jeanette's in *Re B.* The additional factor in *Re M.* was that there was said to be a 50 per cent chance that if M. did conceive her child would also suffer from some degree of mental disability. Bush J affirmed that eugenic considerations are irrelevant to the decision of whether or not M. should be sterilized. He went on to say that none the less it was relevant that, if M. did become pregnant, an abortion on the grounds of foetal handicap would be likely to ensue. Repeated abortions would harm M.'s health, strengthening the case for sterilizing her. Eugenics, forbidden to enter the debate by the front door, slipped in through the back entrance.

Another novel feature in *Re M.* was evidence given by the expert gynaecologist to the effect that, with improvements in tubal surgery, sterilization operations had a 50 to 75 per cent chance of reversibility. Evidence of reversibility was crucial in *Re P.*[59] P. was much less severely disabled. At seventeen she was said to have a mental age of six but unlike M. and Jeanette, she had good communication skills and could cope with her own bodily needs. She seemed to have some maternal feelings, she understood what was involved in sexual intercourse and said she thought it sounded horrid and painful. Her mother feared that as she was of an attractive 'normal' appearance she would be vulnerable to seduction, and that if she became pregnant she might well refuse to have an abortion. The judge acknowledged that P. was a borderline case and even accepted that she might well have the capacity to marry, yet he still authorized her sterilization. In *Re B.* Lord Oliver had agreed with Dillon LJ in the Court of Appeal that '. . . jurisdiction in Wardship proceedings to authorize such an operation is one which should be exercised only in the last resort . . .'[60] Was P. really a case of this magnitude? The judge said that it no longer need be proved that sterilization was the 'last resort'. Professor Robert Winston had testified that reversal of sterilization carried out by clips on the Fallopian tubes achieved a 95 per cent success rate. The House of Lords in *Re B.* had regarded sterilization as irreversible. If that were not so, judges could properly accept less draconian criteria for authorizing 'reversible' surgery. Unfortunately not many gynaecologists do think that they could attain a 95 per cent success rate for reversal of sterilization – and how realistic is it to expect even a mildly disabled woman to be offered reversal surgery? P. understood enough about childbearing for her mother to fear that she would oppose any proposal for an abortion if she became pregnant. True, pregnancy might well be a disaster for P. and her child, but if that is the criterion for involuntary sterilization we are a long way down that slippery slope!

La Forest J in the Canadian Supreme Court declared in *Re Eve*:

The importance of maintaining the physical integrity of a human being ranks high in our scale of values, particularly as it affects the privilege of giving life. I cannot agree that a court can deprive a woman of that privilege for purely social or other non-therapeutic purposes without her consent. The fact that others may suffer inconvenience or hardship from failure to do so cannot be taken into account.[61]

Disquiet about involuntary sterilization in England is even greater where the woman concerned is over eighteen, for as we saw in Chapter 5 (page 117) the House of Lords in *F. v. West Berkshire HA*[62] found that there was no jurisdiction enabling them to *require* doctors to seek a declaration before sterilizing an adult woman. As a matter of good practice their Lordships declared that doctors contemplating such radical surgery should choose to seek a declaration confirming that sterilization was in the woman's interests and in conformity with responsible medical opinion. A Practice Note of the High Court confirms this advice and sets out the procedure for such a declaration.

In practice, the majority of doctors seek a declaration for their own protection. When a court reviews a decision to proceed with involuntary sterilization, do judges much more than rubber stamp the medical decision to sterilize the woman? A swelling tide of recent judgments suggest that judges are beginning to take a more proactive role. In *Re S. (Medical Treatment: Adult Sterilization)* (1998),[63] a twenty-two-year-old woman lived with her parents. She was meticulously cared for and well supervised. The arrangements for her care at home, at the day centre that she attended, and when she was in respite care, meant that the risk of her engaging in sexual intercourse or being subject to sexual assault was exceptionally low. However, her mother feared that S. might be a victim of a sexual assault, and that especially, as her parents grew older and less able to care for her, some care worker might take advantage of her. Johnson J refused to authorize sterilization. Citing Thorpe J in *Re LC (Medical Treatment: Sterilisation)*,[64] he held that the risk of pregnancy must be balanced against the risks and distress of surgery. That risk in S.'s case was, at the time of the hearing, no more than speculative. The case that S.'s interests and welfare demanded immediate surgery was not made out.

In *In Re S. (Adult Patient: Sterilisation)* (2000)[65] the Court of Appeal firmly endorsed a proactive approach to applications to sterilize mentally disabled women. The patient in question was twenty-nine and had severe learning disabilities. She was cared for by her mother but at some point as her mother aged she would have to move into local authority accommodation where she might be at risk of pregnancy. S. also suffered from menstrual problems involving heavy periods, which she did not understand and which distressed her. Her mother sought a declaration that S. could lawfully be sterilized and/or a hysterectomy performed. Medical experts offered a range of views. One option was to fit S. with a Mirena coil, an intra-uterine device that would both prevent pregnancy and alleviate menstrual bleeding. The Court of Appeal refused to authorize sterilization or hysterectomy. Medical opinion was crucial in identifying the responsible options for treating the woman. The choice of which option best met the woman's needs was one for the court. The *Bolam* test is relevant to the first stage of a process of assessing the patient's interests to ensure that any option for treatment proposed conforms to responsible medical opinion. It has no relevance to the second stage of assessing what is best for this patient. The patient's welfare must be the paramount consideration. 'That embraces issues far wider than the medical. Indeed it would be undesirable and probably impossible to set borders on what is relevant to a welfare determination.'[66]

Another important question arose in *In Re S*. Prior judgments[67] had suggested that if a hysterectomy was performed on a mentally disabled woman for therapeutic reasons, no application to court was needed (see page 120). The appeal court made it clear that only where it was absolutely clear that hysterectomy was necessary, for example to deal with uterine cancer or inoperable fibroids, should doctors go ahead without the sanction of the court. 'Borderline' cases should be subject to independent review.[68] One of the expert witnesses in *In Re S.* considered that her heavy periods were not outside normal limits and in 'a woman of normal intelligence no doctor would contemplate a hysterectomy as a means of treating the condition'.[69]

Could a mentally disabled man be subjected to a non-consensual vasectomy? In *F. v. Berkshire Health Authority*, a woman patient in a hospital was, as we saw, sterilized in her 'best interests' after she embarked on a sexual relationship with a fellow (male) patient. Evidence that emerged later suggested that the male patient had a number of other 'girlfriends' in the hospital. Some of these other women were also sterilized in 'their own interests'. Could the man have been sterilized instead? The question never reached the courts at that time. In *Re A. (Medical Treatment: Male Sterilisation)*,[70] A. had Down's Syndrome and suffered from significant learning disabilities. He lived with his elderly mother. He had no understanding of the link between sexual intercourse and pregnancy. While at home he had shown no interest in sex, nor was there much chance of him establishing sexual relationships. His mother feared that when she could no longer care for him and he moved into local authority care, he might form a sexual relationship and father a child. He would be unable to understand the concept of paternity and unable to undertake any sort of responsibility as a father. Thus an application was made to sterilize A. The heart of the problem before the court was whether vasectomy could be said to be 'necessary' for A.'s welfare. He would not become pregnant or face the risks and discomfort a woman with similar disabilities confronts as a possible consequence of sexual intercourse. The Court of Appeal refused to authorize a vasectomy for A. They did not rule out the possibility that a case might be made out to justify non-consensual sterilization of a man with mental disabilities. In A.'s case the risk of his entering into a sexual relationship was assessed as low. Like S. he was carefully supervised. Dame Elizabeth Butler Sloss P wisely noted:

If sterilization did take place, it would not save A from the possibility of exploitation nor help him cope with the emotional implications of any closer relationship that he might form[71]

The Court of Appeal rightly rejected any notion that sexual 'equality' required that if women could be sterilized in their 'best interests', men must be treated 'the same'. They focused on the welfare of A. himself. In recognizing that preventing pregnancy does not protect men from potentially adverse consequences or sexual relationships do the courts open the way to an equivalent view of cases involving women?

12

Assisted Conception[1]

It is estimated that one in ten, or even as many as one in six couples, have difficulty conceiving naturally and seek medical help. The ability of doctors to give that help has made incredible progress. The development of *in vitro* fertilization (IVF) and the birth of the first 'test-tube' baby, Louise Brown, in 1978 gave hope to thousands of childless couples. The advent of surrogacy offered the chance of children even to women who had undergone hysterectomy. Yet for every man or woman who rejoiced at what the doctors could now do, there were those who condemned the technical advances as unnatural and contrary to the will of God. These reproductive technologies have brought heartbreak too, for success rates remain low. Reproductive technologies cannot work miracles.

The advances in medicine resulting in Louise Brown's birth did not just generate moral controversy. Concerns arose about the safety of the 'new' technologies. Fears grew about the competence of practitioners and basic issues such as the hygienic storage of human gametes.[2] Such was the furore created that the government established a committee under Dame Mary Warnock (now Baroness Warnock) to consider:

. . . recent and potential developments in medicine and science related to human fertilization and embryology; to consider what policies and safeguards should be applied, including consideration of the social, ethical and legal implications of these developments; and to make recommendations.

The Warnock Report was published in 1984.[3] It fuelled rather than stilled controversy. Media attention focused on the Report's recommendation to permit research on embryos of up to fourteen days' development. Three members of the committee dissented. The status to be accorded to the human embryo cannot help but be an emotive and complex question. Alas, the publicity accorded to that one part of the Warnock Report distorted debate on the Report as a whole, and contributed to the shameful delay in implementing any of Warnock's proposals. The central plank of the Report was its insistence that the burgeoning business of reproductive medicine should be regulated and the status of children born as a result of all the new and various forms of assisted conception should be clarified. Infertile patients needed protection against charlatans. Medical practitioners needed a framework within which to practise legally and ethically. Children were entitled to a proper family structure, above all to know who in law were their mother and father. Warnock's practical recommendations on all these matters remained in abeyance until enacted in a modified form in the Human Fertilisation and Embryology Act 1990. The Act reached the statute book only after vitriolic debate in Parliament and the publication of two further reports by the government, a general consultation document early in 1987[4] and a White Paper[5] later that year. Both were designed as well-meaning attempts to secure an impossible consensus.

The 1990 Act remains the principal plank for legal regulation of reproductive technologies in the United Kingdom. Developments in medicine and a plethora of legal challenges to the Act over the last twelve months cast doubt on whether, in 2003, 1990 legislation meets society's needs. Alas, enduring controversy surrounding the creation of embryos outside women's bodies and debate about who should have access to assisted conception means that rational debate is rare. Politicians of today are no more enthusiastic than their predecessors to re-open debates on embryo research or, for example, gay couples' rights to have children.

Avoiding questions of reproductive rights will become more difficult as the impact of the Human Rights Act 1998 becomes apparent. Article 8 requires respect for private and family life. Article 12 guarantees the right to marry and found a family.[6] Could a lesbian couple denied access for fertility treatment argue violation of Articles 8, 12 and 14 (prohibiting discriminatory treatment)? If British clinics in the main continue to refuse to treat women over fifty five might a woman of sixty succeed in challenging such a policy?

The Human Fertilisation and Embryology Authority

The Human Fertilisation and Embryology Authority (HFEA), is a statutory licensing authority, established by section 5 of the Human Fertilization and Embryology Act.[7] Schedule I of the Act prescribes the authority's membership. Neither the chairman nor the deputy chairman may be a medical practitioner or anyone else professionally involved in embryo research or assisted conception. At least one third, but fewer than half, of the members must be persons so involved in research or infertility treatment. Interestingly the Secretary of State for Health, who appoints members of the HFEA, is directed to '. . . have regard to the desirability of ensuring that the proceedings of the Authority, and the discharge of its functions are informed by the views of both men and women'. This has resulted in a substantial number of female members of the HFEA.

The HFEA is endowed with impressive powers. Section 3 of the Act makes it a criminal offence to bring about the creation of an embryo outside the human body except in pursuance of a licence granted by the HFEA. Any infertility treatment requiring the creation of an embryo by means of *in vitro* fertilization (IVF), that is the creation of a 'test-tube' embryo, *must* be licensed. Section 4 prohibits any storage of gametes (sperm or eggs), and the use of donor sperm or eggs, without a licence from the HFEA. Any infertility treatment involving artificial insemination by donor (DI)[8] or egg donation is generally unlawful unless licensed by the HFEA. Sections 3 and 4 also outlaw a number of specific procedures, for example, creating human/animal hybrids. Those issues will be dealt with further in the next chapter. This chapter concentrates on the role of the HFEA in relation to, and the legal principles governing, assisted conception.

Any clinic that offers IVF or DI is subject to the control of the HFEA. It cannot operate lawfully without a licence and its staff and procedures are strictly monitored and controlled. Failure to comply with HFEA guidelines about, for example, safety procedures, numbers of embryos to be implanted, selection of donors or assessment of patients may lead to forfeiture of that licence. However, one key area of reproductive medicine is beyond the ambit of the Act and the control of the HFEA. Gametes Intra-Fallopian Transfer (GIFT) is a procedure whereby eggs are taken from an infertile woman and sperm from her partner. Eggs and sperm are mixed together in the laboratory and returned to the woman's body before the process of fertilization begins. There is no creation of an embryo outside the body of a woman, which would require to be licensed. There are arguments that a provision in section 1, the section defining embryo (section 1(2)(a)), which provides that the Act does apply to an embryo created partly *in vitro* and partly in the body, may 'catch' GIFT.

But this is unlikely as, in GIFT, fertilization does not even begin until the eggs and sperm are returned to the woman's body. Section 1(2)(a) is designed to cover a procedure whereby if a woman undergoes IVF at a clinic with no facilities to store embryos, the 'surplus' embryos are collected in a minute glass tube, which is then placed in the woman's vagina. She acts as an 'incubator', and goes to a clinic with storage facilities. There 'her' embryos are removed and frozen. Attempts in Parliament to include GIFT expressly within the 1990 Act failed. This is despite evidence that GIFT is more likely than IVF to result in multiple pregnancies, with attendant risk to mother and children, and so to overstretched neonatal facilities.[9]

How is the HFEA financed? By enacting the Human Fertilisation and Embryology Act the government appears to be giving official blessing to IVF and other means of assisted conception. It is a pretty empty blessing for the Authority's budget derives primarily from fees from licences granted to clinics. So far little extra money is allocated from the NHS budget to fund assisted conception, albeit better NHS provision is promised. The money it will cost a clinic to get a licence means that assisted conception will continue to be offered mainly in the private sector, with few NHS clinics offering a full service. The cost of paying for a licence could constitute an incentive for poorer clinics to offer only GIFT, which does not require a licence.

Whatever its demerits, however, the Human Fertilization and Embryology Act 1990 made significant changes in the law governing the various forms of assisted conception.

Donor insemination (DI)

Where it is the man who is infertile, a couple may be offered the opportunity to have a child by another man, by artificial insemination by donor (DI). As a procedure, DI is far from new and is so simple that it can be, and often is, performed without medical assistance. The problems are legal and ethical, not medical. Let us look first at DI in its simplest, least controversial, setting. Until 1987 a child born as a result of DI was born into a legal limbo. Even if his mother was a married woman whose husband, the 'social' father, had agreed to DI, the child was in law the illegitimate child of his mother and the donor. He had no legal relationship with his 'social' father. Should the 'social' father leave the child's mother before the birth, the child had no claim to maintenance against him. If his 'social' father died intestate, 'his' child had no claim on his estate. Moreover, should the 'social' father seek to assert parentage by registering the child as his, he committed perjury! No wonder DI developed as a procedure shrouded in secrecy. The first attempt to clarify the status of DI children came in the Family Law Reform Act 1987. Section 27 of that Act provided that where a married woman received DI with her husband's consent, the child was in law the child of the woman and her husband. Section 28 and 29 of the Human Fertilization and Embryology Act go a stage further. They apply not just to DI but to any treatment involving the use of donor sperm. So if a couple undergo IVF using donor sperm, not the man's own gametes, section 28 governs his, and the donor's, relationship with the child. Section 28(2) re-enacts the provision relating to DI children born within marriage, deeming the child to be the husband's child[10] and giving the husband all the usual privileges of fatherhood, including an entitlement to contact with his child should the marriage break down.[11] Section 28(3) extends that provision to children born to unmarried couples seeking DI together because the male partner is infertile. Whenever DI is provided for a woman and a man together by a person to whom a licence applies, the man is to be treated as the father of the child. That means he is subject to the same rights and obligations as any other natural father not married to the mother of his child.[12] The apparent simplicity of these provisions about legal paternity is misleading. What 'together' means has triggered a shower of judicial activity. Evidence that at the time the mother received DI she was living with a male partner is not sufficient. He must be an active participant in the process.[13] What happens if a couple have been treated 'together', but their relationship subsequently breaks down? *In Re R. (Parental Responsibility: IVF Baby)*[14] an unmarried couple were treated with IVF using donor sperm and several embryos were created. An unsuccessful attempt at implantation took place and the remaining embryos were frozen. The couple parted and the woman embarked on a new relationship. She returned to the clinic and was successfully treated with embryos taken from storage. Hedley J upheld her former partner's claim to be legal father of the child! The Court of Appeal restored some common sense to the law. Where the man was neither married to the mother nor was he the genetic father of the child, the relevant date determining whether the couple were treated together is the date the embryos were placed in the woman. At that date this couple were no longer together, and the former partner had no legitimate claim on the child.

Further complexities relating to section 28 (3) will become apparent later in this chapter when we examine the law relating to surrogacy.

Section 28(4) provides that wherever the woman's husband or partner is to be treated as the child's legal father, no other person is in any sense the legal father of the child, that is all links between the donor and the child are severed. Even when no husband or partner is to be deemed to be the child's father, where a donor donates sperm and gives the appropriate consent to donation required by the Act in Schedule 3, he is not to be treated as the child's father.[15] Thus, whenever DI is provided in a licensed clinic, in accordance with the rules laid down in the Act, the donor has no legal relationship to the child. The child has no claim on the donor. The donor can never assert any parental rights.

The tragic and extraordinary case of *Leeds Teaching Hospitals NHS Trust* v. *Mr and Mrs A.*[16] posed a dilemma for the courts. Mr and Mrs A. were undergoing fertility treatment at the same clinic as Mr and Mrs B. An error resulted in Mrs A.'s eggs being fertilized with Mr B.'s sperm. The mistake probably only came to light because Mr and Mrs A. were white and Mr and Mrs B. were black. Mr A. argued that section 28 meant that he, as Mrs A.'s husband, was the legal father of the twins to whom Mrs A. gave birth. The President of the Family Division disagreed. Mr B. was not a sperm *donor*. The clinic's mistake undermined the whole purpose of section 28, which was designed to address paternity where a man donated his sperm to be used in the treatment of a woman not his wife or partner. Mr B. intended his sperm to be used to treat Mrs B. and only Mrs B.

However, section 28 (3) and (4) rules severing the link between the sperm donor and his genetic offspring apply only when insemination takes place under medical supervision in a licensed clinic. Should a woman find a willing sperm donor prepared to donate fresh sperm and then she inseminates herself, the donor remains in law the child's father. Should a couple seek medically supervised DI abroad, the 'social' father has no obligations to or claims to the child. A couple sought treatment in Rome using donor sperm as part of IVF. The woman gave birth to twins. Alas, the relationship between the couple broke down. When the mother sought support for the children under the Child Support Act, her former partner denied any responsibility for children who he contended were not his. The court reluctantly found in his favour. Section 28 (3) applied only to treatment in clinics licensed in this country.[17]

The limited application of section 28 (3) and (4) provokes a number of questions. Insofar as the principles clarifying the child's relationship to his 'social' father, the man who jointly with his mother sought his birth, are territorially limited, is this justifiable? Should the father have been able to reject his children? The provisions of section 28 also force us to consider why self-insemination remains totally unregulated. Where DI is provided in a licensed clinic, stored sperm are used and subjected to rigorous testing including HIV screening. Using fresh sperm is a risky business. But could the simple process of self-insemination be outlawed when very obviously no restrictions surround sexual intercourse? Women and couples may prefer the privacy of self-insemination, by-passing intrusive assessment of their personal circumstances and parental fitness. Could it be argued that Article 8 of the Human Rights Convention protecting the right to respect for private and family life would be incompatible with attempts to police self-insemination? On a practical level, it is difficult to see how any rules banning self-insemination could ever be enforced.

DI and single mothers

An increasing number of women who have no male partner want to have a child. Such women may reject as distasteful the prospect of a 'one-night stand' to get pregnant, and not want a transient partner to have any legal claim on 'her' child. The woman may prefer not to engage in heterosexual intercourse. During the passage of the Human Fertilisation and Embryology Act, attempts were made in Parliament to outlaw DI for women without a male partner. They were nearly successful. A compromise was embodied in section 13(5) of the Act. Section 13(5) provides, apparently innocuously, that a licence holder treating a woman must take into account the welfare of any child who may be born as a result of treatment, *including the need of that child for a father*. This is a mandatory condition of any licence granted by the HFEA. A number of MPs and peers hoped that the HFEA would ban DI, and other forms of assisted conception, for all single women save in the most exceptional circumstances. The HFEA Code of Practice will disappoint them. The HFEA directs clinics to assess the prospective welfare of the child with 'skill and sensitivity'. Account should be taken of the mother's ability to provide a stable and supportive environment, her health and ability to look after the child, her age and overall capacity to meet the child's needs. The presence of other people within the mother's family and social circles willing and able to support her and share in the child's upbringing must be addressed. What the HFEA requires is that clinics consider whether the woman seeking to have a child outside a conventional heterosexual relationship can provide an environment for the child in which he can flourish. In making such an assessment no doubt the mother's ability to provide from among her family and friends a male role model, a quasi-father figure, may be important.

Should a woman be helped to have a child who will have no father? The effect of section 28(6) severing all links between a DI donor and child is that a child born to a woman with no partner is literally father-less. It is argued that society cannot allow fatherless children to be born by DI because children need parents of both sexes to develop properly. Yet countless children are born by natural means to women alone, and countless more lose contact with their 'legal' father. If it is asserted that a woman unable to have children by the usual means must be denied help via assisted conception, unless she has a male partner, a case must be made out that her child's welfare is likely to be imperilled by father-lessness. Perhaps never having a father is less traumatic than losing one. A woman who sets out to have a child alone is not misled into think-ing she can always rely on a man for support. Finally, whenever argu-ments are advanced to ban DI for women without a male partner, those arguments should be analysed carefully. Is the essence of the argument that *any* woman without a male partner should not be helped, or that lesbians must not be allowed to use DI to have children? I suspect that it is often the latter. We should not forget that banning single women or lesbian couples from licensed clinics does not prevent them practis-ing self-insemination. It simply bars access to DI in safer, supervised conditions.

Artificial insemination by husband (AIH)

There are rare cases where a woman's husband or partner is fertile, but cannot beget a child because he is incapable of normal intercourse. His sperm may be used to impregnate his wife by artificial means. Or the man may not produce sufficient healthy and mobile sperm to achieve fertilization in the usual way. Such a man may be helped by Intra Cytoplasmic Sperm Injection (ICSI). A single sperm is injected into the cytoplasm (outer casing) of the woman's egg. IVF is combined with AIH (artificial insemination using the husband's or partner's sperm). The child's legal status will be just the same as if she were conceived naturally.

Where a marriage has never been consummated because normal intercourse was not possible, AIH will not prevent the wife from petitioning the court to annul the marriage,[18] although on policy grounds the court may refuse a decree if they consider that in having the child the wife approbated the marriage. The child will remain legitimate even if his parents' marriage is later annulled, for they were married when he was conceived and non-consummation only renders a marriage voidable by the court. It does not mean that the marriage was never valid at all.

The facility to store sperm by freezing may cause further problems if a man banks sperm for later insemination of his wife or partner. He may choose to do so before undergoing vasectomy, or treatment that might damage his fertility, or treatment that might pose a risk to children later conceived. Chemotherapy for cancer is an obvious example. To whom do the sperm belong if the man dies? May the wife ask for insemination then, and if so, what is the child's status? As long ago as 1984 in France, a court ordered a sperm bank to release her deceased husband's sperm to his widow.[19] The attempt at AIH failed and she did not conceive. In the United Kingdom, the Warnock report recommended that posthumous AIH should be actively discouraged.[20] No express provision limiting posthumous AIH is to be found in the Human Fertilization and Embryology Act, but section 28(6)(b) provides that where the sperm of any man, or an embryo created from his sperm, is used after his death, he (the deceased man) is not to be treated as the father of the child. If a widow is inseminated with her dead husband's sperm, a child resulting from AIH has no claim on his natural father's estate. Again he is a child who is legally fatherless.

The issue of whether a wife has a 'right' to posthumous AIH arose in the poignant case of Diane Blood. Diane and Stephen Blood had been married for four years before Mr Blood was struck down with meningitis. He lapsed into a coma and died. Shortly before his death, at Mrs Blood's request, doctors used electro-ejaculation to take sperm from her dying husband which was then stored at a licensed fertility clinic. The HFEA instructed the clinic not to treat Mrs Blood, nor to release her husband's sperm to her so that she could seek treatment abroad. The HFEA ruled that the recovery and storage of Stephen Blood's sperm was unlawful. The taking of sperm did not comply with Schedule 3 of the 1990 Act, which imposes a mandatory requirement for *written* 'effective' consent. No such formal consent had ever been given by Mr Blood, although his widow argued that they had planned to start a family, and that Stephen had told her that in the kind of tragic circumstances that ultimately overtook him she should do just as she did.

Mrs Blood went to court to challenge the HFEA by way of an application for judicial review alleging that it was the HFEA who were acting unlawfully. The High Court upheld the HFEA, but Mrs Blood succeeded in the Court of Appeal.[21] The appeal court agreed that the taking of sperm without Mr Blood's written consent was unlawful as it contravened the 1990 Act, and constituted a common law assault. However, the court expressed sympathy with Mrs Blood's agonizing situation, believing that she had acted in good faith and there could be no question of prosecution. Treatment in the United Kingdom would be unlawful but the Court of Appeal held that the HFEA had failed to give sufficient consideration to European Union Law.[22] Section 24 (4) of the 1990 Act permits the HFEA to issue directions authorizing the export of sperm. Articles 59 and 60 of the Treaty of Rome guarantee certain fundamental freedoms, which include a right to receive services. Such a right is not absolute, but any limitations on that right must be justified. Given that the court had ruled that taking sperm without written consent was unlawful, the circumstances of Mrs Blood's case would not be repeated. The Court of Appeal directed the HFEA to reconsider Mrs Blood's request to export sperm. They did so and granted her permission to take her husband's sperm to Belgium where she finally received treatment and gave birth to a healthy son, Liam. A second son was born to her after further treatment abroad in 2002.

Liam's birth is not the end of the story. The narrow grounds of the appeal court's ruling in Mrs Blood's favour left domestic law unchanged. No woman in a similar position would benefit. The law was clear. Unless the deceased had given formal written consent to storing and use of his sperm,[23] no British clinic could treat his widow or former partner. The fertility specialist Lord Winston introduced a Bill to allow for exceptional cases where written consent could be dispensed with. The Bill did not proceed. Professor Sheila McLean conducted an extensive review of the law on consent and removal of gametes but recommended that no change in the law should be made.[24] Mrs Blood persuaded an MP to attempt to introduce a Bill to change the law regarding legal paternity of a posthumous AIH child so that his genetic father's name could appear on his birth certificate.[25] The government undertook to amend the law relating to registering posthumous AIH births, but has not yet done so. A court ruling that section 28(6)(b) is incompatible with Article 8 of the Human Rights Convention should concentrate its mind!

The *Blood* case leaves more questions unanswered than it resolves. If Stephen Blood's sperm had been lawfully stored, would Diane Blood have been able to demand treatment? It seems unlikely as the ultimate decision remains with the clinician.[26] In the context of private treatment a widow might seek to argue that she has a contractual right to AIH. The possibility remains that attempts will be made to contend that the frozen sperm form part of the deceased husband's estate. Should a court accept that sperm can be classified as 'property' and 'inherited' by the wife, it would logically follow that she could demand 'her' sperm, but she could still not require the DI clinic to inseminate her.[27] In the light of the underlying philosophy of the 1990 Act, it seems unlikely such a 'property' argument would succeed.

Female infertility

Female infertility poses greater medical problems in many cases. IVF, egg donations and surrogacy are just some of the many developments in treatment. All were primarily designed to overcome female infertility but some have also proved useful where it is the man who is sub-fertile.

Test-tube babies (IVF)

A woman who ovulates normally, but whose Fallopian tubes are absent or damaged, will never conceive naturally because the eggs that she produces cannot travel to meet sperm and be fertilized. The test-tube baby procedure (*in vitro* fertilization or IVF) offers such women the chance of their own child. Eggs are removed from the woman and fertilized in the laboratory with sperm taken from the woman's husband or partner. The embryo, or embryos, thus created are carefully tested and then implanted in the mother's womb. IVF is also resorted to in cases of 'unexplained infertility' where the woman ovulates, her Fallopian tubes are clear and her partner provides healthy sperm, yet no pregnancy results. No questions of family law arise from IVF. The child has the same relationship to her parents as if she were naturally conceived. If the parents are married at the time of fertilization or marry before the birth, the child is a marital child and both parents share parental responsibility. When the parents are unmarried, the father is in the same position as any unmarried father, that is he may apply to the court to share parental responsibility with his partner. It is the possible variations of IVF, where eggs or sperm (or both) are provided by a third party, which raise questions of family law. A woman may be infertile because of blocked Fallopian tubes *and* have an infertile male partner. Donor sperm can be used to fertilise her eggs, again returning the resulting embryo or embryos to her womb. As we have seen, a child born as a result of this combination of IVF and DI is to be treated in law just like any other DI child. If the woman is married, and her husband consents to IVF and DI, the child is a child of the marriage. The husband, not the donor, is the legal father. If the couple are unmarried but seek treatment together, again the male partner, the 'social' father, is the legal father of the child.[28]

Egg donation and embryo transplants

Some women, by reason of congenital defect or as a result of disease, do not ovulate at all. They can never conceive naturally. Intensive hormone treatment helps many women to start or re-start ovulation, but for a number that treatment proves fruitless. They can be helped by egg donation but they can never have a child that is genetically theirs. Where the woman carries a genetic disease, egg donation may also be used to avoid transmitting that disease to her children. Eggs can be taken from a fertile woman (the donor), fertilized in the laboratory with the infertile woman's partner's sperm, and the resulting embryo or embryos implanted in the infertile woman's (the recipient's) womb. Should both partners be infertile, or both be carriers of genetic disease, egg and sperm donors may be used, and an embryo created and implanted in the woman's womb that is genetically unrelated to either partner.

The first question arising from egg donation is: who is the legal mother of the child? Is it the donor, or the woman who carries and bears the child? Section 27(1) of the Human Fertilisation and Embryology Act gives a clear answer:

The woman who is carrying or has carried a child as a result of the placing in her of an embryo or of sperm and eggs, *and no other woman* [my italics], is to be treated as the mother of the child.

The woman who gives birth to the child is its mother. The genetic 'mother' has no legal claim on the child, nor has he any claim on her.

When the infertile woman's partner provides the sperm, the legal status of the child is identical to a child naturally conceived by that woman. If donor sperm are used, the same rules deeming the male partner to be the legal father apply as they would in any use of DI in a licensed clinic.

As the Human Fertilisation and Embryology Act clarifies the legal status of a child born as a result of egg donation or embryo transplant, are there any remaining legal or ethical problems related to the procedure? The Warnock Committee saw no ethical objection to egg donation. They regarded it as the female counterpart of DI. Clearly anyone objecting to the separation of sexual intercourse and procreation, or to the use of third parties for reproductive purposes, will object to egg donation as they oppose DI. But such objections are confined to a relatively small sector of society.

Unlike DI, however, egg donation is attended by some risk to the donor. Egg donation requires a surgical procedure, an invasion of the donor's body. Her consent is essential if her doctor is to avoid liability for battery. Two problems exist with consent to egg donation. First, to collect only one egg at a time is a pretty futile exercise. Standard IVF practice is to give a woman drugs to induce her to supra-ovulate, to produce several eggs at once. A number of eggs are fertilized, the best embryos are implanted, defective embryos are disposed of, and 'spare' embryos are frozen for future use. Supra-ovulation carries risks to the health and in a very, very few cases to the life of the woman. A woman undergoing IVF runs identical risks. She does so to have 'her' baby. Egg donors are asked to be a means to an end. They are asked to risk harm with no prospect of benefit to themselves. Healthy volunteers who agree to participate in medical research are invited to act in a similarly altruistic manner. It could not be right to prohibit altruism, but what is quite clear is that there must be no doubt that the donor has given full and free consent. She should be given as much information as possible about the risks of egg collection. Egg donors remain in short supply[29] and scientists are keen to explore new sources. Three possibilities are on the horizon.

First, women will soon be able to store their own eggs for future use. A woman about to undergo chemotherapy could store eggs to preserve her fertility. A woman who at the peak of her fertility does not yet want to embark on childbearing might choose to store eggs for future use. Freezing eggs has proved more difficult than freezing sperm.[30] More damage is caused when the eggs are thawed. It is likely that freezing sections of ovarian tissue will be more successful. When the woman wishes to contemplate pregnancy the ovarian tissue (with eggs intact) is simply re-implanted.

Most of the problems surrounding storing eggs and ovarian tissue taken from the intending mother herself are generated by questions about the safety of the procedure. For example, if ovarian tissue is taken from a woman about to undergo chemotherapy for cancer, is there a risk of re-implanting cancer cells in her? Legal and ethical dilemmas are not absent. If a child of seven is about to undergo chemotherapy, can her parents authorize surgical removal of ovarian tissue in case their daughter, once an adult, wants to have children? Is such a procedure in the child's interests? Perhaps that will depend on the depths of the immediate risk and distress posed to the child by additional surgery. The prospect of adult women choosing to 'bank' eggs for future use appals some people but nothing in the 1990 Act forbids such a procedure.

Secondly, it seems that it may be technically possible to collect immature eggs from aborted foetuses and subject them to a process of maturation.[31] Controversy over such a possibility led to a rare amendment of the Human Fertilisation and Embryology Act. Section 3a now bans treatment using eggs derived from foetuses, although research can still lawfully continue.

Finally, ovarian tissue might be taken from dead women, just as kidneys and other organs are taken from cadaver donors. Such a process would need to meet the legal conditions currently provided for by both the Human Tissue Act 1961 *and* Schedule 3 of the 1990 Act. Express consent to donation of ovarian tissue must be required. Proxy consent by surviving relatives will not suffice. The inadequacy of the Human Tissue Act discussed in Chapter 19 needs to be remedied before any such 'transplant' is contemplated.

Post-menopausal motherhood[32]

Egg donation offers women the opportunity to extend their reproductive lives. Several babies have been born to women who have undergone the menopause. Eggs are collected from a donor and implanted in the post-menopausal mother whose womb has been restored to a premenopausal state by hormone treatment. In the United Kingdom a woman of fifty-eight gave birth to twins in 2002. Her partner of sixty-four tragically died of a heart attack a few weeks after the birth. France prohibits treatment of women past the normal age of childbearing. Post-menopausal motherhood causes controversy here. The crux of the question is not the post-menopausal state itself. Some women suffer a premature menopause in their twenties and few argue that they should be denied help. The question is whether women over fifty, or even sixty should be assisted to have a child.

Those opposed to treating older women focus on the child. If a woman gives birth at fifty-eight, she will be seventy-six before the child is legally an adult. It is more likely that her health may decline or the child face the death of his mother than if she were merely forty. Others point out that men fairly often beget children naturally in their fifties and later. Is it discriminatory to prohibit helping women to do what nature permits men to do? Perhaps what we should ask is whether it is morally responsible for either men or women to create a child at an age when the ability to care for that child is diminishing. In that case we need to consider if it is ethical to assist another person to do something irresponsible.[33]

Recruiting donors: encouraging vendors

What else could be done to encourage recruitment of donors? In its submission to Warnock, the RCOG suggested that eggs might 'conveniently' be collected from patients undergoing sterilization or hysterectomy. Such action might be seen as avoiding unnecessary surgical interference by using women already scheduled for surgery. The procedure for collecting eggs is itself now relatively simple and risk-free. The risks centre on supra-ovulation. A woman asked to donate eggs concurrently with other surgery is in effect asked to agree to a further risky and, for her, unnecessary procedure. Will she be in a proper state of mind to give a full and free consent? Will she feel constrained to 'help out' the doctor treating her? Of particular concern has been the practice of some clinics in offering free sterilization to women who agree to be donors. Waiting lists for NHS sterilizations can be lengthy. For a woman to be offered a private sterilization free of charge is a powerful inducement to agree to donate eggs. The Human Fertilisation and Embryology Act prohibits payments, of money or other benefits, for eggs and sperm (gametes), unless authorized by directions from the HFEA.[34] It has not outlawed such non-financial incentives. Another sort of inducement to egg 'donation' is 'egg-sharing'. A private clinic offers free IVF to a woman prepared to donate half her eggs to a paying client. 'Egg sharing' avoids subjecting the donor to risks unrelated to her own treatment. It raises questions of free consent, however. Does 'egg sharing' subject the potential donor to a nigh on unbearable pressure to agree because otherwise she may have no chance at all of treatment by IVF? How will she feel if the recipient has a successful pregnancy and she does not?

If 'inducements' to donate eggs are permitted, it may be argued overt payments should be allowed. Sperm is also now in short supply. The availability of healthy mobile sperm from UK donors is falling. The HFEA have had to resort to permitting the import of sperm. Currently section 12(e) of the 1990 Act prohibits payment for gametes (eggs or sperm) or embryos unless payment is authorized by directions from the HFEA. Payments for eggs or embryos have never been permitted. Payments for sperm became routine. Advertisements appear in local and student newspapers, in teaching hospital areas, and private DI clinics offering £15 per 'donation'. That may seem a small sum but represents a visit or two to the pub for an impecunious student. In 1998 the HFEA announced its intention of withdrawing directions permitting such payments. The outcry from clinics prompted the Authority to back down, continuing to allow £15 payments plus expenses.[35] Clinics fear that without payments sperm donors will become a scarce commodity. Is it right to pay sperm donors? In the UK the governing philosophy for donation of all other bodily products has historically rested on the 'gift relationship'.[36] Blood is given freely. It is a criminal offence to buy or sell a kidney.[37] It can scarcely be ethical to pay for sperm but not eggs, when egg donors face greater risk and trauma. For a market in eggs to work, payment would need to be substantial. Donation of eggs or sperm should be allowed only as a considered act of altruism. There may be no physical risk in donating sperm, but have young donors considered the implications of their act? How might they feel if later in life they are unable to have children of their own? None the less powerful voices now argue for permitting payment and letting the market regulate supply.[38]

If the main argument *for* paying for sperm is the problem of supply, maybe British clinics should look to a wider source of donors than, as at present, students, and mainly medical students at that. In France all donations are made without payment. The donor must be a mature man who has proved his fertility. Normally the consent of his partner will also be obtained. Donation becomes a 'couple-to-couple' donation and there seem to be no problems finding suitable donors. In relation to supply of eggs, other strategies should be explored. A number of women appear to be prepared to donate eggs to an infertile sister or close friend, but not to the world at large. In the United Kingdom, reservations are expressed about the ethics of sister-to-sister donation, or the use of known donors, including close relatives. There are concerns about problems of identity for the child, and potential conflicts between its 'mothers'. No prohibition on such donations is made by the Human Fertilisation and Embryology Act; perhaps positive encouragement is called for.

Freezing gametes and embryos

It is possible to freeze and store eggs, sperm and embryos. The first British baby to 'start life' as a frozen embryo was born in Manchester in 1985. Storage of gametes and embryos is lawful only if licensed by the HFEA.[39] The Act originally prescribed a maximum statutory storage period of ten years for gametes and five years for embryos.[40] The technology to freeze gametes and embryos is central to advances in techniques of assisted conception. A couple undergoing IVF can have several embryos created, and the 'surplus' stored for later attempts at pregnancy if the first effort fails, or for a second child if all goes well. Several sets of IVF 'twins', born years apart, have now been delivered.

The problems arising from freezing embryos are these. Is the process safe and, if so, for how long can gametes and embryos safely be stored? Is the process acceptable to society? Who decides the ultimate fate of stored gametes and embryos? Experience has established that healthy babies can be born from frozen sperm and embryos. How long such material can safely be stored remains in dispute. In opting for maximum storage periods of ten years for gametes and five years for embryos the Act sought to impose limits recognized as safe in 1990. Freezing inevitably means that at the end of the storage period there will be embryos left unused. The Act requires that such embryos be 'allowed to perish'.[41] In 1996 the five-year storage period came to an end, and thousands of embryos were to be disposed of. In many cases clinics had lost all contact with the gamete donors (or parents). A public outcry greeted the fate of what the media styled the 'orphan embryos'. Finally the government used powers under the 1990 Act to extend the storage period for embryos from five to ten years in certain cases.[42] The furore around orphan embryos highlights paradoxical attitudes to embryos. If embryos can be equated to orphan children, they should not be created doomed to die. If children, these 'orphans' should have been offered to other infertile couples for adoption. If embryos are morally insignificant, they should be put to some good use, whether that use was to help other infertile couples or forward research.

As to the fate of embryos in storage prior to their expiry date, the Act requires anyone storing gametes or embryos to decide what may or may not be done with those embryos before any treatment begins. The donors of the genetic material decide its fate in foreseeable circumstances.

Regulating assisted conception

The Human Fertilisation and Embryology Act only provides a basic framework of rules governing assisted conception in the United Kingdom. The Act entrusts to the Human Fertilisations and Embryology Authority (HFEA) powers to fill in the details of those rules and to regulate the practical and ethical problems of assisted conception. Central to the Act are its provisions on consent.

Schedule 3 expressly endorses the crucial importance of free and informed consent in assisted conception. Before a valid consent can be given, be it to IVF treatment, or the storage of gametes (eggs or sperm) or embryos, or donation of gametes, the potential patient or donor must be '. . . given a suitable opportunity to receive proper counselling about the implications of taking the proposed steps'.[43] He or she must also be provided with such relevant information as is proper. Consent to the use of any embryo must specify whether it is for the use only of the couple seeking treatment, or may be used to treat another couple, or may be used for research purposes.[44] The capacity to fertilize several embryos and freeze 'surplus' embryos means that once a couple seeking IVF have completed their family, 'surplus' embryos will not be needed by them. 'Their' embryos cannot be given to another couple or used for research purposes without their consent. Similar rules apply to the storage of gametes.[45] Consent given to the storage of gametes must specify what is to be done with the gametes if the donor dies.

The rules detailing the matters that consent under the Act must cover serve three purposes. First, they assign to the people providing embryos or gametes the right to decide what is done with their genetic material, allaying fears that by agreeing to IVF treatment they give up any right to control the fate of 'their' embryos. Second, they ensure that provision is made to decide on the fate of embryos and gametes should the donors meet with death or disaster.[46] In Australia just such a dilemma arose when a wealthy couple died in an air crash, leaving several embryos in storage in the state of Victoria. The husband's children by his first marriage vehemently opposed use of the embryos, fearing any child might claim a share in their inheritance. No child born in England could claim from his dead 'parents' estate. Whether he should ever have the chance to be born at all is a decision his genetic parents are required to take before any attempt at his creation is begun. Third, they should avoid any dispute about 'custody' of embryos if a relationship breaks down.[47]

Alas this laudable aim has not been fulfilled. The rules governing 'consent' to use of embryos or gametes require that at the date when any fertility treatment is to be initiated, there must be an *effective* consent from the man or woman whose gametes are stored, or from whose gametes the frozen embryo was created. In *Mrs U. v. Centre for Reproductive Medicine*,[48] Mr U. had consented to removal and storage of his sperm for use in IVF treatment of Mrs U. Initially, his consent specifically extended to authorizing posthumous use of his sperm by Mrs U. should he die prematurely. The clinic's policy was opposed to posthumous insemination and, after a conversation with a member of the clinic's staff, Mr U. changed his mind and altered the consent form. Not long afterwards Mr U. died suddenly. The Court of Appeal held that his widow could not lawfully be treated using his sperm. There was no consent for such use current at the time of her husband's death. The judges rejected Mrs U.'s claim that her husband's original consent for posthumous insemination remained valid because his withdrawal of that consent was obtained via undue influence.

Two subsequent cases highlighting the problems of effective consent are before the courts. Both concern couples who commenced fertility treatment together and later split up. In one case, the woman had had eggs retrieved before a course of chemotherapy that was likely to render her infertile. Embryos were created with her eggs and her then partner's sperm and frozen so that IVF treatment could be attempted at a later date. When their relationship broke down the man withdrew his consent to storage of 'his' embryos and demanded that the embryos be destroyed. His former partner is challenging his right to do so and indeed the provisions of the 1990 Act mandating effective consent. She contends that her right to found a family, protected by Article 12 of the Human Rights Convention, is violated by the 1990 Act.

The HFEA has to operate within the framework set by the Act, but many decisions are left to them. We have seen some examples already. Should ovarian tissue be harvested from foetuses? Should sister-to-sister egg donation be banned? Should egg collection concurrent with sterilization be allowed? The developments in the techniques of assisted conception continually pose new problems for the HFEA. The ethics of sex selection continues to trouble the HFEA as have the wider problems generated by pre-implantation genetic diagnosis (PIGD). PIGD enables doctors to test embryos and exclude either embryos of a particular sex or embryos suffering from some particular genetic disease. At its simplest if a woman is known to be the carrier of a sex-linked disease, such as haemophilia, clinics ensure only female embryos are re-implanted. If a couple are at risk of having a child suffering from cystic fibrosis, embryos can be tested for the affected gene and embryos carrying cystic fibrosis will not be re-implanted. The HFEA allows PIGD to enable couples to avoid having children carrying a serious genetic disease. Sex selection for preference is not permitted. Fears are voiced that PIGD opens the doors to the creation of designer babies. Allowing couples to select the kind of child they want. Even if this becomes possible, it is unlikely that the HFEA will allow me to demand that a clinic re-implants only male embryos with genes indicating high intelligence minus my long sightedness.[49] One very real question does arise in terms of using PIGD positively to ensure certain genes are present in the child. Say an existing child is mortally ill with leukaemia and only a bone marrow transplant can save his life. No current relative proves to be a suitable donor. Should parents be allowed to use PIGD to 'create' a child who will be a tissue match to his sibling? It may be that cells taken from the newborn baby's umbilical cord will be sufficient to 'cure' the existing child. Early in 2002, the HFEA granted a clinic permission to use PIGD to try to help parents seeking to have a baby who would be a tissue match for his dying brother. The brother was afflicted by a genetic disease which could also affect any sibling. PIGD would be used (a) to ensure any embryo was not so affected and (b) to attempt a tissue match with his or her brother.

Later in 2002, the HFEA refused permission to use PIGD to find a tissue match for a child dying of Fanconi's anaemia. Fanconi's anaemia is not a genetic disease. The HFEA argued that PIGD could only be used where screening was necessary to screen out 'unhealthy' embryos and where the possibility of a tissue match for a sibling could be seen as a fortuitous side-effect. The distinction was seen as pretty artificial by many commentators. The HFEA faced attack on all fronts. A Parliamentary committee criticized their presumption in allowing PIGD at all. Others condemned their decision not to allow the second set of parents to attempt to save their fatally ill son as heartless.

Other ethical dilemmas facing the HFEA fade almost into insignificance in comparison with the debate surrounding human cloning. The pros and cons of cloning are dealt with more fully in the next chapter. Suffice it to say here that the HFEA has set its face against reproductive cloning in no uncertain fashion.[50]

Grand ethical issues face the HFEA. Their everyday difficulties are apparently more mundane. How often should gametes from one donor be used? The more often sperm from one donor is used the higher the risk grows of unwitting incest. No single donor is to be used for more than ten inseminations.[51] The HFEA limits the number of embryos that may be replaced in the woman. The current limit is three,[52] with pressure to reduce that number further to two. The more embryos replaced in the woman, the greater the risk of multiple pregnancy. Such pregnancies vastly increase the risk of premature labour with adverse consequences for mother, infants and over-stretched neonatal units within the NHS. Some fertility specialists vehemently oppose what they see as paternalistic interference with clinical freedom. If the woman considers that increased chances of pregnancy outweigh the risk of multiple pregnancy, those doctors argue that the number of embryos replaced is none of the HFEA's business. An attempt to strike down this policy by way of judicial review failed.

Another dilemma for the HFEA surrounds clinics with poor success rates. Live birth rates in the best centres remain around 20 to 25 per cent but small, less well-equipped centres achieve less than 5 per cent success, some centres having virtually nil births to their credit. The HFEA publishes information enabling patients to know about the track record of each clinic. All clinics are regularly inspected.

The HFEA is often criticized. It is an easy target. The kinds of ethical decisions entrusted to it go to the heart of differences in our society. The fundamental role of the HFEA as a regulator of fertility practice is sometimes overlooked. The HFEA never got much credit for the job it does in ensuring 'quality control' of reproductive medicine.[53] The last year however has seen the HFEA beset by a series of disasters threatening its reputation as an effective regulator. The most notorious example resulted in an embryologist's conviction for assault. He had caused, or allowed, several frozen embryos to thaw. Rather than admit his wrongdoing, he provided doctors with empty tubes. The women receiving treatment did not receive any embryos for implantation but were 'injected' with a harmless, but useless, saline solution. The disaster resulted in part from inadequate monitoring procedures at clinics. Now every step of the process must be checked by at least two members of staff. Criticism of the HFEA should none the less reflect that the Authority's funding has always been less than generous and that some fertility clinics are resistant to what they see as undue interference with their clinical freedom.

What should the child be told?

Does a child born after the use of donor gametes have a right to know the identity of his genetic parents? An adopted child has at eighteen a right of access to his original birth certificate and so has the opportunity to trace his natural parents.[54] DI tended to be shrouded in secrecy. The provisions of the Human Fertilisation and Embryology Act deem a child to be the child of the woman who carries him and of her husband or partner, whatever his true genetic origins. Yet if an adopted child may trace his birth mother and genetic father, why should children born from gamete donation be denied a similar right?

Warnock recommended that donors should retain their anonymity for two reasons. First, infertile couples seek to have 'their' child, not to adopt someone else's. Fertility treatment and legal rules governing treatment should respect their wishes. Second, fears were expressed that donors would not come forward if they face the prospect of years later being confronted by their 'children', with consequent disruption to any family they may by then have founded. Warnock did consider that children might have a need for basic genetic information to protect their health or that of their own offspring. For one thing steps had to be taken to prevent siblings unwittingly marrying each other.[55] The Human Fertilisation and Embryology Act adopts a compromise. Section 31 provides that the HFEA shall keep a register detailing the provision of treatment services and the use of gametes. At the age of eighteen a person may, after proper counselling, request information from that register. Section 31(4)(b) provides that information *will* include information about whether or not the applicant and a person whom he proposes to marry are related. Section 31(4)(a) provides that such other information relating to the applicant 'as the Authority is required by regulations to give' shall be made available to him. Thus, the HFEA will decide later exactly how much information children born from gamete or embryo donation may be entitled to. The wording of section 31(4)(a) is such that the HFEA would be free to decide that the information should include the identity of the child's genetic parents, the gamete donors.

Section 31(4)(a) caused uproar among DI practitioners. Prohibiting payments to sperm donors would be bad enough, destroying anonymity was regarded as a near fatal blow for DI. Hence at a late stage in the Act's passage through Parliament, section 31(5) was inserted, ensuring that any removal of anonymity cannot be retrospective. If anonymity prevailed when sperm was donated, a later change in the rules will not give children access to the identity of the donor. Baroness Warnock has changed her mind. She now considers that children have a right to information about their genetic parents. The debate about whether anonymity should be preserved for all time goes on. The Department of Health is carrying out a consultation exercise to review the status quo. Now that donors can never be legally liable to maintain any child born as a result of donation, the case for preserving anonymity seems less strong. If donation is seen as an ethical, altruistic act why must it be kept secret? Above all it must be recognized that what should be paramount are the rights and interests of the child, not those of the parents or the donors. If adopted children need to know the identity of their genetic parents, why are the needs of children born from gamete or embryo donation less pressing?[56] Granting a young man who had spent a miserable childhood in care access to all the files held on him, the European Court of Human Rights declared that '. . . everyone should be able to establish details of their identity as individual human beings'.[57]

Pressure to alter the law increased after the judgment in *Rose* v. *Secretary of State for Health and the Human Fertilisation and Embryology Authority*.[58] Both claimants were born as a result of donor insemination. They sought at least access to non-identifying information about their genetic fathers and the establishment of a contact register. They challenged the Secretary of State's refusal to make regulations under the 1990 Act to meet their demands and argued that the provisions of the Act itself violated their right to family life by denying them information about their heredity. The judges held that Article 8 did create a *prima facie* case to take their claim forward.

Access to assisted conception

In 1990 Parliament, as we saw, sought to discourage provision of any form of assisted conception to single women. Section 13 (5) admonishing clinics to take into account the welfare of the child may be seen as impeding access to treatment. The liberal interpretation of section 13 (9) by the HFEA means that in practice no absolute bar to treatment operates to exclude single women, or couples in unconventional or lesbian relationships. What it does is to entrust a very broad discretion to doctors. It has been powerfully argued that section 13 (5) makes little difference in practice to the range of patients private clinics will treat.⁵⁹ IVF treatment is largely provided in the private sector, with limited NHS facilities for those who cannot pay for treatment. NHS clinics have to make hard choices. Practice varies widely but many clinics operate criteria based on the likelihood that patients will be good parents.⁶⁰ Some follow adoption guidelines used by local social services departments. Most will offer treatment only where neither partner has any existing children. Many operate upper age limits that may be as low as thirty-five for the women. Section 13 (5) is used as a rationing device. Mrs Harriott was a patient at St Mary's Hospital, Manchester. She was ultimately refused IVF because of a criminal record for prostitution offences and because she and her husband had been rejected as prospective adoptive or foster parents by Manchester social services department. The clinicians referred her case to the hospital's informal ethical advisory committee, who endorsed their decision. She sought judicial review of that decision, alleging that the grounds for refusing her treatment were unreasonable and unlawful. The judge held that decisions on IVF treatment could be reviewed by a court. If a patient was refused treatment on grounds, say, of religion or ethnic origin, that could be clearly unlawful. Public bodies and officials, including clinicians taking decisions within the NHS, must act reasonably and not on the basis of irrational prejudices. In Mrs Harriott's case the judge found that the grounds for regarding her to be an unsuitable parent were reasonable.⁶¹ Mrs Seale and her husband were refused NHS treatment because at thirty-seven she was outside the health authority's age limit. The authority argued that thirty-five was a sensible cut-off point because the older the woman, the less the chances of establishing a successful pregnancy. Given a tight budget the NHS should concentrate on treating women who were most likely to benefit from treatment. The judge agreed.⁶² British patients have considerable freedom if they can pay but in practice enjoy no right to be assisted to reproduce. They may some-times look with envy at France where generous public funding for fertil-ity treatment is provided. Income is not an impediment in France and couples of childbearing age are unlikely to be turned away.[63] However, treatment is limited to heterosexual couples of reproductive age. Single women, lesbian couples or post-menopausal mothers are excluded. The government in England has declared its intention of providing more generous funding for fertility treatment on a fairer basis. The National Institute of Clinical Excellence is soon to provide guidelines on NHS treatment.

Liability for disability

What if an attempt to help a patient overcome infertility results in the birth of a disabled infant? This could happen for several reasons. In DI, the donor may turn out to be the carrier of some disease or congenital defect. Babies have been born abroad suffering from HIV contracted from donor sperm. An error may be made in the laboratory, damaging an IVF embryo. Or perhaps there is negligence in the process of screen-ing embryos and a defective embryo is returned to the womb. Finally, the very process of IVF and freezing might in years to come be shown to produce abnormalities manifesting themselves only when the children reach maturity or try to have children themselves. The legal questions are:

(1) Can the parents and/or the child bring an action against the doctors and the clinics concerned?
(2) Will they be able to prove negligence?
(3) Are there specific defences available to the defendants?

The parents' right to sue is unproblematic. Parents will be able to maintain an action against the doctors and the clinic if mother or child is injured by negligence. Clearly if the mother herself suffers any injury, for example, in the course of collecting eggs, she may recover compen-sation for that injury. The hospital or clinic will be in breach of its duty of care to her. That duty extends beyond the mother's immediate phys-ical health to the safety of her child. The woman accepted for treatment expects care, not only in relation to herself, but also in the 'production' of a healthy infant. If, by negligence, the child is born disabled, damage to the parents is readily foreseeable. Both mother and father will suffer emotional trauma and face the added expense of bringing up a disabled child. Is there a problem if the parents cannot pinpoint exactly who was negligent? It may be impossible for them to know if the embryo was damaged by the gynaecologist removing the eggs and implanting the embryo, or by the scientists in the laboratory. In NHS clinics, the NHS trust owes a direct duty to the parents and is responsible if it negligently fails to discharge that duty. In the private sector patients should ensure that the clinic similarly undertakes a contractual duty to provide and underwrite the whole course of treatment. Exactly what the contractual terms agreed with a private clinic entail may be crucial. A couple successfully sued a private clinic who implanted three embryos in the woman after she had specifically stated that no more than two embryos should be replaced. The clinic was held liable for breach of contract and responsible for the birth of a third child. One final point relating to actions by parents is that while they may have legal redress if a damaged baby is born, there will be no legal remedy if no baby is born. Success rates for IVF remain low, neither NHS nor private clinics undertake more than to attempt to assist conception using all due skill and care.

What of an action by the child itself? He will need to rely on the right of action in respect of pre-natal injuries enacted in the Congenital Disabilities (Civil Liability) Act 1976. On the original wording of the 1976 Act it was doubtful whether negligence in assisted conception fell within the ambit of the Act. The Act covered cases where injury resulted from a parent being harmed in his or her reproductive capacity, or the child suffering injury in the womb or course of its birth. Damage in the actual process of conception was hard to fit into either category. The Human Fertilization and Embryology Act expressly amends the 1976 Act to allow for an action arising out of negligence in the process of assisted conception. Section 44 inserts into the 1976 Act a new section 1a that provides for an action if a child carried by a woman as a result of the placing in her of an embryo, or sperm and eggs, or DI, is born disabled, and the disability results from negligence in the selection, or keeping or use outside the body, of the relevant embryo or gametes. Providing the defendant is answerable in tort to one or both parents, he is liable to the child. The sorts of cases envisaged by this new section 1a are just the sort of examples mentioned earlier – the child born HIV positive because doctors failed to screen donors adequately, the child born damaged by some technical error in his creation, and the child born disabled because a defective embryo was negligently implanted in the mother. A further extension to the rights of the child is made in section 35(4) of the 1990 Act, again amending the 1976 Act, to provide that injury to the reproductive capacity of the genetic parent gives rise to a derivative action under the 1976 Act for the child. Section 34 and 35 of the 1990 Act make extensive provision for the disclosure of information necessary to any action by parent or child for damages occasioned by assisted conception.

One difficulty facing an action by the child remains. If the essence of his action is for 'wrongful life', not 'wrongful disability', then, as we shall see from the Court of Appeal's judgment in *McKay* v. *Essex AHA*,[64] no action can lie (see pages 378–9). Much will then turn on *how* it is alleged the child came to suffer injury. If it is claimed that gametes and embryo were originally healthy, but damaged by some act of the doctors or scientists treating the mother, the claim is for 'wrongful disability'. It is on a par with a claim that a healthy foetus was damaged *in utero* by drugs given to the mother. But what if the alleged negligence is that infected sperm was used to inseminate the mother or a defective embryo implanted in her? Such a claim must logically be classified as a 'wrongful life' claim. Assume these facts. A DI clinic negligently fails to check donors for HIV. Baby X is born with HIV from contaminated sperm. Had the clinic exercised due care in the collection of sperm, that individual, Baby X, would never have been born at all. Similarly if a defective embryo is not screened and discarded in the laboratory, any action the child brings is for 'wrongful life'. His parents could, 'but for' the relevant negligence, have had a healthy child, but he would have been a different child.

Both parents and children seeking compensation for disability will face acute problems proving negligence where it is difficult to isolate the cause of the damage to the child. A baby resulting from DI that is born HIV positive or clearly afflicted by a genetic disease carried by the father poses no legal problem in a claim by his parents. Competent screening should have discovered the disease or defect and that sperm should never have been used to inseminate the mother. Linking a defect to an error in the laboratory will be far from easy. An action based on abnormalities manifesting themselves later in life is almost bound to fail. If, say, in 2015 it is shown that freezing embryos produces cancer in the late teens and early twenties, the defence to any claim in negligence will be that responsible professional opinion, endorsed by countless official reports, believed freezing to be safe in 1995 when the child was born.

Finally, if parent or child has a right to sue and proves negligence, are there defences open to the doctor based on the parents having agreed to run the risk of a damaged child or the mother's refusal to terminate the pregnancy when the defect was diagnosed *in utero*? Section 44(3) provides that an action by the child shall fail if either or both parents knew of the risk of their child being born disabled '. . . that is to say, the particular risk created by the act of omission'. So if the mother is known to carry a genetic disease herself and is counselled that it would be better to use donor eggs for an IVF pregnancy yet insists on a child who is genetically hers, she cannot turn round and sue the doctors who carried out her wishes if her genetic problem is inherited by her child. However, it would be no defence for a defendant simply to say, 'Well, parents know that this is a relatively new and risky process, so I am not liable.' The parents must be aware of the particular risk of harming their child. Often the risk of harm to an IVF or GIFT baby arises from the increased danger of a multiple pregnancy. A parent who was not fully counselled on this risk might argue that not warning of that particular risk was negligent. Of course, to succeed in an action she would then have to prove that had she been warned she would not have gone ahead with the treatment.

IVF pregnancies are carefully monitored. Abnormality in the foetus is likely to be discovered well before birth in which case the mother will be offered an abortion. The Court of Appeal in *Emeh* v. *Kensington, Chelsea and Fulham AHA*,[65] strongly endorsed in *McFarlane* v. *Tayside Health Board*,[66] held that refusal to terminate a pregnancy did not constitute either a *novus actus* or contributory negligence where the mother sued for the birth of a child subsequent to a negligently performed sterilization. In the context of IVF it might be argued that *Emeh* is distinguishable because the purpose at abortion here is to prevent the birth of a damaged child. Slade LJ in *Emeh* did leave open the question of whether it might be unreasonable to refuse an abortion for which there were 'medical' grounds; Doctors might also argue that mothers will have been told of the extensive screening and monitoring programme in IVF pregnancies and have in effect agreed to the whole package. It remains my view that an argument that a mother can be held contributorily negligent, or responsible for the birth of her disabled child, because she refuses to abort is neither good law nor good ethics.

Surrogate mothers

I have left until last one of the most emotive issues, surrogacy. Surrogacy can take a number of forms. The most common arrangement remains this. A surrogate agrees with the commissioning couple to artificial insemination with the male partner's sperm. She agrees to carry any resulting child and to hand the child over to the genetic father and his wife or partner, immediately she is born. The surrogate practises self-insemination privately.[67] This practice is often styled 'partial surrogacy'. IVF offers a couple where the woman ovulates, but cannot safely carry a child to term, the chance of a baby who is genetically theirs. Eggs are taken from the woman, fertilized in the laboratory with sperm from the man, and the embryo implanted in the surrogate. The surrogate once again carries the child and agrees to hand it over at birth. The surrogate is merely a 'hostess' for the couple's embryo. This practice may be styled 'full surrogacy'. Surrogacy in all its forms attracts controversy. Particular concern was aroused by commercial surrogacy where a couple approach and pay an agency to find the surrogate and make all necessary arrangements. After the Warnock Report the one swift response from government was to ban commercial surrogacy.[68] Warnock went further, and would have prohibited any third party, commercial agency or doctor, from assisting a couple to arrange a surrogate pregnancy, regardless of whether what was envisaged was full or partial surrogacy.[69]

What are the legal issues arising out of surrogacy? Can it ever amount to a crime to arrange a surrogate pregnancy? What happens if the surrogate changes her mind and refuses to hand the baby over? Where the baby is genetically that of the wife and implanted in the surrogate via IVF, what are the rights of the genetic parents? What rights can the father assert? Should surrogacy be better regulated?

Surrogacy where no money changes hands is lawful in the sense that no crime is committed. If payment is made to an agency, however, an offence is committed. The Surrogacy Arrangements Act 1985 makes it a criminal offence for anyone to play any part in setting up a surrogacy arrangement on a commercial basis. Advertising or compiling information to promote or assist surrogacy arrangements are also made criminal. Offenders face a punishment of a fine and/or up to three months in prison. Under the Act, no offence is committed by a woman herself seeking to become, or becoming, a surrogate, nor is any offence committed by the man or the couple who persuade her to carry a child. The Act is limited to banning the activities of any commercial agencies or individuals aiming to make a profit out of surrogate motherhood. A fertility specialist who helps in establishing a full surrogacy incurs no criminal liability so long as he does not involve himself in arranging the introduction of couple and surrogate. The Warnock proposal that any third-party intervention should be made illegal, including professional help from a doctor that was intended to set up a surrogacy arrangement, was not acted on. The 1985 Act does, however, embrace all forms of surrogacy, be they 'partial' or 'full' surrogacy.[70]

Although the surrogate and the couple engaging her services do not commit any offence under the 1985 Act even if she is paid for what she does, all three parties may be guilty of an offence under the Adoption Act 1976 if the surrogate is offered an overt payment for her services.[71] For it is a criminal offence, punishable by a fine or up to six months in prison, to give or receive any payment in relation to the adoption of a child, the grant of consent to adoption, or the handing over of a child with a view to its adoption, unless that payment is authorized by a court. In order to make the baby born to the surrogate legally theirs, the commissioning couple must ultimately obtain a 'parental order', or adopt the child. In theory, any payment beyond 'reasonable expenses' will debar the couple from obtaining a parental order. If they try to adopt the child and money paid to the surrogate is found to include a sum in payment for her agreement to the adoption and handing over of the child, the surrogate and the couple may face prosecution. Moreover, the Adoption Act further provides that the court may order the infant to be removed to a place of safety 'until he can be restored to his parents or guardians or until other arrangements can be made for him'. A child could in theory be removed from all those involved in the surrogacy arrangements. Would such drastic action make any sort of sense if the surrogate was happy to hand over the baby, and there was no reason to believe that the commissioning couple were unfit to care for the child? How to respond to such a surrogacy case was a dilemma that confronted Barnet Social Services in 1985. A baby girl was born in their area amid great publicity. Her mother (Kim Cotton) had agreed to carry her for a childless couple from abroad. She was artificially inseminated with the husband's sperm. The arrangements were made through an agency who were paid £13,000 by the father, of which the surrogate received £6,500. At the relevant time the Surrogacy Arrangements Act had not yet been enacted. The baby was born and the mother prepared to hand her over. Barnet Social Services stepped in and the child was made a ward of court. Latey J[72] had to decide on her fate. He said that the crucial issue before him was what was best for this baby. The methods used to create the child and the commercial aspects of the case raised delicate problems of ethics, morality and social desirability. They were not for him to decide. Careful inquiries showed that the father and his wife were eminently suitable to be parents. The judge granted them custody of the baby and permission to take her abroad with them to their home. The question of adoption and so the illegality of any payment under the Adoption Act did not arise in that case.

Two years later Latey J was called on again to adjudicate on the consequences of a surrogacy arrangement where all the parties desired to abide by that arrangement.[73] Mr and Mrs A. arranged for Mrs B. to carry a child for them. The child was conceived by natural sexual intercourse between Mr A. and Mrs B. Mrs B. was to be paid £10,000.[74] A baby was born and handed over to Mr and Mrs A. after birth. They sought to adopt the child, as they then had to do to acquire parental rights. Were they in breach of the Adoption Act and so at risk of losing their child? Latey J found they were not. He held that the payments were *not* to procure Mrs B.'s consent to adoption. At the time of the agreement this was not in the parties' minds. The payments were in the nature of expenses for Mrs B., recompense for her time and inconvenience. Furthermore, the judge held that, even if he were wrong and the payments *were* illegal payments, he had power to ratify those payments retrospectively. Payments authorized by the court are not unlawful. As a matter of pure legal reasoning Latey J's grounds for finding that the payments made by Mr and Mrs A. to Mrs B. were lawful may well be faulty. What is clear is that the judge saw no reason to upset an arrangement that had worked, or to remove the child, now two, from the only parents it had known. What else could he do? If Parliament wanted to ban surrogacy, it should have done so outright.

If the surrogate is content to hand the baby over, the courts will help the commissioning couple to keep the baby. What if she changes her mind? First, it is absolutely clear in England that surrogacy agreements are not enforceable as contracts. The commissioning couple cannot sue the surrogate for breach of contract, or ask a court to order performance of a contract. Nor, can the surrogate sue if she does not receive any agreed payments. Section 36(1) of the 1990 Act inserts a new section 1a in the Surrogacy Arrangements Act 1985, providing quite simply that:

No surrogacy arrangement is enforceable by or against any of the persons making it.

It does not matter by what means the child was created, be it sexual intercourse, DI or IVF, the arrangement is not an enforceable contract.

That still leaves open the question of what happens if the surrogate wants to keep the baby. In the notorious *Baby M.* case in New Jersey, USA, a surrogate mother, Mary Beth Whitehead, fought a long, bitter and public battle with her child's genetic father, William Stern, and his wife, Betsy. The Supreme Court of New Jersey[75] quashed the first-instance finding that Mary Beth was bound by her contract with Mr and Mrs Stern. She still lost her baby. It was found to be in the child's best interests that she be brought up by the Sterns.

In England if the surrogate changes her mind and refuses to surrender the child, she will usually be allowed to keep the child. In *A.* v. *C.*[76] as long ago as 1978, a young woman agreed to have a baby by DI and hand over the child to the wealthy father and his partner. She was to be paid £3,000. When the child was born she refused to give him up. The father sought care and control. The trial judge found that the mother should be allowed to keep the child, but granted the father limited access. The Court of Appeal removed his rights of access, condemning the whole arrangement as 'irresponsible, bizarre and unnatural'. Nor does it seem that greater tolerance of surrogacy has altered judicial policy where surrogates change their minds. In *Re P. (Minors) (Wardship: Surrogacy)*[77] Sir John Arnold P refused to order a surrogate mother to hand over twins born as a result of her artificial insemination by the father. It would seem that in England a surrogate would be deprived of her baby only if she were an unfit mother who would not be allowed to keep the child however it had come to be conceived. Surrogacy is an arrangement couples enter into at their peril. If all goes to plan, they will get 'their' baby. If the arrangement breaks down, the law will not assist them in a battle with the surrogate, save in one exceptional situation. If the surrogate hands over the child, who is settled into the couple's home, but later changes her mind about consent to adoption or a parental order, the court has on two occasions at least overruled the surrogate's refusal of consent.[78] The welfare of the child once he or she is established in a 'new' family will override any claims of the surrogate.

Is the position any different where the surrogate is *not* the genetic mother, and the child was created by IVF from the eggs and sperm of the commissioning couple? Prior to the Human Fertilisation and Embryology Act the genetic mother might have argued thus. I am this baby's mother. I do not need to adopt my own child. She (the surrogate) has no right to keep my child from me. That argument is killed stone dead by section 27 of the Act. Section 27 provides, as we have seen, that the woman who carries the child *and no other woman* is to be treated as the mother of the child.

Late in its passage through Parliament a new section, section 30, was inserted in the 1990 Act to help some commissioning couples in surrogacy cases. It provides for a procedure, other than adoption, by which some couples will be able to acquire parental rights over 'their' child. The section was introduced by a Cumbrian MP after representations from a couple in his constituency who objected to having to adopt 'their' IVF child.[79] Section 30 gives the court power to order that the commissioning couple be treated in law as the parents of the child, but *only* in a limited number of circumstances. (1) The couple must be married. (2) The child must have been conceived from either the placing of the embryo (IVF) or sperm and eggs (GIFT) in the woman, or by DI. Eggs or sperm or both must come from the couple. Children conceived by natural intercourse between the surrogate and the husband are not within the ambit of section 30.[80] (3) At the time of the making of the order the child must be living with the couple, and the surrogate (and the 'legal father') must have given full and free consent not less than six weeks after the birth. Section 30 is of no relevance if the surrogate changes her mind and is not willing to hand over the child. Nor is it a backdoor route to enforcing a surrogacy contract. (4) No payments (other than for expenses reasonably incurred) must have been made to the surrogate unless authorized by the court. In effect, section 30 is a statutory embodiment of what might be called the Latey approach to surrogacy. If it has worked out and a child is settled with 'her parents', the law should give legal effect to the actual family circumstances prevailing.

Section 30 is limited in scope. Could the male partner in the commissioning couple assert paternal rights by other means? How do the provisions of the 1990 Act defining paternity affect surrogacy? Section 28 deems the husband of a woman treated with donor sperm to be the father of the child and designates any man treated together with the woman as the father if the couple are not married. Its impact on surrogacy is complicated. If the surrogate is married, her husband will be treated as the child's father! Section 30 will then require his consent to the grant of a parental order to the commissioning couple. If the surrogate is not married, and is treated in a licensed clinic, could it be argued that she and the commissioning father are treated together? If so could the surrogate and the child's genetic father agree to share parental responsibility with the father seeking a residence order? It seems not.[81] If partial surrogacy is established by self-insemination, however, the commissioning father is the legal father of the child. He could, with the surrogate's concurrence, simply seek a residence order. The couple could have the child in their home but the commissioning mother would have no legal relationship with the child.

Surrogacy developed pragmatically after Warnock. Keep commercial agencies at bay and otherwise deal with each case as it arose seemed to be the policy. Difficult questions remain unanswered. What happens if the baby is born disabled and no one wants it? What if the commissioning couple split up? Surrogacy is fraught with risk.

The number of surrogacy arrangements is impossible to ascertain accurately. The evidence suggests that the incidence of surrogacy is rising in the United Kingdom. 'Partial surrogacy' remains the most 'popular' form of surrogacy. Payments are rising with evidence that payments of up to and beyond £12,000 are (sometimes reluctantly) sanctioned as expenses by courts authorizing parental or adoption orders. At least two voluntary agencies provide a well publicized service for couples seeking surrogates. It is relatively common for women to act as surrogates on a number of occasions. Concerns about surrogacy resurfaced in the final years of the twentieth century. In one well publicized case a young woman agreed to carry a child for a Dutch couple in return for £12,000 expenses. She changed her mind and first she told them that she had had an abortion. Later she said that she was still pregnant but planned to keep the baby. Around the same time one of the leading US surrogacy agents arrived in Britain advertising his commercial surrogacy service. The government set up a review[82] of payments for and regulation of surrogacy chaired by myself working with the distinguished ethicist Alastair Campbell and an eminent psychologist, Susan Golombok.

The *Surrogacy Review* made a number of recommendations for law reform. None have yet been acted on. The most controversial proposal is that the prohibition on paying surrogates for their services should be maintained and given teeth. A new Surrogacy Act should define expenses to exclude covert payments. Unless pregnancy causes the surrogate to give up work, it is difficult to see how genuine expenses resulting from pregnancy can add up to more than a couple of thousand pounds. Any agency that introduced couples and surrogates or offered advice on surrogacy would have to be registered with the Department of Health. A Code of Practice would be developed that agencies must abide by in setting out a model of good practice for couples and surrogates. The Code would seek to ensure frank exchanges of information and offer independent counselling to all involved. Multiple surrogacy would be discouraged. Parties who complied with the Code would be able to obtain a parental order swiftly. Where the Code was not followed, the lengthier process of adoption would be required with provision for a full investigation of the circumstances of the arrangement. The proposed Surrogacy Act would reinforce a philosophy of surrogacy as a gift relationship and set in place regulations that would seek to safeguard the interests of all parties.

Prohibition on payments was vigorously opposed by the major surrogacy agency COTS (Childlessness Overcome Through Surrogacy) and a number of eminent scholars. The most telling criticism of the *Surrogacy Review* came from Michael Freeman[83] who argued, first, that surrogates are entitled to payment and, second, that a ban on payment will drive surrogacy underground increasing risks of exploitation and harm the children.

There is agreement that some sort of regulation of surrogacy is needed. The form of regulation will never be settled, however, unless the vexed question of payment is resolved. The arguments are finely balanced. I expect and receive payment for the use of my brain. Why should a surrogate not be paid for the use of her uterus? But should bodily services or body parts be traded? Can you buy children?[84] Proponents of payment argue that paying a surrogate for reproductive labour is not buying a child. Yet what couple would pay if the child is not surrendered? Most pro-payment campaigners argue that surrogacy contracts should remain unenforceable.[85] Is that logical? If the use of the uterus is no different from manual or intellectual labour why should the surrogate not be obliged to honour her contract?

A right to reproduce?

The particular controversies raging around assisted conception have at their heart a simple question. Is there a fundamental human right to reproduce? For if you agree there is, then measures that impede access to assisted conception will be seen as violating that right. Future legal challenges to the HFEA and legal cases surrounding reproduction will continue to invoke Articles 8 and 12 of the Human Rights Convention.[86] Does respect for my private and family life exclude the state from vetting my ability to meet the needs, the welfare, of my child if I seek IVF as an elderly single mother-to-be? Does Article 12 granting me a right to found a family allow me to define the nature of that family and the nature of my child? Human rights arguments will not make the debate any less complex. Remember Article 8(1) entitling me to respect for my privacy and family life is heavily qualified by Article 8(2). The protection of my prospective child may be what justifies outside 'interference' to check my maternal qualifications. Whether Article 12 creates any positive obligation to help me have a child when nature decrees my childbearing days are done remains to be seen.

13

Abortion and Embryo Research

Few medico-legal issues provoke as much bitter controversy as the status of the human embryo. For, if a life given by God begins at conception, the deliberate destruction of any embryo, be it in the course of embryo research, or by abortion, is the equivalent of murder. The killing of the embryo can only be justifiable, if at all, where the mother's life is at risk. If the human embryo has, as others contend, no greater moral status than a mouse embryo, neither research nor abortion is morally wrong. For many feminists a right to abortion is part and parcel of the woman's rights over her own body. The present law on abortion represents an attempt to reach a compromise in a debate in which there is no consensus. In 1990, Parliament in the Human Fertilisation and Embryology Act sanctioned embryo research up to fourteen days, and permitted abortion in certain cases up to the moment of birth. 'Pro-life' campaigners continue to fight to ban research and restrict abortion. The law is controversial and complex. There is little hope that the legal and ethical problems surrounding the human embryo will ever be satisfactorily resolved. I shall examine the law relating to early abortion first, and then return to the vexed question of embryo research, including the furore about cloning.

Criminal abortion

The law relating to criminal abortion is still to be found in section 58 of the Offences Against the Person Act 1861. Proposals to reform the 1861 Act and update the law await Parliamentary time. The 1861 Act makes it a criminal offence punishable by a maximum of life imprisonment for any woman, being with child, unlawfully to do any act with intent to procure a miscarriage, and for any other person unlawfully to do an act with intent to procure the miscarriage of any woman. Self-induced abortion by the woman herself is criminal only if the woman is in fact pregnant. Any act by a third party is criminal regardless of whether or not the woman can be proved to be pregnant. This limited protection afforded to the woman extends only to cases where she acts entirely alone. If she seeks help from a doctor, or any other person, she may be charged with aiding and abetting that person to commit the offence of criminal abortion[1] or of conspiracy with him to commit that offence.[2] The law embodied in the 1861 Act was applied rigorously up to 1967. In 1927, a girl of thirteen was prosecuted for attempting to induce an abortion on herself by taking laxative tablets and sitting in a hot bath. The rigour of the law was tempered by a defence to a charge of criminal abortion by a doctor that he acted to preserve the life or health of the mother.[3] At no time in England was abortion so absolutely prohibited as to require the mother to be sacrificed for her unborn child. Indeed, in *R. v. Bourne*,[4] acquitting a doctor of a charge of criminal abortion, the judge suggested that there might be a *duty* to abort to save the 'yet more precious' life of the mother. The extent of the defence available to doctors was unclear. Some doctors interpreted this defence liberally to include the mother's mental health and even happiness. Others would intervene only to prevent a life-threatening complication of pregnancy endangering the woman. Illegal abortion flourished. Several thousand women were admitted to hospital for treatment after back-street abortions. The Abortion Act 1967 was introduced to bring uniformity into the law, to clarify the law for the doctors, and to stem the misery and injury resulting from unhygienic, risky, illegal abortions.

The Abortion Act 1967

This Act provides that abortion may be lawfully performed under certain conditions. A pregnancy may be terminated by a registered medical practitioner if *two* registered medical practitioners are of the opinion, formed in good faith, that grounds specified in the Act are met. They are, first, that the continuance of the pregnancy would involve risk to the life of the pregnant woman, or of injury to her physical or mental health, or that of the existing children of her family, greater than if the pregnancy were terminated, and, second, that there is a substantial risk that if the child were born it would suffer from such physical or mental abnormalities as to be seriously handicapped. In assessing any risk to the health of the woman or her children, account may be taken of the woman's actual or reasonably foreseeable environment. Exceptionally one registered medical practitioner may act alone when he is of the opinion that an abortion is immediately necessary to save the life of the woman or to prevent grave permanent injury to her physical or mental health. Section 4 of the Act provides that no person shall be under any duty to participate in the performance of an abortion if he has a conscientious objection to abortion, save where immediate treatment is necessary to save the life of the woman or to prevent grave permanent damage to her health.[5]

The furore surrounding the 1967 Act has not abated. Pro-life critics argue that women can obtain abortions on request. On the other hand, counter-claims are made that there are areas of the country where the Act is so restrictively interpreted that abortions are not much easier to obtain than before 1967. In the latter case the only legal remedy would be for a woman to sue if she did in fact suffer damage to her health as a result of the continuance of a pregnancy, or gave birth to a disabled child, and successfully persuaded a court in a claim for wrongful birth that the refusal of the abortion was negligent and unreasonable.

Abortion on demand or request?

Gynaecologists who admit that they are prepared to perform an abortion simply on the request of the pregnant woman rely on statistics that appear to show that the risk of abortion in the first twelve weeks of pregnancy is always less than the risk of childbirth. Therefore any abortion performed in that period meets the requirement of the Act that the continuance of the pregnancy poses a greater risk to the health of the woman than does termination. The medical profession itself is divided on the validity of the statistics and the issue has never been tested in court. Doctors performing abortions have to make a return to the Department of Health stating the grounds for the operation. Some returns simply stated 'pregnancy' as the grounds. The Department changed its forms in 1982 in an attempt to tighten up on the rules for legal abortions. The new form demanded to know the main *medical* condition justifying abortion. Pro-choice doctors continued to return 'pregnancy' as the grounds justifying an operation. No prosecutions were brought. A successful prosecution against a doctor performing an abortion on demand would have to establish (a) that the statistics indicating that abortion posed less risk than childbirth were invalid, and (b) that the doctor on trial did not believe them to be valid and so failed to act in good faith. In view of the fact that only one successful prosecution has ever been brought against a doctor for performing an abortion purportedly under the 1967 Act in bad faith,[6] such a course would appear to be a clumsy means of regulating or eliminating abortion on demand or request. Frequent attempts by Private Members' Bills to amend the Act to require the risk of pregnancy to be *substantially* greater than that of abortion have also failed. The Abortion Act confers no right to abortion. Making doctors the 'gatekeepers' for the Act, means that abortion in England is a privilege granted or withheld at the doctors' discretion.[7]

Post-coital birth control

The 1967 Act envisaged that once a diagnosis of pregnancy had been made, the doctor faced with a request for an abortion would then consider and weigh any risk to the woman or the child. Post-coital contraceptive drugs will, if taken by a woman within seventy-two hours of intercourse, ensure that any fertilized egg will not implant in the womb. This, inaptly named, 'morning-after' pill is not the only means by which a fertilized egg may be disposed of at a stage before pregnancy can be confirmed. An intra-uterine device (IUD) fitted within a similar time after intercourse will have the same effect.[8] Menstrual extraction can be used around the time of the woman's next period to remove all the contents of the uterus, including the products of unwanted conception.

Are such methods lawful? They raise the question of where the line is drawn between contraception and abortion. A distinction must be made between post-coital contraception and menstrual extraction. Post-coital contraception works before the fertilized egg can implant in the womb. By the time menstrual extraction is utilized, the egg will have become an implanted embryo. The action taken to remove that embryo constitutes an induced abortion. The crucial legal issue, in relation to the use of post-coital contraception is whether a drug or a procedure that prevents implantation is an act done to procure a miscarriage. The argument that prevention of implantation falls outside abortion laws runs thus. There is no carriage of a child by a woman before implantation takes place, and so to prevent that event even occurring cannot be an act done to procure a miscarriage. Many fertilized eggs fail to implant naturally and no one then suggests that a miscarriage has occurred. The opponents of post-coital birth control reply that the fertilized ovum is present within the body of the woman; she carries it within her. Therefore there is a carriage of a child, and any act removing that child from her womb is an act done to procure a miscarriage.[9] Up to 40 per cent of *implanted* embryos also abort spontaneously. Thus arguments based on spontaneous loss of the fertilized egg are irrelevant.

No successful prosecution has ever been brought in respect of post-coital birth control, nor is criminalization likely now. In 1983[10] the Attorney-General expressed his opinion that prior to implantation there is no pregnancy and so means used to prevent implantation do *not* constitute procuring miscarriage. In 1991 a judge dismissed a prosecution for criminal abortion based on the insertion of an IUD agreeing with the Attorney-General that until implantation there is no pregnancy.[11] Controversy continues to rage. In 2000, Levonelle, a version of the 'morning after' pill was deregulated to allow sale over the counter in pharmacies. Women no longer need a prescription to obtain post-coital birth control. The Pro-Life Alliance unsuccessfully sought judicial review arguing that the free availability of such a drug contravenes the 1861 Act because the drug procures miscarriage. Munby J poured scorn on their case, and forcefully held that in 2002 no pregnancy was established until the fertilized egg implanted in the uterus.[12]

Menstrual extraction has fallen out of fashion. It was once lauded by feminists as a means of self-abortion, albeit a dangerous one. The development of mifepristone (RU-486), the 'abortion pill', may render menstrual extraction obsolete. Mifepristone is a drug that is administered orally in the first twelve weeks of pregnancy, and will, in most women, induce a complete miscarriage within forty-eight hours or so. A small percentage of women require a surgical abortion to complete the evacuation of the uterus.[13] Clearly the use of mifepristone is lawful only within the conditions laid down in the 1967 Act. The development of the drug does not liberalize the law on abortion. 'Pro-life' campaigners fear that by making abortion 'easier', mifepristone will contribute to the rise in the number of abortions. Section 37(3) of the Human Fertilisation and Embryology Act clears the way for its routine use in England by authorizing the Secretary of State for Health to approve clinics prescribing the drug. 'Pro-life' campaigners will no doubt continue to believe that the 'abortion pill' is the ultimate development of a pro-abortion, 'anti-life', mentality. What mifepristone does do is to place responsibility for ending her pregnancy on the woman taking the drug.

She cannot evade responsibility by seeing the abortion as something done to her. The procedure involves experiencing the pain and distress of a miscarriage. The loss of the embryo will be very evident to her. It is no more likely to be used lightly than recourse to surgical abortion.

Embryo research: the debate[14]

It cannot '. . . be morally preferable to end the life of an embryo *in vivo* than it is to do *in vitro*'.[15] The law regulating abortion in England sanctions the killing of thousands of embryos every year. Advocates of embryo research ask how society can logically accept abortion yet ban research. If the embryo can be destroyed at its mother's request, how can it be unethical to destroy it in the course of beneficial scientific research? Both camps in the debate on embryo experiment link the questions of abortion and research.[16] Are they right to do so?

At the heart of the debate lies the question of the moral status of the developing embryo. When does it acquire the same right to protection as you and I enjoy? Is it at fertilization, when a new unique genetic entity comes into being? Or is it at some later stage in embryonic development? This might be at fourteen days, when the primitive streak forms,[17] or when brain activity is first discernible at eight to ten weeks.[18] Or is it much, much later, indeed after birth? One school of philosophy argues thus.[19] Humanity is just another species and as such has no greater moral status than any other animal. What gives rise to moral rights is not being a human animal, but being a *person*. It is the capacity to value your own existence that gives a person rights, including the right to life. Embryos, and newborn infants, lack that capacity and so are *not* persons.

Each ethical school of thought marshals impressive arguments in support of its thesis. Argument that the embryo enjoys full human status from fertilization is an argument often resting on theological grounds. If you believe that human life is divinely created in the image of God, and that human beings possess an immortal immaterial soul, you are unlikely to find any argument based on personhood acceptable. The crucial moment when the embryo acquires humanity becomes ensoulment. Traditionally that moment might be seen as fertilization, but a number of eminent Christian theologians have argued for a later date – either the appearance of the primitive streak as marking clear individuality, or the beginning of brain life.[20] Any concept of human life as special *per se* is irrelevant to those who support the personhood thesis.

How does the law respond to such a divergence of moral opinion? Consensus is impossible to attain. Proponents of embryo research argue that no one is compelled to participate in research. A liberal democracy should respect divergent moral views but that is anathema to 'pro-life' groups. It is rather like saying that if a sufficient number of people decide redheads are not human and have no moral claim on society, anyone who holds that belief may kill off any redhead he meets. Of course, no 'pro-redhead' will be *required* to join in the slaughter! So what is the difference between redheaded adults and embryos? On any analysis the redhead enjoys moral and legal rights. She is without doubt a person. The embryo's true nature is unprovable. I happen to believe that from fertilization the embryo is *very probably* of the same moral value as myself. It is a unique being created in the image of God, in whom I believe. I cannot prove that belief. But then nor can those who maintain that humanity is just another animal species prove their contention. The verdict on the nature of the embryo must be 'not proven'.

What consequences should the 'not-proven' nature of the embryo have for its legal status? It must be accorded recognition and respect. If its claims to rights conflict with the claims of an entity whose status is beyond doubt, its claims may be subordinated to that entity's. Thus if there is a conflict between the rights of the embryo and the rights of the mother, an indubitably legal person, the mother's rights take precedence. My belief that the embryo must be respected as fully human from fertil-ization requires that I reject abortion as an option for myself. As that belief is unprovable, I cannot legitimately enforce it on other women.[21] Embryo research, by contrast, gives rise to no such direct conflict of rights. The question becomes whether society can legitimately destroy an entity that *may* be fully human in nature and status. The embryo must be given the benefit of the doubt. Of course, justifications have always been advanced for permitting the killing of indubitably human persons in certain cases. It might be argued that the public 'good' expected from embryo research justifies destruction of these 'may be' human persons. At the very least the onus of proof lies on those who advocate research.

What are the benefits that, it is argued, flow from research? They include improvement in fertility treatments, particularly IVF, the devel-opment of more effective means of contraception, the detection and 'cure' of genetic defects and disease, and, if we allow 'therapeutic cloning', the use of early embryonic tissue for transplantation into sick adults and children. How much could be achieved without research on live human embryos, is hotly disputed. It is difficult for a layperson to evaluate the scientific debate, mainly because scientific opinion on the merits of research seems to depend on what stance the scientist takes on the ethics of research. However, if the 'pro-research' camp confront some difficulty in establishing that the manifest benefit of research justifies the destruction of arguably human embryos, the 'anti-research' camp has a fundamental problem of its own. If an embryo is arguably human, it is wrong to destroy it, or to experiment on it for a purpose not designed to benefit it, so that it must ultimately perish. If it is wrong to destroy embryos for research purposes, it must also be wrong to destroy them in the course of infertility treatments using IVF. As long as 'spare' embryos are created, the surplus embryos are doomed to die. To return to a practice of harvesting only one egg from the woman, and so creating and implanting just one embryo, would probably deal a fatal blow to IVF. It is difficult to argue that it is ethical to destroy embryos to alleviate infertility and yet unethical to destroy embryos in order to improve our knowledge and treatment of genetic disease. Those who oppose research should logically also oppose IVF.[22]

Embryo research: the Human Fertilisation and Embryology Act 1990

The 1990 Act permitted licensed research up to fourteen days. It is a criminal offence punishable by up to two years' imprisonment to bring about the creation of an embryo (outside the human body) or to keep or use an embryo except in pursuance of a licence.[23] No embryo may be kept or used after the appearance of the primitive streak, that is fourteen days from the day the gametes were mixed, '. . . not counting any time during which the embryo was stored'.[24] Certain activities are expressly prohibited. Human embryos or gametes may not be implanted in animals, nor may animal embryos be inserted in humans.[25] Replacing the nucleus of a cell *of an embryo* with a cell taken from any person or embryo is outlawed.[26] This was intended to outlaw cloning. Trans-species fertilization, the attempt to create human/animal hybrids, is forbidden save for the 'hamster' test to establish the fertility or normality of sperm, when any resulting embryo must be destroyed at the two-cell stage.[27] The genetic structure of an embryo may not be altered '. . . except in such circumstances (if any) as may be specified in . . .' regulations to be made by the HFEA.[28]

The original rules governing embryo research in the Act centred on two principles. First, the Act implicitly accepts that respect is due to the embryo from fertilization, but that up until the development of the prim itive streak, the 'goods' to be expected from research outweigh the inter ests of the embryo. The Act grants full protection to the embryo only from fourteen days. Secondly, the Act sought to allay fears of a science-fiction nightmare in which scientists freely create all sorts of clones, hybrids and other monsters. It should be noted that until the enactment of the Human Fertilisation and Embryology Act embryos *in vitro* enjoyed no legal protection at all. The wording of abortion legislation prohibit ing 'procurement of miscarriage' meant that in theory 'test-tube' embryos could then be grown and destroyed at will.

Subject to these express prohibitions, researchers were given a remark ably free hand by the Act. Schedule 2 outlined what a research licence could authorize. Five specific purposes were outlined.[29]

(1) promoting advances in the treatment of infertility;
(2) increasing knowledge about the causes of congenital disease;
(3) increasing knowledge about the causes of miscarriage;
(4) developing more effective techniques of contraception;
(5) developing methods for detecting the presence of gene or chromo somal abnormalities in embryos before implantation.

Those five specific purposes may be seen, perhaps, as justification for the destruction of embryos, aimed at improving medicine and increas ing human happiness, designed to reassure those who are doubtful about, but not adamantly opposed to, research. To those named purposes is added an apparently innocuous phrase 'or for such other purposes as may be specified in regulations'.

Embryo research and cloning

From 1990 to about 1998 the fury of the embryo research debate abated. The birth of Dolly, the cloned sheep, changed all that. Dolly was created by a process of cell nucleus replacement (CNR). The nucleus of an adult cell was inserted into an emptied egg cell. The egg cell was then subjected to an electrical impulse so it began to divide and develop as an embryo. The embryo was implanted in a surrogate 'mother'. There is no scientific reason why this process could not (in theory) be replicated in humans. Two principal purposes could drive the development of CNR in humans, albeit mammalian cloning has proved an uncertain process. First, obviously attempts could be made to create a child, a copy of its lone parent sharing his or her DNA. Many British scientists abhor the notion of 'reproductive cloning'. However, a number of eminent ethicists argue that no case has been made out sufficient to justify banning it.[30] Secondly, stem cells could be collected from the cloned embryo. Embryonic stem cells retain their pluripotency. That means they can be cultured to develop into different sorts of tissue, or even grown into organs. 'Therapeutic cloning', or stem cell therapy offers the following scientific benefits. Assume that a patient has a neurological disease. An embryo could be created by CNR using DNA from one of the patient's own cells. Stem cells taken from the resulting embryo could be used to create tissue to repair her damaged brain.

The HFEA joined the Human Genetic Advisory Commission to consider the ethics of cloning. Their Report[31] recommended that regulations under the 1990 Act should be extended to allow the HFEA to authorize procedures:

(a) to extract embryonic stem cells for research on the possible treatment benefits in a wide range of disorders by replacing cells that have become damaged or diseased: and

(b) to conduct research into the treatment of some rare but serious inherited disorders carried in maternal mitochondria.

A further consultation led by the Chief Medical Officer[32] endorsed the recommendations of the HFEA and HGAC. Both ruled out reproductive cloning as beyond the pale. 'Good' cloning would be allowed. 'Bad' cloning would be banned. Regulations to permit stem cell therapy were approved by Parliament in January 2001.[33] These regulations purported to authorise the following additional research purposes:

- increasing knowledge about development of embryos;
- increasing knowledge about serious disease;
- enabling such knowledge to be applied in developing treatment for serious disease.

Alas the position was not so simple. The assumption was made that CNR fell within the 1990 Act. But it is not covered by section 3(3)(d), which had been intended to ban cloning. Section 3(3)(a) only bars replacing a nucleus of a cell taken from an embryo with a nucleus taken from any person or an embryo. CNR removes the nucleus from an egg cell, not an embryo. The government argued that none the less reproductive cloning was effectively outlawed because the HFEA would never license any attempt at reproductive cloning. It would be a crime, because creating an embryo without an HFEA licence is a crime. Embryo for the purpose of the 1990 Act is defined as follows:

embryo means a live human embryo where fertilization is complete.[34]

If CNR is used to create the embryo, *fertilization* never takes place.[35] CNR involves propagation not fertilization. Does it fall outside the 1990 Act in which case CNR 'cloning' could take place without a licence?

The All-Party Pro-Life Alliance challenged the regulations allowing stem cell therapy. They argued that the regulations were *ultra vires* because an embryo created by CNR was not an embryo within the definition provided in the 1990 Act. Crane J agreed that an embryo created otherwise than by fertilization fell outside the Act.[36] The government rushed through a new statute, the Human Reproductive Cloning Act 2001. That Act made implanting a CNR embryo in a woman a criminal offence. Creating such an embryo and implanting it abroad would not fall within that Act! The Court of Appeal came to the government's rescue. They ruled that, whatever the literal wording of the 1990 Act, had Parliament foreseen the development of CNR it would have intended such embryos to be within the 'genus covered by the legislation' and 'the clear purpose of the legislation would be defeated if the extension were not made.' The judges strained statutory interpretation to its outer limits. None the less, the Law Lords endorsed the appeal court's decision.[37]

As someone deeply sceptical about the legitimacy of embryo research, should it follow that I should be outraged by cloning? Cloning perturbs me, but in many senses it is no more than a logical outcome of permitting research at all. If the 'goods' of more successful fertility treatments justify destroying embryos, it is difficult to say that the 'good' of helping seriously ill patients does not. The argument may be raised that use of embryos is not essential to achieve that end. Adult stem cells could be treated to recover pluripotency. It might just take longer to do the research. Evaluating that debate is difficult for the non-scientific observer.

Cloning forces me to consider the basis of my opposition to embryo research. Embryos created from the fertilization of egg by sperm result (normally) in the creation of a unique new genetic entity. What is the nature of an embryo created by CNR using my nucleus, my DNA? If used solely for stem cell therapy, is it different from taking a skin graft from my leg to treat burns on my arm? Intuitively I think it is. Intellectually I flounder.

Embryo to foetus: foetus to baby

For the present, the embryo *in vitro* (be it created by fertilization or propagation) may not be allowed to develop beyond fourteen days from fertilization. What of the embryo *in vivo* growing and developing in his mother's womb? By twelve weeks the embryo will, if seen on an ultrasound scan, look distinctly human and from then on will be termed a foetus. In many legal systems the protection given to the embryo/foetus is extended as the pregnancy progresses, and the foetus develops. Thus, in France, abortion is allowed on demand up to ten weeks' gestation, and from then is permissible only on the ground of risk to the mother's health. In the USA the Supreme Court in *Roe* v. *Wade*[38] declared that any restriction on abortion in the first twelve weeks of pregnancy was unconstitutional. States may regulate abortion to protect maternal health from twelve to twenty-four weeks, and from viability (between twenty-four and twenty-eight weeks) the interests of the foetus take precedence over the interests of the mother. US law adopts a gradualist approach to the conflict of rights between the mother and her unborn child.

In England, the Abortion Act 1967 originally set no limit to the time when an abortion might lawfully be performed. Section 5(1) provided instead that nothing in the Act should affect the provisions of the Infant Life (Preservation) Act 1929 protecting the viable foetus. Under that Act any person who with intent to destroy the life of a child capable of being born alive causes the child to die before it has an existence independent of the mother is guilty of child destruction. The foetus was deemed to be capable of being born alive at twenty-eight weeks.[39] The objective of the 1929 law was to protect the foetus in the course of delivery,[40] and to safeguard any foetus who but for improper intervention could have been born alive.

Controversy raged over when a baby is 'capable of being born alive'. In *C.* v. *S.*[41] a young man, seeking to stop his girlfriend aborting their child at eighteen weeks, argued that at eighteen weeks a foetus was 'capable of being born alive'. It is fully formed and its heart may beat for a second or so after expulsion from the mother. But at eighteen weeks there is no prospect of a baby breathing independently of its mother even with the aid of a ventilator. The Court of Appeal found that to be 'capable of being born alive' a foetus must be able, on delivery, to breathe either naturally or with mechanical aid. The fight to limit late abortions returned to Parliament. Anti-abortion campaigners persuaded the government to agree to the introduction of an amendment to the Human Fertilisation and Embryology Bill designed to reduce the time-limit for abortions. Their attempt misfired, and after a night of confusion, section 37 of the Human Fertilisation and Embryology Act emerged. Section 37 produced a liberalization, rather than restriction, of abortion laws in England.

Section 37 amends the Abortion Act 1967 to provide that the time-limit for lawful abortions carried out on grounds of risk to the physical or mental health of the woman or her existing children shall be twenty-four weeks. In three cases, section 37 further provides that there shall be *no* time-limit, i.e. an abortion may be performed right up to the end of the pregnancy. Abortion up to birth is lawful when (1) termination is necessary to prevent grave permanent injury to the physical or mental health of the mother or (2) continuance of the pregnancy threatens the life of the mother or (3) there is a substantial risk that if the child is born it would suffer from such physical or mental abnormalities as to be seriously disabled. It is the third of these cases that is controversial. The Infant Life (Preservation) Act always permitted action necessary to save the life of the mother, even if doing so inevitably entailed the destruction of the child. Moreover, preventing grave permanent injury to her health was also almost certainly permissible.[42] Such cases of a stark choice between mother and child are few and far between in modern medicine. The third case permitting abortion up to forty weeks on grounds of foetal handicap was novel. In debate in Parliament that provision seemed to be regarded as covering only the most grave and horrifying of disabilities, perhaps where a woman was found late in pregnancy to be carrying an anencephalic child incapable of surviving more than a few hours after birth. However, the wording of section 37 is identical to the general foetal handicap ground provided for in the 1967 Act. Hence, if Down's syndrome or spina bifida are diagnosed, however late into pregnancy, the foetus may lawfully be destroyed. The impact of section 37 of the Human Fertilisation and Embryology Act is that in England children capable of being born alive may be killed providing they are disabled. The protection afforded to the viable foetus by the Infant Life (Preservation) Act is withdrawn from the disabled foetus. A medical practitioner acting within the provisions of the amended and extended Abortion Act cannot be convicted of child destruction. The 1929 Act remains in force, but is applicable only to unlawful late abortions, and those cases where a violent attack on a pregnant woman kills the child within her.

There is one crucial practical consequence of the current laws on abortion. Doctors aborting disabled foetuses late on in pregnancy must ensure that they use means that will destroy the foetus before it emerges from the mother. For if a child is born alive nothing in the Abortion Act or the Human Fertilisation and Embryology Act authorizes its destruction. On occasion, whatever the foetus is subjected to, a living child is born. Horror stories abound of premature infants left to die in the sluice room adjacent to the operating theatre where an abortion was attempted. What legal rules are applicable when an attempted abortion results not in a dead foetus, but a living albeit sick infant? The child once born alive is protected by the law of murder. Any positive act to destroy it is murder. Failure to offer the child proper care *with the intention that it shall die* on the part of persons with an obligation to care for the child is once again murder. In 1983 a consultant gynaecologist was charged with attempted murder. The prosecution was brought after pressure from anti-abortion campaigners. Police had been informed that a baby had been left on a slab to die for some time before being transferred to a paediatric unit. The allegation against the doctor was that he performed an abortion on the basis of an estimate of twenty-three weeks' pregnancy and, when the baby proved to be of thirty-four weeks' gestation, left it without attention intending it to die. The prosecution was dismissed by magistrates for lack of evidence. Failure to offer the child proper care out of incompetence or carelessness is manslaughter. The theory is clear. Reality is more problematical. A doctor who embarks on an abortion undertakes the care of the mother and undertakes to relieve her of her unwanted child. Yet the criminal law imposes on him an obligation to the child. His position none the less is clearly distinct from that of the doctor undertaking safely to deliver a mother of a desired child. And what of the child born disabled? The doctor sets out to abort on the grounds of the substantial disablity to the child, but if it survives must he then use all his efforts to save it? This leads us into the whole issue of medical care of the disabled newborn baby, his rights and those of his parents, a minefield I enter in chapter 14.

Selective reduction: selective feticide

So far, discussion of the legality of abortion has proceeded on the basis that the procedure used terminates the woman's pregnancy completely. There are cases where only selected foetuses in a multiple pregnancy are destroyed, and the pregnancy continues to term when the woman delivers her surviving children. Selective reduction, or selective feticide, may be advised either when the woman has a multiple pregnancy and is unlikely to carry all the foetuses safely to term, or when one of two or more foetuses is disabled. The 'surplus' or disabled foetuses will, using fetoscopically directed procedures, be killed. The dead foetuses are not expelled from the uterus, but may become 'foetus papyraceous', flattened and mummified, and emerge on delivery of their healthy brothers and sisters. Selective reduction to destroy a disabled twin was quietly practised for years. The development of IVF and consequent increase in multiple pregnancies brought the procedure to public attention. In a number of clinics, several embryos were routinely implanted to maximize the woman's chances of pregnancy. If she conceived quadruplets or more, the risk was that the several infants would be delivered prematurely and in the worst case scenario *all* might fail to survive. Selective reduction offered the prospect of one or two healthy children being born safely.

The deliberate destruction of selected foetuses raised ethical and legal problems. Legal debate focused on whether selective reduction could ever be lawful.[43] Some doctors tried to argue that as the dead foetus was not expelled from the mother's body, selective reduction was outside the ambit of the abortion laws altogether, for what the Offences Against the Person Act prohibits is 'procuring a miscarriage'. Other commentators contended that selective reduction was within the Offences Against the Person Act and so prima facie a crime, but beyond the ambit of the Abortion Act 1967. The 1967 Act provided lawful grounds for 'terminating a pregnancy'. Selective reduction did not terminate the pregnancy. Section 37(5)[44] of the Human Fertilisation and Embryology Act provides a relatively clear legal regime for selective reduction. Selective reduction is unlawful unless performed for one of the grounds on which termination of the whole pregnancy is lawful. Thus, if foetuses are destroyed on grounds of foetal handicap, or because a multiple pregnancy poses a risk to the mother's health, selective reduction of the chosen foetal victims is as lawful as ending the pregnancy altogether would be. The anomalous situation is this. Where multiple pregnancy occurs the underlying reason for wanting to destroy foetuses A and B is to maximize the prospects of a healthy birth for foetuses C and D. The ground that would need to be invoked is that of permitting abortion to safeguard the health of any 'existing children' of the pregnant woman. Can foetuses be regarded as 'existing children'? The whole philosophy of English law relating to the status of the foetus is that a foetus is not for legal purposes a child!

What section 37(5) does do is to give legal recognition to a much disputed procedure.[45] If foetuses can be selected and destroyed in effect as part and parcel of infertility treatment, the message from Parliament seems to be that unborn life is little more than a means to an end. The foetus itself counts for little. The parents' desire for children justifies its destruction. Selective killing of disabled foetuses with legal blessing reinforces the second-class status of the disabled foetus.

Nurses and abortion

Some nurses find abortion distasteful and distressing. A number have exercised their right of conscientious objection to refuse to participate in abortions. Some complain that doing so has prejudiced their careers. Occasionally doctors have complained of 'disloyalty' by nurses reporting irregularities in performing abortions, particularly late abortions. The nurses' greatest concern related to mid-trimester terminations, abortions in the middle months of pregnancy. The Abortion Act provides for circumstances when a pregnancy may lawfully be terminated by a registered medical practitioner, a doctor. In 1967 all lawful abortions were carried out by surgical means. The surgeon removed the foetus and ended the pregnancy. By 1972 medical induction of abortion was introduced as the standard method of terminating pregnancies in the middle months of pregnancy. Nurses play the leading role in this treatment. A doctor inserts a catheter into the woman's womb. Later, a nurse attaches the catheter via a flexible tube to a pump, which feeds the hormone prostaglandin through the catheter and induces premature labour. The nurse administers another drug via a drip in the woman's arm to stimulate her contractions. The immature foetus is born dead. The substances that cause the abortion are administered by the nurse, so she in effect terminates the pregnancy.

The Royal College of Nursing became concerned about the legality of medical inductions of abortion. They argued that a pregnancy terminated by a nurse was not lawfully terminated and that nurses might therefore face prosecution for conducting criminal abortions. The Department of Health and Social Security issued a circular upholding the legality of medical inductions of abortion. The Royal College of Nursing went to court for a declaration that the circular was wrong in law. The College lost in the High Court, won in the Court of Appeal and finally lost by three to two in the House of Lords.[46] A total of five judges out of nine agreed with the College, but it is the House of Lords' decision that counts. The majority of their Lordships held that the Act must be construed in the light of its social purposes, first, to broaden the ground on which abortions may lawfully be obtained, and second, to secure safe and hygienic conditions for women undergoing abortion. The Act contemplated the participation of a team of hospital staff involved in the overall treatment of the woman, and exonerated them all from criminal liability if the abortion was carried out within the terms of the Act. It was not necessary for a doctor to perform every physical act leading to the termination of the pregnancy. Provided a doctor accepts full responsibility for every stage in the treatment, a nurse acting under his instructions and in conformity with accepted medical practice does not act unlawfully when she administers the drugs that terminate the pregnancy in an induced abortion.

Conscientious objection

A vital component of the compromise on which the Abortion Act 1967 was based is the right of conscientious objection. Section 4 provides that no person shall be under any duty 'to participate in any treatment authorized by this act to which he has a conscientious objection'. Section 38 of the Human Fertilisation and Embryology Act confers a similar right to refuse to participate in embryo research or any of the infertility treatments regulated by that Act. It is for the person objecting to prove that their objection rests on grounds of conscience. And, in the case of abortion, the professional's conscience does not relieve him of any duty to intervene to save the life of the mother or to prevent grave permanent injury to her health.

In *Janaway* v. *Salford AHA*[47] the House of Lords was asked to determine who was entitled to rely on the right of conscientious objection. Mrs Janaway was a devout Roman Catholic employed as a secretary. She refused to type abortion referral letters and the authority dismissed her.

She challenged her dismissal as unlawful because, she argued, she was entitled to rely on the right of conscientious objection provided for by section 4. Her action failed. The Law Lords ruled that the term 'participate' in section 4 meant actually taking part in treatment designed to terminate a pregnancy. Mrs Janaway was not asked to do anything that involved her personally in the process of abortion. Yet she was an essential cog in the wheel. Abortion was as repugnant to her as murder. As far as Mrs Janaway was concerned, however irrational others might perceive her views to be, her employers were asking her to type out a death warrant.

The House of Lords' restrictive interpretation of the right to conscientious objection has other consequences too. A health care professional may legitimately refuse to carry out, or assist at, an abortion, but he cannot withdraw from any contact with abortion advice. Consider this example. A woman of over thirty-five receives her ante-natal care from an obstetrician who is adamantly opposed to abortion. The prevalence of Down's syndrome increases in mothers over thirty-five but the obstetrician never discusses with her whether in view of her age she should undergo amniocentesis to test for Down's syndrome. If she gives birth to a Down's baby, the mother may sue the obstetrician for negligence. If, as I strongly suspect, the overwhelming body of responsible professional opinion regards amniocentesis (or other available tests for Down's) as routine for pregnant women over thirty-five the obstetrician's right to conscientious objection will be of no avail to him. If his duty of care (as defined by his peers) extends to advice on amniocentesis, then even though that advice is almost inevitably an act preparatory to abortion, he must fulfil that duty, for it involves no active participation in the process of ending a pregnancy.

The right to conscientious objection is limited in scope and in practice difficult to exercise. Hospitals are not unnaturally somewhat wary of staff who will not participate in what has become a fairly common operation. It is said to be near impossible in most hospitals to gain a post in midwifery or gynaecology if you declare your conscientious objection to abortion.[48] Yet there remain areas of England where abortion within the NHS is nigh on unattainable. Is that a violation of women's rights caused by giving undue precedence to the professional's right to his conscience? The irony is that consultants and general practitioners can avoid involvement in abortion without having to invoke the right to conscientious objection. The doctor simply refuses to certify that a ground specified in the Act is made out. The woman's only recourse then is to find another more sympathetically inclined doctor. Her only remedy against the first practitioner would lie if she could prove that to refuse her an abortion was a breach of the duty of care owed to her. If the doctor is a consultant or a GP, no one can order him to participate in an abortion.

Fathers and abortion[49]

Has the father of the unborn child any say in whether or not the child should be aborted? In 1978 in *Paton* v. *British Pregnancy Advisory Service*,[50] a husband tried to prevent his wife having an abortion. She had been concerned about her pregnancy and consulted her doctor, but did not consult her husband. She obtained a certificate from two registered medical practitioners that the continuance of the pregnancy would involve risk to her health. So an abortion could lawfully proceed. Her husband intervened. He went to court to ask for an injunction (an order) to prevent the abortion from being carried out without his consent. The court refused an injunction. The judge said that the 1967 Act gave no right to the husband to be consulted. In the absence of such a right under the Act, the husband had 'no legal right enforceable at law or in equity to stop his wife having this abortion or to stop the doctors from carrying out the abortion'.

The abortion went ahead. The husband went to the European Commission on Human Rights, arguing that the Act and the judge's decision infringed the European Convention on Human Rights. He argued that his right to family life and the unborn child's right to life had been infringed. The Commission dismissed his claim.[51] They said that where an abortion was carried out on medical grounds, the husband's right to family life must necessarily be subordinated to the need to protect the rights and health of the mother. The unborn child's right to life was similarly subordinate to the rights of its mother, at least in the initial months of pregnancy. The Commission's decision suggests that a rather different view might be taken of abortions performed later in pregnancy and of abortions performed other than to protect the mother's health. However, in *C.* v. *S.*[52] the Court of Appeal, having held that the abortion of a foetus at eighteen weeks did not contravene the Infant Life (Prevention) Act 1929, refused the father any right *qua* father or as guardian of the unborn child to challenge the proposed abortion. It is clear that in England husbands have no standing to oppose an abortion agreed to by the wife, nor has a father any right to intervene to 'save' the foetus, nor can anyone argue that the foetus itself has legal personality so enabling him to act as its 'guardian' and stop an abortion.

One issue remains open. The father in *Paton* reluctantly accepted that the doctors' certificate as to the need for the abortion was issued in good faith. Had he challenged the certificate, could he have asked for an injunction to prevent an unlawful abortion taking place? The judge in *Paton* did not have to decide this point. He expressed the view that an injunction would not be granted. The supervision of abortion and the issue of the doctors' good faith is left to the criminal law and a jury. The Court of Appeal in *C.* v. *S.*[53] endorsed that opinion. A remedy that consists of the prosecution of the doctor after the event is not one to bring much comfort to fathers.

Girls under sixteen

The Abortion Act makes no special provision for abortion involving girls under sixteen. Must her parents consent to such an abortion? In 1981 a sad case was reported.[54] A fifteen-year-old girl who already had one child became pregnant again while in local authority care. She wanted an abortion. Her doctors believed that the birth of a second child would damage her mental health and endanger her existing child. The girl's father objected on the grounds that abortion was contrary to his religion. The local authority applied to have the girl made a ward of court and thereby seek the consent of the court to the operation. Butler-Sloss J authorized the abortion. She said that while she took into account the feelings of the parents she was satisfied that the girl's best interests required that her pregnancy be ended. Her decision was approved by the House of Lords in *Gillick* v. *West Norfolk and Wisbech AHA*.[55] *Gillick* would suggest that as long as the girl is mature enough to understand what abortion entails physically and emotionally, the doctor may go ahead on the basis of her consent alone. If the girl is insufficiently mature to make a decision for herself, the doctor must act in her best interests. Should her parents refuse consent to abortion, doctors and social workers may seek to go to court[56] and ask a judge to decide on the conflict between medical and parental opinion. Her wishes will be considered, but not treated as decisive. A doctor who ignores parental views will not be guilty of an offence of criminal abortion though. He may face legal action by the girl's parents in the civil courts, or, in an extreme case, prosecution for an assault on her.

What of a case where a girl's parents want their daughter to have an abortion but she refuses? The Court of Appeal in *Re W. (A Minor) (Medical Treatment)*[57] ruled that a doctor may lawfully proceed with treatment of any young person under eighteen with parental consent. He simply needs a valid consent either from his young patient herself or from her parents. *Gillick competent* children and minors under eighteen can authorize their own treatment but not veto treatment. In theory a gynaecologist could elect to override his patient's refusal to terminate her pregnancy as long as her parents endorsed the abortion. However to force an abortion on a girl must call into question whether either doctor or parents are acting in her interests. Lord Donaldson in *Re W.* thought it unthinkable that doctors would use the law to coerce young girls into abortion.[58] The vexed question of adolescents' rights to refuse treatment is explored further in Chapter 14.

Mentally disabled women

In *T. v. T.*[59] a woman of nineteen became pregnant. She was said to have a mental age of two, was doubly incontinent and incapable of any comprehensible speech. The problem for her mother and her doctors was that T. was quite incapable of giving her consent to the proposed abortion and, as she was an adult, no one else could authorize treatment on her behalf. Wood J granted a declaration that performing an abortion on T. was not unlawful if that operation was considered to be in her best interests and in conformity with good medical practice. Wood J's judgment was confirmed in *F. v. West Berkshire HA*.[60] The general questions about treatment of mentally disabled patients are fully dealt with in Chapter 5. In cases of disputed abortions the crucial factor should be whether the woman understands that she is pregnant and what the proposed abortion entails. If she has that degree of understanding, she is likely to be competent to make the decision for herself on whether or not to end the pregnancy. In other cases ultimately courts will decide for her.[61]

A moral mess?

The debate on the morality of abortion continues. Consensus on the moral claims of the human embryo is unattainable. The law in England is clear on one matter: the embryo/foetus has no legal personality or rights of its own until birth. It is recognized as an entity whose status deserves protection but not as a legal person with rights equal to yours or mine. The question thus becomes how much protection should the embryo/foetus be afforded and at what cost to maternal rights and interests? And should the level of protection increase with gestational age? Today the law recognizes two classes of foetus. Disabled foetuses are denied any protection from destruction even ones capable of surviving birth. 'Normal' foetuses acquire a qualified right to birth at twenty-four weeks dependent on their survival posing no grave risk to the mother. Up to twenty-four weeks the fate of the 'normal' foetus rests in the hands of its mother's doctors. Whatever the intentions of the 1967 Act, in practice it has conferred the authority to grant or withhold abortion on the medical profession. If the fate of the embryo/foetus cannot in our community be decided on the basis of consensus as to its moral status, would it be better to leave women to make the decision on abortion? Can it be right on any analysis that a woman's entitlement to abortion and her child's claim to life should depend on where in the country a woman happens to live?

14

Doctors and Children

In this chapter, I examine the law governing doctors' relationships with their child patients. The courts are often asked to determine the fate of sick children when doctors and parents disagree about how best to care for the child. Often what is at stake is the very life of the child. One tragic case involving the separation in 2000 of conjoined twins provided a heartrending challenge to doctors, parents and the courts.[1] The courts continue to struggle with the question of blood transfusions for the children of Jehovah's Witnesses. May a doctor insist on administering a transfusion against the parents' wishes? Some cases involve, not disagreement between doctors and parents, but disputes between parents themselves. Should a little boy be circumcized as his Muslim father wishes, when his mother vehemently opposes circumcision? On the opposite side of the coin, are there limits to treatment to which a parent may agree on behalf of the child? For instance, may a mother, learning that her four-year-old daughter is a likely carrier of haemophilia, have the child subjected to genetic testing for carrier status or even sterilized? As a child matures, common sense dictates that she be allowed to take more decisions for herself. *Gillick*[2] appeared to establish a right to adolescent autonomy. It proved to be an odd sort of 'right', a right to say yes but not to say no.[3]

I begin this chapter by looking at the legal position where everyone would agree that the child is too young to make any sort of decision about medical treatment for herself. I go on to explore the vexed issues surrounding adolescents.

The neonaticide debate

The birth of a severely disabled baby is a tragedy that most of us prefer to imagine will never happen to our family. The joy of normal childbirth is replaced by fear for the infant's and the family's future. Until relatively recently, two factors to some extent mitigated the parents' dilemma. Many severely disabled infants survived only a few weeks or months after birth. Their parents suffered the pain of bereavement, but were spared anxiety about the child's future. In any case, whether the child lived or died, the decision was made by 'God or nature'. The parents could do nothing about it. Advances in neonatal care have changed the picture. Doctors are able to prolong the lives of many, very sick, infants. At first they applied their skills to save the maximum number of babies. Some paediatricians voiced doubts about the wisdom of that policy. Some ethicists contend that in extreme cases the most gravely disabled babies should be actively put to death. The parents of a disabled baby may be faced with agonizing decisions about the treatment of their baby within hours of her birth.

It is not only in relation to disabled infants that doctors question the wisdom of always applying the full range of available treatments to prolong life. The problem arises equally acutely in relation to the terminally or chronically ill adult, or an older child irreversibly injured in an accident. None the less there are special features surrounding discussion of the care of sick infants. The conscious adult patient can speak for himself. The decision about any continuation of treatment may be his. Even if unconscious, he may earlier have expressed his wishes should the question arise. The baby cannot express any preference. Should parental wishes be decisive in this case? Parents' views are crucial, but children have rights too. The baby's plight is different from that of a newly-disabled adult. She does not move from full health to disability. She does not experience a dramatic drop in her expectations of life. A life of disability is all she can know. A body of opinion has developed among doctors, philosophers and lawyers that the treatment of sick adults and disabled babies raise somewhat separate issues.[4] The term neonaticide[5] has been coined. Proposals have been made for specific legislation on neonaticide.

Why is the treatment, or non-treatment of newly-born children such a vexed question? For paediatricians, one major factor is that the universal application of sophisticated medicine and surgery had disappointing long-term results. This is best illustrated by the example of babies born suffering from spina bifida. The development of surgery to effect external repairs, and of 'shunts' to drain water from the brain where hydrocephalus was present, was hailed as a landmark in the treatment of spina bifida. Virtually all affected babies were operated on within hours of birth. Research demonstrated that barely 41 per cent of the children treated reach their tenth birthday.[6] Of the survivors, only about 7 per cent could hope to lead something approximating to a normal life. All the children faced repeated painful surgery and hospitalization.

The Abortion Act permits the termination of pregnancy when there is a substantial risk that the child, if born, will be severely disabled. Amniocentesis is increasingly used to test mothers at risk for spina bifida or Down's syndrome. The amendment of the Abortion Act by section 37 of the Human Fertilisation and Embryology Act allows the abortion of such a child right up to the end of the pregnancy. Parents may find it difficult to understand why a child who could have been actively destroyed if his disability had been diagnosed in pregnancy must be the subject of intensive life-saving measures if his disability goes unnoticed until birth.

The concept of the sanctity of each and every human life is under attack. Forceful arguments are advanced that the value of life lies in its quality and its contribution to society, rather than in any intrinsic merit in life itself.[7] The newborn infant is no more a 'person' than the embryo or the foetus. Such arguments are equally forcefully rebutted,[8] but seem to have commanded a measure of support among the medical profession as far as severely damaged babies are concerned.

Proposals for legislation

Legislation on neonaticide has been proposed on two grounds. First, the law should be clarified. As we shall see in the case of Dr Arthur (p. 344), doctors may find themselves charged with the offence of murder. Second, the law should more readily permit doctors to withhold treatment, where parents concur, from children whose objective quality of life is low.[9]

A draft 'Limitation of Treatment Bill'[10] proposed that no criminal offence would be committed where a doctor refused or ceased treatment of an infant under twenty-eight days, provided that (1) the parents gave their written consent, and (2) two doctors, both of at least seven years' standing and one of them being a paediatrician, certified in writing that the infant suffered from severe physical or mental handicap that was either irreversible or of such gravity that after receiving all reasonably available treatment the child would enjoy no worthwhile quality of life. The Bill directed doctors to consider a number of factors in assessing the child's likely quality of life. They should consider (*inter alia*) the degree of pain and suffering likely to be endured, the child's potential to communicate, and also the willingness of the parents to care for him and the effect that that may have on *their* physical and mental health.

Mason and McCall Smith now suggest[11] that, if legislation were introduced to deal with adults in a permanent vegetative state, a specific clause addressing neonates should be included:

In the event of positive treatment being necessary for a neonate's survival, it will not be an offence to withhold such treatment if two doctors, one of whom is a consultant paediatrician, acting in good faith and with the consent of both parents if available, decide against treatment in the light of a reasonably clear medical prognosis which indicates that the infant's further life would be intolerable by virtue of pain or suffering or because of cerebral incompetence.

Both proposals apply only to the most severely damaged babies. The baby must have 'no worthwhile quality of life' or his quality of life must be 'intolerable'. Neither would excuse non-treatment of a Down's baby with no additional defect or deformity likely to lower his quality of life. The term 'severe cerebral incompetence' in the second proposal suggests a total inability to appreciate one's surroundings or communicate with others. It is a phrase that could cause endless difficulties of interpretation. Both stop short of sanctioning active measures to end the baby's life.

In the first edition of their celebrated text,[12] Mason and McCall Smith came close to proposing a limited form of active euthanasia, permitting doctors in the first *seventy-two hours* of life to 'arrange . . . for the termination of the life of an infant because further life would be intolerable by virtue of pain and suffering or because of severe cerebral incompetence'. Active euthanasia remains a minefield. Proposals in relation to neonates that focus exclusively on *withholding* treatment leave untouched what Mason and McCall Smith[13] describe as a 'critical dilemma', the fate of the terribly damaged infant who is not treated but none the less hangs on to life for a considerable period of time. Is actively ending such babies' lives an issue that ought to be faced, however distressing it is? For the argument goes: if it is permissible to stand by and watch the baby die slowly, why is it impermissible to end his life swiftly and painlessly? The intention in both cases is the same, that the baby die.

If legislation is to be enacted, society must take a series of deeply difficult and divisive decisions. Do we accept some distinction in the value of the life of the newborn, and the older child or adult? If so, where is the line to be drawn? Is it seventy-two hours, or twenty-eight days, or later? The Abortion Act altered our perception of the sanctity of life. Debate has ebbed and flowed for centuries as to the status and humanity of the unborn. Abortion, although severely punished, was never equated with murder. Birth is a clear dividing line. No other distinction can be as clear. Do we regard the parents as standing proxy for their child in any decision as to treatment? If so, why draw the line at twenty-eight days? Children may develop chronic diseases, be disabled in accidents, or are discovered to suffer from severe disabilities much later in childhood.

1981: Baby Alexandra

The fundamental principle governing withholding life-saving treatment from young children was settled in 1981. It concerned an infant girl, Baby Alexandra, who was born in 1981 suffering from Down's syndrome and an intestinal obstruction. In a normal child, simple surgery would have been carried out swiftly with minimal risk to the baby. Without surgery the baby would die within a few days. Her parents refused to authorize the operation. They argued that God or nature had given their child a way out. The doctors contacted the local authority and the child was made a ward of court. A judge was asked to authorize the operation. He refused to do so. The authority appealed, and the Court of Appeal ordered that the operation go ahead.[14] Counsel for the parents submitted that in this kind of decision the views of responsible and caring parents must be respected and that their decision should decide the issue. The Court of Appeal rejected the submission, holding that the decision must be made in the best interests of the child.

Templeman LJ said:

It is a decision which of course must be made in the light of the evidence and views expressed by the parents and the doctors, but at the end of the day it devolves on this court in this particular instance to decide whether the life of this child is demonstrably going to be so awful that in effect the child must be condemned to die, or whether the life of this child is still so imponderable that it would be wrong for her to be condemned to die. There may be cases, I know not, of severe proved damage where the future is so certain and where the life of the child is so bound to be full of pain and suffering that the court might be driven to a different conclusion, but in the present case the choice which lies before the court is this: whether to allow an operation to take place which may result in the child living for twenty or thirty years as a mongoloid or whether (and I think this brutally must be the result) to terminate the life of a mongoloid child because she also has an intestinal complaint. Faced with that choice I have no doubt that it is the duty of this court to decide that the child must live.

The trial of Dr Arthur

In the same year[15] that the Court of Appeal held that Alexandra must be treated and live, Dr Leonard Arthur, a distinguished paediatrician, faced trial for murder.[16] A baby suffering from Down's syndrome was born in the hospital where Dr Arthur was consultant paediatrician. His parents did not wish the baby to survive. He died sixty-nine hours after his birth. The prosecution alleged that Dr Arthur ordered nursing care only and prescribed a drug to suppress the baby's appetite and so starve him to death. They claimed that apart from being a Down's baby the baby was otherwise healthy, and that his death resulted from starvation and the effect of the drug causing him to succumb to bronchopneumonia. Defence evidence established that (1) the baby suffered from severe brain and lung damage, (2) Dr Arthur followed established practice in the management of such an infant, (3) that in the first three days of life normal babies take in little or no sustenance and usually lose weight (which the dead baby had not done). The baby patently did not starve to death. The judge directed that the charge be altered to attempted murder. Summing up on the law for the jury, the judge stressed that there is '. . . no special law in this country that places doctors in a separate category and gives them special protection over the rest of us.' He emphasized that however severely disabled a child may be, if the doctor gives it drugs in an excessive amount so that the drugs will cause death then the doctor commits murder. He highlighted the distinction between doing something active to kill the child and electing not to follow a particular course of treatment that might have saved the infant. Considering the ethical arguments on terminating newborn life, the judge reminded the jury that if ethics and the law conflict, the law must prevail. His lordship concluded:

. . . I imagine that you [the jury] will think long and hard before deciding that doctors of the eminence we have heard in representing to you what medical ethics are and apparently have been over a period of time, you would think long and hard before concluding that they in that great profession have evolved standards which amount to committing crime.

The jury acquitted Dr Arthur.

A confused picture emerged. A baby girl with Down's syndrome was ordered to be saved. Dr Arthur was not guilty of a crime in relation to his treatment of a severely damaged Down's infant. In attempting to reconcile these decisions, the starting point must be that the jury's acquittal of Dr Arthur tells us little about the law. The confusion over the pathological evidence may have irretrievably prejudiced the jury against the prosecution's case. The baby's multiple abnormalities should have been irrelevant to the reduced charge of attempted murder. When Dr Arthur ordered nursing care only, he thought that he was dealing with a 'normal' Down's baby. Did the jury see it that way? Above all a charge of murder, with its emotional baggage and a mandatory life sentence, was always going to be difficult to sustain against a defendant renowned as a dedicated and caring paediatrician. As Mason puts it: 'Murder, in the popular sense of the word, was the one thing of which Dr Arthur was certainly innocent.'[17] Subsequent judgments need to be explored to understand the parameters within which doctors and parents can lawfully determine whether and how to treat a severely disabled child. The implications of the complex judgment in the tragic case of the conjoined twins have to be assessed.

Deliberate killing

In all but the exceptional instance illustrated by the case of the conjoined twins it is indisputable that neither doctor, nor parents, nor anyone else may do any *act* intended *solely* to hasten the death of the disabled baby. The deliberate killing of any human being is murder. The moment that the child has an existence separate from his mother,[18] the moment he has independent circulation, even though the afterbirth may not yet fully have been expelled from the mother's body, he is protected by the law of homicide. It has on occasion been faintly argued that a grossly malformed child, 'a monstrous birth', should not be regarded in law as human. We shall see that this argument was advanced unsuccessfully in the conjoined twins case.[19] No court is likely to accede to such a view. Defining humanity, other than by virtue of human parentage, is an impossible and unacceptable task. Does 'monstrous' refer to appearance, in which case an intelligent infant of appalling mien could legitimately be destroyed? Does it cover lack of intelligence, lack of a brain?[20] Both are almost impossible to measure at birth.

None the less, in *Re A. (Minors) (Conjoined Twins: Separation)* the Court of Appeal authorized the killing of the weaker of two conjoined twins. Jodie and Mary[21] were born in Manchester after a scan in their native Malta revealed their condition. Their parents came to this country in the hope of surgery to separate and save both children. The girls were joined at the pelvis. Each had her own arms and legs as well as a brain, heart and lungs. Mary's brain was said to be 'primitive', her heart was defective, and she had no functioning lung tissue. Mary remained alive only because a common artery allowed Jodie's heart to circulate oxygenated blood to both infants. Left conjoined, the strain on Jodie's organs would result in the death of both children within three to six months. Surgery to separate the girls would result in Mary's death within minutes of separation.[22] Doing nothing would result in the death of both girls. The twins' parents were devout Roman Catholics. They refused to consent to surgery because they believed that it would be a sin to 'murder' Mary and that their children's fate must be subject to God's will. The hospital applied to the court for authority to overrule the parents' objections.

The Court of Appeal ruled that surgery should go ahead. Their judgment runs to over seventy pages and what follows can only be a summary of their Lordship's complex, and not always unanimous, reasoning. Let us deal first with the question of how it could be said to be lawful to kill Mary. Mary, all the judges agreed, was in law a person whose right to life was entitled to respect. She was not to be regarded as non-human, a monster or, as some had suggested, a 'tumour' attached to Jodie's body. Ward and Brooke LJJ[23] accepted that surgery to separate the twins constituted killing Mary. However much their doctors wished the case to be different, in cutting off Mary's blood supply by clamping the common artery, they 'intended' Mary's death. Unless some lawful excuse justified their conduct the doctors were exposed to liability for murder.

The Court found such lawful excuse in the doctrine of necessity.[24] Brooke LJ cited the analogy of the captain of a ship about to capsize who had to choose who entered the lifeboats. The judge continued

He would not be guilty even though he kept some of the passengers back from the boat at revolver-point and he would not be guilty even though he had to fire the revolver.[25]

Surgeons caring for the conjoined twins had duties to both girls. Surgery would involve a fatal assault on Mary but to save Jodie it was justifiable. It was necessary to avoid an inevitable and irreparable evil. It was no more than what was necessary to preserve Jodie's life. Given Mary too would die without surgery, the evil of her inevitable death was not disproportionate.

A finding that surgery did not constitute murder did not conclude the question of the twins' fate. The more important question revolved around who had the right to make the crucial decision. Doctors wanted to operate. The parents objected. Before going on to look at the question of who decides, we must first consider the more common case, where what is at stake is not actively killing a child but withholding treatment from her.

Withholding treatment

To what extent does the law require parents and doctors to provide treatment to prolong the baby's life? The bare bones of the law can be stated simply. Before any failure to treat a child can engage *criminal* liability, it must be established that a duty to act was imposed on the accused. Parents are under a duty to care and provide for their dependent children. Failing to provide proper care, including medical aid where necessary, will result in a conviction for wilful neglect of the child, provided that the parent was aware of the risk to the child's health.[26] Should the child die, the parents may be convicted of manslaughter.[27] Parents who are aware of the danger to a child's health but who do not seek medical aid because of religious or other conscientious objection to conventional medicine have no defence to criminal prosecutions for neglect or manslaughter.[28] Parents who deliberately withhold sustenance and care from a child intending him to die may be guilty of murder.[29] Finally, a range of other legal remedies are available to local authority social services departments. Failure to provide medical aid, risking significant harm to the child, is a ground for taking a child into care.[30]

What of the doctor? If he is under a duty to treat a baby then he too could be prosecuted for manslaughter if the child dies as a result of his neglect, or for murder if he intended the infant to die. Once the doctor accepts the baby as a patient he assumes a duty to that baby to give him proper medical care. Nor is it likely that a paediatrician could, should anyone ever want to, evade responsibility by refusing to accept a child as a patient after his birth. His contract with the NHS imposes on him an obligation towards the children born in his hospital, giving rise to a duty to the individual infant.[31]

Parents and doctors have a duty to provide medical aid, but what is the scope of that duty? Where a child is suffering from severe disabilities, may proper medical care be defined as keeping her comfortable but deliberately withholding life-prolonging treatment? Two factors play a vital role in deciding whether to treat an acutely ill child. What do her parents desire? What is the practice of the medical profession in the management of her kind of illness or disability? The answer to the second question is that in many instances doctors will explain the treatment available, give a prognosis as to the child's future, and accept the decision taken by the parents. Yet, as we have seen, in the case of Alexandra the Court of Appeal ordered surgery to remove an intestinal blockage against her parents' wishes. How can that judgment be reconciled with Dr Arthur's acquittal? The conditions of the two children were different. Baby Alexandra suffered from the mental and physical disabilities attendant on Down's syndrome. If treated, she could expect the same quality of life as any one of the many other Down's babies born each year. She would suffer no pain from her disability, and the evidence suggests that properly cared for Down's children lead happy lives. The surgery needed to save Alexandra was simple and without risk. Dr Arthur's infant patient was severely damaged over and above his condition as a Down's baby. Whether Dr Arthur should have actively intervened to save him once he developed bronchopneumonia was never properly examined at his trial.

Is the legality of withholding treatment dependent on the degree of a child's disability and the degree of suffering continued life may cause him? Need a severely disabled child whose existence appears to give him no pleasure of any sort and to cause him pain not be treated? That some sort of balance between the pain of prolonged life and the finality of death has to be struck seems to emerge from the immediately post-1981 case law.

'Best interests': a balancing exercise

In *Re C*.[32] a severely disabled baby had been made a ward of court shortly after birth on the grounds of her parents' inability to care for her. She suffered from an exceptionally severe degree of hydrocephalus, and the brain itself was poorly formed. She appeared to be blind and virtually deaf. At sixteen weeks she was, apart from her enlarged head, the size of a four-week baby. It was said to be inevitable that she would die in a matter of months at most. The issues put before the court were these. If it became impossible to go on feeding her by syringe, must she be fed naso-gastrically or intravenously? If she developed an infection, must she be treated by antibiotics? The judge asked the Official Solicitor to intervene and sought the advice of an eminent professor of paediatrics, who examined C. He advised that those caring for C. should not be *obliged* to resort to artificial feeding, or treat C. with antibiotics, simply to prolong her life. The judgement on how to treat C. should depend primarily on relieving her suffering. The judge therefore made an order that leave be given to 'treat the ward to die'. This infelicitous phrase caused an outcry, being wrongly interpreted by some of the media as sanction for active euthanasia. The Court of Appeal affirmed his judgment, deleting the unfortunate phrase. Lord Donaldson MR saw C.'s case as very different from that of Baby Alexandra in *Re B*. C. was inevitably dying. Her life appeared to offer her no pleasures. The court ordered: 'The hospital authority be at liberty to treat the minor to allow her life to come to an end peacefully and with dignity . . .'

A year later in *Re J*.[33] the Court of Appeal confronted a more difficult case. J. had been born thirteen weeks premature and with a birth weight of 1.1 kg. He nearly died several times but was saved by medical skill. He was found to have very severe brain damage: 'A large area of fluid filled cavities where there ought to have been brain tissue.' J. was said to be likely to develop paralysis, blindness and probable deafness. Unlike C., he was not imminently dying and his life expectancy might extend to his late teens. If he developed an infection, must he be treated? If he suffered a further episode of cyanosis and collapse, must he be resuscitated? The Court of Appeal found he need not. Lord Donaldson regarded *Re B*. as near to binding authority that a balancing exercise should be performed in assessing the course to be adopted in the best interests of the child. The exercise must seek to reflect the 'assumed' view of the child. In deciding whether the prolonged life of the child will be 'demonstrably awful', the child's perspective on life is the crucial test. He will know no other life, and the amazing adaptability and courage of disabled people must be considered.

But in the end there will be cases in which the answer must be that it is not in the interests of the child to subject it to treatment which will cause increased suffering and produce no commensurate benefit, giving the fullest possible weight to the child's, and mankind's, desire to survive.[34]

Note that in *Re J.* there was no disagreement between J.'s parents and doctors. The application to the court was undertaken to ensure that any decision to withhold treatment was lawful and neither parents nor doctors would risk prosecution.

In the case of the conjoined twins, *Re A.*,[35] there was disagreement. Having decided that ending Mary's life was not unlawful, the court had to address *whose* judgement on the interests of the two little girls should determine their fate. Their Lordships stressed that while the decisions of devoted and responsible parents should be treated with respect, the court retained power to intervene to protect the paramount welfare of the child. The conjoined twins case was unique because Jodie's welfare depended on Mary's demise. The parents, however, had other separate concerns about Jodie. They feared that she would be profoundly handicapped, unable to walk, possibly doubly incontinent, and likely to have to undergo several more operations during her infancy.[36] Their view was that it was not in the interests of either child to operate. The Court of Appeal disagreed. There was a reasonable prospect that Jodie could lead a relatively normal life. Mary, Ward LJ said, was 'beyond help'. Surgery might shorten her brief life. Without surgery she would still die. The '. . . least detrimental choice, balancing the interests of Mary against Jodie and Jodie against Mary permits the operation to be performed.'[37]

Jodie's prospects, it might be said, were not 'demonstrably awful'. Even had the worst prognosis proven right, Jodie would enjoy a quality of life not available to C. or J. Will the courts then always rule in favour of continuing a child's life unless it is either likely to involve unbearable suffering or will be such that the child will have virtually no ability to enjoy any of the senses or use any of her abilities? *Re T.*[38] (1997) poses a problem. A little boy was born with biliary atresia, a life-threatening liver disease. Without a liver transplant, he would die at about two and a half years of age. Earlier less radical surgery when he was three-and-a-half weeks old had failed and the baby suffered great pain and distress. His parents, both health professionals, adamantly opposed transplant surgery. Fearing intervention by social services, the parents fled abroad to a country without facilities for a liver transplant. The local authority intervened seeking a court order requiring the family's return to England and that the transplant go ahead. The parents argued that if their son had the transplant, even if the operation was successful, he would be subjected to further pain and distress, he would have to take anti-rejection drugs for the rest of his life and might face repeated surgery. They thought that his best interests were better served by a short, happy life and a peaceful death. The Court of Appeal ruled that the parental views should prevail. The parents in *Re T.* were entitled to withhold life-saving treatment from their child.

The essence of the court's ruling in *Re T.* was that on the 'unusual facts' of the case any presumption that the best interests of the child are to prolong his life was rebutted. The trial judge, ordering the transplant, had given insufficient weight to the mother's views. If the operation was ordered against her will, her son's welfare would be compromised. Her commitment to his care was an integral part of any successful recovery post-transplant. Deprived of her care (i.e. taken into care) he would suffer. If she reluctantly complied with the court order, family problems would beset child and parents. The mother would have to return to, and remain in England reluctantly. It was not clear whether the father would give up his job and return with her. If not, problems would arise in terms of financial and emotional support for mother and son. Butler-Sloss LJ finding that the mother's view could not be considered unreasonable said this:

The mother and child are one for the purposes of this unusual case and the decision of the court to consent to the operation jointly affects the mother and it also affects the father. The welfare of the child depends on his mother. The practical considerations of her ability to cope with supporting the child in the face of her belief that this course is not right for him, the requirement to return probably for a long time to this country, either to leave the father behind and lose his support or to require him to give up his present job and seek one in England were not put by the judge into the balance when he made his decision.[39]

Is *Re T.* an aberration? Consider Butler-Sloss LJ's language. She says 'mother and child are one' and that the child's welfare depends on his mother. Where the child remains with loving parents, is this not usual rather than unusual? A sick child always requires extra parental commitment. Why you might ask did a similar analysis not apply to Jodie, the stronger of the conjoined twins? Are there other features of *Re T.*? All the judges emphasize that the parents were themselves health professionals. Did this give their views extra weight? More importantly, and what is truly unusual about *Re T.*, is that any court order would also have needed to drag the family back from the other side of the world. Would *Re T.* have had the same outcome if the parents had never left England?[40]

Scruple or dogma?[41]

Re T. is an uncommon case. Much more common are cases where parents who are Jehovah's Witnesses refuse to consent to blood transfusions for their children. Transfusion violates a fundamental tenet of Witnesses' faith.[42] The kinds of case that reach the courts are well illustrated by *Re S.* (1993).[43] S was four-and-a-half and suffering from R-cell leukaemia. His parents agreed to intensive chemotherapy. Doctors argued that transfusion of blood products was essential to maximize the prospects of successful treatment and so of saving S.'s life. Without resort to blood the chances of successful treatment were significantly reduced. His parents objected not only on religious grounds, but also raised concerns about the safety of blood products. Their lawyers argued that S.'s relationship with his family might suffer for his parents would believe that his life had been prolonged by an 'ungodly act'. Thorpe J dismissed the parental objection. The child's welfare required he be given the best chance of prolonged life. He was unimpressed by talk of problems in the family later in life.

Reconciling *Re S.* and *Re T.* is nigh on impossible. In a whole series of cases, while judges now show some understanding of the dilemma that Jehovah's Witness parents' face, in the end the English courts endorse continuing life and overrule parental objections.[44]

Perhaps part of the key to apparently contradictory decisions about parents' rights to determine the treatment of their young children can be found in the judgment of Waite LJ in *Re T.* (1997).[45] He contrasts cases where parental opposition to treatment is '. . . prompted by scruple or dogma of a kind that is patently irreconcilable with principles of health and welfare widely accepted by the generality of mankind' and '. . . highly problematic cases where there is a genuine scope for a difference of opinion'. Ward LJ in the conjoined twins' case says[46] that

that was not a case where the parents' opposition to surgery to separate the girls was 'prompted by scruple or dogma'.

How much weight should parents' religious beliefs carry? Parents will argue that Article 8 of the Human Rights Convention (endorsing their right to family life) and Article 9 (guaranteeing religious freedom) mean that their views should be conclusive. Both Articles are qualified. The parents' 'rights' must be balanced against the children's interests. Caroline Bridge has argued that prolonging a child's suffering by delaying treatment, in attempts to meet parents' convictions, undervalues the child's interests.[47]

Responsibilities not rights?

One consistent message can be elicited from the case law about the medical treatment of young children. The common law only confers on parents those rights they need to fulfil their undoubted responsibilities to provide adequate medical care for their children. Failure to provide such care exposes parents to possible criminal liability.[48] Lord Templeman sums up the position succinctly in *Gillick* v. *West Norfolk and Wisbech AHA*.

Where the patient is an infant, the medical profession accepts that a parent having custody and being responsible for the infant is entitled on behalf of the infant to consent or to reject treatment if the parent considers that the best interests of the infant so require. Where doctor and parent disagree, the court can decide and is not slow to act, I accept that if there is no time to obtain a decision from the court, a doctor may safely carry out treatment in an emergency if the doctor believes the treatment to be vital to the survival or health of the infant and notwithstanding the opposition of a parent or the impossibility of alerting the parent before the treatment is carried out.[49]

In emergency[50] doctors may proceed without parental consent or court authority. So if a child is brought into casualty bleeding to death after a road accident and his Jehovah's Witness parents refuse to agree to a blood transfusion, the hospital can overrule them if delay threatens the child's life. Dire necessity justifies their action.

Judicial intervention to overrule parental judgements of a child's interests is becoming more common. Two key cases, both confusingly entitled *Re C.*, illustrate the issues. In *Re C. (A Minor) (Medical Treatment)*,[51] Orthodox Jewish parents argued that their sixteen-month-old daughter with spinal muscular atrophy should continue to be ventilated. Doctors argued that continued ventilation was futile. The child was dying and ventilation would only prolong her life by a few days. The parents' faith dictated that every effort be made to preserve the spark of life. The court declined to interfere with the doctors' clinical judgement. *Re C.* can be explained in several ways. Consistently English courts have refused to order doctors to carry out treatment that in their clinical judgement they consider inappropriate.[52] It can be argued persuasively that prolonging a child's suffering cannot be in her interests.[53] Is *Re* C., however, another case where judges may have been tempted to dismiss the parents' case as 'scruple and dogma'?

Re C. (HIV Test)[54] is very different on its facts. A baby was born to an HIV positive mother. The mother had refused conventional treatment for HIV, refused treatment in pregnancy that might have diminished the risk of transmitting HIV to the child, and intended to breastfeed. Both parents refused to agree to an HIV test for their baby. They argued that any possible treatment for the child (were she HIV positive) could be more toxic than beneficial and that sero-positive status would stigmatize the child. The local authority, applying for an order to test the child, relied on medical opinion that the child was at a 25 per cent risk of having contracted HIV and that effective medical care of the child required knowledge of her HIV status. The Court of Appeal upheld the trial judge's view that the child's interests should allow the HIV test.

In judgment after judgment, with the notable exception of *Re T.* (1997), courts prefer medical opinion to parental judgement. Nor does it seem that the Human Rights Act will make too much of a difference. In *Re C. (HIV Test)* the parents sought to assert their right to respect for family life enshrined in Article 8 of the European Convention on Human Rights. But, as the trial judge noted, such a claim is swiftly countered by consideration of the child's own rights and the needs of his health and welfare expressly recognized in Article 8 (2).

Resolving 'conflicts of rights' is far from easy. Disputes between parents can be just as complex as disagreements between doctors and parents. In *Re J. (Child's Religious Upbringing and Circumcision)*[55] a devout Muslim father sought a court order to circumcize his five-year-old son. The child's non-Muslim mother objected. The couple were estranged. The father argued that circumcision would identify child with father and establish the boy within the Muslim community. He invoked his right under Article

9 of the European Convention on Human Rights to freedom of religion. The mother's religious adherence to Christianity was said to be notional only. There were no medical grounds for circumcision. The courts found for the mother, influenced by the pain and distress circumcision might cause the boy.

Re J. (1999) came to court because the parents disagreed about circumcision. It illustrates one of the anomalies of the law. If the principle is that treatment necessary for the welfare of the child should be carried out and nothing contrary to his interest should be done, is circumcision even with both parents' agreement lawful?

The limits of parental consent

As parental rights to determine medical treatment of their children derive from the parental duty to obtain adequate medical care for them, those rights cannot be unfettered. In Skegg's words a parent may give '. . . a legally effective consent to a procedure which is likely to be for the benefit of the child, in the sense of being in the child's best interests'.[56] Routine treatment or surgery for an existing physical condition, diagnostic procedures, preventative measures such as vaccination, pose no problem. The likely benefit is there for all to see. More intricate and even risky procedures cause little difficulty. Not all parents might agree to complex heart surgery on a baby, but if doctors and parents weigh risk and benefit and conclude in favour of going ahead, they have exercised their respective duties properly.

Where problems do surface is in relation to medical or surgical procedures not immediately called for to treat or prevent ill-health. Two classic issues are dealt with later – whether a child can donate organs or tissue (chapter 16) and when children can be used for medical research purposes (chapter 17).

In 1976 the case of *Re D.*[57] came before Heilbron J. It concerned a girl aged eleven. She suffered from Soto's syndrome and was afflicted by epilepsy and a number of other physical problems. The girl was also to some extent emotionally and mentally disabled. Her mother was anxious about her future and considered that she might all too easily be seduced and would be incapable of practising any form of contraception. If she had a child she would never be capable of caring for it and that having a child would damage her. Accordingly she sought to have her sterilized before these risks should materialize. The girl's paediatrician agreed, and a gynaecologist was found who was ready to perform the operation. An educational psychologist involved with the child disagreed and applied to have the child made a ward of court. Heilbron J ordered that proposals for the operation be abandoned. Her function, she said, was to act as the 'judicial reasonable parent', with the welfare of the child as her paramount consideration. She found that medical opinion was overwhelmingly against sterilization of such a child at eleven. The irrevocable nature of sterilization, the emotional impact on the girl when she discovered what had been done to her, her present inability to understand what was proposed, coupled with evidence that her mental development was such that she would one day be able to make an informed choice for herself on childbearing, all led the judge to conclude that the operation was '. . . neither medically indicated nor necessary. And that it would not be in [the girl's] best interests for it to be performed'.[58]

None the less eleven years later in *Re B*.[59] (1987) the House of Lords sanctioned the sterilization of seventeen-year-old Jeanette. Jeanette was much more profoundly disabled than D. She was said to have a mental age of five or six, with a much more limited capacity to communicate. She had no understanding of the link between sexual intercourse and pregnancy. Those caring for her testified that, apart from sterilization, no means of reliable contraception would be suitable for Jeanette. If she became pregnant, delivery might well have to be by Caesarean section, and the girl had an unbreakable habit of picking and tearing at any wounds. Despite her profound disability, Jeanette was sexually mature and provocative. The Law Lords held that the legality of the proposal to sterilize Jeanette depended only on whether sterilization would '. . . promote the welfare and serve the best interests of the ward'.[60] Consideration of eugenics, and whether sterilizing Jeanette would ease the burden on those caring for her, were irrelevant.[61] Their Lordships concluded that as Jeanette (1) would never be capable of making any choice for herself on whether to have a child, (2) would never even appreciate what was happening to her, and (3) would suffer damage to her health if she ever became pregnant, she could lawfully be sterilized by occlusion of her Fallopian tubes (not hysterectomy). Lord Templeman, however, suggested that the radical nature of sterilization was such that a girl under the age of eighteen should never be sterilized without the consent of a High Court judge.

A doctor performing a sterilization operation with the consent of the parents might still be liable to criminal, civil or professional proceedings. A court exercising the wardship jurisdiction emanating from the Crown is the only authority which is empowered to authorize such a drastic step as sterilization after a full and informed investigation.[62]

Following *Re B.* a number of subsequent cases appeared to evidence judicial willingness to authorize sterilization of young girls fairly readily. If a girl required surgery to treat some separate health problem, for example menstrual difficulties, it was suggested no application to the court was required. Parental consent alone authorized the surgery, albeit an inevitable result of the operation was to render the girl sterile. Recent decisions relating to the proposed sterilization of adult women indicate that judges are more ready to scrutinize any proposal to sterilize a woman more rigorously and that cases where other surgery, such as hysterectomy, will result in infertility and where reasonable people might disagree on what was best for the patient ought to go before a judge (see page 279).[63]

What *Re B.* re-affirms in the context of children's treatment generally is that parental powers are limited. Albeit parents honestly believe they are acting in their child's interests, if they propose to authorize some irreversible or drastic measure, their authorization alone will not make that measure lawful. It must be shown to be in the child's interests. No mother could authorize the sterilization of her four-year-old daughter because that daughter was a haemophilia carrier. She has no right to deprive her child of the right to make that decision herself. The child's best interests include her potential right to autonomy. It seems unlikely that parents could authorize a vasectomy on even the most severely mentally disabled son (see pages 280).[64] Such an operation would not be in his interests, albeit it benefited society. Similarly no parent, however strong or genuine his commitment to medical research might be, could lawfully authorize the entry of his healthy child into a research trial posing real and substantial risk to that child's health.

Other examples could be debated endlessly. Just one more will be considered here, cosmetic surgery. May a mother put her son through painful surgery to advance his career as a male model? Certainly not. That cannot be said to be in the interests of the child, rather than the mother's vicarious ambition. Yet surgery on boys with 'bat ears' is common and lawful. The pain of surgery is balanced by the child's misery at being taunted for his deformity. Parents are allowed to judge the outcome of the 'balancing exercise'. Difficult questions are posed by cosmetic surgery on Down's children. Cosmetic surgery may make the child more socially acceptable. Is that in the interests of the child?

Procedures to protect children

I do not examine in any detail the procedural means by which disputes about the care of treatment of a child come before the courts. One or two brief points about parental responsibility and family law procedures should be noted here.

Where a child's parents are married both parents share parental responsibility for her.[65] Normally in relation to medical treatment the consent of one parent to the treatment of their young child suffices. If I take my five-year-old for a booster vaccination, the doctor does not need to delay matters by ensuring that my husband also agrees to her vaccination. The courts have, however, made it clear that where some major or irreversible decision needs to be made about a child's treatment or where there is disagreement between the parents, both parents' consent is required and/or the case must be referred to the court.[66]

Where parents are not married, it used to be the mother alone who had parental responsibility for her child unless the parents had either entered into a formal agreement to share parental responsibility or the father had obtained a court order conferring parental responsibility on him. The Adoption and Children Act 2002 confers parental responsibility on unmarried fathers who jointly register the child's birth. Should a father without parental responsibility, another relative such as a grandparent, local social services, or any other third party show concerns about a child's medical treatment, a number of means exist by which a dispute concerning the child's welfare can be adjudicated by a court. The child could be taken into care or made a ward of court.[67] but that is rare these days. The inherent jurisdiction of the Court can be invoked or an order sought under section 8 of the Children Act 1989.[68] Section 8 orders are diverse in kind.[69] Of particular relevance here are 'specific issue orders' and 'prohibited steps orders'. If a grandfather[70] strongly believes that surgery to correct a hideous birthmark is in the child's interests and her mother opposes surgery solely because she believes that her child's deformity was 'God's will – a punishment for being born out of wedlock' he may seek a 'specific issue order'. Should he seek to prevent the performance of purely cosmetic surgery, which the child's mother wants because she wants the child to be a model, he could apply for a 'prohibited steps order' to prevent surgery.

Sadly the machinery to protect children from inappropriate 'treat-ment' operates fairly randomly. In the course of the judgment in *Re D.* (above), it emerged that two similar sterilization operations on mentally disabled girls had already been performed in Sheffield. D. was lucky. Her psychologist was persistent. Chance took D.'s dilemma to the High Court. This is often the case when parents and doctors agree. Despite judicial pronouncements that sterilization of girls under eighteen must always be a matter for the courts, girls have been sterilized by hysterectomy for 'hygienic' reasons without judicial approval. These cases involve girls who cannot in any sense cope with menstruation. They may refuse to wear their sanitary towels, or in extreme cases may eat them. It is not clear beyond doubt that such an operation is in the girl's interests, though it is certainly in her carers' interests. The Court of Appeal considers that such 'borderline' cases should always go before a judge. However, the problem in protecting such girls is that it is only if some interested third party intervenes that the matter will reach the light of day in time to prevent the procedure going ahead. Nor is the law much of a deterrent to doctors or parents. Technically, if a procedure is not medically indi-cated and/or in the child's best interests it amounts to a civil battery against the child and may be a criminal assault. In debates on the prohi-bition of female circumcision Lord Hailsham argued that genital muti-lation was already a crime, assault occasioning actual bodily harm. But who will tell the authorities; who will prosecute? Besides which, had the common law been faced with the question of female circumcision, difficult questions would have been set in answering the question of the girl's best interests. What if she agreed, wishing to fall in with the custom of her community? What of arguments that the girl's mental well-being required that she meet the customs of her people? If ritual male circum-cision is permissible, why not female circumcision, if carried out by surgeons in aseptic conditions?

Child abuse

The complexities of the law relating to child abuse are also beyond the scope of this book. Again one or two issues of especial concern should be mentioned.

A doctor treating a child whom he suspects may have been abused faces a dilemma. He may wish to examine the child in such a way as to confirm or dispel his suspicions, and he will know that the accompanying parent is likely to veto any such examination and whisk the child away out of the surgery. The dilemma is particularly acute if sexual abuse is suspected. In Cleveland,[71] several children were removed from their families after paediatricians diagnosed sexual abuse on the basis of an intimate examination of the child's vagina and/or anus (the anal dilation test). Legal proceedings against the doctors were settled without judicial resolution of the many legal issues at stake. In what circumstances may a child be so examined without parental consent?

The doctor cannot rely on implicit consent based on the parent presenting the child for examination of some other unrelated, as far as the parent is concerned, medical condition. If a mother takes her asthmatic son to the doctor to have his chest examined, it cannot be implied that she also consents to an anal examination. However, if the doctor has reasonable grounds to believe that the child's asthma and failure to thrive results from abuse, and that if he alerts the mother to his suspicions, she will refuse to co-operate and the child may be abused again, he may do what is immediately necessary to safeguard the child. It will be lawful to examine the child, even against the mother's will, so that the doctor can decide what further steps to take. The onus of proving reasonable grounds for his suspicions, and the necessity of acting immediately, falls on the doctor. Where there is no immediate risk of the child being further abused or disappearing, the doctor should look to the Children Act 1989 for remedies to protect the child. These will include contacting social workers, who may seek an emergency protection order,[72] or assessment order. Child assessment orders, introduced by section 43 of the 1989 Act, should be especially useful in cases of suspected abuse and neglect. Prior to that Act there was no power to require parents to present their child for a medical examination. If a doctor or health visitor had some, but no compelling, grounds to suspect that a child's failure to thrive related to neglect or abuse, she faced a cruel choice. Do nothing and the child might suffer. Activate the social services department and the child may be taken away from his parents on a place of safety order,[73] with all the trauma of separation, and on examination the doctor's suspicions might be proved incorrect. The child assessment order enables health care and social services professionals to require parents to co-operate in assessing the cause of the child's mental or physical condition without at that stage breaking up the family.

One further question affects doctors dealing with suspected child abuse. Do they risk action for breach of confidence by the parents if they disclose information to the police or social workers. First, where that information related to the child, there is no breach of any confidential relationship with the parent. And even where information derived from the relationship with the parent is disclosed, if it is done to prevent imminent danger to the child that disclosure is justified on the principles discussed in Chapter 3.

The views of the child

One matter not so far discussed concerns the child's own wishes on treatment. Once a child can communicate she will in many cases have an opinion of her own. Most four-year-olds object robustly to injections, dental treatment and anything likely to cause them discomfort. At four, the case that the child cannot form any sensible judgement about the pros and cons of treatment may well be made out. At eight, ten and twelve the child acquires greater maturity, albeit most doctors and parents would be reluctant to bow to the child's judgement. What must be remembered, however, is that the balance of the child's best interests will be (radically) affected by his willingness or otherwise to participate in treatment. Obtaining assent even from very young children looks like good practice.[74] Forcible treatment, which may involve restraining, even detaining the child, requires strong justification. And as the child reaches her teens, and becomes what is rather pompously called a 'mature minor', the legal picture changes.

Family Law Reform Act 1969

The Family Law Reform Act 1969 reduced the age of majority from twenty-one to eighteen. When the 1969 Act was before Parliament it was unclear what effect, if any, a consent to medical treatment given by a minor might have. Many sixteen and seventeen-year-olds live, or spend considerable periods of time, away from their parents. Some are married and parents themselves. Section 8 of the 1969 Act clarified the law concerning sixteen to eighteen-year-olds and empowered them to consent to their own medical treatment. Sub-sections (1) and (2) of section 8 are clear. They provide:

(1) The consent of a minor who has attained the age of sixteen years to any surgical, medical or dental treatment which, in the absence of consent, would

constitute a trespass to his person shall be as effective as it would be if he were of full age: and where a minor has by virtue of this section given an effective consent it shall not be necessary to obtain any consent for it from his parent or guardian.

(2) In this section 'surgical, medical or dental treatment' includes any procedure undertaken for the purposes of diagnosis, and this section applies to any procedure (including, in particular, the administration of an anaesthetic) which is ancillary to any treatment as it applies to that treatment.

So far, so good; once a person is sixteen, providing he is mentally competent, he can consent to treatment himself. That does not mean that any parental consent relating to their children under eighteen is always ineffective. If the child of sixteen or seventeen is incapable of giving consent, for example, because of mental disability, his parents may still act on his behalf until he comes of age. Section 8 went on in subsection (3) to provide:

(3) Nothing in this section shall be construed as making ineffective any consent which would have been effective if this section had not been enacted.

The majority of lawyers and doctors interpreted section 8(3) in this way. The common law had never directly determined when, if at all, a child could give effective consent to medical treatment. The assumption was that the law gave effect to consent by a minor provided she or he was sufficiently mature to understand the proposed treatment or surgery.[75] Sixteen was the average age at which doctors judged patients to be old enough to give consent without consulting parents on every occasion. Nevertheless, many doctors regarded themselves free to treat children under sixteen without parental approval if the individual child appeared sufficiently intelligent and grown up to take the decision on treatment alone. The issue before 1969 in every case turned on the doctor's assessment of the particular minor in his surgery. The 1969 Act freed the doctor from doubt and risk where the patient was over sixteen. He no longer had to consider the maturity of a patient over sixteen. He could assume adult status and capability. Sub-section (3), it was argued, simple preserved the *status quo* for the under-sixteens. Doctors could continue to treat a child under sixteen as long as that child was mature enough to make his own judgement. This assumption, that there had always been a limited freedom to treat children under sixteen without parental consent, and that what sub-section (3) did was preserve that freedom, was at the heart of the *Gillick* saga and its sequels in *Re R.* and *Re W.*

The Gillick Case

The Gillick saga has its origins in a circular issued by the DHSS in 1974, outlining arrangements for a comprehensive family planning service within the NHS. Statistics on the number of births and induced abortions among girls under sixteen led the DHSS to conclude that contraceptive services should be made more readily available to that age group. The essence of their advice was that the decision to provide contraception to a girl under sixteen was one for the doctor. He might lawfully treat, and prescribe for, the girl without contacting her parents. Indeed, he should not contact parents without the girl's agreement. In 1980 the DHSS revised its advice. The revised version stressed that every effort should be made to involve parents. If the girl was adamant that her parents should not know of her request for contraception, the principle of confidentiality between doctor and patient should be preserved. The parents must not be told. This amended advice from the DHSS did not satisfy critics appalled at the prospect of young girls being put on the Pill in their parents' ignorance. Victoria Gillick wrote to her local health authority seeking an assurance that none of her daughters would be given contraceptive or abortion advice or treatment without her prior knowledge and consent until they were sixteen. The assurance was refused, and Mrs Gillick went to court seeking declarations against her health authority and the DHSS to the effect that their advice that children under sixteen could be treated without parental consent was unlawful and wrong, and against her health authority to the effect that medical personnel employed by them should not give contraceptive and/or abortion advice and/or treatment to any child of Mrs Gillick's under sixteen without her prior knowledge and consent.

Mrs Gillick's concern was with contraception and abortion for under-sixteens. She had no axe to grind in respect of other forms of medical treatment. The trouble was that contraception cannot be isolated from more general questions. There was another legal problem to bedevil the debate. Mrs Gillick's counsel pursued a two-pronged attack. First, they challenged the assumption that the common law had ever permitted medical treatment of children under sixteen in the absence of parental consent. Second, they argued in relation to contraception specifically that as it is a crime for a man to have sexual intercourse with a girl under sixteen, providing her with contraception amounts to the crime of causing or encouraging sexual intercourse with a girl under sixteen.

Children under 16 and consent to treatment: *Gillick competence*

Woolf J rejected both Mrs Gillick's claims.[76] He endorsed the view that once a child was able to understand what was entailed in proposed treatment, he or she could consent to such treatment. Any physical contact involved in treatment would not constitute battery. Mrs Gillick appealed and, in a complex judgment, the Court of Appeal[77] found for her. Not only was any treatment of a child under sixteen potentially battery unless authorized by a parent, but giving children advice or information about contraception without parental knowledge could constitute an infringement of parental rights. After the Court of Appeal decision no doctor could (save in emergency) safely see a child under sixteen in her clinic or surgery without parental knowledge.

The DHSS appealed to the House of Lords. By a majority the House of Lords held that the original advice circulated by the DHSS was not unlawful and that a child under sixteen can in certain circumstances give a valid consent to medical treatment including contraception or abortion treatment without parental knowledge or agreement.[78] To consider the implications of their decision for doctors, parents and children, the Law Lords' judgment will be dissected into three parts: (1) the general issue of consent by children to medical treatment, (2) the special problems of contraception and abortion and consent thereto, and (3) the criminal law as it affects contraception.

The general problem of consent

The majority of their Lordships rejected the Court of Appeal's finding that consent given by a child under sixteen was of no effect. Like Woolf J they accepted the view that the Family Law Reform Act had left that question open. The matter was for the common law to determine. The common law was not static, fossilized in eighteenth-century notions of the inviolable rights of the paterfamilias. Judge-made law must meet the needs of the times. Parental rights derived from parental duties to protect the person and property of the child. Modern legislation qualified and limited parental rights by placing the welfare of the child as its first priority. Parental rights being dependent on the duty to care for and maintain the child, they endured only so long as necessary to achieve their end. As Lord Scarman put it: '. . . the parental right yields to the child's right to make his own decisions when he reaches a sufficient understanding and intelligence to be capable of making up his own mind on the matter requiring decision'.[79]

Their Lordships argued that the common law had never regarded the consent of a child as a complete nullity. Were that the case intercourse with a girl under sixteen would inevitably be rape. That is not so. Provided the girl is old enough to understand what she is agreeing to, intercourse with her consent will not be rape. Parliament, to protect girls under sixteen from the consequences of their own folly, enacted a separate offence of unlawful sexual intercourse with girls under sixteen in the commission of which the girl's consent is irrelevant. If the girl validly consented, that is the only offence committed, and not the more serious crime of rape.[80]

Moving from the general issue of consent by children to the problem of consent to medical treatment, the House of Lords saw no reason to depart from the general rule. Lord Fraser thought it would be ludicrous to say that a boy or girl of fifteen could not agree to examination or treatment for a trivial injury. Importantly, Lord Templeman, who dissented on the specific issue of contraceptive treatment, agreed that there were circumstances where a doctor could properly treat a child under sixteen without parental agreement. He concurred that the effect of the consent of the child depended on the nature of the treatment and the age and understanding of the child. A doctor, he thought, could safely remove tonsils or a troublesome appendix from a boy or girl of fifteen without express parental agreement. *Gillick* establishes a child below sixteen may lawfully be given general medical advice and treatment without parental agreement, provided that child has achieved sufficient maturity to understand fully what is proposed. The doctor treating such a child on the basis of her consent alone will not be at risk of either a civil action for battery or criminal prosecution

The special problems of contraception and abortion

Lord Templeman, however, departed from his brethren's views on the specific issue of contraception. He did not accept that a girl under sixteen has sufficient maturity and understanding of the emotional and physical consequences of sexual intercourse to consent to contraceptive treatment. His Lordship put it thus:

> I doubt whether a girl under the age of sixteen is capable of a balanced judgement to embark on frequent, regular or casual sexual intercourse fortified by the illusion that medical science can protect her in mind and body and ignoring the danger of leaping from childhood to adulthood without the difficult formative transitional experiences of adolescence. There are many things a girl under sixteen needs to practise but sex is not one of them.[81]

The majority of his colleagues disagreed. They conceded that a request by a girl under sixteen for contraception coupled with an insistence that parents not be told posed a problem for the doctor. Assessing whether she is mature enough to consider the emotional and physical consequences of the course she has embarked on is not easy. But that question is to be left to the clinical judgement of the doctor. Lord Fraser set out five matters the doctor should satisfy himself on before giving contraceptive treatment to a girl below sixteen without parental agreement. They are:

> ... (1) that the girl ... will understand his advice; (2) that he cannot persuade her to inform her parents ...; (3) that she is very likely to begin or continue having sexual intercourse with or without contraceptive treatment; (4) that unless she receives contraceptive advice or treatment her physical or mental health or both are likely to suffer; (5) that her best interests require him to give her contraceptive advice or treatment or both without the parental consent.[82]

Lord Fraser's formula failed to satisfy Mrs Gillick. She regarded it as inadequate in two respects. First, in a busy surgery or clinic has any doctor sufficient time to embark on the investigation and counselling of the girl necessary to fulfil the criteria laid down? Second, underlying the judgments of the majority is acceptance of the view that, as significant numbers of young girls under sixteen are going to continue having sexual intercourse regardless of whether they have lawful access to contraception, it may be in their best interests to protect them from pregnancy by contraceptive treatment. Mrs Gillick disagreed. She contended that if access to contraception without parental agreement were stopped, at least the majority of young girls would (a) be deterred from starting to have intercourse so young by fear of pregnancy and/or parental disapproval, and (b) would have a defence against pressure from their peers to 'grow up' and sleep with someone. Both sides in the debate on 'under-age' contraception agree that early sexual intercourse increases the danger of disease to the child, be it cervical cancer or venereal disease. Most agree about the emotional damage the child risks. They are no nearer agreement as to how girls under sixteen may best be protected than on the day Mrs Gillick first went to court. The decision to allow emergency contraception ('morning after pill') to be sold over the counter in local pharmacies re-ignited controversy.

What about abortion? The greater part of the Law Lords' decision concentrated on contraception. The rules for abortion on girls under sixteen are the same. If a girl is intelligent and mature enough to understand what is involved in the operation, the doctor, if the girl insists on not telling her parents or if they refuse to agree to an abortion, may go ahead on the basis of the girl's consent alone. The House of Lords endorsed the approach of Butler-Sloss J in an earlier case.[83] A fifteen-year-old girl, with one child already, became pregnant again while in the care of the local authority. She wanted an abortion. Doctors considered that the birth of a second child would endanger the mental health of the girl and her existing child. Her father objected as abortion was contrary to his religion. The local authority applied to have the girl made a ward of court and so seek the court's consent to the operation. The judge authorized the operation. She said the decision must be made in the light of the girl's best interests. She took into account the parents' feelings but held that they could not outweigh the needs of the girl.

The criminal law, sexual intercourse and contraception

So far I have examined only the issues relating to a child's capacity to consent to treatment. The second prong of Mrs Gillick's argument related to the criminal law, which renders it a crime to have sexual intercourse with a girl under sixteen regardless of her consent or encouragement. Section 28 of the Sexual Offences Act 1956 provides further that it is an offence '. . . to cause or encourage . . . the commission of unlawful sexual intercourse with . . . a girl for whom [the] accused is responsible'. The majority of the Law Lords found that a doctor who *bona fide* provided a girl with contraception in the interests of her health to protect her from the further risks of pregnancy and consequently abortion or childbirth, committed no crime. He was not encouraging the continuance of sexual intercourse and implicitly the crime of unlawful sexual intercourse, but offering '. . . a palliative against the consequences of crime'. Doctors should, however, tread carefully. For while a doctor commits no crime by giving a young girl contraceptive treatment, the judgment makes it clear that any doctor who fails to assess his patient carefully and make a judgement based on medical indications as to her health may face prosecution. Lord Scarman said:

Clearly a doctor who gives a brief contraceptive advice or treatment not because in his clinical judgement the treatment is medically indicated . . . but with the intention of facilitating her having unlawful sexual intercourse may well be guilty of a criminal offence.[84]

This limb of the judgment also failed to satisfy Mrs Gillick. For her, contraception for young girls cannot be medically indicated.

A right to say no?

For several years *Gillick* was assumed to have established that once young people acquired the necessary maturity to consent to treatment, what Lord Donaldson was later to style *Gillick competence*,[85] they acquired a right to determine what medical treatment they received. They had a right to say no, as much as a right to say yes. Recall Lord Scarman's words in *Gillick*[86] '. . . the parental right yields to the child's right to make his own decision when he reaches a sufficient understanding and intelligence to be capable of making up his own mind on the matter requiring a decision'. Subsequent judgments of the Court of Appeal reject that apparently logical conclusion. Adolescent autonomy is little more than a myth, for no young person, no minor, under eighteen has a right to refuse treatment.[87] Parental powers to authorize treatment against their offspring's will live on, concurrently with extensive judicial powers to order minors to submit to treatment others deem necessary for their welfare.

The first of a long line of cases is *Re R.*[88] R. was a fifteen-year-old girl suffering from acute psychiatric problems. Her condition fluctuated. At times she appeared rational and lucid. However she lacked insight into her illness. During her lucid phases she refused medication and became psychotic once again. R. was in care and the local authority responsible for her sought judicial guidance seeking authority to administer anti-psychotic drugs without R.'s consent. The Court of Appeal agreed with the trial judge that R. was not *Gillick competent*. Her illness prevented her from fully understanding the need for drugs to control her condition. R. could lawfully be treated against her will. In this particular case the court authorized her treatment via its wardship jurisdiction. But the local authority as her legal guardian could equally have provided a proxy consent on R.'s behalf. The interest of *Re R.* lies in Lord Donaldson's *dicta*. He went on to say that even were R. *Gillick competent*, she would still have no power to veto treatment. A *Gillick competent* minor could consent to, but not refuse, treatment. Consent was akin to a key that 'unlocked the door to treatment' making the doctor's action lawful but not obligatory. Once a young person became *Gillick competent* she became a keyholder. Her parents remained keyholders until she reached eighteen. They could still authorize treatment on her behalf. Doctors faced with willing parents but unwilling children were not obliged to treat the child, indeed might choose not to, but they could lawfully elect to act on the basis of the parents' consent alone. The problem was one of ethical and clinical judgement for the physician.[89]

Re R. was not well received.[90] In *Re W.*[91] Lord Donaldson was unperturbed by his critics. W. was a sixteen-year-old girl. She was critically ill with anorexia nervosa and had had a tragic childhood. The local authority sought guidance whether W. could, if it proved necessary, be moved to a specialist unit and force-fed. As W. was sixteen, she was empowered to consent to treatment by virtue of section 8 of the Family Law Reform Act 1969. The Court of Appeal ruled that section 8 on its wording solely empowered a minor over sixteen to give an 'effective consent' to treatment. Section 8(3)[92] preserved the concurrent parental power to authorize treatment and the inherent powers of the courts to act to protect a minor's welfare.

Lord Donaldson regretted only one part of his *dicta* in *Re R.*: his use of the keyholder metaphor. For, as he acknowledged, keys can lock as readily as unlock. In *Re W.* he preferred to compare consent to a flak jacket, saying pithily.

. . . I now prefer the analogy of the legal 'flak jacket', which protects from claims by the litigious whether [the doctor] acquires it from his patient who may be a minor over the age of sixteen, or a '*Gillick competent*' child under that age or from another person having parental responsibilities which include a right to consent to treatment of the minor. Anyone who gives him a flak jacket (i.e. consent) may take it back, but the doctor only needs one and so long as he continues to have one he has the legal right to proceed.[93]

Re R. and *Re W.* make nonsense of *Gillick*. They are explicable on their facts. There are powerful grounds to argue that neither R. nor W. were mentally competent regardless of their age. Their illness deprived them of the understanding and capacity to make a decision about treatment. They would fail the *Re C.* test for mental capacity (see page 409). The same is true of the young people involved in a number of similar cases where judges ruled that an adolescent could not veto treatment.[94]

The crunch case is *Re E.*[95] E. was fifteen and shared his parents' Jehovah's Witness faith. He was seriously ill with leukaemia. Doctors advised that to maximize the prospects of successful chemotherapy, E should receive transfusions of blood products. E., like his parents, refused to agree to transfusions. The boy was made a ward of court and the judge authorized transfusion. He acknowledged that E. was highly intelligent, mature for his age and well informed about his illness. None the less he held that E. was not *Gillick competent*. He lacked insight into the process of dying. He could not turn his mind to the effect of the manner of his death or its effect on his family. How many adults enjoy such insight?

Understandably courts seek to protect young people from decisions that may endanger their life. In E.'s case the outcome was tragic. Treatment at fifteen resulted in a temporary remission. At eighteen he relapsed, refused treatment, and died believing that he had participated in an ungodly act.

The courts have distorted common sense and ethics in attempts to avoid the implications of *Gillick*. Judges have even gone so far as authorizing restraint and detention of young people to ensure that they comply with treatment.[96] All this is done without resort to the Mental Health Act 1983, which at least builds in some safeguards for adult patients.[97]

Confidentiality and children under sixteen

Do young people seeking treatment independently of their parents have any right to confidentiality? A young girl, embarking on a sexual relationship and considering seeking contraception, probably does not think so much about her capacity to give consent to treatment, as 'Will the doctor tell my mum?' The thought that a doctor may be free to give contraceptive advice to a child without the parents even knowing of what is proposed was perhaps at the heart of Mrs Gillick's concern. The disruption of family life, and the danger that the girl might omit to give the doctor information on other drugs she might be taking, horrified many caring parents.

In *Gillick*, the courts paid little attention to confidentiality. The Law Lords held that in exceptional cases the doctor was free to treat the girl without parental knowledge. The question that remains is whether a doctor *must* preserve confidentiality in his dealings with his young patient. By implication the House of Lords endorsed the view that the doctor owed a duty of confidentiality to his patient under sixteen. They upheld DHSS guidelines, laying down the rule that if the girl was adamant that her parents must not be contacted, confidentiality must be preserved. Will a doctor, faced with a girl of fifteen who tells him she has started sexual relationships, be at risk of an action for breach of confidence by the girl if he refuses her contraception and telephones her mother?

The first question that will arise is whether the child is *Gillick competent*. If she lacks the capacity to consent to treatment because she is insufficiently mature to assess her own interests, she may also lack the capacity to give or withhold consent for the disclosure of information about her condition and circumstances. In such a case doctors are advised by the GMC[98] to try to persuade their patient to agree to involving her family, but ultimately the doctor may disclose information to an appropriate person (i.e. the child's parents). Note that this is a decision that must be taken with care. Disclosure must be essential in the child's medical interests. A doctor who simply tells a girl's mother because she thinks the girl is a 'bad girl' or who recklessly informs a violent father of his daughter's relationship could still face disciplinary action. The *Gillick competent* child poses a greater dilemma. If a fifteen-year-old is able to say yes to taking the Pill or having an abortion and her parents have no right to veto her decision, how can disclosure in her interests be justified? The doctor is entitled to refuse the treatment requested. Justifying letting the parents know what their daughter is contemplating is harder. Perhaps the doctor could invoke public interest. He could argue that he is acting to disclose to those most closely concerned with the girl's welfare the commission of a crime, unlawful sexual intercourse, upon her. We saw (page 64) that the extent to which a doctor may lawfully breach his patient's confidence to disclose crime is uncertain. Where the doctor suspects a girl (or boy) is being subjected to abuse, his case will be strengthened.[99]

15

Pregnancy and Childbirth

Medical care begins long before a baby is born. Research into the growth of the foetus in the womb has established the crucial importance of good antenatal care. The thalidomide tragedy highlighted the vulnerability of the developing foetus. Thalidomide was prescribed to a number of pregnant women to help them sleep. It was described as non-toxic and safe for use by pregnant and nursing mothers. It was not safe. Many children were born without limbs and with other awful disabilities. The drug company denied negligence. A settlement was eventually reached, but not all children received compensation because of a dispute as to whether their disabilities related to the mothers taking the drug.[1] A further difficulty for the children was that at the time of the birth of children disabled by thalidomide, the English courts had never decided whether doctors, or drug companies, or anyone at all, could be sued by children for injuries suffered by them before their birth.[2] Parliament enacted the Congenital Disabilities (Civil Liability) Act 1976 to govern claims by children born after 1976. The Act governs the child's rights only.

Can parents sue?

The parents of a child injured before birth may be able to recover for their loss at common law. The doctor caring for the mother in pregnancy owes her a duty in relation to her own health and in respect of the health of the developing foetus. The damage that she will suffer if she bears a disabled child, the emotional trauma[3] *and* the financial burden of the extra expense such a child entails are readily foreseeable and recoverable. But will she be able to prove negligence, and to prove that the child's disability resulted from that negligence? Proving negligence is, as we have seen, no easy task in any malpractice claim. A claim in relation to the birth of a disabled child has two special problems of its own. First, if the claim lies against the doctor, it has to be established that he should have been aware of the risk posed to the foetus by drugs he prescribed or treatment he gave. Second, where a mother becomes ill in pregnancy, or the pregnancy itself is complicated, the interests of mother and child may conflict. An ill or injured pregnant woman may need treatment known to carry risk to the child. For example, a woman injured in an accident may need surgery that can only be carried out under a general anaesthetic that may harm the baby. The doctor's duty to the mother, his patient, is this. He must consult and advise her, giving her sufficient information about her needs and the risk to her baby. If she chooses to reject a particular course of treatment for the sake of the baby he cannot impose it. He must in any case aim at a course of action that will benefit the mother with minimum risk to the child. Even if it can be shown that the doctor has failed in his duty to the mother, that he was negligent, establishing that the infant's disability resulted from that negligence is likely to be even more difficult.[4] Despite immense advances in knowledge concerning the development of the embryo, pinpointing the exact cause of the birth defect remains extremely difficult. Success in a claim for negligence depends on proof that it is more likely than not that the relevant negligence caused the injury. All a claimant with a damaged child is likely to be able to prove is that a drug she took or treatment she received *may* have caused the defect in the baby. However, the cause may be inherited disease, a problem that the mother suffered in pregnancy, or some unknown cause. The parents may well fail to satisfy the burden of proof.

Congenital Disabilities (Civil Liability) Act 1976

This Act, passed to give rights and a remedy to children born disabled as a result of human fault, is ambitious, complex, and largely irrelevant. It is ambitious in that it sought to provide a scheme to protect children not just against injury in the womb but against any act at any stage of either parent's life that might ultimately result in a disability affecting a child. I will outline its complexity in succeeding sections. It is irrelevant because it fails to address the central problem in this type of claim. How do you prove that the disability resulted from an identified act of negligence? Just as his mother's claim is likely to founder for lack of proof of the cause of the disability so is the child's. If Parliament intends and desires to give children disabled by human act a remedy, it must consider whether retaining the normal burden of proof in actions by mother and child is practical.

The Act only applies to births after 1976,[5] and purports to provide a comprehensive code of liability for disabled children in respect of damage caused to them before birth. Under the Act the child's mother is generally exempt from any liability to her child.[6] The father is offered no such immunity. The Act entirely replaces the common law and it would not be possible for a child unable to recover under the Act to argue that liability exists at common law. So, for example, a child seeking to sue his mother, exempt under the Act, must fail, however reckless her conduct in pregnancy and however clear it might be that she caused him to be born disabled.

The scheme of the Act is this. The child must be born alive.[7] He must establish that his disabilities resulted from an 'occurrence' that either (1) affected the mother or father in her or his ability to have a normal healthy child (pre-conception event), (2) affected the mother during her pregnancy, or (3) affected mother or child in the course of its birth. At this first hurdle, proving the cause of the disability, many claims will fail. Where proof of cause is forthcoming the child faces further obstacles. It is not enough to show that the person responsible for the occurrence was negligent. The child must prove that the person responsible for the occurrence was liable to the affected parent. The child's rights are derivative only. The likelihood is that the occurrence at the time caused the parent no harm. Thalidomide's original effect was to sedate anxious mothers-to-be. The Act provides that it is no answer that the parent affected suffered no visible injury at the time of the occurrence providing there was '. . . a breach of legal duty which, accompanied by injury, would have given rise to the liability'. The breach of duty is the negligence of the defendant in relation to the affected parent's reproductive capacity. Sandra Roberts recovered £334,769 in compensation for catastrophic damage she suffered during her mother's pregnancy.[8] A blood transfusion administered to her mother seven years before her birth rendered her parents rhesus incompatible, creating danger for any child of theirs. The hospital knew of Mrs Roberts's condition but failed to act to prevent or minimize the risk to Sandra. This was negligent care for the mother and thus created a right to compensation for mother and via her for Sandra. Other cases are less straightforward.

Drugs and damage to the foetus

Let us take first what appears to be a simple case, the sort of case the Act was intended to remedy. A pregnant woman takes a drug prescribed for her by her GP that damages her baby so that he is born disabled.

The child can prove that his disability results from the effect of the drug on the foetus. He will have to show that the doctor was negligent towards his mother. It must be proven that (1) the doctor knew or ought to have known that she was pregnant, and therefore was in breach of duty to her in prescribing a drug that might damage her baby, and (2) that he ought to have been aware of the risk posed by the drug. It will be no defence for the doctor to answer that far from injuring the mother the primary effect of the drug benefited her by ameliorating the symptoms of some common ailment, or helping her to relax or sleep. The doctor's responsibility to her embraces taking care to avoid harm to the child she carries. Two difficulties arise from this. First, a general practitioner is judged by the standard of the reasonable, average GP. He is not expected to be an expert on embryology or drug-related damage. Proving that he ought to have been aware of the risk of the drug may be awkward. Second, the doctor may be aware of the risk to the baby but argue that the risk to mother and child of not prescribing the drug is greater. Perhaps the mother might argue that given the uncertainty surrounding the effect of medicines on foetal development only exceptionally should *any* drug be prescribed to a pregnant woman by her GP. Advice should be sought from the specialist obstetrician. However, is it reasonable to deny pregnant women basic medicine for minor ailments and is the cost to the NHS of multiple referrals to obstetricians justifiable? The focus ought to be on ensuring that all doctors give women adequate advice about the potential risks of drugs in pregnancy.

Doctors are not the only potential source of compensation for a drug-damaged child. Could the child sue the drug company? Providing the relevant drug was marketed after 1 March 1988, the company's liability would be governed by the Consumer Protection Act 1987. The crucial questions will be is the drug defective, and did it cause the relevant injury to the foetus? There can be little doubt that if the company can be shown to be aware of a risk of foetal damage, yet still marketed the drug with *no* warning of that risk, the drug is defective. The unborn baby is most vulnerable to harm in the earliest stages of pregnancy when the mother may not even know that she is pregnant. Warnings about the use of many non-prescription medicines in pregnancy are routine, but futile if a woman is unaware of her pregnancy. Might a drug be defective simply because it poses a risk of foetal harm? Clearly that cannot generally be the case with many prescription drugs. The benefit such drugs offer when properly prescribed outweight the remote chance of unwitting foetal harm. Over-the-counter, non-prescription, medicines might be looked at differently. If a cough remedy poses a substantial risk of harm, greater than other similar products, for relatively small benefit, that product might be found to be defective. A further difficulty in establishing liability under the 1987 Act arises where the company can show that it was unaware of any risk of foetal harm. The Act allows the defendant to rely on the development risks defence, and it is at least arguable that such a defence would have enabled the manufacturers of thalidomide to escape liability (see page 211).

Suing a doctor

I have already mentioned the potential liability of the mother's GP in prescribing drugs for her. She will meet other doctors during ante-natal visits. One special feature of suing a doctor under the Act needs note: section 1(5) of the 1976 Act, 'the doctors' defence'. Section 1 (5) of the Act provides:

The defendant is not answerable to the child, for anything he did or omitted to do when responsible in a professional capacity for treating or advising the parent, if he took reasonable care having due regard to the then received professional opinion applicable to the particular class of case; but this does not mean that he is answerable only because he departed from received opinion.

The aims of those who sought the inclusion of those words 'then received professional opinion' were probably twofold. First, they quite reasonably wanted it made clear that hindsight as to the effect of a drug or course of treatment should not prejudice a doctor, and second, less reasonably, they did not want the courts to adjudicate on the adequacy of received opinion. As the defendant's standard of care will always be tested by what was expected of the competent practitioner at the time of the alleged breach of duty, that first objective was met at common law. Second, perhaps doctors sought to ensure courts would not seek to evaluate 'received professional opinion'. In 1976, it is likely that no court would have done so. The judgment of the House of Lords in

Bolitho v. *City & Hackney HA*[9] (see page 149) now requires that responsible professional opinion be demonstrably 'logical and defensible'. I see no reason why section 1 (5) should not be susceptible to similar judicial scrutiny.

Ante-natal screening[10]

Ante-natal screening to diagnose foetal abnormalities has become routine. Just some of the more common procedures are looked at here. In amniocentesis a needle is inserted through the mother's abdomen and the uterine wall into the sac surrounding the foetus. A small amount of the amniotic fluid surrounding the baby is removed. Tests on the fluid will indicate whether a number of abnormalities are present, including spina bifida and Down's syndrome. Cultures from the fluid may be grown that will disclose the child's sex. A mother who underwent amniocentesis and was told that she carried a spina bifida or Down's syndrome baby could then opt for an abortion. A mother who knew she was a carrier of haemophilia and learned that she carried a male child might similarly seek a termination. There are medical problems with amniocentesis. It cannot be performed before the fourteenth week of pregnancy and is usually delayed until the sixteenth week. It carries about a 1 per cent risk of causing a miscarriage. It sometimes causes the mother an acute if short period of discomfort. It is an expensive procedure, reserved largely for mothers at special risk of producing a disabled infant, in particular those over thirty-five or where blood tests suggest some abnormality in the baby. Chorionic villus testing, whereby early placental cells are removed and analysed, is possible earlier in pregnancy, at about eight to ten weeks. So far, though, chorionic villus testing can be used only for a more limited group of genetic defects than amniocentesis and carries a higher risk of precipitating miscarriage. Increasingly doctors are seeking to limit the number of women who need to undergo invasive tests of this sort by using simple blood tests to identify high-risk pregnancies. A blood test to discover raised alpha-protein levels, an indication of possible spina bifida, has been available for several years. A blood test identifying increased risk of Down's syndrome is available. Only women whose blood tests indicate possible foetal abnormalities will then have to undergo the invasive procedures of amniocentesis or chorionic villus testing. Finally, ultra-sound scans are now routinely used to check on the growth and development of the foetus and will in certain cases reveal the presence of such deformities as spina bifida without the need to submit the pregnant woman to risky or invasive tests.

What are the legal implications of amniocentesis and chorionic villus testing? First, they involve an invasion of the mother's body. Her consent is essential and should be obtained expressly and in writing. Second, the risk that a healthy baby may be lost should be communicated to the parents. The duty of the obstetrician caring for the mother must embrace offering her the information on which to make such a crucial decision. Tests should be carried out and analysed with due care. Negligence in offering or carrying out ante-natal screening may result in claims by both mother and child. They will contend that had adequate care been provided for the mother in pregnancy, she would have elected to terminate the pregnancy. The mother would have avoided the burden of a disabled child. The child would have avoided the harm of her disabled existence. In neither case is the essence of the claim a claim for wrongful disability. Unlike the examples discussed earlier in this chapter the defendants' negligence is not responsible for causing disability to a foetus normal at conception. The defendants' negligence is responsible for the birth of a child who, but for their negligence, would not have been born. The mother seeks compensation for a wrongful birth, a birth that she would have chosen to avoid if properly advised. The child sues in respect of wrongful life, a life, her counsel argues, she would have chosen not to endure.

Wrongful life

A classic claim for wrongful life is recounted in *McKay* v. *Essex AHA*.[11] The plaintiffs in *McKay* were a little girl, born disabled as a result of the effect of rubella suffered by her mother early in pregnancy, and her mother. When Mrs McKay suspected that she had contracted rubella in the early weeks of her pregnancy, her doctor arranged for blood tests to establish whether she had been infected. As a result of negligence by either her doctor or by laboratory staff, Mrs McKay was wrongly informed that she had not been infected by rubella. She continued with the pregnancy. Had she known the truth she would, as her doctor was well aware, have requested an abortion under the Abortion Act 1967. The little girl was born in 1975, before the Congenital Disabilities Act was passed. The Court of Appeal had to decide the position at common law. They said that no action lay where the essence of the child's claim was that but for the negligence of the defendant she would never have been born at all. The child's claim was thrown out, although her mother's claim was allowed to proceed. The case is not solely of historical interest. The judges further said that under the Act no child born after its passing could pursue such a claim.

In the view of the Court of Appeal, the Act can never give rise to a claim for 'wrongful life'.[12] Ackner L J considering section 1(2)(b) of the Act, said that the relevant 'occurrence' has to be one that affected the mother in pregnancy 'so that the child *is born* with disabilities which would not otherwise have been present'. Clearly under the Act, then, where the breach of duty consists of carelessness in the conduct of the pregnancy or the birth, the claim must relate to disabilities inflicted as a result of the breach of duty by the defendants. Where the essence of the claim is that the child should never have been born at all, it lies outside the scope of section 1(2)(b). A claim by the child that amniocentesis should have been performed, or that subsequent tests were negligently conducted so that the pregnancy continued and he was born disabled, will fail.

The effect of the judgment in *McKay* is that in England a child injured before birth may claim compensation only for *wrongful disability*, that is against a defendant whose conduct actually caused his disability. He cannot sue for *wrongful life*. The Court of Appeal gave three main reasons for ruling out such claims. (1) It was not possible to arrive at a proper measure of damages representing the difference between the child's disabled existence and non-existence.[13] (2) The law should not impose a duty on doctors to abort, to terminate life *in utero*.[14] (3) To impose any duty to abort would be to violate the sanctity of life and to devalue the life of handicapped persons.[15] The second and third reasons are difficult to sustain in the light of the fact that the court did allow Mrs McKay to pursue her *wrongful birth* action.

Wrongful birth

Until the controversial decision of the House of Lords in *McFarlane v. Tayside Health Board*,[16] it appeared that in English law parents of a child born in circumstances akin to those in *McKay* could (like Mrs McKay) sue for the wrongful birth of a disabled child.[17] The Law Lords in *McFarlane* rejected a claim for wrongful conception, insofar as that claim sought damages for the cost of bringing up an unplanned and healthy child. Negligent advice following the husband's vasectomy resulted in the unwanted and unexpected conception of the couple's fifth child. As we saw in Chapter 11, Mrs McFarlane was awarded compensation for her pain and suffering in pregnancy and immediately consequential financial losses. The more substantive part of the claim for damages, the cost of rearing her child was ruled inadmissible as irrecoverable economic loss. The reasons advanced by their Lordships for their ruling were widely diverse. They sought to avoid categorizing the question as one of policy but, as I argue in Chapter 11, it is difficult to make any sense of their decision except in terms of judicial repugnance against compensating parents for the birth of a healthy infant.

Will *McFarlane* affect a claim by parents of a disabled child who can establish that, had the child's disability been diagnosed *in utero*, the mother would have terminated the pregnancy? The Law Lords in *McFarlane* expressly restrict their decision to claims concerning normal, healthy infants. Yet consider the approval Lord Steyn bestows on the following statement from an Australian textbook:

> . . . it might seem inconsistent to allow a claim by the parents, while that of the child, whether *healthy or disabled*, is rejected (my emphasis). Surely the parents' claim is equally repugnant to ideas of the sanctity and value of human life and rests, like that of the child, on a comparison between a situation where a human being exists and one where it does not.[18]

Lord Steyn comments '. . . the reasoning is sound. Coherence and rationality demand that the claim by the parents should also be rejected'.[19]

So can a distinction between a claim for wrongful birth of a healthy child and wrongful birth of a disabled child be sustained? The Court of Appeal have endorsed such a distinction. In *Parkinson* v. *St James and Seacroft University NHS Hospital Trust*[20] it was held that where a disabled child is born as a consequence of clinical negligence his parents may recover the additional costs occasioned by his disability. The relevant negligence in *Parkinson* ensued from a bungled operation to sterilize the mother. The case for compensation covering the costs resulting from a child's disability when the alleged 'wrong' is a failure to prevent the birth of a disabled infant looks stronger. Doctors expressly advising potential parents about the risks of conception, and screening women in pregnancy, undertake that responsibility expressly to avoid the birth of a disabled child. The 'harm' to the parents of the birth of a child with spina bifida, or damaged by rubella,[21] is just what the doctors seek to prevent.

The distress of the parents when their expectations of a healthy child are confounded, combined with the financial cost of raising a disabled child, are directly related to the relevant negligence. The parents' damages, however, will be limited to the additional costs of raising a child with his particular disability. Before *McFarlane*, English courts awarded such parents the whole cost of childrearing.[22] Compensation in such cases of wrongful birth will now relate only to the additional cost of caring for the disabled child.[23] Compensation may still be considerable. It can and should include cost of care beyond the child's minority.[24] 'Good' parents will seek to provide for their disabled children into adulthood.

The tangled web of case-law following *McFarlane* may be morally disturbing to some people. Refusing to compensate parents for the unplanned birth of a healthy child Lord Millett said:

There is something distasteful, if not morally offensive, in treating the birth of a normal healthy child as a matter of compensation.[25]

He regarded childbirth as akin to a balance sheet. The joys of parenthood offset financial costs. Mutual support of parent and child, the support perhaps of the parent in old age offset the burdens of parenting. Distinguishing the healthy and disabled child might seem to suggest the latter is a 'curse' not a 'blessing'. In *Parkinson*, Hale LJ takes a pragmatic approach. She says of the disabled child that:

This analysis treats a disabled child as having exactly the same worth as a non-disabled child. It affords him the same dignity and status. It simply acknowledges that he costs more.[26]

Children damaged by pre-conception events

The 1976 Act purports to protect children against pre-conception injury, not just injury *in utero*. This could happen where the father or mother is affected by radiation or drugs so that the sperm or egg carries a serious defect. Or if doctors mismanage a previous pregnancy, for example if they fail to take note of and treat Rhesus incompatibility in the mother, a second child could be born brain damaged.[27] The Act was intended to cover such cases, providing as it does that the relevant occurrence may be one that affected either parent in his or her ability to have a healthy child. But it may be argued that if the claim is that the child was born disabled because one of his parents is incapable of creating a healthy infant, his claim is essentially that he should never have been born at all and that, as an action for 'wrongful life', is barred under the Act. I think this is a mistaken view of the Act. The child's claim in the case of a pre-conception occurrence rests on the hypothesis that *but for* that occurrence he would have been born normal and healthy, and that his actionable injury is therefore the difference between the life he might have had and the life he must now perforce endure. In *McKay* the child sought to maintain that her actionable injury was life itself, and as such her claim was not and would not be sustainable. What *McKay* does clarify in cases of pre-conception injury is that a doctor, not responsible for that original injury, cannot be liable under the Act if he fails to diagnose the child's disabilities in pregnancy and fails to perform an abortion in such circumstances.

What if a parent realises the risk?

Alas further problems confront the child whose claim is based on pre-conception injury. Section 1 (4) of the Act provides that in such cases if the affected parent is aware of the risk of the child being born disabled the defendant is not liable to that child. Responsibility for knowingly running the risk of creating a disabled baby rests with his parents, and whatever the degree of fault, the original creator of the risk is relieved of liability to the child. There is one exception to this rule. Where the child sues his father, the fact that the father is aware of the risk of begetting an abnormal child will not defeat the child's claim as long as his mother is ignorant of the danger. This raises a nice question. A young man suffers contamination by toxic chemicals at work through the negligence of his employers. He is warned that his reproductive capacity has been damaged, that he is likely to beget abnormal offspring and is advised never to have children. He ignores the warning, marries and tells his wife nothing. A disabled child is born. The child cannot sue his father's original employers. Even if they were in breach of duty to his father, 'the affected parent', the father's knowledge of the risk is a defence. Can the child sue his father? The answer has to be no. This child, like the plaintiff in *McKay* can only claim against his father that he should never have been born at all. His father's condition at the time of the relevant 'negligence', begetting the child, was such that he could not beget a normal child. The father's 'negligence' was in creating him, not in inflicting a disability that but for some act or omission on his part would not have been present. We will consider a little later if fathers can ever be liable for causing pre-natal injury to their own children.

Must a mother consider abortion?

Section 1 (7) of the 1976 Act offers a partial defence whereby if the affected parent shared responsibility for the child being born disabled, the child's damages may be reduced. For example, the child's disabilities may be diagnosed when the mother has an ultra-sound scan, or amniocentesis, before his birth. Once the mother knows of the potential damage to her child, she will, under the 1967 Abortion Act, be entitled to an abortion on the grounds that there is substantial risk that the child if born would be seriously handicapped. Assuming that it is the mother who is the affected parent, does she share responsibility for the child being born disabled if she refuses an abortion? In *McKay* v. *Essex AHA*, refusing to allow the child's claim that she should have been aborted, Ackner LJ said that he could not accept:

... that the common law duty of care to a person can involve, without specific legislation to achieve this end, the legal obligation to that person, whether or not *in utero*, to terminate his existence. Such a proposition runs wholly contrary to the concept of the sanctity of human life.[28]

Applying Ackner LJ's proposition, a submission advanced by the defendant responsible for inflicting the disabilities suffered by the child, that a mother should have accepted abortion must fail. To impose an *obligation* on a mother to undergo an abortion is more repugnant to the concept of the sanctity of human life than to impose an obligation to abort on a doctor.

In *Emeh* v. *Kensington, Chelsea and Fulham AHA*,[29] the plaintiff brought a wrongful conception claim long before *McFarlane*. An operation to sterilize her was carried out negligently by the first defendant and she became pregnant again. She was offered, but refused, an abortion. The trial judge held that once she elected to continue the pregnancy, the pregnancy ceased to be unwanted, and that the birth of the child was the result of her own actions and not a consequence of the defendant's negligence. Her refusal to consider an abortion was so unreasonable as to eclipse the defendant's wrongdoing. The Court of Appeal overruled him.[30] Mrs Emeh did not become aware of her pregnancy until it was about seventeen to eighteen weeks advanced. Refusing an abortion at that stage in pregnancy could not be considered unreasonable. Whether the Court would have taken a different view had the pregnancy been less advanced remains open to question. Waller LJ laid great stress on the increased risk, discomfort and hospitalization entailed in abortion at twelve weeks plus.[31] Slade LJ was emphatic that abortion should generally never be forced upon a woman. He said:

Save in the most exceptional circumstances, I cannot think it right that the court should ever declare it unreasonable for a woman to decline to have an abortion in a case where there is no evidence that there were any medical or psychiatric grounds for terminating the particular pregnancy.[32]

Slade LJ's condemnation of judicially enforced abortion is endorsed in *McFarlane* by Lords Slynn,[33] Steyn[34] and Millett. Lord Millett declares[35] that it is morally repugnant to suggest that it is unreasonable not to have an abortion.

Some slight doubt, however, lurks in the kind of cases we are currently considering. If a foetal abnormality is diagnosed in pregnancy, and caused by the defendants' prior negligence, does this constitute *medical* grounds to terminate the pregnancy and constitute the sort of exceptional circumstances Slade LJ refers to? Certainly the foetal injury would entitle the mother to choose to abort the child. I cannot see that it could require her to do so or risk a reduction to her child's compensation for the disability he suffers. Section 1(7) of the 1976 Act envisages the sort of case where a pregnant woman ignores medical advice and exacerbates her child's disability by drinking, smoking or failing to take precautions advised by her doctors. The mother actively contributes to the disability. That is very different from refusing abortion. Assume a court was prepared to entertain this defence, how will they assess the mother's decision? Is it what the hypothetical reasonable woman in 2003 would do? Or must the woman's own moral views and religious affiliation be considered? Given that the Court of Appeal has finally confirmed that no women can be forced to undergo a Caesarian section to protect the life or health of the foetus, to 'force' a woman to 'kill' her foetus would be illogical.[36] Maternal autonomy demands that pregnant women's choices in this delicate arena of moral controversy should be respected.

Maternal immunity: discriminating against fathers?[37]

I noted earlier that save in respect of road accidents on public roads mothers remain immune from claims under the 1976 Act. Fathers enjoy no such formal immunity. A pregnant woman who drinks so heavily that her child is born with foetal alcohol syndrome or whose drug habit is such that her baby is born addicted to crack cannot be sued by her child. The Law Commission,[38] recommending that mothers be exempted from claims for prenatal injury, offered a number of reasons for maternal privilege. They considered that a claim against the mother would have little practical utility. She, unlike the father, was unlikely to have funds to meet an award of damages. Suing 'mum' would disturb the parental bond and in practice would only happen where a father used his child's claim as a weapon in a parental dispute. The first of these two reasons looks rather outdated now when many more women have independent means. The second applies equally to fathers. Other reasons remain more compelling.[39]

How could an equitable standard of reasonable pregnancy conduct be set? Women are beset by contradictory advice about what they should and should not eat, drink or do. Though, objectively one might agree that the reasonable mother-to-be should give up smoking, for example, achieving that aim is more difficult for some than others. The harassed mother of four struggling alone in poverty may know that she ought to quit smoking but struggles to do so. Most importantly, potential liability for foetal injury would in practice constitute a significant invasion of a pregnant woman's liberty and privacy. The threat of possible redress by the child could be used by partners and doctors to impose their judgement of foetal welfare. Given evidence of the foetus's vulnerability in early pregnancy, when a woman may not know she is pregnant, as Sheila McLean has said the law would in effect demand that '. . . fertile, sexually active women of childbearing age should act at all times as if they were pregnant'.[40] Finally, pragmatically, we should remind ourselves that a claim under the 1976 Act can only arise if a child is born alive. Maternal liability under the 1976 Act could simply provide an incentive to abort. A woman fearing, perhaps for little reason, that she has harmed her child could ensure that he was never born at all.

If there remains a case for maternal immunity, consideration must at least be given to paternal immunity. In 1976 the kind of harm that men might do their unborn children was perceived as pretty crude and obvious wrongdoing. A father who beats his partner up so badly that he injures both her and the child in the womb elicits little sympathy. What science can now tell us about how lifestyle from an early age may affect human gametes is cause for concern. Studies have shown that heavy smoking in teenage years could increase the risk of a man having a child who later succumbs to certain cancers. Whether fathers ought to be constrained by law in their pre-conception conduct must be questionable. Paternal liability unearths a further quirk of the 1976 Act. Even absent maternal immunity, in what sort of circumstances could either parent be liable for pre-conception injury? Liability under the Act is derivative only. The defendant must be liable in tort to the affected parent. Consider this example. A man is a heavy drug user in his youth in an era when such drug use is known to damage sperm. Later he begets a child born disabled because of his damaged gametes. To be liable to the child he must be liable to her mother. To be liable to the mother the courts would have to find that men have a duty of care to their future partners to ensure that they protect those partners' reproductive health. Imagine the outcry if the law declared that women must order their lives to safeguard their husbands' right to have healthy children.

Criminal liability

Before concluding that pregnancy conduct can never be subjected to legal redress, the decision of the House of Lords in *Attorney-General's Reference No. 3 of 1994*[41] must be looked at briefly. A father attacked his pregnant girlfriend and injured his child in the womb. The little girl was born alive but subsequently died of her pre-natal injuries. The father was charged with his daughter's murder. Following his acquittal, the Attorney-General referred the case to the Court of Appeal to determine whether murder or manslaughter can be committed where a foetus is injured *in utero* but is subsequently born alive only to die later of pre-natal injuries. In a convoluted judgment the Court of Appeal answered yes to both questions.[42] The House of Lords partially upheld their judgment on very different grounds. The Law Lords endorsed earlier judgments[43] that a charge of murder or manslaughter can be sustained where a foetus injured *in utero* is born alive and later dies as a consequence of those injuries. On the facts of this case their Lordships held that a charge of murder could not be sustained but that a charge of manslaughter could. Murder could not be committed in this case because there was no express design to harm the foetus 'or the human person which it would become'.[44] However manslaughter could be established in this case. In his assault on the mother, the father committed an unlawful and dangerous act likely to cause harm to the child and in the event resulting in her death. Such conduct constituted unlawful act type manslaughter. The implications of *Attorney-General's Reference No.3 of 1994* are that (a) a person whose unlawful and dangerous conduct results in foetal injury followed by the birth of a child 'doomed to die' commits manslaughter; (b) gross and culpable negligence in relation to the foetus may similarly, where the child is born alive and subsequently dies, constitute manslaughter; (c) a deliberate attempt to harm or kill the foetus directly could in such cases amount to murder. Finally Lord Mustill[45] suggests any violence against the foetus resulting in harm short of death may engage criminal responsibility.

At no point do any of the Law Lords consider maternal criminal responsibility. Their reasoning leaves pregnant women open to such liability in a range of scenarios. The pregnant woman who continues to abuse illegal drugs so that her child is born damaged by those substances and subsequently dies of their effect could be said to commit unlawful act type manslaughter. The woman whose heavy abuse of alcohol results in a child so dreadfully harmed by foetal alcohol syndrome that he lives only a short while, could be seen as criminally negligent. If Lord Mustill's statement about harm short of death is right, even if her child does not die the mother could be charged with causing him grievous bodily harm.

The sorts of illegal or reckless behaviour that might engage criminal liability might seem to create a case for endorsing criminal responsibility for egregiously bad behaviour in pregnancy. The moral obligation to have due regard for the welfare of a child whom a mother elects to bring to term is incontrovertible. Whether the invocation of the criminal law would in practice enhance foetal welfare or simply offer a means of coercing pregnant women and stigmatizing unfortunate mothers is to be doubted.[46]

Pre-pregnancy advice and genetic counselling

It is becoming common for women planning a child to seek advice before allowing themselves to conceive. For a healthy woman this may be simply a check that she is immune from rubella. If contracted in early pregnancy this can damage the foetal nervous system, causing the child to be born with severe disabilities. Another may seek reassurance that pregnancy will not damage her own health, for example if she has a history of cardiac disease. Couples in whose family genetic disease is prevalent or couples who already have a child with a genetic disease may need specialized genetic counselling.

In all these cases, those counselling the woman undertake a duty to her in relation not only to her own health and welfare but also in relation to the birth of a healthy child. If she is given the green light to go ahead with a pregnancy and suffers at the end of it the trauma and additional financial burden of a damaged child, she may have a claim in negligence.[47] She and the child's father will be able to claim the additional cost to them of caring for a disabled child. However, proving negligence may not be easy. Not only must she show that the doctor failed to take into account factors relating to her medical history or genetic background, or failed to conduct tests, that would have alerted him to the danger, she must also show that a reasonably competent doctor would have discovered the risk. If a woman requests a test for immunity from rubella, is brushed aside, and subsequently contracts the disease in pregnancy, her claim should succeed. The enormous publicity given to the Department of Health campaign to eradicate the risk to the unborn child posed by rubella is such that any GP must be aware of and guard against the risk. If the sister of a haemophiliac consults her doctor and explains her brother's condition, and he fails to refer her for counselling with the result that she bears a haemophiliac son, she too should succeed.[48] Beyond these obvious examples of want of competence the medical profession is much divided on the value of pre-conception advice. Some doctors run special clinics and advise special diets and total abstinence from alcohol when attempting to conceive. Significant evidence of the relationship of such regimes to the reduction of risk to the child, and their acceptance by the profession at large, will be needed before a claim based on the lack of such detailed guidance could succeed. Finally, the claimant must also establish that had she received proper advice she would not have allowed herself to become pregnant when she did.

Has the disabled child a remedy? We must distinguish three types of cases where negligent pre-pregnancy advice results in the birth of a disabled child.

In the first case the relevant negligence may be that the woman was encouraged to become pregnant when, had proper care been taken, she could have been advised never to contemplate pregnancy because of the risk to *any* child she might bear. The child's action in such a case will fail because the essence of his claim is that he should never have been born at all. It is a claim for 'wrongful life'.

In the second instance, the negligence may have been in failing to counsel the mother properly on precautions to take or the timing of pregnancy. Such a claim may raise an awkward problem. For example, a woman is not tested for immunity to rubella, or the test is negligently conducted. She is wrongly told that she has immunity. She becomes pregnant, contracts the disease and the child is born disabled. Had she been properly advised, she would have been vaccinated against the disease and advised in the strongest of terms to delay pregnancy for three months after the vaccination. The child would never have been born at all. The particular set of genes in the egg and sperm that went to create him would never have met. A literal interpretation of *McKay* would deny the child a remedy on the grounds that that unique individual would never have been born had his mother had proper advice. It would seem a harsh result, but the conclusion that this follows from the interpretation of the Act by the Court of Appeal in *McKay* is difficult to resist. Examples of this sort could be multiplied endlessly. A parent undergoing treatment for venereal disease is carelessly advised that pregnancy is safe before treatment is complete. The child born disabled would not have been born at all had proper advice been given. A woman knows a little of a family history of genetic disease affecting the males in her family. She seeks counselling. She should have been advised of the risks to male children and been offered pre-implantation genetic diagnosis or amniocentesis in pregnancy, so that she could, if she wished, have ensured she did not give birth to a male child. A disabled male child cannot sue under the Act, for had PIGD or amniocentesis been offered and accepted that boy would not exist.

Finally, there is only one limited class of case where the child's action based on allegedly careless pre-pregnancy advice may succeed. That is where adequate advice and counselling would have enabled that very child to be born hale and hearty. Realistic examples are difficult to think of. Perhaps one example concerns the relationship between maternal diet before conception and spina bifida. There is evidence that folic acid supplements may reduce the likelihood of spina bifida. The child could contend that had his mother been advised to follow that regime his disability would not have developed. He would have been born, but not born disabled. Such a child claims for his disabilities, not wrongful life. He overcomes the first problem in his claim against medical staff, but will he be able to prove that the treatment if given would have prevented his disability?

Genetic counselling and confidentiality

The genetic counsellor's legal problems are not confined to his obligations to the woman seeking his advice. For example, if he discovers that she is, or is likely to be, the carrier of a sex-linked disease, he will be aware that her sisters are also at risk as carriers, and so to a lesser degree are other female relatives. Obviously he will ask her permission to inform her sister or her sister's doctor. What if the woman refuses permission arguing that the counsellor owes her an obligation of confidence? If the sister later bears a damaged child the consequences to her are dreadful and she might sue the counsellor. The sister could contend that the risk to her was readily foreseeable and the counsellor had a duty to warn her. I would suggest that in such circumstances the counsellor exceptionally may be justified in breaking his obligation of confidence. The Court of Appeal[49] has held that information obtained in a confidential relationship may be disclosed if disclosure is in the public interest. Is the interest in preventing the birth of damaged children sufficient to merit disclosure? Does it depend on the degree of disability afflicting the child?

Childbirth: how much choice?

Our grandmothers gave thanks if they survived the perils of childbirth. Our mothers were the first generation to have general access to hospital confinement and skilled attention if things went wrong. Today medical technology offers a whole range of sophisticated devices to monitor mother and baby and ensure safe delivery. Increasingly many women reject the panoply of machinery found in many hospital labour wards. Accepting the necessity of 'high-tech' birth for a minority of difficult cases, the natural childbirth movement has campaigned for the medical profession to be more willing to let nature take its course. For a number of women the ideal would be delivery of their baby at home in the comfort of familiar surroundings.

The debate around childbirth is largely medical and social. Obstetricians in many areas of the country have accepted the ideas propounded. Hospital birth today is usually substantially less interventionist and impersonal than it was twenty-five years ago. Home delivery remains more difficult to obtain. Few general practitioners deliver babies at home. There are insufficient NHS community midwives to meet demand. Progress is being made, but the laywoman is left with the overall impression that while doctors make considerable efforts to meet women's demands for more natural childbirth in hospital, all but a few in the profession are opposed to home delivery.

What role does the law play in the debate? Childbirth remains a professional monopoly. The law denies a woman, unable to persuade a doctor or midwife to attend her at home or a hospital to comply with her wishes concerning the birth, the choice of seeking alternative help.[50] For it is a criminal offence for a person other than a registered midwife or a registered medical practitioner to attend a woman in childbirth. And any person means any person. In 1982 a husband was convicted of delivering his own wife and fined £100.[51] Nor is the unqualified attendant the only potential 'criminal'. The mother herself, if she procures the other's services – in ordinary English, if she asks for help – may be guilty of counselling and procuring a criminal offence. So her choice is to accept the medical help available or give birth alone. Giving birth alone is not an attractive option and one not free of legal hazard, not to speak of medical risk. For if the baby dies the mother may face prosecution for manslaughter (see page 387).[52] Gross negligence by attendants in the delivery of a baby has resulted in criminal conviction where the baby died.[53] The issue where an unattended mother was on trial would be whether refusing medical attendance was sufficiently culpable negligence in relation to the safety of her child.

The rationale for legislation that makes professional attendance at childbirth compulsory may appear self-evident. If a person refuses to seek medical help for any other life-threatening condition she physically harms herself alone. A woman refusing medical attention in childbirth puts her baby at risk. Yet she can lawfully refuse attention for the nine months up to delivery. Proposals that maternity grants and benefits should be made dependent on ante-natal visits have been made. Nobody has yet suggested that it should be a criminal offence to fail to attend the ante-natal clinic. There is no express and considered policy on the respective rights and liberties of mother and baby. The legislation originally enacted to require professional attendance at childbirth was intended to outlaw the 'Sarah Gamps', elderly and often dirty local women who made their living as unqualified midwives.[54] Today's legislation has moved a long way from that point. It may by chance be correct, but it needs proper consideration whether a husband delivering his wife, or a mother her daughter, should be branded as criminal when all goes well and mother and baby thrive.

Hospital birth

How far does a woman retain control of her labour? In 1984 Eekelaar and Dingwall wrote of the woman in labour.

Apart from any express prohibition she might make, if she receives substantially that form of treatment, a lack of explicit consent to particular details will not make it unlawful, providing that those details relate reasonably to the treatment according to the prevailing professional standards.[55]

Such a statement of the law will strike fear into women who actively seek to participate in and, as far as possible control, their labour. I would suggest that today, save in an emergency, explicit consent is required for any invasive examination or procedure in labour. That does not mean that the midwife must obtain a written consent for every vaginal examination or that explicit consent to wiping the woman's brow is called for. Any significant procedure must where possible proceed with the woman's agreement. Most midwives regard treating mothers as partners in labour as simply good practice. One of the most controversial issues of hospital birth is the use of episiotomy. A small cut is made in the vagina to assist delivery and prevent tearing. One of its advantages is said to be that the deliberate cut will heal better than a random tear. In some hospitals episiotomy became routine. It was performed regardless of any necessity for it. The number of episiotomies has fallen. The law, as Eekelaar and Dingwall make clear, will render such a procedure unlawful if the woman *expressly* bans it. Many women will enter the labour ward confused and a little overwhelmed. They will have given no express instructions. Episiotomy without express consent is unlawful. It is not an inevitably necessary invasion of the mother's body, as are the contacts by the midwife when she feels the abdomen and assists the baby's exit. Episiotomy is a greater invasion of the body than any contacts implicitly authorized simply by seeking professional aid. The skin is cut. A wound, however small, is made. The law should uphold the mother's right to control what happens to her.

Childbirth can be an unpredictable process. Midwives and obstetricians may sometimes have to respond swiftly to an unforeseen emergency. The woman may at this stage be in acute pain, perhaps a little panicky, or significantly affected by doses of painkilling drugs that cause some mental confusion. Doubts may surface about her decision-making capability, and/or time to seek consent may truly be limited. The Court of Appeal[56] has suggested that if the woman is temporarily incompetent to make decisions for herself, health professionals may do whatever is required in her best interests. Defining the borderline between capacity and mental incapacity in such cases is tricky. It is too easy to assume women are incompetent. 'Birth plans' offer a partial solution to such dilemmas. Women, ideally in consultation with their midwives, outline how they wish to be treated if certain emergencies materialize. 'Advance directives' should have just as great force and authority at childbirth as in the life-threatening circumstances in which they are more usually invoked. The controversy over whether the law should compel medical attendance in childbirth would be much less substantial if the woman's rights in hospital were fully protected.

It goes without saying that a mother suffering injury as a result of carelessness in the management of childbirth is entitled to compensation for negligence. She will recover compensation for her pain and suffering and for the shock and grief consequent on the death of a baby, or the birth of a disabled child. Her damages may also include any effect of the mismanaged delivery on her prospects of future childbearing.[57] Where obstetric negligence results in the birth of a disabled infant, the child too has a claim. The most common kind of case centres on allegations that the baby suffered brain damage resulting in cerebral palsy as a consequence of oxygen starvation during delivery. The parents argue that the obstetric team failed to act on signs of foetal distress and perform a Caesarean section as swiftly as the circumstances required. Very often the core of the dispute is not whether clinical negligence can be proven, but whether causation can be established. Such cases are expensive, slow and worryingly common. A survey by the National Audit Office[58] demonstrates that cerebral palsy and birth injury claims account for 80 per cent of outstanding claims against the NHS in terms of value and 26 per cent in crude numbers (see page 172). Little wonder the government is giving serious thought to a special no-fault scheme to compensate birth injuries.

Maternal autonomy/foetal welfare

The child injured by obstetric negligence will have a claim against doctors and midwives who failed him. What are his rights if his mother refuses a course of action that will benefit him and thus causes him injury?

In theory the child's rights are now governed by the Congenital Disabilities (Civil Liability) Act 1976, albeit the Act appears to go unnoticed in the relevant case-law. The 1976 Act covers not just injury to the child in the womb but also any occurrence that *affected mother or child in the course of its birth*. It has been argued that the 1976 Act reduced the child's rights.[59] Liability under the Act arises only where the defendant would have been liable in tort to the affected parent. A failure by the defendant caring for the mother, for example failure to proceed quickly enough to Caesarean section, is in no way the responsibility of the mother. The duty to the mother embraces care of her child. A breach of duty to her that injures the child creates rights for both her and her child.

The thrust of the argument that the Act reduces the child's rights lies in these sorts of circumstances. If a doctor recommends a Caesarean section because the child is believed to be at risk and the mother refuses, resulting in the child suffering brain damage, the child will not be able to sue the doctor. The doctor is not liable to the mother in this case. The child cannot sue his mother, for the Act grants immunity to mothers.[60] If there is no duty directly to the child a doctor cannot after the 1976 Act advance his duty to the child as a defence against acts done to the mother.[61] Were there still a direct duty to the child, the doctor might contend that in exceptional circumstances he could, for example, proceed to Caesarean section without consent in order to save the baby. That begs the fundamental question of whether doctors ought ever to be allowed to place the child's welfare above his mother's right to make her own choices about her childbirth. Will the law force women to submit to surgery to protect the child?

In 1998 the Court of Appeal in *St George's Healthcare NHS Trust* v. *S.*[62] finally ruled that in English law no mentally competent woman could be required to submit to a Caesarean section or any other form of obstetric intervention to which she objected. Neither pregnancy nor labour diminished the woman's rights of self-determination. Judge LJ put the position succinctly:

. . . while pregnancy increases the personal responsibilities of the pregnant woman it does not diminish her entitlement to decide whether or not to undergo medical treatment.[63]

Six years of uncertainty were ended. In 1992 in *Re S*,[64] the then President of the Family Division, had ruled that doctors could carry out a Caesarean on a woman whose own life and that of her child were imminently imperilled by an obstructed labour. Several other cases[65] followed where courts, often in hurried hearings in circumstances of dire emergency, ordered Caesarean surgery despite maternal objections. In a number, but not all, of these cases the mother's mental capacity was questionable. In 1997 in *Re MB (An Adult: Medical Treatment)*[66] the Court of Appeal said that if a woman retained mental capacity she retained the right to make decisions about surgery for herself but found on the facts that MB's needle phobia rendered her temporarily incompetent.

The theory of the law is this. Unless a woman lacks the mental capacity to make her own decisions about labour, her freedom to determine what is and is not done to her is unimpaired. In practice the temptation to seek grounds to find her capacity to be impaired is great. Judge LJ in *St George's* is emphatic in his endorsement of maternal autonomy. The mother's wishes should be respected even if her thinking process is '. . . apparently bizarre and irrational and contrary to the views of the overwhelming majority of the community at large'. Yet in *Re MB* Butler-Sloss LJ suggested a woman might suffer temporary incapacity induced by fear, confusion, shock, pain or drugs. Finding any of these factors in childbirth will not be hard.

Is the theory right? Or ought the foetus at the point of birth to be more highly valued? The difficulties of using law to enforce a duty to the foetus are well illustrated in *Re F. (In Utero)*[67] where a local authority unsuccessfully tried to make a foetus a ward of court. The mother was a thirty-six-year-old woman who suffered from severe mental disturbance, but she was not 'sectionable' under the Mental Health Act 1983. She refused antenatal care and had disappeared by the time the local authority started proceedings to make the foetus a ward of court. There was concern for the child's welfare. Refusing to extend the wardship jurisdiction to unborn children, the court advanced the following reasons for their decision. (1) In English law the foetus has no legal personality until it is born and has an existence independent of the mother. (2) To extend the wardship jurisdiction to the foetus with its predominant principle that the interests of the ward are paramount would create inevitable conflict between the existing legal interests of the mother and her child. Is the mother to be 'sacrificed' for the child? (3) There are immense practical difficulties in enforcing any order against the mother. If she is, for example, refusing to consent to an elective Caesarean and is not already in hospital, will the police be called on to go and arrest her? (4) There would be problems with the limit of such a jurisdiction. Mothers can do most harm to their unborn children early in pregnancy by, for example, alcohol and drug abuse. Yet up to twenty-four weeks in pregnancy a mother may well be able to obtain a legal abortion. Would a woman who wants her baby be subject to coercive measures in the baby's interests, yet free to destroy it should she change her mind? May LJ concluded that in the light of these problems any such radical extension of the wardship jurisdiction was a matter for Parliament and not for the courts themselves. In the event, and unbeknownst to the court, while they were hearing the action the mother had already safely given birth to a healthy child.

Parliament should firmly reject any proposal to extend the wardship jurisdiction to unborn children or to endorse non-consensual obstetric interventions.[68] Over and above those reasons given by the Court of Appeal, such a proposal should be thrown out on the grounds of the damage it would do to antenatal care generally. Obstetricians, knowing that they could in the end coerce their patients, would become less willing to inform and persuade, to rely on patience rather than compulsion. Women, knowing that ultimately they could be forced against their will to submit to blood transfusion or surgery, may opt out of formal obstetric care and far more babies could be born damaged as a result. The law must continue to recognize the pregnant woman's autonomy and *her* sovereignty over *her* own body. In no other circumstances can one person be required to submit to any medical procedure to benefit another. Once a child is born neither of his parents could be forced to donate even a drop of blood to him, however trivial the discomfort to them or great the child's need may be. Caesarean surgery remains major invasive surgery with significant risks and pain for the patient.[69]

Instinctive support for such a principle gains further credence from the evidence of how forced Caesareans actually work in the USA. Of the women subjected to forced obstetric intervention 81 per cent belonged to an ethnic minority, 44 per cent were unmarried and none were private patients.[70] Moreover in a startling number of cases where a court ordered a 'necessary' intervention, the woman, having evaded the court officials seeking to enforce the order, went on to give birth to a healthy child without that intervention.[71] Very, very few pregnant women refuse to follow their doctors' advice. Giving the courts legal powers to enforce medical orders would do far more harm than good to the principles and practice of obstetric care.

16
Medical Research

In 1981 an elderly widow, Mrs Wigley, died from the effects of an experimental drug she had been given subsequent to an operation for bowel cancer. She died not from bowel cancer but from bone-marrow depression induced by the drug. Without her knowledge or consent she had been entered in a clinical trial of the new drug. In 2001, a twenty-four-year-old volunteer died in the course of a clinical trial in Washington.[1] More recently inquiries have been held into allegations that research was carried out on newborn babies without parental consent in a hospital in North Staffordshire (see page 402). Evidence emerged in Bristol and Liverpool of children's body parts being retained for research without their parents' consent or knowledge (see page 470). Medical research was acquiring a bad reputation. Yet every time any one of us receives a prescription for antibiotics we benefit from research performed on others in the past. It is becoming a human guinea pig oneself, or letting one's child be so used, that is an unattractive prospect. However, if medicine is to make progress against cancer and continue the battle against diseases such as diabetes and multiple sclerosis, new drugs and procedures must be subject to trials.

In this chapter,[2] we examine the role the law does and should play in the control of medical research involving human participants. There are four fundamental legal questions. (1) How far, if at all, should there be statutory regulation of clinical research? Anyone wishing to undertake a research project using animals may do so only under a licence from the Home Secretary.[3] An embryologist experimenting on a human embryo of up to fourteen days' development may do so only with the sanction of the Human Fertilization and Embryology Authority (see page 324). Yet a doctor may lawfully carry out research on a human adult or child with no such equivalent authority. (2) The authority to carry out research on the human adult derives from that person's consent. The second crucial question thus becomes: how satisfactory are the principles governing consent to participation in clinical research? (3) The law on medical treatment demands that the physician respects the confidences of his patient. How does this translate into medical research? (4) Finally, what provision does the law make for an individual suffering injury in the course of his participation in such clinical research?

Clinical research[4] may be classified in a number of ways. Non-intrusive research involves no direct interference with the participant, for example, research into medical records, or epidemiological research. Intrusive research may be non-invasive, for example, psychological inquiries, or invasive, involving actual contact with the patient's body, for example, taking blood, administering drugs, testing new surgical techniques. Therapeutic research involves research on patients in the hope that it will benefit those patients. Non-therapeutic research involves volunteers who agree to participate in a research project not likely to confer any personal benefit to themselves. The boundaries between these categories are difficult to draw. The more invasive the research the greater are the ethical problems. Non-therapeutic research generates particular difficulties.

Research ethics committees

In the absence of formal statutory regulation of medical research on humans, akin to the detailed control exercised over animal research, the responsibility for regulating medical research is entrusted largely to research ethics committees. A number of informal ethics committees exist outside the NHS. These include ethical review committees set up by universities, private hospitals and pharmaceutical companies. Within the NHS, Department of Health policy in 1975 required each district health authority to set up and administer one or more local research ethics committees (LREC). Formal guidance was issued in 1991[5] establishing the independent nature of such committees, which comprise lay and medical individuals who advise on the ethics of any health care research using NHS premises, staff or patients. From October 2002, NHS reforms reduced the number of health authorities to create twenty-eight larger strategic health authorities (StHA). Strategic health authorities take on the responsibility of supporting

LRECs. Within the geographical boundaries of each StHA, there will normally be more than one LREC. Researchers should apply to their most local committee for approval, but if that committee is overloaded or the researcher has just missed a deadline, he can apply to another LREC within the StHA boundaries.

Very often major clinical trials are conducted in several different parts of the United Kingdom. In 1997 special arrangements were put in place to review research taking place in more than one research site.[6] Multi-centre research ethics committees (MRECs) were introduced to reduce delays and bureaucracy for multi-centre researchers.[7] For example, an epidemiological researcher looking into the effects of smoking across the UK would, before 1997, have had to submit applications to a substantial number of LRECs. Now the ethics of the proposal will be reviewed by a single MREC and the relevant LRECs will consider only issues that relate to the particular locality (such as the suitability of the researcher and facilities at the research site).

Although a researcher contravenes no law in carrying out research without ethics committee approval, other sanctions deter any such practice. An NHS employee failing to seek approval from the relevant REC is likely to be disciplined by his employing trust. Outside the NHS, conducting research without ethical review may well constitute 'serious professional misconduct'. The RCP guidelines state unequivocally:

All medical research involving human subjects should undergo ethical review before it commences, in accordance with the principles that investigators should not be the sole judge of whether their research raises significant ethical issues.

An NHS LREC was formerly a sub-committee of its local health authority, and is presumably now such a sub committee of the StHA. There can be little doubt that the authority is therefore legally responsible for the decisions of the committee. The authority *and* each individual member of the committee owe a duty of care to all those who participate in research approved by the ethics committee. Although there has as yet been no case in England where an ethics committee has been sued by a research participant, it is important to recognize that ethics committees have direct legal responsibilities to research participants.[8]

The practices and effectiveness of ethics committees have been much disputed. LRECs were introduced with limited guidance, which resulted in significant variations between them. A proposal accepted without reservations in Brighton, might be subject to amendments in Birmingham, and be rejected outright in Manchester. As a result researchers' confidence in the system quickly diminished.[9] The introduction of MRECs in 1997 countered a number of criticisms but generated new problems.[10] The lack of researcher confidence in the NHS ethics committees was matched by public concern. The Department of Health responded in 2001 with fresh guidance in the *Research Governance Framework for Health and Social Care*.[11] It outlines the allocation of responsibilities, demands more rigorous monitoring of research and imposes high scientific, ethical and financial standards and transparent decision-making processes. Concurrently the Clinical Trials Directive[12] was promulgated by the European Parliament in order to encourage consistency in the ethical review of clinical trials across Europe. The Central Office for Research Ethics Committees (COREC) was set up by the Department of Health to coordinate the development of operational systems for RECs, to manage MRECs, to act as a resource for the training of REC members and to advise on matters of operation and policy. COREC issued its *Governance Arrangements for NHS Research Ethics Committees*[13] in July 2001. This guidance had been long awaited by researchers and ethics committee members alike.

The *Research Governance Framework*, together with the COREC guidance, mean that LRECs and MRECs should now receive greater support, training and monitoring. LRECs must include up to eighteen members from a balanced age and gender distribution. There should be a mixture of expert and lay members, the latter constituting at least one third of the membership. New time limits have been introduced to ensure that researchers will receive a timely response to their applications. By April 2002, LRECs and MRECs must have complied with these substantial changes, ensuring the protection of the dignity, rights, safety and well-being of research participants whilst recognising the crucial contribution of medical research to modern and effective health and social care. Ethics committees must review:

1. the scientific design and conduct of the study;
2. recruitment of research participants;
3. care and protection of research participants;
4. confidentiality issues;
5. the informed consent process;
6. community considerations.

At the heart of the ethics committee's difficult job lies a balancing exercise. Any NHS research ethics committee is instructed to consider carefully:

The justification of particular risks and inconveniences against the anticipated benefits for the research participants and concerned communities.

The quality of the people who volunteer to serve on NHS ethics committees, and their ability to exercise judgement, is fundamental to the process. It should be noted that, somewhat surprisingly, the COREC guidance does not require ethics committees to concern themselves too much with the law. It provides:

RECs should have due regard for the requirement of relevant regulatory agencies and of applicable laws. It is not for the REC to interpret regulations or laws, but they may indicate in their advice to the researcher and those institutions where they believe further consideration needs to be given to such matters.

Given that legislation requires the grant of a licence before research can be undertaken on non-human animals or embryos, it is perhaps surprising that these new governance arrangements were introduced via administrative measures in preference to introducing at last statutory regulation of the ethics committee system. Such legislation recently received support from the Scottish Working Group on Organ Retention.[14] The case for statutory ethics committees is particularly strong in the light of the Clinical Trials Directive, which must be incorporated into UK law by 2004. The Directive requires that research ethics committees approving clinical trials be given independent statutory authority. The Directive defines an ethics committee as:

An independent body in a Member State, consisting of healthcare professionals and non-medical members, whose responsibilities it is to protect the rights, safety and wellbeing of human subjects involved in a trial and provide public assurance of that protection by, among other things, expressing an opinion on the trial protocol, the suitability of the investigator and the adequacy of the facilities, and on methods and documents to be used to inform trial subjects and obtain their informed consent.

It would be technically possible to implement the Directive without a new Act of Parliament. Regulations can be made under the European Community Act 1972. However, if all the government does is to implement the Directive as narrowly as possible chaos will ensue. The Directive does not embrace all forms of medical research, only clinical trials, defined essentially as trials of new pharmaceutical products. Simply implementing the Directive by regulations would result in statutory authority to review drug trials, but not other research proposals (such as those investigating surgical techniques, epidemiology, complementary medicine, or psychology). Non-NHS drug trials, which are currently often reviewed by private ethics committees, would come within the remit of the new statutory REC. NHS research other than drug trials could be remitted to the statutory committee by directions from the Secretary of State. Stitching together a coherent system to implement the Directive without legislation and without creating a plethora of different sorts of LRECs and MRECs is a complicated task.

Why has the government abjured legislation? Statute would grant undoubted authority to RECs emphasizing the importance of protecting human research subjects while promoting ethical research. The independence of RECs, required by the Clinical Trials Directive, could be addressed. Are ethics committees truly independent if they operate, as LRECs do, as sub-committees of an NHS health authority, or as MRECs do under the aegis of COREC? Drafting a *Research Ethics Act* would also be a technically difficult task, and there are those who argue that inflexible legislation might prevent ethics committees responding adequately to the evolutionary nature of medical research. Yet much of the groundwork has been accomplished with the introduction of detailed guidance from COREC. In the light of the Clinical Trials Directive it seems an opportune time to implement such changes.

Consent to participation in trials

In 2000 allegations were made, albeit later largely not proven, surrounding research carried out a decade before on premature babies at North Staffordshire Hospital.[15] It was claimed the research was conducted without parents' consent.[16] Since 1964 the Declaration of Helsinki has sought to protect research participants' rights by demanding rigorous consent procedures. The fall-out from disputes surrounding this controversial research contributed to the impetus for the 2001 Department of Health *Research Governance Framework for Health and Social Care*. This states that informed consent is at the heart of ethical research and demands 'appropriate arrangements' for obtaining consent, and the review of those arrangements by an ethics committee.[17] It should be noted this was by no means a new requirement. Prior NHS guidelines placed equal emphasis on the need for consent.

Though informed consent of the participant is a prerequisite for ethical approval in most types of medical research, there are ethical codes of conduct that accept limited circumstances where alternative safeguards are acceptable. Self evidently someone may be unable to consent by virtue of being a child or suffering from mental disability. In such circumstances, we shall see (page 405) that other safeguards are put in place to protect the research participant. Even in relation to competent adult subjects there may be trials where the risks to the participant might be minimal and the impracticalities of gaining consent tremendous. Thus, in some cases of epidemiological research (such as the collection of statistics on measles, for example) where the individual participant cannot be identified, an ethics committee might decide that obtaining consent is unnecessary.[18] Even in epidemiological trials consent must be obtained when data is not fully anonymized. The 2001 COREC guidance requires that consent should usually involve a written consent form and information sheet, in addition to an oral explanation. The Declaration of Helsinki is often seen as the 'Bible' of ethical research practice. It was revised for the fifth time in October 2000.[19] Article 20 provides that 'the subjects must be volunteers and informed participants in the research project.' Article 22 outlines the importance of adequate information and Article 23[20] stresses the importance of voluntariness. What does this mean in practice?

In any research on human beings, each potential subject must be adequately informed of the aims, methods, sources of funding, any possible conflicts of interest, institutional affiliations of the researcher, the anticipated benefits and potential risks of the study and the discomfort it may entail. The subject should be informed of the right to abstain from participation in the study or to withdraw consent to participate at any time without reprisal. After ensuring that the subject has understood the information, the physician should then obtain the subject's freely-given informed consent, preferably in writing. If the consent cannot be obtained in writing the non-written consent must be formally documented and witnessed.

The requirement of adequate information for consent to treatment has already been addressed in Chapter 4. We have seen that, very gradually, the English courts are moving away from an exclusively professional standard of information disclosure. In the context of research, we would argue that the 'prudent patient' test governs what researchers must disclose to research participants.[21] The formal guidance offered to researchers is overtly patient-centred. The medical profession endorses that guidance. Only rarely, we would suggest, could it be logical or defensible[22] to depart from such unequivocal guidance.

Setting a stringent test for disclosure in the context of clinical research in Canada in *Halushka* v. *University of Saskatchewan* Hall JA declared:

> There can be no exception to the ordinary requirements of disclosure in the case of research as there may well be in ordinary medical practice. The researcher does not have to balance the probable effect of lack of treatment against the risk involved in treatment itself. The example of risks being properly hidden from a patient when it is important that he should not worry can have no application in the field of research. The subject of medical experimentation is entitled to a full and frank disclosure of all the facts, probabilities and opinions which a reasonable man might be expected to consider before giving his consent.[23]

Self-evidently Hall JA's principle must be applied to volunteers. No one but the volunteer can be allowed to assess what risk he is prepared to accept for the community's welfare. This applies equally to patients who agree to become research participants. Of course, the doctor in such cases hopes that the patient may benefit from the experimental treatment but the patient is exposed to additional, unquantifiable risk, at least in part to benefit others, not himself.

In the case of non-therapeutic research, however, a further problem is whether the volunteers are truly volunteers. Do medical students feel under compulsion to assist in trials mounted by their teachers? Do patients feel obliged to 'help' their doctor if he asks them to participate in non-therapeutic research?[24] Where resort is had to volunteers outside the medical schools and hospital patients, payments are often made in this country. Amounts paid are relatively modest but may still constitute an inducement to impoverished students and the unemployed.[25] The principles of law are clear. Any degree of compulsion renders any written consent invalid.[26] Proving compulsion might be difficult for a medical student. For an unemployed 'volunteer', economic compulsion arising from his circumstances rather than any misconduct by the research team is as yet unrecognized in English law. Article 23 of the Declaration of Helsinki is clear that where any *suspicion* of duress might arise, an independent physician unconnected with the research project should seek the subject's consent.

The issue of free and full consent is central to the propriety and legality of clinical trials.[27] Should the public, and patients in particular, come to believe that there is a real likelihood of being involved in a trial unknowingly, or, having agreed to participate, discovering that they have been given inadequate or inaccurate information, the supply of volunteers for research will dry up and patients' confidence in general health care will be seriously undermined. The definition of what constitutes a proper consent is, as we have seen, far from easy.[28]

There is another difficulty too. The line between experimenting on a patient and doing your utmost for him is blurred. For example, if a doctor caring for patients with new variant CJD attempts a novel treatment as a last resort, knowing that there is no conventional treatment that will prolong the patient's life, has he crossed that line and made his patient a research-subject?[29] The thorny problem of consent and medical research should not be left for a *cause célèbre* to be fought through the courts. Attempts should be made to work out in advance a statutory code of practice, based on guidance from the Department of Health, Medical Research Council and General Medical Council,[30] that both safeguards the rights of, and protects the interests of, patients and research subjects, and ensures that properly regulated research can continue and flourish.

Children in medical research programmes

Very real difficulties beset the question of consent to clinical trials by adults. The problems are even greater where children are concerned. When can a child give his own consent to participation in a trial? When can he withhold that consent? If the child is incapable of giving an effective consent, may a parent give consent on his behalf?

The House of Lords' ruling in *Gillick*[31] (see page 363) empowers a minor to consent to medical treatment when he or she has reached an age and individual maturity to judge what the treatment entails and assess its benefits and disadvantages. In the case of therapeutic research where the child may expect to benefit from the procedure, the test might be the same. If the child is over sixteen, the Family Law Reform Act 1969, statutorily empowering minors over sixteen to consent to medical treatment, will offer protection to the medical team. Legal requirements for consent of minors in research are supplemented with guidance from august bodies such as the Medical Research Council and the British Paediatric Association.[32] In 1991 Department of Health guidance to research ethics committees demanded that, despite a child satisfying the *Gillick* test, 'even for therapeutic research purposes it would . . . be unacceptable not to have the consent of the parent or guardian where the child is under sixteen'.[33] It further required parental consent for sixteen- and seventeen-year-olds 'unless it is clearly in the child's best interests that the parents should not be informed'.[34] The current COREC guidance is surprisingly silent about the consent requirements for children.[35] More concrete guidance has been issued by the Royal College of Paediatrics and Child Health[36] that advises that where a child satisfies the *Gillick* test, he should also be able to consent to participation in research.

Non-therapeutic research poses a more awkward problem. Could the *Gillick* ruling apply to a procedure of no immediate benefit to the minor? There is no apparent reason why it should not. The basis of the judgment is not limited to medical treatment alone but concerns the general capacity of older children to make decisions for themselves. Provided the child or young person truly appreciates what he is agreeing to, provided he is sufficiently mature to make the judgement on whether the benefit to the community justifies any risk to himself, one might expect that he could give consent as an adult may to participation in a research project. What the medical team would have to assess is the maturity and understanding of that individual child or young person. Indeed whenever researchers wish to include in a trial a research subject under eighteen, only the *Gillick* test can grant the minor herself authority to consent to participate in the trial. Section 8 of the Family Law Reform Act 1969, empowering young people between sixteen and eighteen to consent to medical treatment, is strictly limited to therapeutic and diagnostic interventions.[37] Indeed Lord Donaldson has doubted whether any minor can authorize a non-therapeutic procedure for herself. He considered it to be 'highly improbable'[38] that a *Gillick competent* minor could consent to a procedure of no benefit to himself. The safest course of action where people under eighteen are to be involved in clinical trials remains to seek a dual consent from both the older child and her parents.[39]

What about younger children or an older child robbed of mental capacity by illness? Therapeutic research poses little difficulty. The agreement of the parents to a procedure, albeit novel, which it is hoped will benefit the child will authorize the doctors' action. Parental consent is legally effective to authorize any treatment of the child aimed at promoting the best interests of that child. In *Simms* v. *Simms*[40] the parents of a sixteen-year-old girl suffering from new variant CJD sought a ruling that it would be lawful for doctors to attempt an experimental treatment which just might arrest her decline. Butler-Sloss P held that where no alternative therapy was available and it was reasonable to suggest that the experimental treatment might have some benefit but would not pose a risk of increased suffering to the child her parents could lawfully consent to such treatment.

Non-therapeutic research on a child offers no immediate benefit to the child. On the present state of authority in England, it is unclear whether parental consent to such research on a child is of any effect.

The arguments on the present law can be put in this way. The test of the legality of procedures performed on children centres on the individual child. What will benefit him? What are the pros and cons as far as he is concerned? So in *Re D.*,[41] sterilization of an eleven-year-old girl was prohibited because it was an invasion of her right to choose for herself on reproduction, and because of the emotional damage early sterilization might cause her. Social questions, for example the risk that any baby she had might be a burden on the community or be disabled himself, were barely touched on. And, although the House of Lords authorized the sterilization of seventeen-year-old Jeanette in *Re B.*,[42] their Lordships stressed that that operation was lawful only on the grounds that it benefited Jeanette. The benefit to her carers and to society in general was to be totally disregarded. By analogy then, is one forced to say that non-therapeutic research on any child must be barred because the risk to the child, however slight, cannot be justified in the absence of some immediate benefit to him? In 1962 that was the advice given to doctors by the Medical Research Council.[43]

Quite rightly, paediatricians emphasize the need for some degree of carefully controlled research on children.[44] Children respond differently to drugs, they suffer from illnesses not afflicting adults and, above all, their suffering when afflicted is particularly poignant. The Royal College of Paediatrics and Child Health[45] considers non-therapeutic research on children to be neither unethical nor illegal. They have laid down guidelines centring on the principles that research should never be done on children that could adequately be done on adults and that the benefit/risk ratio must be carefully assessed.[46]

The Royal College's belief that non-therapeutic research on children is legal can only be right if the courts were prepared to accede to the following argument. Parental rights to consent to procedures involving their young children are often said to be dependent on the procedure being in the child's best interests. That embraces any procedure, not just strictly medical matters; for example taking blood to ascertain paternity is allowed.[47] The best interests of the child include the interests of the community. The child benefits from serving the community and may in the long term benefit himself. For example, a three-year-old from whom blood is taken as part of a control group to be compared with blood from a group of diabetic children may develop diabetes himself, or his own child may. Hence may he be said to benefit indirectly from research into the disease? A further argument may be advanced to this effect. The case-law from which the 'in the best interests' of the child test derives concerns radical and major treatment decisions. Should a young girl be sterilized? May parents withhold consent from surgery necessary to prolong their newborn infant's life?[48] Such decisions touch on matters which may be seen as involving acts and omissions positively 'against the interests' of the child. The House of Lords in *S. v. S.*[49] were asked to authorize a blood test on a child to determine his paternity. Lord Reid described the parental power to authorize such a test in this way:

Surely a reasonable parent would have some regard for the general public interest and would not refuse a blood test unless he thought that would clearly be *against the interests of the child* [our italics].

In other words, where any risk to the child is minimal, parents may authorize any procedure that is not perceived as *against* the interests of the child. It is by no means certain that in all cases such an argument will succeed. Of crucial importance will be the extent to which the parents genuinely participated in the decision. Did they have the information and understanding to weigh the benefit of the programme against the risk to the child? The slighter the risk to the child, though, the more likely a court will accept parental judgement as the arbiter of their child's interests and welfare. The law does not require that children be molly-coddled from every conceivable physical risk.[50]

This matter is too vital to be left to the unpredictability of the common law. Statutory force should be given to a code of practice that will determine when consent may be given, and who may give effective consent, to research on children, and provide for independent expert scrutiny of research proposals involving young children.[51]

Mentally disabled adults

The question of research involving mentally ill, mentally disabled or unconscious patients is as problematic as that involving children. The first issue to establish is whether or not the individual has the capacity to consent to medical research. Many individuals suffering from psychiatric illnesses will be competent to consent, and this should be the presumption. Some will temporarily lose and then regain their capacity; others will never have it. On the basis of *Re C. (Refusal of Medical Treatment)*[52] a three-fold test establishes that a person has capacity if he is able to comprehend and retain the information, to believe it and to weigh it up so as to arrive at a choice. In most cases, the doctor will apply the test and it is quite conceivable that this will be the same doctor who has an interest in recruiting the participant to his medical research project. Guidance from the Medical Research Council[53] requires that the inclusion of individuals unable to consent should be subject to the agreement of an informed, independent person who will testify that the individual's welfare and interests are properly protected. This requirement has not been translated into law.

Once it is established that an individual is indeed incapacitated, the legality of treatment of such patients depends on proof that the doctor acted in the patient's best interests and in conformity with responsible professional opinion.[54] A similar test might be applied to therapeutic research. Guidance from the Medical Research Council provides that incapacitated patients should never be involved in research that could equally well be carried out using competent participants; all projects should be approved by a research ethics committee; and those included in research should not object in either words or actions.[55] The matter is more complex in relation to non-therapeutic research. However, ethical guidance sanctions such research where risk is minimal and the research offers the prospect of substantial benefit to patients suffering from the same illness or disability as the participant.[56]

In 1995 the Law Commission proposed legislative reform, including the establishment of a statutory Mental Incapacity Research Committee.[57] Scotland enacted the Adults with Incapacity (Scotland) Act 2000, section 51 of which prescribes in detail a number of circumstances and conditions that must be fulfilled before research on incapacitated individuals can proceed. In England and Wales, however, legislation now seems unlikely (see Chapter 5). Guidance from the GMC[58] encourages the use of advance statements and recommends further measures for the protection of mentally incapacitated individuals. The research should only take place if it could not be so conducted on a non-vulnerable research population and should either benefit the participants' health or the health of others with a similar condition. Furthermore, the research should cease at the first sign of distress or pain.

Further guidance can be found in the draft additional protocol to the Convention on Human Rights and Biomedicine, released for consultation by the Steering Committee on Bioethics in July 2001. Article 18 of this protocol on *Biomedical Research*[59] provides protection for persons unable to consent to research. Yet, the Convention is not legally binding in the UK and contrary to the advice of the Law Commission it seems that England is destined to continue without formal statutory protection for the mentally incapacitated subject in research. This might lead to their inclusion in trials under circumstances that do not adequately safeguard their rights. Equally worrying, it might also lead ethics committees to withhold their approval to valuable research due to sparse legal and ethical guidance. This may well have a dire effect on the development of treatment for debilitating psychiatric and neurological illnesses. If a new Mental Incapacity Bill does soon see the light of day let us hope that this issue will be addressed.

Randomized controlled trials[60]

At the heart of much modern medical research lies the randomized controlled trial (RCT). Patients suffering from the same illness are divided into two groups and subjected to different treatments. Most commonly, either one group will receive the conventional treatment, and another be given the experimental and hopefully more effective treatment, or one group will be given a new drug, and the other a placebo. For an outsider there are a number of worrying features to RCTs. First, there is again the question of consent. Second, there is concern that the control group is denied a chance of superior treatment. In particular, public anxiety was highlighted by a trial involving 3000 women at risk of conceiving a spina bifida baby. Studies had shown that similar women appeared to suffer a reduced incidence of carrying a spina bifida baby if treated with special vitamin supplements. The trial involved randomizing the women into four groups. One group received the full treatment under trial, another part only of the supplement, a third the other element of the supplement, and the fourth a placebo. Why should any woman at risk be denied a treatment that *might* help her avoid a spina bifida conception? Further criticism of randomized trials includes this point, that while the control group in a test may be denied a benefit, the experimental group may be at some risk. Finally, who controls and monitors RCTs?

The law's involvement in the control of RCTs can only be peripheral unless specific legislation is introduced. The role the law plays now is largely restricted to the need to obtain, and the difficulty of obtaining, consent to an RCT. There are doctors and researchers who believe that the RCT is most effective if conducted 'blind', that is the patient is told nothing at all. The issue then is whether consent to treatment given generally is negated by unwitting participation in the RCT. The law will decide the issue on how closely related the RCT is to the condition under treatment and whether consent to treatment implies consent to what was done in the trial. At best, when a patient is asked to take part in an RCT the nature of the trial and the purpose of random allocation may be explained. Exactly what will be done to the patient cannot be explained, by virtue of the very nature of an RCT. Consent on the strength of a proper explanation of the trial and free acceptance by the patient of its random basis would appear both sufficient and necessary. Entering the patient in a random test with no explanation and no consent places the doctor at risk of an action for battery if the patient finds out. Fears that patients if properly informed will refuse to participate are natural. The erosion of personal freedom resulting from allowing 'blind' trials is not justified by those fears. A patient who will not agree to, or cannot understand the implications of, a trial should not be entered in that trial.[61]

Apart from the questions of consent, the other means by which the courts may be invoked to consider the RCT arise when something goes wrong, and a participant suffers injury. Will the law enable him to obtain compensation? We move on to this next, and later consider general procedures to monitor clinical trials.

Compensation for mishap

At present, compensation for personal injury suffered as a participant in a clinical trial is only available either to a participant who can prove negligence on the part of the operator of the trial, or on an *ex gratia* basis. A claim in negligence may arise in two contexts in an RCT. A participant from the control group may complain that he was denied an improved prospect of cure. Participants from the experimental group may allege that unjustifiable risks were taken. Neither is likely to succeed. As long as conventional treatment of the control group remains proper medical practice, the control has no claim in negligence. As long as the novel procedure was a properly conducted piece of research, carried out in conformity with a well-founded and responsible body of medical opinion, the subject of that procedure is likely to fail. One interesting speculation may be made. In the spina bifida trial, might a court be prepared to consider whether, if there was a realistic hope of benefit, the trial was really necessary? Could a mother denied the full vitamin supplement allege that the doctor treated her negligently? Or would the issue return full circle to the question of whether she freely consented to take part in the trial?

Next, what about the case where something goes disastrously and unexpectedly wrong? The participant will not know why. There may be an inherent risk in the trial, it may be that the staff conducting the trial were negligent. In principle, carelessness by the research team, be it in their selection of participants on the basis of their previous medical history, or in the conduct of the trial or in their monitoring of the effects of the trial, creates a remedy for the patient. Moreover, he also may have in theory a possible remedy against the ethics committee that approved the trial. Did that committee act negligently in approving a hazardous trial and fail in its duty to safeguard the interests of patients and volunteers? His problems lie in proof of negligence, just as any other patient-claimant's do (see Chapter 7), but they are more acute. If proving negligence in the operation of standard procedures is difficult, it is much more difficult to prove negligence where novel procedures are concerned.

No-fault compensation again!

One issue on which lawyers, doctors and drug companies do agree is that the present law is inadequate as a means to provide compensation for injury suffered while participating in medical research. Well over twenty years ago the Pearson Commission (see Chapter 10), which inclined towards retaining the law of negligence for medical accidents generally, recommended that

Any volunteer for medical research or clinical trials who suffers severe damage as a result should have a cause of action, on the basis of strict liability, against the authority to whom he has consented to make himself available.[62]

No change in the law has yet been effected. The Department of Health and the pharmaceutical industry operate *ex gratia* compensation schemes. The injured participant's legal rights remain, in general, dependent on the vagaries of the law of negligence. When a research participant suffers injury in a drug trial he may, of course, gain some slight advantage from the regime of strict liability imposed on drug companies by the Consumer Protection Act 1987. He still has to prove that his injury resulted from a defect in the drug, and that it was that defect that caused his injury. If the drug company chooses to dispute liability, once again the matter is clumsily resolved by adversarial proceedings (see Chapter 8). An individual, volunteer or patient, who agrees to subject himself to risk in the cause of medical science and the better health of the community deserves better than this.

Extra-legally, drug companies in the United Kingdom recognize the research participant's moral right to compensation independent of proof of fault. The Association of British Pharmaceutical Companies (ABPI) operates an *ex gratia* scheme whereby any healthy volunteer in a drug trial mounted by an ABPI member will receive compensation for any injury arising from that trial. However, many drug trials relate to drugs manufactured by foreign companies. Such companies may well not be ready to accept the ABPI guidelines. Department of Health guidance provides that ethics committees should be adequately reassured about 'whether there is provision in proportion to the risk for compensation/treatment in the case of injury/disability/death of a research participant attributable to participation in the research: the insurance and indemnity arrangements.'[63] Further, the Royal College of Physicians[64] advises research ethics committees that they should require from such companies a written agreement to provide for research participants 'at the least the same protection' as that offered by the ABPI. Such advice raises the interesting question of whether a failure by a research ethics committee to obtain such assurances to safeguard research participants might constitute negligence on the part of the committee.

Patients agreeing to participate in research, and volunteers involved in non-drug trials, remain outside this informal no-fault provision. The *ex gratia* nature of the ABPI scheme also means that compensation remains dependent on the drug companies' generosity and is in no sense a right enjoyed by research participants.

The case for no-fault compensation of persons injured in the course of research has long received wide support among doctors too.[65] The burden of compensating those injured in the course of research to benefit us all should have a wide base. A fund could be financed from all bodies promoting research, from the medical profession, the pharmaceutical industry and the Department of Health. The prospects for the introduction of a scheme to compensate medical research victims along these lines may be brighter than the prospects for a general no-fault scheme for all victims of medical accidents. Practical problems of definition, administration and finance will be faced, but with a will most difficulties could be overcome. Change is in the wind. In July 2001 the Health Secretary announced that the Chief Medical Officer for England would chair a committee to look at suggestions to make the clinical negligence compensation system faster and fairer for both patients and doctors (see Chapter 10). A White Paper is expected to be published shortly.

However, a scheme limited to injury suffered as a research participant will confront one very real problem. Exactly who would be entitled to benefit under the scheme? Would eligibility be confined to volunteers for non-therapeutic research? The moral case for automatic compensation for that group is overwhelming. These volunteers put their health on the line with no hope of personal benefit. Yet as patients may be used as participants in non-therapeutic research into conditions unrelated to their illness, the line between therapeutic and non-therapeutic research may be blurred. If the compensation scheme is to extend to all research participants, the problem of determining eligibility moves to deciding whether a patient has suffered injury as a result of a research enterprise, or in the course of general health care that has included resorting to some novel procedure. Neither of these potential problems is insuperable. They illustrate perhaps that a general scheme of compensation embracing all victims of medical mishap is to be preferred.

Monitoring research programmes

In the absence of specific legislation, the law's role in the control of medical research is limited to intervention when disaster has struck. At present it is only in relation to new drugs that legislation provides machinery that seeks to prevent disasters (see Chapter 8).

New drugs must be licensed in most cases before being granted a limited clinical trial certificate. The company seeking a licence must disclose results of preliminary research and animal tests. Only if the Committee on Safety of Medicines (CSM), established under the

Medicines Act 1968, is satisfied with the information submitted by the company may clinical trials on patients begin.

Provision is made for reporting back of adverse reactions to the CSM via the 'yellow card' system. This aspect of the process has been much criticized. The evidence is that the wider the trial, and the more doctors and patients involved in the trial, the less reliable is the reporting system. The continuing list of anti-rheumatic drugs withdrawn only after several patients have suffered serious reactions and even death is a poignant instance of the partial failure of the system to monitor drugs.

Research ethics committees were concerned that monitoring was so ineffective that their advice to researchers might be ignored. In some cases they even took it upon themselves to monitor research.[66] In 2001 the Department of Health *Research Governance Framework*[67] outlined new monitoring measures, including a new system for monitoring adverse events. Regulations will be introduced in compliance with the *Clinical Trials Directive*, article 15 of which demands that Member States appoint a system of inspection of clinical trial sites. Consequently, by 2004 inspection by the new MHRA will become mandatory but only in relation to pharmaceutical trials. New guidance gives no general authority to RECs to monitor other research projects.

What should now be asked is whether central legal control of research programmes concerning new procedures should be imposed. A possible pattern for legislation is provided for by the Medicines Act in its regulation of clinical trials of new drugs. All research procedures could be made subject to approval by a body responsible to the Secretary of State for Health. Research would be permitted only under licence from the government. Such a proposal would be anathema to the medical profession who would see it as undermining their clinical freedom. And it would. Drawing a distinction between providing optimum care for a patient and experimenting would cause endless dispute. The additional burden in terms of money and time spent obtaining licences would eat into the public purse and valuable professional time. The case is not made out yet. Research ethics committees play a valuable role in representing the public's and the patient's views. Bodies within the medical profession, especially the Medical Research Council, act as central brakes on individual over-enthusiasm.

There are two areas of danger. The first is that a series of incidents in which research victims die or suffer serious injury may lead to litigation. As we have seen, the law, be it on consent or compensation, is unclear and unsatisfactory. Litigation may be bitter. If the reaction of the medical staff involved is to go on the defensive, saying nothing and defending the claim to the bitter end, the probity of medical research in general may be questioned. The second is, paradoxically, that pressure for the introduction of no-fault compensation is successful, and the threat of litigation is removed without the introduction of stringent measures to ensure accountability. In New Zealand in 1988 a public inquiry revealed a horrific tale. An individual gynaecologist was convinced that orthodox opinion on cervical smear tests was wrong. A positive smear, he believed, was not a precursor of cervical cancer. No action should be taken until an actual malignancy was apparent. He recruited thousands of women into his trial using manifestly inadequate consent procedures. Many, many women suffered dreadfully when cancer did develop as by that stage of the disease they had to undergo painful invasive surgery. For years no other doctor dared speak out and challenge the investigator. New Zealand operates a no-fault system of compensation. The cervical smear trial started before that system was introduced. It will never be possible to know whether the knowledge that no patient could sue for their injuries reinforced the investigator's blind faith in his misguided theory, or deterred his colleagues from taking action earlier, even if only out of self-protection. Recourse to court is a clumsy weapon, but it must not be taken from the research participant without affording him other safeguards. Litigation may provoke distrust, leading to public demand for all-embracing and stringent statutory controls on research. Abolishing legal liability in clinical research may provoke a scandal that will have the same effect unless existing controls are seen to operate effectively.

Monitoring guards against research misconduct, which has been the subject of public outcry in recent years.[68] Career promotions are dependent on research publications and competition is fierce. In 1995 a high-ranking obstetrician and gynaecologist made headline news when it was discovered that he had forged a number of papers.[69] Two years later a former secretary of the Royal College of Physicians in Edinburgh was struck off the medical register for research misconduct.[70] In 2002 a GP falsified research data.[71] In response to the obvious failure of self-regulation, the Department of Health *Research Governance Framework* offers only limited reassurance. The Department of Health will consider 'the possibility of a co-ordinating group or body to take responsibility for investigating on behalf of all relevant stakeholders.' At present the Director of Counter Fraud Service continues the effort to counter fraud within the NHS. Fraud, however, is only one species of research misconduct. Subjects deserve the reassurance of a much more comprehensive monitoring system.

Confidentiality and medical research

The Data Protection Act 1998 (implementing the European Directive 95/46/EC on the processing of personal data into UK law) came into effect in March 2000. An Information Commissioner registers the names of data controllers and a description of the processing of data by each. Medical researchers are among those who must in most cases register with the Commissioner. In addition to registration, researchers must also comply with the complex provisions of the Act, which demand special conditions to be attached to the processing of 'sensitive data' (including all personal health data). The Act requires that explicit consent is obtained before personal health data is processed, but an exception is made in the case of medical research. However, the Act demands that 'personal data shall be processed fairly and lawfully'. This clearly places a duty on the researcher to apply the principles enshrined in the common law duty of confidentiality. Arguably it goes further still.

The common law duty of confidentiality, which applies independently of the Act, is equally open to misinterpretation in relation to medical research. To advance the development of medicine and to enable research when completed to benefit other patients, the results of research must be published. Does publication of research findings amount to a breach of confidence to the patient? First, the patient, if he has given full and free consent to his participation in a trial may at the same time agree to information about him being disclosed once the trial is completed and a report is prepared. This must be the preferable course of action. Whether in law disclosure in the course of a research project of confidential information about a patient without his consent amounts to an actionable breach of confidence depends yet again on the nebulous test of whether that disclosure can be justified by the public interest in the advancement of the relevant research.

The General Medical Council[72] requires that, where practicable, researchers seek consent and anonymize data, and always keep disclosures to a minimum. It provides special requirements for researchers dealing with medical records and advises on the reporting of research data. Prior to 1999 it was generally assumed that it was not necessary to obtain the participant's consent to release data, provided that data was fully anonymized. In such a case neither the researcher nor any other individual can trace the data to a given research participant. The Data Protection Act 1998 does not apply when data is fully anonymized because the data is not considered 'personal'. The matter was put to the test in *R. v. Department of Health, ex p. Source Informatics Ltd*[73], which involved pharmacists who sold fully anonymized data to industry. Latham J held at first instance that such disclosure might breach confidentiality on the basis that consent could not be implied because the data was used for commercial purposes and was therefore not in the public interest. However, researchers breathed a sigh of relief when the decision was overturned in the Court of Appeal, where it was held that confidence would not be breached where the confider's identity was not disclosed.

What is clear, is that disclosure should be limited to information strictly necessary to the project and that the anonymity of the patient must be protected. The NHS Ombudsman upheld a complaint from a young man who discovered in a medical textbook a full-face frontal picture of his naked body! There are various means of achieving anonymity. Full anonymization offers the greatest protection to research participants' confidentiality, however the research cannot then be linked to either the individual's past medical history or his future treatment. In most research projects a system of data coding is preferred. The codes can be broken in the event of adverse reaction and results can be linked to the individual's past medical history. Some researchers regard coded data as anonymized, but in fact the data is 'personal', the Data Protection Act 1998 applies and the common law duty of confidentiality will be breached if consent (be it express or implied) is not obtained before results are published.[74]

The way forward

Medical research is constantly evolving and the law needs to retain a sufficient degree of flexibility to react to those changes. The system must both protect the research participant whilst fostering ethical research. The new guidance for research ethics committees will help to streamline the ethical review process. Yet, in order to protect the rights and interests of the research participant and to give the medical researcher a greater degree of certainty, further reform is needed. Four fundamental legal issues remain. (1) The current failure to place the ethical review system on a statutory basis warrants concern. To comply with the Clinical Trials Directive, it will be necessary to give statutory authority to ethics committees reviewing clinical trials. That authority should be extended to incorporate non-clinical trials and all non-NHS research. (2) The case for automatic compensation for injury suffered in forwarding the public good must be met. (3) Consent requirements, particularly in cases where the participant lacks capacity due to age or mental disability are clearly lacking in certainty. This has potential to prohibit valuable research where it is most sorely needed. (4) In the context of medical research the Data Protection Act 1998 has added to the confusion that already surrounded the common law duty of confidentiality. Guidance from august professional bodies is invaluable but until the common law tests the boundaries of the duty of confidentiality and the relevant provisions of the Data Protection Act, a measure of uncertainty will persist.

17

Organ and Tissue Transplantation[1]

This chapter explores legal questions surrounding organ and tissue transplantation. It focuses solely on transplantation. The vexed and painful issues arising out of organ retention are dealt with in Chapter 19. Both chapters must be accompanied by a 'health warning'. Radical new legislation to reform the law relating to all users of human organs and tissues will shortly be forthcoming.

Certain sorts of tissue transplantation such as blood donation and skin grafts, have been routine for years. Tens of thousands of lives have been saved by bone marrow transplants. Despite the number of lives saved, organ donation has had a stormy history. Debates involving clinical, ethical, scientific, financial and resource considerations continue to rage. Public attitudes towards what have become standard procedures, such as kidney transplants, are affected from time to time by more controversial matters, for example, controversy concerning the use of foetal tissue and recent revelations about organ retention (see pages 470–72). Public response to transplantation has been erratic, influenced by publicity given to dramatic success and failures. For example, in the early days of heart transplants publicity given to declarations that described transplant surgeons as 'human vultures', and headline stories of organs allegedly removed from bodies before 'real death' had occurred, all excited public concern and hostility. On the other hand, the media can be effective in publicizing the benefits of transplantation and creating maximum favourable public awareness on the subject. At the height of media coverage of organ retention, publicity given to the plight of a baby called Margaux dying of heart disease helped to ensure that a donor heart was made available for her.

The scientific developments in transplantation in the past two decades have been amazing. The principal problems continue to be the discrepancy between supply and demand.[2] There are an insufficient number of kidneys, hearts, livers and other organs to meet demand. In 2000, for example, there were 1487 cadaver kidney transplants in the United Kingdom but 6824 people waiting for a kidney.[3] Much ink has been spilled exploring strategies to increase the supply of organs for transplant. Increasingly the advantages of live donation, where that is feasible, are recognized. Live heart donation is self-evidently impossible. Techniques to develop transplantation of lobes of the lung and segments of the liver are advancing fast. A market in organs from live 'donors' has powerful advocates today. Debates about how best to increase the availability of cadaver organs embrace moving to an opt-out system of 'donation', and the use of elective ventilation to increase the supply of viable organs. The potential of xenotransplantation, using genetically modified organs harvested from non-human animals, is much talked about. In all these debates law plays a role, though not always a helpful one.

Live donor transplantation

For one person to subject himself to an unnecessary procedure for the benefit of another requires courage and altruism. A distinction must be made between donation of regenerative and non-regenerative organs. Blood and bone marrow are regenerative tissue. The blood donor undergoes temporary discomfort and his body replaces the blood he has lost. Non-regenerative organs such as the heart are, as noted above, impossible for a living donor to donate in normal circumstances.[4] The major non-regenerative organ that is a candidate for live donation remains the kidney, with increasing hopes that techniques allowing transplants of lobes of the lung and segments of the liver will increase the utility of live donations.[5] The donor agrees to major surgery and accepts a significant risk to his own health. The law should be designed to ensure that such a donation is truly voluntary, informed and not the result of coercion. The British tradition has been that the donation of body products should be just that, not a sale. No part of a person's body should be treated as a commodity subject to the pressures of the market.[6] In 1989, the Human Organs Transplant Act 1989 gave legal effect to that tradition, outlawing payments for non-regenerative organs. As we shall see, in 2001 the debate was re-opened with powerful voices advocating permitting sale of organs to help bridge the gap between supply and demand.

We have noted elsewhere that there is no specific legal ruling that determines what limits, if any, are set to permissible surgical operations. In general, inflicting actual bodily harm on another person constitutes a crime regardless of his consent.[7] None the less, surgical operations are lawful, where a patient properly consents, because the intrusive procedures are for the benefit of the patient.[8]

There is now a consensus that a donor can, in law, give consent to a regenerative organ or part of an organ being taken from his body; albeit the transplant is of no physical therapeutic benefit to the donor, and in some cases could prove to be harmful. The Law Commission have declared '. . . there is no doubt that once a valid consent has been forthcoming, English law now treats as lawful donation of regenerative tissue, and also non-regenerative tissue that is not essential to life'.[9]

Thus a person is permitted to consent to surgeons taking an organ from his body in certain circumstances. There is, of course, the problem of the genuineness of consent. Live donors are often closely related to the potential recipient. The potential donor may be the only person whose compatibility is such that the relative's life can be saved.[10] In such circumstances the psychological pressure that exists on a person can be enormous, and if the consent is not really free the surgeon may well be exposed to moral and legal censure. Full discussion and counselling are essential before a donor is asked to sign an appropriate consent form.

Child donors

More difficult are cases where organs or tissue are to be taken from young children. Can children lawfully be organ donors?[11] A young child will not have the capacity to give consent herself for medical treatment for her own benefit. Consent must usually be given by a parent or guardian. Can parents go further and give proxy consent to 'non-therapeutic' procedures?

In the USA, the courts sanctioned such a course of action long ago. The cases involved three sets of minor twins, two sets aged fourteen and one set aged nineteen. In each case the healthy twin was willing to donate a kidney to his dying brother, but it was not clear whether the law permitted this. Applications were made to the court for guidance. The court focused on the psychiatric evidence given to show that each donor had been fully informed about the nature of the procedure and also that, if it were not possible to perform the operation and the sick twin were to die, there would be a resulting grave emotional impact of the surviving twin. This enabled the US court to be satisfied in each case that the operation was for the benefit not only of the recipient but also of the donor, and that accordingly a parent was capable of giving consent to such a 'therapeutic' procedure.[12]

Would an English court be prepared to sanction a kidney donation, or transplant of a liver segment from a child? It seems unlikely.[13] In any case renal transplant surgeons in this country appear of their own volition to have ruled out kidney donations by minors. Bone marrow donations by children, however, including very young children, to help treat siblings suffering from leukaemia are routine, as are skin grafts. Nor is judicial authorization sought for such procedures. Parental consent is assumed to authorize the removal of bone marrow from one child to benefit the other. The legality of bone marrow donations by young children can depend only on reasoning analogous to that used to authorize twin-to-twin kidney transplants in the USA. The healthy child 'benefits' by the survival of her sibling. Taking bone marrow from the healthy sibling is a relatively minor procedure attended by very little risk or pain to the donor. Removing a kidney is major surgery and so it is that much harder to argue that a presumed psychological benefit outweighs the manifest physical risk. In any instance of organ or tissue donation involving a young child donating to a sibling concern must revolve around the role of parents as decision-makers in this context. Can a parent be expected to make an impartial evaluation of the interests of one child when the life of another of her children is at stake?[14]

The age of the child or young person may well be thought crucial in this context. The younger sets of American twins were fourteen. Even if legally not of an age to give independent consent, at fourteen the child can be a party to the decision. Many fourteen-year-olds would be considered *Gillick competent* in this country if therapeutic treatment was at issue. The Family Law Reform Act 1969 section 8 empowers minors at sixteen to give effective consent to medical treatment. In *Re W.*,[15] however, the Court of Appeal made it clear that the 'medical age of majority' of sixteen does not allow minors to authorize organ donation.[16] Lord Donaldson doubted that a court would be ready to find a minor sufficiently *Gillick competent* to give an independent consent to any non-therapeutic procedure.[17] In such cases, a dual consent from parent and minor must be advisable and careful consideration given to an application to the courts for guidance.

Mentally disabled 'donors'

In the USA, in *Strunk* v. *Strunk*[18] a twenty-eight-year-old married man who was dying of a fatal kidney disease sought the permission of the court for a kidney donation from his twenty-seven-year-old brother, who was said to have a mental age of six and who was detained in a mental institution. The Kentucky court emphasized the emotional and psychological dependence of the mentally disabled sibling on his brother, and that his well-being would be jeopardized more severely by the loss of his brother than by the removal of a kidney. Accordingly, it applied a doctrine of 'substituted judgment', to allow the court to act as they believed the mentally disabled brother would have acted had he possessed all his faculties, and gave consent on behalf of the donor. Subsequent cases in the USA[19] have stressed that in authorizing organ donation on behalf of a mentally disabled adult the court must be fully satisfied that the interests of the donor will be served by the transplant. The benefits to him of his sibling's or relative's survival must be real, not speculative.[20]

What would be the position in England if doctors proposed to use a mentally disabled adult as a live organ donor? No one can give proxy consent on an adult's behalf. Following the House of Lords judgment in *F.* v. *West Berkshire HA*[21] a hospital, together with the family, could seek a declaration that the 'donation' was not unlawful. In the Court of Appeal, Neill LJ implied that organ 'donation' by a mentally disabled patient was not inevitably unlawful. He argued that such radical surgery should require judicial authority but seemed to accept that there might be circumstances where such sanction would be forthcoming.[22]

In *Re Y.*,[23] Connell J granted a declaration that bone marrow donation from a severely mentally disabled woman of twenty-five to her thirty-six-year-old sister, who was dying of leukaemia, was lawful. The mentally disabled sister, who proved to be the only compatible donor was quite incapable of giving any kind of consent to the procedure. The relationship between the sisters themselves was not especially close. The older sister's illness had meant that visits had become fewer. The mother had a close relationship with both of her daughters. The judge found that if the older daughter died, her death would have an adverse impact on the mother. She would be less able to visit Y and much occupied in caring for her grandchild if the child's mother died. If the transplant went ahead the 'positive relationship' between Y and her mother would be enhanced, as would the relationship between the sisters. The risk and discomfort to Y would be minimal. Accordingly it was in Y's best interests to allow the bone marrow transplant to go ahead. Connell J made it clear that he was not setting a precedent for kidney 'donation' by a mentally disabled person. He said:

It is doubtful that this case would act as a useful precedent where the surgery involved is more intrusive than in this case . . .

Should he have sanctioned what amounts to enforced donation at all? The 'benefit' to Y seems somewhat tenuous on the facts of the case.

The Human Organs Transplant Act 1989

In 1989 a scandal relating to the sale of kidneys and a private London hospital prompted Parliament to enact the Human Organs Transplant Act in record time. Four medical practitioners were found guilty of serious professional misconduct by the GMC. Evidence was presented that established that money had been paid to poor Turkish citizens in return for their agreement to come to London, where a kidney was removed from each of them for transplantation into wealthy private patients. Allegations were made by one of the Turkish 'donors' that he was not even aware that he had agreed to the removal of a kidney. He believed that he had consented to an operation for his own benefit. If those allegations were true, clearly the doctors involved acted without consent and were guilty of the crime of causing grievous bodily harm and the tort of battery. It may even be the case that *any* purchase of organs amounts to an assault. The public policy reasons justifying altruistic donation may not necessarily apply to trafficking in organs, if a court were to find such traffic unethical. Complex arguments that the sale of organs may be illegal as an assault on the donor are rendered largely otiose by the Human Organs Transplant Act. Section 1 of the Act makes it clear beyond peradventure that making or receiving any payment for the supply or offer of an organ is illegal and punishable by a substantial fine or up to three months' imprisonment. The Act prohibits the sale of organs regardless of whether the 'donor' is living or dead. Any commerce in a non-regenerative organ is illegal. The Act applies to kidneys, hearts, pancreas, lungs and livers, to '. . . any part of a human body consisting of structured arrangement of tissues which, if wholly removed, cannot be replicated by the human body'.[24] It does not ban payments for regenerative body products such as blood or bone marrow. Payments for gametes 'semen or eggs' are, as we have seen (page 295) prohibited by the Human Fertilisation and Embryology Act except with the authorization of the Human Fertilisation and Embryology Authority.

The Human Organs Transplant Act goes further than its original purpose of prohibiting commerce in organs. Section 2 makes it a criminal offence to remove a non-regenerative organ from a living person intended for transplantation into another person, or to transplant such an organ removed from a living person into someone else, unless the donor and the recipient are closely genetically related. For the purpose of the Act[25] you are closely genetically related to your natural parents or children, your siblings of the whole or half blood and your nephews and nieces, and your uncles and aunts, again of the whole or half blood. Regulations made under the Act specify how such a relationship must be proved.[26] In the absence of such close genetic relationship, removal of a non-regenerative organ from a donor and its transplant into the recipient is lawful only with the permission of the Unrelated Live Transplant Regulatory Authority (ULTRA). Such permission for the use of unrelated living donors will be granted only if ULTRA is satisfied that no payment has been made in contravention of section 1 of the Human Organs Transplant Act 1989[27] and that a full and informed consent has been given by the donor.[28] Note, that spouses are not included in the 'genetic relationship' category. Permission must be sought from ULTRA for one spouse to donate an organ to another.

The need to ensure tissue-matching between donor and recipient means that doctors have normally preferred a living donor closely related to the recipient. Close genetic relationship maximizes the prospect of a successful transplant. Developments in anti-rejection therapy now mean doctors are more prepared to consider unrelated donors, so why ban unrelated donations save with the permission of ULTRA? The primary reason is to enforce the ban on commerce in organs. If section 1 of the Act, prohibiting sale of organs, stood alone, 'donors' and desperate recipients might seek to mislead health care professionals, claiming to be siblings or close friends involved in an altruistic donation when in fact the recipient is buying a kidney. The Act requires proof of the sibling relationship, and outlaws the friend's donation except where ULTRA is prepared to give its blessing.[29] By allowing unrelated live transplants only with the sanction of ULTRA, the Act seeks to protect donors from coercion or exploitation. Donating a kidney is no trivial matter in terms of the pain of surgery or its risks. ULTRA was established to ensure that donors fully appreciate what they are doing and cannot be made use of save of their own informed volition. The anomaly is that coercion, at any rate emotional coercion, is most likely where donor and recipient are closely related. Imagine the pressure a family could put on one brother to save the life of another when the latter is dying from renal failure. Having decided to create an unprecedented system of regulation for live organ transplants, should Parliament have required that all live donations be authorized by ULTRA?

Cadaver transplantation – the Human Tissue Act 1961

The majority of organs for transplantation are taken from persons who have died rather than from living donors. As we shall see later (pages 471–9) a person has no legal right at common law to determine what shall happen to his body after his death. A body, or part of it, cannot ordinarily be the subject matter of ownership, and normally it is the legal duty of the close relatives of the deceased person or those who are in 'lawful possession' of the body to arrange for its disposal at the earliest opportunity. So it is not legally possible for a person to impose a duty upon others that he be cremated after death. All he can do is indicate that he desires to be cremated, and his executors or family are free to comply with or ignore such a wish as they see fit. It follows, technically, that a person has no legal power to donate organs from his body after his death under the common law: equally nobody has any right to interfere with a corpse, and any such interference would be a criminal act.[30]

Cadaver transplantation is governed by statute. In 1952, the Corneal Grafting Act, now amended by the Corneal Tissue Act 1986, authorized the use of eyes for therapeutic purposes in some circumstances. This statute attracted little publicity at the time; nor was there much more public interest when, in 1961, the Human Tissue Act widened the law to cover any other parts of the body. It is this Act that governs the use of organs for transplantation purposes and retention of organs for purposes of education and research (see Chapter 19) and, although it served as a model for similar legislation in many other countries, it has proved to be unsatisfactory in almost every respect. In 2002 the Department of Health launched a wide-ranging consultation on law reform designed to result in new legislation to fit the needs of the twenty-first century.[31]

Authority for the removal of parts of the body may be obtained in two ways under the Human Tissue Act. First, there is a 'contracting-in' provision whereby any person may in writing at any time, or by word of mouth in the presence of two or more witnesses during his last illness, express a request that his body be used after his death for therapeutic purposes (or for purposes of medical education or research). If such a request is made, then the person lawfully in possession of his body after his death has the power (though not the duty), unless he has reason to believe that the request was subsequently withdrawn, to authorize the removal from the body of any part or, as the case may be, a specified part, for use in accordance with the request.[32] The problems arising from this provision are mainly practical. The usual way in which a person determines what should happen after his death is by will. Relying upon a will would rarely be of much use in transplantation. It is essential to remove organs within a short time of death taking place. By the time the will was obtained and read, the relevant organs would be useless for transplantation purposes. Are donor cards the answer? The card, signed by the holder, will specify which organs may be removed, or may state that 'any part of my body be used for the treatment of others'. The holder's signature and the telephone number of the next of kin are required. Several problems afflict the use of donor cards. First, the number of people carrying donor cards remains disappointingly low. Second, even if someone has signed a donor card there is a significant risk that it will not be on his person when needed. In 1992 a survey showed only 27 per cent of people had donor cards and only one in five carried their card with them at any time.[33]

The second method provided for in the Act, and which does not depend upon the express consent of the deceased, enables a person 'lawfully in possession' of the body of a deceased person to give permission for organs to be removed if, 'having made such reasonable inquiry as may be practicable', he has no reason to believe either that the deceased had expressed an objection to his body being so dealt with after his death, and had not withdrawn it; or that the surviving spouse or any surviving relative of the deceased objects to the body being so dealt with.[34] This particular provision bristles with difficulties and ambiguities. It is also capable of causing serious distress to close relatives unless its exercise is handled with care.

First, who is regarded in law as the person 'lawfully in possession of the body'? Take an example, by no means unusual, where a young man who has been fatally injured in a motorcycle accident is brought into hospital and there is delay in identifying him. In those circumstances, it would appear that it is the hospital that is lawfully in possession of his body until such time as the relatives can be traced and can carry out their normal duties in connection with its disposal. This point has never been tested in the courts, however.[35] The hospital authorities may wish to use the organs of that person, and the law provides that they may do so if 'having made such reasonable inquiry as may be practicable' they have no reason to believe that the deceased or close relatives object. It is not clear whether the practicability of such inquiry relates to the interests of the relatives or the interests of the hospital. For example, in order to trace relatives and establish their views, it would not be unreasonable to take days or even weeks; the family of the deceased may be on holiday and may not be traceable for some time. If the requirement is concerned primarily with the need to establish their views, it would be unlawful for the hospital to act before those relatives were contacted; and so the body would be 'wasted' for transplantation purposes. Alternatively, the need to make such reasonable inquiry as may be practicable may be interpreted in relation to the particular use for which the parts of the body are required, bearing in mind the short time in which it is possible to make effective use of a deceased person's organs. Thus, it has been argued that if the hospital is unable to trace the relative within a few hours then it has made such reasonable inquiries as it could and is free to act. Those who regard the Human Tissue Act as being far too restrictive in any event would regard the latter interpretation as the better one.[36] One may doubt, though, whether that is the correct interpretation.[37]

Which relatives should be consulted to establish whether or not they object raises a further problem.[38] The 1961 Act specifies the surviving spouse *or any* surviving relative of the deceased. If there is a surviving spouse, does that mean that it is not necessary to consult any other relatives should that spouse agree to the body being used? If there is no surviving spouse, *any* relative suggests, on a literal reading, that the person lawfully in possession of the body, must make inquiries of *all or any* of the relatives, so that even a distant second cousin would have the power to object. In most cases the hospital authorities would act sensibly and so also would close relatives; and it may be, therefore, that some of the technical difficulties created by the rather wide wording of the section may not raise problems in practice. However, difficulties have arisen from time to time. One woman, who had been separated from her husband for more than six years and who had not been consulted before his kidneys had been removed upon death, afterwards maintained that he had indicated a very strong objection during his life to any organs being transplanted from his body.[39] In other cases, serious distress has been caused to parents who were not approached before organs were removed from their children's bodies. Greater clarity in the law is desperately needed.

The role of the coroner

Where there is reason to believe that an inquest may have to be held on a body, or a post-mortem examination may be required by the coroner, it is necessary to obtain the consent of the coroner for the removal of any part of the body. This, too, may delay the opportunity to remove organs. This may be the case particularly where a coroner regards his duty to act as coroner as being of greater importance than the secondary power which he has to authorize the use of organs before his coroner's duties are complete. In a controversial case in Leicester in 1980, the father of a girl who had died in a road accident gave surgeons permission to use any of her organs, including her heart. At a subsequent inquest, the coroner complained that he had not given permission for the heart to be removed since permission had been sought from him only for the removal of a kidney. He therefore directed that in future written permission would have to be obtained from him and countersigned by a pathologist. This incident highlighted the problem that coroners, acting in pursuance of what they regarded as their legal duties, could adversely restrict the use of organs even where parents or other relatives had consented. It was for such reasons that the Home Secretary circularized coroners, stressing that it was not part of a coroner's function to place obstacles in the way of the development of medical science or to take moral or ethical decisions in this matter, and that the coroners should assist rather than hinder the procedure for organ removal. A coroner should refuse his consent only where there might be later criminal proceedings in which the organ might be required as evidence, or if the organ itself might be the cause or partial cause of death, or where its removal might impede further inquiries.[40]

Life must be extinct [41]

The Human Tissue Act 1961 is concerned exclusively with the removal of parts of a body *after death*. What is death? The Act simply states that 'no . . . removal shall be effected except by a fully registered medical practitioner, who must have satisfied himself by a personal examination of the body that life is extinct'. Prompted initially by the need, to act as soon as possible after death has occurred[42] the traditional medical definition of death has been reformulated, and the implications of this generally will be examined in Chapter 19. The difficulty in persuading the public that 'brain-stem death' truly constitutes the death of a person has beset organ transplantation for decades. Fears have been voiced that doctors might have conflicting interests in that, on the one hand, their duty would be to act in the best interests of the ill or dying patient and yet, on the other, there might be pressures to certify a potential donor's death at the earliest possible moment to enable organs to be removed for the benefit of potential recipients. Unease was exacerbated by the need in some cases to maintain a person who is 'brain-stem dead', and thus dead clinically and legally, on what was confusingly described as a 'life-support' machine to ensure that the organ to be removed is kept in good condition.

In 1975 the British Transplantation Society (BTS) sought to allay public fears by recommending a *Code of Practice for Organ Transplantation Surgery* (finally agreed in 1979) to provide safeguards (beyond those contained in the Human Tissue Act) for those who needed reassurance about possible abuses of practice by over-zealous transplant teams. The Royal Colleges of Medicine added their authority to the prescription of detailed rules on diagnosing death.[43] Now, a Code of Practice (see page 466) from the Department of Health sets out the procedure to establish 'brain-stem death'. The BTS Code provides:

(1) Before organs are removed from a body for transplant, death should be certified by two doctors, one of whom has been qualified for at least five years; and neither of these doctors should be members of a transplantation team.

(2) In cases of irreversible and total brain death, where respiration is dependent on mechanical ventilation, the decision to stop ventilation must have no connection with transplantation considerations. Brain-stem death must be established using agreed criteria (as discussed later). Two sets of tests should be carried out, separated by a twenty-four-hour interval.

(3) Where it has been decided that death of the brain has occurred and mechanical ventilation is to be stopped, the question of organ

removal should be discussed fully and sympathetically with available relatives so that their informed consent is obtained for the removal of organs either before or after mechanical ventilation is finally stopped.

(4) If available relatives objected to the use of the deceased's organs for transplant, even if it were established that the deceased himself has not objected, the relatives' wishes would be followed.

Elective ventilation

More recently controversy has surrounded a procedure known as 'elective ventilation'. Patients dying from strokes or similar conditions are transferred to the intensive care unit and ventilated until brain-stem death occurs. In this way, their organs are maintained in optimum condition for organ retrieval. Patients are brain-stem dead when organs are removed, but are not legally dead when ventilated. Ventilation is performed solely to enable the patient to become a potential organ donor and confers no benefit on him. Is elective ventilation lawful? Probably not.[44] The 'treatment' of the still living patient is not in his best interests and fails the test of legality set in *F. v. West Berkshire Health Authority* (see page 117).[45] Should elective ventilation be lawful? The Law Commission's original report on the treatment of mentally incapacitated adults suggested that with proper safeguards such a procedure could be ethical and lawful. Perhaps the two cases should be differentiated. If I choose, not just to carry a donor card but to indicate that, were I to suffer a stroke or other cerebral accident and recovery of consciousness was impossible, I should be ventilated to maximize my utility as an organ donor, that advance directive is as entitled to respect as any other. If I have expressed no such wish, should I, while still alive, be used as means to other ends even with my family's concurrence?

Violating the Human Tissue Act

Given the concern about possible abuse of transplantation, it is extraordinary to note that violation of the Act may not give rise to any criminal penalty or civil remedy. The Act itself creates no specific criminal offence.[46] The dire consequences of the toothless nature of the 1961 Act are illustrated only too well by its failure to police tissue retention (see Chapter 19).

Options for reform

The most radical option for reform is that advanced by the philosopher John Harris. Organ retrieval, he argues, should be permissible without the consent of the deceased or her family.[47] Such a proposal is unlikely to gain Parliamentary support. Reform proposals in general focus on moving to an opting out model (presumed consent) or introducing laws requiring doctors to request permission to remove organs for transplant.

Let us consider opting out (presumed consent) first. This means in effect that the law should allow organs to be removed for transplant unless the deceased had expressly put on record, for example, on a public register, that he had objected to such use. Relatives would lose any right of veto. A Private Member's Bill to introduce such a scheme was unsuccessfully presented to Parliament in March 2002. Such a law, which now exists in a number of European countries, should, in theory, enable surgeons to acquire all the organs they need, unless large numbers of people went to the trouble of registering their objections. In France the change in the law made little difference in practice.[48] Doctors remained unwilling to remove organs without the consent of the deceased's family.

Other jurisdictions,[49] notably Belgium, have seen law reforms introducing contracting out rules for organ donation result in a significant increase in the number of cadaver organs transplanted. Belgium offers a particularly interesting test case for such law reform. Laws implementing an opting out system were implemented in one part of the country but not universally. The available supply of organs rose sharply in the region where opting out prevailed but not elsewhere. The Belgian model prompted a number of distinguished lawyers, doctors and ethicists to renew the campaign for similar reform of the law in the United Kingdom.[50]

A further option for reform of the Human Tissue Act would be a system of 'required request'. It is suggested that one of the main reasons for the shortfall in donor organs is the failure by doctors to ask relatives to agree to cadaver organ donations. A number of American states[51] have thus enacted legislation requiring hospital staff to request permission from the deceased's family to remove suitable organs. The most comprehensive analysis of possible systems of organ retrieval is pessimistic about prospects of success. The King's Fund Report[52] suggests it is unlikely to work and might result in undue pressure being placed on families. In the current climate generated by the scandals surrounding organ retention legislation overriding relatives' wishes or coercing families is scarcely appropriate.

A market in organs?

The tradition that has so long held sway in the United Kingdom that bodily products should be freely given and not traded is now under attack.[53] The Human Organs Transplant Act bans payments for live or cadaver organs. The European Convention on Human Rights and Biomedicine states forcefully:

The human body and its parts shall not give rise to financial gain[54]

In support of maintaining a prohibition of a market in organs are a cluster of arguments. They centre on four questions. (1) Would financial incentives to sell your own, or your deceased relative's organs, risk endangering the safety of organ transplants? In their anxiety to obtain payment might people conceal medical conditions that could endanger the recipient?[55] (2) Is there a risk that financial pressure on potential vendors is such that they would give a less than voluntary and informed consent? Certainly there is ample evidence from the developing world that economic duress operates to pressure the poor into selling organs to the rich. (3) Is it intrinsically wrong that, even if properly informed, poorer people should 'have' to 'earn' part of their living by selling off body parts? (4) In sum, do markets degrade?[56]

Those proposing markets do so cautiously. They stress the vulnerability of the person needing the transplant.[57] They argue that a regulated market[58] would both ensure the quality of organs 'sold' and rigorously monitor the consent process. Provision would be made to ensure that the vendor was adequately informed and acted freely. Fears of exploitation could be met in a regulated market. As to the distastefulness of the poor becoming organ banks, it is contended that worldwide the rich have benefits denied the poor. In the end the debate comes down to an assessment of whether markets do degrade. Mason and McCall Smith while (without enthusiasm) sanctioning live donor 'sales' are uncomfortable with families selling off the organs of the dead.[59] Janet Radcliffe Richards, leading the advocates for markets, sums up the debate.

The weakness of the familiar arguments suggests that they are attempts to justify the deep feelings of repugnance which are the real driving force of the prohibition, and feelings of repugnance among the rich and healthy, no matter how strongly felt cannot justify removing the only hope of the destitute and dying. This is why we conclude that the issue should be considered again, with scrupulous impartiality.[60]

Liability for mishaps[61]

A number of questions about potential liability arise if organ transplantation goes awry. A failed transplant does not of itself give rise to any legal claim by the recipient. The renal surgeon does not guarantee success any more than any other medical practitioner. But what if, for example, donated blood or kidneys prove to be infected, perhaps with HIV? Might the donor or the transplant team be liable in tort? It would seem unchallengeable that donors owe a duty of care to recipients that is breached when a donor donates organs or tissue when he is aware that he is infected by, say, hepatitis or HIV. The recipient's problem will be tracing the donor. Public policy grounds for protecting the anonymity of donors may be found to outweigh the recipient's individual right of action.[62]

Realistically any claim in respect of contaminated body products will be brought against the hospital supplying those products. Actions in negligence against the Department of Health by haemophiliacs who contracted HIV from contaminated Factor 8 were settled out of court (see page 216). The Pearson Commission recommended that strict liability should be imposed on authorities responsible for the supply of human blood and organs. It is now clear the Consumer Protection Act 1987, imposing strict liability for defective products, includes human tissue in its definition of a product.[63]

Foetal tissue transplants

The potential for the use of foetal tissue for transplantation has aroused much ethical debate. Foetal brain cells can be taken from aborted foetuses and transplanted into the brains of patients with Parkinson's disease, in the hope of improving the recipient's condition. In 1989 a committee chaired by the Rev. Dr Polkinghorne reported and recommended a Code of Practice for the use of foetuses and foetal material in research and treatment.[64] Many of the fears about the use of foetal tissue focus on concern that women with relatives suffering from Parkinson's disease might deliberately become pregnant, intending to abort the foetus to provide the needed brain cells. The ethical implications of breeding a human 'medicine' are frightening. The law is relatively simple. Any abortion must conform to the provisions of the 1967 Act. The Code of Practice mandates that any question of the use of foetal tissue must be independent of decisions relating to the management of the pregnancy. The only remaining question is whether the mother's consent is needed before doctors may make use of the aborted foetus. BMA guidelines require such consent, as does the code of practice, but whether consent is mandatory in law is less clear. Does the mother own the foetus, so that 'misuse' of it is an interference with her property? Even if the foetus is 'property', which I doubt, has she in making the decision to abort abandoned her property? The development of stem cell therapy may in any case overtake the debate regarding the use of foetal tissue.

Xenotransplantation

A further much vaunted development in the field of organ transplantation involves the use of animals. Animal to human transplant attempts are not new. Early efforts resulted in disastrous rejection episodes. Now scientists are working on procedures to modify the genetic make-up of pigs to provide tailor-made organs suitable to transplant into humans. The technical progress with xenotransplantation has been slow. The range of problems associated with it is vast.[65] Is it right to use non-human animals in this way?[66] What about infection risks? How will the first human volunteers be recruited? The government responded cautiously, setting up an interim regulatory body, the United Kingdom Xenotransplantation Interim Regulation Authority (UKXIRA).[67]

Transplantation: the future

The most important single issue in the context of organ and tissue transplantation is to find means of ensuring an adequate supply of organs. New possibilities for extending live donor transplantation will have to be explored. Means of ensuring a more adequate supply of cadaver kidneys will continue to be sought. In the end society will have to decide what price can be paid to improve supply. Are the ethical doubts about, for example, sale of organs, elective ventilation, foetal tissue transplants and xenotransplantation sufficiently grave to rule out their use?

18
Death, Dying and the
Medical Practitioner

Society has never been comfortable with issues surrounding the process of dying. As health care staff are involved with the dying, they inevitably become involved in ethical as well as medical dilemmas. These dilemmas are, first, whether efforts should always be made to keep a dying person alive in spite of the additional suffering incurred by that person and the cost in terms of human dignity; and, second, when, if ever, attempts may be made to hasten death when there is excessive suffering and when the cause is hopeless.

The practice of what some regard as 'striving officiously to keep alive' has been facilitated by the increase in high-technology equipment, much of it capable of being used to postpone inevitable death for a time. The benefits of such equipment may often be great; yet there is a cost, both in human and economic terms. Further treatment may sometimes be said to be futile. A vast literature has developed around the concept of medical futility[1] The very word generates controversy. Mason and McCall Smith[2] prefer to talk of non-productive treatment, treatment that cannot offer even a minimal likelihood of benefit to the patient. Part of the difficulty in this debate is the problem of separating human and economic considerations. Refusing to order doctors to continue to ventilate a severely injured infant, Balcombe LJ said openly:

... [A]n order which may have the effect at compelling a doctor or health authority to make available scarce resources and to a particular child ... might require the health authority to put J on a ventilator in an intensive care unit, and thereby possibly deny the benefit of those limited resources to a child who was much more likely than J to benefit from them.[3]

Language invoking medical futility could be seen as disguising rationing decisions, or even covert euthanasia. Whatever the economic considerations, few would deny the personal cost to the patient and to those close to the patient in terms of human dignity. Do the 'rights' of patients include the right to die with dignity? If so, does that 'right' extend to being 'helped to die'? In preserving and sustaining the life of a patient with a hopeless prognosis, is it in the interests of the patient, the family, or the doctor, to prolong his suffering? Unlimited access to technology may sometimes be as cruel as the illness itself. Doctors concerned with terminally ill patients must make professional and human decisions to give up treatment that may be merely sustaining the function of the organs, and turn to appropriate care at the terminal stage.

In 1993 the tragic case of Tony Bland thrust this question into the public domain.[4] Did the law demand that a young man grievously injured in the horrific disaster at Hillsborough football stadium should continue to be kept alive by artificial means? The Law Lords concluded that it did not. The *Bland* judgment rekindled debates on euthanasia, albeit their Lordships and many commentators[5] vehemently rejected suggestions that the decision to allow Tony Bland to die was in any sense sanctioning euthanasia.[6] Two recent cases re-opened society's ambivalent response to death, dying and the law. The House of Lords denied Diane Pretty access to assisted suicide.[7] The President of the Family Division resoundingly endorsed a tetraplegic patient's right to demand that doctors switch off the ventilator keeping her alive.[8]

The *Concise Oxford Dictionary* defines euthanasia as 'Gentle and easy death; bringing about of this, especially in case of incurable and painful disease'. It is a term much used, and misused. It may be popularly invoked to include conduct characterized as 'mercy killing', when somebody, usually a relative, deliberately and specifically performs some act, such as administering a drug, to accelerate death and terminate suffering. Prosecutions for mercy killing, while rare, are sometimes reported, and the courts deal with such cases with compassion. Thus, in one case, a man who had for eleven years devotedly nursed his wife, who suffered from disseminated sclerosis, was convicted of her manslaughter but received a conditional discharge. In another case, a mother who shot her six-year-old-son, who suffered from cystic fibrosis, was put on probation for three years.

Such cases of mercy killing, where doctors are not usually directly involved may also be termed active euthanasia, in contrast to 'passive euthanasia', which might describe, for example, withholding of life-support treatment. The terminology of the debate is complex and confusing.[9] Active euthanasia involves a deliberate act designed to shorten life, by however short a span. *Active* euthanasia may involve *voluntary* euthanasia where the act done, the killing of the patient, is done at his specific request. *Non-voluntary euthanasia*[10] may be the term used to refer to ending the life of someone who cannot express a view on the prolongation of his life at the relevant time. A proxy speaks on his behalf and what is done is at least purportedly done for the patient's own good. *Involuntary* euthanasia involves killing a person without her own or any proxy authority. The patient's life may be ended for what others perceive as her good, or could be terminated because of the burden her continued life places on society. *Passive* euthanasia can itself be voluntary, non-voluntary or involuntary. As we shall see any boundary between passive and active euthanasia is a lot less clear than might at first be thought.

Attitudes to euthanasia in all its forms are changing rapidly. Legislation in the Netherlands to affirm the informal sanction given for years to limited active euthanasia in that country has influenced opinion across the world. Physicians themselves are more disposed to accept in theory some limited form of active euthanasia, or at least physician assisted suicide. Surprisingly large numbers of doctors are prepared to confess in private that they have participated in active voluntary euthanasia.[11] Set against what may appear a more favourable public response to euthanasia are the fears generated by the conviction of Harold Shipman for the murder of fifteen of his patients and the unfolding evidence that the true death toll may be well over 300.

The uncertainties and doubts that affect public attitudes towards the euthanasia debate are compounded by misunderstanding about, and lack of clarity in, the relevant law. We must now examine the present state of the law in England to see how it applies to the various situations in which the medical profession becomes involved.

Murder, suicide and assisting suicide

Deliberately taking the life of another person, whether that person is dying or not, constitutes the crime of murder. Accordingly, any doctor who, no matter how compassionately, practises voluntary euthanasia or mercy killing can be charged with murder, if the facts can be clearly established.[12] As Lord Mustill puts it.

. . . 'mercy killing' by active means is murder . . . that the doctor's motives are kindly will for some, although not for all, transform the moral quality of his act, but this makes no difference in law.[13]

The doctor convicted of murder faces a mandatory life sentence. Mrs Lillian Boyes suffered unbearable pain from rheumatoid arthritis and begged her doctor, Dr Cox, to end her suffering. He injected her with potassium chloride, a drug that stops the heart and has no therapeutic or painkilling properties. Before Dr Cox's action came to the attention of the police, Mrs Boyes was cremated. It could not therefore be proved beyond reasonable doubt that the injection administered by Dr Cox killed her. Dr Cox was convicted only of attempted murder. The judge imposed a suspended sentence, and the GMC allowed him to continue to practise subject to certain conditions.[14] Dr Cox was lucky. Had the link between his action and Mrs Boyes's death been clearly established, no such merciful course would have been open to the judge. Active euthanasia, whatever the circumstances, equals murder in English law.

The only exception to that rule was spelt out by Devlin J in the case *R. v. Adams*[15] in 1957. Dr Adams was charged with the murder of an eighty-one-year-old patient who had suffered a stroke; it was alleged that he had prescribed and administered such large quantities of drugs, especially heroin and morphine, that he must have known that the drugs would kill her. In his summing-up to the jury, Devlin J first stated:

. . . it does not matter whether her death was inevitable and her days were numbered. If her life was cut short by weeks or months it was just as much murder as if it was cut short by years. There has been much discussion as to when doctors might be justified in administering drugs which would shorten life. Cases of severe pain were suggested and also cases of helpless misery. The law knows no special defence in this category . . .

However he went on to say

. . . but that does not mean that a doctor who was aiding the sick and dying had to calculate in minutes, or even hours, perhaps, not in days or weeks, the effect on a patient's life of the medicines which he would administer. If the first purpose of medicine – the restoration of health – could no longer be achieved, there was still much for the doctor to do and he was entitled to do all that was proper and necessary to relieve pain and suffering even if the measures he took might incidentally shorten life by hours or perhaps even longer. The doctor who decided whether or not to administer the drug could not do his job, if he were thinking in terms of hours or months of life. Dr Adams's defence was that the treatment was designed to promote comfort, and if it was the right and proper treatment, the fact that it shortened life did not convict him of murder.

Devlin J introduced into English law a version of the 'double-effect' principle, whereby if one act has two inevitable consequences, one good and one evil, the act may be morally acceptable in certain circumstances. His ruling is endorsed in *Bland*.[16] It is not crystal clear in its meaning. In one passage Devlin J referred to the incidental shortening of life by hours and, in another passage, he referred to the shortening of life by hours or months. It must be a matter of judgement in each case. Clearly he was dealing with terminally ill patients where, in order to alleviate pain, it is permissible to disregard the fact that the treatment involved may accelerate the patient's death.

Since the Suicide Act 1961 it is no longer a criminal offence to commit, or attempt to commit, suicide. However, the Act does provide that 'a person who aids, abets, counsels or procures the suicide of another or an attempt by another to commit suicide, shall be liable on conviction ... to a term not exceeding fourteen years'. In order to achieve consistency in bringing prosecutions, it is necessary for the consent of the Director of Public Prosecutions to be obtained. It is a crime that may be committed for diverse reasons, ranging from the avaricious to the compassionate. In *R.* v. *McShane*,[17] a daughter was found guilty of trying to persuade her eighty-nine-year-old mother in a nursing home to kill herself so that she could inherit her estate. A secret camera installed by the police showed the daughter handing her mother drugs concealed in a packet of sweets, and pinning a note on her dress saying 'Don't bungle it!' Equally, if a doctor were to be shown to have supplied drugs, with similar intent, whatever his motive may have been, an offence would have been committed. However, in practice it would be difficult to prove that a doctor who had supplied drugs to a patient was responsible for the patient taking an overdose.

Clear evidence of aiding and abetting a particular act of suicide is necessary before a prosecution can be successful. In *Attorney-General* v. *Able*,[18] the court was asked to declare that it was an offence for the Voluntary Euthanasia Society to sell a booklet to its members aged twenty-five and over, setting out in some detail various ways in which individuals could commit suicide. The Society, which campaigned for the introduction of voluntary euthanasia legislation, claimed that, pending such legislation, they saw no alternative to supplying on request the necessary information to enable its members to bring about 'their own deliverance': the Society neither advocated nor deplored suicide; it had a neutral stance and regarded such decisions as matters of personal belief and judgement. Evidence in the case suggested that over a period of eighteen months after the first distribution of the booklet there were fifteen cases of suicides linked to the booklet and nineteen suicides where documents were found that showed that the deceased was a member of, or had corresponded with, the Society. The court concluded that in most cases the supply of the booklet would not constitute an offence. Normally, a member requesting the booklet would not make clear his intentions, and the booklet would be supplied without any knowledge by the supplier of whether it was required for general information, research, or because suicide was contemplated. To establish an offence it would have to be proved that the Society distributed the booklet to a person who, at the time of the distribution, was known to be contemplating suicide, with the intention of assisting and encouraging that person to commit suicide by means of the booklet's contents, and, further, that that person was in fact assisted and encouraged by the booklet to commit or attempt to commit suicide.

The application of laws relating to murder and suicide are central to an understanding of the legal issues concerning treatment of the dying. It will be appropriate to consider first the case of the 'competent' patient, that is a person with full legal and mental capacity, who is aware of what is happening and who may wish to make decisions himself about his quality of life, the way he will be treated and how he will continue to live or die. Second, the case of the 'incompetent' patient will be considered: the infant, and the unconscious or mentally disabled person who does not have the mental or physical capacity to make his own wishes known at the relevant times.[19]

Competent patients: is there a 'right' to die?

Does a patient have a 'right' to die? The answer will depend on the circumstances in which she seeks to exercise such a 'right'. The Court of Appeal in *Re T*.[20] made it clear that an adult, mentally competent patient enjoys an absolute right to refuse further treatment even where refusing treatment means certain death. The patient who is terminally ill, or who, even if not terminally ill, suffers from intractable pain or unbearable disability can refuse further treatment. The only *caveat* is that the evidence that her refusal of treatment was free and informed must be unequivocal. Her reasons to refuse treatment are not material. A patient dying of cancer has the right to say 'no more', however strongly her doctor may argue that more chemotherapy would offer her some additional months of life. A person paralysed by multiple sclerosis can refuse to be ventilated. A patient whose condition is no longer bearable to her can take her own life if she has access to the means to do so and is still independently capable of such action. There is a right to prevent others forcing you to live.

The first major difficulty surfaces in this context. A patient who wishes to die is already receiving life sustaining treatment in the form of life support. She is hooked up to a ventilator or receiving artificial nutrition via a naso-gastric tube or intravenous drip. She wants her life support withdrawn and to be permitted to die. Intrinsically her position seems indistinguishable from the patient who refuses further chemotherapy or instructs her doctors not to ventilate her. However, someone else will have to intervene to switch off the ventilator or remove the feeding tube. Will a doctor who does so risk prosecution for murder or assisting suicide?

The decision in *Airedale NHS Trust* v. *Bland*[21] made it clear that if a doctor disconnects a patient from life support at her specific request, that act does not constitute either murder or assisting suicide. *Bland* exposes the fragility of distinctions made between active and passive euthanasia. Three principles emerge from the speeches of the Law Lords. (1) Treatment involving any invasive procedure constitutes a battery, unless authorized by the patient, or if he is unable to authorize his own treatment, by other lawful authority. (2) Continuing invasive treatment once justification for that treatment is withdrawn becomes a battery and therefore unlawful. (3) Artificial feeding constitutes treatment as much as drug therapy or ventilation. If a patient instructs doctors to switch off a ventilator or withdraw a naso-gastric tube, failure to act on those instructions renders continuing treatment unlawful.

In *B.* v. *An NHS Trust*[22] Ms B. suffered a haemorrhage in the spinal column in her neck. Her condition deteriorated rapidly. Within two years she was paralysed from the neck down and could only breathe supported by a ventilator. Doctors told her that she was unlikely to recover. Rehabilitation programmes to allow her to live outside hospital on the ventilator were proposed to her. Ms B. was adamant that she did not want to survive in such a condition. She instructed doctors to switch off the ventilator. The doctors treating her refused, citing conscientious objections to such a course of action and challenging Ms B.'s mental capacity to refuse further treatment. Butler-Sloss P held that Ms B. remained mentally competent (see page 124). That being the case, continuing to ventilate her against her will was unlawful. She was entitled to demand that the ventilator be switched off, though not to require an individual clinician to act contrary to his conscience.

None the less there can be no doubt that switching off a ventilator or removing a naso-gastric tube is an act hastening death. Should a passer-by wander into the hospital and switch off a ventilator, his act would constitute murder, however perilous the patient's prior state, however benevolent the person's motive. The Law Lords skirt around the logical implications of their findings. Lord Browne-Wilkinson is honest in his appreciation of the dilemma. He says:

Mr Munby QC . . . submits that the removal of the naso-gastric tube necessary to provide artificial feeding and the discontinuation of the existing regime of artificial feeding constitute positive acts of commission. I do not accept this. Apart from the act of removing the naso-gastric tube, the mere failure to continue to do what you have previously done is not, in any ordinary sense to do anything positive; on the contrary it is by definition an omission to do what you have previously done.

The positive act of removing the naso-gastric tube presents more difficulty. It is undoubtedly a positive act, similar to switching off a ventilator in the case of a patient whose life is being sustained by artificial ventilation. But in my judgment in neither case should the act be classified as positive, since to do so would be to introduce intolerable fine distinctions. If instead of removing the naso-gastric tube, it was left in place but no further nutrients were provided for the tube to convey to the patient's stomach, that would not be a positive act . . . if the switching off of a ventilator were to be classified as a positive act, exactly the same result can be achieved by installing a time-clock which requires to be reset every twelve hours; the failure to reset the machine could not be classified as a positive act. In my judgment, essentially what is being done is to omit to feed or ventilate; the removal of the naso-gastric tube or the switching off a ventilator are merely incidents of that omission.[23]

Eliding acts and omissions enable the Law Lords to achieve the desired result. Consider its implications. A disabled relative who is sustained by a ventilator asks me to switch it off because his doctor refuses to do so. He rejects my advice to seek a declaration from the courts to overturn his doctor's advice. Reluctantly I pull the switch and he dies. Am I exempt from a charge of murder, or is a *Bland* defence exclusive to doctors? In the light of *B. v. An NHS Trust* could I argue thus? Continuing to ventilate my relative against his will constitutes the tort of battery and the crime of assault. When I switched off the ventilator all I did was use reasonable measures to prevent a crime. Then there is the most awkward question of all. What of the patient whose illness renders their life intolerable but who is not reliant on treatment or life support to survive? Their condition is none the less such that they cannot take their own life.

The sad case of Diane Pretty illustrates the dilemma. Mrs Pretty was dying of motor neurone disease. Gradually she had lost all ability to use her muscles. She could barely speak and could not swallow and had to be fed by a tube. Mrs Pretty sought an assurance from the Director of Public Prosecutions that no charge would be brought against her husband should he help her to die at a time of her choice. The DPP refused to give any such assurance. Mrs Pretty brought an application for judicial review. She argued that the DPP had acted unlawfully having failed to pay due regard to Mrs Pretty's fundamental human rights. Her application failed before the Divisional Court,[24] as did her subsequent appeal to the House of Lords.[25] She took her case to the European Court of Human Rights at Strasbourg, but lost again.[26] The Law Lords held that the decision not to promise immunity to Mr Pretty should he help his wife to die was not, in the circumstances, amenable to judicial review.[27] The crux of Mrs Pretty's case turned on the alleged violation of her human rights. Mrs Pretty's counsel argued that a blanket prohibition on assisted suicide contravened Articles 2, 3, 8, 9 and 14 of the European Convention on Human Rights. The Suicide Act 1961 was incompatible with the Human Rights Convention. All the judges disagreed. It was put to them that Article 2 endorsing the right to life carried with it the corollary of a right to die at a time and in a manner of one's own choosing. The Law Lords were unimpressed. They could read nothing into Article 2 to confer a right to be helped to die. Lord Bingham regarded Article 2 as embodying the traditional doctrine of the sanctity of life. He put it thus:

Whatever the benefits which, in the view of many, attach to voluntary euthanasia, physician-assisted suicide and suicide without the intervention of a physician, these are not benefits which derive protection from an article framed to protect the sanctity of life.[28]

Nor did an argument based on Article 3 prohibiting inhuman or degrading treatment find any greater favour. Dignity in sickness and dying should be protected. Nothing in Article 3 conferred a positive obligation to help an individual end her life. The Divisional Court declared:

... far from having the effect contended for by Mr Havers, Articles 2 and 3 between them are aimed at the protection and preservation of life and the dignity of life, because of its fundamental value, not only to the individual but also to the community as a whole. It is to stand the whole purpose of these articles on its head to say that they are aimed at protecting a person's right to procure their own death.

In the Lords, Lord Bingham[29] doubted whether any positive obligation to prevent citizens being subjected to degrading treatment could translate into a duty to ensure a person could seek help to die. Lord Steyn was clear that: '. . . article 3 was not engaged'. It was

... singularly inapt to convey the idea that the state must guarantee to individuals a right to die with the deliberate assistance of third parties. So radical a step, infringing the sanctity of life principle, would have required far more explicit wording.[30]

Lord Hope[31] was not convinced that Mrs Pretty's condition met the minimum level of severity required in Article 3. Since she could not be compelled to accept treatment and, in his view, palliative treatment was available, Lord Hope doubted that her state was degrading.

Arguments centred on Article 8, the right to respect for private and family life, fared little better. The Divisional Court did concede that Article 8 could extend to embrace a right to bodily integrity, including a right to refuse life-saving treatment. They were even prepared to assume Article 8 (1) could extend to a right to be allowed to take one's own life.

In some of their speeches, the Law Lords suggest Article 8 does not even go that far. Lord Steyn puts it bluntly:

... article 8 prohibits interference with the way in which an individual leads his life and it does not relate to the manner in which he wishes to die.[32]

All their Lordships concurred with the Divisional Court that even if some sort of right to choose one's manner of dying can be inferred from Article 8 (1), Article 8 (2), placing restrictions on privacy rights, justifies the State in criminalizing assisted suicide. The need to afford protection for vulnerable people, especially the elderly justifies the provisions of the Suicide Act as they stand. Lord Bingham says:

It is not hard to imagine that an elderly person, in the absence of any pressure, might opt for a premature end to life if that were available, not from a desire to die or a willingness to stop living, but from a desire to stop being a burden to others.[33]

Arguments grounded on Articles 9 and 14 of the Convention also failed. No doubt the detailed arguments to the several speeches in *Pretty* will be dissected and debated for years. Two policy questions perhaps drive all the judges in the Divisional Court and the Lords. First note that Mrs Pretty did not seek physician-assisted suicide but her husband's help to die. The Divisional Court noted:

We are not being asked to approve physician-assisted suicide in carefully defined circumstances with carefully defined safeguards. We are being asked to allow a family member to help a loved one die, in circumstances of which we know nothing, in a way of which we know nothing, and with no continuing scrutiny by any outside person.[34]

Second, the Law Lords were much exercised by the European scope of the Convention. Lord Steyn made this point:

The fact is that among the forty-one member states . . . there are deep cultural and religious differences in regard to euthanasia and assisted suicide. The legal-isation of euthanasia and assisted suicide as adopted in the Netherlands would be unacceptable in predominantly Roman Catholic countries in Europe. The idea that the European Convention requires states to render lawful euthana-sia and assisted suicide (as opposed to allowing democratically elected legis-latures to adopt measures to that effect) must therefore be approached with caution.[35]

None the less the last (judicial) word on physician-assisted suicide may still be to come. Judges' hopes that Parliament will take this burden from them are unlikely to be realized. For Diane Pretty, any change in the law comes too late. She died shortly after her final appeal failed before the European Court of Human Rights.

The unconscious patient

What of the fate of the patient whose illness or injury has rendered him unconscious and unlikely ever to regain consciousness? This was the issue in the seminal American case of Karen Quinlan,[36] a young woman who, suddenly stricken with illness, lay in a coma attached to a life-support machine. Although she was not brain-stem dead, her doctors were satisfied that there was no hope that she would ever recover a cognitive state: she was characterized as being in a 'chronic, persistent, vegetative condition' kept alive only with the assistance of a ventilator. Karen's parents decided that it would be best for her to be removed from the life-support machine. Accordingly, her father applied to the court to be appointed her guardian and claimed that, as guardian, he would be entitled to authorize the discontinuance of all 'extraordinary' medical procedures sustaining Karen Quinlan's life.

The Supreme Court of New Jersey upheld the father's claim. First, had Karen Quinlan been conscious and lucid, she would have had a right, just like Ms B., to decide to discontinue life-support treatment in circumstances where it was simply prolonging for a short period a terminal condition. She was not conscious or lucid. Second, because of her condition, her father was appointed guardian and the question then arose whether he could make a decision of that kind on her behalf. He was entitled to go to the court to seek assistance; and the court was prepared to 'don the mental mantle of Karen Quinlan' to make a decision for her that she would have made had she been able to do so. Thus, by applying a 'substituted judgement' test, the court decided that if, upon the concurrence of the guardian and the family of the patient, the attending physicians should conclude that there was no reasonable possibility of her ever emerging from her comatose condition to a cognitive state they should consult with the Hospital Ethics Committee and, if that body agreed, the life-support system might be withdrawn, without any civil or criminal liability on the part of any participant. Following that judgment, a Hospital Ethics Committee was convened and the decision was taken to remove life support. It is an interesting reflection on the fallibility of human judgement that withdrawal of the life-support system did not lead to a swift death and Karen Quinlan survived for ten long years after falling into the coma.

Bland: Crossing the Rubicon? [37]

In England a similar tragedy befell the Bland family. At seventeen, Anthony Bland suffered crush injuries at Hillsborough football stadium. He suffered catastrophic and irreversible damage to his brain. The condition from which he suffered is known as a persistent vegetative state (PVS). He had lost all cortical (higher brain) function but his brain stem continued to function. PVS patients continue to breathe independently and their digestion continues to function. Tony Bland was incapable of voluntary movement and could feel no pain. He could not see or hear, taste or smell. 'The space which the brain should occupy is full of watery fluid.'[38] He remained alive, fed through a tube. All his excretory functions were managed mechanically. Doctors were agreed that there was no hope of recovery of any sort. In this condition the young man existed for two years until, with the concurrence of his family, the hospital applied for a declaration that they might lawfully discontinue artificial feeding and hydrating Tony Bland. The House of Lords unanimously granted that declaration.

We have seen (pages 443–4) how their Lordships managed to find that withdrawing the naso-gastric tube was not an act hastening death such as to expose doctors to liability for murder. Tony Bland, however, could not instruct his doctors to cease treatment. Unlike in the Karen Quinlan case in the USA, nor could his family seek to be appointed as guardians of their adult son. The Law Lords fell back on *F.* v. *West Berkshire Health Authority* (see pages 117–21).[39] When a patient was incapable of deciding for himself whether to continue treatment, what could lawfully be done to him depended on what constituted treatment in his best interests and had to conform to responsible medical practice. For Lords Goff, Keith and Lowry the evidence of medical opinion and professional guidelines on diagnosis and confirmation of PVS assisted them to conclude that, as Tony Bland received no benefit from treatment, it was not in his best interests to continue naso-gastric feeding. They reasoned that the regime of artificial feeding constitutes treatment, and an overwhelming body of medical opinion supported withdrawing artificial nutrition and hydration from patients confirmed in PVS. Therefore withdrawing 'treatment' was lawful.

Lord Mustill acknowledged the complexity of best interests in this context.[40] Tony Bland was not suffering; he felt no pain.

By ending his life the doctors will not relieve him of a burden become intolerable, for others carry the burden and he has none. What other considerations could make it better for him to die now rather than later? None that we can measure, for of death we know nothing. The distressing truth, which must not be shirked, is that the proposed conduct is not in the best interests of Anthony Bland, for he has no best interests of any kind.

Lord Mustill turned traditional analyses of best interests on their heads. He looked at the justification for what was being done to Tony Bland's body; the tubes feeding him, the tubes excreting his waste. Absent evidence that such invasive treatments were necessary to promote his best interests, they were themselves unlawful, a trespass on the youth's unconscious body. Thus treatment not in his interests could and must be withdrawn.

Bland is an exceptional, difficult case. No one could fail to sympathize with his family whose child was breathing, but effectively a 'living corpse'. Yet where does *Bland* lead?[41] Can something as basic as feeding be withheld to bring about death? Would this mean staff could stop spoon feeding a patient in advanced stages of dementia who did not demand food?

The Law Lords saw the dangers in their decision. They advised that before treatment was discontinued a declaration should be sought from the courts. They warned that their ruling covered only patients in PVS. They sought to restrain any slide down slippery slopes. Withdrawal of artificial nutrition and hydration required evidence that (1) every effort should have been made to provide rehabilitation for at least six months; (2) diagnosis of irreversible PVS should not be considered confirmed until at least twelve months after the injury; (3) diagnosis should be agreed by two independent doctors and (4) generally the views of the patient's immediate family will be given great weight.[42]

Bland is a limited and cautious decision. Even on its own facts it provokes numerous questions. The experts who gave evidence in *Bland* expressed total confidence in medical ability to judge that a patient was irreversibly in PVS. Others are more dubious, concerned that diagnosis may be mistaken and arguing that in some cases intensive treatment can result in limited recovery.[43] The *legerdemain* by which their Lordships classified removal of a feeding tube as an omission not an act provokes charges of covert legalization of euthanasia.[44] If Tony Bland's life was sacred, for itself, not its quality, how can withholding basic food and water be acceptable?

After *Bland*: PVS to 'near PVS'

The series of decisions that followed *Bland* indicate that it has led to radical change in the law governing the ending of life. The carefully constituted limitations built into *Bland* to keep that decision within bounds have been eroded step by step. In *Frenchay Healthcare NHS Trust* v. *S.*[45] the patient was said to have been in PVS for two and a half years following a drug overdose. His feeding tube was accidentally disconnected. The hospital immediately sought a declaration that it could lawfully refrain from re-inserting the tube. The Court of Appeal granted the declaration in haste and without any independent medical opinion confirming that *S.* was irreversibly in PVS. The court recognized that the evidence as to *S.*'s condition was neither as unanimous nor as emphatic as in *Bland*. The judges found that in the emergency that had arisen because of the disconnection of the tube, there was no benefit conferred on *S.* by re-inserting the tube. Indeed following Lord Browne-Wilkinson's reasoning in *Bland* it might be construed as an assault on *S.* to do so. In these circumstances the further inquiry necessary to take an independent medical opinion could be dispensed with. A fortuitous event affected the criteria set out in *Bland* to protect patients. On the facts of *S.* some doubt exists as to whether *S.* was truly in PVS. There was evidence of restlessness and distress for which *S.* was receiving medication.[46] The third condition set by Lord Goff in *Bland*, independent evidence confirming PVS, survived barely a year.

Subsequent decisions erode the *Bland* limitations yet further. In *Re D.*[47] the patient had suffered serious brain damage after a road accident. As in *Frenchay*, her feeding tube became disconnected. Stephen Brown P accepted evidence that *D.*'s condition did not fully conform to guidelines for the diagnosis of PVS laid down by the Royal College of Physicians. He was satisfied that there was 'no evidence of any meaningful life whatsoever' and held that it was lawful to refrain from re-inserting the tube. In *Re H.*[48] a forty-three-year-old woman had suffered brain injuries in a car crash. She retained some rudimentary awareness and like *D.* did not fit squarely within the RCP definition of PVS. The President of the Family Division authorized cessation of artificial feeding. He was: '. . . satisfied that it is in the best interest of this patient that the life sustaining treatment currently being artificially administered should be brought to a conclusion.'[49]

In *Bland, Frenchay, D.* and *H.* the patient's family fully supported the doctors' judgement to cease treatment. *Re G*[50] revealed a difference of opinion among the family. *G.* suffered serious injuries while riding his motorcycle. In the course of attempts to resuscitate him, he suffered a heart attack, which resulted in the interruption of blood flow to his brain. In 1992 he was diagnosed as being in PVS, a state in which he had lain for nearly two years at the time of the application to court to withdraw feeding. *G.*'s wife and mother remained devoted to him and visited regularly. *G.*'s wife somewhat reluctantly supported the application to withdraw feeding from *G.* His mother opposed the application. Stephen Brown P said that he was satisfied that doctors had taken into account all the views of *G.*'s family. The mother's views could not prevail against what was considered to be the best interests of the patient. It might be argued that the wife's judgement should be preferred. This is not the basis of the finding in *G.* The judge seems to give relatively little weight to any relative's views. He says:

It would indeed be an appalling burden to place upon any relative to transfer as it were the responsibility for making a decision in a case of this nature to that relative. In this case, the responsibility must ultimately remain with the doctors in charge of the case, albeit taking fully into account the views of relatives.[51]

Mason and McCall Smith[52] comment that the '. . . heavy and continuing emphasis placed on medical assessment rather than on a robust and principled approach to individualized human and patients' rights may mean that an expansionist development of clinical discretion is inevitable.'

After *Bland*: beyond PVS?

Another lesson that may be drawn from the line of post-*Bland* cases on PVS or near PVS is that PVS cases are no longer 'special'. Nor is withdrawal of feeding seen as much more of a dilemma than withdrawal of any other form of treatment, such as dialysis.[53] The *Practice Note*[54] setting out procedures to obtain court sanction to withdraw treatment from a mentally disabled adult embraces PVS within a wider range of medical and welfare disputes leading to litigation. Each case turns on the best interests of the patient. 'Best interests' is a phrase easy to utter and difficult to interpret. It inevitably involves judgements of quality of life. In *Re D*.[55] a patient who had been hospitalized for much of his life with serious psychiatric illness developed renal failure and required dialysis. He lacked the mental capacity to consent to treatment and often would not be co-operative in dialysis treatment, sometimes having to be anaesthetized. The judge ruled that it was not in the patient's interest to impose dialysis on him where in the doctors' opinion 'it is not reasonably practicable to do so'. Whether they like it or not, the effect of the long series of judicial decisions relating to withdrawal of treatment is that judges are making life or death decisions.

The entry into force of the Human Rights Act raised questions about the legality of the reasoning in *Bland* and the cases that followed. Were decisions to cease feeding, especially to withdraw artificial feeding, lawful? Or did they contravene Article 2 of the Human Rights Convention protecting the right to life? In *NHS Trust* v. *M*.[56] the President of the Family Division ruled that in the circumstances of cases such as *Bland* where a recovery allowing the patient to enjoy any sort of cognitive abilities was nigh on impossible, nothing in Article 2 required measures to ensure prolongation of survival.

DNR orders

Much controversy surrounds DNR (do not resuscitate) orders. What is at issue is not withdrawing treatment but whether or not a patient who suffers a cardiac arrest should be resuscitated. Should the patient's notes instruct hospital staff not to resuscitate? Whose decision should determine whether or not a DNR order is made? Guidelines developed jointly between the British Medical Association and the Royal College of Nursing[57] suggest that it is appropriate to consider a DNR order if the following conditions are met. (1) The patient's condition is such that effective cardio-pulmonary resuscitation (CPR) is unlikely to be successful. (2) CPR is not in accord with the recorded sustained wishes of the patient who is mentally competent. (3) If successful, CPR is likely to be followed by a quality of life that the patient would find unacceptable. Where a DNR order has not been made and the wishes of the patient are unknown, CPR should be attempted if cardiac or pulmonary arrest occurs. Responsibility for a DNR decision rests with the consultant in charge but decisions should be made on the basis of appropriate consultation with other staff and the patient's family. Fears about DNR orders focus on *who* makes the decision about life or death and whether such decisions may be made arbitrarily or in a discriminatory fashion. Public perception is that doctors use DNR orders rather like death warrants and that age is a key factor.[58] Undoubtedly DNR orders are made more often in relation to elderly patients. That of itself may not be surprising. It is the quality of decision-making that counts and how prospects of successful resuscitation and future quality of life are assessed. A greater number of very elderly patients who are also gravely ill may be more unlikely to recover than their grandchildren in their twenties and thirties. If, before you became critically ill, you were young and fit, a DNR order will be made only after vigorous efforts to improve your condition and once there can be little doubt that continued treatment will be futile or non-productive. If you are over eighty, you have had your innings, the feeling goes. The criteria governing the assessment of the patient and the weight given to his or her family's wishes should not vary with age.

Current guidelines on DNR also make it clear that decision-making is not an exclusively medical role. The patient's wishes if known must be respected. The family must be consulted. The validity of DNR orders came before the English courts in *Re R. (Adult: Medical Treatment)*.[59] R. was twenty-three. He was born with a severe malformation of the brain and developed epilepsy in infancy. He suffered from multiple disabilities and had no real means of communicating with others. He had severe and debilitating intestinal troubles including ulcers 'all the way through his guts'. His only real response to others seems to have been to being cuddled. He appeared to experience quite acute pain. He was not in PVS or anything akin to 'near PVS'. Since he was nineteen, he had lived in a nursing home, attending a day centre and going home to his devoted family most weekends. In the year before the court proceedings R. had been hospitalized five times. His doctors, with the full agreement of R.'s parents, issued a DNR order. Should R. suffer from a life-threatening condition involving a cardiac arrest he should not be resuscitated. Staff at R.'s day centre were concerned about the use of DNR orders in R.'s case and made an application for judicial review of the order. The NHS Trust responsible for R.'s care sought a declaration both to declare the DNR order lawful and to support a wider non-treatment policy, including withdrawing nutrition and hydration. This part of the Trust's application was later withdrawn.

Sir Stephen Brown P upheld the DNR order. He was persuaded that the evidence established that, in cases such as R., CPR was unlikely to succeed. Indeed the very process might do *R.* further injury. Condition (1) in the BMA/RCN guidance was met. Conditions (2) and (3) focus in part on the patient's wishes. *R.* had never been able to articulate any such wishes. None the less the judge concluded that it was permissible to consider the patient's quality of life in assessing his best interests. DNR orders do not involve measures to terminate life or accelerate death. Where continued existence involved a life 'so afflicted as to be intolerable',[60] policies designed to limit lifesaving intervention could be approved.

Advance directives[61]

Cases discussed so far in this chapter illustrate the intractable difficulty that doctors, courts and families face in trying to decide what is best for someone else. The English courts have largely rejected the fiction of 'substituted judgement' whereby decision-makers seek to reach the decision a person, who is now unable to make her own decisions, might have made herself. None the less most people would agree that if there is concrete evidence of the wishes of a patient these should have effect, as policy on DNR orders seeks to do. Hence the case is made to give legal effect for advance directives.

Advance directives take two forms. First, you may execute a *living will* whereby you outline the circumstances in which those caring for you should cease any life-sustaining treatment. A 'living will' may provide, *inter alia*, that if you develop cancer, but are no longer competent and your condition is irreversible, you should not be given antibiotics to combat any life-threatening infection, nor should you be artificially fed.

Secondly, you may execute a *continuing power of attorney*, nominating a proxy to make treatment decisions on your behalf should you become incompetent. Generally living wills and continuing powers of attorney will be complementary. The patient will use the living will to indicate his general wishes, and nominate a proxy to interpret the 'will'.

The common law in England already gives effect to living wills providing that there is unequivocal evidence that the patient intended to refuse life-saving treatment in the circumstances that have materialized, and that she did so freely, and on the basis of adequate information.[62] The older and vaguer any document embodying the living will, the less its force may be. For a continuing power of attorney to have legal force in

England, legislation is required.[63] Most American states have enacted legislation expressly giving binding force to both living wills and continuing powers of health care attorney. A Working Party set up by the King's College Centre of Medical Law and Ethics and Age Concern recommended that similar legislation be enacted in the United Kingdom. In an excellent report the Working Party canvasses the pros and cons of advance directives.[64]

When the Law Commission reviewed the law governing decision making on behalf of mentally incapacitated patients generally,[65] they endorsed legislation to give statutory force to living wills. Advance refusals of treatment should be executed in writing, signed and witnessed. If such an advance refusal prohibits life-saving treatment, it must do so specifically. Advance refusals could not preclude continuation of 'basic care' such as measures to ensure cleanliness, alleviate pain or ordinary feeding and hydrating. The Law Commission considered that the interests of others, including staff and fellow patients who might have to witness the pain and degradation of the patient refusing such basic care, outweighed the individual's right to prohibit that sort of treatment. The Law Commission also supported legislation to give effect to continuing powers of attorney.

In the event,[66] the Lord Chancellor's Department concluded at that time that legislation in relation to living wills was not necessary or desirable. Current law and practice gave sufficient force to such documents. Legislation to give effect to continuing powers of attorney should be introduced as part of a broader Mental Incapacity Bill. That Bill will be brought forward when the parliamentary timetable allows. There is some hope that this much needed law reform may soon be forthcoming.

The advantages of advance directives are self-evident. None the less, there are problems and pitfalls. Over 50 per cent of Britons never execute a conventional will. Will living wills prove more popular? Nominating a health care proxy, someone you trust to take life and death decisions for you, is easy in middle life, less easy in old age. There may be no close friends or family left alive when you actually face terminal disease in extreme age. Is there a risk that proxies would abuse their power? Consider this scenario. A woman of sixty-three is acting as proxy for her ninety-year-old mother who has suffered from senile dementia for ten years. The mother is doubly incontinent, has vicious temper tantrums and no longer recognizes her daughter. Is there an understandable risk that the daughter will refuse treatment for her mother's pneumonia, motivated in part by a desire to be rid of an intolerable burden?

However, the greatest problem with living wills and continuing powers of health care attorney is this. Your advance directive can only authorize any act that you, if still competent, could lawfully authorize. Thus it may authorize cessation of treatment within the limits, and subject to the caveats, earlier discussed. What the advance directive cannot do is authorize an act that would hasten your death, that is to say any act of active euthanasia. The nightmare for many of us is that we may end up in a geriatric ward with our mental faculties gone, our dignity destroyed. However, patients afflicted with dementia are often physically fit and survive for years. No advance directive can direct the geriatrician, or anyone else, to kill you. A prohibition on killing, whatever the beneficent motive, remains in place.

The euthanasia debate[67]

English law is imprecise and uncertain. Doctors cannot always be given clear advice about the legality of various procedures. Is this fair to the medical profession? Is it right that some doctors, even acting with the best of motives, may under a screen of silence do things that they believe may be unlawful? There is certainly some evidence that doctors practise covert euthanasia. If what is taking place in medical practice is acceptable to society then, it is argued, the law should be changed to set out clearly the parameters within which these actions take place. If society disapproves of certain procedures, how can they be controlled? Should the law be left obscure when prosecutors may elect not to proceed against clear evidence of euthanasia? On the other hand there are those who oppose legislation on the grounds that the current fudge allows for maximum flexibility for a caring medical profession. McCall Smith has argued that:

The current state of the law can be defended as the embodiment of a moral compromise which satisfies the needs of a delicately nuanced problem.[68]

Any proposal to clarify the current fudge polarizes opinions sharply. Pro-life campaigners have sought unsuccessfully to reverse the decision in *Bland*[69] and to encourage police and prosecutors to pursue vigorously any evidence of covert euthanasia. Supporters of voluntary euthanasia argue the contrary case with equal passion. As Kennedy and Grubb note

'. . . whenever the topic of voluntary euthanasia is broached, rational argument becomes an early casualty'.[70]

The case for voluntary euthanasia is deceptively simple. It rests on the principle of autonomy. The individual is the '. . . final determinant of his or her destiny'.[71] We enjoy the right to control our death just as we enjoy the right to control our lives. Moreover, dignity and welfare, it is contended, impel us to allow the individual the right to end an intolerable life. A compassionate society should not force people dying, or living, with pain and disability, to continue to live. The patient in the terminal stages of motor neurone disease should not be compelled to suffer all the consequences of a drawn out death. Human rights are invoked in support of the pro-euthanasia case. Article 3 prohibits inhuman and degrading treatment. Does the absence of a euthanasia option in effect impose such degrading treatment? Article 8 protects our private and family lives. Do laws preventing my doctor, or indeed my husband, from helping me to end an intolerable life violate my privacy? We have seen that the Law Lords, and the European Court of Human Rights, in *Pretty* (see page 445) were unmoved by such legal arguments. The ethical debate continues.

Those opposed to legislation permitting voluntary euthanasia advance several objections. For many though not all opponents of euthanasia, central to their opposition to euthanasia is their commitment to the doctrine of sanctity of life.[72] But other concerns are voiced. Just how voluntary would such euthanasia be? Would the introduction of such laws result in a change of attitude by society towards the sanctity of life generally, towards the elderly, infirm, and the mortally sick? Would the existence of such laws impose pressures upon elderly and terminally ill patients to seek euthanasia rather than remain a burden on relatives or on society? Would the existence of such legislation provide opportunities for fraud and abuse and undermine the relationship of trust between doctor and patient? How easy would it be to apply such a law?

Let us examine what form legislation might take. Two rather different sorts of laws might be envisaged – both of which have models in other jurisdictions. Legislation could sanction physician-assisted suicide (as is now the case in Oregon, USA) or could allow full-blown active euthanasia (as is the case in the Netherlands).

Physician-assisted suicide

As we have seen, while suicide itself was decriminalized in 1961, it remains a criminal offence to assist someone else to end her life. The doctor who knowingly provides me with sufficient tablets with which to end my life and advises me how best to take them risks prosecution. The well-informed and able may kill themselves. The patient dying of degenerative disease or in the terminal throes of cancer may need help to do so. Mason and McCall Smith[73] rightly castigate the definitional niceties of the current law. If I can breathe only with the aid of a venti-lator I can require my doctor to switch off the ventilator. If I am slowly choking to death with motor neurone disease, but can still swallow enough lethal sleeping tablets I can end my misery. If I am so weak-ened by the disease that I cannot reach for the tablets I must endure my suffering.

An increasing number of commentators now advance the case for legalizing physician-assisted suicide.[74] But what does this mean? The Oregon Death with Dignity Act 1994[75] allows doctors to comply with a patient's request for medication to end their life. Will this meet the truly hard case where the patient, even if supplied with medication, cannot take the lethal dose independently? The draft Bill proposed by Meyers and Mason envisaged the doctor 'providing or *administering* a lethal dose of medication'. A lethal injection performed by the doctor must surely be killing, not simply assisting suicide. Do we have to resort to complex mechanical devices whereby the doctor sets up a machine that allows the patient to trigger the mechanism delivering the lethal injection? The line between assisted suicide and killing becomes as frag-ile as the artificiality of the current law. In *Pretty*, Lord Bingham exposed the dilemma.

If article 2 does confer a right of self-determination in relation to life and death, and if a person were so gravely disabled as to be unable to perform any act whatsoever to cause his or her own death, it would necessarily follow in logic that such a person would have a right to be killed at the hands of a third party . . .[76]

Mason and McCall Smith frankly acknowledge:

The chances of legislation which legalizes active euthanasia being accepted in the United Kingdom are very slim, but opposition might be very much less were it possible to legislate for PAS alone – an electorate that, rightly, could not accept the doctor as an executioner might be less hostile to a doctor who could be regarded as a friend in need.[77]

Active euthanasia

So should the law go further and sanction active euthanasia in some circumstances? If a patient voluntarily requests help to die, should doctors be authorized to give such help directly by, for example, injecting the patient with a lethal dose of morphine? In the Netherlands an informal agreement between the prosecution authorities and the medical profession allowed active euthanasia for several years. The prosecution authorities agreed not to prosecute any doctor who ended his patient's life within the parameters set by agreed guidelines. The patient must have freely requested 'help in dying' and the physician must assure himself that that request is truly voluntary and well considered. The patient and his doctor must be satisfied that there are no other means of relieving the patient's suffering. A second doctor must be consulted. It is estimated that thousands of patients each year have opted for active euthanasia in the Netherlands, perhaps 2 per cent of all reported deaths.[78] None the less, until 2000, euthanasia remained formally unlawful in the Netherlands. Legislation to give legal effect to the earlier informal arrangements was enacted in 2000.[79] The impact of Dutch practice and their new laws is much debated. Opponents argue (*inter alia*) that the incidence of active euthanasia is under-reported; there is evidence of termination of life without an explicit request from the patient (in perhaps as many as one in five cases); withdrawal of treatment with minimal safeguards is common; depressed and mentally disturbed patients are helped to die.[80] The nub of the case is that what is supposed to be a limited provision to allow free and informed choices by competent patients to end their lives has become a convenient means of disposing of the elderly and grievously sick. Supporters of the Dutch 'experiment' equally passionately refute these allegations.[81] Dispassionate analysis of how voluntary euthanasia 'works' in the Netherlands is hard to find.

The history of euthanasia reform in this country is not encouraging for those who favour legislation. The first Euthanasia Bill in 1936 was designed to deal with a situation in which the doctor could no longer control a patient's pain. The patient had to be over twenty-one, suffering from an incurable and fatal illness, and had to sign a form in the presence of two witnesses asking to be put to death. This form and two medical certificates were then to be submitted to a 'euthanasia referee', whose task it was to interview the patient to ensure that he understood the nature of his request. The referee might then also question doctors and relatives. If the referee gave his certificate of approval, the matter would go to a special court, which had the right to question any parties and consider objections; if the court was satisfied, it would issue an appropriate certificate, which would authorize a practitioner to administer euthanasia, which would have to be effected in the presence of an official witness. This Bill was quickly rejected.

Another Voluntary Euthanasia Bill, introduced in 1969, was designed to allow a person to sign in advance a declaration requesting the administration of euthanasia if he was believed to be suffering from a fatal illness or was incapable of rational existence. Again, the Bill was severely criticized by some as being inadequately thought out, ill-drafted and riddled with loopholes and ambiguities of the most dangerous kind; and above all 'because it failed in what it chiefly sought to do . . . it provided no reliable safeguards for the patient'. The *coup de grâce* was applied with the following comment:

Such a Bill is medically unnecessary, psychologically dangerous and ethically wrong. Unnecessary, because legal rigidity should not be substituted for medical discretion. Dangerous, because this Bill would diminish the respect for life, blurring the line between crime and medicine. Ethically wrong, because it infringes on the absolute value of life.

Subsequent Bills in the mid-1970s were more modest and attempted to avoid being seen as attempts to legalize euthanasia or 'mercy killing'.

In the wake of the decision in *Bland*, the House of Lords set up a Select Committee on Medical Ethics to investigate legal, ethical and social issues surrounding treatment decisions at the end of life.[82] In a lengthy report of almost amazing banality the Committee endorsed the judges' ruling in *Bland* itself, and commended but refused to endorse legislation to give effect to advance directives. In effect they recommended no change and that such difficult questions be left to the doctors. The report came out firmly against legalizing voluntary euthanasia. Their Lordships considered that argument based on autonomy, the right to choose to die constituted '. . . insufficient reason to weaken society's prohibition on intentional killing'. It was not, in their view possible to set secure limits on voluntary euthanasia and vulnerable people might be pressured into requesting early death. Moreover there was good evidence that palliative care could relieve pain and distress in the majority of cases.

The Select Committee Report rehearsed the 'old' arguments around euthanasia. The debate intensifies but it does not seem to move on. The Bill currently promoted by Lord Jaffe in the House of Lords is unlikely to meet with any more success than its predecessors.

19
Death and Retention
of Body Parts

The ending of a patient's life does not bring to an end legal questions relating to that person. First, as we shall see, a legal definition of death is required for several purposes. Second, a host of questions surround what may lawfully be done with the dead body and its parts. Revelations that organs and tissue were in the past regularly retained by hospitals after post mortem examinations created a controversy almost unparalleled in the history of the NHS.

Defining death

Biologically, death is a process and not an event. Different organs and systems supporting the continuation of life cease to function successively and at different times. Historically, the key factors used to determine whether death had occurred were the cessation of breathing and the cessation of heartbeat, matters that could be verified with simplicity. Thus, the irreversible cessation of heartbeat and respiration implied death of a patient *as a whole*, although that did not necessarily imply the immediate death of every cell in the body.

The need to determine an exact or, at best, approximate time of death is important for many reasons. The law not infrequently requires such a finding.[1] Establishing the date of death may be important for property purposes: until death is established, steps cannot be taken to obtain probate or letters of administration to that person's estate; the interest of a beneficiary under a will is usually dependent upon the beneficiary surviving the testator. In some cases, where the testator and the beneficiary die at around the same time, it is important to know when each death took place. When two relatives die in a common accident, there may be a presumption that the elder died before the younger, unless evidence can be established as to the precise time of death of either; and the property consequences of this decision are significant.[2] There may also be tax factors: if a person gives away property before his death, that property may be free from tax, or be subject to less tax, only if he survives the gift for a specified period. There have been many stories written involving relatives of such a donor going to great lengths to postpone or conceal the 'true moment' of death so that he 'survives' beyond the relevant statutory period for tax purposes! Another possibility may be that the spouse of a person who is either dead or dying may wish to remarry. In the absence of clear evidence as to whether or not death has occurred, there may be a risk of bigamy. Finally, if a victim has a claim for damages for injuries sustained, the amount of damages will differ substantially between cases where the victim is comatose, yet living, or dead.[3]

Determining whether a person was dead once posed little difficulty. Doctors accepted and used traditional methods of establishing death. When someone's heart stopped beating and he stopped breathing, he was dead. Advances in medicine gradually demonstrated that this was not a valid test for all purposes. The heart could be stopped deliberately during open-heart surgery, for example, and there were cases of spontaneous cardiac arrest followed by successful resuscitation. Mechanical ventilators or respirators have effected major improvements in techniques of resuscitation and life support for those who are desperately ill or injured. Where these efforts are successful and the patients recover satisfactorily, one may praise the advances in medical techniques. Sometimes such measures do not provide any satisfactory outcome, for example where the person's heart continues to beat on the machine long after breathing has stopped and his brain is irreversibly damaged.

In such circumstances, keeping a person 'alive' on a machine can be as undesirable as it is pointless. It is distressing to relatives. It can have an adverse effect on nursing staff morale; the cost of maintaining the patient in such intensive care is high and, indeed, the use of machines in these cases can mean that other patients, better able to benefit from them, may be denied access to them. However, the principal trigger to rethinking our definition of death was the development of transplantation, which highlighted the need for speed in diagnosing death and taking organs from the body.

Thus, pressures developed to produce a redefinition of death based upon a new concept of 'irreversible brain damage' or 'brain death'. This concept can be illustrated dramatically by considering a guillotine victim. Nobody would consider the body, after the head has been severed, to represent an individual living being; yet the body could be resuscitated and the organs kept 'alive' for a considerable period.[4] Thus, whereas in most cases brain death follows the cessation of breathing and heartbeat in the dying process, occasionally the order of events is reversed. This occurs as a result of severe damage to the brain itself, from, perhaps, a head injury or a spontaneous intercranial haemorrhage. In such cases, instead of failure of such vital functions as heartbeat and respiration eventually resulting in brain death, brain death results in the cessation of spontaneous respiration, normally followed within minutes by cardiac arrest. If, however, the patient is supported by artificial ventilation, the heartbeat can continue for some days and this will, for a time, enable other organs, such as the liver and kidneys, to be maintained.

This condition of a 'state beyond coma' or 'irreversible coma' or 'brain death' was first advanced as a new criterion of death in 1968 in an influential report of an *ad hoc* Committee of the Harvard Medical School.[5] In such cases a doctor could pronounce as dead a comatose individual who had no discernible central nervous system activity; and then the ventilator could be switched off. It was stated that judgement of the existence of the various criteria of death was solely a medical issue.

Public opinion was unwilling to surrender control of such matters lightly to the medical profession! Unease was expressed with the relationship between the attempt to redefine death and the needs of transplant surgeons. From the surgeon's point of view, it is important that organs taken from a deceased person should be taken as soon as possible after death. In 1975 the British Transplantation Society expressed concern at the poor quality of cadaver kidneys being transplanted, mainly because of delay between the determination of death and the removal of the kidneys from the body. It was also important that the body be kept on the life-support machine to preserve the quality of the organs until they were required. Two major fears were voiced. First, was death being redefined simply to enable transplant surgeons to obtain better results? For example, might potential transplant donors be designated 'dead' earlier than if they were not potential donors? Second, was it ethically or legally permissible to remove organs from a donor before the ventilator had been turned off? Because of doubts such as these, the

British Transplantation Society, as we have seen in an earlier chapter, recommended that the death of a potential organ donor should be certified by two doctors; that neither should be a member of the transplant team and, most importantly, that the decision to stop a ventilator should be made quite independently of transplant considerations.

From the late 1970s the medical establishment in Britain agreed that 'brain death' or, preferably, 'brain-stem death' (which is the 'irreversible loss of brain-stem function')[6] could be diagnosed with certainty; and, in these circumstances, the patient is dead whether or not the function of some organs, such as the heart, is still maintained by artificial means.[7] Controversy continued.

Were patients being diagnosed as brain dead who were not 'really' dead? Or were, the few reported examples simply cases where the appropriate criteria for determining brain death had not been properly implemented? Was it possible that organs were being taken for transplant before a patient had died? As late as 1986 anxieties were once again being voiced publicly. The validity of procedures to establish 'brain death' had never, some argued, been rigorously tested. Short cuts in procedures were too often prompted by pressure from the transplant team anxious to 'get at' organs swiftly.[8]

Official endorsement of 'brain stem death' is to be found in both the Report of the Conference of the Royal Colleges of Medicine,[9] and now the Department of Health's Code of Practice,[10] which defines death as follows:

Death entails the irreversible loss of those essential characteristics which are necessary to the existence of a living human person . . . [The] definition of death should be regarded as 'irreversible loss of the capacity for consciousness, combined with irreversible loss of the capacity to breathe'. The irreversible cessation of brain stem function (brain stem death) whether induced by intra-cranial events or the result of extra-cranial phenomena, such as hypoxia, will produce this clinical state and therefore brain stem death equates with the death of the individual.

The law

There is still no statutory definition of death in the United Kingdom. There is, however, little doubt that there is now sufficient judicial authority to support a definition of death based on 'brain-stem death'. The early cases arose where persons accused of murder claimed that it was not they who killed the victim, but the hospital team who disconnected the life-support machine. The courts did not react favourably, even though they side-stepped the issue as to what, in law, constitutes death. In *R. v. Malcherek*[11] the Court of Appeal dealt with two such cases. In the first, the defendant had stabbed his wife, who was taken to hospital and put on a life-support machine. When it was found she had irreversible brain damage, the ventilator was disconnected and shortly after that all her bodily functions ceased. The second defendant attacked a girl, causing her multiple skull fractures and severe brain damage. She was taken to hospital and put on a life-support machine, which was disconnected when the doctors concluded that her brain had ceased to function. The Court of Appeal upheld the trial judges' decisions in each case not to leave the issue of causation to the jury, pointing out rather tartly that it was not the doctors, but the accused, who were on trial. The Court took the crucial evidence to be that the original criminal acts by the defendants were continuing, operating and substantial causes of the death of their victims. In the ordinary case where treatment is given bona fide by competent and careful medical practitioners, evidence is not admissible to show that the treatment would not have been administered in the same way by other medical practitioners. Without exploring the definition of death, the Court was not prepared to allow assailants to shelter behind technical arguments challenging standard medical procedures. Lord Lane CJ did go slightly further saying,

. . . whatever the strict logic of the matter may be, it is perhaps somewhat bizarre to suggest . . . that where a doctor tries his conscientious best to save the life of a patient brought to hospital *in extremis*, skilfully using sophisticated methods, drugs and machinery to do so, but fails in his attempt and therefore discontinues treatment he can be said to have caused the death of the patient.

The sad case of *Re A.*[12] ultimately settled the matter. A two-year-old boy suffered a serious head injury. Doctors struggled to save his life and he was put on a ventilator. His condition deteriorated and tests established that he was, undoubtedly, brain-stem dead. His parents vehemently opposed the decision to switch off the ventilator. The hospital sought a declaration that doctors in disconnecting the child from the ventilator did not act unlawfully. Endorsing the definition of brain-stem death now encapsulated in the Department of Health Code of Practice, the judge declared that the child was for all purposes legally dead. The House of

Lords in *Airedale NHS Trust* v. *Bland* (see page 449–51)[13] lent further authority to a legal definition of death dependent on proof of 'brain-stem death'.

Should there be a statutory definition of death?

In 2002, the Department of Health launched a major consultation paper to seek views on reform of the laws governing (inter alia) organ transplantation and organ retention.[14] The case for a statutory definition of death is less compelling today than when such arguments were first advanced.[15] The courts have introduced a degree of certainty into the debate. Had there been a *statutory* definition of death in 1970, based upon the long-standing medical criteria of irreversible cessation of breathing and heartbeat, then the medical redefinition of death as irreversible cessation of brain function would have no legal effect until the existing statutory definition was changed. As long as the matter is treated as a question of medical fact, changes in medical approach can be accommodated within the law without any requirement for further legislation.

Those in favour of legislation, however, regard the very ease with which, without legislation, definitions of death can and have altered as a source of disquiet. Doctors, supported by judges, are moving the goalposts. People who a generation ago were regarded as still alive, albeit dying, are now declared dead. Visceral fears that doctors continue to be eager to declare A dead to give B her organs have not gone away. A debate on a statutory definition of death would allow wide public involvement in that debate, and an opportunity for public education.

Such a debate could also encompass other difficult issues surrounding defining death. There are those who argue that Tony Bland was not dying but dead.[16] The destruction of the cortex and consequent loss of all cognitive function rendered him, in that ghastly phrase, a 'human vegetable'. He had irreversibly lost personhood, and those capacities that made him distinctively human. It would not be a far cry to modify the definition of death so that comatose patients in this state are also regarded as dead.[17] Some argue that this is the most sensible and most compassionate way of dealing with these persons. Criteria based on 'brain-stem death' would be replaced by a concept of 'cognitive death'. But is this a decision that unelected judges should take by choosing to endorse flexible and developing definitions of death as valid if they accord with medical practice? The House of Lords in *Airedale NHS Trust* v. *Bland*[18] rightly did not explore this avenue. Public debate and democratic legitimacy is essential if, in effect, a limited form of euthanasia is to be endorsed in England and Wales.

Public debate on what we mean by death is called for but it must be noted that formulating a statutory definition of death is not itself straightforward. Early attempts provided for alternative definitions; the long-established traditional definition and the new definition. This, it was said, would lead the public to believe that there are two separate phenomena of death, one being primarily for transplantation purposes. The American Uniform Brain Death Act (1978) has served as a model for a number of states in the USA. It provides simply that 'for legal and medical purposes, an individual who has sustained irreversible cessation of all functioning of the brain, including the brain stem, is dead. A determination under this section must be made in accordance with reasonable medical standards.'

It is difficult to see what this would add to English law, were it to be enacted. Such a statute would simply repeat and reinforce the Code of Practice currently operated voluntarily by the medical profession. Any doctor currently violating the Code by operating a concept of 'cognitive death' in relation to his patients would have difficulty in justifying his action in any subsequent legal or disciplinary proceedings. The more flexible means of regulation by a Code of Practice enable criteria for defining death to be examined and where necessary modified without the need to resort to amending legislation. None the less it is crucial that any such modification is fully and openly discussed if the public is to have confidence in the profession's own Code of Practice. Care must be taken that criteria for defining death are not used as a backdoor means of legalizing active euthanasia. Public confidence in the definition of death is crucial. If that confidence is betrayed, legislation will be needed. Loss of confidence generated by controversies over organ retention graphically illustrated now damaging this can be.

Open debate would allow two other questions to be explored properly, the tragic cases of anencephalic infants and pregnant women.

In relation to anencephalic babies, criteria for 'brain-stem death' are unworkable.[19] An anencephalic baby is born lacking a higher brain. He is bound to die, usually in a matter of days, and were his interests alone to be considered such an infant would not be ventilated. Other babies will be born with intact brains, but defective hearts or kidneys. Doctors may want to use organs from the anencephalic baby to save the life of a baby with other defective organs. If they allow the anencephalic baby to die 'normally', simply by ceasing to breathe, his organs will deteriorate so rapidly as to be useless. If the anencephalic baby is to be used as an organ donor he must be ventilated. That poses a problem in defining when he dies. Tests for 'brain-stem death' are not yet properly applicable to newborn babies. Moreover, there is some evidence that if ventilated an anencephalic infant's brain stem may remain active, 'alive', for some considerable period of time. If 'brain-stem death' is inapplicable to anencephalic babies should we accept that the lack of any higher brain function renders the baby, so to speak, born dead?[20] Or is that again confusing active euthanasia with defining death?

One objection, regardless of how we define death in such cases, is that in ventilating an anencephalic baby to retrieve her organs we use her solely as a means to an end. A similar problem surrounds ventilating brain-dead pregnant women.[21] If a pregnant woman suffers head injuries during pregnancy and brain-stem death is diagnosed, should her corpse be ventilated to allow the foetus the opportunity to be delivered alive? Who should make such decisions? Where a woman has herself contemplated such a possibility and in an advance directive expressed her wish that her body be sustained so her child can live, the outcome seems clear. She has authorized the use of her body for that purpose. Few women contemplate such a tragic outcome in pregnancy. Absent such instruction from the woman herself, do her husband or parents have a right to determine whether or not the foetus survives? Or is this a case where an independent foetal interest can be asserted?

Removal of body parts

The consequences for patients and doctors of loss of trust in medical integrity is graphically illustrated by the controversy generated by revelations about organ retention. In the course of the Inquiry established in 1998 to investigate the paediatric cardiac service at Bristol Royal Infirmary, evidence emerged of a widespread practice of organ and tissue-retention.[22] Over a long period of time, organs and tissue had been taken at, or after, post mortem from children's bodies and used '. . . for a variety of purposes, including audit, medical education and research, or had simply been stored'. The Bristol Inquiry Team, led by Professor Ian Kennedy issued an Interim Report, *Removal and Retention of Human*

Material,[23] in May 2000. The report notes that this had become an '. . . issue of great and grave concern' generating an outcry not confined to the Bristol parents. Worse was to follow. Almost in passing, one of the witnesses to the Bristol Inquiry, Professor R. H. Anderson, in explaining the benefits of retaining hearts for educational purposes, noted the existence of many collections of children's hearts elsewhere. The largest collection, he commented, was at the Royal Liverpool Children's Hospital (Alder Hey). His evidence prompted the Department of Health to set up an Independent Confidential Inquiry under section 2 of the National Health Service Act 1977. The inquiry was instructed to investigate the removal and disposal of human organs and tissue following post mortem examinations at Alder Hey.

The *Alder Hey Report* published in January 2001 proved to be political dynamite.[24] It revealed longstanding practices of removing and retaining children's organs without the consent or even knowledge of their grieving parents. In some cases infants were literally stripped of all their organs and what was returned to their families was an 'empty shell'. In a horrifying number of cases, organs and tissue retained were simply stored. They were put to no good use. In some of the most tragic instances, the whole of a foetus or stillborn infant was kept and stored. The *Alder Hey Report* is 535 pages long. It addresses not just the original wrong of retaining organs, but subsequent mishandling of organ return and a range of other appalling practices and mismanagement. In this chapter, I concentrate on the legal issues arising out of organ retention.

Simultaneously with the publication of the *Alder Hey Report*, the Chief Medical Officer issued his own advice to Ministers,[25] and published a census carried out to ascertain the extent of organ retention since 1970 across the NHS in England and Wales.[26] What became apparent was that practices whereby pathologists simply took and retained human material after post mortem were routine. The extent to which the deceased's family was involved at all in such decisions varied radically. What was clear was that adequate and free consent was rarely obtained, or even thought necessary. Nor was this a practice limited to dead children. Many families were to learn about organs stripped from adult relatives.[27]

Before examining the law governing this troubled issue, a number of points must be clarified. The value of taking and retaining organs after post mortem in certain cases should not be doubted. Ascertaining the cause of death is self-evidently important. Often, especially with infants, tests on organs and tissue may have crucial value to the child's

family. Investigations that reveal genetic disease may be the key to helping that family have further healthy children. In the wider public interest, medical research is dependent on access to human organs and tissue.
Medical education requires such material. One simple example may
illustrate the educational use of human organs. If a child dies tragically and is found to have a grossly abnormal heart, it makes sense to
retain that heart so that paediatric surgeons can examine it before
attempting to operate on and save the life of a child with a similar
abnormality. It can only be ethical to do so with the family's consent.
For the devout Jew or Muslim, there is a religious imperative to bury
the body intact. For other families, the pain of not laying their relative
to rest complete is overwhelming. However, for many families involved
in the organ retention scandal what motivated their anger was the loss
of control over their relative's burial or cremation. Many relative have
said publicly that had they been consulted they would have agreed to
doctors retaining the organs of the dead child or other relative. They
would have been content to 'gift' some parts of the body to achieve
good ends, if these ends were fully explained to them. What they abom-
inate is the lack of respect shown to them and their relative. They feel
that someone whom they loved dearly has been treated as a mere
convenience, treated with contempt.

The law[28]

Doctors, especially pathologists, have endured odium in the wake of revelations at Bristol and Alder Hey. The law should share the blame. The
Bristol Interim Report says simply but tellingly:

'. . . we have no doubt that the complexity and obscurity of the current law will
be manifest to all. Equally we have no doubt that there will be general agreement
that this state of affairs is regrettable and in need of attention.'[29]

The starting point for any analysis of the present law must be the
longstanding assumption that no one can own a human body or its parts.
The common law has several times asserted that there is 'no property in
a corpse'.[30] When a family member dies his next of kin have no claim by
which they can assert 'this is now our body and we have unfettered rights
to dispose of it or its parts'. Control of the body rests with whoever is at
the relevant time in lawful possession of the body. Where a person dies
in hospital this will be the hospital. The executors or administrators of

the deceased's estate are subject, ultimately, to a common law duty to dispose of the body decently. This duty confers on them a right to possession of the body to fulfil that duty of decent disposal of the body.[31] A number of prior events may delay the family taking possession of the body for burial or cremation.

Several Acts of Parliament touch on the lawful use of dead bodies. The three key statutes are the Anatomy Act 1984, the Human Tissue Act 1961 and the Coroners Act 1988.

The Anatomy Act can be dealt with fairly swiftly. Put simply, the Act enables people to donate their bodies or their parts for use for anatomical examination.[32] People give their bodies to medical schools to assist in medical education, pre-eminently to educate medical students in anatomy and train them in dissection. The details of the 1984 Act are in some ways fuzzy, as we shall see is also the case with the Human Tissue Act. The criteria governing authority to take and use the body are largely identical to those we shall examine in the Human Tissue Act. The framework for the use of donated bodies is, however, closely regulated. The performance of any anatomical examination and possession of bodies or body parts donated under the Anatomy Act must be licensed by the Secretary of State. Bodies may be retained for no more than three years. HM Inspector of Anatomy controls the use of bodies under the 1984 Act and regularly inspects anatomy departments.[33] At the end of the three years, there are arrangements for respectful disposal of the bodies and many medical schools regularly hold a public service of memorial and thanks to the donors and their families. The Act does permit retention beyond the three-year period of certain body parts but only provided that the donor originally authorized such retention.[34] No parts may be retained that would enable the deceased to be recognized by that part, for example, the head.[35] Violation of the Anatomy Act creates criminal liability. Unlicensed possession of an anatomical specimen (a body or body part taken under the Anatomy Act) constitutes a criminal offence punishable by up to three months imprisonment.[36]

It is that vast majority of cases not regulated by the Anatomy Act that provoked the controversy around organ retention. First, a distinction must be made between removal of organs and tissue after a hospital post mortem, and removal of body parts subsequent to a coroner's post mortem. The Human Tissue Act 1961, already examined in the context of transplants, governs removal and retention of organs after a hospital post mortem. The 1961 Act is primarily concerned with the removal of body parts 'for therapeutic purposes [i.e. transplant] or for purposes of medical education or research'.[37] Section 2(2) provides that, where no coroner's inquiry is likely, the person lawfully in possession of the body (the hospital) may authorize a post mortem if the following conditions applicable to the lawful removal of body parts are met. These are that the hospital may authorize removal and retention of body parts if after

... such reasonable enquiry as may be practicable, there is no reason to believe: (a) that the deceased had expressed an objection to his body being so used after his death ... or (b) that the surviving spouse or any surviving relative objects to his body being so dealt with.[38]

In relation to transplants, doctors have shown themselves reluctant to exercise the powers granted by the 1961 Act. In the context of organ retention, the opposite ethos seems to have prevailed. The 1961 Act is obscure. It does not mandate that body parts may only be removed and retained with explicit consent. Rather it sets up a 'no objection' rule. Put crudely, hospitals thought that they could take organs and tissue for purposes of education and research if no family member voiced dissent. The *Bristol Interim Report* suggests that even where families were asked their views and expressed no objection, 'agreement' both to hospital post mortems and subsequent removal of body parts was often given with little understanding of what was entailed. It might be an 'agreement' given at a time of great personal trauma, shortly after the death of a child for example. In some cases, families, knowing nothing of the distinction between hospital and coroners' post mortems did not realize that they had a right to object. The use of the word 'tissue' confused people. Understandably, lay people assumed that in agreeing to the removal of tissue, they agreed to doctors taking small specimens from organs, not whole organs. The *Alder Hey Report* revealed a bleaker picture. Organs had been taken and stored without even a pretence of seeking the family's views. The flaws within the Human Tissue Act became patent. What it required was obscure. Even if it could be shown to have been flouted, the lack of sanctions punishing violation of the Act rendered it tooth-less (see page 432).

The position in relation to coroners' post mortems was no better. The overwhelming majority of post mortems are performed on the orders of the coroner. Put briefly[39] a coroner may order a post mortem if he is informed that the body of the deceased is lying within his district and there is reasonable cause to suspect that the deceased:

(a) died a violent or unnatural death; (b) has died a sudden death of which the cause is unknown; or (c) has died in prison or such a place or in such circumstances as to require an inquest under any other Act.[40]

Regulations made under the Coroners Act elaborate on the rules governing which deaths must be reported to the coroner, placing an emphasis on reporting surgical deaths or deaths where some medical negligence may have occurred.[41] A pathologist carrying out a coroner's post mortem acts under the coroner's authority. Rule 9 of the Coroner's Rules places a duty on the pathologist to remove and preserve 'materials' that in his opinion bear on the cause of death. If a baby dies in the course of cardiac surgery, the pathologist may lawfully remove and retain his heart, until it is possible to ascertain why the infant died. This may take time. In criminal cases, retention of organs over an extensive period of time may be justified. However, after coroners' post mortems there is no power to retain organs for research or teaching purposes. Once the cause of death is established, neither the coroner nor the pathologist have any further legal power to retain body parts. Such 'material' should be disposed of, unless the relatives of the deceased authorize retention for research or teaching purposes. In practice it seems that coroners simply allowed pathologists to do what they wished with human material no longer required for the purposes of verifying cause of death. Pathologists, in ignorance of the law in many cases, retained organs and tissue over long periods of time and for a multiplicity of purposes.

By 2001, NHS hospitals were in possession of literally tens of thousands of organs and vast collections of blocks and tissue slides. Leading teaching hospitals and medical museums such as the Royal College of Surgeons had extensive archival material of body parts, some including collections long predating the NHS. The legal basis of such collections was obscure. The ethics of organ retention appear to have been ignored.

The rights of the families

The grievances of families, especially where organs had been taken from infants without their parents' knowledge, received great publicity. The political and media response to the controversy was unprecedented. The Secretary of State described the state of affairs revealed in the *Alder Hey Report* as 'grotesque'. The lack of clarity about families' legal rights and redress exacerbated their anger and grief. Several families started legal

claims against NHS Trusts who had removed and retained their relative's organs. The cause of action was, in many cases, not founded on
the initial wrong done in removing organs or retaining organs without
legal authority. Families sued hospitals for negligently causing them
psychiatric harm in their bungled response to disclosures about organ
retention. Families were given misleading information. In a number of
instances, a family was told, for example, that a hospital had retained
certain of a child's organs, perhaps the heart. The heart was returned to
the family and a second burial or cremation arranged. The parents were
assured that no other organs were retained, only to be told a little later
that other organs had been found. A third burial had to be arranged and
endured by traumatized relatives. The way in which organs were returned
was not always sensitive. Nor was information about what had happened
always given with proper empathy and compassion.[42] A settlement has
been made in most of the Alder Hay claims. The outcome of other claims
is still awaited.

What, however, of the initial wrong? Could there be a cause of action
for taking or retaining body parts without authority? In an attempt to
answer that question we need to explore the complex issue of ownership
of body parts.

Ownership of body parts[43]

We noted earlier the ancient common law assumption that there is no
property in a corpse. That statement must be qualified. Consider the
Egyptian mummies held in the British Museum. Do they belong to the
British Museum? Or might I lawfully help myself to them? The case of
R v. *Kelly*[44] confirmed that, once a body or body parts had been changed
by work done on them, such parts become capable of being property.
A technician was accused of stealing body parts from the Royal College
of Surgeons and selling them to an artist who wished to use the parts
as moulds for his sculptures. Both were charged with theft. Their
defence was the College did not own the parts and so they could not
steal them. Upholding the convictions, the Court of Appeal found that
body parts became capable of being property for the purposes of the
Theft Act because they had '. . . acquired different attributes by virtue
of the application of skills, such as dissection or preservation technology, for exhibition or teaching purposes'. The notion of 'property',
however, is complex in this context. The Court of Appeal in Kelly did

not find that the Royal College of Surgeons *owned* the stolen body parts. A right to lawful possession of property is all that is required for that property to be stolen from you. The English Court of Appeal concurred with their Australian brethren in *Doodeward* v. *Spence*;[45] in that case Griffith CJ spoke of a body or its parts becoming the subject of property '. . . when a person has by the lawful exercise of work or skills so dealt with a human body or part of a human body that is has acquired some attributes differentiating it from a mere corpse awaiting burial he requires a right to retain possession of it, at least as against any person not entitled to have it delivered to him for the purpose of burial.'

Does it follow from *R.* v. *Kelly* that whenever organs or tissue have been retained and, for example, have been preserved in formalin or put in blocks, the hospital in possession of the specimen can assert a property right of it? *Dobson* v. *North Tyneside Health Authority*[46] undermines such an argument. The family of a woman who had died of a brain tumour brought a claim in clinical negligence against the health authority alleging failure to diagnose her condition sufficiently swiftly to offer her effective treatment. To succeed in their claim, they needed to ensure that their expert witnesses could examine samples of the brain. The brain had been removed at a coroner's post mortem, preserved in paraffin, and later disposed of. The family sued the hospital for conversion, alleging unlawful disposal of the brain. They argued that on completion of the coroner's investigation the family were entitled to return of the brain. They enjoyed ownership, or at least a right of possession, of the deceased's brain. The Court of Appeal dismissed their claim. Fixing the brain in paraffin was not a sufficient exercise of skill or labour to give that brain any different attributes to the organ initially removed from the body in the course of post mortem. There was

. . . nothing . . . to suggest that the actual preservation of the brain after the post mortem was on a par with stuffing or embalming a corpse or preserving an anatomical or pathological specimen for collection or with preserving a human freak such as a double-headed foetus that had some value for exhibition purposes.[47]

Identifying exactly what must be done to transform an organ taken from a body into property is difficult. It must though be noted that at one point in *Kelly*,[48] Rose LJ suggests that the common law could develop to recognize a body part as property even without the acquisition of different attributes if it had acquired '. . . a use or significance beyond . . . mere existence'. Rose LJ even suggests in such a case outright ownership may be recognized. Reconciling *Kelly* and *Dobson* is not straightforward.[49] Even if it is established that a body part has become capable of being property, or even being owned, that of itself will not assist families aggrieved by organ retention. The application of skill sufficient to transform the body part into property vests that property in the person doing the requisite work on the part, providing he possesses it lawfully. The body part belongs to the pathologist not the family.

A family seeking redress for the removal and retention of an organ needs to establish their right to possess or control the destiny of the organ. They could seek to rely on the duty to bury their deceased relative, and argue that duty carries with it a right to custody and possession of the body until decently interred. Several problems surface with this approach. First kinship itself confirms no such duty or right. The duty to bury the body rests in the executor or administrator of the deceased's estate. If at the time an organ is taken, there is no executor, nor has an administrator been appointed, there is nobody who has an immediate right of possession, a right to claim the body from the hospital.[50] This will often be the case with children where there is no 'estate' to be dealt with.

Where there is an executor entitled to claim the body for burial, the next question is this. Was the original removal of organs lawful? If there was no coroner's post mortem and no compliance with the Human Tissue Act the answer should be no. If absolutely no authority to remove organs was granted, the initial act was unlawful. However, if removal of organs was ordered by the coroner, what was done intially may be lawful. The two sorts of cases must be distinguished.

Let us consider first a case where the removal of organs was neither authorized by the coroner, nor lawful by virtue of the Human Tissue Act. The final hurdle faced by the executors arguing that removal of organs violates their right to custody and possession of the body is what is meant by body. If a corpse is returned without a heart, does that infringe the executors' rights to possession of the body? Is that right a right to return of the body complete with all organs? The line is difficult to draw. To say a body returned after a few cells have been removed for DNA testing is not a 'body' might sound ludicrous. To say a body returned stripped of all its internal organs is a body sounds equally bizarre. But is even the removal of a few cells entirely unproblematic? The Human Genetics

Commission is exploring possible criminal sanctions against those who steal DNA.

Families whose relatives' organs were initially removed legally confront an additional hurdle. The executors will need to argue that their right to custody and possession of the body entitles them to demand return of any organs lawfully removed once legal authority to retain those organs expires. After a coroner's post mortem this means, once the cause of death is established, the executors have a right to repossess those parts of the body retained after the rest of the body has been interred or cremated.

Families involved in organ retention will find the law not only obscure but also offensive in its language of property. Their focus is on consent and respect. What was done should not have been done without consent. What was done should have demonstrated respect for their dead relative and for them. Families see what happened in many cases as 'criminal'. Discerning a criminal offence under existing law is difficult however. Ancient common law offences such as wrongful desecration of a corpse or outraging public decency or causing a public nuisance might be invoked. Successful prosecution is far from certain. Unlike the Anatomy Act, neither the Human Tissue Act nor the Coroners Act, provide for specific criminal liability.

Towards a gift relationship[51]

There is little dissent from the view that law reform is urgent. The confused and tangled web of different statutes and outdated common law principles must be clarified, preferably in a single Act of Parliament. Explicit consent of the deceased or her family should determine the legality of organ removal and retention save for exceptional and clearly defined cases where the public interest mandates non-consensual retention. Guidelines from the Chief Medical Officer, the Royal College of Pathologists, and most recently the Department of Health, seek to move rapidly towards such a position extra–legally. The Medical Research Council[52] has promulgated guidance on the use of human tissue in research. Law reform is taking a little longer.[53] Who has authority to consent to organ removal is not always straightforward. If parents disagree, should a mother's consent override a father's objection or vice-versa?[54] What forms of redress and sanctions are available will need thought.

In 2002 the Department of Health launched a consultation on wide-ranging law reform.[55] In the same period a fundamental review of the coroners' system[56] is under way. With luck, by 2004 new legislation will be in place regulating organ retention whether it follows a hospital autopsy or a corner's post mortem.

Epilogue

Medical law has altered beyond recognition in the sixteen years since the first edition of this book was published in 1987. The sheer quantity of case-law and literature is daunting. For many doctors, their increasing involvement with the law is frightening and, they often believe, damaging to good medical practice. The financial burden that malpractice litigation imposes on the NHS must be a matter of concern to everyone. Patients are not much happier with the state of the law. Success rates in claims for clinical negligence remain low. Complaints procedures still provoke complaint. And patients still feel their rights are too readily defined by what doctors think best.

The past decade has witnessed a host of initiatives, including reforms of civil procedures, 'new' complaints processes and radical changes to the General Medical Council. More is in the pipeline. 'No fault' compensation is on the agenda. A 'no blame' culture is much talked about. The worrying feature of so many well-meaning attempts at reform is that often there seems to be little coordination between the several different initiatives. In particular, no rigorous analysis is applied to consider just what role the law should play in regulating medical practice and what the limits of the law's remit should be. Consideration of the principles of clinical negligence and the processes of litigation tends to be divorced from debates about the ethical framework of good medical practice. Black letter lawyers address malpractice litigation. Ethicists and more philosophically inclined lawyers join doctors and theologians in debating the grand moral dilemmas of medicine. Ordinarily, patients and lay people do not get much of a chance to have their say until some heated controversy breaks, such as the scandal around organ retention.

Legal innovation remains to too great an extent *ad hoc* and reactive.

The political will to drive through potentially controversial reform seems lacking. Thus I remain convinced that there is still a case to establish a Commission on Health Care, Law and Ethics. While such a commission would share some of the features of a National Bioethics Council, similar to those august bodies already established in France and Denmark, I would see its remit as somewhat different, and much more practically focused. My hope would be that such a commission would be a United Kingdom body. That is not to say that Scotland will not on a number of occasions wish to regulate matters of medical practice and medical ethics differently. Difference could be a blessing. Evaluating how different approaches to ethical dilemmas actually work is an opportunity to be grasped. Examining how different sets of rules succeed or fail will help us develop better rules. For example, Scotland has already grasped the nettle of decision-making on behalf of mentally incapacitated patients. Evaluating how the Adults with Mental Incapacity Act (Scotland) 2000 succeeds in meeting its objectives will result in better laws all round.

At the heart of many of the problems in medical decision-making discussed throughout this book lies the question of the patient's right to determine what treatment he receives, how to reconcile that right with the doctor's duty to give the patient the best treatment available, and increasingly how we reconcile the rights of one patient with those of her fellows and the legitimate interests of society. The belated recognition granted to patient autonomy by recent judgments can only be part of the story. More attention now needs to be paid to responsibilities as well as rights. How the law safeguards those people unable to articulate and promote their own rights must be considered. The current climate of 'rights' could all too easily end in a world where medical law became difficult to differentiate from consumer law. The age-old power of the doctor might be replaced by power vested in the most vociferous and well-connected consumers.

Perhaps to suggest that a multi-disciplinary commission begins by revisiting patient autonomy and patients' rights and responsibilities sounds too mundane? The closest model the United Kingdom currently has to a national bioethics council is the Nuffield Council on Bioethics. The Nuffield Council expressly focuses on ethical problems arising out of innovation. It charts the waters in novel dilemmas. So the Nuffield Council has produced reports on (*inter alia*) genetic screening, use of human tissue and xenotransplantation. Of course, a national commission should review the ethical problems posed by, for example, cloning, pre-implantation genetic diagnosis, tissue banks and all the frightening array of possibilities medical technology now presents to us with their potential for good and evil. There will be those who say that rather than waste time on the old chestnut of 'autonomy and responsibility', what needs consideration are such questions as whether the technology can be used to order 'designer babies' or therapeutic cloning used to produce transplant organs. Investigation of the ethics of medicine must truly be vigorously proactive not reactive. Such an approach is misguided. Many of the 'problems' posed by advances in medicine are not new – just old problems in a new guise. The implications of our growing ability to screen for genetic disease, to use genetic knowledge itself as medicine often raise once more the old questions of the status of the embryo, the rights of its progenitors, and above all individuals' rights to mandate their medical treatment. If we can settle more 'old' questions of rights and responsibility, 'new' problems may more readily settle themselves. The distribution of power and responsibility for decision making remains at the heart of most medico-legal problems. Then there is the added dimension to the commission's work, defining the limits of what society should tolerate.

How would any such commission be constituted? Who would sit on it? The membership must have a wide base. Clearly doctors and other health professionals, should be represented. The consumers of health care, patients and their families, must be given a voice. The disciplines of philosophy and theology have a contribution to make, helping to identify proper criteria for decision making and the formulation of the rights and obligations of those involved in decision making. And as the legal framework for medical practice and the application of medical ethics would be central to the work of the commission, lawyers cannot be excluded.

In practical terms, even before the selection of members for the commission comes the question of its formal status. The commission could either be established by means of a statute creating it, or in the first instance a committee of inquiry along the lines of the Warnock committee could be set up by the Department of Health. That committee could consider the appropriate formal constitution for pursuit of its purpose. My preference, tentatively, is for establishment by statute from the start, with Parliament giving its seal of approval to the process of review and having a stake in the provision for membership and terms of reference of the commission.

The commission's terms of reference will need careful drafting.

Initially, fundamental questions of the nature of patients' rights as they operate in so many areas of medical care and medical research should be referred to the commission. Maybe a genuine Charter of Patients Rights could be considered. The impact of the Human Rights Convention on medicine could be fully explored. Other European and international documents such as the *Bioethics Convention* would be examined. Decisions then need to be taken as to which other of the issues surveyed in Part III of this book, and many others outside the scope of this work, require immediate examination. Maybe those that put the doctor at risk of criminal liability should be given priority. Thereafter the Secretary of State for Health should be empowered to refer specific issues to the commission for consideration and the commission should be empowered to propose to the Secretary of State questions that it believes require attention. What I envisage is not a short-term institution that would conduct a limited inquiry, make recommendations and then be wound up. After completing its initial review of problems apparent today, the commission would be there to deal with problems that arise as medicine and technology advance, and it would keep the law relating to medical practice and medical ethics under review. The commission would be expressly instructed to ensure that the practical consequences of case law and legal developments were fully evaluated.

The commission's powers should be two-fold, to investigate and to recommend. Investigation is the keynote of its function. The commission would examine the present constraints that the law places on medical practice, including the feasibility and application of the principles relating to consent developed by the courts. The role families should play where an individual cannot herself make a decision needs further study. The impact of clinical negligence claims needs evaluating. The spectre of defensive medicine must be confronted to see whether it has substance. The commission must extend its remit beyond the issues already litigated or debated in the context of existing common law. The time available for, and the manner of, communications with patients, and the role nursing staff do and can play, must be looked at. From investigation, the commission would move on to reports and recommendations. The commission would have three options. First, it may simply issue a report on its findings and outline its views of the appropriate development of the common law. The report should relate general principles to specific practice, distinguishing between and illustrating various spheres of medical ethics and practice. The Law Commission's work on *Mental*

Incapacity offers a model for this kind of work. Secondly the commission could go further and append to its report recommended codes of practice. A commission created by Act of Parliament could be empowered to make proposals on codes of practice to the Department of Health, so that by ministerial directions those codes could be given statutory force in the NHS. Finally, the commission would in appropriate cases recommend specific legislation.

It is the second possibility, that the commission be empowered to propose codes of practice, that needs some further consideration. Codes of practice have the attraction of introducing a greater degree of practical certainty into health care decision making. They can distinguish between different areas of medical enterprise, providing, for example, for a separate discrete code on research. None the less Codes of Practice can create problems for the doctor, the patient and the lawyer. A code of practice may often represent negotiated compromise. It offers the doctor greater precision in the legal framework within which he practises, but its provisions may not command uniform support for each and every clause in the code.

Two questions about the legal effect of codes of practice call for consideration. First, what force would the codes have to bind medical staff in their practice of health care? At the lowest they could be advisory only. Breach of the code would be a factor to be taken into account in investigating complaints and deciding on any disciplinary action against health care staff. Codes might be incorporated in NHS contracts of employment. If litigation were in progress, the codes would offer evidence of what constitutes logical and defensible practice. To give further force to the codes of practice, the statute creating the commission could empower Ministers to give statutory force to a code of practice. In appropriate cases, criminal sanctions would attach to breach of the code.

So far I have concentrated on the commission's role in examining and developing the law. The commission's task must be wider than this. It must also consider ethical standards, and when it is appropriate for the ethical standard to be set higher than the law. The law can never be more than a crude base-point in deciding what is proper and ethically accepted. Just as the commission should liaise with the Law Commission in devising a legal framework for decision making in medical practice, it should also liaise with the General Medical Council in advising on ethics. Nor must the commission confine itself to formal procedures, whether via legal regulation or the control exercised over professionals by the GMC and other professional bodies. Health Service procedures must be examined. The education of doctors and other health professionals should be kept under review. The commission offers a forum for general debate, for coordination between groups working in this field, throughout the UK. This is an opportunity that should not be missed for all those involved in and concerned about health care to cooperate with rather than to confront each other.

Since 1987 support for such a commission has grown apace. Ian Kennedy[1] is no longer a lone voice demanding that society plays its part in ethical decision making in medicine. The tradition of self-regulation by the profession alone has been eroded; reproductive medicine, genetics, and transplant surgery are now subject to statutory authorities such as the Human Fertilization and Embryology Authority (HFEA), the Human Genetics Commission (HGC) and the Unrelated Live Transplant Regulatory Authority (ULTRA) all with lay representation. Yet the Department of Health seems unconvinced by any case for a Commission on Healthcare, Law and Ethics. They might perhaps quite reasonably argue that there are now a number of bodies that provide advice on the ethics of certain areas of evolving medical practice and regulate controversial fields of medicine. Who needs a commission when we have the HFEA, the HGC and ULTRA? Moreover, almost daily new kinds of inspectorates, commissions and councils are set up, such as the Commission for Healthcare Audit and Inspection and the Social Care Standards Commission. When a gap in the coverage of controversial medical problems is exposed, the department will set up a special body to deal with it, such as the Retained Organs Commission. A Commission on Health Care, Ethics and Law would just be unnecessary bureaucracy. I disagree. The plethora of different bodies creates a duplication of effort and yet leaves fundamental questions unaddressed. The pool of individuals to sit on so many bodies must be running dry. Contradictory results often ensue from different bodies addressing similar problems, but in different guises. Over time the proposed commission could rationalize this plethora of other committees, commissions and councils. That is not to say a discrete regulatory body for embryology and genetics will no longer exist. But it would exist under the umbrella of the commission. Its debate would feed into the wider context of the commission's work. When gaps in its powers emerged, the commission would be there to fill the gaps with no need to set up an *ad hoc* body in haste.

Finally, medicine is an international enterprise. Doctors and scientists are not limited by national boundaries. More and more of the debates discussed in this book take place in the international arena. The proposed commission could represent the United Kingdom effectively in such debates and ensure *our* national perspective on medicine, law and ethics is not driven by the vagaries of political fashion.

Notes

1 The Practice of Medicine Today

1 *Learning from Bristol*, The Report of the public inquiry into children's heart surgery at the Bristol Royal Infirmary 1984–1995 CM 5207 (1) 2001 (hereafter *Learning from Bristol*).

2 Interim Report *Removal and Retention of Human Material* (available at www.bristol-inquiry.org.uk.

3 *Royal Liverpool Children's Inquiry Report* HC 12–11 2001 (hereafter the *Alder Hey Report*).

4 Female doctors rarely attract the same levels of public acclaim.

5 *Learning from Bristol* at p. 1.

6 Ian Kennedy, *The Unmasking of Medicine*, Allen & Unwin, London, 1981, Chapter 1, pp. 9ff.

7 ibid., p. 8.

8 The report of the Legal Service Ombudsman for 1999–2000 described the solicitors' complaints system as having 'lurched from one self-destruction strategy to another'. *Guardian* 12 July 2000.

9 Medical Act 1983, s. 49; and see *Younghusband* v. *Luftig* [1949] 2 KB 354; *Wilson* v. *Inyang* [1951] 2 KB 799. Unregistered practitioners are expressly prohibited from certain fields of practice, e.g. venereal disease (Venereal Disease Act 1917), and they are barred from holding certain positions (Medical Act 1983, s. 47).

10 Medical Act 1983, s. 46.

11 Theft Act 1968, s. 15.

12 See Sixth Report of the Select Committee on Science and Technology *Science and Technology of Complementary and Alternative Medicine* (HL 2000).

13 Osteopaths Act 1993.

14 Chiropractors Act 1999.

15 See J. Stone and J. Mathews, *Complementary Medicine and the Law*, OUP, 1996.

16 He was initially sentenced to six years' imprisonment. His sentence was reduced on appeal to eighteen months! See also *R.* v. *Tabassum* [2000] Lloyd's Rep. Med 404 CA.

17 *R.* v. *Brown* [1993] 2 All ER 75, HL; and see *Consent in the Criminal Law*, Law Com. Consultation Papers No. 139 Part XIII (1995).

18 Medical Act 1983, Sched. I.

19 *GMC News* (August 2001); and see *Effective, inclusive and accountable: reform of the GMC's structure, constitution and governance*, GMC, March 2001.

20 And see General Medical Council (Constitution) Order, 2002, SI 2002/3136; Medical Act 1983 (Amendment) Order 2002 SI 2002/3135.

21 Medical Act 1983, s. 2, and see ss. 30–34.

22 ibid., s. 35.

23 *Revalidating Doctors: Ensuring Standards: securing the future*, GMC, 2000.

24 See *Acting fairly to protect patients: reform of the GMC's fitness to practise procedures*, GMC, 2001.

25 ibid., s. 37. And see *Crompton* v. *GMC (No.1)* [1981] 1 WLR 1435 and *(No. 2)* [1985] 1 WLR 885.

26 ibid., s. 36.

27 ibid., s. 40.

28 See R.G. Smith, *Medical Discipline: The Professional Conduct Jurisdiction of the General Medical Council 1858–1990*, OUP, 1994.

29 See J. Robinson, *A Patient's Voice at the GMC: A Lay Member's View of the GMC* Report I (Health Rights), 1992.

30 See *McCandless* v. *GMC* [1995] 30 BMLR 53 (PC).

31 See *Doughty* v. *General Dental Council* [1987] 3 All ER 843 (PC); and see *Hossack* v. *General Dental Council* [1997] 40 BMLR 97 (PC).

32 See *Good Medical Practice*, 1995.

33 *Bhandari* v. *Advocates' Committee* [1956] 1 WLR 1442, PC.

34 See *Roylance* v. *GMC* [1999] Lloyd's Rep. Med 139, PC.

35 The Medical Act 1983 (Amendment) Order 2002.

36 *Ibid*

37 See R. G. Smith above at Note 28.

38 See s. 30.

39 See *Learning from Bristol*, pp. 349–50.

40 I. Kennedy and A. Grubb, *Medical Law* (3rd edn), 2000, p. 3.

41 Lord Irvine of Lairg, 'The Patient, the Doctor, their Lawyers and the Judge: Rights and Duties' (1999) 7 Med. L. Rev 255 at p. 261.

42 An excellent introductory text to the Act is: J. Wadham and H. Mountfield, *Blackstone's Guide to the Human Rights Act 1998*, Blackstone, 1999.

43 s. 3.

44 ss. 6–8.

45 s. 7.

46 For a clear introductory account of how the Act works see K. Ewing, 'The Human Rights Act and Parliamentary Democracy' (1999), 62 *Modern Law Review* 79.

47 See later at p. 291

48 *Secretary of State for the Home Department* v. *Wainwright, The Times*, 14 January, 2002.

49 Albeit an argument rejected in *R (Heather)* v. *Leonard Cheshire Foundation* [2001] EWHC Admin 429.

50 *Douglas* v. *Hello Magazine* [2001] 2 All ER 289, CA; *A* v. *B* (A Company) [2002] 2 All ER 545, CA; *Campbell* v. *MGN Ltd* [2003] 1 All ER 224 CA.

51 op. cit., p. 41.

52 *R (Heather)* v. *Leonard Cheshire Foundation* [2001] EWHC Admin 429; might the very detailed regulation of licensed private fertility clinics bring such clinics within the scope of the Act?

53 *Dudgeon* v. *United Kingdom* (1982) 4 EHRR 149.

54 *Open Door and Dublin Well Women* v. *Ireland* (1992) 15 ECHR 244.

55 See *Osman* v. *United Kingdom* (1998) 29 EHRR 245.

56 Ibid

57 *Airedale NHS Trust* v. *Bland* [1993] 1 All ER 821 HL.

58 [2000] 1 All ER 811. And see *NHS* v. *D* [2002] 2 FCR 577.

59 [1998] 3 All ER 673.

60 See *Bruggeman and Scheuten* v. *Federal Republic of Germany* [1977] EHRR 24; *Paton* v. *BPAS* [1981] 2 EHRR 408.

61 See *R* v. *North West Lancashire Health Authority ex p. A. & B.* [2000] 1 WLR 977, CA.

62 See *The Queen (Pretty)* v. *DPP*, [2002] 1 All ER 1, HL and see *Rodriguez* v. *British Columbia A-G (1993) 82 BCLP* (2d) 273.

63 *Pretty* v. *United Kingdom* [2002] 2 FLR 45.

64 See *Herczegfalvy* v. *Austria* (1992) 18 BMLR 48. See *R. (N.)* v. *M.* [2003] 1 WLR 562, CA.

65 May *F* v. *West Berkshire Health Authority* need review? Article 5 certainly casts doubts on *R* v. *Bournewood Community and NHS Trust ex p. L.* [1999] AC 458 HL. This decision is now being appealed to the European Court on Human Rights in Strasbourg.

66 See *Osman* v. *United Kingdom* (above at Note 55).

67 Could lowering the standard of proof of serious professional misconduct violate Article 6? And see *Ghosh* v. *GMC* [2001] Lloyds Rep. Med, 433.

68 See *R.* v. *North West Lancashire Health Authority ex p. A. & B.* (note 61 above).

69 *Z.* v. *Finland* (1997) 25 EHRR 371, *MS* v. *Sweden* (1997) 45 BMLR 133, *Brown* v. *United Kingdom* [1997] 24 EHRR 39.

70 *Rees* v. *United Kingdom* [1986] 9 EHRR 56, *Cossey* v. *United Kingdom* [1990] 13 EHRR 622, *B* v. *France* (1992) 16 EHRR.

71 Graphically illustrated in *H. (A Healthcare Worker)* v. *Associated Newspapers*

Ltd and N. (A Health Authority) [2002] Lloyd's Rep. Med 210 CA; see later at p. 68.

72 See Kennedy and Grubb op. cit. at pp. 42–4.

73 See C. Newdick, *Who Should We Treat? Law Patients and Resource in the NHS*, Clarendon Press, 1995.

74 *R. v. Secretary of State for Social Services, ex p. Hincks.* The first instance judgment is reported (1979) 123 Sol. J. 436. The appeal judgment remains unreported but is discussed by Finch, op. cit., pp. 38–9.

75 *R. v. Central Birmingham HA ex p. Walker, The Times,* 26 November 1988; *R. v. Central Birmingham HA ex p. Collier, The Times,* 6 January 1988 CA.

76 [1995] 2 All ER 129, CA.

77 *R. v. St Mary's Ethical Committee ex p. Harriott* [1988] 1 FLR 512.

78 (1994) 25 BMLR 1.

79 [1997] 8 Med LR 327.

80 [2000] 1 WLR 977, CA.

81 Case C-157/99.

82 And see s. 8 of the National Health Service Reform and Health Care Professions Act.

83 *R. v. Lord Saville of Newdigate ex p. A.* [1998] 4 All ER 860, HL.

2 Medicine, Moral Dilemmas and the Law

1 See J.K. Mason and R.A. McCall Smith, *Law and Medical Ethics,* (6th edn) Butterworths, 2002, chapter 11; G.H. Mooney, 'Cost-benefit Analysis and Medical Ethics' (1980) 6 J. Med. Ethics 177.

2 Excellent texts on medical ethics include T. L. Beauchamp and J.F. Childress, *Principles of Biomedical Ethics* (5th edn) OUP, 2001; R. Gillon, *Philosophical Medical Ethics,* John Wiley, 1996; J.M. Harris, *The Value of Life,* Routledge, 1985; and see generally *A Companion to Bioethics* H. Kuhse and P. Singer (eds.), Blackwell, 1998.

3 This model of 'ethics' was initiated by the Manchester physician Thomas Percival in his book on *Medical Ethics,* first published in 1808; see C.D. Leake (ed.) *Percival's Medical Ethics,* Williams & Wilkins, 1927.

4 See Gillon op. cit. Chapter 5.

5 See for example GMC 'Bluebook', *Professional Conduct: Fitness to Practise* (April 1985).

6 See also R.M. Veatch, *A Theory of Medical Ethics,* Basic Books Inc, 1981; H.T. Engelhard, & *The Foundation of Bioethics* (2nd edn) OUP, 1996.

7 e.g. K. Clouser and B. Gert, 'A Critique of Principalism' (1996) 15 *Journal of Medicine and Philosophy* 219.

8 Gillon op. cit. at p. viii.

9 p. 80.

10   See *Re A. (Minors) (Conjoined Twins: Separation)* [2000] Lloyd's Rep. Med 425, CA.

11   See generally C. Newdick, *Who Should We Treat? Law Patients and Resources in the NHS*, Clarendon Press, 1995.

12   Gillon op. cit. p. 87.

13   She can of course simply opt for private care. Is it unjust that those who can pay can obtain whatever treatment they desire?

14   See, e.g., M. J. Underwood and J. S. Bailey, 'Should Smokers be Offered Coronary Bypass Surgery?' (1993) 306 BMJ 1047.

15   Newdick op. cit. p. 22. See generally R. Cookson and P. Dolan, 'Principles of Justice in Health Care Rationing' (2000) 26 *Journal of Medical Ethics* 323.

16   Given her mother's longevity this does not seem an unreasonable assumption.

17   Gillon op. cit. Chapters 7 and 8.

18   See J. Finnis, *Natural Law and Natural Rights*, OUP, 1980; O.O'Donovan, *Begotten or Made*, OUP, 1984.

19   See for example the debate between J. Finnis and J. Harris in J. Keown (ed.), *Euthanasia Examined: Ethical, Clinical and Legal Perspectives*, CUP, 1995.

20   See, for example, Keith Ward, 'An Irresolvable Debate' in A. Dyson and J. Harris (eds), *Experiments on Embryos*, Routledge, 1989, Chapter 7.

21   HL Official Report, 15 January 1988, cols. 1461–6.

22   See the correspondence in *The Times*, 27 August to 2 September 1985, following an article by Paul Johnson (*The Times*, 26 August) calling for a ban on abortion and embryo research but for a return of the death penalty.

23   See G. Dworkin, R.G. Frey and S. Boy, *Euthanasia and Physician Assisted Suicide For and Against*, CUP, 1998.

24   See M. Phillips and J. Dawson, *Doctors' Dilemmas*, Harvester Press, London, 1984, pp. 22–6; and see that same work generally for its support of the 'middle ground' of the debate.

25   See in particular two persuasive and lively works: Jonathan Glover, *Causing Death and Saving Lives*, Penguin, Harmondsworth, 1977; J. M. Harris, *The Value of Life*, Routledge & Kegan Paul, London, 1985.

26   Glover, op.cit., Chapter 3.

27   Harris, op cit., Chapter 1.

28   See Gillon, op. cit.

29   For the Declaration of Geneva, the Hippocratic Oath and other codes of medical ethics, see Mason and McCall Smith, op.cit., Appendices A-F pp. 663–72.

30   See Phillips and Dawson, op. cit., p. 26.

31   Note the current challenge to the legality of making post-coital contraception available for purchase in pharmacies; see later at p. 321.

32   ibid., pp. 47–9, 82–5; Mason and McCall Smith, op. cit., pp. 146–50.

33   *Re A.* [1992] 3 Med L.R. 303.

34 See Chapter 19 and also Ian Kennedy, *The Unmasking of Medicine*, Allen & Unwin, London, 1981, Chapter 7. And see the *Guardian*, 6 August 1986, expressing disturbing doubts on brain death.

35 Glover, op. cit., pp. 43–5.

36 See *Airedale NHS Trust* v. *Bland* [1993] AC 789 HL; discussed on p. 438ff.

37 See Chapter 18, and also Phillips and Dawson, op. cit., pp. 33–4

38 ibid., p. 34.

39 See the case of James Lawson set free after being convicted for the manslaughter of his mentally ill daughter: the *Independent* 14 June 2001.

40 Indeed see Lord Browne-Wilkinson in *Airedale NHS Trust* v. *Bland* [1993] AC 785 at p. 885.

41 *B.* v. *An NHS Hospital Trust* [2002] 2 All ER 449; and see I. Kennedy, 'Switching Off Life Support Machines: The Legal Implications' [1977] Crim. L.R.443.

42 See I. Kennedy, 'The Karen Quinlan Case: Problems and Proposals' (1976) 2 J. Med. Ethics.

43 Glover, op. cit., Chapters 7 and 15; Harris, op.cit., Chapter 4.

44 See Phillips and Dawson, op. cit., p. 34, and BMA, *Philosophy and Practice of Medical Ethics*, 1988, p. 90.

45 See D. Abrahams, 'A Doctor's Justification for Withdrawing Treatment' (1985) Vol. 135 NLJ 48.

46 See Glanville Williams, *The Sanctity of Life and the Criminal Law*, Faber & Faber, London, 1958; P.D.G. Skegg, *Law, Ethics and Medicine*, Clarendon Press, Oxford, 1984; Mason and McCall Smith, op. cit.

47 But ultimately resulted in a 'liberalization' of the law on late abortions; see s. 37 of the Act.

48 J. Havard, 'Legislation Is Likely to Create More Difficulty Than It Resolves' (1983) 9 J. Med. Ethics 18.

49 [1981] BMJ 569.

3 A Relationship of Trust and Confidence

1 For a lively discussion of the complex ethical dilemmas faced by doctors in relation to confidentiality, see M. Phillips and J. Dawson, *Doctors' Dilemmas*, Harvester Press, London 1984, Chapter 5, 'Secrets'. And see J.K. Mason and R.A. McCall Smith, *Law and Medical Ethics* (6th edn), Butterworths, London, 2002, Chapter 8.

2 See J.E. Thompson, 'The Nature of Confidentiality' (1979) 5 J. Med. Ethics 57.

3 See F. Gurry, *Breach of Confidence*, Clarendon Press, Oxford, 1984.

4 See Law Commission Report No. 110, *Breach of Confidence*, para. 3.1 (Cmnd 8388), and see G. Jones, 'Restitution of Benefits Obtained in Breach of Another's Confidence' (1970) 86 LQR 463.

5   Gurry, op. cit., Chapters 8 and 9.

6   *Argyll* v. *Argyll* [1967] 1 Ch. 302.

7   *Stephens* v. *Avery* [1988] 2 All ER 477.

8   *Attorney-General* v. *Jonathan Cape Ltd* [1976] 1 QB 752.

9   *W.* v. *Egdell* [1990] 1 All ER 835, 846, CA.

10   *Wyatt* v. *Wilson* [1820], unreported but referred to in *Prince Albert* v. *Strange* [1849] 41 ER 1171, 1179.

11   *Hunter* v. *Mann* [1974] 1 QB 767, 772.

12   *Gartside* v. *Outram* [1856] 26 LJ Ch. 113, 114.

13   *Lion Laboratories Ltd* v. *Evans* [1984] 2 All ER 417, 433.

14   *X.* v. *Y.* [1988] 2 All ER 648.

15   *W.* v. *Egdell* [1990] 1 All ER 855, CA.

16   Law Commission Report No. 110, paras. 6–106, but see the Scottish decisions *A.B.* v. *C.D.* [1851] 14 Dunl. (CT of Sess.) 177; *A.B.* v. *C.D.* 1904 7F (Ct of Sess.) 72; discussed in Mason and McCall Smith, op cit., pp. 265–6.

17   See *X.* v. *Y.* [1988] 2 All ER 648; *W.* v. *Egdell* [1990] 1 All ER 835, 843 and 850.

18   GMC *Confidentiality: Protecting and Providing Information* (2000) and see BMA *Philosophy and Practice of Medical Ethics*, 1988, pp. 19–27. And see P. Moodie and M. Wright, 'Confidentiality, Codes and Courts' [2000] 29 *Anglo-American Law Review* 39.

19   *Confidentiality: Protecting and Providing Information* (above) paras 40–42. The publication of memoirs by Lord Moran, physician to Winston Churchill during the Second World War, provoked a great furore: see Mason and McCall Smith, op. cit., pp. 267–8.

20   Doctors do not act unlawfully if they disclose information when required to do so by statute or under court order. The law cannot condemn a doctor for conduct compelled by the law. And see *Confidentiality: Protecting and Providing Information* (above note 18) paras. 43–6.

21   The courts have stressed that care must be taken to limit information to those who 'need to know' and to ensure that the recipients of that information understand the requirements of confidentiality; see *W* v. *Egdell* [1990] 1 All E.R. 835, 850.

22   See *F.* v. *West Berkshire Health Authority* [1989] 2 All E.R. 545, H.L.

23   For the test used to establish decision-making capacity in health care see *Re C. (Adult: Refusal of Treatment)* [1994] 1 All E.R. 819.

24   Criminal Law Act 1967, s. 5(5).

25   ibid., s. 5(1).

26   e.g. s. 172 of the Road Traffic Act 1988 (information identifying the driver of a car involved in a road accident).

27   *Kitson* v. *Playfair* (1896), *The Times*, 28 March.

28   Birmingham Assizes (1914) 78 JP 604; see Mason and McCall Smith, op. cit., p. 245.

29   *Initial Services Ltd* v. *Putterill* [1968] 1 QB 396, 405.

30 At para 37.
31 *W.* v. *Egdell* [1990] 1 All ER 835, 849.
32 See *Hubbard* v. *Vosper* [1972] 2 QB 84; *Church of Scientology* v. *Kaufman* [1973] RPC 635 (disclosure of matter threatening the health of members of the public), see Gurry, op. cit., pp. 334–8.
33 [1988] 2 All ER 648. And see *H. (A Healthcare Worker)* v. *Associated Newspapers Ltd and N. (A Health Authority)* [2002] Lloyd's Rep. Med 210 CA.
34 Ibid., p. 653.
35 [1990] 1 All ER 835; applied in *R.* v. *Crozier*, [1991] Crim. L.R. 138, CA.
36 GMC. *Serious Communicable Diseases* (1997).
37 See *R.* v. *Gaud* (unreported); discussed in M. Mulholland, 'Public nuisance – a new use for an old tool? (1995) *Professional Negligence* 70; M. Brazier and J. Harris,' Public Health and Private Lives' (1996) 4 Med. Law Rev. 171.
38 Similar arguments prevail where other forms of disease may impair the doctor's judgement. If a doctor has reason to believe that a patient, who is also a health-worker, is so mentally disturbed that he poses a threat to his own patients, once again the appropriate authority should be alerted to the risk.
39 Law Commission Report No. 110 (Cmnd 8388), paras. 6–94 to 6–96.
40 [2002] Lloyd's Rep. Med 210, Ca
41 Fully and eloquently discussed in Mason and McCall Smith op.cit., Chapter 7. And see Nuffield Council on Bioethics, *Genetic Screening: The Ethical Issues*, London, 1993; G. T. Laurie, *Genetic Privacy: A Challenge to Medico-Legal Norms,* 2002.
42 *Carmarthenshire CC* v. *Lewis* [1955] AC 549.
43 *Tarasoff* v. *Regents of University of California* [1976] 551 P 2d 334.
44 See *Smith* v. *Littlewoods Organisation Ltd* [1987] 1 All ER 710, HL. Nor is there in English law, unlike Continental civil law, a 'duty to rescue': See A. McCall Smith, 'The Duty to Rescue and the Common Law', in M. Menlowe and A. McCall Smith, *The Duty to Rescue,* Dartmouth Press, 1993. And note the restrictive approach of many American courts to *Tarasoff*; see de Haan, 'My Patient's Keeper' (1986) 2 *Professional Negligence* 86.
45 *Peabody Donation Fund* v. *Parkinson* [1984] 3 All ER 86, HL.
46 Law Commission Report No. 110.
47 See J. V McHale, *Medical Confidentiality and Legal Privilege*, Routledge, 1993.
48 [1977] 1 All ER 589.
49 1993 SLT 36.
50 *Hunter* v. *Mann* [1974] 1 QB 767.
51 Police and Criminal Evidence Act 1984, ss. 8–14 and Sched. 1.
52 The National Health Service (Veneral Diseases) Regulations 1974 make provision for the tracing of sexual contacts but also seek to ensure that the identity of patients and contacts remains confidential.

53 The Public Health (Infectious Diseases) Regulation, 1985.
54 But powers must be used with proper regard for the patient's right to privacy under Article 8 of the Human Rights Convention; see *A Health Authority v. X.* [2001] Lloyds Rep.Med 349.
55 See Health Service (Control of Patient Information) Regulations SI 2002/no. 1438.
56 See I. Kennedy & A. Grubb *Medical Law* (3rd ed), Butterworths, 2000, pp. 1021–46.
57 s.. 68 (2).
58 s. 69.
59 The Act does include osteopaths and chiropractors. The definition would appear to cover all health professionals subject to statutory regulation.
60 s. 10.
61 s. 13.
62 See generally on the implications of record keeping for medical confidentiality, *Report on the review of patient-identifiable information (The Caldicott Report*, HMSO, 1997); *The Protection and Use of Patient Information*, Department of Health, 1996
63 See also the Access to Medical Reports Act 1988 granting access to reports supplied to employers and insurers.
64 *R.* v. *Mid-Glamorgan Family Health Services ex p. Martin* [1995] 1WLR 110.
65 See s. 30 (1).
66 Data Protection (Subject Access Modification) (Health) Order 2000 (S1 2000 No. 413) Article 5 (1).
67 s. 7.
68 GMC, *Confidentiality: Protecting and Providing Information*, 2000, paras 4–6.
69 *Pearce* v. *United Bristol Healthcare NHS Trust* [1991] PLQR. 53.
70 s. 3 (1) (f).
71 See GMC op. cit. above.
72 [2000] 1 All ER 786, CA.
73 See Pheby, 'Changing Practice on Confidentiality: A Cause for Concern' (1982) 8 J.Med. Ethics 12.
74 *The Protection and Use of Patients Information*, Department of Health, (1996)
75 *Z.* v. *Finland* (1997) 25 EHRR 371.
76 *MS* v. *Sweden* (1997) 45 BMLR 133.
77 [2001] 2 All ER 289, CA. In *Secretary of State for the Home Department* v. *Wainwright, The Times*, January 4, 2002, the Court of Appeal held that at common law there was no tort of invasion of privacy.
78 At 320; and see per Keene LJ at p. 330.
79 [2001] 1 All ER 908.
80 At p. 933.
81 See also *Hellewell* v. *Chief Constable of Derbyshire* [1995] 4 All ER 473; *R.* v. *Chief Constable of North Wales Police ex p. AB* [1997] 4 All ER 691, CA.

82 See *Campbell* v. *MGN Ltd* [2003] 1 All ER 224, CA; *A.* v. *B. (A Company)* [2002] 2 All ER 545, CA.
83 See *Venables* v. *News Group Newspapers Ltd* above at pp. 918–19.
84 See *Inside Information: Balancing Interests in the Use of Personal Genetics Data* (HGC, 2002).

4 Agreeing to Treatment

1 *Allan* v. *New Mount Sinai Hospital* [1980] 109 DLR (3d) 536.
2 *Devi* v. *West Midlands* AHA [1980] 7 CL 44.
3 *Bartley* v. *Studd* (1995) 2 *Medical Law Monitor* July 15 1997 (the surgeon was disciplined by the GMC)
4 *Freeman* v. *Home Office* [1984] 2 WLR 130.
5 See for example the judgment of Lord Alverstone in *Leigh* v. *Gladstone* [1909] 26 TLR 139 authorizing forcible feeding of a suffragette prisoner.
6 [1992] 4 All E.R. 645, CA. And note the endorsement of autonomy in *Airedale NHS Trust* v. *Bland* [1993] 1 All ER 825, HL.
7 At p. 652–3.
8 At p. 663.
9 On undue influence see *Mrs U.* v. *Centre for Reproductive Medicine* [2002] Lloyd's Rep. Med. 259 CA
10 See *Secretary of State for the Home Department* v. *Robb* [1995] 1 All ER (forcible feeding of a mentally competent prisoner is unlawful); *Re C. (Adult: Refusal of Medical Treatment)* [1994] 1 All ER (patient entitled to order prohibiting amputation of leg even if leg became gangrenous).
11 [2002] 2 All ER 449.
12 At 653.
13 [1992] 4 All ER 671.
14 *Rochdale Healthcare (NHS) Trust* v. *C.* [1997] 1 FCR 274.
15 *Re MB (Caesarian Section)* [1997] 8 Med LR 217, C.A; *St George's Healthcare NHS Trust* v. *S.* [1998] 3 All ER 673.
16 *St George's Healthcare NHS Trust* v. *S.* (above) at p. 692.
17 *O'Brien* v. *Cunard SS Co.* (Mass. 1891) 28 NC266.
18 Special forms are provided, for example, to cover surgery where there are doubts about the patient's mental capacity or in relation to sensitive procedures such as sterilization.
19 See *Chatterton* v. *Gerson* [1981] 1 All ER 257.
20 [1981] 1 All ER 257. The nature and purpose test for battery is cogently criticized by Tan Ken Feng, 'Failure of Medical Advice: Trespass or Negligence' [1987], *Legal Studies* 149.
21 See *Potts* v. *NWRHA*, the *Guardian*, 23 July 1983. This case is further discussed in Chapter 11.
22 *Appleton* v. *Garrett* [1996] PLQR P1. Contrast with *R.* v. *Richardson (Diana)*,

(1998) 43 BMLR 21 CA (dentist acquitted of criminal assault even though she failed to inform her patients that she had been struck off the dental register).

23 *R.* v. *Tabassum* [2000] Lloyd's Rep. Med 404 CA.

24 *Hills* v. *Potter (note)* [1984] 1 WLR 641, 653.

25 [1984] 1 All ER 1081, 1018 at 1026 and *Freeman* v. *Home Office* [1984] 1 All ER 1036.

26 *Sidaway* v. *Board of Governors of the Bethlem Royal and the Maudsley Hospital* [1985] 1 All ER 643.

27 *Reibl* v. *Hughes* [1980] 114 DLR (3d) 1.

28 Though note that in *R* v. *Richardson (Diana)*, above at note 22, the Court of Appeal rejected such a proposition

29 Discussed elegantly in J. Keown, 'The Ashes of AIDS and the Phoenix of Informed Consent' [1989] 52 MLR 790.

30 *R.* v. *Clarence* [1888] 22 QBD 23.

31 *R.* v. *Richardson (Diana)* [1998] 43 BMLR 21, CA; and see generally Kennedy and Grubb op. cit. at pp. 658–72.

32 [1957] 2 All ER 118

33 *Hatcher* v. *Black, The Times*, 2 July 1954, and see *O'Malley-Williams* v. *Board of Governors of the National Hospital for Nervous Diseases* [1975] BMJ 635

34 (1972) 464 F. 2D 772, 780.

35 *Reibl* v. *Hughes* (above).

36 [1993] 4 Med L.R. 79: discussed in D. Chalmers and R. Schwartz, 'A Fair Dinkum Duty of Disclosure' (1993) 1 Med. Law Rev. 189.

37 *Sidaway* v. *Board of Governors of the Bethlem Royal and the Maudsley Hospital* [1985] 1 All ER 643; In the High Court Mrs Sidaway also sued for battery. Both claims were dismissed and she appealed on the issue of negligence alone.

38 ibid., at p. 663.

39 ibid at p. 663.

40 ibid at p. 654.

41 ibid at p. 654.

42 *The Times*, 24 May 1985.

43 *Blyth* v. *Bloomsbury HA* [1993] 4 Med LR 151 CA.

44 [1987] 3 WLR 649, CA.

45 See generally the case-law on failed sterilization in Chapter 11.

46 *The Times*, 17 June 1986.

47 [1987] 2 All ER 884.

48 And see *Moyes* v. *Lothian Health Board* [1990] 1 Med L R 471 where Lord Caplan could see nothing in *Sidaway* to suggest that the extent and quality of warning to be given by a doctor to his patient should not in the last resort be governed by medical criteria.

49 At p. 657.

50 *Seeking Patients' Consent: The Ethical Considerations*, GMC, 1999.

51 [1994] 5 Med. L.R. 334; and see *McAllister* v. *Lewisham and North Southwark*

Health Authority [1994] 5 Med. L.R. 343; *Newall and Newall* v. *Goldenberg* [1995] 6 Med. L.R. 371; *Williamson* v. *East London & City Health Authority* [1997] 41 BMLR 85; *Lybert* v. *Warrington Health Authority* [1996] 7 Med. L.R. 71, CA; *Chester* v. *Afshar* [2002] 3 All ER 552, CA.

52 [1998] A.C. 232

53 At p. 243.

54 See M. Brazier and J. Miola, 'Bye-Bye Bolam: A Medical Litigation Revolution?' (2000), 8 Med. L. Rev 85 at pp. 107–10.

55 [1998] 48 BMLR 118, CA.

56 [2002] 3 All ER 552 CA; and see *Chappel* v. *Hart* [1999] Lloyd's Rep. Med 223 (Australia).

57 It has been argued that informed consent claims are the thin end of the wedge, opening the door for no fault liability see A. Meisel, 'The Expansion of Liability for Medical Accidents: From Negligence to Strict Liability by Way of Informed Consent' (1977) 56 Neb. L. Rev. 51.

58 At pp. 658–9 See M. Brazier 'Patient Autonomy and Consent to Treatment: The Role of the Law? [1987] 7 *Legal Studies* 169.

59 See in particular *Making Health Care Decisions*, President's Commission for the study of Ethical Problems in Medicine, US Govt Printing Office, 1982, and '*What Are My Chances Doctor?*': *A Review of Clinical Risks*, Office of Health Economics, 1986.

60 Alas, such a proposition was rejected by both the Court of Appeal, and the Law Lords in *Sidaway*. See M. Brazier, op. cit., pp. 189–91.

61 See A. Grubb, 'The Doctor as Fiduciary' (1994) *Current Legal Problems* 112; P. Bartlett, 'Doctors as Fiduciaries' (1997) 5 Med. L. Rev. 193; M. Brazier and M. Lobjoit, 'Fiduciary Relationship: An Ethical Approach and a Legal Concept', in R. Bennett and C. Erin (eds), *HIV and AIDS Testing, Screening and Confidentiality*, OUP, 1999, p. 170.

62 See H. Teff, 'Consent to Medical Procedures, Paternalism, Self-Determination or Therapeutic Alliance' (1985) 101 LQR 432.

63 *Sidaway* v. *Royal Bethlem Hospital at* pp. 650–51; *R.* v. *Mid-Glamorgan FHSA ex p. Martin* [1995] 1 All ER 356, CA.

64 See *R.* v. *Tabassum* [2000] Lloyds Rep. Med 404 CA (above at Note 23). But what if the doctor is qualified, but has been erased from the register? See *R.* v. *Richardson (Diana)* on p. 101.

65 *Government Response to the Bristol Inquiry*.

66 *F.* v. *West Berkshire Health Authority* [1989] 2 All ER 545 HL.

67 Ibid at p. 566.

68 Ibid at p. 567.

69 (1988) 63 OR (2d) 243 (Ontario High Court).

70 Discussed in (1990) 5 *Professional Negligence* 118.

71 [1992] 4 All ER 649, CA.

5 Competence, Consent and Compulsion

1 Law Commission Report No. 231 *Mental Incapacity*, HMSO, 1995, extensively reviewed in a dedicated edition of the *Medical Law Review*; see (1994) 2 Med L Rev. pp. 1–91.

2 Predominantly proposals relating to medical research (see p. 409) and withdrawal of artificial nutrition and hydration (see p. 449).

3 *Who Decides? Making Decisions on Behalf of Mentally Incapacitated Adults* (Cmd 1803, 1997).

4 *Making Decisions:* (Cmd 4465, 1999).

5 *F. v. West Berkshire Health Authority* [1989] 2 All ER 545 HL.

6 Section 34 provided that the guardian enjoyed all the powers of the parent of a child under fourteen.

7 See B.M. Hoggett, *Mental Health Law*, (4th edn), Sweet & Maxwell, 1996, p. 218. And see G. Richardson, 'Autonomy, Guardianship and Mental Disorder: One Problem, Two Solutions' (2002) 65 MLR 702.

8 Part VII; see sections 92–6.

9 *F. v. West Berkshire HA* [1989] 2 All ER 545, 554, HL.

10 For a history and evaluation of the *parens patriae* jurisdiction see B.M. Hoggett, 'The Royal Prerogative in Relation to the Mentally Disordered: Resurrection, Resuscitation or Rejection', in M.D.A. Freeman (ed.), *Medicine, Ethics and Law*, Stevens, London, 1988.

11 See *F. v. West Berkshire HA* [1989] 2 All ER 545, 552, HL.

12 *T. v. T.* [1988] 1 All ER 613.

13 *B v. Croydon Health Authority* [1995] 1 All ER 683, CA; *Riverside Mental Health NHS Trust* v. *Fox* [1994] 1 FLR 614.

14 *Tameside and Glossop Acute Services Trust* v. *CH (a patient)* [1996] 1 FLR 762.

15 *Re T.* (14 May 1987, unreported); *Re X. The Times*, 4 June 1987; *T. v. T.* [1988] 1 All ER 613.

16 See *Re B. (A Minor) (Wardship: Sterilization)* [1987] 2 All ER 206, HL, discussed further in Chapters 15 and 17.

17 *T. v. T.* [1988] 1 All ER 613, at p. 625.

18 [1989] 2 All ER 545, HL.

19 p. 551.

20 [1989] 1 All ER 764, CA.

21 Lord Griffiths dissented. He argued that a grave decision such as sterilization with all its implications should not be left to doctors alone. He believed that it was open to the House of Lords to develop a common law rule that prior judicial approval was required before an operation as radical as sterilization could be performed (pp.561–2).

22 See J. Bridgman, 'Declared Innocent?' (1995) 3 Med L Rev. 117.

23 See *Bolam* v. *Friern Hospital Management Committee* [1957] 1 WLR 582 discussed fully in Chapter 6.

24 See M.A. Jones, 'Justifying Medical Treatment without Consent' (1989) 5
    Professional Negligence 178.
25 p. 567.
26 At 3.27.
27 See in *Re A. (Medical Treatment: Male Sterilization)* [2000] 1 FCR 193 CA.
28 At p. 200.
29 [2000] 3 WLR 1288. And see *Re SS (Medical Treatment: Late Termination)*
    [2002] 1FLR 445.
30 At p. 1299.
31 See *Re GF* [1993] 4 Med L.R. 77.
32 *In Re S. (Adult Patient: Sterilization)* [2000] 3 WLR 1288 at 1303; and see *Re
    Z. (Medical Treatment: Hysterectomy)* [2000] 1 FCR 274.
33 [1998] 3 All ER 299, HL.
34 See P. Fennell, 'Doctor Knows Best? Therapeutic Detention Under Common
    Law, the Mental Health Act and the European Convention' (1998) 6 Med L.
    Rev. 322.
35 See *St George's Healthcare NHS Trust* v. *S.* [1998] 3 All ER 673.
36 [1998] 3 All ER 613.
37 [1994] 1 All ER 819.
38 [1954] p. 112.
39 See Note 37 (above). And see *R.* v. *Collins and Ashworth Hospital Authority
    ex. p. Brady* [2000] Lloyds Rep. Med 355.
40 [1997] 8 Med L. Rev 217, CA.
41 Law Commission Report No. 231, *Mental Incapacity*, at 3.3.
42 A point graphically illustrated in *B.* v. *An NHS* Trust [2002] 2 All ER 449.
43 A number of cases authorizing the forcible treatment of anorectic patients
    also illustrate the problems of establishing ability to make a decision: see
    Re W. (Minor) (Medical Treatment) [1992] 4 All ER 627 at 637; *Riverside
    Mental Health NHS Trust* v. *Fox* [1994] 1 FLR 614; *B.* v. *Croydon Health
    Authority* [1995] 1 All ER 683 CA.
44 In *Re MB* itself and in *St George's Healthcare NHS Trust* v. *S.* [1998] 3 All
    ER 673 CA.
45 [2002] 2 All ER 449.
46 See K. Keywood, S. Fovargue and M. Flynn, *Best Practice? Health Care
    Decision-Making, By With and For Adults with Learning Disabilities*, NDT,
    1999.
47 See Mason and McCall Smith op. cit. Chapters 21 and 22; B. M. Hoggett,
    Mental Health Law (4th edn), Sweet & Maxwell, 1996; P. Fennell, *Treatment
    Without Consent*, Routledge, 1996.
48 Cm 5538–1 (accessible at www.doh.uk/mental health/draftbilljune02.pdf)
49 See s. 2. An emergency application founded on the recommendation of a
    medical practitioner may be made under s. 4 and authorizes detention for
    up to seventy-two hours.

50 A successful application for admission for treatment authorizes detention for an initial period of six months.

51 Even though the Court of Appeal has developed a fairly broad definition of treatment to include group therapy and nursing care in a structured environment; see *R. v. Canon Park Mental Review Tribunal ex p. A.* [1994] 2 All ER 659, CA; *R. v. Mental Health Review Tribunal ex p. Macdonald*, 1998, Crown Office Digest 205.

52 *R. v. Hallstrom ex p.W. (No.2)* [1986] QB 824.

53 [1995] 1 All ER 683 CA. And see *R. v. Collins and Ashworth Hospital Authority ex p. Brady* [2000] Lloyds Rep. Med 355.

54 See K. Keywood, 'B. v. Croydon Health Authority: Force-Feeding the Hunger Striker under the Mental Health Act 1983' [1995] 3 Web JCL1.

55 [1996] 1 FCR 753.

56 See s. 57(1).

57 See s. 57(2); and the Mental Health (Hospital Guardianship and Consent in Treatment) Regulations 1983 (SI 1983 No. 893) reg. 16(2). S 57(2) empowers the Secretary of State to bring other treatments within the ambit of s. 57(2).

58 See generally *R. (Wilkinson) v. RMO Broadmoor Hospital Authority* [2002] 1 WLR 419.

59 See s. 58(1) and SI 1983 No. 893 reg. 16(2). Again the Secretary of State is empowered to bring further treatments within the ambit of s. 58(1).

60 See s. 58(2).

61 See above at note 48 and see *Report of the Expert Committee, Review of the Mental Health Act 1983* (Department of Health 1999); *Reform of the Mental Health Act 1983 Proposals for Consultation* (HMSO 1999) Cm 4480; discussed in J. Laing, 'Rights versus Risks: Reform of the Mental Health Act 1983', 2000 8 Med L. Rev. 210.

62 See Law Commission Report No.231 *Mental Capacity* 3.1 to 3.23.

63 See *Re AK (Medical Treatment: Consent)* [2001] 2 FCR 35.

64 See Law Com. No. 231 Part IV.

65 See *In Re Quinlan* (1976) 355 A. 2d 647.

66 See Law Com. No 231 Part V.

67 See *Making Decisions* (Cm 4465) CLCD 1999 paras 12–20

68 See Law Com. No 231, 3.24–3.37.

69 See *Making Decisions* 1.12. The government proposes adding two further factors to the 'best interests' checklist (1) whether there is a reasonable expectation of the person recovering capacity to make the decision in the reasonably foreseeable future (2) the need to ensure that the wishes of the person without capacity were not the result of undue influence.

70 See Law Com. No.231, Part VI.

71 *Making Decisions* op.cit. para 12.

72 See A. Grubb, 'Treatment Decisions, Keeping it in the Family', in A. Grubb (ed.), *Choices and Decisions in Health Care*, Wiley, 1993.

73 See Law Com No. 231 Part VIII; Making Decisions 3.2–3.34.

74 A number of decisions will be outside the manager's powers.

75 Under the Enduring Powers of Attorney Act 1985.

76 See Law Com No. 231 Part VII.

77 See Law Com No. 231 Part VIII.

78 See *Making Decisions: Helping People Who Have Difficulties Deciding for Themselves*, April 2002.

79 For discussion of compulsory sterilization laws in the USA see M.D.A. Freeman, 'Sterilizing the Mentally Handicapped', in *Medicine, Ethics and Law*, Stevens, London, 1988.

80 See ss. 10, 11, 16.

81 See s. 38.

82 See s. 35.

83 See S. H. Bronitt, 'Spreading Disease and the Criminal Law', [1994] Crim L.R 21; K.M. Smith, 'Sexual Etiquette, Public Interest and the Criminal Law' (1991) 42 NILQ 309.

84 *R.* v. *Clarence* [1888] 22 QBD 23; *Hegarty* v. *Shine* (1878) 14 Cox CC 124. But note prosecution for causing grievous bodily harm of a doctor who allegedly infected his lover with herpes; see *The Times*, 12 January, 2002.

85 *R.* v. *Gaud* (unreported); analysed in M. Mulholland, 'Public nuisance – a new use for an old tool' (1995) *Professional Negligence* 70.

86 Draft Offences Against the Person Bill.

87 See M. Brazier and J. Harris, 'Public Health and Private Lives' (1996) 4 Med L. Rev. 171.

88 Unreported 23 February 2001; discussed in J. Chalmers, 'The Criminalization of HIV Transmission (2002) 28 *Journal of Medical Ethics* 160.

89 Section 47 of that Act (as amended the National Assistance (Amendment) Act 1951) empowers community health physicians to remove from their homes and place in a suitable hospital a person 'suffering from chronic disease or being aged, infirm or physically incapacitated' and unable to care for themselves. The CHP may apply to a magistrates' court for an order removing such a person to hospital either in his own interests or to 'prevent injury to the health of, or serious nuisances to, other persons'. Section 47 is highly controversial and many geriatricians refused to invoke such powers. The Law Commission proposals recommended repeal of s. 47.

90 See P. Lewis, 'Procedures that are Against the Interests of Incompetent Adults' (2002) 22 OJLS 575.

6 Clinical Negligence

1 See generally V. Harpwood, *Negligence and Healthcare: Clinical Claims and Risk*, Informa, 2001.

2 *Barnett* v. *Chelsea and Kensington HMC* [1969] 1 QB 428.

3 Though note the standard of care that she must attain in such a case will take account of the conditions in which she volunteers to offer treatment.

4 *Barnett* v. *Chelsea and Kensington HMC* (above).

5 [2000] 2 All ER 74, CA.

6 See, for example, *Capital & Counties plc* v. *Hampshire County Council* [1997] QB 1004 CA.

7 See *R.* v. *Central Birmingham HA ex p. Collier*, *The Times*, 6 January 1988, CA, above, p. 30.

8 For a thorough survey of problems *re* duties to patients see I. Kennedy and A. Grubb, *Medical Law: Text and Materials*, Butterworths, 2000, pp. 277–369

9 See generally Harpwood op. cit. at pp. 14–17, 23–7.

10 [2001] 57 BMLR 158; *Walters* v. *North Glamorgan NHS Trust* [2002] Lloyd's Rep Med 227

11 On which see *Alcock* v. *Chief Constable of South Yorkshire* [1991] 4 All ER 907, HL.

12 See *Sion* v. *Hampstead Health Authority* (1994) 5 Med. L.R. 170, CA. And see P. Casen, 'Curiouser and Curiouser: Psychiatric Damage Caused by Negligent Misinformation' (2002) 18 *Professional Negligence* 248

13 See Harpwood op. cit. at pp. 18–21 and see D.M. Kloss 'Pre-employment Health Screening' in *Law and Medicine: Current Legal Issues* Vol. 3 (M. Freeman and A. Lewis eds), OUP, 2000.

14 *Baker* v. *Kaye* [1996] 39 BMLR 12.

15 *Kapfunde* v. *Abbey National plc* [1998] 46 BMLR 176 CA.

16 *Phillips* v. *William Whiteley Ltd* [1938] 1 All ER 566.

17 [1957] 1 WLR 582, 586, 188.

18 *Maynard* v. *West Midlands RHA* [1984] 1 WLR 634, 638.

19 *Nettleship* v. *Weston* [1971] 2 QB 691, CA.

20 [1986] 3 All ER 801, CA.

21 [1988] 1 All ER 891; see, p. 163.

22 See *Jones* v. *Manchester Corporation* [1952] 2 QB 852, 871. Note that in *Wilsher* (p. 145), Dr Wyeth, the house officer, was found not negligent.

23 *Bolam* v. *Friern HMC* [1957] 1 WLR 582, 587–8.

24 See, for example, *Edward Wong Finance Co. Ltd* v. *Johnson, Stokes & Master* [1984] A.C. 296, PC.

25 See the account of the first instance decision in *Bolitho* v. *City & Hackney Health Authority* [1998] AC 232 HL.

26 Graphically illustrated in *Whitehouse* v. *Jordan* [1981] 1 All ER 246, HL.

27 [1984] 1 WLR 634 HL.

28 At p. 639.

29 [1993] 4 Med. L.R. 281, CA.

30 M.A. Jones 'The *Bolam* Test and the Responsible Expert' (1999) Tort Law Review 226.

31 *Sidaway* v. *Royal Bethlem Hospital* [1984] 2 WLR 778, 752, CA. And see Lord

Bridge [1985] 1 All ER 643, 663 IIL.

32 Reported [1993] 4 Med LR 393 CA.

33 [1998] AC 232 HL.

34 At p. 242.

35 As Andrew Grubb so nicely put it '"Eureka!" The courts have got it at last. Expert evidence, whether of professional practice or otherwise is not conclusive in a medical negligence case that the defendant has not been careless!' A. Grubb, 'Negligence, Causation and Bolam' (1998) 6 Med L.Rev. 378, 380.

36 See N. Glover, 'Bolam in the House of Lords' (1999) 15 PN 42.

37 At p. 226.

38 See M. Brazier and J. Miola, 'Bye-Bye Bolam: A Medical Litigation Revolution' (2000) 8 Med. L. Rev. 85.

39 [1999] Lloyd's Rep. Med 23

40 see, for example, *Penney* v. *East Kent* AHA [2000] Lloyds Rep. Med.41; *Reynolds* v. *North Tyneside Health Authority* [2002] Lloyd's Rep Med 453.

41 Lord Irvine of Lairg, 'The Patient, the Doctor, their Lawyers and the Judge: Rights and Duties' (1999) 7 Med.L.Rev 255.

42 See Lord Woolf, 'Are the Courts Excessively Deferential to the Medical Profession?' (2001) 9 Med.L Rev. 1.

43 A Maclean, 'Beyond Bolam and Bolitho' (2001) 5 *Medical Law International* 205.

44 [1998] Lloyd's Rep Med 223 CA.

45 Brazier and Miola op.cit. at p. 106.

46 *Hunter* v. *Hanley* [1955] SC 200.

47 *Bolam* v. *Friern HMC* [1957] 1 WLR 582, 587.

48 See *Gascoine* v. *Ian Sheridan & Co* [1994] 5 Med. L.Rev. 437.

49 *Crawford* v. *Board of Governors of Charing Cross Hospital, The Times*, 8 December 1953, CA

50 *Whiteford* v. *Hunter* (1950) 94 Sol. J. 758. HL.

51 *Roe* v. *Ministry of Health* [1954] 2 KB 66, p. 84.

52 See V. Harpwood, 'NHS Reform. Audit Protocols and the Standard of Care in Medical Negligence' (1994) 1 *Medical Law International* 1; V. Harpwood, 'The Manipulation of Medical Practice in Law and Medicine'; H. Teff, 'Clinical Guidelines, Negligence and Medical Practice' both in M. Freeman and A. Lewis (eds), *Law and Medicine: Current Legal Issues*, Vol. 3, OUP, 2000.

53 See ss. 18–25.

54 See J. Warden, 'NICE to Sort our Clinical Wheat from Chaff' (1999) 318 BMJ 416.

55 See Brazier and Miola op. cit. at Note 38.

56 *Hunter* v. *Hanley* 1955 SLT 213, 217.

57 *Newton* v. *Newton's New Model Laundry, The Times*, 3 November 1959.

58 For details of a number of unreported recent cases see Harpwood op. cit. at pp. 98–102.

59   *Wood* v. *Thurston, The Times*, 25 May 1951.

60   *Langley* v. *Campbell, The Times*, 6 November 1975; and see *Tuffil* v. *East Surrey Area HA, The Times*, 15 March 1978, p. 4. (Failure to diagnose amoebic dysentery in a patient who had spent many years in the tropics.)

61   Annual Report of the MDU, 1990, pp. 26–7.

62   *Serre* v. *De Filly* (1975) OR (2d) 490; and see Annual Report of the MDU, 1982, pp. 22–3; and 1983, p. 24.

63   See Harpwood op. cit.

64   *Maynard* v. *West Midlands RHA* [1984] 1 WLR 634.

65   Annual Report of the MDU, 1982, p. 24.

66   *Chin Keow* v. *Govt of Malaysia* [1967] 1 WLR 813.

67   *Hucks* v. *Cole* (1968) [1993] 4 Med. LR 395, CA.

68   Annual Report of the MDU 1984, p. 18.

69   *Dwyer* v. *Roderick* (1983) 127 SJ 806, and see J. Finch, 'A Costly Oversight for Pharmacists' (1982) 132 NLJ 176.

70   [1989] 1 Med L.Rev. 36.

71   Annual Report of the MDU, 1989, p. 32.

72   See Annual Report of the MDU, 1988, pp. 28–9, 1989, pp. 20–21.

73   e.g. *Taylor* v. *Worcester and District Health Authority* (1997) 2 Med. L.Rev. 215.

74   Annual Report of the MDU, 1984, pp. 34–5.

75   *Collins* v. *Hertfordshire Corporation* [1952] 2 QB 852.

76   *Jones* v. *Manchester Corporation* [1952] 2 QB 852.

77   [1954] 2 QB 66, CA.

78   *Ashcroft* v. *Mersey AHA* [1983] 2 All ER 245, 247.

79   *Urry* v. *Biere, The Times*, 19 July 1955.

80   *Corder* v. *Banks, The Times*, 9 April 1960.

81   *Wilsher* v. *Essex AHA* [1986] 3 All ER 801, CA.

82   See *Cassidy* v. *Ministry of Health* [1951] 2 KB 14; and see Chapter 7.

83   [1986] 2 All ER 801, pp 833–4.

84   *Knight* v. *Home Office* [1990] 3 All ER 237. But such an argument was firmly rejected in *Brooks* v. *Home Office* [1999] 48 BMLR 109.

85   *Johnstone* v. *Bloomsbury HA* [1991] 2 All ER 293.

86   See, for example, *Nickolls* v. *Ministry of Health, The Times*, 4 February 1955 (surgeon working on while fatally ill).

87   See *Marriott* v. *West Midlands Area Health Authority* above, at note 39.

88   *Chin Keow* v. *Government of Malaysia* [1967] 1 WLR 813.

89   *Coles* v. *Reading and District HMC, The Times*, 30 January 1963.

90   *Dwyer* v. *Roderick* (1983) 127 SJ 806. Recounted in 'A Costly Oversight for Pharmacists' (1982) 132 NLJ 176.

91   [1990] 1 Med. L.Rev. 36.

92   See National Health Service Act 1977; National Health Service (General Medical Services) Regulations 1992 (SI 1992 No. 635) (as amended); National

Health Service (Primary Care) Act 1997. The complex statutory rules governing GP services are fully discussed in Kennedy and Grubb *Medical Law* (3rd
edn), Butterworths, 2000, pp. 60–88.

93 National Health Service (General Medical Services) Regulations para 4.
94 ibid., para. 4(h). Note limited exceptions to this obligation in current
Regulations.
95 *Barnes* v. *Crabtree, The Times*, 1 and 2 November 1955.
96 P.C. Nathan and A.R. Barrowclough, *Medical Negligence*, Butterworths,
London, 1957, p. 38.
97 *Edler* v. *Greenwich and Deptford HMC*, The Times, 7 March 1953.
98 *Kavanagh* v. *Abrahamson* [1964] 108 Sol. J. 320.
99 Because of the doctrine of vicarious liability; see Chapter 7. As to liability where
a deputizing service is used see Kennedy and Grubb op. cit. at pp. 66–8.
100 [2002] Lloyd's Rep Med 361.
101 [1987] 2 All ER 417. And see *Loveday* v. *Renton* [1990] 1 Med L.Rev. 117.
102 ibid., p. 421.
103 [1988] 1 All ER 871, HL.
104 See *per* Lord Bridge, pp. 882–3.
105 [2002] Lloyd's Rep Med 361
106 At p. 386.
107 [1998] AC 232, HL; see M. A. Jones, 'The Bolam Test and the Responsible
Expert' (1999) Tort Law Review 226; A. Grubb, 'Negligence Causation and
Bolam' (1998) 5 Med. L. Rev. 378.
108 At p. 240.
109 [1987] 2 All ER 909, HL. See T. Hill, 'A Lost Chance for Compensation in
the Tort of Negligence in the House of Lords' (1991) 54 MLR 111.
110 [1985] 3 All ER 167.
111 [1987] 2 All ER 909, HL.
112 See *Pearman* v. *North Essex Health Authority* [2000] Lloyd's Rep. Med 174.
113 See *Smith* v. *National Health Service Litigation Authority* [2001] Lloyd's Rep.
Med 90.
114 For an example of a successful claim of this type, see *Sutton* v. *Population
Services Family Planning Ltd, The Times*, 7 November 1981. And see *Falcon*
v. *Memorial Hospital* [1996] 462 NW 2d 44 (Michigan), *Herskovits* v. *Group
Health Co-operative of Paget Sound* 604 2d 474 (Washington).
115 [2003] Lloyd's Rep. Med 105.
116 Unfair Contract Terms Act 1977, s. 2.
117 *Eyre* v. *Measday* [1986] 1 All ER 488; *Thake* v. *Maurice* [1986] 1 All ER 497,
CA. And see Kennedy and Grubb, *Medical Law*, op. cit. at pp 273–6.
118 [1925] 41 TLR 557.
119 [1993] 4 All ER 935, CA.
120 The third appeal, *R* v. *Holloway*, involved an electrician whose faulty wiring
caused a death.

121 *R* v. *Adomako* [1995] 1 AC 171, HL.

122 At p. 188.

123 See A. McCall Smith, 'Criminal Negligence and the Incompetent Doctor' (1993) 1 Med. L. Rev 336.

124 See generally A. Merry and A.McCall Smith, *Errors, Medicine and the Law*, 2001, CUP.

7 Malpractice Litigation

1 And see Montgomery, op. cit., Chapter 8.

2 C. Ham, R. Dingwall, P. Fenn and D. Harris, *Medical Negligence, Compensation and Accountability*, King's Fund Institute/Centre for Socio-Legal Studies, Oxford, 1988.

3 See Hansard 24 March 1998, cols 165–6.

4 National Audit Office, *Handling Clinical Negligence Claims in England*, 2001.

5 17 per cent of claims overall succeeded in 1996–7 (see Note 3).

6 See *The Guardian* 30 April 1998.

7 *Bolam* v. *Friern HMC* [1957] 1 WLR 582.

8 [1998] AC 232 HL.

9 But see J. Harris, 'The Injustice of Compensation for Victims of Medical Accidents' (1997) 314 *BMJ* 182.

10 See M.A. Jones and A.E. Morris, 'Defensive Medicine: Myths and Facts' (1989) 5 *Journal of the Medical Defence Union* 40.

11 See Ham et al. op.cit., pp. 14–15, and note in particular Fig.6.

12 Caesarean Section: the National Sentinel Audit Report (RCOG, 2001) (www.rcog.org.uk).

13 HL Official Report, 10 November 1987, cols. 1350–51.

14 See generally P. Danzon, *Medical Malpractice*, Harvard University Press, Cambridge, Mass, 1985.

15 Hence Ian Kennedy argues eloquently that what is required to defuse any 'crisis' is better information about the law for doctors so that they will not feel constrained to practise 'defensive medicine' see 'Review of the Year 2. Confidentiality, Competence and Malpractice', in P. Byrne (ed.), *Medicine in Contemporary Society*, King's Fund, London, 1987.

16 See generally Ham et al, op.cit., pp. 19–20. And note too suggestions that any US malpractice crisis is at least in part a creation of the medical insurers seeking to protect their profits. See N. Terry, 'The Malpractice Crisis in the United States: A Dispatch from the Trenches' (1986) 2 *Professional Negligence* 145.

17 See now s. 27 Access to Justice Act 1999.

18 *Heil* v. *Rankin* [2000] 2 WLR 1173.

19 Law Commission Report No. 247 *Aggravated, Exemplary and Restitutionary Damages* (1997).

20 See generally V. Harpwood, *Negligence in Healthcare: Clinical Claims and Risk*, Informa, 2001, pp. 215–20.

21 The Act also replaces the Legal Aid Board with the Legal Service Commission and established a Community Legal Service.

22 Access to Justice Act s. 7.

23 See National Audit Office *Handling Clinical Negligence Claims* (above at Note 4).

24 op. cit. at p. 218.

25 See s. 27 of Access to Justice Act 1999.

26 Although the currently maximum uplift of normal fees allowed as a success fee is 25 per cent.

27 *Callery* v. *Gray, The Times*, 24 October 2001, CA.

28 HC (89) 34 'Claims of Medical Negligence Against NHS Hospitals and Community Doctors and Dentists'; as amended by HGG (96) 48; see M. Brazier, 'NHS in Indemnity: The Implications for Medical Litigation', (1990), 6 *Professional Negligence* 88.

29 See s. 21 NHS and Community Care Act 1990.

30 Established as a Special Health Authority under s. 21(3) National Health Service and Community Care Act 1990.

31 For the first three years of its life the CNST was administered by the Medical Protection Society. The NHSLA also runs the Existing Liabilities Scheme dealing with claims prior to April 1999; see Harpwood at pp. 222–3.

32 Membership of a defence organization is no longer required of hospital doctors. Most doctors retain membership of such a body to ensure access to individual legal advice.

33 Consider also the problem of agency nurses. They are not employed by the hospital.

34 See *Wilsher* v. *Essex AHA* in Chapter 6, p. 197; *Bull* v. *Devon Area Health Authority* [1993] 4 Med LR 117, CA.

35 See *Cassidy* v. *Ministry of Health* [1951] 2 KB 343, per Lord Denning at pp. 359–60, and *Roe* v. *Ministry of Health* [1954] 2 QB 66, 82.

36 [1998] Lloyd's Rep. Med 157.

37 At p. 161.

38 Note the Supply of Goods and Service Act 1982, s. 13 (implied term that service will be carried out with care and skill); and Part I of that Act imposing conditions as to goods supplied in the course of a contract for services; see A.P. Bell, 'The Doctor and the Supply of Goods and Service Act 1982' (1984) 4 LS 175.

39 If the deputizing service actually employs the doctor working for it, the service may be sued. This is unlikely; deputies are usually engaged on a 'casual labour only' basis.

40 Harpwood op. cit. pp. 161–73.

41 e.g. did not know for some years that he had been given blood infected by CJD; *N* v. *UK Medical Research Council* [1996] BMLR 83.

42 See, for example, *Smith* v. *Leicestershire Health Authority* [1996] 36 BMLR 23.

43 *Access to Justice: Final Report to the Lord Chancellor on the Civil Justice System in England and Wales*, HMSO, 1996.

44 See generally *Civil Justice Reforms Evaluation Further Findings* (LCD, 2002).

45 Civil Procedure Rules (SI 1998 No.3132); see generally O'Hare and Hill, *Civil Litigation* (10th edn), Sweet and Maxwell, 2001.

46 See M.A. Shaw, 'Pre-action protocol for the resolution of clinical disputes' (1999) *New Law Journal* 252.

47 And see *Civil Procedure Rules*, Rule 31.16.

48 And see *Civil Procedure Rules*, Rule 31.7.

49 *MacIvor* v. *Southern Health and Social Services Board, Northern Ireland* [1978] 2 All ER 625.

50 *Dunning* v. *Liverpool Hospitals' Board of Governors* [1973] 2 All ER 454.

51 *Waugh* v. *BRB* [1980] AC 521; and see Diana M. Kloss (1984) 289 BMJ 66.

52 *Lee* v. *South West Thames RHA* [1985] 2 All ER 385.

53 *Naylor* v. *Preston AHA* [1987] 2 All ER 353.

54 Supreme Court Act 1981, s. 35.

55 *HIV: Haemophiliac Litigation, Guardian*, 28 September 1990, CA.

56 See O'Hare and Hill op. cit. pp. 368–405.

57 *Ashcroft* v. *Mersey AHA* [1983] 2 All ER 245.

58 [1981] 1 All ER 287, HL.

59 [1980] 1 All ER 650, p. 655.

60 Rule 35(3).

61 Rule 35(1).

62 Rule 35(7).

63 See Harpwood op. cit. at p. 234.

64 Ibid at p. 233.

65 See *Street on Torts* (M. Brazier and J. Murphy eds), 10th edn, Butterworths 1999, pp. 258–63.

66 *Mahon* v. *Osborne* [1939] 2 KB 14.

67 *Roe* v. *Ministry of Health* [1954] 2 QB 66.

68 *Cassidy* v. *Ministry of Health* [1951] 2 KB 343.

69 (1985) 82 Law Soc. Gaz. 1491.

70 *Ratcliffe v Plymouth & Torbay HA* [1998] Lloyd's Rep.Med 162, CA.

71 *Roe* v. *Ministry of Health* [1954] 2 QB 66, p. 82.

72 For fuller treatment of this topic see Harpwood op. cit. Chapter 8.

73 This is known as compensation for the 'lost years'; see *Pickett* v. *BRB* [1980] AC 136.

74 Fatal Accidents Act 1976 as amended by the Administration of Justice Act 1982.

75 Inserted by the Administration of Justice Act 1985, s. 6. For the procedure relating to a claim for provisional damages, see RSC Ord. 37 rr. 8–10.

76 Where the patient is completely incapable of managing his own affairs the award may be managed by the Court of Protection.

77 Law Reform (Personal Injuries) Act 1948, s. 2(4).

78 *Geest plc* v. *Monica Lansiquot* [2002] Lloyds Rep Med 482, PC

79 [1986] 1 All ER 332, CA.

80 Law Commission Report No 257 *Damages for Personal Injury: Non-Pecuniary Loss* (1999).

81 [2000] 3 All ER 138.

82 At p. 150.

83 See *Wells* v. *Wells* [1999] 1 AC 345, HL; Damages Act 1996; discussion in Harpwood op. cit. at 178–83.

84 See *Mansell v Dyfed Powis Health Authority*, 13 October, 1998, noted in Harpwood op. cit. at p. 381.

85 Discussed in Harpwood op. cit. at pp. 191–2.

86 See Harpwood op. cit. at pp. 192–4; R. Lewis, *Structured Settlements*, Sweet & Maxwell, 1996.

87 See *B.* v. *Liverpool Heath Authority ex p. Hopley* [2002] Lloyd's Rep. Med 494.

8 Medical Products Liability

1 See generally P.R. Ferguson, *Drug Injuries and the Pursuit of Compensation*, Sweet & Maxwell, 1996; J. Stapleton, *Product Liability*, Butterworths, 1994.

2 Though see H. Teff and C. Munro, *Thalidomide: The Legal Aftermath*, Saxon House, London, 1976, pp. 101–4, discussing the doubts expressed about the 'pharmaceutical miracle' and suggesting that eradication of disease had as much to do with improved standards of living and hygiene as with the invention of new drugs.

3 See Ferguson op. cit. at pp 1–20.

4 See J. Braithwaite, *Corporate Crime in the Pharmaceutical Industry*, Routledge & Kegan Paul, London, 1984; S. Adams, *Roche versus Adams*, Jonathan Cape, London, 1984.

5 See *Re HIV Haemophiliac Litigation* [1990] 41 BMLR 171, CA; *N* v. *Medical Research Council* [1996] 7 Med LR 309; *The Creutzfeldt–Jakob Disease Litigation* [1997] 41 BMLR 157; *A* v. *National Blood Authority* [2001] Lloyd's Rep. Med 187.

6 For a full and lively history of the events surrounding the thalidomide tragedy, see Teff and Munro, op. cit.

7 See, for example, *Davies* v. *Eli Lilly and Co.* [1987] 1 All ER 801, CA.

8 In *Davies* v. *Eli Lilly and Co* [1987] 2 All ER 94, CA it was held that the costs of litigation must be borne proportionately by all claimants. Legally

aided claims could not be used to provide 'lead' cases so that the costs would be borne by the legal aid fund.

9 *Nash* v. *Eli Lilly and Co., The Times*, 13 February 1991. For a full analysis of the Opren litigation, see Ferguson op. cit. at p. 14.

10 Indeed no reported English case of an award of damages for personal injury for drug-induced injury can be discovered: see H. Teff, 'Regulation under Medicines Act 1968', 1984 47 MLR 303, 320–22.

11 *Richardson* v. *LRC Products Ltd* [2000] Lloyd's Law Reports; *Abouzaid* v. *Mothercare (UK) Ltd, The Times*, 20 February 2001; *A* v. *National Blood Authority* [2001] Lloyd's Rep. Med 187.

12 In contrast to West Germany which, after the thalidomide disaster, enacted a special regime of liability for injury caused by drugs.

13 In *A* v. *National Blood Authority* (above at Note 11) Burton I. prefers the terminology *standard* and *non-standard* products.

14 A particular difficulty here has been establishing which manufacturer made the actual drug taken by the mother. There were several brands of the same drug on the market; see *Sindell* v. *Abbott Laboratories* [1980] 26 Cal. 3d. 588, *Mindy Hymowitz* v. *Eli Lilly & Co.* (1989) 541 NYS 2d 941 (NY CA) and see generally Ferguson op. cit. at pp. 135–47; Newdick, 'Liability for Defective Drugs' (1985) 101 LQR 405. But consider the possible impact of *Fairchild* v. *Glenhaven Funeral Services Ltd*, [2002] Lloyd's Rep. Med 361 HL.

15 See *Sindell* v. *Abbott Laboratories* (above).

16 See Teff, 'Regulation under the Medicines Act 1968' (1984) 47 MLR 303; Stewart and Wibberley, 'Drug Innovation – What is Slowing It Down?', (1980), 284 *Nature* pp. 118–20.

17 Sale of Goods Act 1979, s. 14(2)(b) (as amended by the Sale and Supply of Goods Act 1999; see Ferguson op. cit. at pp. 77–93).

18 ibid., s. 14 (2) (B); see Ferguson ibid.

19 Unless she can show that her husband bought the medicine for her as her agent.

20 See D. Prayle and M. Brazier, 'Supply of Medicines: Paternalism, Autonomy and Reality' (1998) 24 *Journal of Medical Ethics* 93.

21 *Pfizer* v. *Ministry of Health* [1965] AC 512; *Appleby* v. *Sleep* [1968] 1 WLR 948.

22 See the Supply of Goods and Service Act 1982; A.P. Bell, 'The Doctor and the Supply of Goods and Service Act' [1984] *Legal Studies* 175.

23 *Prendergast* v. *Sam and Dee*, [1985] 1 Med LR 36. And see *Dwyer* v. *Roderick* (1988) 127 Solicitors' Journal 805.

24 *Donoghue* v. *Stevenson* [1932] AC 562, 599.

25 *Watson* v. *Buckley and Osborne, Garrett & Co. Ltd* [1940] 1 All ER 174 (duty imposed on distributors of hair dye).

26 Teff and Munro, op. cit., Chapters 1 and 2.

27 *Wright* v. *Dunlop Rubber Co. Ltd* [1972] 13 KIR 255; *Hollis* v. *Dow Corning Corporation* [1995] 129 DLR (4th) 609 (Canada) and see Forte, 'Medical Products Liability', in S.A.M. McLean (ed.), *Legal Issues in Medicine*, Gower, Aldershot, 1981, p. 67.

28 Notably the Law Commission in their report 'Liability for Defective Products', 1977, Law Com. No. 82, Comnd 6831, and the Royal Commission on Civil Liability and Compensation for Personal Injury, 1978, Comnd 7054 (the Pearson Report).

29 The pharmaceutical industry repeatedly argued that drugs should remain exempt from any regime of strict liability, mainly on the grounds that (1) scientific research and innovation would be adversely affected; (2) the nature of drug disasters meant that strict liability could have catastrophic results for the industry; (3) the difficulty of defining defect in a drug: these arguments have been consistently rejected; see Law Com. No. 82 (above), pp. 19–21; Pearson Report, para. 1274.

30 See ss. 1–2.

31 Even if the importer is not an English company, but a company based in another EU state, the victim will be able to sue here in England if he suffered injury here; see the Civil Jurisdiction and Judgements Acts 1982 and 1991.

32 This includes pharmacists dispensing NHS drugs even though they do not sell NHS drugs to patients.

33 Council Directive of 25 July 1985.

34 See the thorough and excellent discussion of this problem in Newdick, op.cit. pp. 409–20.

35 *The Times*, 20 February 2001, CA.

36 [2000] Lloyd's Law Report 280.

37 [2001] Lloyd's Rep. Med 187.

38 At p. 216.

39 See s. 4(1)(e). The remainder of s. 4 outlines a number of defences that will only rarely be relevant in claims for drug-abused injuries.

40 The European Directive Article 7(e) permitted states to incorporate a development risks defence.

41 *Commission* v. *UK* (Case C-300/95) [1997] All ER (EC) 481.

42 Discussed in C. Hodges, 'Development Risks: Unanswered Questions' (1998), 61 MLR 560; M. Mildred and S. Howells, 'Comment on Development Risks: 'Unanswered Questions' (1998) 61 MLR 570.

43 And see *Richardson* v. *LRC Products Ltd* above.

44 At pp. 220–21.

45 Pearson Report, para 1259; and see Law Com. No. 82 (above).

46 See HC Deb. Vol. 1357 Col. 808.

47 [2002] Lloyds Rep Med 361, HL.

48 (1980) 607 P 2d 924.

49 At p. 386.

50 For a fuller account see Ferguson op.cit. K. Mullan, *Pharmacy Law and Practice*, Blackstone, 2000 at pp. 21–40; G. Appelbe and J. Wingfield, *Dale and Appelbe's Pharmacy, Law and Ethics* (7th edn), Pharmaceutical Press, 2001.

51 A voluntary scheme preceded the Act. For details see Teff and Munro, op. cit., pp. 111–18.

52 Medicines Act 1968, s. 6.

53 ss. 7 and 35; for limited exemptions to the requirement for a clinical trial certificate see Medicines (Exemption and Licences) (Clinical Trials) Order 1981 SI No. 164.

54 s. 2.

55 s. 4.

56 s. 20(3).

57 s. 19(1).

58 s. 19(2).

59 s. 24.

60 s. 38.

61 s. 21(5).

62 See D. Longley, 'Who is Calling the Piper? Is there a Tune? The New Regulatory Systems for Medical Devices in the United Kingdom and Canada' (1998) 3 Medical Law International 319.

63 See D. Prayle and M. Brazier (above at Note 20)

64 Discussed fully in Teff, 'Regulation under the Medicines Act 1968' (above).

65 H C Deb. Vol. 847 Col. 440–41, 29 November 1972.

66 The claim against the CSM was dropped.

67 See Ferguson op. cit. pp. 6–8.

68 Civil Procedure Rules: Sched I; RSC Ord. 11. R.1(f); Civil Jurisdiction and Judgements Conventions; Art. 5(3).

69 *Distillers Co. [Biochemicals] Ltd.* v. *Thompson* [1971] AC 458 (New Zealand mother allowed to sue the British company Distillers in New Zealand over thalidomide manufactured here; essence of the negligence alleged was failure to warm her, in New Zealand, of the danger to her baby).

70 See in particular the Pearson Report, Chapter 25.

71 Though parents in Ireland succeeded see *Best* v. *Wellcome Foundation* [1993] 2 IR 421.

72 [1990] 1 Med L. Rev. 117.

73 Tribunals, however, clearly do not accept *Loveday* v. *Renton* as gospel.

74 See Newdick, op. cit., p. 429.

9 Hospital Complaints Procedures

1 See L. Mulcahy *Mediating medical negligence claims: an option for the future*, HMSO, 2000.

2 *Being Heard – The Report of a Review Committee on NHS* Complaints Procedures, London, DoH, 1994.

3 See NHSE *Complaints – Listening – Acting – Improving: Guidance on Implementation of the NHS* Complaints Procedures, London, DoH, 1996, (hereafter *NHSE Guidance*). On the detail of implementation of this guidance see J. Montgomery, *Health Care Law*, OUP, 2002, pp. 114–18.

4 Select Committee on Health Sixth Report: *Procedures Related to Adverse Clinical Incidents and Outcomes in Medical Care* HC 549, (1999); and see D. Longley, 'Complaints After Wilson: Another Case of Too Little Too Late?' (1997) 5 Med L. Rev 172.

5 See Report of the House of Commons Health Committee, *The Regulation of Private and other Independent Healthcare* (5th Report, 1998–9 HC 281–1); and note measures to introduce complaints procedures in the private sector in the Care Standards Act 2000 and Health and Social Care Act 2001.

6 s. 18(1) Health Act 1999.

7 See *An Organisation with a Memory* (2000) HMSO; http:/www.doh.gov.uk/orgmemreport

8 See *Supporting Doctors: Protecting Patients: Assuring the Quality of Medical Practice* (2000) http://www.doh.gov.uk/cmconsult.htm; and 'Assuring the Quality of Medical Practice: Implementing Supporting doctors protecting patients', http:/www.doh.gov.uk/assuringquality

9 See s. 19 *et seq.* Health Act 1999. And see ss. 12–14 National Health Service Reform and Health Care Professions Act 2002.

10 For further information on regulatory measures to minimize adverse outcomes in health care see Harpwood op. cit. pp. 250–65.

11 For analogous requirements in relation to general practice see Montgomery op. cit. at p. 118.

12 For example, if a patient was too ill or distressed to consider bringing a complaint in that time span.

13 See *NHSE Guidance* para 4–32.

14 *NHSE Guidance* paras 4.37–4.39.

15 Ibid. para 5.12.

16 Ibid. para 4.17.

17 Ibid. para 7.9.

18 See Harpwood op. cit. at p. 241.

19 See *Cause for Complaint: An Evaluation of the Effectiveness of the NHS Complaints Procedures*, Public Law Project, 1999.

20 Sixth Report of the Select committee on Health (see above at Note 4); and see Harpwood op. cit. at pp. 240–47.

21 National Health Service Reorganisation Act 1973.

22 Health Service Commissioners Act s. 4(1)(b).

23 See V. Harpwood 'The Health Service Commissioner: The Extended Role in the New NHS (1996) 3 *European Journal of Health Law* 207.

24 Health Service Commissioners Act 1993 s. 3. The Ombudsman has a discretion to extend this time limit.

25 ibid. s. 10.

26 See ibid., ss. 11, 12.

27 Annual Report for 2000–2001 (HC 3 2000–2001).

28 Health Service Commissioners Act 1993 s. 3(1).

29 See Harpwood above Note 22.

30 Annual Report for 1999–2000.

31 Case E. 2087/99–00.

32 Case W 24 84–5; HC 428 (1984–5) p. 41.

33 Case E. 1579/98–9

34 Case E. 1860/98–9

35 Annual Report for 1989–90.

36 See tables at p. 23, Annual Report for 1989–90.

37 Annual Report for 2000–2001 p. 1.

38 Case E. 1860/98–99.

39 Case E. 1212/99–00.

40 Annual Report for 1999–2000.

41 Case W 309 83–4; HC 33 (1984–5), p. 99.

42 Case E. 1095/98–9.

43 Case W 236/75–6; HC 160 (1976–7), p. 23.

44 Case W 241/79–80; HC 51 (1982–3).

45 See Harpwood, op. cit. at pp. 242–4.

46 Such a philosophy lies at the heart of proposals currently being developed by the Clinical Disputes Forum.

47 Under HC 66 (15) generally, in serious cases this responsibility fell to regional health authorities now long abolished and replaced by strategic health authorities.

48 See *Learning from Bristol* – The Report of the Public Inquiry into children's heart surgery at the Bristol Royal Infirmary 1984–95 CM 5207 (1) (2001).

49 Note that the Alder Hey Inquiry was not a public inquiry but an Independent Confidential Inquiry set up under s. 2 of the National Health Service Act. See *Royal Liverpool Children's Inquiry Report* HC 12–11 2001.

50 See *The Times*, 7 February 2001.

51 At p. 31.

52 For Mrs Savage's own account of the 'affair', see *The Savage Inquiry*, Virago, London, 1986.

10 No Fault Compensation?

1 See *Compensation for Adverse Consequences of Medical Intervention*, RCP, 1990, BMA.

2 Litigation is a 'beanfeast' for lawyers: see Frank Dobson, then Secretary of State for Health, in evidence to the House of Commons' Select Committee on *Procedures Related to Adverse Clinical Incidents and Outcomes in Medical Care* (1998–9) HC 549-II (at p. 233).

3 See *Learning from Bristol* at p. 367.

4 *Clinical Negligence: What are the Issues and Options for Reform*, Department of Health, 2001.

5 See in particular P.S. Atiyah, *Accidents, Compensation and the Law*, (4th edn), Weidenfeld & Nicolson, 1987; T.C. Ison, *The Forensic Lottery*, Staples Press, London, 1967.

6 The Pearson Report (Report of the Royal Commission on Civil Liability and Compensation for personal Injury), Cmnd 7054 Vol. 1 paras. 246–63.

7 [1988] 1 All ER 871, HL.

8 National Audit Office, *Handling England Clinical Negligence Claims in England*, 2001.

9 [1981] 1 All ER 287, HL.

10 [1983] 2 All ER 245. And see *Nash* v. *Richmond Health Authority* [1996] 36 BMLR 123.

11 At p. 246. And see *Wilsher* v. *Essex AHA* [1986] 3 All ER 801 *per* Mustill LJ, p. 810.

12 Pearson Report, Vols. 1–3.

13 ibid., paras. 1304–71.

14 ibid., paras. 1372–413; and see Chapter 8.

15 ibid., paras. 1340–41 (opinion among the medical profession and the drug industries has moved towards favouring a centrally funded no-fault scheme for injury sustained by volunteers in clinical trials; see CIBA Foundation Study Paper (1980) BMJ 1172).

16 ibid., paras. 1193–278. The Commission's proposals related to all defective products and not drugs alone. And see Chapter 8.

17 ibid., paras. 1488–535.

18 ibid., paras. 1370–71.

19 See C. Ham, R. Dingwall, P. Fenn and D. Harris, *Medical Negligence: Compensation and Accountability*, King's Fund Institute/Centre for Socio-legal Studies, Oxford, 1988.

20 See Note 4.

21 See Ham et al., pp. 30–32.

22 For detailed studies of the New Zealand and Swedish schemes in the 1970s see the Pearson Report, Vol. 3.

23 For a favourable account of the operation of the original New Zealand scheme, see Richard Smith (1982) 284 BMJ 1243–5, 1323–5, 1457–9; for a highly critical analysis of the scheme as it affects medical accidents, see S.A. McLean, 'No Fault Liability and Medical Responsibility', in M.D.A. Freeman (ed.), *Medicine, Ethics and Law*, Stevens, London, 1988, p. 147; and for a

detailed survey, G. Palmer, *Compensation for Incapacity: A Study of Law and Social Change in New Zealand and Australia*, OUP, Wellington, 1979. And see Vennell (1989) 5 *Professional Negligence* 141.

24 See K. Oliphant, 'Defining "Medical Misadventure": Lessons from New Zealand', 1996, 4 Med. L. Rev 1.

25 [1990] NZAR 481; and see *Childs* v. *Hillock* [1994] 2 NZLR 65.

26 See Oliphant op.cit.

27 *Bridgeman* v. *Accident Compensation Commission* [1995] NZAR 199.

28 See C. Oldertz, 'The Swedish Patient Insurance Scheme: Eight Years of Experience', 1984, 52 *Medico-Legal Journal* pp. 43–59; C. Oldertz, 'Security Insurance, Patient Insurance and Pharmaceutical Insurance in Sweden', 1986, 34 Am. J. Comp. Law 635.

29 See Brahams, op. cit.

30 ibid.

31 Treatment would be defined to include treatment given to a pregnant mother and injuring the child. Consideration of the implications of ante-natal treatment would be required, e.g. would treatment necessary for the mother but injuring the child be excluded? What about pre-conception injury to either parent?

32 K. Oliphant, 'Defining Medical Misadventure: Lessons from New Zealand', 1996, 1 Med L. Rev 1 at pp. 30–31.

33 See Ham et al., op.cit., pp. 31–2.

34 In New Zealand a maximum limit of 80 per cent of actual earnings up to a limit of about £350 a week is now placed on compensation for loss of income.

35 For detailed discussion of proposals for a no-fault scheme for drugs see A.L. Diamond and D.R. Lawrence, 'Product Liability in Respect of Drugs' (1985) 290 BMJ 365–8.

36 See the proposals of the Clinical Disputes Forum.

37 A. Merry and A. McCall Smith, *Errors, Medicine and the Law*, CUP, 2001, p. 248.

38 See Note 4.

11 Family Planning

1 *Sutherland* v. *Stopes* [1925] AC 47, p. 68.

2 *Bravery* v. *Bravery* [1954] 3 All ER 59, pp. 67–8.

3 *The Queen (on the application of SPUC)* v. *Secretary of State for Health* [2002] 2 FLR 146.

4 See National Health Service (Family Planning) Act 1967 as amended by the National Health Service (Family Planning) Amendment Act 1972.

5 See note 3.

6 *R* v. *Donovan* [1934] 2 KB 498, and see *R* v. *Brown* [1993] 2 All ER 75 HL.

7 See the discussion on this matter in the essay 'Sterilisation' by S.A.M. McLean

and T.D. Campbell in S.A.M. McLean (ed.), *Legal Issues in Medicine*, Gower, Aldershot, 1981.

8 *Baxter* v. *Baxter* [1948] AC 274.

9 See N. Lowe and G. Douglas, *Bromley's Family Law* (9th edn), Butterworths, London, 1998, p. 91.

10 *Bravery* v. *Bravery* (above), at p. 62.

11 *Baxter* v. *Baxter* (above).

12 *The Times*, 19 April 1972; see Bromley, op. cit., p. 186.

13 *Sullivan* v. *Sullivan* [1970] 2 All ER 168, CA.

14 *The Times*, 7 November 1981.

15 See the *Guardian*, 27 July 1983, p. 4.

16 [1997] 4 All ER 771.

17 [1999] PIQR p. 53 see pp. 107–8

18 But see *Vadera* v. *Shaw* (unreported) 22 July, 1998.

19 *Buchan* v. *Ortho-Pharmaceuticals (Canada) Ltd* [1986] 54 OR (2d) 92, 100.

20 See again *Vadera* v. *Shaw* above.

21 See *McFarlane* v. *Tayside Health Board* [1999] 4 All ER 961, HL.

22 [2000] Lloyd's Law Reports 280.

23 See H. Draper, 'Women and Sterilisation Abuse', in M. Brazier and M. Lobjoit (eds), *Protecting the Vulnerable*, Routledge, 1991, Chapter 6.

24 [1980] 7 Current Law S. 4.

25 *Wells* v. *Surrey Area Health Authority*, *The Times*, 29 July 1978.

26 See M. Puxon and A. Buchan, 'Damages for Sterility' (1988) 138 NLJ 80.

27 *Udale* v. *Bloomsbury AHA* [1983] 2 All ER 522.

28 See *Thake* v. *Maurice* [1984] 2 All ER 513, CA; *Emeh* v. *Kensington & Chelsea Health Authority* [1993] 1 All ER 651.

29 [1999] 4 All ER 961, HL. See also *Greenfield* v. *Irwin (A Firm)* [2001] 1 FLR 899.

30 Se J.K. Mason, 'Unwanted Pregnancy: A Case of Retroversion?', (2000), 4 ELR 191.

31 Lord Millett dissented on this point.

32 At p. 978.

33 At p. 985.

34 At p. 990.

35 At p. 998.

36 Ibid.

37 At p. 998.

38 At p. 1005.

39 See Lord Steyn at p. 979.

40 *Rand* v. *East Dorset Health Authority* [2000] Lloyd's Rep. Med 181; *Hardman* v. *Amin* [2000] Lloyds Rep. Med 498.

41 [2001] Lloyds Rep. Med 393.

42 For guidance on what constitutes 'disability', see Hale LJ at p. 323.

43 At p. 318; and see Hale LJ at p. 323.

44 Note Hale LJ's analysis of the nature of the loss and injury. Are the costs consequent on the birth of an unplanned child, disabled or not; truly pure economic loss?

45 [2002] 2 All ER 177, CA. Note though that there must be a real financial burden imposed on the claimant as a result of struggling to bring up a child and cope with her own disabilities; see *AD* v. *East Kent Community NHS Trust* [2002] Lloyd's Rep Med 424.

46 Note the difference in reasoning between Hale and Robert Walker LJJ. Consider whether poverty is a 'disability' deserving at least some compensation for an unplanned child.

47 See for example *Danns* v. *Department of Health* [1998] PIQR p. 226.

48 [1984] 2 All ER 513.

49 [1986] 1 All ER 497, and see *Eyre* v. *Measday* [1986] 1 All ER 488.

50 [1996] 2 All ER 161 CA.

51 At p. 170.

52 [1987] 2 All ER 266.

53 [1989] 2 All ER 545, HL.

54 At p. 219.

55 See M.D.A. Freeman, 'Sterilising the Mentally Handicapped', in M.D.A. Freeman (ed.) *Medicine, Ethics and Law*, Stevens, London, 1998.

56 See *T.* v. *T.* [1988] 1 All ER 613 discussed earlier at p. 117.

57 See *Re B.* [1987] 2 All ER 266.

58 [1988] 2 FLR 997.

59 [1989] 1 FLR 182; see M. Brazier, 'Sterilization: Down the Slippery Slope' (1990) 6 *Professional Negligence* 25.

60 At p. 218.

61 (1986) 31 DLR (4th) 1.

62 [1989] 2 All ER 545, HL.

63 [1998] 1 FLR 944.

64 [1997] 2 FLR 258.

65 [2000] 3 WLR 1288 CA.

66 At p. 1302 per Thorpe LJ.

67 See *Re G F (Medical Treatment)* [1999] 1 FLR 293.

68 And see *Re Z. (Medical Treatment: Hysterectomy)* [2000] 1 FCR 274.

69 At p. 1294.

70 [2000] 1 FCR 193, CA.

71 At p. 203.

12 Assisted Conception

1 For an authoritative and comprehensive account of law, ethics and policy see R. Lee and D. Morgan, *Human Fertilisation and Embryology: Regulating*

the Reproductive Revolution, Blackstone, 2000. For an excellent critique of law and policy see E. Jackson, *Regulating Reproduction: Law Technology and Autonomy*, Hart, 2001.

2 There is a (possibly apocryphal) story about one clinic storing sperm in the same fridge as the milk for staff coffee breaks.

3 *Report of the Committee of Inquiry into Human Fertilisation and Embryology*, Cmnd 9314 (1984) (The Warnock Report).

4 *Legislation on Human Infertility Services and Embryology* Cm 46 HMSO, 1987.

5 *Human Fertilisation and Embryology: A Framework for Legislation* Cm 259 HMSO, 1987.

6 See *R* v. *Secretary of State for the Home Department ex p. Mellor* [2001] 3 WLR 533.

7 Replacing the Interim Licensing Authority [ILA] set up by the medical profession itself in the long period of limbo between the publication of the Warnock Report and the 1990 Act coming into force. The reports of the ILA and its predecessor the Voluntary Licensing Authority (VLA) are invaluable sources of information about the development of assisted conception from 1985 to 1991.

8 Though note that if self-insemination using fresh sperm is practised by a couple the Act does not apply; see p. 287.

9 For a discussion of the political horsetrading that resulted in GIFT being omitted from the 1990 Act see Lee and Morgan op. cit. at pp. 142–5.

10 In cases where the husband's consent is disputed it would be for him to prove that he did not consent.

11 *Re CH (Contact: Parentage)* [1996] 1FCR 768.

12 He does not automatically share parental responsibility with the mother. Section 4 of the Children Act 1989 enables him to apply to the court to share parental responsibility with the mother, or he and the mother may expressly agree to share parental responsibility. The child enjoys the same rights of inheritance as a child born within marriage. The Adoption and Children Act will (once in force) provide that any unmarried father whose name appears on the child's birth certificate will automatically share parental responsibility for his child.

13 *Re B. (Parentage)* [1996] FLR 15; and *see R.* v. *HFEA ex p. Blood* [1997] 2 All ER 687 CA.

14 [2003] 2 All ER 131, CA.

15 See s. 28(6).

16 [2003] 1 FLR 412.

17 *U.* v. *W. (Attorney-General Intervening)* [1997] 2 FLR 282.

18 *L.* v. *L.* [1949] p. 211.

19 *Parpalaix* v. *CECOS;* Gazette du Palais 15 September 1984 (Court de Cassation)

20 At p. 55.

21 [1997] 2 All ER 687, CA; See D. Morgan and R. Lee, 'In the Name of the Father? Ex parte Blood Dealing with Novelty and Anomaly' (1997), 60 MLR 84.

22 See T. Hervey, 'Buy Baby: The European Union and Regulation of Human Reproduction' (1998) 18 OJLS 207.

23 A number of children have been born after posthumous AIH where the requisite written consent had been given. See *Mrs. U.* v. *Centre for Reproductive Medicine* (2002) Lloyd's Rep Med 259 CA where a widow argued that the clinic used undue influence to persuade her deceased husband to withdraw his consent.

24 *Review of Common Law Provision Relating to the Removal of Gametes and of the Consent Provision in the Human Fertilisation and Embryology Act* 1990 (July 1958).

25 The Human Fertilisation and Embryology (Deceased Fathers) Bill.

26 Who must presumably take into account 'the need of the child for a father' as required by *s*. 13(5).

27 See the discussion in I. Kennedy and A. Grubb, *Medical Law: Text and Materials* (2nd edn), Butterworths, London, 2000, pp. 1308–15.

28 See s. 28, discussed on page 284.

29 See A. Plomer and N. Martin-Clement. 'The Limits of Beneficence: Egg Donation Under the Human Fertilisation and Embryology Act 1990' (1995) 15 *Legal Studies* p. 434.

30 Though note that children have been born using frozen eggs.

31 See HFEA, *Donated Ovarian Tissue in Embryo Research and Assisted Conception*, July 1994.

32 See F. Fisher and A. Somerville, 'To Everything there is Season? Are There Medical Grounds for Refusing Treatment to Older Women?', In J. Harris and S. Holm (eds), *The Future of Reproduction* Oxford, Claredon Press, p. 203.

33 See M. Brazier, 'Liberty, Responsibility Maternity', (1999), 52 *Current Legal Problems*, 359.

34 See s. 12(e).

35 *HFEA Directions*. (Ref D 1998/1).

36 See Richard Titmuss's seminal book *The Gift Relationship: From Human Blood to Social Policy*, Allen & Unwin, London, 1971.

37 See the Human Organs Transplant Act 1989, discussed fully in Chapter 17.

38 See N. Duxbury, 'Do Markets Degrade?' (1996) MLR 331.

39 *s*. 4.

40 See s. 14(4)(5). Section 14(5) allows for reduction or extension of these periods by regulations.

41 s. 14(1)(c).

42 Human Fertilisation and Embryology (Statutory Storage Period for Embryos) Regulations 1996 (SI 1996 No. 375)

43 Sched, 3, para, 3.

44 Sched. 3, para 2.
45 Sched. 3, para 3.
46 The HFEA may give further directions as to what additional matters must be covered in the patients' consent. The fate of embryos on divorce for example is not required to be dealt with by the Act.
47 As has happened frequently in the USA; see for example *Davis* v. *Davis* [1992] 842 SW 2d.
48 [2002] Lloyds Rep. Med 259 CA.
49 On the ethics of PIGD generally see HFEA/ACGT Consultation Document *Pre-Implantation Genetic Diagnosis*, 1999 and see S. Holm, 'Ethical Issues in Pre-Implantation Diagnosis; in J. Harris and S. Holm (eds) *The Future of Human Reproduction*, OUP, 1998.
50 HFEA/HGC, *Cloning Issues in Reproduction, Science and Medicine*, 1998.
51 See HFEA Code of Practice.
52 HFEA Code of Practice 7.9.
53 See M. Brazier, 'Regulating the Reproduction Business?' (1999) 7 Med. L. Rev p. 166.
54 Adoption Act 1976, s. 51.
55 See the Report, pp. 24–5.
56 But see K. O'Donovan, 'What Shall We Tell the Children? Reflections on Children's Perspectives and the Reproduction Revolution', in R. Lee and D. Morgan, *Birthrights: Law and Ethics and the Beginning of Life*, Routledge, 1989.
57 *Gaskin* v. *United Kingdom* [1990] 1 FLR 167.
58 [2002] 2 FLR 962.
59 G.Douglas, 'Assisted Reproduction and the Welfare of the Child' (1993) *Current Legal Problems* 46.
60 See D. Savas and S. Treece, 'Fertility Clinics: One Code of Practice?' (1998) 3 *Medical Law. International* p. 243.
61 *R.* v. *St Mary's Hospital Ethical Committee ex p. Harriott* [1998] 1 FLR 512.
62 *R.* v. *Sheffield Area Health Authority ex p Seale* [1994] 25 BMLR 1.
63 See M. Latham, 'Regulating the New Reproductive Technologies: A Cross-Channel Comparison', 1998, *Medical Law International* p. 89; M. Latham, *Regulating Reproduction*, MUP, 2002.
64 [1982] 2 All ER 771, CA.
65 [1984] 3 All ER 1044.
66 [1999] 4 All ER 961, HL.
67 See M. Brazier, A. Campbell and S. Golombok, *Surrogacy: Review for Health Ministers of Current Arrangements for Payments and Regulation* (CM 4068), HMSO, 1998 (hereafter referred to as *Surrogacy Review*).
68 Surrogacy Arrangements Act 1985.
69 p. 46.
70 The 1985 Act will apply however the embryo came to be created, be it by

GIFT or IVF; see s. 36 of the Human Fertilisation and Embryology Act 1990.

71 s. 57.

72 *Re C. (A Minor)* [1985] FLR 846.

73 *Re an Adoption Application (Surrogacy)* [1987] 2 All ER 826. And see *Re Q (Parental Order)* [1996] 1 FLR 369.

74 In the event Mrs B. accepted only £5,000 of the agreed fee, having co-authored a book on her experience of surrogacy.

75 *In the Matter of Baby M.* (1988) 537 A 2d 1227, extracted in Kennedy and Grubb, op. cit., p. 1375, and see on p. 1364 the detailed 'contract' agreed between Mary Beth Whitehead and the Sterns.

76 [1985] FLR 445 (FD and CA).

77 *Re P. (Minors) (Wardship: Surrogacy)* [1987] 2 FLR 421.

78 *Re MW (Adoption: Surrogacy)* [1995] 2 FLR 759; *C. v. S.* (1996) SLT 1387.

79 And see *Re W. (Minors Surrogacy)* [1991] 1 FLR 385.

80 As was the case in *Re an Adoption Application (Surrogacy)* (above, note 73).

81 *Re Q. (Parental Order)* [1996] 2 FCR 395.

82 The *Surrogacy Review* (see Note 68).

83 M. Freeman, 'Does Surrogacy Have a Future after Brazier?', (1999), 7 Med. L. Rev 1.

84 See M. Brazier, 'Can You Buy Children?' (1999) 11 *Child and Family Law Quarterly* 345.

85 With the honourable exception of COTS.

86 See *Rose* v. *Secretary of State for Health and the Human Fertilization and Embryology Authority* [2002] 2 FLR 962; *R. (Mellor)* v. *Secretary of State for the Home Department* [2001] 3 WLR 533.

13 Abortion and Embryo Research

1 *R. v. Sockett* [1908] 72 JP 428.

2 *R. v. Whitchurch* [1890] 24 QBD 420.

3 *R. v. Bourne* [1939] 1 KB 687.

4 ibid., p. 693.

5 See *Janaway* v. *Salford AHA* [1988] 3 All ER 1051, HL.

6 *R. v. Smith (John)* [1974] 1 WLR 1510 CA.

7 Indeed, the history of abortion in England from well before the 1967 Act is marked by 'medicalization'; see J. Keown, *Abortion, Doctors and the Law*, CUP, 1988.

8 In *R. v. Price* [1969] 1 QB 541, a prosecution for criminal abortion was brought against a doctor who inserted an IUD into a woman who was some months pregnant. The prosecution failed because it was not proved that he knew her to be pregnant.

9 See J. Keown, 'Miscarriage: A Medico Legal Analysis' [1984] Crim L.R. 604.

10 HC Official Report, 10 May 1983, Col. 238–9. A prosecution under the

Abortion Act requires the consent of the DPP. The DPP is answerable to the Attorney-General, so as long as that officer concurs with the opinion given by Sir Michael Havers a prosecution is unlikely to get off the ground; see the Prosecution of Offences Regulations 1985.

11 *R* v. *Dhingra* (unreported) (1991).

12 *The Queen (on the application of SPUC)* v. *Secretary of State for Health* [2002] 2 FLR 146

13 The woman will be asked to agree to undergo surgical abortion should the drug fail to work before being given mifepristone. She cannot of course be forced to go through with the surgical procedure should she later change her mind. But, providing she has been properly warned of the risk of failure and possible adverse effect on the embryo, neither she nor any child damaged by the drug could sue in respect of their injuries. See 'Unfinished Feticide' (1990) 16 J. Med. Ethics 61–70.

14 See generally A. Dyson and J. Harris (eds.), *Experiments on Embryos*, Routledge & Kegan Paul, London, 1989.

15 J.M. Harris, *The Value of Life*, Routledge & Kegan Paul, London, 1985, p. 117.

16 See M. Brazier, 'Embryos' "Rights": Abortion and Research', in *Medicine, Ethics and Law*, M.D.A. Freeman (ed.), Stevens, 1988, pp. 9–23.

17 See the Warnock Report, pp. 63–4.

18 See in particular M. Lockwood, 'When does a life begin?', in M. Lockwood (ed.), *Moral Dilemmas in Medicine*, OUP, 1988.

19 See J.M. Harris, op. cit., pp. 18–25; and 'Embryos and Hedgehogs', in Dyson and Harris (eds.), op. cit., p. 65; and see Jonathan Glover, *Causing Death and Saving Lives*, Penguin, Harmondsworth, 1977.

20 See G.R. Dunstan, 'The Moral Status of the Human Embryo: A Tradition Recalled' (1984) 10 J. Med. Ethics, 38; Keith Ward, 'An Irresolvable Debate?', in Dyson and Harris, op. cit., p. 106.

21 For a powerful argument that even if the embryo is presumed to enjoy full human status abortion remains defensible, see J. Jarvis Thompson, 'A Defence of Abortion', in R.M. Dworkin (ed.), *The Philosophy of Law*, OUP, 1977, p. 112. But note the response by J.M. Finnis, 'The Rights and Wrongs of Abortion', in the same book, p. 129.

22 See M. Brazier, 'The Challenge for Parliament: A Critique of the White Paper on Human Fertilization and Embryology', in Dyson and Harris (eds), op.cit., p. 142.

23 See s. 3(1). Any prosecution under the Act will require the consent of the DPP; s. 42.

24 s. 3(3)(a).

25 See s. 3(2) and s. 3(3)(b).

26 s. 3(3)(d).

27 s. 4(1); Sched. 2 para. 3(5).

28 Sched. 2 para. 3(4).

29 Sched. 2 para 2.

30 See, for example, J. Harris, 'Goodbye Dolly? – The Ethics of Human Cloning' (1997) 23 *Journal of Medical Ethics* 353; and see Kennedy and Grubb op. cit. pp. 1239–68.

31 HFEA/HGAC *Cloning Issues in Reproduction, Science and Medicine* (1998). And see J. Harris, *Clones, Genes and Immortality*, OUP, 1998.

32 Expert Group of the CMO *Stem Cell Research: Medical Progress and Responsibility*, 2000.

33 The Human Fertilisation and Embryology (Research Purposes) Regulations 2001. And see the report of a select committee of the House of Lords: *Stem Cell Research* (HL Paper 83ii) 2002

34 S. 1 (1) (a).

35 See M. Brazier, 'Regulating the Reproduction Business?' (1999) 8 Med. L. Rev. p. 166.

36 *R. (Quintavalle)* v. *Secretary of State for Health* [2001] 4 All ER 1019.

37 *R (Quintavalle)* v. *Secretary of State for Health* [2002] All ER.

38 [1973] 93 S Ct. 705.

39 Albeit at twenty-eight weeks the foetus was deemed to be capable of being born alive, that did *not* mean an earlier abortion was necessarily lawful. It would be for the prosecution to prove *that* foetus was capable of being born alive.

40 Thus closing a lacuna in the abortion laws.

41 [1987] 1 All ER 1230.

42 See *R.* v. *Bourne* [1939] 1 KB 687.

43 See J. Keown, 'Selective Reduction of Multiple Pregnancy' (1987) 137 NLJ 1165; D.P.T. Price, 'Selective Reduction and Feticide: The Parameters of Abortion' [1988] Crim. L.R. 199.

44 Section 37(5) amends s. 5(2) of the Abortion Act 1967 which now reads: for the purposes of the law relating to abortion, anything done with intent to procure a woman's miscarriage (or, in the case of a woman carrying more than one foetus, her miscarriage of any foetus) is unlawfully done unless authorized by section 1 of this Act and, in the case of a woman carrying more than one foetus, anything done with intent to procure her miscarriage of any foetus is authorized by that section if:
(a) The ground for termination of the pregnancy specified in subsection (1)(d) of that section applies in relation to any foetus and the thing is done for the purpose of procuring the miscarriage of that foetus (foetal handicap ground).
(b) Any of the other grounds for termination of the pregnancy specified in that section applies.

45 See Morgan and Lee, op.cit., pp. 252–6.

46 *Royal College of Nursing* v. *DHSS* [1981] AC 800.

47 [1988] 3 All ER 1051, HL.

48 See Mason and McCall Smith op. cit. at p. 140.

49 See M. Fox 'Abortion Decision-Making – Taking Men's Needs Seriously' in E. Lee (ed.) *Abortion Law and Politics Today*, Macmillan, 1998, p. 198.

50 [1979] QB 276.

51 [1980] 3 EHRR 408. And see *Bruggeman and Scheuten* v. *Federal Republic of Germany* [1977] 3 EHRR 244.

52 [1987] All ER 1230. And see *Kelly* v. *Kelly* 1997 SLT 896 (Scotland).

53 At p. 1243.

54 *Re P. (A Minor)* (1981) 80 LGR 301.

55 [1985] 3 All ER 402, HL.

56 See *Re B. (A Minor) (Wardship: Abortion)* [1991] 2 FLR 226 (Hollis J authorized abortion for twelve-year-old-girl).

57 [1992] 4 All ER 627.

58 [1992] 4 All ER 627 at p. 635.

59 [1988] 1 All ER 613.

60 [1989] 2 All ER 545, HL.

61 See *Re SS (Medical Treatment: Late Termination)* [2002] 1 FLR 445 (judge refused to authorize abortion close to 24-week limit).

14 Doctors and Children

1 *Re A. (Minors) (Conjoined Twins: Separation)* [2000] Lloyd's Rep. Med 425.

2 *Gillick* v. *West Norfolk and Wisbech AHA* [1985] 3 All ER 402 HL.

3 See *Re R. (A Minor)* [1991] 4 All ER 177, CA; *Re W. (A Minor) (Medical Treatment)* [1992] 4 All ER 627, CA.

4 See A. Goldworth W. Silverman *et al.*, *Ethics and Perinatology*, OUP, 1995.

5 See, in particular, J.K. Mason and R.A. McCall Smith, *Law and Medical Ethics*, (6th edn), Butterworths, London, 2002, at pp. 471–509.

6 J. Lorber, 'Results of the Treatment of Myelomengole', *Developmental Medicine and Child Neurology*, 1971; and 'Spina Bifida Cystica', *Archives of Disease in Childhood*, 1972.

7 See Jonathan Glover, *Causing Death and Saving Lives*, Penguin, Harmondsworth, 1977, Chapter 12. And see earlier in Chapter 2 of this book.

8 See, in particular J.K. Mason, *Human Life and Medical Practice*, Edinburgh University Press, 1988, Chapter 6.

9 See Rachels (1975) 292 New Eng. J. Med. 78.

10 (1981) 78 Law Soc. Gaz. 1342.

11 Mason and McCall Smith op. cit. at p. 502.

12 1st edn at p. 89.

13 5th edn at p. 502.

14 *Re B. (A Minor) (Wardship: Medical Treatment)* [1981] 1 WLR 1421.

15 In October, the DPP announced that it would not prosecute a doctor alleged to have taken no action to preserve the life of a spina bifida baby, Stephen

Quinn; see *The Times*, 6 October 1981.

16 See 'Dr Leonard Arthur: His trial and its Implications' (1981) 283 BMJ 1340; H. Benyon, 'Doctors as Murderers' [1982] Crim. L.R. 17; M.Gunn and J.C.Smith, 'Arthur's Case and the Right to Life of a Down's Syndrome Child' [1985] Crim L.R. 705.

17 *Human Life and Medical Practice*, Edinburgh University Press, 1988, p. 63.

18 Some dispute exists as to the moment in childbirth when this occurs. The child need not have breathed apparently. See *R.* v. *Poulton* [1832] 5 C & P. 329, and *R.* v. *Brain* [1834] 6 C. & P. 349; *Attorney General's Reference (No.3 of 1994)* [1997] 3 All ER 936, HL.

19 *Re A. (Minors) (Conjoined Twins: Separation)* [2000] Lloyd's Rep. Med 425 at pp. 464–5.

20 How would you classify the status of a baby born with anencephaly? See Mason and McCall Smith op. cit. at pp. 495–6.

21 [2000] Lloyd's Rep. Med 425. The names given to the girls to preserve their anonymity. The ban on identifying the family was later lifted

22 For an eloquent discussion of the issues raised by surgery to separate conjoined twins prior to *Re A* see S. Sheldon and S. Wilkinson, 'Conjoined Twins: The Legality and Ethics of Sacrifice' [1997] 2 Med L.Rev. 149.

23 At p. 456 and pp. 466–7 Robert Walker LJ sought to argue that Mary's death resulted not from surgery but her own inability to sustain life (at p. 510).

24 Ward LJ also advanced, and preferred, a doctrine of quasi-self defence.

25 At p. 474.

26 Children and Young Persons Act 1933, s. 1(1).

27 *R.* v. *Lowe* [1973] QB 702.

28 *R.* v. *Senior* [1899] 1 QB, 823.

29 *R.* v. *Gibbons and Proctor* [1918] 13 Cr. App. Rep. 134.

30 Children Act 1989 s. 31 (2).

31 See Beynon, op. cit., pp. 27–8.

32 [1989] 2 All ER 782, CA.

33 [1990] 3 All ER 930, CA.

34 At p. 938.

35 [2000] Lloyd's Rep. Med 475.

36 The latest news on Jodie's progress suggests that these fears will not materialize. Surgeons expect her to be able to walk, to avoid incontinence and even to be able to bear children.

37 At p. 455.

38 *Re T. (A Minor) (Wardship: Medical Treatment)* [1997] 1 All ER 906 CA (discussed in M. Fox and J. McHale 'In Whose Best Interests?' (1997) 60 MLR 600).

39 At pp. 914–15.

40 This seems to be the tenor of Roch LJ's judgment.

41 See C. Bridge, 'Religion, Culture and Conviction – the medical treatment

of young children' (1999) 11 CFLQ 1, and 'Religion, Culture and the Body of the Child' in A. Bainham, S.D. Sclater and M. Richards *Body Lore and Laws*, OUP, 2002 p. 265.

42 Albeit the Council of Elders does seem recently to have softened slightly its opposition to transfusions, leaving the matter more to the conscience of the believer.

43 *Re S. (A Minor) (Medical Treatment)* [1993] 1 FLR 376.

44 *Re E. (A Minor)* (1990) 9 BMLR 1; *Re O. (A Minor) (Medical Treatment)* (1993) 4 Med L.R 272; *Re R. (A Minor)* [1993] 2 FLR 757.

45 [1997] 1 All ER 906 CA.

46 *Re A.* [2000] Lloyds Rep. Med 425 at p. 454; and see *Re C. (A Minor) (Medical Treatment)* [1998] 1 FLR 384.

47 See C. Bridge 'Parental Powers and the Medical Treatment of Children' in C. Bridge (ed.) *Family Law: Towards the Millennium*, Butterworth, 1997, p. 321.

48 Prosecution for wilful neglect under the Children and Young Persons Act 1933 s. 1(1) or even manslaughter if the child dies; see *R v. Senior* [1899] 1 QB 283.

49 [1985] 3 All ER 402 at p. 432.

50 As Lord Scarman put it in *Gillick* (above) at p. 410, 'Emergency, parental neglect, abandonment of the child or inability to find the parent are examples of exceptional situations justifying the doctor proceeding to treat the child without parental knowledge or consent.'

51 [1998] 1 FLR 384. And see *Royal Wolverhampton Hospitals NHS Trusts v. B.* [2000] 2 FLR 953; *A National Health Service Trust v. B.* [2000] 2 FCR 577; *R. v. Portsmouth NHS Trust ex p. Glass* [1999] 2 FLR 205; *Re MM (Medical Treatment)* [2000] 1 FLR 224.

52 See Mason and McCall Smith op. cit. at p. 318.

53 See *Re Superintendent of Family and Child Services and Dawson* [1983] DLR (3d) 610.

54 [1999] 2 FLR 1004 CA.

55 (1999) 52 BMLR 82, CA.

56 See Skegg, op.cit, p. 377.

57 [1986] 1 All ER 376.

58 At p. 335.

59 [1987] 2 All ER 206.

60 *Per* Lord Bridge, p. 213.

61 See *per* Lord Oliver, p. 219.

62 p. 214.

63 See *In Re S. (Adult Patient: Sterilization)* [2000] 3 WLR 1288.

64 See *Re A. (Medical Treatment: Male Sterilization)* [2000] 1 FCR 193 CA discussed above.

65 See generally N. Lowe and G. Douglas *Bromley's Family Law* (9th edn) (Butterworths, 1998) Chapter 10.

66 See *Re J. (Child's Religious Upbringing and Circumcision)* [1999] 2 FLR 1004 CA.

67 In which case the court will acquire control over all aspects of the child's life and upbringing.

68 See generally Kennedy and Grubb op. cit. at pp. 774–8.

69 See Lowe and Douglas op. cit. at Chapter 12.

70 Or the local authority or in certain cases other relatives.

71 See *Report of the Inquiry into Child Abuse in Cleveland* 1987, Cm. 412 (1988).

72 See s. 44 of the Children Act 1989.

73 The predecessor to the emergency protection order.

74 See P. Alderson *Children's Consent to Surgery*, Open University Press, 1995.

75 See P.D.G. Skegg, 'Consent to Medical Procedures on Minors' (1973) 36 MLR 370, pp. 370–75.

76 [1984] 1 All ER 365.

77 [1985] 1 All ER 533.

78 [1985] 3 All ER 402.

79 p. 422.

80 In another context, just a year before the *Gillick* hearing, the House of Lords had considered the crime of kidnapping as it related to children under sixteen. They held that the central issue was the agreement of the child, not either parent, to being taken away by the accused. In the case of a young child absence of consent could be presumed. With an older child the question was whether he or she had sufficient understanding and intelligence to give consent. See *R. v. D.* [1984] 2 All ER 449.

81 p. 432.

82 p. 413.

83 *In Re P. (A Minor)* [1981] 80 LGR 301.

84 p. 425. For trenchant criticism see Glanville Williams, op. cit.

85 See *Re R. (A Minor)* [1991] 4 All ER 441 CA.

86 At 422; see above at p. 365.

87 See C. Bridge and M. Brazier, 'Coercion or Caring: Analysing Adolescent Autonomy' (1996) 15 *Legal Studies* 84.

88 *Re R. (A Minor)* [1991] 4 All ER 177 CA.

89 See *Re R.* (above) at p. 184.

90 See for example, A. Bainham, 'The Judge and the Competent Minor' (1992) 108 LQR 104.

91 [1992] 4 All ER 627.

92 See Balcombe LJ at p. 639.

93 At p. 635.

94 E.g. *South Glamorgan County Council v. B. & W.* [1993] 1 FLR 574; *Re S. (A Minor) (Consent to Medical Treatment)* [1994] 2 FLR 1065; and see Bridge and Brazier op. cit.

95 *Re E. (A Minor)* [1990] 9 BMLR 1. *Re M. (Child: Refusal of Medical Treatment)* (2002) 52 BMLR 124.

96 See *Re C. (Detention: Medical Treatment)* [1997] 2 FLR 180.

97 See C. Bridge, 'Adolescents, and Mental Disorder: Who Consents to Treatment' (1997) 3 *Medical Law International* 51.

98 GMC, *Confidentiality: Protecting and Providing Information*, 2000, para 38.

99 GMC op. cit. para 38.

15 Pregnancy and Childbirth

1 For a thorough discussion of the legal implications of the thalidomide tragedy see H. Teff and C. Munro, *Thalidomide: The Legal Aftermath*, Saxon House, London, 1976. And see Chapter 8.

2 Sixteen years after the 1976 Act, the Court of Appeal held that a duty was owed at common law to a child born in 1967; *Burton* v. *Islington HA* [1992] 3 All ER 833; see A. Whitfield, 'Common Law Duties to Unborn Children', 1993, 1 Med. L. Rev. 28

3 *S.* v. *Distillers Co.* [1970] 1 WLR 114.

4 On the difficulties in proving causation of birth defects see the Report of the Royal Commission on Civil Liability and Personal Injury (Pearson Report) Cmnd 7054 (1978) paras. 1441–52, and see the essay 'Ante-Natal Injuries' by S.A.M. McLean in S.A.M. McLean (ed.), *Legal Issues in Medicine*, Gower, Aldershot, 1981.

5 But a child born before 1976 could sue at common law, see *Burton* v. *Islington HA* above Note 2.

6 She is liable for injuries caused through negligent driving of a vehicle on the road; s. 2. A claim against the mother was in general seen as not likely to be pursued by the child within a happy family relationship. The mother would not proceed against herself. The father would do so only where the marriage had broken down, and women are subject to such contradictory advice as to the management of pregnancy that establishing negligence would be extremely difficult. Negligence while driving a car, by contrast, is easy to prove, and in reality the claim would be against the mother's insurers.

7 Where the child is not born alive, the mother may be able to claim for the pain and suffering of miscarriage or stillbirth.

8 *The Times*, 26 July 1986; the hospital conceded liability.

9 [1997] 4 All ER 771.

10 For a more comprehensive account of ante-natal screening and genetic counselling see Mason and McCall Smith op. cit. Chapter 6.

11 [1982] 2 All ER 771.

12 It has been argued that the Act does not apply to a 'wrongful life' claim. The Act provides a scheme to compensate for disability inflicted by human error, not to a claim for allowing a disabled foetus to be born at all. See J. Fortin, 'Is the "Wrongful Life" Action Really Dead'? [1987] J. Soc. Welfare Law 306. The Court of Appeal were adamant that at common law no such action lay either.

13 pp. 782, 787 and 790. See the American judgments in I. Kennedy and A. Grubb, *Medical Law: Text and Materials*, Butterworths, London, 2000.
14 p. 787.
15 p. 781.
16 [1999] 4 All ER 961.
17 e.g. *Salih* v. *Enfield Health Authority* [1991] 3 All ER 400 (where only the amount of compensation was disputed)
18 Trindade and Cane *The Law of Torts in Australia* (2nd edn), 1993, at p. 434.
19 At p. 978.
20 [2001] Lloyds Rep Med. 309 CA; And see *Rees* v. *Darlington Memorial Hospital NHS Trust* [2002] 2 All ER 177, CA; *AD* v. *East Kent Community NHS Trust* [2002] Lloyd's Rep Med 424, discussed fully on p. 271.
21 As in *Hardman* v. *Amin* [2000] Lloyds Rep. Med. 498.
22 *Salih* v. *Enfield Health Authority* (thought note that, if the parents would in any case have gone on to have a healthy child, the damage would be restricted to the costs incurred by the child's disability).
23 *Rand* v. *East Dorset HA* [2000] Lloyd's Rep. Med. 181; and see *Anderson* v. *Forth Valley Health Board* [1997] 44 BMLR 108 (Scotland).
24 *Nunnerley* v. *Warrington Health Authority* [2000] Lloyd's Rep.Med. 170.
25 At p. 1003.
26 At p. 325; it should be noted Hale LJ seems less than convinced of Lord Millett's general reasoning that the joys of a healthy child outweigh the costs. And see *Hardman* v. *Amin* [2000] Lloyds Rep. Med. 498.
27 See *Lazenvnick* v. *General Hospital of Munro City Inc.* Civ. Act 78–1259 Cmnd Pa., 13 August 1980.
28 p. 787.
29 *The Times*, 3 January 1983.
30 [1984] 3 All ER 1044.
31 See p. 1048.
32 At p. 1053.
33 At p. 970.
34 At p. 976.
35 At p. 1004.
36 See *St George's Healthcare NHS Trust* v. *S* [1998] 3 All ER 673 (CA).
37 See generally R. Scott, 'Maternal Duties toward the Unborn? Soundings from the Law of Tort' (2000) 8 Med. Law Rev. 1. And see E. Jackson, *Regulating Reproduction: Law Technology and Autonomy*, Hart, 2001, pp. 140–60.
38 Discussed fully in P. Pace, 'Civil Liability for Pre-Natal injuries' (1977) 40 MLR 193.
39 See M.Brazier, 'Parental Responsibilities, Foetal Welfare and Children's Health', in C. Bridge (ed.), *Family Law: Towards the Millennium*, Butterworth, 1997.
40 See S.A.M. McLean, *Old Law, New Medicine*, Pandora Press, London, 1999 at p. 66.

41 [1997] 3 All ER 936. See S. Fovargue and J. Miola, 'Policing Pregnancy: Implications of the Attorney-General's Reference (No. 3 of 1994)' (1998), Med. L Rev 265.

42 [1996] 2 All ER 10 CA; discussed in M. Seneviratne, 'Pre-Natal Injury and Transferred Malice: The Invented Other' (1996) 59 *Modern Law Review* p. 884.

43 *R.* v. *West* [1848] 175 ER 329; *R.* v. *Senior* [1832] 168 ER 1298.

44 See Lord Mustill at p. 949.

45 At p. 942.

46 See Fovargue and Miola (above at Note 41); M. Brazier (above at Note 39); M. Brazier, 'Liberty Responsibility and Maternity' (1999) 52 *Current Legal Problems* 359.

47 See *Parkinson* v. *St James and Seacroft University NHS Hospital Trust* [2001] Lloyds Rep. Med 309 CA; *Hardman* v. *Amin* [2000] Lloyd's Rep. Med. 458.

48 See *Anderson* v. *Forth Valley Health Board* [1998] 44 BMLR 108.

49 *W.* v. *Egdell* [1990] 1 All ER 835; *Lion Laboratories Ltd* v. *Evans* [1984] 2 All ER 417. Consider also the implications of the Data Protection Act 1998 and Article 8 of the Human Rights Convention. And see Mason and McCall Smith, op. cit., pp 209–17.

50 Nurses, Midwives and Health Visitors Act 1979, s. 17. An exception is made to protect family, policemen and ambulance crew from liability for helping in emergencies. For thorough discussion of the monopoly on childbirth see J.M. Eekelaar and R.W.J. Dingwall, 'Some Legal Issues of Obstetric Practice' [1984] JSWL p. 258, and J. Finch, 'Paternalism and Professionalism in Childbirth' (1982) 132 NLJ pp. 995 and 1011.

51 For further discussion of this case see Finch, op. cit.

52 See *Attorney-General's Reference (No.3 of 1994)* [1997] 3 All ER 936.

53 *R.* v. *Senior* [1832] 1 Mood. CC 346; and see *R.* v. *Bateman* [1925] 19 Cr. App. R. 8.

54 See Finch, op. cit., pp. 995–6.

55 Eekelaar and Dingwall, op. cit.

56 *Re MB (An Adult) (Medical Treatment)* [1997] 8 Med. LR 217 CA.

57 *Kralj* v. *McGrath* [1986] 1 All ER 54.

58 National Audit Office, *Handling Clinical Negligence Claims*, 2001.

59 Eekelaar and Dingwall. op cit., pp. 264–6.

60 S. 1(2).

61 Eekelaar and Dingwall, op cit., p. 265.

62 [1998] 3 All ER 673.

63 At p. 692.

64 [1992] 4 All ER 671.

65 *Rochdale Healthcare NHS Trust* v. *C* [1997] 1 FCC 274; *Norfolk and Norwich NHS Trust* v. *W.* [1996] 2 FLR 613; *Re L. (An Adult: Non Consensual Treatment)* [1997] 1 FCR 609; *Tameside & Glossop Acute Services Trust* v. *CS* [1996] 1 FLC 762.

66 [1997] 8 Med L.R. 217.

67 [1989] 2 All ER 193.

68 As the Royal College of Obstetricians and Gynaecologists itself has done; see RCOG, *A Consideration of the Law and Ethics in Relation to Court-Ordered Obstetric Intervention*, 1994 (revised 1996) London

69 See L. Miller, 'Two Patients or One? A Problem of Consent in Obstetrics', 1993, *Medical Law International* p. 97.

70 See L. Msiah-Jefferson, 'Reproductive Laws, Women of Color and Low-Income women', in Cohen and Tubb, op cit., p. 39.

71 See J. Gallagher, op. cit.

16 Medical Research

1 See J. Savelescu, 'Two deaths and two lessons' (2002) 28 *Journal of Medical Ethics* pp. 1–4.

2 On the general background to the debate on research see I. Kennedy and A. Grubb, *Medical Law: Text and Materials*, (3rd ed.), Butterworths, London, 2000, pp. 1665–86.

3 See the Animals (Scientific Procedures) Act 1986.

4 This chapter focuses on clinical research. Wider aspects of health care research (including sociological research) are not covered here. See N. Mays and C. Pope (eds), *Qualitative Research in Health Care*, BMJ Publishing Group, London, 1996. Also I.K. Crombie and H.T.O. Davies, *Research in Health Care*, Wiley, London, 1996.

5 See Department of Health *Local Research Ethics Committees*, HSG(91)5. Replaced by the Central Office for Research Ethics Committees (COREC), *Governance Arrangements for NHS Research Ethics Committees* (2001). See http://www.doh.gov.uk/research/documents/gafree.pdf.

6 COREC *Governance Arrangements for NHS Research Ethics Committees* ibid., at paragraph 3.5 define 'research site': 'For the purposes of ethical review of the research proposal, a research 'site' is defined as the geographical area covered by one Health Authority, whether the research is based in institutions(s) or in the community. Even when the research may physically take place at several locations within that geographical boundary, a favourable ethical opinion of the research protocol is required from only one NHS REC within that Health Authority boundary.'

7 Department of Health, *Multi-centre Research Ethics Committees*, HSG(97) 23. Replaced by the COREC *Governance Arrangements for NHS* Research Ethics Committees, ibid.

8 On the liability of ethics committees, see M. Brazier, 'Liability of Ethics Committees' (1990) 6 *Professional Negligence*, 186 and E. Pickworth and M. Brazier, 'Fees and Research Ethics Committees' (1999) 151 *Bulletin of Medical Ethics*, 18.

9 See Z.J. Penn, and P.J. Steer, 'Local research ethics committees; hindrance or help?' (1995) 102 *British Journal of Obstetrics and Gynaecology*, pp. 1–2; P. Garfield, 'Cross district comparison of applications of research ethics committees' (1995) 311 BMJ, pp. 660–1; T.W. Meade, 'The trouble with ethics committees' (1994) 28 *J R Coll Phys Lond*, pp. 102–3; U.J. Harries, P.H. Fentem, W. Tuxworth, W. Hoinville, 'Research ethics committees: widely differing responses to a national postal survey' (1994) 28 *J R Coll Phys Lond*, pp. 150–4.

10 K.G.M. Alberti, 'Multicentre research ethics committees: has the cure been worse than the disease?' (2000) 320 BMJ, pp. 1157–58.

11 Department of Health, *Research Governance Framework for Health and Social Care*, Department of Health, London, 2001.

12 Directive 2001/20/EC of the European Parliament and of the Council of 4 April 2001 'on the approximation of the laws, regulations and administrative provisions of the Member States relating to the implementation of good clinical practice in the conduct of clinical trials on medicinal products for human use' (2001) L 121 *Official Journal of the European Communities*, pp. 34–41.

13 See note 5.

14 *Independent Review Group on Retention of Organs at Post Mortem*, Final Report, Scottish Executive, 2001, para. 99.

15 See Editorial, 'Babies and consent: yet another NHS scandal' (2000) 320 BMJ, pp. 1285–6.

16 M.P. Samuals, D.P. Southall, 'Negative extrathoracic pressure in treatment of respiratory failure in infants and young children' (1989) 299 BMJ, pp. 1253–7. There was a subsequent NHS review: NHS Executive, *West Midlands Regional Office report of a review of the research framework in North Staffordshire Hospital NHS Trust*. http://www.doh.gov.uk/wmro/north-staffs.htm.

17 ibid., para 2.2.3.

18 General Medical Council *Research: The Role and Responsibilities of Doctors*, GMC, February 2002, para 34.

19 World Medical Association Declaration of Helsinki: *Ethical Principles for Medical Research Involving Human Subjects*, WMA General Assembly, Edinburgh, Scotland, October 2000.

20 Article 23 Declaration of Helsinki ibid., 'When obtaining informed consent for the research project the physician should be particularly cautious if the subject is in a dependent relationship with the physician or may consent under duress. In that case the informed consent should be obtained by a well-informed physician who is not engaged in the investigation and who is completely independent of this relationship.'

21 COREC, *Governance Arrangements for NHS Research Ethics Committees*, Department of Health: London, 2001, paragraphs 9.17, 10.6. Under the NHS

plan the 'good practice in consent initiative' seeks to review consent procedures to ensure a patient-centred standard.

22 'The use of these adjectives – responsible, reasonable and respectable – all show that the court has to be satisfied that the exponents of the body of opinion relied upon can demonstrate that such opinion has a logical basis.' Per Lord Browne-Wilkinson, *Bolitho* v. *City and Hackney HA* [1998] AC 232.

23 (1965) 52 WWR 608.

24 Department of Health and the Royal College of Physicians of London guidelines both require patient consent forms to state expressly that whether or not the patient agrees to take part in the trial will not affect his medical care and that the patient is free to withdraw from the trial at any time.

25 Wilkinson and Moore 'Inducements in Research' (1997) 11(5) *Bioethics*, 373 argue that inducements are acceptable and promote individual autonomy.

26 *Re T. (Adult: Refusal of Medical Treatment)* [1992] 4 All ER 649.

27 See L. Doyal, J.S. Tobias, (eds.), *Informed Consent in Medical Research*, London, BMJ Publishing, 2000.

28 On the problem of the development of a doctrine of 'informed consent' in the research context see J.K. Mason and R.A. McCall Smith, *Law and Medical Ethics* (6th edn) Butterworths, London, 2002, pp. 586–90.

29 See *Simms* v. *Simms* [2003] 1 All ER 669.

30 Department of Health, *Consent to Treatment: Summary of Legal Rulings*, HSC 1999/031 and *Good Practice in Consent*, HSC 2002/023. See also General Medical Council, *Seeking Patients' Consent: The Ethical Considerations*, GMC, November 1998; *Research: The Role and Responsibilities of Doctors*, L, GMC, February 2002 and Medical Research Council, *Good Clinical Practice in Clinical Trials*, MRC, 1998; *Good Research Practice*, MRC, 2000.

31 *Gillick* v. *West Norfolk and Wisbech Area Health Authority* [1985] 3 All ER 542.

32 Medical Research Council, *The Ethical Conduct of Research on Children*, MRC, 1991; British Paediatric Association, *Guidelines for the Ethical Conduct of Medical Research Involving Children* British Paediatric Association, 1992.

33 HSG(91)5 para 4.

34 This guidance has since been replaced by the COREC *Governance Arrangements for NHS Research Ethics Committees*, op. cit., which is silent on the issue.

35 COREC *Governance Arrangements for NHS Research Ethics Committees* ibid., para 9.17c requires that the committee is satisfied as to 'clear justification for the intention to include in the research individuals who cannot consent, and a full account of the arrangements for obtaining consent or authorization for the participation of such individuals'.

36 Royal College of Paediatrics and Child Health, 'Guidelines for the Ethical Conduct of Medical Research Involving Children', 2000 82 *Ethics Advisory Committee in Archives of Disease in Childhood*, pp. 177–82.

37 *Re W. (A Minor) (Medical Treatment)* [1992] 4 All ER 177 CA at pp. 635 and 647.

38 ibid. at p. 635.

39 It is highly unlikely that a court would sanction including a *Gillick competent* minor in a trial against her will. Albeit no minor can veto treatment, refusal is always a very important consideration for doctors making judgements whether to proceed against the minor's wishes; *Re W.* (above at pp. 640, 645 and 648–9.

40 [2003] 1 All ER 669

41 *Re D* [1976] 1 All ER 326.

42 [1987] 2 All ER 506.

43 'Responsibility in Investigation on Human Subjects' (1964) 2 BMJ p. 178.

44 See S. Conroy, J. McIntyre, I. Choonara, T.J. Stephenson, 'Drug trials in children: problems and the way forward' (2000) 49 *Br J Clin Pharmacol* pp. 93–7

45 Royal College of Paediatrics and Child Health, op. cit.

46 See generally Kennedy and Grubb, op. cit., pp. 1727–31.

47 See P.D.G. Skegg, 'Consent to Medical Procedures on Minors' (1973) 36 MLR 370, pp. 379–80.

48 As in *Re B. (A Minor) (Wardship: Medical treatment)* [1981] 1 WLR 1421.

49 [1972] AC24.

50 R.R. Nicholson (ed.), *Medical Research and Children: Ethics, Law and Practice*, OUP, Oxford, 1986.

51 'On experimentation on Children' (1977) 2 *Lancet* pp. 754–5; G. Dworkin, 'Legality of Consent to Non-Therapeutic Medical Research on Infants and Young Children' (1978) Vol. 53, *Archives of Disease in Childhood*, pp. 443–6.

52 [1994] 1 WLR 290.

53 Medical Research Council, *The Ethical Conduct of Research on the Mentally Incapacitated*, MRC, 1993, para. 6.1.3.

54 See now *Simms* v. *Simms* [2003] 1 All ER 669.

55 ibid.

56 The Convention for the Protection of Human Rights and Dignity of the Human Being with Regard to the Application of Biology and Medicine (1997) at Article 17 sanctions non-therapeutic research that 'has the aim of contributing, through significant improvement in the scientific understanding of the individual's condition, disease or disorder, to the ultimate attainment of research conferring benefit on the person concerned or on other persons in the same age category or afflicted with the same disease or disorder or having the same condition; and the research entails only minimal risk and minimal burden for the individual concerned.'

57 Law Commission, *Mental Incapacity*, Law Com. 231, 1995.

58 *Research: The Role and Responsibilities of Doctors*, GMC, February 2002, paras 43–50.

59 Council of Europe Steering Committee on Bioethics, *Draft Additional*

Protocol to the Convention on Human Rights and Biomedicine, on Biomedical Research CDBI/INF 2001

Article 17(3). Where the capacity of the person to give informed consent is in doubt, arrangements must be in place to verify whether or not the person has such capacity.

Article 18 Protection of persons not able to consent to research

1. Research on a person without the capacity to consent to research may be undertaken only if all the following specific conditions are met:

i) the results of the research have the potential to produce real and direct benefit to his or her health,

ii) research of comparable effectiveness cannot be carried out on individuals capable of giving consent,

iii) where possible, the persons undergoing research have been informed of their rights and the safeguards prescribed by law for their protection,

iv) the necessary authorisation has been given specifically and in writing by the legal representative or an authority, person or body provided for by national law, and after having received the information required by Article 19, taking into account previously expressed wishes or objections. An adult not able to consent shall as far as possible take part in the authorisation procedure. The opinion of a minor shall be taken into consideration as an increasingly determining factor in proportion to age and degree of maturity,

v) the person concerned does not object to participating in the research.

2. Exceptionally and under the protective conditions prescribed by law, where the research has not the potential to produce results of direct benefit to the health of the person concerned, such research may be authorised subject to the conditions laid down in paragraph 1, subparagraphs ii, iii, iv, and v above, and to the following additional conditions:

i) the research has the aim of contributing, through significant improvement in the scientific understanding of the individual's condition, disease or disorder, to the ultimate attainment of results capable of conferring benefit to the person concerned or to other persons in the same age category or afflicted with the same disease or disorder or having the same condition,

ii) the research entails only minimal risk and minimal burden for the individual concerned; and any consideration of additional potential benefits of the research shall not be used to justify an increased level of risk or burden.

3. Objection to participation, refusal to give authorisation or the withdrawal of authorisation to participate in research shall not prejudice the right of the individual concerned to receive appropriate and timely medical care.

60 For trenchant criticism on ethical and legal grounds of randomized clinical

trials, see Carolyn Faulder, *Whose Body Is It?*, Virago, London, 1985, Chapters 5–7.

61 See the useful discussion by S.J. Edwards, R.J. Lilford, D.A. Braunholtz, J.C. Jackson, J. Hewison and J. Thornton, 'Ethical issues in the design and conduct of randomized controlled trials', *Health Technology Assess* 2(15), 1998, p. 1.

62 Royal Commission on Civil Liability and Compensation for Personal Injury, Cmnd 7054, HMSO, 1978, paras. 1340–41.

63 COREC *Governance Arrangements for NHS Research Ethics Committees*, op. cit., para. 9.15(1).

64 Royal College of Physicians of London, *Research Involving Patients*, (1991).

65 See the deliberations and recommendations of the CIBA Foundation Study Group (1980) BMJ pp. 1172–5. There has also been long-standing support for a no-fault compensation scheme from the British Medical Association: http://web.bma.org.uk.

66 See J. Berry, 'Local Research Ethics Committees can audit ethical standards in research' (1997) 23 *J Med Ethics*, pp. 379–81 and E. Pickworth, 'Should local research ethics committees monitor research they have approved?' (2000) 26 *J Med Ethics*, pp. 330–33.

67 *Research Governance Framework for Health and Social Care*, op. cit., para 5.

68 See M. Farthing, R. Horton, R. Smith, 'Research misconduct: Britain's failure to act' (2000) 321 BMJ, pp. 1485–6.

69 S. Lock, 'Lessons from the Pearce affair: handling scientific fraud' (1995) 310 BMJ, pp. 1547–8.

70 C. Dyer, 'Consultant struck off over research fraud' (1997) 315 BMJ, p. 205.

71 C. Dyer, 'GP who falsified research data found guilty of professional misconduct' (2001) 323 BMJ, p. 1388.

72 *Research: The Role and Responsibilities of Doctors*, GMC, February 2002.

73 [1999] 4 All ER 185; [2000] 1 All ER 786, C.A.

74 See J. Strobl, E. Cave, T. Walley, 'Data protection legislation: interpretation and barriers to research' (2000) 321 BMJ, pp. 890–92.

17 Organ and Tissue Transplantation

1 See generally D. Price *Legal and Ethical Aspects of Organ Transplantation*, CUP, 2000; G. Dworkin, 'The Law Relating to Organ Transplantation in England' (1970) 33 MLR 353.

2 For an excellent analysis of the issue see B. New, M. Solomon, R. Dingwall, J. McHale, *A Question of Give and Take? Improving the supply of donor organs for transplantation*, Kings Fund Institute, 1994.

3 See Mason and McCall Smith, op. cit., at p. 439.

4 Although 'swaps' of hearts and lungs (known as domino transplants) have taken place with the recipient of a double heart/lung transplant donating her heart to another patient.

5 See Price op. cit. pp. 217–25.
6 See R.M. Titmuss; *The Gift Relationship: From Human Blood to Social Policy*, Allen & Unwin, London, 1971.
7 *R* v. *Brown* [1993] 2 All ER 75, HL.
8 Law Commission Consultation Paper No 139 *Consent in the Criminal Law*, HMSO, 1995.
9 Ibid at para 8.32.
10 In one American case a court, not surprisingly, refused to order the only possible donor to submit to a bone-marrow transplant; *McFall* v. *Shimp* [1978] 10 Pa D & C 3d.
11 See D. Price and A. Garwood-Gowers 'Transplantation from Minors: Are Children Other People's Medicine?', 1995, 1 *Contemporary Issues in Law 1*.
12 Curran, 'A Problem of Consent: Kidney Transplantation in Minors', 1959, 34 NY Univ. L. Rev. 891.
13 Though note that the Article 20 of the European Convention on Human Rights and Biomedicine does recognize that 'exceptionally' sibling donations may be authorized.
14 See Price op. cit. at pp. 359–62.
15 *Re W. (A minor) (Medical Treatment)* [1992] 4 All ER 627.
16 At pp. 635 and 647.
17 At p. 635.
18 [1969] 35 ALR (3d) 683.
19 See generally Price op. cit. pp. 347–50.
20 See *Re Pescinski* 226 N.W. 2d 180 at p. 181 (Wisconsin); *Re Richardson* [1973] 284 So 2d p. 185.
21 [1989] 2 All ER 945; discussed in Chapter 5.
22 [1989] 2 WLR 1025 at pp. 1051–3.
23 *Re Y. (Mental Incapacity: Bone Marrow Transplant)* [1997] Fam. 110.
24 s. 7(2). It is an open question whether this definition extends to lobes of lungs or segments of liver.
25 See s. 2(2).
26 See the Human Organs Transplant (Establishment of Relationship) Regulations SI 1989, No. 2107.
27 See s. 2(3).
28 See the Human Organs Transplant (Unrelated Persons) Regulations SI 1989, No. 2480.
29 Section 3 of the Act also requires detailed information to be supplied to the Department of Health about *all* transplant operations. See the Human Organs Transplant (Supply of Information) Regulations SI 1989, No. 2108.
30 In *R.* v. *Lennox-Wright* [1973] Crim. L.R. an unqualified person removed eyes from a cadaver for further use in another hospital. He was successfully prosecuted for contravening s. 1(4) Human Tissue Act 1961, which prohibits removal save 'by a fully registered medical practitioner'. But see

Kennedy, 1976, 16 Med. Sci. Law 49. And see Chapter 19.

31 See *Human Bodies, Human Choices: The Law on Human Organs and Tissues in England and Wales*, DoH, 2002, (available at www.doh.gov.uk/tissue)

32 Human Tissue Act 1961, s. 1(1).

33 Kings Fund Report at 66. See above Note 2.

34 ibid, s. 1(2)

35 This was the view of the DHSS, who require the NHS hospitals to designate one of their officers to exercise the function. DHSS 1975 HSC 15 (156). And see s. 1(7) Human Tissue Act 1961.

36 See P.D.G. Skegg 'Human Tissue Act 1961' (1976) 16 Med. Sci Law p. 197.

37 See Dworkin at Note 1.

38 See Skegg op. cit.

39 *The Times*, 8 September 1976.

40 HC (77) 28 August 1975.

41 And see the debate on non-heart-beating donors in Mason and McCall Smith op. cit. pp. 442–4.

42 A kidney which is removed from the body and 'cooled' may be kept for at least twelve hours and may function satisfactorily for as long as two days, but the longer the delay the greater the damage to the kidney.

43 See 'Diagnosis of Brain Stem Death' [1976] 2 BMJ p. 1187; 'Memorandum on the Diagnosis of Death' [1979] 1 BMJ p. 332.

44 See J.V. McHale, 'Elective Ventilation – Pragmatic Solution or Ethical Minefield' [1985] 11 *Professional Negligence* 23. And see Mason and McCall Smith op. cit. at pp. 443–4.

45 [1989] 2 All ER 545 HL.

46 See P.D.G. Skegg, 'Liability for the Unauthorised Removal or Cadavers Transplantation Material' (1974) 14 Med Sci & Law p. 153; I. Kennedy, 'Further Thoughts on Liability for Non Observance of Provisions of the Human Tissue Act 1961' (1976) 16 Med Sci & Law p. 49

47 See J. Harris, 'The Survival Lottery' (1975) 50 *Philosophy* p. 81.

48 See Redmond-Cooper, 'Transplants Opting Out or In – the Implications', (1984) 134 NLJ p. 648.

49 See generally Price op. cit. pp. 83–126.

50 See Kennedy et al. 'The Case for, "Presumed Consent", in Organ Donation' (1998) 351 *Lancet* p. 1650.

51 See Kennedy and Grubb, op. cit., pp. 1048–57.

52 Op. cit. pp. 60–63.

53 J. Radcliffe-Richards et al. 'The Case for Allowing Kidney Sales' (1998) 351 Lancet p. 1950.

54 Article 21.

55 At the heart of Titmuss's argument in *The Gift Relationship* (see Note 6).

56 See M. Radin, 'Market – Inalienability', 1987, 100 Harvard L. Rev 1849;

N. Duxbury 'Do Markets Degrade?' (1996) 59 MLR 331.

57 See J. Harris, *Clones, Genes and Immortality: Ethics and the Genetic Revolution* (2nd ed.) 1998, at pp. 147;

58 See Harris ibid and see C. Erin and J. Harris, 'A Monopsonistic Market?' in I. Robinson (ed.), *The Social Consequence of Life and Death under High Technology Medicine*, Manchester University Press/Fulbright Commission, 1995.

59 At p. 446.

60 See Note 51.

61 Note the interesting case of *Urbanski* v. *Patel* [1978] 84 DLR (3d) 850, where the donor claimed that the defendant's negligence in removing his daughter's only kidney caused injury (the loss of his kidney) to him!

62 A Scottish court so found in relation to a claim against a blood donor; see *AB* v. *Scottish Blood Transfusion Service* [1990] SLR 203.

63 See *A.* v. *The National Blood Authority* [2001] Lloyds Med Rep. 187 discussed fully on p. 210.

64 *Review of the Guidance on the Research Use of Fetuses and Fetal Material* Cm 762, 1989, HMSO.

65 See M. Fox and J. McHale 'Xenotransplantation: The Ethical and Legal Ramifications' (1998) 6 Med L. Rev 42; Nuffield Council on Bioethics, *Animal to Human Transplants*, 1996.

66 See W. Cartwright, 'The Pig, The Transplant Surgeon and the Nuffield Council' (1996) 4 Med.L.Rev p. 250.

67 'Animal Tissue into Humans', *Report of the Advisory Group on the Ethics of Xenotransplantation*, 1996: *The Government Response to 'Animal Tissue into Humans'*, 1997.

18 Death, Dying and the Medical Practitioner

1 Mason and McCall Smith op. cit. Chapters 16 and 17.

2 ibid at p. 366.

3 *Re. J. (A Minor)* [1992] 4 All ER 614 at 625 CA.

4 *Airedale NHS Trust* v. *Bland* [1993] 1 All ER 821, HL.

5 Mason and McCall Smith op.cit. at p. 393.

6 See in particular *Airedale NHS Trust* v. *Bland* [1993] 1 All ER 821 at p. 856 per Hoffman LJ.

7 *R. (Pretty)* v. *DPP* [2002] 1 All ER 1, HL.

8 *B* v. *An NHS Trust* [2002] 2 All ER 449.

9 See Mason and McCall Smith at pp. 529–35.

10 Albeit Mason and McCall Smith prefer to regard non-voluntary euthanasia as a 'sub-variety of voluntary euthanasia'.

11 Note Mason and McCall Smith's scepticism at p. 530.

12 *R.* v. *Lodwig, The Times*, 16 March, 1996

13 *Airedale NHS Trust* v. *Bland* [1993] 1 All ER 821 at p. 850.

14 *R.* v. *Cox* [1992] 12 BMLR 38.

15 *R.* v. *Adams* [1957] Crim. L.R. 773.

16 *Airedale NHS Trust.* v. *Bland* [1993] 1 All ER 821 at 868, HL.

17 (1977) 66 Cr. App. R. 97.

18 [1984] QB 795.

19 It should be noted, of course, that it may not always be an easy issue to determine whether a person is clinically or legally competent. See Chapter 5.

20 *Re T. (Adult: Refusal of Treatment)* [1992] 4 All ER 465, CA. See pp. 93–5.

21 [1993] 1 All ER 821 HL; and see *Nancy B.* v. *Hôtel Dieu de Québec* [1992] 86 DLR (4th) 385 (Canada); *Auckland Area Health Board* v. *A-S* [1993] 1 NZLR 235 (New Zealand); *Bouvia* v. *Superior Court* [1986] 225 Cal. Reptr 297.

22 [2002] 2 All ER 449.

23 At p. 881.

24 [2001] All ER (D) 251.

25 [2002] 1 All ER 1, HL.

26 *Pretty* v. *United Kingdom* [2002] FLR 45.

27 Although at least some of their Lordships left open the question whether on different facts such an application might succeed.

28 At p. 7.

29 At p. 11–12.

30 At p. 29.

31 At p. 37.

32 At p. 29.

33 At p. 18.

34 And see Lord Bingham at p. 21.

35 At p. 27.

36 *In Re Quinlan* [1976] 355 A. 2d. 647. And see *Cruzan* v. *Director Missouri Department of Health* [1990] 110 S Ct. 2841 (USA Supreme Court).

37 *Airedale NHS Trust* v. *Bland* [1993] 1 All ER 821, HL.

38 This incontrovertible physical evidence and irreparable damage to the brain distinguishes *Bland* from some subsequent cases.

39 [1989] 2 All ER 545.

40 At p. 894.

41 For critical appraisal of Bland see J.M. Finnis, 'Bland: Crossing the Rubicon?' (1993) 109 LQR 329; J. Keown, 'Restoring Moral and Intellectual Shape to the Law after *Bland*' (1997) 113 LQR 481.

42 See BMA, *Withholding and Withdrawing Life-Prolonging Medical Treatment: Guidance for Decision-making, 1999, GMC, Withholding and Withdrawing Life Prolonging Treatments Good Practice in Decision-Making,* 2002.

43 See K. Andrews, 'Recovery of Patients after Four Months or More in the

Persistent Vegetative State' (1993) 306 BMJ 1597; 'Patients in the Persistent Vegetative State: Problems in their Long-Term Management' (1993) 306 BMJ 1600.

44 See the incisive arguments of Finnis and Keown above at Note 41.

45 [1994] 2 All ER 403. And see *Re S. (Adult Incompetent: Withdrawal of Treatment* (2001) 65 BMLR 6

46 See J. Stone, 'Withholding of Life Sustaining Treatment' (1995) NLJ 354.

47 *Re D. [Medical Treatment]* [1998] FLR 411.

48 *Re H. (A Patient)* [1998] 2 FLR 36.

49 At p. 41.

50 *Re G. (Persistent Vegetative State)* [1995] 2 FCR 46.

51 At p. 51.

52 op. cit. at p. 401

53 e.g. *Re D. (Medical Treatment: Mentally Disabled Patient)* [1998] 2 FLR 22.

54 *Practice Note (Official Solicitor: declaratory proceedings: medical and welfare decisions for adults who lack capacity)* [2001] 2 FLR 569

55 See above at Note 52.

56 [2001] 1 All ER 801 and see E. Wicks, 'The Right to Refuse Medical Treatment under the European Convention on Human Rights' (2001) 9 Med. L. Rev 17.

57 See now BMA/RCN *Decisions Relating to Cardio-Pulmonary Resuscitation*, 1999.

58 See Mason and McCall Smith, p. 565.

59 [1996] 31 BMLR 127.

60 See *Re J. (A minor) (Wardship: Medical Treatment)* [1990] 3 All ER 930, CA.

61 See D. Morgan, 'Odysseus and the binding directive: only a cautionary tale' (1994) 14 *Legal Studies* p. 411.

62 See *Re T.* (Adult: Refusal of Treatment)[1992] 4 All ER 649 discussed fully on page 93.

63 The Enduring Powers of Attorney Act 1985 does not extend beyond powers to manage property and finance.

64 *The Living Will*, Edward Arnold, London, 1988.

65 Law Commission Report No. 231 *Mental Incapacity*, 1995, HMSO. See Chapter 5.

66 See LCD *Who Decides?* (Cm. 3803, 1997); LCD *Making Decisions* (Cm 4465, 1999) discussed fully in Chapter 5.

67 See generally J. Keown (ed.), *Euthanasia Examined: Ethical, Legal and Clinical Perspectives*, CUP, 1995 J. Keown, *Euthanasia, Ethics and Public Policy: An Argument Against Legalization*, CUP, 2002; M. Otlowski, *Voluntary Euthanasia and the Common Law*, OUP, 1997.

68 See A. McCall Smith, 'Euthanasia: The Strengths of the Middle Ground', (1999) 7 Med.Law Rev 198.

69 In the Medical Treatment (Prevention of Euthanasia) Bill discussed in

J.Keown, 'Dehydrating Bodies: the *Bland* Case, the Winterton Bill' in A. Bainham, S.D. Sclater, M. Richards (eds), *Body Lore and Laws* Hart Publishing, 2002, p. 245.

70 op. cit. at p. 1997.

71 See M. Otlowski op.cit.

72 See L. Gormally (ed.), *Euthanasia, Clinical Practice and the Law*, Linacre Centre for Health Care Ethics, 1994.

73 At p. 536.

74 Notably and eloquently D. W. Meyers and J.K. Mason, 'Physician Assisted Suicide': A Second View from the Mid-Atlantic' (1999) 29 *Anglo-Am Law Review* 39.

75 See Kennedy and Grubb op. cit. 1950.

76 At pp. 6–7.

77 At p. 537. See also J. K. Mason and D. Mulligan, 'Euthanasia by Stages' (1996) 347 *Lancet* p. 810.

78 See Mason and McCall Smith op. cit. at p. 533.

79 Termination of Life on Request and Assisted Suicide (Review Procedures) Act 2000. Discussed in J. de Haan, 'The New Dutch Law on Euthanasia' (2002) 10 Med L. Rev 57.

80 See J. Keown, 'The Law and practice of Euthanasia in the Netherlands', 1992, 108 LQR 51; H. Jochenson and J. Keown, 'Voluntary Euthanasia under Control? Further Empirical Evidence from the Netherlands' (1999) 25 *Journal of Medical Ethics* 16.

81 J.M. Van Delden, 'Slippery Slopes in Flat Countries – a Response' (1999) 25 *Journal of Medical Ethics* 22.

82 *Report of the Select Committee on Medical Ethics* (1993–4) HL-21.

19 Death and Retention of Body Parts

1 The old common law, 'year and a day', rule which required that if a person was charged with murder his victim must have died within a year and a day of the unlawful act was abolished by the Law Reform (Year and a Day Rule) Act 1996.

2 See Law of Property Act 1925, s. 184.

3 e.g. *Lim Poh Choo* v. *Camden and Islington AHA* [1980] AC 174.

4 British Transplantation Society [1985] BMJ, pp. 251, 253.

5 'A Definition of Irreversible Coma' (1968) 205 JAMA p. 337.

6 For an excellent analysis of the confusing terms and debates on 'brain death' see Mason and McCall Smith op. cit., pp. 328–33. And see D. Price, *Legal and Ethical Aspects of Organ Transplantation*, CUP, 2000, Chapter 1.

7 'Diagnosis of Brain Death' [1976] 2 BMJ 1187 and 'Memorandum on the diagnosis of death' [1979] 1 BMJ 332; see also I. Kennedy and A. Grubb, op

cit, Chapter 15; C. Pallis and D.H Harley, *ABC of Brainstem Death* (2nd edn), BMA, 1996.

8 See the *Guardian*, 6 August 1986, p. 11; in particular, concern was expressed that the twenty-four-hour gap between sets of tests for 'brain death' was not always observed.

9 See above at Note 7.

10 *Code of Practice for Diagnosis of Brain Stem Death*, DoH, 1998.

11 [1982] 2 All ER 422.

12 [1992] 3 Med LR 303; and see *Mail Newspapers plc* v. *Express Newspapers plc* [1987] FSR 90.

13 [1993] 1 All ER 821, HL.

14 Department of Health *Human Bodies, Human Choices. The Law on Human Organs and Tissue in England and Wales: A Consultation Report* (2002), available at www.doh.gov.uk/tissue

15 See Skegg (1976) 2 J. Med. Ethics 190–91; Kennedy (1977) 3 J, Med. Ethics 5. And see 14th Report of the Criminal Law Reform Committee *Offences Against the Person* (Cmnd 7844, 1980).

16 See Price op. cit. at pp. 61–72.

17 See the arguments discussed in P.D.G. Skegg, *Law, Ethics and Medicine*, Clarendon Press, Oxford, 1988.

18 [1993] 2 All ER 821, HL.

19 See Kennedy and Grubb op. cit. pp 2225–37.

20 See the Report of the Working Party of the Medical Royal Colleges, *Organ Transplantation in Neonates*, 1988, sanctioning such a course of action.

21 See Mason and McCall Smith op. cit. at pp. 419–20.

22 *Learning from Bristol*: The Report of the Public Inquiry into children's heart surgery at the Bristol Royal Infirmary 1984–1995 CM 5207 (1), 2001.

23 The Inquiry into the management of care of children receiving complex heart surgery at the Bristol Royal Infirmary Interim Report *Removal and Retention of Human Material* (available at www.bristolinquiry.org.uk) hereafter *Bristol Interim Report*.

24 *The Royal Liverpool Children's Inquiry Report* (HC 12–11 2001) hereafter the *Alder Hey Report*.

25 *The Removal, Retention and Use of Human Organs and Tissue from Post-Mortem Examination*. Advice from the Chief Medical Officer, DoH, 2001.

26 *Report of a Census of Organs and Tissue Retained by Pathology Services in England*, DoH, 2001.

27 The *Bristol Interim Report*, the *Alder Hey Report* and the Chief Medical Officer all made extensive recommendations about how the NHS should seek to manage and resolve the process of informing families about organ retention and organ return, about support for families and how to resolve past controversies as well as how the law should be reformed. The Secretary

of State established a special health authority, the NHS Retained Organs Commission, to manage the process by which NHS trusts provided information to families about organ retention, oversee the process of organ return, act as an advocate for families and develop a new regulatory framework for organ and tissue retention.

28 See generally the Nuffield Council on Bioethics, *Human Tissue: Ethical and Legal Issues*, 1995; A. Grubb, 'I, Me, Mine: Bodies, Parts and Property' (1998) *Medical Law International* p. 299.

29 At p. 20.

30 *Doodeward* v. *Spence* [1908] 6CLR 906.

31 *Williams* v. *Williams* [1882] 20 Ch.D 659.

32 S. 1 defines anatomical examination as '. . . the examination by dissection of a body for the purposes of teaching or studying, or researching into, morphology; and where parts of a body are separated in the course of an anatomical examination, such examination includes the examination by dissection of the parts for those purposes'.

33 The Inspector of Anatomy advises the Secretary of State on the licensing of anatomical examinations, the possession of anatomical specimens and the licensing of premises where such examinations are carried out; s. 3.

34 See ss. 5,6.

35 S. 5(4) (b).

36 s.11; on the overlap between the Anatomy Act and the Human Tissue Act see generally P. D. G. Skegg 'Use of Corpses for Medical Education and Research (1991) 31 *Medicine, Science and the Law* p. 345.

37 S. 1(1).

38 S. 1(2).

39 For a much fuller account, see the *Bristol Interim Report*, Annex B, *Law and Guidelines*.

40 S. 8(1) Coroners Act 1988.

41 Regulation 41(e)

42 See the *Alder Hey Report*.

43 Similarly difficult questions surround ownership of parts taken from living people. These are not addressed in this work; see Mason and McCall Smith, op. cit. Chapter 20.

44 [1998] 3 All ER 741.

45 [1908] 6 CLR 406 at pp. 413–44.

46 [1996] 4 All ER 479.

47 At p. 479 (per Peter Gibson LJ).

48 At p. 750.

49 See *Bristol Interim Report* at pp. 75–6

50 *Dobson* v. *North Tyneside HA* [1996] 4 All ER 474 at p. 478.

51 For diametrically opposed views about the ethics of organ retention see J. Harris, 'Law and regulation of retained organs: the ethical issues' (2002)

22 *Legal Studies* p. 527; M. Brazier, 'Retained Organs: ethics and humanity' (2002) 22 *Legal Studies* p. 550.

52 Medical Research Council *Human Tissue and Biological Samples For Use in Research: Operational and Ethical Guidance*, April 2001.

53 For an argument as to how a regulatory framework based around professional codes of practice offers the best way forward, see M. McLean, 'Letting Go: Retention of Human Material after Post Mortem', in A. Bainham, S.D. Sclater, M. Richards, *Body Lore and Law*, Mart Publishing, 2002, p. 70.

54 See M. Brazier, 'Organ retention and return: problems of consent' (2003) 29 *Journal of Medical Ethics* 30.

55 Department of Health *Human Bodies, Human Choices The Law on Human Organs and Tissue in England and Wales: A Consultation Report*, 2002, available at www.doh.gov.uk/tissue

56 See *Certifying and Investigating Deaths in England, Wales and Northern Ireland*: A Consultation Paper by the Fundamental Review of Death Certification and the Coroner Service 2002.

Epilogue

1 See Ian Kennedy, *The Unmasking of Medicine*, Allen & Unwin, London, 1981.

Index